FARMERS' CYCLOPEDIA

Farmers' Cyclopedia

Abridged Agricultural Records

IN SEVEN VOLUMES
AND A GUIDE

From the Publications of the

UNITED STATES DEPARTMENT OF AGRICULTURE

AND

THE EXPERIMENT STATIONS

---

*A compilation of such Bulletins and Reports
as are Indispensable to the Practical Farmer*

VOLUME III

DISEASES OF CATTLE, SHEEP, GOATS, CATS, DOGS. THEIR PREVENTION AND CURE

SEE VOLUME VII FOR COMPLETE INDEX

GARDEN CITY   NEW YORK
DOUBLEDAY, PAGE & COMPANY
1916

ACKNOWLEDGMENT

THE WRITINGS of the following authorities were consulted or abridged, or both, in the preparation of this volume:

United States Department of Agriculture.—George M. Rommel, R. P. Steddom, U. G. Houck, A. D. Melvin, A. M. Farrington, E. H. Webster, C. B. Lane, R. W. Hickman, Marion Dorset, John R. Mohler, E. C. Schroeder, J. A. Emery, Morris Wooden, R. A. Ramsay, Albert E. Behnke, H. J. Washburn, B. H. Ransom, B. H. Rawl.

Alabama.—C. A. Cary, D. T. Gray.

Arizona.—F. W. Wilson, A. E. Vinson.

Arkansas.—R. R. Dinwiddie, W. Lenton, A. K. Short.

California.—A. R. Ward, E. W. Major, M. E. Jaffa.

Canada.—L. Caesar, W. H. Peters, J. W. Mitchell, F. Torrance, J. H. Reed, H. H. Dean, C. A. Zovitz, F. C. Harrison, L. G. Jarvis, C. W. Nash, F. W. Foster.

Connecticut.—E. H. Lehnert, W. A. Stocking, Jr., C. L. Beach, W. H. Conn, L. F. Rettger, G. H. Lamson, J. M. Trueman, F. H. Stoneburn.

Colorado.—G. H. Glover, J. O. Williams, W. E. Vaplon, W. G. Sackett, H. M. Cottrell, Dr. Barnes, Dr. Knapp, W. J. Carlile, C. J. Griffith, B. C. Buffum.

Delaware.—Charles F. Dawson.

Florida.—Charles F. Dawson, John M. Scott.

Georgia.—P. N. Flint, L. J. Herring, H. J. Wing, J. H. McClain.

Hawaii.—H. H. Simpson.

Idaho.—H. T. French, John S. Burd.

Illinois.—William Dietrich, A. J. Glover, W. C. Coffey, J. M. Barnhart, H. W. Mumford, J. M. Trueman, C. H. Yates, L. D. Hall.

Indiana.—John H. Skinner, Robert A. Craig, J. H. Skinner, A. W. Bitting.

Iowa.—John A. Craig, John J. Repp, G. L. McKay, Carl W. Gay, W. J. Kennedy, J. H. McNeil, H. G. Van Pelt, Milliken Stalker.

Kansas.—Roland J. Kinzer, Francis S. Schoenleber, Oscar Erf, D. H. Otis.

Kentucky.—E. S. Good, D. W. May.

Louisiana.—W. H. Dalrymple, W. G. Owen, W. R. Dodson.

Maine.—Fremont L. Russell, G. M. Gowell, Gelman A. Drew, Walter Anderson, Raymond Pearl.

Maryland.—Samuel S. Buckley (who abridged Volume III of this series), R. H. Waite, G. E. Gage.

Massachusetts.—James B. Paige.

Michigan.—L. M. Hart, C. E. Marshall.

ACKNOWLEDGMENT

Minnesota.—M. H. Reynolds, T. L. Haecker.

Mississippi.—Archibald Smith, J. A. McLean.

Missouri.—J. W. Connaway, Paul Paquin, Paul Evans, F. B. Mumford, C. A. Willson.

Montana.—Robert W. Clark, W. J. Taylor.

Nebraska.—A. T. Peters, H. R. Smith, A. L. Haecker.

Nevada.—R. H. McDowell, N. E. Wilson, Peter Frandsen, G. H. True, W. B. Mack.

New Hampshire.—T. R. Arkell, H. H. Lamson, I. C. Weld, Fred Rasmussen.

New Jersey.—T. Earle Budd, F. C. Minkler.

New Mexico.—J. D. Tinsley, H. H. Simpson, W. A. Lassell.

New York.—James Law, H. H. Wing, James S. Rice, George C. Watson, J. A. Foord, O. F. Hunziker, George A. Smith, R. A. Pearson, W. A. Stocking, M. W. Harper, C. A. Rogers, W. P. Wheeler, H. A. Harding.

North Carolina.—G. A. Roberts, F. P. Williamson, J. C. McNutt, J. S. Jeffrey, R. S. Curtis, John Michels.

North Dakota.—L. Van Es.

Ohio.—B. E. Carmichael, C. E. Thorne, J. W. Hammond, R. E. Caldwell.

Oklahoma.—W. T. McDonald, L. L. Lewis.

Oregon.—F. L. Kent, E. F. Pernot, A. L. Kinsely, James Dryden.

Pennsylvania.—H. P. Armsley, W. A. Cochel, G. C. Watson, H. C. Jackson, C. W. Larson.

Rhode Island.—Leon J. Cole, Cooper Curtice, George W. Field, Thomas H. Taylor.

South Carolina.—M. R. Powers, D. A. Nourse.

South Dakota.—E. L. Moore, C. Larsen.

Tennessee.—Moses Jacob, W. G. Shaw.

Texas.—M. Francis, John C. Burns.

Utah.—R. W. Clark, F. B. Linfield, H. J. Frederick, John T. Caine.

Vermont.—F. A. Rich, E. H. Gregg, R. M. Washburn, W. F. Hammond, H. A. Edson.

Virginia.—N. S. Mayo, John Spencer, W. K. Brainerd, E. V. Niles, E. A. Smith, Jr., A. P. Spencer, W. D. Saunders.

Washington.—S. B. Nelson, W. T. McDonald, A. B. Nystrom.

West Virginia.—N. J. Giddings, T. F. Watson.

Wisconsin.—D. H. Otis, M. P. Ravenel, G. C. Humphrey, A. S. Alexander, H. L. Russell, W. A. Henry, W. L. Carlile.

Wyoming.—T. F. McConnell, J. A. Hill, A. D. Faville, O. L. Prim

TABLE OF CONTENTS

Part I.

DISEASES OF CATTLE

Part II.

DISEASES OF SHEEP

Part III.

DISEASES OF GOATS, DOGS, AND CATS

ILLUSTRATIONS

VOLUME III.

DISEASES OF CATTLE, SHEEP, GOATS, ETC.

PART I

DISEASES OF CATTLE.

INDICATIONS AND SYMPTOMS OF DISEASE.

INTRODUCTION.

IN THE determination of disease the veterinary physician, in a very large majority of cases, is obliged to rely almost solely upon the objective symptoms, and perhaps in no class of diseases is this more true than in the exploration of those under consideration. This condition of affairs has a strong tendency to develop observation and discernment in the veterinarian, and not infrequently do we find that the successful veterinary practitioner is a very accurate diagnostician. But in order to make a differential diagnosis it is not only necessary to have a knowledge of the structure and functions of the organs in health, but to adopt a rigid system of details of examination, without which successful results can not be reached.

History.—The history of a case should always be ascertained so far as possible. The information obtained is sometimes unsatisfactory and not to be depended upon, but even when such is the case it is advisable to weigh the evidence from every point of view. In connection with the history of every case it is always of primary importance to ascertain the cause of illness. A knowledge of the origin and development of a disease is important, both in making a diagnosis and in formulating the treatment. Exposure to cold and dampness is frequently the exciting cause of affections of the organs of respiration.

The experienced practitioner is always sure to ascertain whether the particular animal he is called on to attend is the only one in the stable or on the premises that is similarly affected. If several animals are similarly affected the disease may have a common cause, which may or may not be of an infectious nature. Another thing that the experienced practitioner ascertains is what previous treatment, if any, the animal has had. Medicine given in excessive doses sometimes produces symptoms resembling those of disease.

The hygienic and sanitary conditions have always to be considered in connection with the cause as well as the treatment of disease. Much of the disease which occurs in large dairies, as well as elsewhere, could be prevented if owners and those in charge of animals had proper regard for the fundamental laws of animal hygiene and modern sanitation.

Attitude and General Condition.—The feeling of pain in animals suffering from serious affections is expressed to the close observer in no uncertain language—by their flinching when the painful part is touched; by the care with which they move or lie down; by walking or standing to "favor" the part; by the general attitude and expression of the eye; by the distress and suffering apparent in the face of the sick animal; and by other evidences.

The general physical condition and attitude of the sick animal tell much to the careful observer that aids him in making a diagnosis and prognosis. Cows suffering from affections of the organs of respiration usually assume a position or attitude that is characteristic, well known to experienced stockmen as well as to veterinarians. When an animal has a fever or is suffering from an inflammation, the skin is one of the first parts of the body to undergo a change that is apparent to the average observer. The skin soon loses its elasticity and tone and the hair becomes dry and staring.

From the general conditions or state of nutrition one is able to judge the effect that the disease has already had upon the animal and to estimate the amount of strength remaining available for its restoration to health; from the amount of emaciation one can approximate as to the length of time the animal has been ill. The age and breed of the animal, as well as its constitution and temperament, are among the things that have to be taken into account in making a diagnosis and in overcoming the disease.

The Mucous Membrane.—The mucous membrane should in all cases be examined. It can be readily seen by averting the eyelids or by an inspection of the lining membrane of the nostrils. Paleness of the mucous membrane indicates weak circulation or poor blood. It may result from inappropriate food, from disease, or from hemorrhage.

In healthy animals increased redness of the mucous membrane occurs from pain, excitement, severe exertion, and in such instances is always transitory. In certain pathological conditions, such as fevers and inflammation, this condition of the mucous membrane will also be found. The increased redness of the mucous membrane lasts during the duration of the fever or inflammation. A bluish or blue mucous membrane indicates that the blood is imperfectly oxidized, and contains an excess of carbon dioxid, and is seen in serious diseases of the respiratory tract, such as pneumonia and in heart failure.

The Secretions.—The secretions may be either diminished, increased, or perverted. In the early stage of an inflammation of a secretory organ its secretion is diminished. In the early stage of pleurisy the serous membrane is dry, and as the disease advances the membrane becomes unnaturally moist. The products of secretion are sometimes greatly changed in character from the secretion in health, becoming excessively irritant and yielding evidence of chemical and other alterations in the character of the secretion.

Cough.—Cough depends upon a reflex nervous action, and may be primary when the irritation exists in the lungs or air passages, or secondary when due to irritation of the stomach, intestines, or other parts having nervous communications with the respiratory apparatus. A cough is said to be dry, moist, harsh, hollow, difficult, paroxysmal, suppressed, sympathetic, etc., according to its character. Cough is a very important symptom, often being diagnostic in diseases of the respiratory organs; but this is a subject which can be more satisfactorily treated in connection with special diseases.

Respiration.—In making an examination of an animal observe the depth, frequency, quickness, facility, and the nature of the respiratory movements. They may be quick or slow, frequent or infrequent, deep or imperfect, labored, unequal, irregular, etc., each of which has its significance to the educated and experienced veterinarian. Sleep, rumination, pregnancy in cows, etc., modify the respiratory movements even in health. Respiration consists of two acts—inspiration and expiration. The function of respiration is to take in oxygen from the atmospheric air, which is essential for the maintenance of life, and to exhale the deleterious gas known as carbon dioxid.

The frequency of the respiratory movements is determined by observing the motions of the nostrils or of the flanks. The normal rate of respiration for a healthy animal of the bovine species is from fifteen to eighteen times per minute. The extent of the respiratory system renders it liable to become affected by contiguity to many parts, and its nervous connections are very important.

Rapid, irregular, or difficult breathing is known as dyspnea, and the animal in all such cases has difficulty in obtaining the amount of oxygen that it requires. Among the conditions that give rise to dyspnea may be mentioned restricted area of active lung tissue, due to filling of portions of the lungs with inflammatory exudate, as in pneumonia; painful movements of the chest, as in rheumatism or pleurisy; fluid in the chest cavity, as in hydrothorax; adhesions between the lungs and chest walls; compression of the lungs or loss of elasticity; excess of carbon dioxide in the blood; weakness of the respiratory passages; tumors of the nose and paralysis of the throat; swellings of the throat; foreign bodies and constriction of the air passages leading to the lungs; fevers, etc.

As already alluded to, it is only the careful and constant examination of animals in health that will enable one properly to appreciate abnormal conditions. One must become familiar with the frequency and character of the pulse and of the respirations, must know the temperature of the animal in health, before changes in abnormal conditions can be properly appreciated.

Temperature.—The temperature should be taken in all cases of sickness. Experienced practitioners can approximate the patient's temperature with remarkable accuracy, but I would strongly recommend the use of the self-registering clinical thermometer, which is a most valuable instrument in diagnosing diseases. It is advisable that a tested instrument be procured, as some thermometers in the market are inaccurate and misleading. The proper place to insert the thermometer is in the rectum. The instrument should be rested against the walls of the cavity for about three minutes. The normal temperature of the bovine is 101° to 102° F., which is higher than that of the horse. A cow breathes faster, her heart beats faster, and her internal temperature is higher than that of the horse. Ordinary physiological influences—such as exercise, digestion, etc.—give rise to slight variations of internal temperature; but if the temperature rises two or three degrees above the standard, some diseased condition is indicated.

Pulse.—The pulse in a grown animal of the bovine species in a state of good health beats from forty-five to fifty-five times per minute. Exercise, fright, fear, excitement, overfeeding, pregnancy, and other physiological conditions, as well as disease, may affect the frequency and character of the pulse. It assumes various characters according to its rapidity of beat, frequency of occurrence, resistance to pressure, regularity, and perceptibility. Thus we have the quick and slow, frequent and infrequent, hard and soft, full and imperceptible, large and small pulses, the characters of which may be determined from their names; also the form known as the intermittent, either regular or irregular. We may have a dicrotic, or double, pulse; a thready pulse, which is extremely small and scarcely perceptible; the venous, or jugular, pulse; the running down pulse, and so on.

In cattle the pulse is conveniently felt over the submaxillary artery where it winds around the lower jawbone, just at the lower edge of the flat muscle on the side of the cheek. If the cow is lying down the pulse may be taken from the metacarpal artery on the back part of the fore fetlock. The pulsations can be felt from any superficial artery, but in order to ascertain the peculiarities it is necessary to select an artery that may be pressed against a bone. There is a marked difference in the normal or physiological pulse of the horse and that of the cow, that of the horse being full and rather tense, while in the cow it is soft and rolling. The pulse is faster in young and in old cattle than it is in those of middle age.

Auscultation.—Auscultation and percussion are the chief methods employed to determine the various pathological changes that occur in the respiratory organs. Auscultation is the act of listening and may be either mediate or immediate. Mediate auscultation is accomplished by aid of an instrument known as the stethoscope, one extremity of which is applied to the ear and the other to the chest of the animal. In immediate auscultation the ear is applied directly to the part. Immediate auscultation will answer in a large majority of cases. Auscultation is resorted to in cardiac and certain abdominal diseases, but it is mainly employed for determining the condition of the lungs and air passages. Animals can not give the various phases of respiration on demand, as can the patients of the human practitioner. The organs themselves are less accessible than in man, owing to the greater bulk of tissue surrounding them and the pectorial position of the fore extremeties, all of which render it more difficult in determining pathological conditions.

The air going in and out of the lungs makes a certain soft, rustling sound, known as the vesicular murmur, which can be heard distinctly in a healthy state of the animal, especially upon inspiration. Exercise accelerates the rate of respiration and intensifies this sound. The vesicular murmur is only heard where the lung contains air and its function is active. The vesicular murmur is weakened as inflammatory infiltration takes place and when the lungs are compressed by fluids in the thoracic cavity, and disappears when the lung becomes solidified in pneumonia or the chest cavity filled with fluid as in hydrothorax. The bronchial murmur is a harsh, blowing sound, heard in normal conditions by applying the ear over the lower part of the trachea, and may be heard to a limited extent in the anterior portions of the lungs after severe exercise. The bronchial murmur when heard over other portions of the lungs generally signifies that the lung tissue has become more or less solidified or the fluid has collected in the chest cavity.

Other sounds, known as mucous rales, are heard in the lungs in pneumonia after the solidified parts begin to break down at the end of the disease and in bronchitis where there is an excess of secretion as well as in other conditions. Mucous rales are of a gurgling or bubbling nature. They are caused by air rushing through tubes containing secretions or pus. They are said to be large or small as they are distinct or indistinct, depending upon the quantity of fluid that is present and the size of the tubes in which the sound is produced. According to their character they are divided into dry and moist. The friction sound is produced by the rubbing together of roughened surfaces and is characteristic of pleurisy.

Percussion.—Percussion is that mode of examination by which we elicit sounds by striking or tapping over the part. It may be direct or indirect. If the middle finger of the left hand is placed firmly on the chest and smartly tapped or struck with the ends of the first three fingers of the right hand, the sound will be noticed to be more resonant and clear than when the same procedure is practiced on a solid part of the body. This is because the lungs are not solid, but are always, in health, well expanded with air. But in certain pulmonary diseases, as in pneumonia, they fill up and become solid, when the sound given out by percussing them is dull, like that on any other solid part of the animal. When fluid has collected in the lower part of the chest cavity the sound will also be dull on percussion. Where there is an excess of air in the chest cavity, as in emphysema or in pneumothorax, the percussion sound becomes abnormally loud and clear. By practice on healthy animals the character and boundaries of the sounds can be so well determined that any variations from them will be readily detected, and will sometimes disclose the presence of a diseased condition when nothing else will.

Percussion is sometimes practiced with the aid of a special percussion hammer and an object to strike upon known as a pleximeter. A percussion hammer is made of rubber or has a rubber tip, so that when the pleximeter, which is placed against the side of the animal, is struck the impact will not be accompanied by a noise. A percussion hammer and pleximeter can be purchased from any veterinary instrument maker.

ADMINISTRATION OF MEDICINES.

Medicines may be administered to cattle in many ways. The channel and method of administration depend on whether a general or local effect is desired, the condition of the animal, and the nature of the medicine that is to be given. It is the easiest method, and therefore customary, to give ordinary remedies by the mouth, either with the food, or with drink, or separately. There are, however, some conditions in which medicines administered in this way will not act promptly enough, or wherein a desired effect of the medicine on a distant part of the body is wholly lacking, unless it is applied in some other way.

The various methods of administering medicines to cattle will be considered below.

By the Mouth.—The simplest way to give medicines by the mouth is to mix them with the food or water. This can be done when the medicine is in the form of a powder or fluid, if but a small quantity is to be given, if it does not have a taste that is disagreeable to the animal and is not so irritant as to injure the lining membranes of the mouth and throat.

The usual method of administering bulky or unpalatable doses is to mix them with a fluid vehicle, such as water, milk, molasses, or beer, and give from a bottle. A dose given in this way is known as a drench. In administering a drench the head of the animal should be elevated a little by an assistant. This is best accomplished when standing on the left side of the cow's head, by grasping the nose with the thumb and fingers of the right hand inserted in the nostrils; then with the left hand beneath the chin the head is further raised and supported. If the animal is unruly, it may be tied in a stall or placed in a stanchion. The medicine can now be poured into the mouth by inserting the neck of the bottle between the lips on the right side. Care must be taken to avoid getting the bottle beween the back teeth. The mouth of the bottle should be inserted as far as the middle of the tongue and the contents poured slowly. If the cow coughs, the head must at once be lowered to permit the fluid to escape from the larynx. If one persists in giving medicine during coughing, some of the dose may pass down the windpipe to the lungs and cause a severe or a fatal pneumonia. This accident is especially to be guarded against when the throat is partly paralyzed or insensitive, as in parturient paresis (milk fever). In this disease it has often happened that drenches have been poured into the lungs, thus killing the cow.

The amount of fluid to be given in a drench depends upon the effect that is sought and the nature of the medicine. In impactions of the stomach very large quantities of fluid may be given—as much as a gallon or several gallons at a time. Usually, however, it is not customary or desirable to give more than from 1 to 2 quarts at a dose, and not more than a pint unless it be necessary on account of the irritant quality of the drug that has to be shielded with a large quantity of the vehicle.

Medicines that are soluble should be completely dissolved before they are given. Insoluble medicines should be finely divided by powdering or by shaking, and should be well agitated and mixed immediately before they are given. In the latter case a menstruum with considerable body, such as molasses or flaxseed tea or milk, will help to hold solids or oils in suspension until swallowed.

Balls are large pills adapted for the larger animals. Powders or gums are sometimes mixed with an adhesive substance and rolled into balls for the purpose of convenience of administration. Balls are not so much used and are not so well adapted to the medication of cattle as of horses. The process of solution is slower in the paunch of a cow than in the stomach of a horse; and if the cow is so sick as to have stopped ruminating, a ball may become covered up and lost in the mass of material in the paunch and so lie for days, producing no effect whatever.

Capsules are shells or envelopes made of soluble gelatine in which powders or liquids may be inclosed. Capsules and balls are administered by being placed on the tongue well back in the mouth while the tongue is drawn forward and the mouth is held open by a block of wood between the back teeth. The ball should be dropped, the tongue released, and the block removed as nearly simultaneously as possible, so that the backward carriage of the tongue will throw the ball into the throat and lead to its being swallowed. Care must be taken to avoid having the hand cut or crushed while introducing the ball. After a little experience it is possible to do away with the block of wood between the teeth for keeping the mouth open.

By the Stomach.—Medicines are introduced directly into the first stomach by the use of an esophageal tube or through the canula of a trocar passed into the paunch through the side. This method is used in the treatment of diseases of indigestion.

By the Rectum.—Medicines are usually administered by the rectum for the purpose of controlling the bowels and for the treatment of local diseases. Sometimes, however, medicines that have a general effect are given in this way when, for any reason, it is not possible or convenient to give them through the mouth. Only drugs that are readily absorbed should be given per rectum for a general effect and in somewhat larger dose or more frequently than when given by the mouth. Such stimulants as ether, alcohol, or the aromatic spirits of ammonia, diluted with from four to six times their bulk of warm water, may be used in this way. Rectal injections, or *enemata,* are used in the treatment of constipation. If it is the purpose of the injection to soften hardened fecal masses, the water should be comfortably warm and it may have a little clean soap in it. If it is the purpose of the injection to stimulate sluggish bowels to contraction, the water may be cold. In giving rectal injections a rectal syringe may be used, or, better, a piece of one-half to three-quarter inch rubber hose 5 feet long with a tin funnel attached to one end. The hose is soaped or oiled and introduced slowly and gently into the rectum 2 or 3 feet. The fluid is then slowly poured into the funnel and allowed to gravitate into the rectum. The same apparatus may be used for feeding by the rectum.

By the Vagina.—Medicines are inserted into the vagina, and through the vagina into the womb, in a manner similar to that of rectal administration. Most of the medication made use of in this way is for the local treatment of these organs. Following calving, during outbreaks of abortion, and in an infectious disease of the vagina, such injections become necessary.

By the Udder.—Injections into the udder are now regularly made in the treatment of parturient paresis (milk fever). In making this injection there are so many precautions necessary in relation to the sterilization of the apparatus and the teats and skin that this work should be left in the hands of a skilled veterinarian. The result of the introduction of even a minute quantity of infectious dirt may be the loss of the udder. For making this injection one may use one of the prepared sets of apparatus or a milking tube and funnel connected by a piece of small rubber hose. The apparatus should be boiled and wrapped in a clean towel until needed. The udder and teats and the hands of the operator must be well disinfected. The udder should be emptied of milk before the injection is made. After all these precautions have been observed the milking tube may be inserted and through it one-half pint of solution introduced by gravity, air pressure or by syringe. There is practically no danger in this mode of treatment if it is properly carried out. Injections into the udder are sometimes made in the treatment of garget, but so far with indifferent success.

By the Nostrils.—An animal may be caused to inhale medicine in the form of gas or vapor or to snuff up a fine powder. Sometimes, for the purpose of local treatment, fluids are injected into the nose. Medicine inhaled may have a local effect alone or a general effect. Medicated steam, carrying the volatile products of creolin, carbolic acid, balsam of Peru, compound tincture of benzoin, tincture of iodine, etc., may be liberated beneath the nostrils of a cow so that she must inhale these soothing vapors; but such treatment is not so common for cattle as for horses. In producing general anesthesia, or insensibility to pain, the vapor of chloroform or ether is administered by the nostrils. As a preliminary to this it is necessary to cast and confine the animal. Great care is necessary to avoid complete stoppage of the heart or breathing.

By the Trachea.—Medicines are injected into the trachea, or windpipe, in the treatment of some forms of diseases of the lungs, and especially in that form of bronchitis or pneumonia that is caused by lungworms. For this injection a large hypodermic syringe is used that is fitted with a very thick, strong needle. The needle is to be inserted about the middle of the neck and between the cartilaginous rings of the trachea.

By the Skin.—Although a number of drugs, notably mercury, are so readily absorbed by the skin of cattle as to render poisoning easy, medicines are not given in this way for their general or constitutional, but only for their local effect. Diseases of the skin and superficial parasites are treated or destroyed by applications in the forms of washes, ointments, dips, and powders. Liniments and lotions are applied to the skin for the relief of some near-lying part, such as a muscle, tendon, or joint. Blisters are applied to the skin for the purpose of obtaining the effect of counter-irritation upon a neighboring region or organ. Cold water may be applied to the skin to reduce the temperature and to diminish congestion or inflammation in a superficial area or to reduce the temperature of the whole body. High fever and heat strokes are treated in this way.

By the Tissue Beneath the Skin.—Hypodermic or subcutaneous injections are often made for the purpose of introducing a drug reagent, or vaccine directly into the connecting tissue beneath the skin. Introduced in this way, the substance is quickly absorbed, none of it is lost, and its whole effect is obtained, often within a few minutes.

There are numerous precautions necessary in making a subcutaneous injection, most of which have to do with cleansing and sterilization. It is also important to select a proper site for the injection, so that blood vessels, joints, and superficial nerves, organs, or cavities may all be avoided. With due regard for the necessary precautions, there is practically no danger in such an injection, but it should be attempted only by those who are able to carry it through in a surgically clean way. Only certain drugs can be given subcutaneously, and dosage must be accurately graduated.

By the Veins.—Certain medicines act most promptly and surely when introduced directly into the blood by injecting them into a vein. The jugular vein is usually selected for this purpose. Some vaccines and antitoxins are administered in this way. Intravenous injection should be practiced only by experienced veterinarians.

MEDICINES USED.

The object of this section is to place before the stock owners who are not in reach of competent veterinarians, a limited amount of information on the subject of Veterinary Materia Medica, and to discountenance the use of obnoxious mixtures, which frequently do more harm than good. Only the most common drugs will be dealt with, giving in a general way their actions and uses. Before entering into a discussion of each drug separately, it will be necessary, in order to make more clear its discussion, to define a few of the terms that will be used in this connection; also to describe the methods of administration, and the manner in which medicines act.

Medicines act both locally and generally. The local effect of a medicine is produced when the medicine is applied directly to a part, and when the effect is limited to the part to which it is applied. The general effect of a drug is produced only when the drug enters the circulation; some medicines may produce such an effect when locally applied as a result of absorption through the tissues. Medicines also act physiologically and therapeutically. The physiological action is said to be gotten when the drug produces the same effect in health as in disease. When such actions are exerted in the cure of disease they are termed therapeutic or curative actions. Medicines, too, have a certain affinity for certain organs or sets of organs; for example, aloes exerts its influence upon the digestive tracts, nux vomica upon the nervous system, aconite upon the heart, spirits of nitrous ether upon the kidneys, etc. Just why a medicine affects one organ more than another has not been satisfactorily explained; that medicines do have such an affinity, however, has been thoroughly proven.

Medicines are said to cure disease in three ways: 1st, by allopathy, whereby effects are produced which overcome the disease; 2d, by antipathy, whereby medicines overcome disease by more powerful and antagonistic force; 3d, by homœopathy. The advocates of this theory claim to cure disease by the administration in small doses of such medicines that in large doses would produce symptoms similar to the disease to be cured. This theory does not meet with as general favor as the other two theories.

Antiseptics are agents which destroy bacteria and arrest putrefaction. They prevent suppuration in wounds, thereby hastening the healing process. Examples, bi-chloride of mercury in solution of 1-1000, lysol, carbolic acid, creolin, etc.

Disinfectants are agents which destroy the specific poisons, bacteria, of contagious diseases. They are used to disinfect buildings in which diseased animals have been kept, for cleansing wounds, etc. The same class of drugs are used as in the above.

Deodorizers are agents which destroy smells. They do so by disguising or destroying the cause of the odor. Permanganate of potash is the best example of this class of drugs.

Counter-irritants are those agents which, when applied to the surface of the body, counteract or allay deeper seated inflammations, or cause the absorption of abnormal enlargements to which they are applied. In acute inflammatory attacks they allay the congestion through reflex action. They may be used beneficially in bronchitis, pneumonia, and in the secondary stages of inflamed joints, counter-irritants stimulate the circulation and hasten resolution.

Astringents contract the living tissue. They may also produce their effect by coagulating or precipitating albumen. They are used to check excessive diarrhœa and to arrest hemorrhage. Acids, salts of iron, chalk and tannic acid are examples.

Demulcents and emollients soothe, soften, relax and ensheathe the parts with which they come in contact. This action is entirely mechanical. They include gums, mucilage and oils. They lubricate and protect abraded or irritable parts from external injury. Given internally they shield the mucous membranes from irritable substances and, to a certain extent, prevent the absorption of poisons.

Narcotics are drugs which disturb the relation of the mental function with the external world. Examples, alcohol, ether, chloroform and opium.

Anodynes relieve pain by diminishing excitability of nerves or nerve centers. They are indicated in cases of colic, pleurisy and pneumonia. Examples, cannabis indica, opium, chloroform and ether.

Antispasmodics are agents which prevent or remove spasm of voluntary or involuntary muscles. Examples, cannabis indica, belladonna, opium, chloroform and ether.

Nerve sedatives are agents which lessen nervous excitability. Bromide of potassium and bromide of ammonium are included in this class of drugs.

Nerve stimulants are agents which increase nervous excitability. Example, nux vomica.

Expectorants facilitate the removal of secretions from the air passages. They are indicated in common colds, pneumonia and bronchitis. Examples, chloride and carbonate of ammonia, squills and dovers powders.

Heart stimulants increase the frequency and force of the pulse, and are indicated in debilitating diseases when the pulse is slow and feeble. Alcohol and the ammonium preparations are examples.

Heart sedatives decrease the frequency and force of the pulse, and are used in febrile diseases when the pulse is rapid and strong. They should not be used when the pulse is weak. Aconite is an example.

Purgatives are agents which cause intestinal evacuations. When their action is mild they are termed laxatives.

Vermicides are agents which destroy parasites, such as round worms and tape worms in the digestive tract. Santonin and areca nut are included in this class of drugs.

Diuretics are agents which act on the kidneys and increase the flow of urine. They are divided into two classes, stimulating and refrigerating. Stimulating diuretics increase the flow of urine by increasing the blood pressure in the kidneys, and should never be used in inflammatory diseases of the kidneys. Refrigerating diuretics act by increasing the cell protoplasm of the kidneys, and have a cooling effect on those organs. They are indicated in febrile diseases when the kidneys are inactive, and in inflammation of the kidneys. The potassium and lithium salts act as refrigerating diuretics, while sweet spirits of nitre, alcohol and other stimulants act as stimulating diuretics.

Tonics are agents which impart tone or strength to the parts on which they specially act. It is a notable fact that all drugs which have a tonic action do not produce their effects in the same manner. Gentian acts as a stomach tonic, aids digestion and, hence, tones up the whole system. Nux vomica acts as a nerve tonic thereby bettering the general condition of the system. Iron acts as a blood tonic, while cinchona acts as a general tonic. Tonics are indicated in feeble digestion, debilitated conditions of the nerves and after all debilitating diseases.

Antipyretics lower the temperature of the body in fever. Examples, quinine and antifebrin.

Antidotes are agents which counteract the effects of poison. They act mechanically and chemically. Such agents as charcoal act mechanically by absorbing the poison and preventing its being taken into the system. In lead poisoning sulphuric acid and the sulphates combine with the lead forming the insoluble (therefore non-poisonous,) sulphate of lead. The dose or quantity of the drug administered affects the degree of its action. Sometimes the nature of the action is also affected. For example, small doses of potassium, sodium and magnesium salts and aloes act as tonics, while large doses act as purgatives. The size of the dose required of any drug will depend upon the size and age of the animal. Owing to the difference in the size of the stomach, the cow will require a much larger dose than the horse. The stomach of the cow being large and constantly filled with a large quantity of food the drug is more tardily absorbed, hence, the dose must be larger to produce the desired effect. When continued effects of a drug are required better results are gotten by giving the drug in small and repeated doses than by single large doses. The doses mentioned are for adult animals. The dose for young animals will necessarily have to be governed by the size and age of the animal.

Medicines are administered in four ways, but as it is not convenient for most stock owners to use all of the methods, only two will be described, viz., by the mouth and by inhalation. Medicines when given by the mouth should usually be given in the fluid state to insure more rapid absorption. When small quantities are to be given the best method is to throw the fluid well back in the mouth by means of a syringe. Larger quantities may be given in the form of a drench through the mouth. *The practice of drenching through the nostrils can not be too strongly condemned.* Serious results follow this cruel method of drenching. In drenching, the head should be elevated only sufficiently high to prevent the fluid from running out of the mouth. If medicines are to be given in a solid form they are best administered in the form of a bolus, which may be made by mixing with the drug a little flaxseed meal or liquorice root, using just water enough to make a stiff mass. The whole is wrapped in tissue paper and placed well back on the roots of the tongue. Medicines may also be mixed with the animal's food. If the animal refuses to eat his food containing the drug a little pinch of the drug placed in his mouth before he has tasted the food so prepared, will give to the animal the taste of the drug and deceive him to such an extent that he will not notice anything wrong with his food. The administration of drugs by inhalation will be spoken of in connection with the drugs that are used in that manner.

TONICS.

Agents that act as tonics are derived from both the vegetable and mineral kingdom. Vegetable tonics that will be described are, gentian, nux vomica and ginger. Mineral tonics, iron and its preparations.

Gentian is the dried root of Gentiana lutea; obtained from druggists in the form of powder and fluid extract. Its color is yellow, shading to brown; bitter in taste which it readily imparts to water, alcohol and ether. Gentian acts as a pure tonic and exerts its influence mainly upon the stomach. It improves the appetite and general tone, and relieves indigestion in young animals, for which purpose it is conjoined with ginger and sodium bicarbonate. In young animals suffering with indigestion and diarrhœa the writer has often gotten excellent effects by the use of gentian and hydrochloric acid. In influenza, distemper and most debilitating diseases gentian improves the appetite and tone of the animal when conjoined with iron and ginger. It exerts its influence on all animals alike and is, therefore, a safe and valuable tonic for the smaller as well as the larger animals. Horses take of the powdered gentian one-half ounce to one ounce; cattle one to two ounces; sheep one to three drachms; pigs one-half to one drachm; dogs five to twenty grains. The fluid extract is given in the same doses. Best results are gotten when the above doses are repeated two or three times daily.

Ginger acts as a mild tonic and is usually conjoined with other tonics for the purpose of increasing their action. It is also conjoined with purgatives for the same purpose, and to relieve the griping.

Nux Vomica is used in the form of powder, fluid extract and tincture. It owes its activity to two alkaloids; *strychnine* and *brucine.* Nux vomica and its alkaloids act as stimulants to the motor centers of the spinal cord and other nerves. Medicinal doses act as nerve tonics and aid digestion, overcome paralysis and improve the general tone. The digestive glands are stimulated, whereby dyspepsia and other forms of indigestion are relieved. In torpidity of the bowels nux vomica acts beneficially by toning up the nerves and increasing the perastaltic action of the bowels. In paralysis following milk fever, canine distemper and other debilitating diseases nux vomica is indicated. Combined with gentian and iron it acts beneficially as a general tonic. Horses take of the powdered drug one-half to one drachm; cattle one to two drachms; sheep ten to thirty grains; pigs ten to twenty grains; dogs one-half to two grains.

Iron and its preparations act as astringents and tonics. They improve the condition of the blood. The sulphate of iron is most commonly used in veterinary practice as a tonic, and is indicated in much the same class of patients as other tonics. The tincture of the chloride of iron is largely used to arrest hemorrhage; also the sub-sulphate, both in powder and solution.

Gamboge is used almost entirely as a purgative for cattle. It is a powerful irritant, and produces copious watery discharges. It is usually prescribed for cattle in impaction of the rumen and other parts of the stomach; also in obstinate cases of constipation conjoined with Epsom or Glauber salts, which increases the activity of the purgative mixture. Cattle take one-half to one ounce of the powdered drug.

Epsom and Glauber Salts act as mild purgatives and are useful in the same class of cases in which the foregoing purgatives are recommended, with the addition that they may be used in febrile diseases, having a tendency in such cases to lower the fever. Conjoined with other purgatives they increase their activity. Salts are used more than any other drug as a purgative for ruminants. In small doses they act as a tonic. The purgative dose for cattle is one to one and one-half pounds.

Castor, linseed, cottonseed, and olive oil act as laxatives. They soothe and ensheathe the mucous membranes with which they come in contact and are valuable in spasmodic and flatulent colic. One-half pint of oil with one and one-half ounce of tincture of opium and one-half ounce cannabis indica is often sufficient to relieve mild attacks of colic in the horse. The dose of the oils for the horse is one-half to one pint; cattle, one to two pints.

Spirits of Nitrous ether (*Sweet Spirits of Nitre*) acts as a stimulating diuretic. It is indicated in torpidity of the kidneys and to hasten excretion of waste matter from the system. In azoturea it hastens the excretion of urea. In gravel of the kidneys, by increasing the flow of urine, it is said to act beneficially by washing the small gravel from the pelvis of the kidney. It should not be given in inflammation of the kidneys, since it belongs to the class of stimulating diuretics and hence increases the blood supply of those organs. Horses take one to two ounces; cattle, one to four ounces.

Nitrate and Acetate of Potassium act as refrigerating diuretics and are used in most febrile diseases. They lower the body temperature in fevers and relieve congestion of the kidneys. Potassium Nitrate placed in the drinking water of fever patients cools the mouth and, to some extent, allays thirst. Horses take one-half to one ounce; cattle, one to three ounces.

STIMULANTS.

Ammonium is a diffusible stimulant and antacid. Owing to its antacid properties it is of value in indigestion and tympanitis, especially in ruminants. Being a stimulant it is also of value in spasmodic colic. Ammonium, and its preparations, promotes bronchial secretions and assists in its expulsion, and is, therefore, a stimulating expectorant. Externally, ammonia is used as a counter-irritant. A stimulating liniment is made by mixing one ounce each of aqua ammonia and oil of turpentine with six ounces of linseed oil. Horses take of the aqua ammonia one to three drachms; cattle three to six drachms. The carbonate and chloride of ammonia are given in about the same doses. Both the aqua and carbonate, being very irritating, must be largely diluted for internal use.

Aconite is a heart sedative and decreases the frequency and force of the heart's action. It reduces abnormal temperature and appears to have some tendency to lessen perception of pain. Aconite is of value in the congestive stage of pneumonia, when the pulse is strong and full, but as soon as the pulse begins to weaken its use should be discontinued. Conjoined with quinine it acts beneficially alike in acute sore throat, laryngitis and pleurisy when accompanied with high fever. In enteritis aconite reduces the high pulse and lowers the temperature. Aconite is often conjoined with belladonna and opium for external application over bruises and sprains. The dose of the tincture for horses is ten to thirty minims. Better results are gotten by giving small and repeated doses than by a single large dose.

Potassium Bromide is a nerve sedative. It allays nervous excitement and relieves spasm, but has little tendency to produce sleep. It is used in epileptic convulsions, chorea and tetanus. In the latter, however, it is of but little value. Horses and cattle take from four drachms to one ounce; dogs five to ten grains.

Chloral Hydrate is an antiseptic and topical irritant. Absorbed, it has primarily a stimulant and, secondarily, a sedative action on the circulation and central nervous system. Medicinal doses are hypnotic, analgesic and feebly anæsthetic. Large doses produce sleep. It quiets irritability and relieves spasms in strychnine poisoning. Chloral hydrate is very irritating and, when given internally, must be largely diluted with water. Horses take from four to eight drachms; cattle one to two ounces; dogs five to twenty grains.

Cannabis Indica is an anodyne and antispasmodic. In large doses it induces pleasing, dreamy narcosis. It relieves spasms and excitability. It has been recommended in tetanus. It does not impair the appetite, interfere with the bowels or produce delirium. Two drachms being given on the tongue every fifteen minutes until relief is obtained, or until two ounces have been given. The fluid extract is the best form in which to use the drug. Horses take one-half to one ounce; cattle one to two ounces; dogs one-half to one drachm.

Areca Nut is an astringent and vermicide, proving of special value for dogs, destroying both round and tape worms. Better results are obtained, however, when it is combined with male shield fern, fl. ext., ten to fifteen minims with ten grains to one drachm of areca nut proving quite effectual in most cases. The drug should be given in milk, to which worms are partial, and followed with a dose of castor oil. If the worms are not gotten rid of by the first dose, it may be repeated in a few days. The addition of a few drops of turpentine will also increase the vermicide effect. Of the powdered areca nut, dogs take fifteen grains to two drachms; horses four to six drachms. Areca nut is an uncertain vermicide for larger animals.

Hyposulphite of Soda is an antiseptic and insecticide. It is given as an internal antiseptic and to expel worms. Such actions are probably due to the hydrogen sulphide given off as a result of the decomposition of the hyposulphite. Two parts of the hyposulphite mixed with one part of powdered charcoal destroy intestinal worms and aid digestion in swine that are suffering from such troubles. Many so-called outbreaks of hog cholera are due entirely to intestinal worms, which are gotten rid of by the above mixture. Horses and cattle take one to three ounces; swine two to four drachms.

Creolin is a coal-tar derivative and acts as an antiseptic and parasiticide. It is non-poisonous and without irritation. When added to water it makes a milky solution. Applied to wounds in three per cent. solution it destroys pus-forming organisms and prevents suppuration, thereby hastening the healing progress. It enters largely in the preparation of dog soaps for the destruction of fleas, for which purpose it is quite effectual. It is equal to carbolic acid as an antiseptic and has the advantage of being non-poisonous.

Lysol is also derived from coal tar and acts as an effectual antiseptic in two to five per cent. solutions. It is used to disinfect wounds, abscesses, buildings, etc.

Pyoctanin is another coal-tar derivative and is said to be an effectual antiseptic in solutions of one to one thousand. It is also sometimes used as an internal antiseptic, but its value as such has not been thoroughly demonstrated. In irritable conditions of the conjunctival membrane of the eye with the formation of pus a few drops of one to one thousand solution three to four times daily proves quite effectual in giving relief.

Quinine is the alkaloid of cinchona and acts as an antiseptic, antipyretic and tonic. In small doses quinine tones up the entire system by improving the appetite and aiding digestion. It destroys micro-organisms in the system and is, therefore, valuable in malarial troubles. It is also said to be of value in Texas cattle fever. In large doses, repeated every two or three hours, it reduces abnormal temperature by preventing oxydation of the tissues. In Texas cattle fever it should be given in two to four drachm doses three to four times daily.

DISINFECTION OF STABLES AND DISPOSAL OF CARCASSES.

In dealing with infectious diseases of live stock it has been found that the average stockman and farmer does not realize the importance of thoroughly disinfecting his premises following an outbreak of contagious disease. There is apparently a widespread lack of information regarding the germicidal power of various substances, commonly termed disinfectants. There is also a lack of knowledge concerning practical and economical methods of proceeding with the work of disinfection. Moreover, the reappearance of a contagious disease on premises from which it was believed to have been eradicated may frequently be traced to careless or imperfect work in connection with the cleaning and disinfection of the place.

THE NECESSITY FOR DISINFECTION.

It is but natural to acknowledge the presence of only such objects as can be seen with the unaided eye. Science has clearly proved the existence of numerous minute animal and vegetable organisms— micro-organisms—and it is a matter of common knowledge that

Cows Affected with Foot-and-Mouth Disease.   Dairy Herd at Westboro, Mass. B. A. I. 1902.

many of these organisms frequently find their way into the animal body and produce disease. It is also well known that these micro-organisms, or germs, vary in form and other characteristics and that for each disease of an infectious nature there is a specific germ.

If these germs could be confined to the animal body and die with it there would be no such thing as an infectious disease. Unfortunately, however, they are thrown off by the animal through the excretions and lie in the earth, in the litter of stables, upon the floor and walls, and in cracks and crevices. Here they may remain and maintain their virulence for an indefinite period, ready at any time to be gathered up by an animal in its feed or to be blown about in dust and drawn into the lungs.

For example, we have tuberculosis in cattle and glanders in the horse. In the former disease the causative agent is a rod-shaped germ (*Bacillus tuberculosis*), which is about one-thousandth of an inch in length. Cattle affected with tuberculosis pass myriads of these germs with the manure, and it is not difficult to understand how in the average stable they would have little difficulty in finding many lodging places. In glanders the causative agent is another rod-shaped germ (*Bacillus mallei*), about the same length as the tuberculosis germ, but somewhat thicker. A characteristic of this disease is the formation of ulcers in the nostrils and other portions of the body, from which there is more or less discharge laden with the glanders germ. And here, again, it is not difficult to understand how one diseased animal may contaminate extensive premises.

As has been stated, some of these minute forms are vegetable organisms. In fact, these vegetable parasites are the cause of some of the most destructive diseases, and some of them are very difficult to destroy, for the reason that they contain spores. A spore may be likened to the seed of a plant, for it bears about the same relation to the bacillus that a grain of wheat does to the plant proper. As the plant may be destroyed and the seed remain latent for an indefintie time, so destruction of the bacillus may be easily accomplished while the spores remain unharmed and retain life for weeks or months.

An example of this class of organisms is seen in the agent which causes anthrax (*Bacillus anthracis*). Ordinary methods for the destruction of the bacillus will not destroy the spore as well, and thus anthrax becomes a most difficult disease to eradicate. Upon farms where animals have died from anthrax and the carcasses have been buried instead of destroyed, repeated outbreaks of the disease may occur from time to time, possibly extending over a period of several years. This condition is due to the existence of the very resistant spores, which under favorable circumstances are carried to the surface of the earth and become infecting organisms—much as the seed of a noxious weed, after remaining in the soil during the winter, finds the conditions favorable in the spring and develops into a plant —except that these minute forms of life multiply with the most wonderful rapidity. Thus it is that our increased knowledge regarding micro-organisms or bacteria as the cause of many animal diseases has emphasized the importance of disinfection.

THE NATURE OF DISINFECTION.

The work of disinfection is based upon our recognition of the presence of disease germs, and disinfection means the act of destroying the cause of the infection. In other words, disinfection is a removal of the cause, and it will be clear to any practical man that in dealing with disease any effort which stops short of a complete removal of the cause is most unwise and unprofitable. To those unaccustomed to the work, disinfection may seem a most complicated process. Any approved method, however, is comparatively simple when carried out carefully, although like many another procedure it is one in which attention to details counts for much. It is important to bear in mind that the causative agents of many diseases are extremely small and may remain for an indefinite time in dust, cracks, and crevices of buildings, so that efforts aiming at the eradication of disease from contaminated premises must be thorough in order to be effective.

DISINFECTANTS.

In the work of disinfection nature has provided man with a most valuable ally—sunlight. It is well known that the direct rays of the sun are destructive to many forms of bacteria, in some cases destroying them and in others lessening their influence. Thus the importance of well-lighted stables is evident. The dark and sunless building will be a favorable breeding place for bacteria, and the structure which admits the greatest amount of sunlight will be the least favorable for their development. Again, heat will destroy the bacteria of disease. By this is not meant the ordinary heat of the sun, but heat as developed in boiling water or in flame. It is upon this principle that the surgeon before operating renders his instruments free from the possible presence of bacteria by boiling, and it is heat which renders a jet of live steam destructive to bacteria. Sunlight, however, can not be considered more than an accessory in the destruction of bacteria, while the application of heat in the form of steam or flame is seldom possible. The result is that in the practical work of disinfection we are dependent upon certain drugs, which have power to destroy the organisms of disease.

Such drugs are known as disinfectants, and, fortunately, we have at hand a number that possess the power of destroying bacteria. It is not the purpose here to consider further the relative values of these drugs, neither will it be necessary to discuss the exact manner in which they act. It is sufficient to know that they possess the power of destroying bacterial life with the same certainty that poisonous drugs destroy animal life. They have only to be brought in contact with the bacteria in order to destroy them. As disinfecting drugs vary more or less in potency and in adaptability to general use, possessing certain advantages as well as disadvantages, it may be well to describe briefly a few of the commoner forms.

FORMALDEHYDE.

Formaldehyde—formic aldehyde—is available on the market as paraform (a sort of condensed formaldehyde, which is sold as a white powder or in the form of pastils) and also in aqueous solution generally known under the name of formalin. The solution is supposed to contain 40 per cent of formaldehyde, though in reality the amount of formaldehyde present rarely exceeds 37 to 38 per cent. Formaldehyde may be used for disinfection in either a liquid or gaseous form.

Liquid Formaldehyde.—Solutions of formaldehyde are best prepared by making a 5 per cent solution of formalin in water. This is applied directly to substances that require disinfection, and in the case of refuse, excreta, and similar substances should be thoroughly mixed with them. A 5 per cent solution of formalin is generally regarded as superior to carbolic acid of the same strength as a general disinfectant.

Gaseous Formaldehyde.—In disinfecting with formaldehyde gas it is essential that the compartments to be disinfected be tightly closed so that a sufficient concentration of the gas may be held in contact with the infected substances a sufficient length of time. The temperature of the air is an important factor in securing efficient action, the formaldehyde being much more energetic in a warm atmosphere than in a cold. The best authorities state that gaseous formaldehyde disinfection should not be attempted if the temperature of the air is below 50° F. The gas is most conveniently secured by liberating it from the concentrated aqueous 40 per cent solution or from the solid paraform. A number of methods for accomplishing this in practice have been devised, the more important of these being as follows:

GAS FROM FORMALIN.

Heating Under Pressure.—Portable autoclaves specially designed for the purpose are charged with a sufficient amount of formalin, the quantity depending upon the cubic air space to be disinfected. The autoclave is closed and heat is applied until the required pressure within the autoclave is attained. The gas which has been liberated from the solution by the heat is allowed to flow through an outlet tube into the closed chamber which is to be disinfected. The room is then kept closed for from two to twelve hours; the shorter time if only smooth surfaces are to be acted upon; the longer if penetration into fabrics is desired. Ten ounces of formalin should be used for each 1,000 cubic feet of air space.

Heating Without Pressure.—This method is similar to that just described. Formalin is placed in a specially designated retort and heated with a lamp. The gas is conducted into the compartment to be disinfected by means of a small tube which passes through the keyhole, or other small aperture. Ten ounces of formalin is required for each 1,000 cubic feet of space. The evolution of gas by this method is less rapid than when generated under pressure and a longer time is required for disinfection. The compartment should remain closed for at least six hours, and for twelve hours if penetration into the interior of fabrics, hay, etc., is required.

Spraying.—In this method the formalin is sprayed upon the surface of objects which require disinfection or upon sheets which are hung up in the compartment containing the infected materials. The gas is liberated by simple evaporation, this liberation being favored by the wide surface which is exposed. The gas is liberated much more slowly by this method than by either of those already described, and the diffusion is also relatively much slower. For these reasons the compartment to be disinfected should not be very large, and should remain closed for at least twenty-four hours. Not less than 10 ounces of formalin should be used for each 1,000 cubic feet of space.

Liberation of the Gas by Chemical Means.—Several methods of liberating formaldehyde from formalin solutions without the use of artificial heat have been proposed in recent years. The most important of these is known as the "permanganate method." Formalin is poured upon crystallized or powdered potassium permanganate. A violent chemical reaction takes place immediately, heat is generated, and a rapid liberation of formaldehyde gas takes place. As will be understood, the heat is caused by the reaction between the formaldehyde in solution and the permanganate, a large portion of the formaldehyde being consumed by the reaction. The amount of gas evolved depends in great measure upon the relative weights of permanganate and formalin employed. Experiments have shown that when the formalin and permanganate are mixed in the proportion of 6 parts of formalin to 5 parts of chemically pure permanganate, by weight, 50 per cent of the formaldehyde employed is liberated in the form of gas. If 10 ounces of formalin are required for disinfection of 1,000 cubic feet of space by the first three methods described, twice that amount is necessary when the permanganate method is employed, as half of the formaldehyde is destroyed by the reaction. For disinfecting 1,000 cubic feet, therefore, use 20 ounces of formalin and 16 2-3 ounces of permanganate. The needle-shaped crystals of potassium permanganate should be employed. Place the required amount of permanganate in a wide-bottomed vessel (an ordinary dish pan is excellent) and pour the formalin on quickly, then close the compartment for from six to twelve hours, depending upon the character of the materials to be disinfected.

GAS FROM PARAFORM AND WOOD ALCOHOL.

Lamps provided with a pan for holding the paraform are obtainable on the market. The paraform is placed in the pan and heat applied by means of an alcohol lamp. The evolution of gas in this manner is slow. Two ounces of paraform is required for the disinfection of 1,000 cubic feet of space, and the compartment should remain closed for at least twelve hours. This method is best suited to the disinfection of small spaces.

Generation of Formaldehyde from Wood Alcohol.—Formaldehyde is readily produced by the oxidation of wood alcohol (methyl alcohol). This fact has been taken advantage of for use in practical disinfection. Lamps have been designed by means of which the vapor of wood alcohol is passed over hot, finely divided platinum. This causes the oxidation of the alcohol to formaldehyde, which is given off in the room to be disinfected. There is somewhat more danger from fire when this method is employed than in those previously described. Not less than 25 ounces of wood alcohol should be employed for disinfecting 1,000 cubic feet of space.

The advantages of formaldehyde may be summarized as follows: (1) It is one of the most powerful germicides known. (2) Its action is not interfered with by albuminous substances. (3) It is not poisonous and may therefore be used for disinfecting hay and grain without destroying these for food purposes. (4) It is not injurious to delicate fabrics, paint, or metals. (Formalin solutions will attack iron, but not other metals).

The disadvantages are, briefly, as below: (1) The gas has a strong tendency to condense in cold weather and is not reliable as a disinfectant when the air temperature is below 50° F. (2) It is necessary to seal tightly, all compartments which are to be disinfected with the gas in order that penetration may be secured and that the required concentration may be maintained for a sufficient length of time.

Carbolic Acid (Phenol).—Pure carbolic acid is solid at ordinary temperatures and crystallizes in long white needles. It may be purchased in this form or as liquefied carbolic acid (Phenol liquefactum, U. S. P.). The latter form is prepared by adding 1 part of water to 9 parts of the crystals and is employed by pharmacists on account of convenience in dispensing. Carbolic acid must not be confused with "crude carbolic acid" and "liquid carbolic acid," which are described below.

For disinfecting purposes carbolic acid is generally used in watery solution, though powder containing it are sold. A 5 per cent solution of crystallized carbolic acid in water is recommended for general use, for, although weaker solutions have been found efficient for destroying many nonspore-bearing bacteria, the conditions found in practice vary widely and in some cases hinder the action of the disinfectant. As carbolic acid dissolves slowly, the 5 per cent solution should be prepared with warm water, using care to see that all is dissolved before use. For disinfecting large surfaces a spray may be used and the disinfectant should be applied liberally. Garments or implements to be disinfected should remain in the 5 per cent solution for at least one hour.

The advantages of carbolic acid are: (1) It is reasonably effective for destroying nonspore-bearing bacteria. (2) its action is only slightly interfered with by albuminous substances. (3) It does not destroy metals or fabrics in a 5 per cent solution. (4) It is readily available at all pharmacies.

The following disadvantages may be mentioned: (1) It can not be depended upon to destroy the spores of such bacteria as anthrax and malignant edema. (2) It is expensive (the pure phenol costs approximately 75 cents per pound).

CRUDE CARBOLIC ACID.

Probably no substance is so widely used in this country as a household and farm disinfectant as crude carbolic acid, and at the same time there is probably no disinfectant that is so uncertain in its effect if used without a proper understanding of its nature. The commercial crude carbolic acid is one of the products of coal-tar distillation, and consists essentially of a mixture of coal-tar oils and so-called "cresylic acid" with little or no phenol. The oils are practically inert as disinfectants, but the cresylic acid, which is a mixture of cresols and similar homologues of carbolic acid, has very marked disinfecting power.

As crude carbolic acid depends almost exclusively upon the cresylic acid which it contains for its disinfecting power, it should not be employed unless the cresylic acid content is definitely known. Even then it must be regarded as of doubtful efficiency if the percentage of hydrocarbon oils is relatively very large, for the oil will prevent to a great extent the solution of the cresylic acid in water when this is mixed with the crude carbolic acid for use as a disinfectant. As is stated in the paragraph dealing with cresol, the cresylic acid is used in 2 per cent solution in water as a disinfectant. When crude carbolic acid is employed, the amount of acid which it contains should be known and the disinfecting solution should be made of such strength that it will contain 2 per cent of cresylic acid. This disinfecting solution or mixture is best applied by means of a spray pump, and while spraying the mixture should be well agitated in order that the oils containing undissolved cresols may be evenly distributed over the surface to be disinfected.

There are found on the market products which are sold as liquid carbolic acid, straw-colored carbolic acid, etc.; these, as a rule, contain from 90 to 98 per cent of cresylic acid and very little coal-tar oil. They are considered in the next section dealing with cresols.

CRESOL.

Cresol (tricresol, straw-colored carbolic acid, liquid carbolic acid), is derived from coal tar and is found in the trade in varying degrees of purity. The cresol of the United States Pharmacopœia is a colorless liquid, having a strong odor resembling that of carbolic acid. It consists of a mixture of three closely related bodies, all of which are superior to carbolic acid as disinfectants. The other grades of cresol usually contain a small percentage of impurities, and are sold as liquid carbolic acid, 95 per cent, straw-colored carbolic acid, etc. These usually contain from 90 to 98 per cent of cresol, and may be purchased under a guaranty to contain certain definite amounts of cresylic acid. Grades containing less than 90 per cent of cresylic acid are not so desirable as those of a higher degree of purity, as the coal-tar oils which are usually found in such products interfere with the solution of the cresols in water, as already stated.

The commercial cresols guaranteed to contain more than 90 per cent of cresylic acid are relatively cheap and well suited to the disinfection of cars, barns, and yards. For general disinfection a 1½ to 2 per cent solution of cresol in water should be used, allowance being made for the impurities when the cheaper grades are employed. Cresol is not easily soluble in water; therefore, in preparing solutions warm water should be used and care taken to see that all is dissolved before applying the solution. A 2 per cent solution of cresol is regarded as being a more efficient disinfectant than a 5 per cent solution of carbolic acid and should be applied in the same way.

Briefly the advantages of cresol are: (1) A 2 per cent solution of cresol is as efficient as a 5 per cent solution of carbolic acid. (2) It it not interfered with by albuminous substances. (3) It is cheaper than carbolic acid. (4) It does not destroy metals or fabrics in a 2 per cent solution. (5) It is more effective than carbolic acid for destroying spores of bacteria, such as anthrax.

The main drawback to the use of cresol is that it is not readily soluble in water, hence may be used in too weak solution unless great care is taken in the preparation of the solution.

COMPOUND SOLUTION OF CRESOL.

This preparation, known as liquor cresolis compositus, United States Pharmacopœia, is recognized as official by the last edition of the United States Pharmacopœia, and is a mixture of equal parts of cresol (U. S. P.) with a linseed-oil-potash soap. The mixture is a thick, dark, amber-colored fluid which mixes readily with water in all proportions to form a clear soapy solution. A very efficient disinfectant may be made from the commercial cresols or liquid carbolic acids of known strength by mixing these with the soap described in the United States Pharmacopœia under the heading Liquor cresolis compositus. When other than United States Pharmacopœia cresol is used a sufficient excess must be added to insure 50 per cent of actual cresylic acid in the mixture. Compound solution of cresol is recommended for use as a general disinfectant in a 3 to 4 per cent solution in water. In this strength it will accomplish the same results as a 1½ to 2 per cent solution of cresol and may be applied in the same manner as a 5 per cent solution of carbolic acid. It may be said in favor of the compound solution of cresol that it possesses all the advantages of cresol, and in addition is far more readily soluble. It is, however, somewhat more expensive than cresol, owing to a stronger solution being required; this is in great measure compensated for by its ready solubility.

CHLORINATED LIME (CHLORID OF LIME).

This substance is prepared by exposing slaked lime to the action of chlorin gas. It is a white powder which gives off a disagreeable odor of chlorin, and decomposes rapidly upon exposure to air. It can not be depended upon unless kept in hermetically sealed containers. It is prepared for use in the general disinfection of cars, pens, or refuse by mixing 6 ounces with a gallon of water. This is applied liberally, and infectious excreta must be mixed thoroughly with the solution to insure disinfection. Chlorinated lime is a powerful deodorant and is valuable for use in foul-smelling cesspools and similar places. As a disinfectant, chlorinated lime possesses no advantage over formaldehyde, carbolic acid, cresol, etc. It has, moreover, certain disadvantages, chief among which are uncertainty of strength and destructiveness to metals and fabrics.

BICHLORID OF MERCURY.

This is a white crystalline substance which is also known as mercuric chlorid and corrosive sublimate. It is usually prepared for use in the form of tablets with ammonium chlorid, which facilitates the solution of the bichlorid in water. The bichlorid is used in solution in water in a strength of 1 to 1,000, though solutions 1 to 500 may be employed with correspondingly quicker action on nonspore-bearing bacteria and much more effective action on the spores of bacteria. Bichlorid of mercury is a violent poison, and has the property of combining with albuminoids to form inert compounds. These facts necessarily limit its usefulness as a general disinfectant. It should never be used to disinfect excreta, or substances containing blood or serous fluids. Bichlorid solutions should not be kept in lead or tin vessels, or poured through lead pipes, as the mercury combines with these metals and injures them, besides affecting the germicidal efficiency of the solution itself.

The chief advantage in the use of bichlorid of mercury lies in its great germicidal power when employed under proper conditions. The disadvantages are its poisonous nature, its tendency to attack certain metals, and the interference by albuminoids and other organic substances.

DETAILS OF DISINFECTION.

In the practical work of disinfection there are three essentials: (1) A preparation of the building that will facilitate reaching organisms of disease. (2) A disinfectant which upon contact can be depended upon to destroy such organisms. (3) A method of applying the disinfectant that will assure the most thorough contact with the bacteria.

Preparation of Building.—Before beginning the use of a disinfectant it is essential that certain preliminary work be done in and about the stable that is to be treated. The various surfaces, such as ceiling, walls, partitions, floors, etc., should be swept until free from cobwebs and dust. Any accumulation of filth should be removed by scraping. In some cases the woodwork may have become softened and so porous as to be a good medium for the absorption of disease germs. Such woodwork should be removed, burned, and replaced with new material.

All refuse, manure, etc., from stable and barnyard should be removed to a place inaccessible to live stock and, if possible, be burned or thoroughly mixed with a solution of chlorid of lime in the proportion of 6 ounces to 1 gallon of water. If the floor is of earth, it will doubtless have become stained with urine and contaminated to a depth of several inches. In such cases 4 inches or more of the surface soil should be removed and treated as above suggested for refuse and excreta. All earth removed should be replaced with soil from an uncontaminated source, or better, a new floor of concrete may be laid, this being the most durable and sanitary material for the purpose.

Selection and Preparation of the Disinfectant.—Having made ready the field of operation, the next consideration should be the se-

Cow Dying from Infestation by the North American Fever Tick.
(Original) Y. B 1910.

A Dangerously Tuberculous Cow. Dept. of Agr.

lection and preparation of the disinfectant. The fact must not be overlooked that many agents used for the destruction of bacteria are likewise poisonous to animals and man. In fact, some drugs, although powerful as germicides, are so poisonous as to preclude their general use in the work of disinfection. Among such, as previously stated, is bichlorid of mercury, which possesses the power of destroying not only bacteria, but spores as well. It is therefore essential in deciding upon an agent to select one having a known germicidal strength, properties of solubility, and at the same time possessing a reasonable degree of safety to animals and man.

All things considered, it is probable that some of the coal-tar products best fulfill these requirements. In this class is the compound solution of cresol, already mentioned, a preparation recognized as official by the United States Pharmacopœia and known as liquor cresolis compositus (U. S. P.). This preparation mixes readily with water and will prove a very efficient disinfectant. It should be used in the proportion of 4 or 5 ounces to each gallon of water.

Another favorable agent is cresol (commercially known as liquid carbolic acid). It is not as soluble as liquor cresolis compositus and should be thoroughly stirred during the process of mixing, which will be facilitated by using hot water. It is advisable to secure a grade of the drug with a guaranty of 95 per cent pure, and such should be used in the proportion of 2 or 3 ounces to a gallon of water.

As an accessory preparation and for use after the application of the disinfectant it may be advisable to make ready a lime wash to each gallon of which there has been added 4 ounces of chlorid of lime, or if it appears desirable to use the disinfectant and lime wash at one application, the following method may be followed in preparing 5 gallons: Slake 7½ pounds of lime, using hot water if necessary to start action. Mix to a creamy consistency with water. Stir in 15 fluid ounces of cresol (commercially known as liquid carbolic acid) at least 95 per cent pure, and make up to 5 gallons by adding water. In case compound solution of cresol (liquor cresolis compositus) is used, add 30 fluid ounces instead of 15 as in the case of cresol (liquid carbolic acid). Stir thoroughly. If to be applied through a spray nozzle, strain through a cloth or very fine wire sieve. Stir frequently when applying and keep covered when not in use. In case a large surface is to be disinfected it will be advisable to prepare a liberal amount of the disinfecting solution before beginning the application. Such solutions, however, should not be permitted to remain in receptacles which are accessible to animals.

Method of Application.—The efficacy and economy of the work will depend in a great measure upon the method of applying the disinfectant. Economy requires that the disinfecting solution be applied rapidly; efficiency requires that it be not only spread in such manner as to cover the entire surface requiring disinfection, but that sufficient quantity and force be used to drive the solution into all cracks and crevices.

Where a very limited surface is to be treated, as, for example one stall, it may be possible to apply the disinfectant in a satisfactory manner by means of a whitewash brush. In all cases, however the best method of applying the disinfectant and the lime wash i by means of a strong spray pump. Such should be equipped witl not less than 15 feet of hose, to which may be attached a 5-foot sec tion of iron pipe of the same caliber. With a spraying nozzle at th end of the pipe the operator will be enabled to proceed with th greatest possible dispatch and the least possible inconvenience.

The entire interior of the stable should be saturated with th disinfectant. Special attention should be given to the feedin troughs and drains. After this has dried the surface may be spraye with lime wash, provided this has not been combined with the dis infectant; and when this process has been completed it will be ad visable to open all doors and windows of the building for the ad mission of air and light.

DISPOSAL OF BODIES OF ANIMALS DYING OF CONTAGIOUS DISEASES.

The bodies of animals dying of contagious diseases are a men ace to the health of other animals, and even in some cases to that o man, if allowed to lie exposed above ground, and it has been foun that in case of certain very virulent diseases, like anthrax, ordinar burying is not an entirely effective safeguard. The germs of sucl diseases retain their virulence for many years, even in the soil, an are thus a constant source of danger. Of course if the disease bodies are left above ground or thrown into a ditch or stream th danger of disseminating the disease is increased many fold. Th most effective means that have been found for disposing of sucl diseased bodies are deep burying with free use of lime and burning

As Professor McDowell, of the Nevada Station, points out, th first method is probably best suited to small animals, like chickens which may be quite effectively disposed of by burying at least a foo deep with about one-half pint of caustic (unslaked) lime. Th second method (burning) Professor McDowell believes will in series of years prove the most thorough and satisfactory. The owne may not always be sure of the cause of an animal's death, but if it i completely destroyed by burning, no matter whether the cause o death is disease or accident, no chances are taken of transmittin disease either to man or animals. In absence of a furnace, o specially prepared place for burning, a hole or trench 2 or 3 fee deep may be dug, a layer of brushwood placed on the bottom, anc on this the body covered with brushwood sprinkled with kerosene Open-air burning of course requires more time and fuel than woul be necessary with a furnace. In a case cited by Professor McDowel the complete destruction of a 1,300-pound body required 5 gallon of kerosene oil, five-eighths of a cord of wood, and the time of tw men, each for 2½ hours.

A neighborhood organization for burning animals, with specia facilities, would, in all probability, decrease the cost of burning eacl animal.

When it is necessary to move a dead animal, either for burning or burying, it is safer, provided the animal died of any contagious disease, not to draw it out on the ground with the chances in favor of scattering disease germs, but to draw the animal on a cheaply made sled, or rock boat. If the animal is to be burned, the boat and all litter and bedding from the stall or yard where the animal has been kept should be burned also.

If the animals are burned in a specially made crematory, with one man doing the work by contract, then the sled or truck used in moving animals may be disinfected.

DISPOSAL OF DAIRY AND FARM SEWAGE.

The health of the public depends upon cleanliness. Since the dairy products of the United States stand first as a food, it is essential that they should be produced under the strictest sanitary conditions. With this in view it is our purpose to give a few suggestions as to the proper manner of disposing of farm sewage from the cow barn, milk house, dairy, and from the dwelling, or any other place that is closely situated to the dairy plant.

This matter is of greatest importance on dairy farms, for if conditions are kept filthy they very soon breed diseases which affect not only people who live on the farm, but consumers as well; for we now know that many diseases are transmitted through milk and other dairy products.

Where many cows are kept in small places, and where the population is large, sanitary improvements are most important to health and prosperity. Where fewer animals are kept and where the country is sparsely settled, sanitary precautions are not so necessary, for nature usually takes care of these conditions. In cities the sanitary conditions of homes and surroundings are chiefly maintained by a system of co-operation and centralization which brings into existence extensive sewage systems, water-supplies, and the collection of house waste by public authority. Rules are prescribed and enforced under which the individual household must avoid all such conditions which are likely to prove dangerous to the health of the immediate neighborhood, and to the entire community.

The principle underlying the disposal of the sewage on the farm should be essentially similar to that of the cities. The proper method of disposing the sewage on the farm eliminates a great many dangers which constantly face the farmer. One of the most serious dangers is contamination of the water-supply. If the water-supply on the dairy farm is contaminated it will be impossible to produce sanitary milk, since utensils washed in impure water will directly affect the milk. The cesspool, so common on dairy farms, quite frequently secures a direct connection with the well, especially if located near it, and thus contaminates the water. Polluted water comes from improper sewage disposal, and is generally infected from household excrements, barn-yard drainage, etc. Its use leads to bowel disturbances, typhoid fever, and dysentery, affecting man and beast alike. The health of large communities of people who draw their food supply from the country is in a measure dependent upon the healthfulness of the farming community. In fact, there is scarcely a city child whose health is not in a degree dependent upon the sanitary condition of the barn and house of the dairyman. Milk has frequently been shown to be the means of disease distribution.

With these conditions before us it is absolutely necessary to have a good sewage-disposal plant on every farm. Health cannot be measured by cost; for a small cost should not stand in the way to any great extent in erecting a plant that is effective for this purpose.

The average cow voids about 20,000 pounds of manure per year, of which approximately 9,500 pounds are liquid and 10,500 pounds solid. If the gutters are properly constructed the liquid manure will take care of itself and will reduce the labor one-half of what it would be were the liquid absorbed by some absorbent like straw and then removed with the solid excrements.

Liquid manure contains a high per cent of nitrogen, the most expensive part of a fertilizer. According to Snyder, liquid manure from cows fed a well-balanced ration contains about 89 per cent water and 1.2 per cent of nitrogen; solid manure contains 76 per cent of water and .5 per cent of nitrogen. This shows the comparative high value of liquid manure, which, on average farms, is allowed to flow into streams and pollute the same.

According to Woll, the value of manure from a cow for one year, fed on a well-balanced ration, is estimated at $29.97. This is a source of income for the farmer which is seldom taken into consideration because his conditions are such that he is not able to take care of it. By means of a proper sewage-disposal system the value of this manure may be fully recovered, besides making conditions on the farm more sanitary.

Manner of Disposing of Sewage.—The disposal of sewage is brought about by the decomposition of the organic matter. All sewage is largely organic matter and water. All organic matter decays. This decaying process is simply the disintegrating action of minute organisms known as bacteria upon the solid parts of the sewage, dividing the same into such a form that it becomes fluid. The superficial layers of soil from six to twelve inches are thoroughly innoculated with bacteria. The action of the bacteria upon any organic material is to reduce the complex organic compounds into simpler compounds. Hence, decay is the destruction of complex substances that have been built up by growth. There are certain kinds of bacteria that can penetrate organic substances to a slight extent only. Some must have air, particularly oxygen, to decay a portion of the mass, while there are other bacteria that have the power of decomposing organic material without the presence of air or oxygen. In the system herein described it is chiefly the last kind of bacteria with which we have to deal. The sewage discharges into a receptacle that is air-tight, known as a septic tank. This sewage is acted upon by these bacteria, which partially decomposes and liquefies the same. Most of the disagreeable odors are liberated by this process, and the liquid can then be discharged into an open stream with a great bulk of the running water, or into an irrigating system.

The process of decomposition in this septic tank is greatly aided by using a great quantity of water. This is an advantage on dairy farms, for water is used in abundance for washing utensils and cleaning the cow barns.

Plan of Disposing of Sewage After Liquefying.—As stated above, the sewage, after once being decomposed in a septic tank, can be discharged into a running stream or river without emitting offensive odors. This is the simplest way to dispose the sewage, but there are many farms which are not located so as to allow the sewage to be discharged into such a stream. For such a farm, in fact for every farm where it can be adopted, the disposal of sewage by irrigation is by far the best method. There are two methods used for irrigation: the surface method and the subsoil method. With the surface method liquid sewage is drained through glazed tile to a piece of ground set apart for this purpose. The ground is ridged and the sewage is allowed to flow over the ground in shallow channels. The liquid slowly disappears by filtering through the soil. Patches of ground that are wet must be carefully under-drained so as to allow the surplus water to be drained from the surface. This method of disposing sewage is objectionable from the standpoint that the sewage flows on the surface and animals crossing such fields may carry sewage on their feet, and if there are any disease germs in the sewage it may be carried from one place to another.

The safest method is sub-soil irrigation. This consists of a system of underground porous tile, laid so as to allow the sewage to seep through the tile. The tile are connected directly with a septic tank and laid so as to leave approximately one-eighth of an inch between each tile in order to allow the sewage to seep through the tile into the soil. The main line should consist of a five-inch tile, depending somewhat upon the sewage. If a great amount of water is used with sewage, four-inch tile may be used. The lateral drains may be four-inch tile, or if the main drain is a four-inch tile the laterals may be three inch. Nothing smaller than a three-inch tile should be used for this purpose.

For irrigation purposes tile should be laid from eight to sixteen inches beneath the surface of the ground, with a gradual incline of one or two inches for every one hundred feet. The depth to which these tile should be laid depends on the nature of the soil. There should be two systems for each septic tank. One of these systems should be laid below the frost line for winter sewage disposal, while the one laid shallow is used for summer disposal. By this method the sewage which is so objectionable on the dairy farm or in the creamery is removed and is used for irrigating and fertilizing purposes.

This surface method of sewage irrigation is particularly profitable for intensive farming and horticulture. The author knows of a number of instances where in one year such a system has paid for itself by the increased crop production which resulted from irrigating and fertilizing the soil. It is authentically stated that a horticulturist in Ohio has grown enough berries on his irrigated and fertilized soil in one year to pay for three such sewage disposal plants.

Construction of a Septic Tank.—There are numerous ways for building septic tanks. Such tanks may be built of any tank material, but for durability it is preferable to construct them of brick, stone, or concrete. The partitions may be built of concrete or wood. It is generally advisable to build them of concrete if convenient to do so. The tank should be built as nearly air-tight as possible, with a slight vent of one-half inch pipe to allow the gas to escape. There should be a trap door in the first compartment so as to allow the same to be cleaned when necessary. The partition should be built in such a way as to allow the water to be taken from the center of the tank, where the sewage is all liquid. The most of the solid particles of sewage either sink or float; consequently, by taking the sewage from the center of the basin only such liquid and particles as are of a semi-solid nature, or have the same density as water, are discharged into the second compartment. Decomposition is carried on still further in this compartment. When transferred to the third compartment it should be thoroughly liquefied. When transferred to the fourth compartment it is ready to be deposited into the irrigating system, where it is to be taken up by the soil. If the sewage is not to be utilized for irrigating purposes, but drained directly into a stream, the sewage may be taken from the top of the tank. In case the tank is to be cleaned, the plugs of the same systems may be removed and thoroughly drained. For irrigating purposes it is advisable to use a siphon. This siphon removes the water from the last compartment of the septic tank automatically at intermittent discharges. The discharge at one time of a quantity of sewage large enough to fill the irrigating system will scour the system of pipe; besides it more uniformly distributes the sewage throughout the whole irrigating system. Without a siphon, on pulling the plug occasionally the same effect can be secured, but if the sewage is allowed to overflow into the tile it will run out into the soil nearest to the septic tank. In the latter case the soil will become over-saturated with the liquid, and the purification of the sewage in the soil is thereby rendered imperfect.

Sewer Connection to Septic Tank.—Sewer connection from the cow barn to the septic tank should be constructed of not less than five-inch glazed sewer pipe, and preferably six-inch pipe. The sewer should be connected directly with the gutters and allowed to enter into a trap. This trap is a small box, in which a pipe bends down into the liquid to prevent the gases or odors coming from the septic tank from going into the stable. Similar traps should be put in when connected with the gutters of a creamery or cheese factory, or to the house or dairy house on the farm. The diameter of the sewer pipe from the house need not be more than four inches, and may connect with the same tile as that coming from the dairy barn.

The Size of Septic Tank and Irrigating System.—The size of the septic tank depends somewhat upon the amount of sewage run through the tank and the consistency of the sewage. For average conditions the last two compartments should hold the average discharge in twenty-four hours, and the irrigating system should be of equal capacity to hold the sewage from this compartment. However, the larger the tank the greater will be the chance for the organic matter to thoroughly decompose, and at the same time the irrigating system can be of greater capacity, irrigating a larger tract of land.

Necessity of Compartments.—Since the decomposition of the sewage depends upon the action of bacteria, it is essential in order to have the process go on effectively that the germs should not be disturbed to any great extent. Sewage, as a rule, when it comes from the house or dairy barn, runs into the tank with a rush, which has a tendency to roil the sewage in the tank. To overcome this sudden rush a partition should be put across the septic tank close to the inlet of the tank, which is supposed to prevent the disturbance in the second, third and fourth compartments. However, it is quite impossible to regulate the force of sewage in such a manner as to prevent any disturbance in the second tank. For this reason it is advisable to put a third partition in the tank, which will give the germs a chance to act thoroughly upon the sewage before it enters the discharge tank, or last compartment.

As the sewage travels from one tank to another it is gradually purified, and as it flows into the discharge tank all organic matter is in a liquid or semi-liquid state. At this point the sewage is practically deprived of any disagreeable odor, and that which is still retained is not objectionable. To prove the efficiency of this method of purification, sewage after passing through the tank, being thoroughly decomposed, can be kept for weeks at a very favorable temperature, showing no signs of the development of putrefactive odors. It should require from three to four days, however, for sewage to pass through this tank to thoroughly deodorize it. Three partitions in a tank, as described above, have proven very efficient. However, a tank with two compartments is very satisfactory, but in no case can a tank without compartments be recommended.

Location of Septic Tank.—There should be a slight fall from the stable to the septic tank, and from this tank to the irrigating system. A septic tank can be located as far as convenient, or as near as desirable, to the traps. This is a matter that depends upon conditions entirely. However, in all cases the inlet and outlet drains of the system, as far as the point of irrigation, should consist of sewer pipe with joints cemented. A preferable location for the tank is about a foot to eighteen inches in the ground. This prevents freezing, which checks decomposition. However, there are instances in which the slope of the ground from the stable to the irrigated field is so slight that the septic tank needs to be put above the ground. In that case it is advisable to cover the tank with earth, straw, or barn-yard manure, to prevent freezing.

Precautions.—Care should be taken that no strong disinfectant, such as corrosive sublimate, is allowed to be run into the septic tank from the stables or house, since any disinfectant prevents the action of the bacteria in the tank; consequently a large part of the sewage will remain in a solid form and the tank will soon fill up.

Cleaning Out the Tank.—The frequency of cleaning this tank depends entirely upon the kind of sewage discharged into the tank. All organic matter is readily decomposed and will flow through the tank, as has been stated before, but inorganic matter, such as sand, crushed rock, cinders, etc., cannot be decomposed and will remain in the same. If due precaution is taken in not allowing too much of this inorganic matter to flow into the tank, there is little need of cleaning it. For a cow barn such a tank need not be cleaned oftener than once in eight months. For creameries and cheese factories these tanks need not be cleaned oftener than once a year.

Siphon.—The siphon to be used in this tank for irrigating purposes can be purchased from any plumbing concern.

Cost of a Septic Tank.—The cost of a tank depends somewhat upon the locality and the price of material in that locality. The following estimate is based on average prices:

Cost of Round Tank (Four Compartments).

Digging	$ 4.00
Concrete and labor	21.00
Lumber, 200 feet of 2-inch plank, @ $30 per M	12.00
Posts, 4x4	.50
Labor	2.00
One 15-inch sewer-pipe	.75
Two 4-inch sewer-pipe bends	1.50
One 4-inch sewer-pipe	.50
One length of sewer pipe	.25
Total	$42.50

Cost of Rectangular Tank.

Concrete and labor	$24.20
Digging	4.00
Lumber	9.00
Labor	2.00
Two sewer-pipe bends	1.00
One 4-inch T	.50
Two 4-inch pipe	.40
Total	$41.10

RELATION OF WATER SUPPLY TO ANIMAL DISEASES.

Water is not a food within the strict meaning of the word, but it is necessary to the maintenance of animal life. It forms a part of every bone, muscle, nerve and tissue in the body, and in such large proportions that it aggregates nearly 60 per cent. of the total weight.

FIG. 1.—A TUBERCULOUS COW OF THE KIND NOT UNCOMMON IN DAIRY HERDS.

[With very few exceptions visibly tuberculous cows scatter enormous numbers of tubercle bacilli, through which their environment, to say nothing of the products from their bodies, becomes dangerous for man and beast.]

FIG. 2.—A VISIBLY TUBERCULOUS COW.

[As tuberculosis is generally a slow, chronic disease, which gives no external signs of its presence in cattle during its earlier stages, it may reasonably be assumed that visibly tuberculous cows have been affected with tuberculosis and have been dangerous disseminators of tubercle bacilli a long time. The propagation of tuberculosis depends absolutely upon the tubercle bacilli that are excreted by tuberculous animals and persons, and hence no tuberculous cow should

In young animals the per cent. is somewhat higher, and in old or very fat animals it is somewhat lower. Water is not only necessary because it is such an important component of the tissues, but also as an aid to digestion. Food can only be assimilated when in a soluble state, and hence a large quantity of water is required to carry on this physiological process.

It is not surprising that a relationship may exist between the water supply and disease. This relationship may exist in two ways; first, by not furnishing an adequate supply of water or not being accessible when needed; and second, by the water being the carrier of matter which may cause disease.

The quantity of water required by the different animals has not been determined for all conditions. The horse requires from sixty-four to eighty pounds, or eight to ten gallons per day, a gallon of water weighing eight pounds. Cattle drink more than horses. The Utah Experiment Station (Bul. 16) found that steers feeding upon dry feed required 83 pounds of water per day, while those fed upon green food consumed only 33 pounds per day.

Cattle drank 72 per cent. of water in the morning and 28 per cent. in the evening. We have conducted no experiments to determine the quantity of water required during the summer months.

No attempt has been made to determine the quantity of water needed daily for sheep, and I find no satisfactory tests recorded. Owing to the close grazing habits of sheep, they drink comparatively little water while upon pasture. They can endure privation as regards water far beyond other domestic animals. This has led to the common belief among farmers that sheep do not need water, and that the dew is sufficient. This is a serious mistake and accounts for the loss of many hundred lambs in this State every year.

The number of times an animal will drink during the day, when allowed full opportunity, is not known, but is indicated in a general way by the stomach. The stomach of the horse is small, and, as might be supposed, does not require much water at a time, but often. The stomach in cattle is very large, and rumination (chewing the cud) is performed. This necessitates saturating the food with water before rumination can take place, and probably explains why so much water is drunk in the morning.

The diseases which arise as a result of supplying water in insufficient quantities, or not providing water in accessible places, are sporadic in character, that is, affect only an occasional animal or a few in a herd or flock. Probably the most serious disease having such cause is mad itch in cattle. This occurs especially in the fall of the year, when the cattle are upon dry pasture, or when turned in upon a dry stalk field. It may occur at other times, and also be due to other causes, but without doubt, 90 per cent. of the cases occurring are directly traceable to this cause. Sheep also suffer from impaction and constipation, and large numbers die for want of proper water supply. Hogs, especially young ones, often succumb from like treatment. Horses probably suffer least loss, because they receive the greatest care in this respect, but no doubt many cases of colic, impaction and constipation are traceable to this source.

It is not the intent to give the symptoms or prescribe treatment for the diseases arising from an insufficient water supply, but to indicate that animals require large quantities of water, and that losses may be expected when not supplied in sufficient quantity or at the proper time. The remedy lies in prevention.

The losses that arise from an insufficient water supply are small compared with the losses that arise from supplying water of an improper character. Whether water will act as an agent for the carrying of the germs of disease, the ova, larvæ and special stages of parasites, will depend upon the source from which the water is obtained. If it comes from a deep well that is properly protected, these organisms will not be present. If it is obtained from the surface, as small ponds, ditches and streams, they may be present. Not all surface waters are dangerous, but all are more or less exposed to infection and may become dangerous at any time. The time it becomes dangerous can not be detected by the eye, and may not be detected by laboratory tests.

The earth acts as a filter for all germs that fall upon it, no matter what may be their character. Only a small per cent. will pass through the first inch of soil, and a very small number will pass through the first ten feet. In the first few feet of soil most disease germs are destroyed by the forms that inhabit it, but should they pass further down they are restrained only by the mechanical action of the earth. If, however, a soil becomes saturated with germs, as for example in a barn yard, or if the pollution is delivered below the surface, as in a cess-vault, little purification will take place, and the germs may find their way into nearby wells. In order to be certain of the water supply, wells should penetrate an impermeable layer of earth, and the sides be perfectly sealed, as with the iron tubular forms, so that no water can gain entrance except from below. A tubular well twenty feet deep, is a much deeper well, from a sanitary standpoint, than a dug well of the same depth. It is also true that a shallow well may produce pure water at one time and afterwards become contaminated because of the saturation of the soil with germs, either by the barnyard or vault.

Drs. Salmon and Smith came to the conclusion in their investigation of hog cholera, that perhaps the most potent agents in the distribution of hog cholera, are streams. They may become infected with the specific germ when sick animals are permitted to go into them, or when dead animals or any part of them are thrown into the water. They may even multiply when the water is contaminated with fecal discharges or other organic matter. Experiments in the laboratory have demonstrated that hog cholera bacilli may remain alive in water for four months. Making all due allowance for external influences and competition with the bacteria in natural water, we are forced to assume that they may live at least a month in streams. This would be time enough to inflect every herd along its course.—(Report upon Hog Cholera, Bureau of Animal Industry, 1889, p. 124.)

Some conception of the number of germs that are present in water and the filtering property of the soil may be obtained from the following. The quantity in each case is one cubic centimeter, or a half thimble full.

Source.	Number of germs per cubic centimeter.	
Very filthy hog wallow	2,680,000	
Ordinary hog wallow	730,000	1,420,000
Wabash river above LaFayette	12,000	32,000
Wabash river below LaFayette	112,000	390,000
Clean looking pond	290,000	
Filthy watering trough	248,000	
Stock troughs	5,000	21,000
Tile drains	8,000	
Six cisterns, without filters	5,000	91,000
Four cisterns, with filters	580	3,000
Dug well receiving surface drainage	420,000	
Dug well 14 feet deep in corner of unprotected barn lot	398,000	
Eight tubular wells 60 to 150 feet deep	4	16

A test upon the filtering properties of the soil is as follows:

Depth.	Number of germs.	Number of germs after a heavy rain.
Surface	518,400	312,000
1 inch	51,200	
2 "	28,800	
3 "	17,600	
4 "	17,600	
5 "	18,600	
6 "	13,200	47,500
8 "	8,000	
10 "	12,800	
12 "	5,200	16,000
18 "	10,400	
24 "	2,000	6,000
30 "	3,600	
36 "	4,000	4,300
42 "	3,600	
48 "	3,000	3,100
54 "	2,800	

The bacteria ordinarily found in water are not injurious, but the number present may always be taken as an index of its unwholesomeness. A larger number indicates that it is easy for contamination to occur, while a smaller number may be accepted as an evidence of difficulty for extraneous germs to find entrance.

If the larger streams have such a marked influence upon the percentage of loss along their courses, it is only reasonable to suppose that the smaller streams and ponds have a like effect. It is common practice to dig out a pond to receive the surface water from buildings and yards, to dam ravines and creeks, to catch the water from tile drains and springs for water for hogs. In such cases it follows that they receive only surface water. It is apparent then, that the first step to be taken in the prevention of hog cholera, is the securing of a wholesome water supply.

All animals are more or less subject to parasitic diseases, and the intestinal tract, owing to its relation to the food and water consumed, becomes the favorite seat of attack. Countless numbers of germs, eggs, larvæ, etc., enter with the food, but only a small part are in a proper state of development when they enter or they do not find suitable conditions for continuing life and therefore perish. Water plays a more important part as a carrier of parasites than does the food.

The life cycle of the parasites that affect animals, nearly always includes a stage of development outside of the body. Some parasites are passed out of the body as eggs. These hatch and after undergoing greater or less change, they may be prepared to again inhabit another animal. Some pass out, as larvæ, and after a certain time may infect an animal if taken in the stomach. A few require an intermediate host, as the liver-fluke, which infects the snail, and most tapeworms must usually pass one period of their existence in a different species of animal before they can again cause disease in another animal. Altogether the number of parasites which again find their way into another host, represent a very small per cent of the eggs produced. The eggs and larvæ of all these parasites contain a great deal of water and are easily killed by drying. Moisture is a necessary factor in their existence outside of the body, and hence it is that they are found in large numbers in surface water and are ingested (taken up) with it. Bacteria can stand drying better than parasites, but must have water in which to multiply. It follows then, that fewer parasitic diseases of stock will occur upon high pasture land when well water is furnished, than upon bottom land where they must depend upon a natural supply.

Among the most destructive parasitic diseases with which we have to contend, is the twisted stomach worm of sheep (*Strongylus contortus*). It is found especially on low lands along creek bottoms and around ponds. It affects sheep of all ages but is particularly fatal to lambs. In seasons of excessive rainfall it may occur upon any pasture, but in ordinary seasons it causes little damage except upon the low pastures. The eggs and embryos are passed from the sheep and fall with the droppings upon the pasture, and may be washed into the streams or ponds from which the sheep drink. Moisture is necessary for their existence outside of the body, and the dryer the pasture, the less the opportunity for conveying the parasite from one sheep to another. In seasons of heavy rainfall, when the grass is kept constantly wet, the danger may be mitigated to a certain extent by changing the sheep from one pasture to another every other day.

Another disease of sheep that is conveyed in the same way, is the nodular disease. It is due to a small worm, and while it does not manifest itself until winter, the time the infection is spread from one sheep to another is during the summer months.

Such parasitic diseases as paper-skin, liver-fluke and lung worm of sheep, and the worms in hogs, horses and cattle, are all conveyed in much the same way and are largely due to surface water. Pure water from deep wells is the prevention.

VENTILATION OF STABLES.

Abundance of sunlight and of fresh pure air is the basis of cure that has been adopted at modern consumptive sanitariums. The prevalence of tuberculosis among both cattle and men is to a considerable extent due to close confinement, for longer or shorter periods, in ill-ventilated and badly lighted rooms. Dark, close basement stables for cattle, and tightly-bottled-up dwellings for men, women, and children, are too often found in this and other countries.

Ventilation is a mattter more of accident than of plan in most of our houses and stables. As a consequence, the inmates are breathing the same air over and over again. This would be bad enough if every inmate of the house were perfectly healthy, for the products of respiration, even of a healthy animal, are a mild poison, which are, however, prevented from doing much harm by being more or less diluted. But when we remember not only that the expired breath of an unhealthy animal contains the usual constituent of carbonic acid, but that its presence is very likely to infect the air with the germs of disease as well, the necessity for frequently changing the air of occupied rooms is quite apparent.

In warm seasons, and in warm climates, the problem of ventilation is a comparatively easy one. We have only to throw open our dwellings to the action of the breeze, and the air is continuously changed. But in the wintry season, and in rigorous climates, the question is one of considerable complexity; for along with the demand for fresh air comes another more immediately urgent—the demand for warmth. In cold weather, these two requirements must necessarily conflict, and the one need is satisfied at the expense of the other. That being the case, we manage to have the more urgent need satisfied, and neglect the remoter necessity. We are more sensitive to cold than to impure air; and in order to secure a proper degree of warmth without too great cost, we are content to ignore the fact that we are breathing impurities.

The question of ventilation involves the question of temperature. We have not only to make provision for bringing fresh air into our dwellings, but we must warm it artificially after it is introduced. Therefore, ventilation, particularly for dwellings, is doubly expensive. We have to provide contrivances for renewing the air in houses and stables. That is one item of expense. In stables we have to guard against too great a reduction of temperature, and hence a system of ventilation in stables requires either careful watching or special appliances for warming the air. In houses, we generally expect to warm the incoming air by the consumption of a little more fuel. That is the second item of expense. It remains for us, therefore, to sit down and count the cost, whether we will put up with the dangers and inconveniences and discomforts of bad ventilation, or pay the charges for introducing and keeping up of a system of changing and purifying the air that we breathe in our dwellings, or that the animals under our charge breathe in their stables.

What Is Ventilation? Theoretically, perfect ventilation consists in removing the unwholesome products that are diffused through the air of occupied rooms, as rapidly as these products are formed. But perfect ventilation exists only in theory. Practically, we are satisfied if we can remove a certain portion of these products,—carbonic acid gas and moisture from the lungs,—and dilute the remainder to a definite standard, by mixing with pure fresh air. An ordinary test of a system of ventilation, is to determine the percentage of carbonic acid gas present in the air of the room, and compare this with the amount of the same constituent that is found in pure air. In any case, ventilation consists in removing certain portions of the air, and continually introducing fresh air. The rate at which this is done will fix the degree of completeness of the ventilating arrangements. For this constant removal and introduction of fresh air, certain forces operate, which forces depend upon certain physical principles. It is important that every man who is thinking of ventilating his house or stables, should understand these principles, in order that he may adapt the suggestions that are made in this pamphlet to suit his own circumstances.

The Problems in Ventilation.—The object to be gained in ventilation is the maximum quantity of fresh air. But with the introduction into a room of large quantities of fresh and generally cold air, we must guard against the possible consequences, viz., drafts, cold, and dripping or condensation of moisture within the room. The problems then are:

(1) To find a force that will keep the air in motion: removing foul air and bringing in fresh. (2) To introduce and distribute the air so as to avoid drafts. (3) To prevent the ventilated room from becoming too cold. (4) To prevent condensation of moisture in the room.

Natural Aids to Ventilation.—Under the first of the above mentioned heads, there are certain natural forces or tendencies in the gases of which air is composed, that aid in ventilating a room or stable. The first of these we shall consider under the head of Gravity.

Gravity.—When the air is warmed, it has a tendency to expand, and will do so if allowed. The result of the expansion is that it becomes lighter, bulk for bulk, than the cooler air. The warm air, as a consequence of its lighter weight, is displaced by the cooler air, and driven upward, on the principle that heavy bodies sink when immersed in fluids that are lighter than themselves. A stone when thrown on the top of water sinks to the bottom on exactly the same principle that cold air flows in underneath or falls down through warm air and forces the latter upward. This sinking of cold air and rising of warm air is called convection, and this convectional movement of air is one of the forces, if we may so speak, that operate in ventilating buildings. In an occupied room or stable, the heat from the bodies of the occupants warms the air and produces the upward tendency. If this tendency is encouraged so far as to allow the rising air to escape altogether, and if at the same time provision is made for the cooler fresh air to find its way into the room or stable, we have ventilation. Whether or not this convectional movement is a sufficient force to give satisfactory ventilation, is a question to be considered later. The second of these natural aids to ventilation is Diffusion.

Diffusion.—The air that we take into the lungs may contain but little water-vapor; and, if pure, it contains a very small percentage of carbonic acid gas. The latter is a chemical compound of carbon and oxygen. It exists in the free atmosphere in very small quantities—the average amount of which has been estimated at $3\frac{1}{2}$ volumes of carbonic acid gas in 10,000 volumes of air. On the other hand, the breath expired from the lungs is saturated with moisture, and contains between 4 per cent and 5 per cent of carbonic acid gas; or, to state it in the same form as above, in 10,000 volumes of expired air there are about 430 volumes of carbonic acid gas. The problem of ventilation is to prevent these two products—moisture and carbonic acid gas—from accumulating in excess within the occupied spaces. Aqueous vapor, at the same temperature and pressure, is lighter than air; carbonic acid gas is considerably heavier. It might be supposed, therefore, that when these products are emitted from the lungs, the aqueous vapor would raise to the ceiling, and the carbonic acid gas settle to the floor. There is a tendency to this movement; but, at the same time a process goes on which is equally as effective as the force of gravity. This process is known as diffusion. A simple illustration of diffusion may be seen by putting a few drops of milk into a glass of clear water. Soon the milk is seen to diffuse through the water, giving a uniform whitish shade to the whole. The same thing goes on with the aqueous vapor and carbonic acid gas. Instead of separating completely according to density, from the air of the room, these products diffuse throughout the whole room; so that wherever the foul air opening is placed, it will find almost uniform proportions of the products that ventilation is required to remove. If any difference, however, exists in the distribution of these gases, the excess of carbonic acid will be found at the floor; while that of water-vapor will be found at the ceiling.

Another aspect of diffusion is the movement of gases through porous walls. Suppose that the air of a room becomes overcharged with carbonic acid gas, and at the same time robbed of its oxygen; then the carbonic acid will diffuse outward through the plaster of the walls, and through the brick or between the clapboards; and the oxygen from the outside will in the same manner diffuse into the room. So that a natural ventilation proceeds at all times, even if the room appears perfectly air tight. This natural ventilation is, of course, most rapid in rooms that have the greatest amount of wall-space exposed to the free outside atmosphere.

A third natural aid to ventilation is the wind. When the fresh air inlets are on the windward side of the building, there will be no question about plenty of ventilation. But when the wind blows from the side opposite the inlets, there is little or no ventilation. To make free use of the wind, therefore, it is necessary, either to have inlets at all sides of the buildings, or to have inlets that always face the wind.

Under the second head, namely, distribution of fresh air in the stable, it is necessary to admit the air directly into the stable through a number of small openings rather than one large opening.

The third point, namely, temperature, constitutes a great difficulty in the ventilation of stables in winter. To introduce fresh cold air into a stable at any considerable rate and to draw off warmer air, necessarily cools the stable, and may cool it below the point of comfort and safety. Without artificial heating, the only safeguards against a temperature too low are: (1) A crowded stable, in which the animal heat given off is sufficient to warm large quantities of incoming air; hence the amount of ventilation may be, as it should be, in proportion to the number of animals in the stable. (2) A naturally warm, tight stable, which allows but little cold or drafts to enter the stable, other than by ventilating arrangements. (3) Shut-offs in the inlet and outlet pipes, so that the amount of ventilation can be controlled according to the temperature of the incoming air, the principle being to get as much fresh air as is consistent with a proper stable temperature—between 35° and 45°. (4) A sub-earth duct, by means of which the fresh air, before being admitted to the stable, is carried for some distance through an underground pipe, 6 feet deep or more. The earth temperature at that depth being much higher than that of the outside air, the air is warmed in passing through the duct, and enters the stable at a much higher temperature than it would if admitted directly. (5) Provision for drawing off the foul air at the floor, as an alternative to ceiling outlets. With floor outlets, the air drawn off is colder than that drawn off at the ceiling, and hence the stable is not chilled so much. Ceiling outlets, however, encourage a more rapid ventilation, and it is therefore advisable to provide both—by extending the foul air box to the floor, leaving the lower end open, and providing a flap in the box near the ceiling, to open or shut as is required.

The fourth problem in ventilation is to prevent dripping, or condensation of moisture in the stable. In an ill-ventilated stable, the moisture from the breath and from other sources often condenses on the cold ceiling or wells. In a well-ventilated stable, the moisture is carried off with the impure air before condensation can occur. There are two cases, however, in which ventilation is sometimes the cause of dripping. First, the moisture may condense on the pipes or boxes carrying the cold fresh air. This is more likely to occur if these pipes are at the ceiling of the stable, and especially if the cold air is admitted at the ceiling—the condensation occurring where the cold air comes in contact with the warm moist air at the ceiling. Sec-

Disinfecting Stable, B. A. I. 1902. (Whitewash Containing Disinfectants, After Being Mixed in a Half Barrel, Is Pumped Through Hose and Applied in Form of Spray.)

ondly, dripping may occur from the outlet boxes, especially if these are long. The preventives of dripping are generally a brisk movement of air, forcing the moist air out before condensation can occur; fresh air inlets at the floor; and outlet pipes as short and direct as possible.

SHOULD DAIRY COWS BE CONFINED IN STALLS?

It is considered axiomatic that the practices of any locality are approximately correct for that region. This, however, is not always the case, for man is by nature a great imitator and it seems natural for him to adopt such practices as he sees his neighbor pursuing. A striking example of this in dairy affairs is found in the little country of Holland, which is only about one-fourth the size of the State of Illinois. In the province of North Holland, the house and stable on each farm are built under one roof, while in the province of Friesland, only a few miles distant, the house and stable are always separate buildings connected by a covered passage. No reason can be given for this difference in construction as both provinces are intensive dairy districts, and the climatic conditions, the kind of cows, and the purpose for which they are kept, are practically the same in both provinces.

In our own country people travel about so freely that we have no such striking example as this in so short a distance, but the same thing exists nevertheless. In the dairy region in the northern section of Illinois the majority of dairy barns are equipped with low mangers and rigid stanchions, while in the dairy region of the southern part of the state practically all dairy barns have high mangers and the cows are tied with chains or ropes. There can be no possible reason for fastening cows differently and having the mangers of such different shapes in two sections of the same state. These examples simply show how prone we are to follow the customs of the community in which we live, adopting their methods and following them for years, apparently without a thought as to whether or not there is a better way.

This does not seem to be a wise policy when dealing with such a delicate animal as a fine dairy cow. Her food and care should be given most thoughtful attention and she should by all means be kept as long as she is profitable because of the great difficulty with which a good producer is obtained.

Three essentials to successful milk production are: 1. An excellent individual obtained by good breeding. 2. Feed of the proper kind and quality, supplied in a well balanced ration. 3. Care of the animal.

This discussion is devoted exclusively to the third essential. If the first two requisites are present in the highest degree and the last is not supplied, the efficiency that should be gained from a good individual, well fed, is largely lost. For this reason the care of the animal is of great importance. A cow that is a good producer does a large amount of work and since the milk is secreted from the blood and is such a delicate product, the cow must be properly cared for that the milk shall be in the best possible condition. To obtain such milk the cow must have an abundance of fresh air and light, as much comfort as possible, and a reasonable amount of exercise, not alone for humane reasons, but that she may produce the most that she as an individual is capable of on the food supplied, as this will mean more dollars and cents in the owner's pocket.

It is a well known fact that cows cannot endure as much exposure as steers and this has given rise to the too common practice of keeping dairy cows shut up in a tightly closed stable, cramped on a platform, and crowded among other cows with their heads fast in rigid stanchions for nearly twenty-four hours in the day for six or eight months in the year, usually with no system of ventilation and with very little light.

The existing state of affairs led to an investigation concerning the best method of keeping dairy cows. The question is: Are we caring for our cows in the best manner possible and if not, how can present methods be improved?

Keeping cows properly in a stable, involves much labor as each cow must be handled and treated individually. Since some dairymen who were known to be allowing their cows the freedom of a closed shed or covered barnyard, using the stable for milking only, were so well pleased with the system, an effort has been made to get the views of as many as possible who have had experience in keeping cows in this manner.

To the question, What are the chief advantages of keeping dairy cows in this way over ordinary stabling? answers are given in full below.

1. It saves labor in cleaning stables and in feeding roughage. Cows are kept more comfortable. As more bedding is required a greater amount of manure is made which is preserved in better shape.

2. Cheaper, as it saves labor, is cleaner, and the cows are more healthy.

3. Saves labor in handling manure, in bedding stock, and in feeding roughage. The stock has access to water at all times and is kept much more comfortable.

4. A larger amount of manure is made and preserved in better condition. By containing much straw all liquid manure is absorbed and when applied to the land, humus is added to very great advantage. The system is good only where straw is abundant that can be so utilized. If the straw is limited in amount the system would be a filthy one and if the herdsman is negligent or careless the cows will become more or less filthy. With a careful man and reasonable attention the system works exceedingly well. We are so well pleased with it that we have no thought of making a change.

5. This method saves a great deal of labor as it is more convenient and there is little stable cleaning to be done. The cows are free, comfortable, and more healthy, giving the owner greater profit.

6. Saves labor in keeping stable clean.

7. The greatest advantage is the saving of labor. One man can handle forty cows except milking. Cows are more healthy and con-

tented. Manure is worth more as all the liquid is absorbed by the bedding and the whole is thoroughly mixed together. The manure has to be handled but once and that may be done at any time most convenient and when no injury is done the land by tramping.

8. From my point of view and experience the chief advantages are: Freedom and ease for the cows in getting up and lying down without having to do so in cramped quarters, the saving of labor in bedding and cleaning stables besides avoiding the necessity of hitching up and hauling out the manure every day. We have a large watering tank which is fed by an underground pipe and from the windmill pump. The tank is incased on the sides and ends with sawdust space and a cover is used in very cold weather when the windmill is not running, which keeps the water from freezing. I have seen cows go to the tank at nine or ten o'clock at night and drink heartily and then lie down. This will be done more frequently than we have any idea unless we watch. It is this freedom to supply any want, with comfort and kindly handling that increases the production and I think makes better milk.

We have a lot adjoining the shed where the cows are allowed to pass out as they wish in pleasant weather to enjoy a sun bath for a few hours. We use the same lot for the cows at night in summer where they may lie and enjoy the cooler air, or if they wish they can crop a little grass in the pasture adjoining.

I know of no way we can save so much manure. Straw with us is abundant and can be used in this way to add to the comfort of our live stock as well as the fertility and better condition of the soil. I venture to predict that the time will come when many of our best farmers will care for their cattle in covered sheds.

9. I consider the chief advantages to be: the sanitary condition of the milking stable, the saving of labor in the more economical handling of manure and feeding of roughage, and, most important, the health of the herd.

10. The advantages of this system are that it saves labor in watering stock and in stable cleaning; the manure can be hauled out at any time or it can be left until needed without waste. The shed is a good place to feed fodder corn or sheaf oats, as the pigs get the shatterings and the refuse may be used for bedding. What long stalks are thrown out of racks have never been noticed in the manure. A water tank with good float valve affords the cows access to water at all times, and the shed is a good place for the cows during the first cold rains in fall.

11. By this method we have cleaner cows and increased milk flow; we save labor in cleaning stables, and in hauling out manure; and the fertility in the manure is preserved more completely.

12. I consider that the chief advantages are, saving of labor in feeding and in double handling of manure; freedom from weather exposure, thus keeping coats dry; giving exercise, which prevents restlessness; and keeping cows and milking stable clean.

13. I consider the chief advantages to be the comfort and cleanliness of the herd and the saving of labor.

14. In any case the closed shed most assuredly saves labor, for the cows do not require so much grooming and there is less work in handling manure. The cows are certainly more comfortable in the shed and what favors the health and comfort of the cows favors the production of milk. I believe that I had two cases of abortion caused by keeping the cows too much in the stanchions.

15. The advantages are saving of labor in cleaning stables, bedding cows and feeding roughage; cleanliness; allowing cows more exercise; and preserving the manure in much better condition.

16. This method saves a great deal of labor in feeding and in stable cleaning and the cows are more at their ease. The same cows in a pen soon become used to each other and never make trouble after being handled in this way for a little time, each one almost invariably stands in the same place while eating. When cows are kept in this way the value of the manure is nearly double as the liquid is saved and no leaching takes place.

17. Our cattle are cleaner than any herd of stalled cattle I ever saw. A soiled cow is a rare sight in our herd. By this method we have increased milk yield and greater healthfulness; have not had a case of milk fever since our dairy started. We consider the system a success.

18. The advantages are, cleanliness, health of the herd, and saving of labor.

The improvement in the capacity for production in cattle has been accomplished through selective breeding, with the production object principally in view, and chest development secondarily considered.

The aim must be directed towards the correction of the system of stabling so that the added features of exercise, fresh air and changing temperatures, will tend to overcome this evil.

It was with a full realization of the benefits obtained in the treatment of human tuberculous patients, that the Maryland Experiment Station planned several years ago the type of stable in use at that place.

The actual plan of stable is of course not material, as long as the principles and practices are similarly carried out; however, reference is made to this structure because it has been in operation long enough to demonstrate its practicability.

OPEN STABLE.

The stable is of solid concrete construction, with slate roof. The stabling portion is 36x58 feet, and the milking room annex 10x30 feet outside measurements.

The walls of the milking room are 12 inches thick of solid concrete, and 9 feet high. Into this room two doors enter from the stable, and one from the outside. It contains four windows 3x3½ feet hinged at the bottom which open inward at the top to 9 inches, and are protected along the sides by galvanized iron cheeks to prevent direct air currents upon the cows and milkers. There are also two 6x18 inch flues in the walls for purposes of ventilation. The floors are of concrete, and slope towards the traps for proper drainage.

The walls of the stabling portion of the building are of 12 inch solid concrete, but only 4½ feet in height. There are two 8 feet openings in the ends, protected by solid gates, and two four feet openings on one side, protected likewise by solid gates. The floor is of concrete and practically level, a slope to the drain being provided should it be found necessary to wash off the floors.

On the top of the outside wall are set 8x8 oak posts properly placed for the support of the plates carrying the roof; and near the corners anchor irons, with turnbuckles, are let into the concrete wall and plates for properly securing the superstructure. The ordinary roof construction is used for closing in the top.

This, it will be observed allows an open space 3 feet 6 inches high around the entire building, with the exception of that occupied by the milking room. There are no blinds, sashes nor curtains to interfere with the free circulation of air and perfect light is had in all parts.

There is a double row of racks built across the stable which divides the room into two compartments 23x34 feet and 33x34 feet respectively. In the 23x34 feet end is a watering trough and hydrant. —(Md. E. S. Rept.)

The capacity of this stable is about twenty-five head of milch cows. The management of these differs from that of cows in closed stables.

The cows are not tied, and are free to move about in the entire enclosure. The racks are kept supplied with the coarse feed, ensilage, roots, etc., to be consumed at their pleasure. Drinking water, too, is accessible at all times.

When ready for milking, all the cows are driven into the smaller compartment and the gates closed. The door to the milking room is opened and sufficient cows are allowed to pass in to fill the stalls. These eat their grain and are milked. They are then let into the larger compartment, and others enter. This is continued until all are milked, when the center gates are opened and the free run of the stable is given until the next milking time.

It is anticipated that objections will be raised to the practice of feeding grain at milking time, but as before stated it is not material that the exact plan and method of feeding be followed so long as the following points be observed, and these are regarded as vital.

1. Air, light and changing temperatures must be supplied as freely and unrestricted as outside conditions will furnish.

2. Food should be plentifully supplied and accessible at all times.

3. Water should be always available.

4. Cows should not be tied except in the milking room.

The reasons for the first requirement have been previously stated.

Accessibility to food and water, constantly, smacks of Fletcherism but it is recommended because it is a natural condition, and cows do well as a result. Pasturage does not produce the largest milk returns solely because of the palatability, succulence and character of the food afforded. It is because food and water being constantly available are naturally consumed and digested under conditions of freedom and abundance of air and light. Probably the greatest criticism against such a practice will be directed at the suggestion for exposure to extreme winter temperatures. The popular notion that "to get milk you must have warm stables" is as fallacious actually, as it has proven pernicious practically. In order to show the results of a severe winter's exposure the following table is presented:

TABLE

	1908 October	1908 Nov.	1908 Dec.	1909 Jan.	1909 Feb.	1909 March	
	Lbs. milk	Lbs. milk	Lbs. milk	Lbs. milk	Lbs. milk	Lbs. milk	
143	674[8]*	614[4]	566[8]	476[6]	359[7]	289[8]	Note—These cows were kept in the open stable, but averaged 3½ hours daily in closed stable when they were milked.
144	665[4]	684[5]	719[6]	669[7]	569[8]	623[9]	
145	687[8]	682[4]	567[8]	509[6]	870[7]	841[8]	
146	....	....	....	593[1]	581[2]	609[8]	

	1909 October	1909 Nov.	1909 Dec.	1910 Jan.	1910 Feb.	1910 March	
Max. Temp.	....	76° F	62° F	51° F	60° F	....	
Min. Temp.	....	24° F	5° F	7° F	5° F	....	
143	1971*	989[2]	980[8]	928[4]	825[5]	844[6]	Note—The same cows as above, but were kept in the open stable, and milked in the milking room of same.
144	2511[10]	1421[17]	209[1]	903[8]	950[8]	783[4]	
145	917[1]	1041[8]	1001[8]	883[4]	755[8]	796[6]	
146	57[10] } 84[1]	865[8]	742[8]	600[4]	491[5]	479[6]	

	1908 October	1908 Nov.	1908 Dec.	1909 Jan.	1909 Feb.	1909 March	
91	542[8]*	520[4]	586[8]	689[6]	553[7]	600[6]	Note—Kept in closed stable.
106	....	....	282[1]	562[2]	516[8]	556[4]	
110	....	86[1]	385[8]	472[8]	488[4]	553[5]	
113	....	25[1]	490[8]	476[8]	454[4]	500[8]	
123	1174[8]	1177[8]	1240[4]	1169[5]	1021[0]	1048[7]	

*Small figures refer to month of milking period.

TABLE (Continued)

	1909 October	1909 Nov.	1909 Dec.	1910 Jan.	1910 Feb.	1910 March	
Max. Temp.	....	76°F	66°F	60°F	72°F	......	
Min. Temp.	....	48°F	32°F	37°F	34°F	....	
91	543[3*]	510[4]	489[5]	369[6]	....	....	Note—Kept in closed stable.
106	817[11]	291[12] / 261[1]	585[2]	459[3]	446[4]	469[5]	
110	349[12]	250[13]	177[14]	58[15]	252[1]	889[2]	
113	472[1]	783[2]	729[3]	657[4]	555[5]	605[6]	
128	616[14]	101[15] / 487[1]	1208[2]	1016[3]	....	....	

*Small figures refer to month of milking period.

Attention is called to the fact that cows 143, 144, 145 and 146 were kept in the open stable during the winter of 1908-9, but were milked in the closed stable. By this arrangement the cows spent the night in the open stable and were brought into the warm closed stable early in the morning to be grained and milked. They averaged about 2½ hours in the warm stable in the morning after which they were again placed in the open stable. In the afternoon they averaged about 1½ hours in the closed stable, before returning to the open stable for the night. This unnatural and sudden change of temperature, probably had some effect in keeping their milking record lower for the winter than they would have shown, had they been confined in either one or the other of the stables regularly.

LIST OF PUBLICATIONS ABRIDGED ABOVE.

Special Report on the Diseases of Cattle: U. S. Department of Agriculture, Washington, D. C.

Veterinary Materia Medica for Farmers: Virginia Agricultural Experiment Station Bulletins 8 and 10, Vol. III.

Practical Methods of Disinfecting Stables: U. S. Dept. Agr., Farmers' Bulletin 480.

Some Common Disinfectants: U. S. Dept. Agr., Farmers' Bulletin 345.

Disposal of Bodies of Animals Dying of Contagious Diseases: U. S. Dept. Agr., Farmers' Bulletin 190.

Sanitary Conditions in the Home and on the Farm: South Carolina Agr. Exp. Station Bulletin 89.

Disposal of Dairy and Farm Sewage, and Water Supply: Kansas Agr. Exp. Station Bulletin 143.

The Relation of Water Supply to Animal Diseases: Purdue Univ. Agr. Exp. Station Bulletin 70, Vol. IX.

Ventilation of Farm Stables and Dwellings: Ontario Agr. Col. and Exp. Farm Bulletin 119.

Should Dairy Cows Be Confined in Stalls? Univ. of Ill. Agr. Exp. Station Circular 93.

Tuberculosis of Animals: Maryland Agr. Exp. Station Bulletin 145.

The Burning of Dead Animals: Nevada Agr. Exp. Sta. Bulletin 53.

DISEASES OF THE DIGESTIVE SYSTEM.
THE MOUTH.

Wounds and Contusions of the Lips, and Snake Bite.—The lips may become inflamed from contusions, which are sometimes produced by a blow from the horns of another animal, or, in the case of working oxen, by a blow from the driver. While cattle are grazing they may be bitten in the lips by either insects or serpents, more especially when they are pastured in woods.

Symptoms.—As a result of a contusion the lips become thick and swollen, and if treatment is neglected the swelling may become hard and indurated, or an abscess may form. This condition renders it difficult for the animal to get food into its mouth, on account of the lips having lost their natural flexibility. In such cases an ox will use his tongue more in the prehension of food to make up for the incapacity of the lips. In cases of snake bite the swelling is soft or puffy and its limits are not well defined.

Treatment.—When we have to deal with a bruise, the affected part should be bathed with hot water two or three times daily. In recent cases no other treatment will be required, but if the swelling is not recent and has become hard or indurated, then the swollen part should be treated each day by painting it with tincture of iodin. In snake bite a straight incision penetrating into the flesh or muscle should be made across the center of the swelling and in the direction of the long axis of the face. After this has been done a small wad of cotton batting should be pressed against the wounds until the bleeding has almost stopped. Afterwards the following lotion may be applied to the wounds several times a day: Permanganate of potash, half a dram; distilled water, 1 pint. As snake bites are usually attended with considerable depression, which may terminate in stupor, it is advisable to give doses of whisky at intervals. Half a pint of whisky mixed with a pint of water should be given, and the dose should be repeated in half an hour if the animal is sinking into a stupefied and unconscious condition. The repetition of the dose must depend on the symptoms which the animal shows. It must be borne in mind that the object of treatment is to ward off the stupor, which is one of the results of snake bite, and that in administering whisky the object is to produce a stimulating and not an intoxicating or stupefying effect. The swelling from an insect bite should be bathed as soon as noticed with ammonia water and then treated with frequent applications of hot water.

Salivation.—Salivation is a symptom of some general or local disorder. It may be a symptom of a general disease, such as rabies or the foot-and-mouth disease, or it may be a purely local trouble, as

FIG. 1.—THREE TUBERCULOUS COWS.

[The one in the center of the picture expels tubercle bacilli from her bowels and probably also from her mouth. The visible condition of the cows is better than that of most dairy cattle; they show no observable symptoms of the disease with which they are affected. Such cows, because of the germs they scatter, are a source of great danger to other animals, and the use of their milk, either as a beverage or in the form of other dairy products, is a menace to public health.]

FIG. 2.—A DANGEROUSLY TUBERCULOUS COW.

[Notwithstanding her excellent bodily condition and bright appearance she is known to expel tubercle bacilli with the ejecta from her bowels and probably also does so with the material slobbered from her mouth. She shows absolutely no symptoms of disease; at the time her picture was taken she had been known to be tuberculous about two years. The enormous tuberculous masses sometimes found on post-mortem examination in the bodies of cows similar to the one in this picture cause great surprise, and demonstrate that life and apparent health can be maintained under extremely adverse conditions that are of slow and gradual development, like tuberculosis or consumption.]

when copious secretion of the salivary glands is produced by the eating of irritating plants, such as wild mustard. In cases where saliva is observed to dribble from the mouth, that part must be carefully examined by introducing an instrument like a balling-iron into the mouth, or, if such an instrument is not at hand, by grasping the tongue and partially withdrawing it from the mouth, and by placing a block of wood between the back teeth, while all parts of the mouth are exposed to a good light, so that the presence of any foreign substance may be detected. The cause will sometimes be found to depend on a short piece of wood becoming fixed on the palate, its two ends resting on the upper molar teeth of each side; or it may depend on a needle, thorn, or splinter of wood becoming embedded in the tongue. Sometimes a sharp piece of tin or other metal may become partially embedded in the inner surface of the cheek. Hay occasionally possesses some quality, usually dependent upon its having heated in the mow or having become moldy, which produces salivation. Second-crop clover and some irritant weeds in the pasture or forage may cause salivation. Cattle rubbed with mercurial ointment may in licking themselves swallow enough mercury to bring about the same result. (See Mercury Poisoning.) Such cases, of course, arise from the constitutional action of mercury, and indicate the danger of using such a preparation externally on account of the common habit which the animals have of licking themselves. Mercury is also readily absorbed through the skin, and, as cattle are very susceptible to its action, it is thus easy for them to be poisoned by it even without licking it from the surface.

Treatment.—If salivation depends on the irritation and inflammation set up by the ingestion of acrid plants, or forage possessing some peculiar stimulating property, the food must be changed and a lotion composed of an ounce of powdered alum dissolved in a quart of water may be syringed into the mouth twice a day, using half a pint of the solution each time. If, however, the salivation depends on the presence of a thorn, splinter of wood, or any other foreign substance embedded in the cheek or tongue, remove the offending object and wash the mouth occasionally with a weak solution (2 per cent) of carbolic acid and tepid water. When salivation is produced by mercurial poisoning or by the foot-and-mouth disease, the treatment appropriate to those general conditions of the system, as well as the local treatment, must be applied.

The Changes Which Take Place in the Teeth of Cattle with Age. —Owing to the character of the teeth of the ox, as well as the somewhat less importance of determining their exact age, the same exactness has not been, and, it may be said, can not be carried to the same degree of perfection as with the horse. However, as will be seen, there are certain periods of the life's cycle that can be more or less definitely determined by the teeth of the ox.

The teeth of the ox are thirty-two in number, twenty-four of which are molars, arranged as in the horse, and eight incisors, belonging to the lower jaw. The latter are replaced in the upper jaw by a thick cartilaginous pad, covered by the mucous membrane of the mouth. This pad forms the gum and furnishes a bearing for the incisors of the lower jaw.

Sometimes, as in the horse, there are found supplementary molars, which, if four in number, will make up the whole to thirty-six, though they are never all present at the same time, as the supplementary ones are shed before the molar dentition is completed. The composition of the teeth of the ox is the same as those of the horse, the only difference being in the arrangement of the several substances.

Incisors.—The incisors, eight in number, are placed like a keyboard at the extremity of a kind of rounded shoulder bone by which the lower maxillary bone terminates; forming around the point a perfect circle, when they have acquired their full development. Instead of being fixed in the alveoli, they possess a certain degree of mobility, sometimes mistaken for a diseased condition. This is necessary in order to prevent their wounding the cartilaginous pad of the upper jaw, against which they press.

They are divided, according to their position, into two centrals, two first laterals, two second laterals, and two corner incisors. Each incisor offers for consideration, two parts; one free, the other incased, the root, and separated by a very marked constriction, the neck. This arrangement gives to the tooth the form of a shovel, the root representing the handle.

The free portions of the incisors are flattened above and below, and are thinnest and widest towards their anterior extremity, and present two faces, an inferior or external, and a superior or internal; also three borders, an anterior and two lateral. The external face, slightly convex, and of milk-white color, is covered with fine, undulating striæ, which disappear with age and leave the surface beautifully polished. The internal face, flatter than the external, presents in its middle a slight conical eminence, whose base widens and is terminated near the free extremity of the tooth, while its sides are circumscribed towards each border by a well-defined groove. The two lateral borders (the internal slightly convex in its length, the external slightly concave in the same direction), make the free portion appear as if it were thrown outwards. The anterior border is sharp and slightly convex from one side to the other; it is the first part of the tooth which is destroyed by wear. The root is rounded, slightly conical, and implanted in the alveolus which is of the same form. In youth, it shows at its extremity an opening communicating with an internal cavity, analogous to that in the teeth of the horse, and prolonged into the interior of the free portion. In the virgin tooth, the enamel forms around the free portion a continuous layer, thinnest on the internal surface, and extending very scantily over a part of the root.

The dentine forms the remainder of the organ, and the (pulp) cavity, which is originally a large space of the same form as the tooth, is filled, as the animal grows old, by a new dentine, which, as in the horse, has a yellower tint than the primitive ivory. When the cavity is completely filled, the tooth ceases to grow, and is not pushed beyond the alveolus during wear, as is the case with the teeth of the horse.

The incisor tooth has scarcely arrived at its perfect development before it begins to be worn. Its horizontal position, and its coming in contact with the pad on the upper jaw, exposes the anterior border and superior face to friction and consequent wear from before to behind. The wear, therefore, chiefly affects its upper face, which really forms the table of the tooth, and which is designated the Avale. When use has worn away the conical eminence and the grooves bordering it, the tooth is levelled. As wear goes on, there appears at first, and at the extremities of the tooth, a yellow band, which is the dentine denuded of its enamel; and later, in the dentine, a yellower transverse band shows itself. With increase of wear, this contracts, then widens, and finishes by forming a mark nearly square, and then round, which is the recently formed dentine that fills the pulp cavity of the tooth. It is a veritable dental star, analogous to that in the horse's teeth, and varying in form according to the incisor in which it appears.

In proportion as the teeth are used, they seem to separate from one another, although they still remain in the same place. This is because these teeth, in use, only touch each other by their extremities, and as they become worn they decrease in width, and are necessarily separated to an extent varying with their degree of wear. Finally, when the tooth has reached its last stage of wear, there only remains the root, the upper portion of which, becoming apparent by the retreat of the gum, stands as a yellow stump, very distant from those which form with it the remains of the incisive arch.

The first incisors (milk teeth) of the ox, like those of the horse, are all deciduous or temporary, and differ from those which replace them by their smaller volume, less width, the transparency of their enamel, and their being more curved outwards. Their roots are much shorter, and are destroyed by the succeeding teeth. The two temporary centrals are always separated by a marked interval, depending on the thickness of the fibro-cartilage in the maxillary symphysis during youth.

Molars.—As in solipeds, the molars are six in number in each side of each jaw, but are much smaller and form a much shorter arch. Their reciprocal volume is far from being uniform, as in the horse, but goes on augmenting from the first to the sixth, and to such a degree that the space occupied by the three anterior molars is only about one-half of that required for the three posterior ones. The last molar alone occupies nearly four times as much space, lengthwise, as the first.

Their wearing surface, constructed on the same system as that of the horse's molar, presents eminences a little more acute. The arrangement of their three constituents is in principle as in the latter animal. As in the horse, the three front molars are deciduous or temporary. The period of dentition is as follows:

Incisors.

Centrals ....Before or some days after birth.
First Laterals...........Before or some days after birth.
Second Laterals......................Fourteen days.
Corners...........................Two to three weeks.

Molars.

First...................Before or some days after birth.
Second.................Before or some days after birth.
Third..................Before or some days after birth.
Fourth.............................Six to nine months.
Fifth............................Two and a-half years.
Sixth..............................Four to five years.

The replacements are as follows:

Incisors.

Centrals ....One and a-half years.
First Laterals....................Two and a-half years.
Second Laterals..................Three and a-half years.
Corners.........................Four and a-half years.

Molars.

First............................One and a-half years.
Second..........................Two and a-half years.
Third..........................Three and a-half years.

The fourth, fifth, and sixth are not replaced.

As has been mentioned in the foregoing table, the calf is sometimes born with the nippers and first lateral teeth, or at least, they are out in the first eight days. Towards the twentieth day, the second lateral teeth appear, and at the end of the month the corners. However, the dental arch is not perfect, or round, or full, until five or six months. The wear of the teeth varies with the mode of feeding; in general, it may be said, that the milk nippers are worn at ten months, the first lateral teeth at one year, the second lateral teeth at fifteen months, and the corners at twenty months.

At this time the milk nippers, or centrals, are shed and are replaced by the permanent nippers, which are at their full growth at two years old.

From two and a-half to three years, the first milk laterals are shed and the permanent ones make their appearance.

From three and a-half to four years, the second lateral permanent incisors make their appearance.

From four and a-half to five years, the appearance of the permanent corners takes place.

From five to six, the jaw is full, and well rounded.

From seven to eight, the nippers or centrals are worn.

From eight to nine the laterals are worn.

At ten years the corners are worn.

At eleven, the teeth begin to become quite short and somewhat separated.

At twelve, the separation of the teeth is well marked, the dental star appears as a white band, and the teeth assume a square rubbing shape.

After this age the characters are only vague and approximative.

Irregularities of the Teeth.—Irregularities of the teeth may be occasioned by the unequal wearing of some of the teeth or by some of the incisors being broken, which may happen when cattle are pastured on sandy or gravelly soil. The molar teeth may also show irregular wear from similar causes, or from a disease or malformation of the jaw. Their edges may become sharp, or it may happen that a molar tooth has been accidentally fractured. It may also occur that a supernumerary tooth has developed in an unusual position, and that it interferes with the natural and regular mastication of the food.

Treatment.—The mouth may be examined by grasping the animal's tongue with one hand and partially withdrawing it from the mouth, so as to expose the incisor and molar teeth to inspection. When it is desired, however, to examine the molar teeth with the fingers, so as to obtain a more precise idea of their condition, and instrument like the balling iron which is used for the horse should be introduced into the mouth, so as to separate the jaws and keep them apart while the examination is being made. Any sharp edges of the molars must be removed by the tooth rasp, such as is used for horses. Any supernumerary tooth which interferes with mastication or any tooth which is fractured or loose should be extracted. In performing such operations it is desirable to throw, or cast, the animal, and to have its head held securely, so as to enable the operator to do what is necessary without difficulty.

Decay of the Teeth, Caries.—The presence of caries may be suspected if the mouth exhales a bad odor and if the animal occasionally stops during mastication as if it were in pain. The existence of caries in a molar tooth may be ascertained by examining the mouth in the manner already described. If one of the molars is found to be carious, it should be extracted. When the crown of the tooth has been destroyed and only the stump or root is left, extraction will be impracticable. In such cases it is best to sell the animal to the butcher unless it have special value, in which case the root stumps may be removed by a veterinarian by the operation of trephining.

SORE MOUTH (MYCOTIC STOMATITIS).

The name stomatitis signifies that there is present in the affected animals an inflammation of the mucous membrane of the mouth. This inflammation, which quickly develops into ulcers, is one of the principal and most frequently observed lesions. Mycotic stomatitis refers to that form of stomatitis which results from eating food containing irritant fungi.

Character of the Disease.—Mycotic stomatitis is a sporadic, noninfectious disease which affects cattle of all ages that are on pasture, but more especially milch cows. It is characterized by inflammation and ulceration of the mucous membrane of the mouth, producing salivation and inappetence, and secondarily affecting the feet, which become sore and swollen. Superficial erosions of the skin, particularly of the muzzle and of the teats and udders of cows, may also be present, with some elevation of temperature and emaciation.

Cause.—This disease, as its name indicates, results from the eating of forage containing fungi or molds. It is probable that more than one fungus is involved in the production of this disease, but no particular species has been definitely proved to be the causative factor.

Symptoms and Lesions.—Among the first symptoms observed in mycotic stomatitis are inability to eat, suspension of rumination, frequent movements of the lips with the formation of froth on their margins, and in some cases a dribbling of saliva from the mouth. There is a desire to eat, and frequent attempts to take food are made, but prehension is very difficult. If, however, food is placed on the back of the tongue it is readily masticated and swallowed. If the mouth is examined at this time it will be found red and hot, and exceptionally small blisters will be seen, which, however, quickly become eroded and develop into active ulcers varying in size from one-eighth to 1 inch in diameter. Where several ulcers have coalesced a large and irregularly indented patch is formed. These erosions are most frequently found on the gums around the incisor teeth, on the dental pad, inside the lips, and on the tip of the tongue, but they also occur on the cheeks, interdental space, and dorsum of the tongue. The ulcers have a hemorrhagic border, a depressed suppurating surface, and contain a brownish or yellowish colored débris, which is soon replaced by granulation tissue. As a result of this sloughing of the tissues and the retention of food in the mouth, a very offensive odor is exhaled. The muzzle becomes dry and parched in appearance, which condition is shortly followed by erosions and exfoliations of the superficial layer of the skin. Adherent brownish crusts and scabs form over the parts, and similar lesions are seen around the nostrils and external surface of the lips.

In some cases there are associated with these alterations a slight swelling and painfulness in the region of the pasterns, at times affecting the fore feet, at other times the hind feet, and occasionally all four feet. In a few cases the swelling may extend above the fetlock, but it has never been observed above the knee or hock. The skin around the coronet may occasionally become fissured and the thin skin in the cleft of the foot eroded and suppurated, but without the formation of vesicles. As a result of these feet lesions, the affected animal may assume a position with its back arched and the limbs propped under the body as in a case of founder and will manifest much pain and lameness in walking. If it lies down the animal shows reluctance in geting up and, although manifesting no inclination to move about, when forced to do so there is more or less stiffness and a tendency to kick or shake the foot as if to dislodge a foreign body from between the claws.

In some outbreaks the milch cows have slight superficial erosions on the teats which at times extend to the udder. The cracks in the skin are filled with serum and form brownish colored scabs. The teats become tender and the milk secretion diminishes; in some cases it disappears.

In mild cases, only the mouth lesions may be observed, or these alterations may be associated with one or more of the other above-described symptoms, but in severe cases where there is a generalized mycotic intoxication one animal may show all these alterations. When the disease is well developed the general appearance of the animal is one of great lassitude, and it either stands off by itself with hind feet drawn under the body and its fore feet extended or it assumes a recumbent position. Owing to the inability to eat and to the general systemic disturbance present, the animal loses flesh very rapidly and becomes greatly emaciated in the latter stages of the disease. The temperature and pulse are somewhat increased, the former two or three degrees, the latter to from 75 to 90 beats per minute. The fever is not lasting, and these symptoms are soon modified. The animal has an anxious look, and in a few cases there is gastro-intestinal irritation, the feces being thin, of a dark color, and of an offensive odor.

Prognosis and Mortality.—Mycotic stomatitis is not a serious disease, and in uncomplicated cases recoveries soon follow the removal of the cause and the application of the indicated remedies. In such cases complete restoration may take place within one week. In mild outbreaks a large percentage of the animals will recover without treatment, but that the disease is fatal is shown by the fact that animals which develop an aggravated form of the affection succumb if not treated. In such animals death occurs in six or eight days, but the mortality in the serious outbreaks thus far investigated has been less than 0.5 per cent. The course of this disease is irregular and runs from seven to fifteen days, the average case covering a period of about ten days.

Treatment.—The treatment of mycotic stomatitis should consist in first removing the herd of cattle from the pasture in which they have been running. The affected animals should, if it is possible, be brought to the barn or corral and fed on soft, nutritious food, such as bran mashes, ground feed, and gruels. A bucket of clear, cool water should be kept constantly in the manger, so that the animal may drink or rinse the mouth at its pleasure, and it will be found beneficial to dissolve 2 heaping tablespoonfuls of borax or 1 tablespoonful of potassium chlorate in each of the first two buckets of water taken during the day. If the animals are gentle enough to be handled, the mouth should be swabbed out daily with antiseptic washes, such as a 2 per cent solution of carbolic acid or of creolin, or a 1 per cent solution of lysol or permanganate of potash, or 1 part of hydrogen peroxide to 2 parts of water. This should be followed by astringents, such as one-half tablespoonful of alum, borax, or chlorate of potash placed on the tongue. Probably a more satisfactory method of administering the antiseptic treatment to a large number of animals would be to mix thoroughly 2 teaspoonfuls of pure carbolic acid every morning in a quart of bran mash and give to each affected animal for a period of five days. Range cattle may be more readily treated by the use of medicated salt placed in troughs accessible to the animals. This salt may be prepared by pouring 4 ounces of crude carbolic acid upon 12 quarts of ordinary barrel salt, after which they are thoroughly mixed. The lesions of the feet should be treated with a 2 per cent solution of carbolic acid or of creolin, while the fissures and other lesions of the skin will be benefited by the application of carbolized vaseline or zinc ointment. If the animals are treated in this manner and carefully fed the disease will rapidly disappear.

Big Jaw, or Lumpy Jaw (Actinomycosis of the Jawbones). [See pages 287-295.]

Inflammation of Mucous Membrane of Mouth (Stomatitis).—The membrane of the mouth may become inflamed by cattle eating some irritating substance or plant, or little vesicles may form in the mouths of calves when they are affected with indigestion, constituting what is termed aphtha.

Symptoms.—The saliva dribbles from the mouth, and when the mouth is examined the surface of the tongue and other parts will appear red and inflamed. When young animals are affected with the form of disease termed aphtha, small red elevations will be observed on the tongue and other parts of the mouth, having little white points on their centers, which consist of the epithelium of the mucous membrane raised into vesicles. These white patches are succeeded by ulcerated surfaces, which are caused by the shedding of the white patches of epithelium.

Treatment.—When there is merely a reddened and inflamed condition of the mucous membrane of the mouth, it will suffice to syringe it out several times a day with 4 ounces of the following solution: Alum, 1 ounce; water, 2 pints. When the edges of the tongue and other parts of the mouth are studded with ulcers, these should be painted over once a day until the affected surface is healed, with the following solution: Permanganate of potash, 20 grains; water, 1 ounce. When indigestion is associated with an ulcerated condition of the mouth, separate treatment is required.

DISEASES OF THE PHARYNX AND GULLET.

Sore Throat (Pharyngitis).—This is an inflammation of the mucous membrane lining the pharynx. It is frequently associated with inflammatory diseases of the respiratory tract, such as laryngitis and bronchitis or pleurisy.

Symptoms.—The muzzle is dry and the saliva dribbles from the corners of the mouth; the animal either does not swallow or swallows with difficulty, and holds its neck in a stiff, straight position, moving it as little as possible. The eyelids are half closed, the white of the eye is bloodshot, and the animal occasionally grinds its teeth. After masticating the food the animal drops it out of its mouth as if to avoid the pain of swallowing, and also evinces pain when pressure is applied on the pharynx externally and tries to prevent such pressure being applied.

Causes.—Pharyngitis may be produced by a sudden cooling of the surface of the body, as when cattle are exposed to a cold wind or a cold rain· or by swallowing irritant substances.

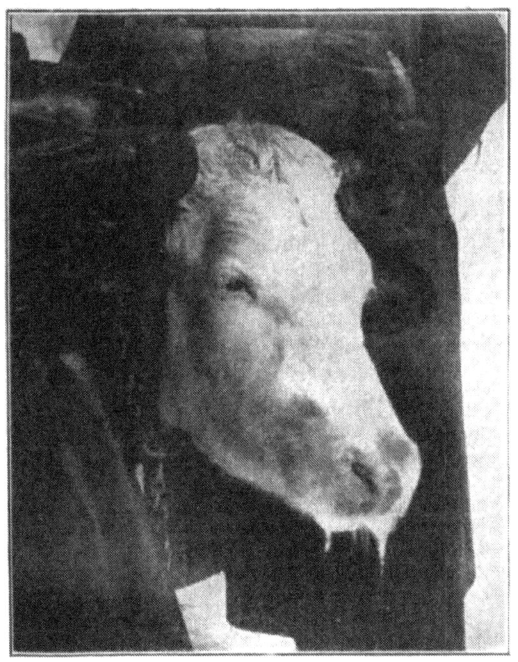

Head of Cow With Foot-and-Mouth Disease.
Dept. of Agr.

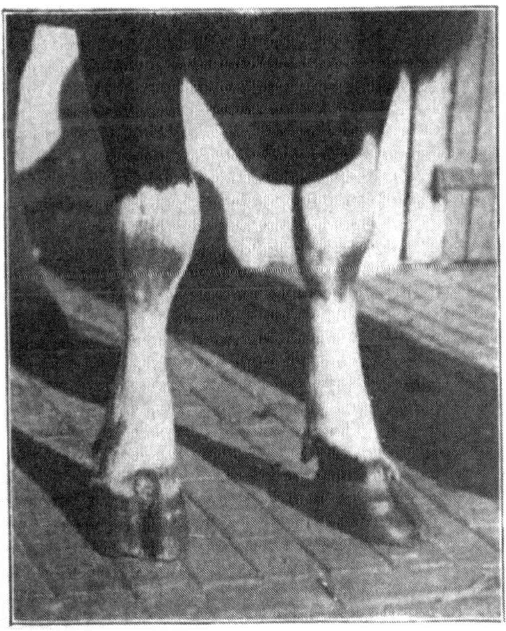

Foot-and-Mouth Disease in Foot of Cow.
Dept. of Agr.

Treatment.—The throat should be syringed three times a day with an ounce of the following solution: Nitrate of silver, 1½ drams, distilled water, 1 pint. Bland and soothing drinks, such as linseed tea or oatmeal and water, should occasionally be offered. Diet should consist of soft food, such as bran mashes with a little linseed meal mixed in them. Dry hay and fodder should be avoided. Fresh green grass or sound ensilage may be fed in small quantities. The upper part of the throat and the space between the jaws should be well rubbed once a day with the following liniment: Liquor ammonia fortior, 4 ounces; oil of turpentine, 4 ounces; olive oil, 4 ounces; mix. When evidence of blistering appears the application of the liniment should be stopped and the skin anointed with vaseline. Under the above treatment the inflammation of the throat will gradually subside and the animal will be able to swallow as usual in five or six days. During its treatment the sick animal should be kept in a comfortable stable.

Mumps (*Parotitis*).—Inflammation of the parotid gland may arise from the inflammation extending to it when an ox is affected with pharyngitis or laryngitis, or the inflammation may commence in the salivary ducts and may depend on some influence the nature of which is unknown. Parotitis sometimes arises from a blow or contusion which is severe enough to set up inflammation in the structure of the gland. Tuberculosis and actinomycosis may infrequently be characterized by the lodgment of their parasitic causes in the parotid glands, in which case parotitis may be a symptom of either of these diseases.

Symptoms.—There is an elongated painful swelling, beginning at the base of the ear and passing downward along the posterior margin of the lower jaw. The swelling is sometimes limited to one side and when both sides are swollen it is generally larger on one side than on the other. The secretion of saliva is increased, the appetite is poor, the neck is stiff, so that it is painful to raise the head, and food is swallowed with difficulty. In many cases the swelling of those glands, when submitted to proper treatment, disappears in a comparatively short time. In other cases, however, the gland remains enlarged, even after the animal recovers its appetite. In tuberculosis, lymphatic glands beneath the parotid glands are sometimes enlarged thus causing the appearance of enlarged parotid glands.

Treatment.—A warm bran poultice, made by mixing bran with a hot 2 per cent solution of creolin in water, should be applied on the swollen gland, maintained in place by means of a bandage. Whenever the poultice has cooled it should be replaced by a new one. This treatment should be continued until the pain is less and the swelling is reduced or until there is evidence of pus formation, which may be ascertained by examining the surface of the gland with the fingers; and when, on pressing any part of the surface, it is found to fluctuate or give, then we may conclude that there is at that place a collection of pus. It is well not to open the abscess until the fluctuation is well marked, as at this stage the pus or matter is near the surface and there is less trouble in healing the wound than if the pus is deep seated. The abscess should be opened with a clean, sharp knife. The poulticing should then be continued for two or three days, but the form of the poultice should be changed, by replacing the bran with absorbent cotton and pouring the creolin solution on the cotton. At all times the wound should be kept clean and the cavity injected once or twice daily with a solution of 1 dram of carbolic acid in 8 ounces of water. Under this treatment the pus may cease and the wound heal without complications. Saliva may issue from the orifice and result in the formation of a salivary fistula. This requires operative treatment, which should be performed by a qualified veterinarian. When poulticing fails to reduce the swelling or produce softening, the inflamed area may be rubbed once daily with camphorated oil, compound iodin ointment, or painted twice daily with Lugol's solution of iodin. The diet should be as recommended under Pharyngitis.

Pharyngeal Polypi.—Tumors form not infrequently in the pharynx, and may give rise to a train of symptoms varying according to their size and location. The tumor may be so situated that by shifting its position a little it may partially obstruct the posterior nares (nostrils), when, of course, it will render nasal breathing very noisy and labored. In another situation its partial displacement may impede the entrance of air into the larynx. In almost any part of the pharynx, but especially near the entrance of the gullet, they will interfere with the act of swallowing. As these tumors are frequently attached to the wall of the pharynx by a pedicle, or stalk, it will be seen that they may readily be displaced in different directions so as to produce the symptoms before described. Enlarged postpharyngeal lymphatic glands are not rare in tuberculosis and by pressing upon the wall of the pharynx and restricting the lumen of this organ they cause difficulty in both breathing and swallowing. Such enlarged glands may be differentiated from tumors by passing the hand into the cow's throat after the jaws are separated by a suitable speculum or gag.

Treatment.—The method of treatment followed in such cases is to separate the animal's jaws with an instrument termed a gag, and then, after drawing the tongue partially forward, to pass the hand into the pharynx and to gently twist the tumor from its attachment. One veterinarian who has had considerable practice in treating this form of disease scrapes through the attachment of the tumor gradually with his thumb nail. In cases where the attachment is too strong to be severed in this way an instrument like a thimble, but possessing a sharp edge at the end, might be used to effect the same purpose, or the base of the tumor may be severed by the use of a crushing instrument known as an écraseur.

Choking.—This accident usually happens from attempting to swallow too large an object, such as a turnip, potato, beet, or an apple or pear, though in rare cases choking may occur from bran, chaff, or some other finely divided food lodging in and filling up a portion of the gullet. This latter form of the accident is most likely to occur in animals which are greedy feeders.

Symptoms.—The symptoms will vary somewhat according to the part of the gullet or throat in which the obstruction is located. In most cases there is a discharge of saliva from the mouth; the animal coughs frequently, and when it drinks the water is soon ejected. The cow stops eating and stands back from the trough, the expression is troubled, breathing is accelerated, and oftentimes the animal bloats as a result of the retention of gas in the paunch. These symptoms, however, are not always present, for ·if the obstacle does not completely close the throat, or gullet, gas and water may pass, thus ameliorating the discomfort. If the obstruction is in the neck portion of the gullet, it may be felt as a lump in the left jugular gutter.

Treatment.—If the object is in the throat, it is advisable to put a gag in the animal's mouth, and, while the head is held in a horizontal direction by two assistants, to pass the hand into the pharynx, grasp the foreign body, and withdraw it gradually and steadily. When the substance is lodged in the upper part of the gullet, pressure should be made by an assistant in an upward direction against the object while the operator passes his hand into the pharynx, and if the assistant can not by pressure dislodge the substance from the gullet, the operator may by passing his middle finger above and partly behind the substance gradually slide the object into the pharynx and ·then withdraw it by the mouth. The presence of an obstructing substance in the cervical portion of the gullet may be ascertained by passing the hand along the left side of the neck, when a hard and painless swelling will be found to indicate the presence of the foreign body. In such cases we must endeavor by gentle and persevering pressure with the thumb and two next fingers to slide the obstructing substance gradually upward to the pharynx. To facilitate this it is well to give the animal a half pint of raw linseed or olive oil before the manipulations described are commenced. When the substance has been brought into or nearly into the pharynx, then the mouth gag should be used, the tongue drawn partially forward with the left hand, and the right should be passed backward into the pharynx to withdraw the obstruction. When bran or chaff causes the trouble it is best to give a small quantity of oil to lubricate the walls of the gullet and then by gentle and persevering pressure to endeavor to separate and divide the mass and to work it downward toward the stomach. This will be assisted by pouring small quantities of oil and water down the animal's throat. It is not advisable to use the probang to push down any soft material, such as oats or chaff, as this generally condenses and renders firmer the obstructing substance by pressing its particles or elements together, so that it forms a solid, resisting mass which can not be moved.

In some cases, either because located in the chest portion of the esophagus, and so beyond reach, or because too firmly seated, the foreign body can not be dislodged from the neck by pressing and

manipulating that part externally. In such an event we must re
sort to the use of the probang. A probang is a flexible instrumen
and adapts itself to the natural curvature of the gullet, so that i
it is used cautiously there is not much risk of injury. Before pass
ing the probang, a gag which has an aperture at each end, fror
which straps pass to be buckled at the back of the head below th
horns, is introduced into the mouth. The probang should then b
oiled, and, the head and neck being held in a straight line by tw
assistants, the tongue must be partly drawn out of the mouth, th
probang cautiously passed along the roof of the mouth into th
pharynx and thence into the gullet, through which it is passe
down. If resistance is met, gentle and continuous pressure must b
employed, under the influence of which the agent will generally i
a short time pass into the stomach. One must be careful not t
pass the probang into the larynx and thence into the windpipe c
the cow. An animal may readily be killed in this way. This acc
dent is indicated by efforts to cough and by violently disturbe
breathing. If such symptoms arise the probang must be withdraw
at once. To avoid a wrong passage, the end of the tube should b
pressed through the throat very slowly until its presence in th
esophagus is assured. After it is once in the esophagus care is sti
necessary, because the walls of this tube may easily be torn.

Some writers have advised that when the obstruction is lodge
in the cervical (neck) portion of the gullet it should be struck wit
a mallet, so as to crush it and thus alter its shape, so that it ma
easily slip down into the stomach. If the obstructing substance i
hard, this will be a dangerous operation, but if soft—as in case o
a ripe pear, for example—this proceeding may be safely adopted.

In all cases where pressure applied on the neck fails to mov
the obstruction and the probang also fails to move it, it may be d
vided by a subcutaneous operation or the gullet may be opened an
the obstructing substance removed through the wound. In suc
cases the assistance of a veterinarian or a surgeon must be obtained

Wounds and Injuries of the Gullet.—Sometimes from the ras
and too forcible use of the probang the walls of the gullet may b
more or less lacerated or abraded, and the animal consequentl
swallows with pain and difficulty. In such cases dry feed must b
withheld for five or six days, so as to allow the injured parts to hea
and the diet must be limited to linseed tea, hay tea, and thin oat
meal gruel and molasses. The same kind of diet must be fed afte
the operation of cutting into the gullet has been performed.

Sometimes the gullet is ruptured and lacerated to such an ex
tent that treatment of any kind is hopeless. This has been know
to occur when the handle of a pitchfork or a buggy whip has bee
pushed down a cow's throat to remove an obstruction. Where suc
treatment has been applied it is best to slaughter the animal with
out delay, as the flesh may be utilized so long as there is no feve
or general disease, and remedial treatment would be hopeless. I
this connection it may be mentioned that whatever substitute ma
be used for a probang, which sometimes is not at hand, it should b

flexible and should possess a smooth surface. A piece of new rope, with the end closely wrapped and waxed and then oiled, or a piece of thin garden hose, or a well-wrapped twisted wire may be used in emergencies.

DISEASES OF THE STOMACH AND BOWELS OF CATTLE.

Hoven, or Bloating (Acute Tympanites).—This disease is characterized by swelling of the left flank, and is caused by the formation of gas in the rumen, or paunch.

Causes.—Tympanites may be caused by any kind of food which produces indigestion. When cattle are first turned into young clover they eat so greedily of it that tympanites frequently results; turnips, potatoes, and cabbage may also cause it; middlings and corn meal also frequently give rise to it. In this connection it may be stated than an excessive quantity of any of the before-mentioned foods may bring on this disorder, or it may not be due to excess, but to eating too hastily. Sometimes the quality of the food is at fault. Grass or clover when wet by dew or rain frequently disorders digestion and brings on tympanites; frozen roots or pastures covered with hoar frost should also be regarded as dangerous. When food has been eaten too hastily, or when it is cold and wet, the digestive process is imperfectly performed, and the food contained in the paunch ferments, during which process large quantities of gas are formed. The same result may follow when a cow is choked, as the obstruction in the gullet prevents the eructation, or passing up, of gas from the stomach, so that the gas continues to accumulate until tympanites results.

Symptoms.—The swelling of the left flank is very characteristic, as in well-marked cases the flank at its upper part rises above the level of the backbone and when struck with the tips of the fingers emits a drumlike sound. The animal has an anxious expression, moves uneasily, and is evidently distressed. If relief is not obtained in time, it breathes with difficulty, reels in walking or in standing, and in a short time falls down and dies from suffocation. The distention of the stomach may become so great as to prevent the animal from breathing, and in some instances the case may be complicated by rupture of the stomach.

Treatment.—If the case is not extreme, it may be sufficient to drive the animal at a walk for a quarter or half an hour; or cold water by the bucketful may be thrown against the cow's sides. In some cases the following simple treatment is successful: A rope or a twisted straw band is coated with pine tar, wagon grease, or other unsavory substance, and is placed in the cow's mouth as a bit, being secured by tying behind the horns. The efforts of the animal to dislodge this object result in movements of the tongue, jaws, and throat that stimulate the secretion of saliva and swallowing, thus opening the esophagus, which permits the exit of gas, and at the same time peristalsis is stimulated reflexly.

In urgent cases the gas must be allowed to escape without delay, and this is best accomplished by the use of the trocar. The trocar is a sharp-pointed instrument incased in a sheath, which leaves the sharp point of the trocar free. In selecting the point for using the trocar a spot equally distant from the last rib, the hip bone, and the transverse processes of the lumbar vertebræ must be chosen. Here an incision about three-fourths of an inch long should be made with a knife through the skin, and then, the sharp point of the trocar being directed downward, inward, and slightly forward, is thrust into the paunch. The sheath of the trocar should be left in the paunch so long as any gas continues to issue from it. If the canula, or sheath, of the trocar is removed while gas is still forming in the paunch and the left flank becomes considerably swollen, it may be necessary to insert it again. It is well, accordingly, to observe the canula closely, and if gas is found to be issuing from it, it should not be removed. When gas issues from the canula in considerable quantity the sound accompanying its escape renders the exact condition obvious. It is occasionally necessary to keep the canula in the stomach for several hours. When this is necessary a piece of stout cord should be passed around the neck of the canula immediately below the projecting rim and then be passed around the animal's body and tied in a secure knot, and a careful attendant must remain with the cow during the entire period that the instrument is in place. The rim surrounding the mouth of the canula should be in contact with the skin. Whenever the person in charge of the cow is satisfied that gas has ceased to issue from the canula the instrument should be removed.

The trocar is to be employed only in extreme or urgent cases, though everyone who has had experience in treating indigestion in cattle will realize that he has saved the lives of many animals by its prompt application. When the tympanitic animal is not distressed and the swelling of the flank is not great, or when the most distressing condition has been removed by the use of the trocar, it is best to resort to the administration of internal medicine. Two ounces of aromatic spirits of ammonia should be given every half hour in a quart of cold water, or half an ounce of chloride of lime may be dissolved in a pint of tepid water and the dose repeated every half hour until the bloating has subsided, or 1 ounce of creolin in 2 parts of tepid water may be given at one dose or carefully injected through the canula directly into the paunch to inhibit fermentation and the recurrent formation of gas. It is generally necessary to give a dose of purgative medicine after bloating has subsided, as animals frequently show symptoms of constipation after attacks of indigestion. For this purpose 1 or 1½ pounds of Glauber's salts may be used.

Chronic Tympanites.—Cattle, especially those which have been kept in the stable all winter, are liable to suffer from chronic tympanites. In this form the animal bloats up after feeding, but seldom swells so much as to cause any alarm. The chronic form of indigestion may also follow an acute attack like that previously described. This is also a symptom of tuberculosis in those cases in which the lymphatic glands lying between the lungs are so enlarged as to press upon and partly occlude the esophagus.

Treatment.—Treatment should be preceded by a moderate dose of purgative medicine: 1 pound of sulphate of magnesia (Epsom salts) or sulphate of soda (Glauber's salts), half an ounce of powdered Barbados aloes, 1 ounce of powdered ginger, and 1 pint of molasses. The salts and aloes should be dissolved by stirring for a few minutes with 2 quarts of lukewarm water, then the molasses should be added; and after all the ingredients have been stirred together for about ten minutes, the dose should be administered. It will generally be necessary after the operation of the purgative to give some tonic and antacid preparation to promote digestion, which is imperfectly performed in such cases. The following may be used: Powdered gentian, 3 ounces; powdered bicarbonate of potash, 3 ounces; powdered ginger, 3 ounces; powdered capsicum, 1 ounce. Mix and divide into twelve powders, one of which should be given three times a day before feeding, shaken up with half a pint of whisky and a pint of water. It is also advantageous in such cases to give two heaped teaspoonfuls of wood charcoal, mixed with the animal's feed three times a day. The animal should also go out during the day, as want of exercise favors the continuance of this form of indigestion. If the dung is hard, the constipation should be overcome by feeding a little flaxseed twice daily or by giving a handful of Glauber's salts in the feed once or twice daily, as may be necessary. Roots, silage, and other succulent feeds are useful in this connection. If tuberculosis is suspected as the cause of the chronic bloating, a skilled veterinarian should be employed to make a diagnosis, using the tuberculin test if necessary. Until it is settled that the cow has not tuberculosis, she should be kept apart from the other members of the herd.

Distention of Rumen, or Paunch, With Food.—This form of indigestion is caused by the animal gorging itself with food, and arises more from the animal's voracious appetite than from any defect in the quality of the food supplied to it. The condition is, however, more severe if the food consumed is especially concentrated or difficult of digestion. In cases of this kind there is comparatively no great formation of gas, and the gas which is formed is diffused through the stomach instead of accumulating in a layer in its upper part. On pressing the flank with the closed fist the indent of the hand remains for a short time in the flank, as if the rumen were filled with a soft, doughy mass.

This form of indigestion should be treated by stimulants, such as alcohol, wine, or aromatic spirits of ammonia.

If the formation of gas is not great and the distention with solid material is somewhat limited, the animal may be drenched through a piece of ordinary garden hose, one end being inserted in the animal's mouth like the neck of a bottle, and the other end fitted with a funnel, giving 1½ pounds of Epsom or Glauber's salts, dissolved in 2 gallons of water, at a single dose. Immediately after this treatment the left side of the animal, extending below the median line of the abdomen, should be powerfully kneaded with the fist, so that the impacted food mass will be broken, allowing the water to separate it into small portions, which can be carried downward for the process of digestion.

But if the treatment applied fails and the impacted or overloaded condition of the rumen continues, it may become necessary to make an incision with a sharp, long-bladed knife in the left flank, commencing at the point where it is usual to puncture the stomach of an ox, and prolong the incision in a downward direction until it is long enough to admit the hand. When the point of the knife is thrust into the flank and the blade cuts downward, the wall of the stomach, the muscle, and the skin should all be cut through at the same time. Two assistants should hold the edges of the wound together so as to prevent any food slipping between the flank and the wall of the stomach, and then the operator should remove two-thirds of the contents of the rumen. This having been done, the edges of the wound should be sponged with a little carbolized warm water, and, the lips of the wound in the rumen being turned inward, they should be brought together with catgut stitches. The wound penetrating the muscle and the skin may then be brought together by silk stitches, which should pass through the entire thickness of the muscle and should be about 1 inch apart. The wound should afterwards be dressed once a day with a lotion and the animal covered with a tight linen sheet, to protect the wound from insects and dirt. The lotion to be used in such a case is made up as follows: Sulphate of zinc, 1 dram; carbolic acid, 2 drams; glycerin, 2 ounces; water, 14 ounces; mix. It is clear that this operation requires special skill and it should be attempted only by those who are competent.

Imaginary Diseases.—It would appear quite in place here, in connection with the diseases of the stomach and bowels of cattle, to consider the three old fallacies or superstitions known as hollow horn, loss of cud, and wolf in the tail. These names, whenever and wherever used, seem to be invariably applied to some form of digestive derangement or disease having its origin in the stomach and bowels.

Hollow Horn.—In the first place it should be noted that the horns of all animals of the ox tribe are hollow. The horn cores are elongations of the frontal bones of the skull, and the frontal sinuses, which are the larger of the air spaces of the head, are prolonged into the horn cores. When a cow is sick, if the horns are hot it is an evidence of fever; if they are cold it indicates impaired circulation of the blood, but these manifestations of sickness are to be regarded as symptoms of some constitutional disorder and do not in themselves require treatment.

The treatment should be applied to the disease which causes the abnormal temperature of the horns. The usual treatment for the supposed hollow horn, which consists of boring the horns with a gimlet and pouring turpentine in the opening thus made, is not only useless and cruel, but is liable to set up an acute inflammation and result in an abscess of the sinus.

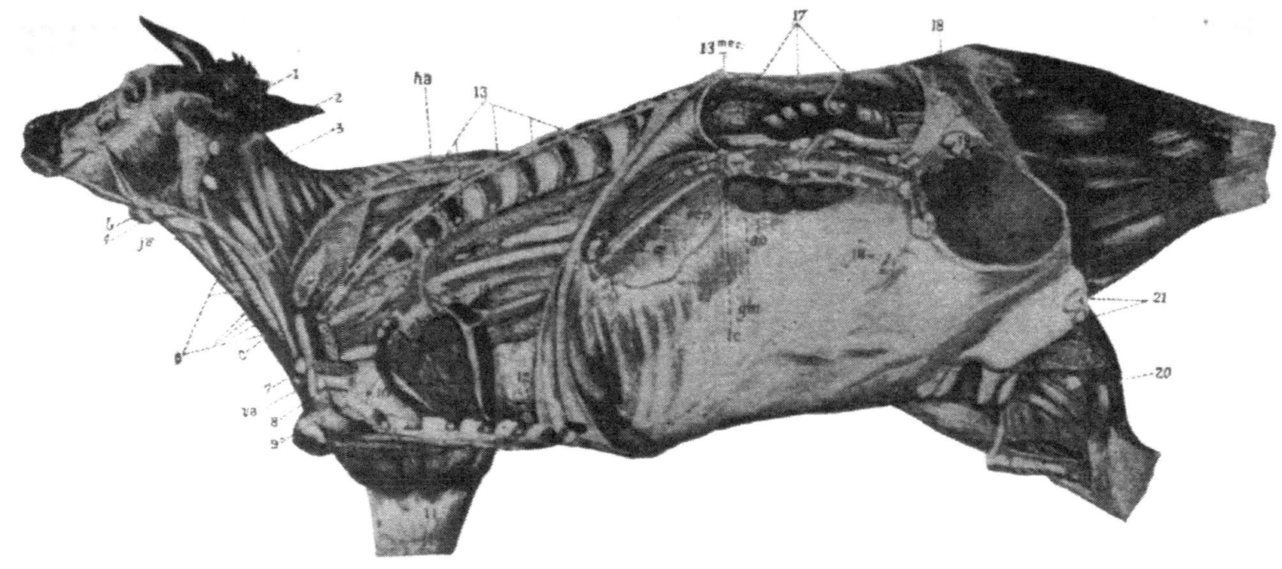

LYMPH GLANDS IN THE COW. B. A. I. 1910.

Loss of Cud.—It is very common among farmers, when a cow or ox is ailing to say that the sick animal has lost its cud. If it is meant that the animal does not ruminate or chew the cud, and that it consequently must be sick, no fault can be found with the expression. In most cases, however, the remark is intended to convey the idea that the loss of cud is a disease in itself. Such is not the case. It is simply a cessation of rumination, and frequently the first indication of some form of sickness, since ruminants stop chewing the cud when feeling much out of condition. Loss of cud is a symptom of a great many diseases, and when its existence is detected it should lead the observer to try to discover other symptoms upon which to base a correct opinion as to the nature of the disease from which the animal suffers. No local treatment is required.

Wolf in the Tail.—The so-called wolf in the tail is most generally treated by those who are possessed of this fallacious belief by splitting the end of the tail with a knife, filling the cut with salt, and binding with a cloth. This imagined trouble is nothing more than a debilitated condition of the system, resulting in a relaxed or softened condition of the tail, especially at its extremity. It is evident that it is the constitutional disorder which requires treatment and not the relaxed tail.

When the immense volume and complicated arrangement of the gastric pouches of the cow are considered, together with the great quantities of aliment required in the elaboration of milk and for the animal's nutrition, it is small wonder, in view of the carelessness so often apparent as to both the kind and quality of food, that disease of the digestive organs in these animals is of more frequent occurrence than other diseases. And it is believed that a recognition of the facts contained in the foregoing statements will not only tend to dissipate any remaining belief in these old fallacies, but to a more humane and rational treatment of the various forms of indigestion or dyspepsia, of which those manifestations giving rise to impressions of hollow horn, loss of cud, and wolf in the tail are but symptoms.

Vomiting.—This is not to be confounded with rumination, though some writers have advanced the opinion that vomiting is merely a disordered and irregular rumination. It is not of common occurrence in cattle, though it sometimes occurs.

Symptoms.—Animals which vomit are frequently in poor condition. After having eaten tranquilly for some time the animal suddenly becomes uneasy, arches the back, stretches the neck and head, and then suddenly ejects 10 or 12 pounds of the contents of the rumen. After having done this the uneasiness subsides, and in a short time the animal resumes eating as if nothing had happened.

Cause.—The cause of this disordered state of the digestive system in cattle is usually obscure, but has in some cases been traced to a partial closure of the opening into the second stomach or to a distention of the esophagus. It has been found to occur when there was cancerous disease of the fourth stomach, and experimentally it has been shown that a suspension of digestion or great derangement of the fourth stomach produces considerable nervous disorder of the rumen and sometimes vomiting, or an attempt to vomit.

Treatment.—Easily digested food and plenty of water should be given. Fear and excitement, chasing, or hurrying animals after eating heartily are apt to bring on an attack. In order to overcome irritation which may produce vomiting, the following draft should be given: Hydrate of chloral, half an ounce; whisky, 8 ounces; water, 1 pint. The dose must be repeated when the condition of the animal seems to require it. As a rule, treatment is not successful.

Depraved Appetite (Pica).—Cattle suffering from this disease have a capricious and variable appetite as regards their ordinary food, but evince a strong desire to lick and eat substances for which healthy cattle show no inclination. Alkaline and saline-tasting substances are especially attractive to cattle having a depraved appetite, and they frequently lick lime, earth, coal, gravel, and even the dung of other cattle. Cows in calf and young cattle are especially liable to develop these symptoms. Animals affected in this way lose condition, their coat is staring, gait slow, and small vesicles containing yellow liquid form under the tongue; the milk given by such cows is thin and watery. Such animals become restless and uneasy, as is indicated by frequent bellowing. The disease may last for months, the animal ultimately dying emaciated and exhausted. Depraved appetite frequently precedes the condition in which the bones of the cattle become brittle and fracture easily, which is known as osteomalacia.

Causes.—It is generally believed, from the fact that this disease is largely one of regions, that some condition of the soil and water and of the local vegetation is responsible for it. It is more prevalent some years than others, and is most common in old countries where the soil is more or less depleted. Cattle pastured on low, swampy land become predisposed to it. It occasionally happens, however, that one individual in a herd suffers though all are fed alike; in such cases the disease must arise from an imperfect assimilation by the affected animal of the nutritive elements of the food which is supplied to it.

Treatment.—The aim in such cases must be to improve the process of digestion and to supply the animal with a sufficiency of sound and wholesome food. The following should be given to the cow three times a day, a heaped tablespoonful constituting a dose: Carbonate of iron, 4 ounces; finely ground bone or bone flour, 1 pound; powdered gentian, 4 ounces; common salt, 8 ounces; powdered fenugreek, 4 ounces; mix. In addition to this, 3 tablespoonfuls of powdered charcoal may be mixed with the animal's food three times a day, and a piece of rock salt should be placed where the animal can lick it at will. German veterinarians have had brilliant results from the treatment of this disease with subcutaneous injections of apomorphine in doses of 1½ to 5 grains daily for three or four days.

Hair Concretions.—These concretions, or hair balls, result from the habit which cattle have of licking themselves or other animals.

The hairs which are swallowed are carried round by the contractions of the stomach and gradually assume the form of a small pellet, or ball. This increases in size as fresh quantities of hair are introduced into the stomach, which become adherent to the surface of the hair ball. These hair balls are found most frequently in the reticulum, or second stomach, though sometimes in the rumen. In calves hair balls are generally found in the fourth stomach.

There are no certain symptoms by which we can determine the presence of hair balls in the stomach, and therefore no treatment can be recommended for such cases. In making post-mortem examinations of cattle, we have sometimes found the walls of the reticulum transfixed with nails or pieces of wire, and yet the animal during life had not shown any symptoms of indigestion, but had died from maladies not involving the second stomach.

Indigestion (Dyspepsia, or Gastro-Intestinal Catarrh).—Tympanites, already described, is a form of indigestion in which the chief symptom and most threatening condition is the collection of gas in the paunch. This symptom does not always accompany indigestion, so it is well to here consider other forms under a separate head. If indigestion is long continued the irritant abnormal products developed cause catarrh of the stomach and intestines—gastro-intestinal catarrh. Or, on the other hand, irritant substances ingested may cause gastro-intestinal catarrh, which, in turn, will cause indigestion. Hence it results that these several conditions are usually found existing together.

Causes.—Irritant food, damaged food, overloading of the stomach, and sudden changes of diet may cause this disease. Want of exercise predisposes to it, or food which is coarse and indigestible may after a time produce this condition. Food which possesses astringent properties and tends to check secretion may also act as an exciting cause. Food in excessive quantity may lead to disorder of digestion and to this disease. It is very likely to appear toward the end of protracted seasons of drought; therefore a deficiency of water must be regarded as one of the conditions which favor its development.

Symptoms.—Diminished appetite, rumination irregular, tongue coated, mouth slimy, dung passed apparently not well digested and smelling badly, dullness, and fullness of the flanks. The disease may in some cases assume a chronic character, and in addition to the foregoing symptoms slight bloating, or tympanites, of the left flank may be observed; the animal breathes with effort and each respiration may be accompanied by a grunt, the ears and horns are alternately hot and cold, rumination ceases, the usual rumbling sound in the stomach is not audible, the passage of dung is almost entirely suspended, and the animal passes only a little mucus occasionally. Sometimes there is alternating constipation and diarrhea. There is low fever in many cases.

The disease continues a few days or a week in the mild cases, while the severe cases may last several weeks. In the latter form the emaciation and loss of strength may be very great. There is no appetite, no rumination, or peristalsis. The mouth is hot and sticky, the eyes have receded in their sockets, and milk secretion is ceased. In such cases the outlook for recovery is unfavorable. The patient falls away in flesh and becomes weaker, as is shown by the fact that one frequently finds it lying down.

Treatment.—Small quantities of roots, sweet silage, or selected grass or hay should be offered several times daily. Very little food should be allowed. Aromatic and demulcent drafts may be given to produce a soothing effect on the mucous lining of the stomachs and to promote digestion. Two ounces of camomile flowers should be boiled for 20 minutes in a quart of water and the infusion on cooling should be given to the affected animal. This may be repeated about three times a day. When constipation is present the following purgative may be administered: One pound of Glauber's salts dissolved in a quart of linseed tea and a pint of molasses. After this purgative has acted, if there is a lack of appetite and the animal does not ruminate regularly, the powder mentioned in remarks on the treatment of chronic tympanites may be given according to directions. The diet must be rather laxative and of a digestible character after an attack of this form of indigestion. Food should be given in moderate quantities, as any excess by overtaxing the digestive functions may bring on a relapse. Ice-cold water should be avoided.

Indigestion From Drinking Cold Water (Colic).—This disorder is produced by drinking copiously of cold water, which arrests digestion and produces cramp of the fourth stomach, probably of the other stomachs, and also of the bowels.

Causes.—It is not customary for the ox to drink much water at once. In fact, he usually drinks slowly and as if he were merely tasting the water, letting some fall out at the corners of his mouth at every mouthful. It would, therefore, seem to be contrary to the habits of the ox to drink largely; but we find that during hot weather, when he has been working, and is consequently very thirsty, if he drinks a large quantity of cold water he may be immediately taken with a very severe colic. Cows which are fed largely on dry hay drink copiously, like the working ox, and become affected in precisely the same manner. In such cases they are seized with a chill or fit of trembling before the cramps come on.

Symptoms.—There is some distention of the abdomen, but no accumulation of gas. As the distention and pain occur immediately after the animal has drunk the water, there can be no doubt as to the exciting cause.

Treatment.—Walk the animal about for 10 minutes before administering medicine, as this allows time for a portion of the contents of the stomach to pass into the bowel, and renders it safer to give medicine. In many cases the walking exercise and the diarrhea bring about a spontaneous cure of this disorder, but as in some instances the cramps and pains of the stomachs persist, one may give 1 ounce of sulphuric ether and 1 ounce of tincture of opium, shaken up with a pint of warm water, and repeat the dose in half an hour if the animal is not relieved. In an emergency when medicine is not to be had, half a pint of whisky may be substituted for medicine, and should be given mixed with a pint of warm water; or a tablespoonful of powdered ginger may be administered in the same way as the remedies already mentioned.

Indigestion in Calves (Gastro-Intestinal Catarrh, Diarrhea, or Scour).—[See Diseases of Young Calves.]

Gastro-Enteritis.—Gastro-enteritis, or inflammation of the walls of the stomach and intestines, follows upon irritations more severe or longer continued than those that produce gastro-intestinal catarrh.

Causes.—Severe indigestion may be followed by gastro-enteritis, or it may be caused by swallowing irritant poisons, such as arsenic or corrosive sublimate or irritant plants. Exposure to cold or inclement weather may produce this disease, especially in debilitated animals or animals fed improperly. It is claimed that if cattle feed on vegetation infested with some kinds of caterpillars this disease may result.

Symptoms.—Dullness; drooping of the ears; dryness of the muzzle; dry skin; staring coat; loins morbidly sensitive to pressure; fullness of the left flank, which is owing to the distention of the fourth stomach by gas. The pulse is small, the gait is feeble and staggering; each step the animal makes is accompanied by a grunt, and this symptom is especially marked if the animal happens to walk in a downward direction. There is loss of appetite, and rumination is suspended. The passages at first are few in number, hard, and are sometimes coated with mucus or with blood. Later a severe diarrhea sets in, when the passages contain mucus and blood and have an offensive odor. There is evidence of colicky pain, and the abdomen is sensitive to pressure. Pain may be continuous. There is fever and acceleration of the pulse rate and respirations. Mental depression and even insensibility occur before death. The disease is always severe and often fatal.

Post-Mortem Appearances.—The mucous membrane of the fourth stomach has a well-marked red color and sometimes presents ulcerations. The wall is thickened and softened, and similar conditions are found in the walls of the intestines. The red discoloration extends in spots or large areas quite through the wall, showing on the outside.

Treatment.—Very small quantities of carefully selected food must be given and the appetite must not be forced. Protect the animal well from cold and dampness. Internally, give linseed tea, boiled milk, boiled oatmeal gruel, or rice water. These protectives may carry the medicine. Tannopin in doses of 30 to 60 grains is good. Subnitrate of bismuth in doses of 1 to 2 drams may be given. If the diarrhea is severe, pulverized opium may be used in 1 to 2 dram doses. If the bowel movements are not free, one may give from a pint to a quart of castor or raw linseed oil.

Diarrhea and Dysentery.—The word dysentery, as it is commonly used in relation to the diseases of animals, signifies a severe form of diarrhea.

Causes.—Diarrhea is a symptom of irritation of the intestines, resulting in increased secretion or increased muscular contractions, of both. The irritation is sometimes the result of chilling from exposure, improper feeding, irritant foods, indigestion, organic diseases of the intestines, or parasites.

Symptoms.—Passages from the bowels are frequent, at first consisting of thin dung, but as the disease continues they become watery and offensive smelling, and may be even streaked with blood. At first the animal shows no constitutional disturbance, but later it becomes weak and may exhibit evidence of abdominal pain by looking around to the side, drawing the feet together, lying down, or moving restlessly. Sometimes this malady is accompanied by fever, great depression, loss of strength, rapid loss of flesh, and it may terminate in death.

Treatment.—When the disease depends on irritating properties of the food which has been supplied to the animal, it is advisable to give a mild purgative, such as a pint of castor or linseed oil. When the secretions of the bowels are irritating, an ounce of carbonate of magnesia and half an ounce of tincture of opium should be shaken up in a quart of linseed tea and given to the animal three times a day until the passages present a natural appearance. When there is debility, want of appetite, no fever, but a continuance of the watery discharges from the bowels, then an astringent may be given. For such cases the following is serviceable: Tannic acid, 1 ounce; powdered gentian, 2 ounces; mix and divide into twelve powders, one powder to be given three times a day until the passages present a natural appearance. Each powder may be mixed with a half pint of whisky or blackberry brandy and a pint of water. Tannopin is a new remedy that is most useful in such cases. The dose is from 30 grains to 2 drams. Useful household remedies are raw eggs, strong coffee, parched rye flour, or decoction of oak bark. In all cases the food must be given sparingly and it should be carefully selected to insure good quality. Complete rest in a box stall is desirable. When diarrhea is a symptom of a malady characterized by the presence of a blood poison, the treatment appropriate to such disease must be applied.

Croupous Enteritis.—Under certain conditions severe irritation of the digestive canal may, in cattle, cause a form of inflammation of the intestines (enteritis) that is characterized by the formation of a false membrane upon the surface of the lining membrane of the intestines, and particularly the large intestines.

Symptoms.—There is fever, depression, loss of appetite, diarrhea, and in the fecal masses shreds of leathery false membrane may be found. These shreds are sometimes mistaken for parasites or for portions of the wall of the intestine.

Treatment.—Give a pound of Glauber's salts, followed by bicarbonate of soda in doses of 2 ounces four times daily.

Constipation.—Constipation is to be regarded rather as a symptom of disease or of faults in feeding than as a disease in itself. It occurs in almost all general fevers unless the bowels are involved in local disease, in obstructions of all kinds, from feeding on dry, bulky food, etc. In order to remove the constipation, the treatment must be applied to remove the causes which give rise to it. Calves sometimes suffer from constipation immediately after birth when meconium that accumulates in the bowels before birth is not passed. In such cases, give a rectal injection of warm water and an ounce of castor oil shaken up with an ounce of new milk. The mother's milk is the best food to prevent constipation in the new-born calf, as it contains a large amount of fatty matter, which renders it laxative in its effects.

It is usually better to treat habitual constipation by a change of diet than by medicine. Flaxseed is a good food laxative. If the constipation has lasted long, repeated small doses of purgatives are better than a single large dose.

Intestinal Worms. [See chapter on "The animal parasites of cattle."]

Ruptures (Ventral Hernia).—Ventral hernia, or rupture, is an escape of some one of the abdominal organs through a rupture in the abdominal muscles, the skin remaining intact. The rumen, the small intestine, or part of the large intestine, and the fourth stomach are the parts which usually form a ventral hernia in bovine animals.

Causes.—Hernia is frequently produced by blows of the horns, kicks, and falls. In old cows hernia may sometimes occur without any direct injury.

Hernia of the Rumen.—Hernia of the rumen is generally situated on the left side of the abdomen, on account of the situation of the rumen. In exceptional cases it may take place on the right side, and in such cases it also generally happens that some folds of the intestine pass into the hernial sac. Hernias have been classified into simple or complicated, recent or old, traumatic (from mechanical injury) or spontaneous.

In recent traumatic hernia there is a swelling on the left side of the lower part of the abdomen. The swelling is greatest in the cases of hernia which are situated on the lower part of the abdomen. Unless an examination is made immediately after the injury has been inflicted it is difficult, and sometimes impossible, to ascertain the exact extent of the rupture, owing to the swelling which subsequently takes place. Frequently there is no loss of appetite, fever, or other general symptoms attending the injury. From the twelfth to the fifteenth day the swelling has generally subsided to such an extent that it is possible by an examination to determine the extent of the rupture.

In old cows what is termed spontaneous hernia may sometimes take place without any direct injury. The occurrence of this form of hernia is explained by the increase in the size of the abdomen, which takes place in an advanced stage of pregnancy, causing a thinning and stretching of the muscular fibers, which at last may rupture, or give way. Such hernias frequently occur about the end of the period of gestation, and in some instances have contained the right sac of the rumen, the omentum, the small and large intestines, a portion of the liver, and the pregnant uterus.

In old hernias the swelling is soft and elastic, and if they have not contracted adhesions to the sides of the laceration, they can be made to disappear by pressure carefully applied. Sometimes this accident is complicated by a rupture of the rumen, constituting a complicated hernia. If a portion of the contents of the rumen escape into the abdomen, the case will be aggravated by the occurrence of peritonitis.

Hernia of the Bowel.—When the intestines form the contents of the hernia, it will be situated at the right side of the abdomen. In an intestinal hernia the swelling is usually not painful, of a doughy consistency or elastic, according as the intestines does or does not contain alimentary matter. This swelling can generally be made to disappear by pressure, and when it has been reduced one can easily recognize the direction and extent of the hernial opening. Hernias of the bowel which are situated at the upper and right side of the abdomen are usually formed by the small intestine. They are less easily reduced than a hernia in a lower situation, but when reduction has been effected they are less readily reproduced than those occurring lower. In hernias of the small intestine, adhesion of the protruding parts to the walls of the opening, or strangulation, are complications which sometimes take place. If adhesion has taken place the hernia can not be reduced by pressure, and when strangulation has occurred the animal shows symptoms of pain—is restless, turns its nose to the painful part, and shows those symptoms which are usually collectively designated under the term colic. If relief is not afforded, the animal will die.

Hernia of the Rennet, or Fourth Stomach.—This disease occasionally occurs in calves and is usually caused by a blow from a cow's horn on the right flank of the calf. After such an accident a swelling forms on the right flank near the last rib. This swelling may be neither hot nor painful, even at first, and is soft to the touch. It can be made to disappear by careful pressure, when the sides of the aperture through which it has passed can be felt. The application of pressure so as to cause the disappearance of the hernia is best made immediately after the occurrence of the accident, or when the edema which accompanies the swelling has disappeared.

Treatment. — When a hernia is reducible — that is, can be pushed back into the abdomen—then, if it is of recent occurrence, it is advisable to maintain the natural position of the parts by bandaging and to allow the walls of the laceration to grow together. The bowels should be kept reasonably empty by avoiding the use of bulky food, and the animal must be kept quiet.

The following method of bandaging is recommended by Bouley: First prepare a bandage (must be of strong material), about 10 yards long and between 3 and 4 inches broad, and a flexible and solid piece of pasteboard adapted in size to the surface of the hernia. The protruding organ must then be replaced in the abdomen and maintained in that position during the application of the bandage.

Vat and Apparatus.

Ducking the Animal.

Animal Walking Out.

CAGE VAT FOR DIPPING CATTLE. Dept. of Agr.

This being done, a layer of melted pitch and turpentine is quickly spread on the skin covering the seat of the hernia, so as to extend somewhat beyond that space. This adhesive layer is then covered with a layer of fine tow, then a new layer of pitch and turpentine is spread on the tow, and the piece of pasteboard is applied on the layer of pitch, its outer surface being covered with the same preparation. Lastly, the bandage, adhering to the piece of pasteboard, to the skin, and to the different turns which it makes around the body, is carefully applied so as to form an immovable, rigid, and solid bandage, which will retain the hernia long enough for the wound in the abdominal walls to heal permanently.

If the hernia is old and small it may be treated by injecting a strong solution of common salt about the edges of the tear. This causes swelling and inflammation, which, respectively, forces the protruded organ back and closes the opening. There is some risk attached to this method of treatment.

In small, old ventral hernias the method of compressing and sloughing off the skin has been used successfully. If the hernia is large a radical operation will be necessary, and this is also true when the symptoms indicate that a hernia is strangulated. This operation is performed by cutting down on the hernia, restoring the organ to the abdominal cavity, and then closing the wound with two sets of stitches; the inner stitches, in the muscular wall, should be made with catgut and the outer stitches, in the skin, may be made with silk or silver wire. The strictest surgical cleanliness must be observed. Bleeding vessels should be tied. Then a compress composed of ten or twelve folds of cloth must be placed smoothly over the seat of injury and a bandage applied around the body, the two ends being fastened at the back. In the smaller kinds of hernia, nitric acid may sometimes be applied with success. This treatment should not be applied until the swelling and inflammation attending the appearance of the hernia have subsided; then, the contents of the hernia having been returned, the surface of skin corresponding to it is sponged over with a solution composed of 1 part of nitric acid to 2 parts of water. This treatment acts by exciting considerable inflammation, which has the effect of causing swelling, and thus frequently closing the hernial opening and preventing the contents of the sac from returning. A second application should not be made until the inflammation excited by the first has subsided. In what is termed spontaneous hernia it is useless to apply any kind of treatment.

Umbilical Hernia.—The umbilicus, or navel, is the aperture through which the blood vessels pass from the mother to the fetus and naturally the sides of this aperture ought to adhere or unite after birth. In very young animals, and sometimes in new-born calves, this aperture in the abdominal muscles remains open and a part of the bowel or a portion of the mesentery may slip through the opening, constituting what is called umbilical hernia. The wall of the sac is formed by the skin which is covered on the inner surface by a layer of cellular tissue, and within this there is sometimes, but not always, a layer of peritoneum. The contents of the hernia may be formed by a part of the bowel, by a portion of the peritoneum, or may contain portions of both peritoneum and bowel. When the sac contains only peritoneum it has a doughy feel, but when it is formed by a portion of the bowel it will be more elastic on applying pressure.

Causes.—In the new-born animal the opening of the navel is generally large, and this opening may sometimes give way to the pressure of the bowel on account of the weak and relaxed condition of the abdominal muscles. This defective and abnormal condition of the umbilicus is frequently hereditary. It may be occasioned by roughly pulling away the umbilical cord; through kicks or blows on the belly; through any severe straining by which the sides of the navel are stretched apart. We may mention in this connection that it is best in new-born calves to tie the umbilical cord tightly about 2 inches from the navel, and then to leave it alone, when it will drop off in a few days in most cases, leaving the navel in a closed condition.

Treatment.—It is well to bear in mind that many, and especially the smaller, umbilical hernias will heal spontaneously; that is, nature effects a cure. As the animal gets older the abdominal muscles get stronger and possess more power of resistance to pressure, the bowels become larger and do not pass so readily through a small opening, so that from a combination of causes there is a gradual growing together or adhesion of the sides of the navel. In cases of umbilical hernia where there are no indications that a spontaneous cure will take place, the calf should be laid on its back, and immediately on this being done the hernia will often disappear into the abdomen. If it does not its reduction may be brought about by gentle handling, endeavoring, if need be, to empty the organs forming the hernia before returning them into the abdomen. After the hernia has been returned the hair should be clipped from the skin covering it and a compress composed of ten or twelve folds of linen or cotton should be applied, first smearing the skin with pitch and then a bandage about 3 inches wide should be passed round the body so as to retain the compress in position. The lower part of the compress should be smeared with pitch, and also those portions of the bandage which pass over it, so as to keep it solid and prevent it from shifting. In some cases it will be found that the contents of the sac can not be returned into the abdomen, and this generally arises from the fact that some part of the contents of the sac has grown to or become adherent to the edges of the umbilical opening. In such a case the skin must be carefully laid open in the long direction, the adhesions of the protruding organs carefully separated from the umbilicus, and after the protruding parts have been returned into the abdomen, the sides of the umbilicus must be freshened if necessary by paring, and then the edges of the opening brought together by catgut stitches; the wound in the skin must then also be brought together by stitches. The wound must be carefully dressed every day and a bandage passed round the body so as to cover and protect the part operated on.

In the small hernias nitric acid has been used successfully in the same manner as has been described in speaking of the treatment of ventral hernia. Sulphuric acid has also been used for a similar purpose, diluting it to the extent of 1 part of acid to 3 or 5 of water. In thin-skinned animals the weaker preparations ought to be preferred, and caution must be exercised in using such preparations so as not to destroy the tissues on which they are applied.

Another method of treatment is, after the contents of the sac have been returned into the abdomen, to tie a piece of strong waxed cord round the pendulous portion which formed the outer covering of the hernia. The string is apt to slacken after two or three days, when a new piece of cord should be applied above the first one. The constriction of the skin sets up inflammation, which generally extends to the umbilicus and causes the edges to adhere together, and by the time the portion of skin below the ligature has lost its vitality and dropped off, the umbilicus is closed and there is no danger of abdominal organs protruding through it. This is what takes place when this method has a favorable result, though if the umbilicus does not become adherent and the skin sloughs, the bowels will protrude through the opening.

Gut-Tie (Peritoneal Hernia).—In peritoneal hernia of the ox a loop or knuckle of intestine enters from the abdomen into a rent in that part of the peritoneum which is situated at the margin of the hip bone or it passes under the remains of the spermatic cord, the end of which may be grown fast to the inner inguinal ring. The onward pressure of the bowel, as well as the occasional turning of the latter round the spermatic cord, is the cause of the cord exercising considerable pressure on the bowel, which occasions irritation, obstructs the passage of excrement, and excites inflammation, which terminates in gangrene and death.

The rent in the peritoneum is situated at the upper and front part of the pelvis, nearer to the sacrum than the pubis.

Causes.—Among the causes of peritoneal hernia considerable importance is attached to a method of castration which is practiced in certain districts, viz, the tearing or rupturing of the spermatic cord by main force instead of dividing it at a proper distance above the testicle in a surgical manner. After this violent and rough method of operating, the cord retracts into the abdomen and its stump becomes adherent to some part of the peritoneum, or it may wind around the bowel and then the stump becomes adherent so that strangulation of the bowel results. The rough dragging on the cord may also cause a tear in the peritoneum, the result of which need not be described. The severe exertion of ascending hills and mountains, drawing heavy loads, or the straining which oxen undergo while fighting each other may also give rise to peritoneal hernia.

Symptoms.—The ox suddenly becomes very restless, stamps with his feet, moves backward and forward, hurriedly lies down, rises, moves his tail uneasily, and kicks at his belly with the foot of the affected side. The pain evinced may diminish, but soon returns again. In the early stage there are frequent passages of dung, but after the lapse of eighteen to twenty-four hours this ceases, the bowel apparently being emptied up to the point of strangulation, and the passages now consist only of a little mucus mixed with blood. When injections are given at this time the water passes out of the bowel without even being colored. The animal lies down on the side where the hernia exists and stretches out his hind feet in a backward direction. These two particular symptoms serve to distinguish this affection from enteritis and invagination of the bowel. As time passes, the animal becomes quieter, but this cessation of pain may indicate that gangrene of the bowel has set in, and may, therefore, under certain circumstances, be considered a precursor of death. Gangrene may take place in from four to six days, when perforation of the bowel may occur and death result in a short time.

Treatment.—The ox should in the first place be examined by oiling the hand and arm and passing it into the rectum; the hand should be passed along the margin of the pelvis, beginning at the sacrum and continuing downward toward the inguinal ring, when a soft, painful swelling will be felt, which may vary from the size of an apple to that of the two fists. This swelling will be felt to be tightly compressed by the spermatic cord. It very rarely happens that there is any similar swelling on the left side, though it is best in such cases to make a thorough examination. The bowel has sometimes been released from its position by driving the ox down a hill, by causing him to jump from a height of 2 feet to the ground, and the expedient of trotting him has been resorted to with the hope that the jolting movement might bring about a release of the bowel. If the simple expedients mentioned have been tried and failed, then the hand being passed into the rectum should be pressed gently on the swelling in an upward and forward direction, so as to endeavor to push the imprisoned portion of the bowel back into the abdomen. While this is being done the ox's hind feet should stand on higher ground than the front, so as to favor the slipping out of the bowel by its own weight, and at the same time an assistant should squeeze the animal's loins, so as to cause it to bend downward and so relax the band formed by the spermatic cord. If the imprisoned portion of gut is freed, which may be ascertained by the disappearance of the swelling, the usual sounds produced by the bowels moving in the abdomen will be heard, and in a few hours the feces and urine will be passed as usual. If the means mentioned fail in releasing the imprisoned portion of the gut, then an incision about 4 inches long must be made in the right flank in a downward direction, the hand introduced into the abdomen, the situation and condition of swelling exactly ascertained, and then a probe-pointed knife inserted between the imprisoned bowel and band compressing it, and turned outward against the band, the latter being then cautiously divided and the imprisoned gut allowed to escape, or, if necessary, the bowel should be drawn gently from its position into the abdomen. The wound in the flank must be brought together in the same way as in the case of the wound made in operating for impaction of the rumen.

Wounds of the Abdomen.—A wound of the abdomen may merely penetrate the skin; but as such cases are not attended with much danger, nor their treatment with much difficulty, we propose to consider here merely those wounds which penetrate the entire thickness of the abdominal walls and expose to a greater or less extent the organs contained in that cavity.

Causes.—Such accidents may be occasioned by falling on fragments of broken glass or other sharp objects. A blow from the horn of another animal may produce a wound which penetrates the abdomen. Exposure and protusion of some of the abdominal organs may also be occasioned by the incautious use of caustics in the treatment of umbilical or ventral hernia. The parts which generally escape through an abdominal wound are the small intestine and floating colon.

Symptoms.—When the abdominal wound is small, the bowel exposed presents the appearance of a small round tumor, but in a few moments a loop of intestine may emerge from the opening. The animal then shows symptoms of severe pain by pawing with his feet, which has the effect of accelerating the passage of new loops of intestine through the wound, so that the mass which they form may even touch the ground. The pain becomes so great that the ox now not only paws but lies down and rolls, thus tearing and crushing his bowels. In such cases it is best to slaughter the animal at once; but in the case of a valuable animal in which tearing and crushing of the bowels has not taken place, the bowels should be washed with freshly boiled water, reduced to the temperature of the body, and returned, and the wounds in the muscle and skin brought together in a manner somewhat similar to that which was described in speaking of ventral hernia.

DISEASES OF THE LIVER AND SPLEEN.

Jaundice (the Yellows, or Congestion of the Liver).—When jaundice exists, there is a yellow appearance of the white of the eyes and of the mucous membrane of the mouth. A similar aspect of the skin may also be observed in animals which are either partly or altogether covered with white hair. Jaundice is then merely a symptom of disease and ought to direct attention to ascertaining, if possible, the cause or causes which have given rise to it. A swollen condition of the mucous membrane of that part of the bowel called the duodenum may produce jaundice, as that mechanically closes the orifice of the biliary duct. In constipation there is an inactive or torpid condition of the bowel, and the bile which passes into the intestine may be absorbed and cause the yellow staining of jaundice. Jaundice is one of the symptoms of Texas fever. It may also arise from the presence of parasites or gallstones in the ducts, forming a mechanical obstruction to the onward flow of bile. The conditions under which jaundice most commonly calls for treatment are when cattle have been highly fed and kept in a state of inactivity. At such a time there is an excess of nutritive elements carried into the blood, which is associated with increased fullness of the portal vein and hepatic artery. When continued high feeding has produced this congested state of the liver, the functions of that organ become disordered, so that a considerable portion of the bile, instead of being excreted and passing into the intestine, is absorbed by the hepatic veins.

Symptoms.—This disease, although rare, occurs most frequently among stall-fed cattle. Pressure along the margin of the short ribs on the right side produces pain; the appetite is poor and the animal shows hardly any inclination to drink; the mucous membranes of the eye and mouth are yellow, the urine has a yellow or brown appearance, the animal lies down much and moves with reluctance, moans occasionally, and has a tottering gait. The ears and horns are alternately hot and cold; in cows the secretion of milk is much diminished, and that which is secreted has a bitter taste; sometimes the animal has a dry, painful cough and presents a dull, stupefied appearance.

Treatment.—In such cases it is advisable to produce a free action of the bowels, so as to remove the usually congested condition of the portal vein and liver. For this purpose we recommend the administration of the following dose: Sulphate of soda, 16 ounces; molasses, 1 pint; warm water, 1 quart. The sulphate of soda is dissolved by stirring it up in tepid water. Following this the animal should have a heaping tablespoonful of artificial Carlsbad salts in the food three times daily. This treatment may be assisted by giving occasional injections of warm water and soap. The diet should be laxative and moderate in quantity, and may consist of coarse bran mash, pulped roots, grass in the season, and hay in moderate quantity.

Inflammation of the Liver (Hepatitis).—Hepatitis is an inflammation of the liver, and usually occurs as a complication of some infectious disease. It may also occur as a complication of gastro-intestinal catarrh, or in the hot weather from over-heating or damaged (putrid or fermented) foods.

Symptoms.—The symptoms are sometimes obscure, and their real significance is frequently overlooked. The most prominent symptoms are yellowness of the white of the eye and of the membrane lining the mouth, the appetite is poor, the body presents an emaciated appearance, the feces are light colored, while the urine is likely to be unusually dark; there is thirst, and pain is caused by pressing over the liver. The gait is weak, and the animal lies down more than usual, and while doing so frequently has its head turned round resting on the side of its chest.

Treatment.—Give a purge of Glauber's salts, and after it has operated give artificial Carlsbad salts in each feed, as advised under "Jaundice." Give green food and plenty of water. Oil of turpentine should be rubbed in well once a day over the region of the liver. The skin on which it should be applied extends from the false ribs on the right side to 6 inches in front of the last one, and from the backbone to 12 inches on the right side of it.

The Fluke Disease. [See pages 368, 370.]

INFLAMMATION OF THE SPLEEN (SPLENITIS).

This disease occurs almost solely as a result of the existence of some infectious disease, and the symptoms caused by it merge with the symptoms of the accompanying causative disease. The spleen is seriously involved, and becomes enlarged and soft in Texas fever, anthrax, and blood poisoning.

DISEASES OF THE PERITONEUM.

Peritonitis.—Peritonitis consists in an inflammation of the peritoneum, which is the thin, delicate membrane that lines the abdomen and covers the abdominal organs.

Causes.—Wounds are the usual cause in cattle. The wound may be of the abdominal wall or of the intestines, stomach, or uterus; or inflammation may extend from one of the organs of the abdominal cavity to the peritoneum; so this disease may complicate enteritis or inflamed womb. A sharp metal body may perforate the second stomach and allow the gastric contents to escape, irritating the peritoneum. This disease may follow castration or operation for hernia.

Symptoms.—A continuous or occasional shivering; the animal lies down, but appears uneasy; it frequently turns its head toward its belly and lows plaintively; pressure on the flanks produces pain; has no appetite; muzzle is dry and no rumination; while standing its legs are placed well under its body; pulse small and hard. The evacuations from the bowels are dry and hard. If this disease is complicated by the presence of inflammation of the bowels, the pain is more severe and the animal is more restless. The skin is cold and dry in the early stage of this disease, but in a more advanced stage this condition may be succeeded by heat of the skin and quick breathing. The fits of trembling, uneasiness, small and hard pulse, and tension of the left flank are symptoms the presence of which should enable one to reach the conclusion that peritonitis exists.

Post-Mortem Appearance.—The membrane lining the abdomen and covering the surface of the bowels is reddened to a greater or less extent, and there is usually considerable serous, or watery, fluid collected in the abdomen.

Treatment.—When we have to do with the form of peritonitis resulting from an injury, as when the horn of another animal has been thrust through the abdominal walls, this lesion must be treated in accordance with directions before given, but the general treatment must be similar to that which follows. Peritonitis resulting from castration or from parturition fever must also be treated in connection with the special conditions which give rise to it, as the general treatment of this disease must be modified to some extent by the exciting cause,

The aim must be to discover and remove the cause. The cause must be treated according to its nature. Harms strongly recommends borax in the treatment of peritonitis. He gives 6 ounces in the first twenty-four hours, divided into three doses, and afterwards he gives 6 drams three times daily. Opium in doses of 2 to 3 drams may be given. To bring on evacuations of the bowels it is better to give rectal injections than to administer purges. The strength may be sustained by coffee, whisky, or camphor.

The body should be warmly clothed, and it is advisable, when practicable, to have a blanket which has been wrung out of hot water placed over the abdomen, then covered by several dry blankets, which are maintained in position by straps or ropes passing round the body. The wet blanket must be changed as it cools—the object of treatment being to warm the surface of the body and to determine as much blood to the skin as possible. The diet should consist of laxative food and drinks, such as linseed tea. If peritonitis assumes chronic form the diet should be nutritious, such as selected clover hay, linseed cake, grass, etc., and iodide of potassium should be given in dram doses dissolved in a pint of water three times a day.

Dropsy of the Abdomen (Ascites).—In this disease there is a serous, or watery, effusion in the cavity of the abdomen. *Causes.*—When old animals are fed on innutritious food or when an animal is reduced by disease, they become anemic; or, in other words, their blood becomes impoverished and dropsy may follow this condition. An innutritious and insufficient diet will produce the same effect in young animals. It is one of the results of peritonitis, and may also arise from acute or chronic inflammation of the liver, such as is of common occurrence when flukes are present in the liver in large numbers. Heart disease and chronic lung disease may be followed by ascites. It is sometimes, in calves, a symptom of infestation with worms.

Symptoms.—A gradual increase in the size of the abdomen at its lower part, while the flanks become hollow; pallor of the mucous membrane of the mouth and eye; weak and sluggish gait; want of appetite, and irregularity in ruminating. On percussion, or tapping the surface of the abdomen with the fingers, a dull sound is produced. If the hand and arm are oiled and passed into the rectum so far as possible, on moving the hand from one side to the other the fluctuation caused by the presence of fluid in the abdomen may be felt.

Treatment.—The cause must be discovered if possible and removed. The diet should be nutritious, and in those cases where we have merely to deal with anemia (the bloodless state) arising from insufficient diet, the use of tonics and diuretics, at the same time keeping the skin warm, may bring about a gradual absorption of the fluid contained in the abdomen. One of the following powders may be mixed with the animal's food three times a day; or, if there is any uncertainty as to its being taken in that way, it should be mixed with sirup, so as to form a paste, and smeared well

DIRTY BARNYARD. DEPT. OF AGR. 1909.

A DANGEROUSLY TUBERCULOUS COW. DEPT. OF AGR.

back on the animal's tongue with a flat wooden spoon: Carbonate of iron, 3 ounces; powdered gentian, 3 ounces; powdered nitrate of potash, 3 ounces; mix and divide into twelve powders. The administration of purgatives which promote a watery discharge from the mucous surface of the bowels, also tends, by diminishing the serum of the blood, to bring about absorption and a gradual removal of the fluid contained in the abdomen. Large doses should not be given, but moderate doses should be administered morning and night, so as to produce a laxative effect on the bowels for some days. To attain this end the following may be used: Sulphate of soda, 8 ounces; powdered ginger, half an ounce; mix in 2 quarts of tepid water, and then give at one dose.

NON-INFECTIOUS DISEASES OF THE ORGANS OF RESPIRATION.

COLD IN THE HEAD (CATARRH).

Nasal catarrh is an inflammation of the mucous membranes of the nostrils and upper air passages. Simple catarrh is not a serious disease in itself, but if neglected is liable to be complicated with laryngitis, bronchitis, pneumonia, pleurisy, and other diseases of the respiratory organs, which are of a serious nature and sometimes fatal. Catarrh is a common disease among cattle. It is often due to sudden exposure to wet and cold after they have been accustomed to shelter. It may arise from inhalation of irritating gases. It is sometimes due to certain specific atmospheric conditions, and may assume an enzoötic form. It is very debilitating, and requires prompt and judicious treatment.

Symptoms.—Redness of the mucous membranes of the nose, redness and watering of the eyes. The mucous membrane first becomes dry; afterwards a watery discharge appears, and later on in severe cases the discharge becomes mucopurulent. In mild cases there is little or no fever, but in severe cases the fever may run high. The animal becomes dull, languid, and is not inclined to move about, and the appetite may become impaired; there is variable temperature of the horns and ears. If in a cow giving milk, the secretion diminishes; the mucus from the eyes and nose becomes thicker and yellower. Afterwards, as the symptoms increase in severity, the discharge becomes mucopurulent.

Treatment.—The animal should be housed in a well-ventilated place, with good hygienic surroundings. In cold and damp weather it should be kept warm with blanketing. Give hot, medicated inhalations in severe cases. If the fever is high this may be reduced by giving nitrate of potassium, from 1 to 2 ounces, in the drinking water, three times daily. Diffusible stimulants are beneficial in most cases. Too much importance can not be attached to good nursing. There is no necessity to resort to the old system of bleeding, purging, or the use of powerful sedatives.

BLEEDING FROM THE NOSE (EPISTAXIS).

Bleeding from the nostrils is rather rare in cattle. It may arise from any one of a variety of causes, but usually results from disease or injury to the mucous membranes, or to violent exertions in coughing and sneezing. It is seldom serious. The bleeding generally occurs in drops from one nostril only, accompanied by sneezing, and without frothing. Bleeding from the lungs comes from both nostrils, is bright red, frothy, and accompanied by a cough.

Treatment.—In many cases the bleeding will cease spontaneously, and all that is necessary is to keep the animal quiet and bathe the head and nostrils with cold water. Ascertain the cause of the bleeding and be governed accordingly in the treatment. In severe and exceptional cases, where the hemorrhage is persistent and long continued, tie the animal's head to a high rack or beam and apply cold water, ice, or have recourse to styptic injections. If the hemorrhage is profuse and persistent, give either a drench composed of 1½ drams of acetate of lead dissolved in a pint of water or 1½ drams of gallic acid dissolved in a pint of water.

SORE THROAT (LARYNGITIS).

Laryngitis consists of an inflammation of the mucous membrane lining the larynx. It may be either a primary or a secondary disease, complicated or uncomplicated. In the majority of cases it is due to some form of exposure, a sudden change from warm to cold surroundings, or exposure to cold storms. It may also arise from inhaling irritating gases. It may be the result of external violence. In an acute attack of laryngitis there is an elevation of temperature, pain on pressure over the region of larynx, violent paroxysms of coughing, difficult and noisy respiration. The nostrils are dilated, the nose extended, and the animal has a frightened expression. There is marked difficulty in swallowing.

Treatment.—This consists of fomentations and hot applications over the throat. Stimulating liniments, mustard mixed with *cold* water and well rubbed in with a stiff brush, or other forms of counter-irritation may be applied in severe cases. Hot inhalations should be frequently resorted to, and often afford much relief to the suffering animal. In this disease medicines should be given so far as possible in the form of electuaries (soft solid), on account of the difficulty of deglutition. Large drafts of medicines have a tendency to produce violent spells of coughing, and in this way retard recovery. The subjoined formula for an electuary will be found to answer the purpose in ordinary cases: Chlorate of potassium, pulverized, 8 ounces; fluid extract of belladonna, 2 ounces; powdered opium, 1 ounce; powdered licorice root, 8 ounces; sirup, sufficient quantity; mix. At frequent intervals place a small tablespoonful of the mixture on the tongue or back teeth. Or the following may be used instead: Aloes, powdered opium, and gum camphor in equal parts; mix. Rub an ounce on the molar teeth every four or five hours. The bowels should be kept open and the diet should be such as the patient can easily swallow. Warm, sloppy mashes, boiled oatmeal gruel, linseed tea, and the like are the most suitable substances. If suffocation be threatened during the course of the disease tracheotomy should be performed without delay. The details of the operation are fully described under the head of Surgical operations.

When the disease assumes a chronic form strong counterirritation is indicated. A cantharides blister may be applied, or the following ointment may be used: Biniodid of mercury 1 part, lard 6 parts; mix. In some cases it will be found necessary to repeat the above application.

BRONCHITIS.

Bronchitis is an inflammation of the mucous membrane of the bronchial tubes. When a primary disease it is generally the result of what is commonly known as catching cold. It may be secondary to or complicated with many of the diseases of the respiratory system. It may also be caused by breathing irritating gases; or by the introduction of foreign bodies into the bronchial tubes, which sometimes results from injudicious and careless drenching when the larynx is in a temporary relaxed state. It may be acute or chronic, and is divided, according to the seat of the inflammation, into bronchitis proper where the large tubes are affected, or capillary bronchitis where the smaller tubes are affected.

Symptoms.—Loss of appetite, elevation of temperature, generally 104° to 105° F. The inspiration is incomplete, short, and painful, and the expiration is prolonged. The pulse is increased in frequency and is hard. A characteristic and painful cough is present, but it is paroxysmal and incomplete. Auscultation and percussion greatly aid us in a diagnosis. A normal sound is observed on percussion. On auscultation, in the early stages, rhonchus rales are detected if the larger tubes are affected, and sibilant rales if the smaller tubes are affected. Later on mucous rales are noted, and sometimes all sounds in certain parts are absent, which is due to the plugging up of the tubes. This plugging of the tubes, if extensive enough, is sometimes the cause of death, or death may result from extension of the disease to the lungs or pleura.

Treatment.—The animal should be placed in a light, well-ventilated box, and the bowels kept in a soft condition by enemas, etc. Avoid violent purgatives. The body should be kept warm by blanketing. In the early stages give three times daily a draft composed as follows: Extracts of belladonna, 2 drams; solution of acetate of ammonium, 4 fluid ounces; water, one-half pint. In the later stage of the disease substitute the following formula, which may be given twice daily. Carbonate of ammonium, 3 drams; liquor hydrochlorate of strychnine, 2 fluid drams; spirits of nitrous ether, 1 fluid ounce; water, one-half pint.

In some cases the following is preferable to either of the above and may be given in a pint of linseed tea every four hours: Spirits of nitrous ether, 1½ ounces; aromatic spirits of ammonia, 2 ounces; powdered camphor, 2 drams. The food should be light and nutritious.

Bronchitis is liable to assume a chronic form if not properly treated in the earliest stage. Remedial treatment is of little value when the disease becomes chronic.

PLEURISY.

Pleurisy is an inflammation of the serous membrane lining the chest cavity and enveloping the lungs. It is somewhat rare as an independent disease, but it often complicates pneumonia; indeed, it is often due to the same germ that causes pneumonia—pneumococcus. It may arise from exposure to cold or wet or from external violence and is usually present in some degree in cases where the ribs have been fractured with or without a penetrated wound.

Symptoms.—In the first stage there is great pain aggravated by movement, and the animal is usually stiff as though foundered, the pulse is quick and hard, the breathing abdominal, the chest being fixed so far as possible, the inspiration short and jerky, the expiration longer. The pain is due to the friction of the dry, inflamed pleural surfaces of the lung and chest on each other. At this stage the ear detects a dry friction murmur resembling somewhat the sound made by rubbing two pieces of sole leather together. Pressure between the ribs gives pain and usually causes the animal to flinch and grunt. The muzzle is hot and dry, the mouth slimy, and the secretions scanty. After a day or two the severity of the symptoms is much lessened, the temperature, which during the first days may have been as high as 106° F., falls to 103° or 104°, the pain decreases, the stiffness disappears, and the patient eats a little. The pulse softens, but remains quicker than normal. Now, day by day the patient loses a little strength, the friction sound disappears as the exudation moistens the pleural surfaces; percussion now shows a horizontal line of dullness, which day by day rises higher in the chest, the respiration grows more frequent and labored, the countenance is anxious and haggard, the eyes sink somewhat in their sockets, and in unfavorable cases death occurs during the second or third week, either from asphyxia or heart failure.

In pleurisy, as in pneumonia, the elbows are usually turned outward. Care must be taken to differentiate pleurisy from traumatic pericarditis (which see). In the latter condition the area of dullness of the heart is much increased, and usually a splashing sound is heard at each beat of the heart. Another diagnostic symptom of value is that in traumatic pericarditis respiration is painful, not difficult, and the respiratory rate is very much increased on movement. In both conditions a considerable swelling of the dewlap may be noticed in the later stages.

Treatment.—Give the same general care as recommended in bronchitis or pneumonia. In the early stages give a febrifuge to reduce the fever, as directed for pneumonia. For relief of the cough give electuary formula, which will be found in the treatment of laryngitis. The bowels must be kept relaxed and the kidneys secreting freely. In the stage of effusion give the following three times daily: Digitalis tincture, 1 ounce; iodid of potassium, 30 to 60 grains; mix. Apply strong counterirritant to chest and put seton in dewlap. (See "Setoning,"). If collapse of the lung is threatened, a surgical operation is sometimes performed, termed *paracentesis thoracis,* which consists in puncturing the chest cavity and drawing off a part of the fluid. The instruments used are a small trocar and canula, which are introduced between the eighth and ninth ribs. Draw the skin forward so that the external wound may not correspond with the puncture of the chest, to prevent the entrance of air. Only a portion of the fluid should be removed. The animal gets immediate relief, but it is generally only temporary, as there is a tendency for the fluid to accumulate again.

PNEUMONIA.

This is an inflammation of the lung substance. It is divided into three different forms, viz: First, croupous pneumonia; second, catarrhal pneumonia; and third, interstitial pneumonia. But these various forms can only be differentiated by the expert, and I therefore deem it necessary for the purposes of the present work to treat the subject under the general head of pneumonia.

The causes of pneumonia in general are the same as those of the various other inflammatory diseases of the respiratory tract. The germ is called the pneumococcus. It mostly follows congestion of the lungs, but may in rare cases have a parasitic origin.

Symptoms.—In the first stage, that of congestion, the disease is usually ushered in by a chill, although this may not always be observed by the attendant. This is followed by an elevation of temperature, usually 105° to 106° F., or it may be even higher. The respirations are quick and shallow; the nostrils are dilated; the pulse is full and hard. Cough may or may not appear in this stage. The nose is hot and dry; the tongue sometimes protrudes and is slimy; the coat is staring, and the skin dry and harsh. The urine is usually diminished in quantity, high colored, and the bowels constipated. The animal stands with the fore legs wide apart to facilitate respiration. On auscultation crepitation will be observed over the portion of the lung affected. The sounds elicited on percussion are practically normal in this stage.

In the second stage the temperature generally drops one or two degrees, and respiration is performed with much difficulty. The cough is frequent and painful. The animal still stands with the fore legs wide apart and the elbows turned outward. If it assumes the recumbent position it rests on the sternum. All secretions are more or less suspended, particularly the milk in cows. The animal has a haggard appearance, and the pulse becomes small and wiry at this period. The extremities are hot and cold alternately; the crepitation which was present in the first stage is now absent, and no sound on auscultation will be heard, except it be a slight wheezing or whistling noise. On percussion dullness over the diseased lung is manifested, indicating consolidation. The lung has now assumed a characteristic liver-like appearance.

In the third stage, if the disease is going to terminate favorably, the cough becomes loose, the animal improves, the appetite returns, and the symptoms above detailed rapidly subside; but if, on the other hand, resolution is not progressing, the lung substance is broken down, is heavy, and will sink in water. In fatal cases the breath has a peculiar fetid, cadaverous odor, and is taken in short gasps; the horns, ears, and extremities become cold and clammy, and the pulse is imperceptible. On auscultation, when suppuration is taking place and the lung structure is breaking down, a bubbling or gurgling crepitation, caused by the passage of air through pus, will be heard.

Treatment.—Good hygienic surroundings and good nursing are essential in connection with the medical treatment. The probability of recovery depends largely on the extent of the lung tissue involved, as well as on the intensity of the inflammatory process. In the early stage, when the fever is high, give febrifuges. If the pulse be strong and full, aconite (Fleming's tincture, 1 to 2 drams, every four or five hours) may be given for a short time, but should be discontinued as soon as the fever begins to abate. Aconite is a valuable drug in the hands of the intelligent practitioner, but my experience leads me to believe that not infrequently animals are lost by its injudicious use, for in many febrile conditions it is positively contraindicated, owing to its action upon the heart. In a plethoric animal, with a strong, bounding pulse, bleeding may be resorted to instead of administering aconite. If the bowels are constipated, give calomel, 1 to 3 drams, which acts as a cathartic and a febrifuge. In the second stage diffusible stimulants are required, viz.: Spirits of nitrous ether, 2 ounces; aromatic spirits of ammonia, 1 ounce; mix, and give in gruel three times daily. If the above is not at hand, give an alcoholic stimulant. Half a pint of brandy or whisky may be given in a quart of gruel three times daily. In some cases carbonate of ammonia, 2 to 5 drams, has been found beneficial. Most practitioners apply counterirritants externally, such as mustard plasters, turpentine, and ammonia liniment, or cantharides.

EMPHYSEMA (HEAVES).

Emphysema consists of a rupture of the minute air vesicles of the lung substance, and may be either interlobular or vesicular. There is an extreme interference with respiration, inspiration being short and expiration prolonged. It is a nonfebrile condition, in which the appetite is not decreased and the milk secretion is kept up. It may be caused by an attack of asthma, or may result from chronic bronchitis. The disease can be diagnosed by the marked interference with respiration. The animal, as a rule, is emaciated, has a staring coat, and is hidebound. If percussion is resorted to, the animal's chest will give a tympanic, drum-like sound. The normal resonant sound is exaggerated.

Treatment.—The disease is incurable, and only a palliative form of treatment can be carried out. The destruction of the animal is often advisable, from a humane as well as from a financial point of view.

PULMONARY CONGESTION.

Cattle that are overdriven or overworked are liable to pulmonary congestion in an acute form, and sometimes pulmonary apoplexy. In such cases the animal should be allowed to rest, and if the weather be hot put in a shady place. Give stimulants internally, unload the venous side of the heart by bleeding, and apply stimulating applications to the legs, and bandage.

HEMOPTYSIS.

This is a term used to signify bleeding from the lungs. The trouble may result from a previous congestion of the lungs, or from a breaking down of the lung substance, or from specific disorders.

Bleeding from the lungs comes from both nostrils and from the mouth. The blood is bright red, frothy, and accompanied by a cough, the flow being somewhat profuse and intermingled with mucus. It may cease of its own accord. Internally hemostatics are indicated, and locally over the sides cold applications have a tendency to check the hemorrhage. Give the animal a drench composed of 1½ drams of gallic acid dissolved in a pint of water.

ABSCESS OF THE LUNG.

Abscesses of the lung sometimes form during the course of or subsequent to tuberculosis or other diseases. An animal affected with abscess of the lung usually has a protracted, feeble cough and a general appearance of emaciation and anemia. The pulse is feeble and the breath foul. An offensive discharge from the lungs frequently occurs. Percussion and auscultation will aid in making a diagnosis in this condition. The appetite is poor. Such animals go from bad to worse, and their prompt destruction would, as a rule, be to the interest of the owner.

HYDROTHORAX.

Hydrothorax, or dropsy of the chest, is not a disease in itself, but is simply a condition where an effusion takes place in the chest cavity, and is the result or effect of some disease, mostly pleurisy. This condition can be easily diagnosed by physical signs. A loss of the respiratory murmur will be noticed on auscultation, and on percussion dullness or flatness on a line as high as the effusion has taken place. When there is a large amount of effusion present, tapping with the trocar and canula is generally resorted to. The proper method of performing this operation will be found under the head of Pleurisy.

PNEUMOTHORAX.

An accumulation of gas in the pleural sac is known as pneumothorax. The presence of air may either result from an injury of the lung or a wound communicating from the exterior. The indications for treatment are to remove any foreign body that may have penetrated, to exclude the further entrance of the air into the cavity by the closure of the external opening, and to employ antiseptics and adhesive dressings. The air already in the cavity will in most cases be absorbed.

VERMINOUS BRONCHITIS.

This is a disease that sometimes attacks young cattle when pastured in low-lying meadows near rivers subject to flood. It is caused by a small worm, *Strongylus micrurus,* which lodges in large numbers in the trachea and bronchial tubes, giving rise to considerable irritation of the air passages and inflammation. Sometimes the strongylus lodge in large numbers in the windpipe, forming themselves into a ball, and thus choke the animal to death.

Symptoms.—It is liable to attack a number of animals at once, and the weakest are the first to give way. The animal has a remarkably forcible cough, distressing, and of a special hacking and paroxysmal character. A stringy mucus is sometimes expelled during the spells of coughing. This mucus contains the *Strongylus micrurus,* which can be detected, or their ova observed, under a low power of the microscope. The attack has a subacute character and proves very exhausting. The parasites, by becoming entwined in balls, seriously impede respiration, which is always remarkably labored in this disease.

Treatment.—The affected calves should be placed in a dry stable, protected from dampness, and subjected to fumigations of sulphurous anhydrid or chlorin gas. The liberation of chlorin gas is brought about by the action of sulphuric acid, either on a mixture of chloride of sodium and black oxid of manganese or on bleaching powder. Sulphurous anhydrid may be procured by burning sulphur. Some practitioners prescribe small doses of spirits of turpentine in linseed oil. The system requires good support, and the diet should therefore be liberal and nutritious. Equal parts of sulphate of iron, gentian, and ginger make an excellent tonic.

Prevention.—Avoid pastures notorious for generating verminous bronchitis.

PLEURODYNIA.

This is a term applied to rheumatism of the intercostal muscles. The apparent symptoms are quite similar to those of pleurisy. The animal is stiff and not inclined to turn around, and the ribs are kept in a fixed state as much as possible. Pleurodynia may be distinguished from pleurisy by the coexistence of rheumatism in other parts and by the comparative absence of fever, cough, the friction sound, and the effusion into the chest. The treatment for this affection is the same as that for rheumatism affecting other parts.

DISEASES OF THE HEART, BLOOD VESSELS, AND LYMPHATICS.

The heart, blood vessels, and lymphatics may be described as the circulatory apparatus.

The heart is located in the thoracic cavity (chest). It is conical in form, with the base or large part uppermost, while the apex, or point, rests just above the sternum (breastbone). It is situated between the right and left lungs, the apex inclining to the left, and owing to this circumstance the heart beats are best felt on the left side of the chest behind the elbow. The heart may be considered as a hollow muscle, containing four compartments, two on each side. The upper compartments are called auricles and the lower ones are called ventricles. The right auricle and ventricle are completely separated from the left auricle and ventricle by a thick septum or wall, so that there is no communication between the right and left sides of the heart.

At the bottom of each auricle is the auriculo-ventricular opening, each provided with a valve to close it when the heart contracts to force the blood into the arteries. In the interval between the contractions these valves hang down into the ventricles.

The muscular tissue of the heart belongs to that class known as involuntary, because its action is not controlled by the will.

The cavities of the heart are lined by serous membrane, called the endocardium. The endocardium may be considered as continued into the veins and the arteries, forming their internal lining. The walls of the ventricles are thicker than those of the auricles, and the walls of the left ventricle are much thicker than those of the right.

The heart is enveloped by a fibrous sac (or bag), called the pericardium, which assumes much of the general shape of the outer surface of the heart.

The action of the heart is similar to that of a pump and its function is to keep the blood in circulation. The auricles may be considered as the reservoirs or receivers of the blood and the ventricles as the pump chambers. During the interval between contractions, the heart being in momentary repose, the blood pours into the auricles from the veins; the auriculo-ventricular orifices being widely open, the ventricles also receive blood; the auricles contract and the ventricles are filled; contraction of the ventricles follows; the auriculo-ventricular valves are forced up by the pressure of the blood and close the auriculo-ventricular openings and prevent the return of blood into the auricles; the contraction of the ventricles forces the blood from the right ventricle into the lungs through the pulmonary artery and its branches, and from the left ventricle into the aorta and all parts of the body through the arteries. After the contraction of the ventricles the heart is again in momentary repose and being filled with blood, while the valves in the aorta and pulmonary artery close to prevent the return of blood into the ventricles.

The average weight of the heart of an ox is said to be from 3½ to 5 pounds, but, of course, the weight must be very variable in different animals, owing to the many breeds and sizes of cattle.

The vessels that convey the blood from the heart to all parts of the body are called arteries; the vessels which return the blood to the heart are called veins. Between the ultimate ramifications of the arteries and the beginning of the veins there is an intermediate system of very minute vessels called capillaries, which connect the arterial with the venous system of the circulation. The walls of the arteries are possessed of a certain amount of rigidity, sufficient to keep the tubes open when they are empty.

The blood leaves the left ventricle through a single vessel, the common aorta, which divides into the anterior and posterior aortas, which in turn give off the large arteries.

The arteries divide and subdivide (like the branches of a tree), become smaller and smaller, and ultimately ramify into every part of the body, terminating in a network of very small tubes called capillaries, which can only be recognized by the aid of a microscope. The capillaries terminate in veins.

The veins take the blood from the capillaries in all parts of the body. They begin in very small tubes, which unite to become larger in size and less in number as they approach the heart.

In its course an artery is usually accompanied by a vein and in many situations by a nerve. The more important arteries are placed deep within the body; but in those cases where they are superficial they are generally found where least exposed to injury, as, for example, on the inner side of the legs. Arteries are less numerous than veins, and the total capacity of the arteries is much less than that of the veins. A great number of veins are in the tissue immediately beneath the skin, and these are not generally accompanied by arteries. The blood throughout its course, in the heart, arteries, capillaries, and veins, is inclosed within these vessels. There is no opening into the course of the blood, except where the large lymphatics empty into the venous blood.

All the arteries, except the pulmonary artery and its branches, carry bright-red blood, and all the veins, except the pulmonary veins, carry dark-red blood. The impure dark-red blood is collected from the capillary vessels and carried to the right auricle by the veins; it passes down into the right ventricle and thence into the pulmonary artery, and through its branches to the capillaries of the lungs, where the carbonic-acid gas and other impurities are given up to the air in the air cells of the lungs (through the thin walls between the capillaries and the air cells), and where it also absorbs from the air the oxygen gas necessary to sustain life, which changes it to the bright-red, pure blood. It passes from the capillaries to the branches of the pulmonary veins, which convey it to the left auricle of the heart; it then passes through the auriculo-ventricular opening into the left ventricle, the contraction of which forces it through the common aorta into the posterior and anterior aortas. and through all the arteries of the body into the capillaries, where it parts with the oxygen and nutritive elements and where it absorbs carbonic-acid gas and becomes dark colored.

The branches of certain arteries in different parts unite again after subdividing. This reuniting is called anastomosing, and assures a quota of blood to a part if one of the anastomosing arteries should be tied in case of hemorrhage, or should be destroyed by accident or operation.

BLOOD.

The various kinds of food, after being digested in the alimentary canal, are absorbed and carried into the blood by the lymphatics, and by the blood to the places where nutrition is required. The blood takes from all parts of the body all that is useless and no longer required, and carries it to the different organs where it is eliminated from the body. It contains within itself all the elements which nourish the body.

The blood may be considered a fluid holding in solution certain inorganic elements and having certain bodies suspended in it. To facilitate description, the blood may be considered as being made up of the corpuscles and the liquor sanguinis. The corpuscles are of two kinds, the red and the white, the red being the most numerous. The color of the blood is due to the coloring matter in the red corpuscles. The red corpuscles are the oxygen carriers. Both kinds are very minute bodies, which require the aid of the microscope to recognize them. The liquor sanguinis is composed of water containing in solution salts, albumen, and the elements of fibrin.

The lymphatics, or absorbents, are the vessels which carry the lymph and chyle in the blood. They begin as capillaries in all parts of the body, gradually uniting to form larger trunks. Placed along the course of the lymphatic vessels are glands, and in some situations these glands are collected into groups; for example, in the groin, etc. These glands are often involved in inflammation arising from the absorption of deleterious matter.

Absorption is the function of the lymphatics. The liquor sanguinis passes from the blood capillaries to supply nutrition to the tissues. All excess of the liquor sanguinis that is not required is absorbed by the lymphatic vessels and conveyed back to the blood by the lymphatic ducts. The lymphatics which proceed from the intestines convey the chyle into the blood during digestion. As a rule, the lymphatic vessels follow the course of the veins. All of the absorbent vessels convey their contents to the thoracic duct and right great lymphatic vein, which empty into the anterior vena cava, where the lymph and chyle mix with the venous blood, and thus maintain the supply of nutritive elements in the blood.

Pulse.—As fully explained, the heart pumps the blood throughout the arterial system. The arteries are always full and each contraction of the ventricle pumps more blood into them, which distends their elastic walls and sends a wave along them which gradually becomes less perceptible as it nears the very small arteries, and is lost before the capillaries are reached. This wave constitutes the pulse. The sensation or impression given to the finger when placed upon the artery shows the force exerted by the heart and some important facts concerning the condition of the circulation. In cattle the average number of pulsations in a minute (in adults) is from 50 to 60. The pulse is faster than normal after exercise, excitement, on hot days from pain, and as a result of fullness of the stomach. In old animals it is slower than in the young and in males slightly slower than in females. In fevers and inflamations and in local diseases of the heart the pulse rate is increased. If the rate is greater than 100 or 110 to the minute the outlook for recovery is not good.

Other variations of the pulse are known as infrequent pulse, which means that the number of pulsations in a given time is less than normal. The irregular or the intermittent pulse is when the pulsations do not follow in regular order. The large pulse and the small pulse refer to the volume of the pulse, which may be larger or smaller than usual. The strong pulse and the feeble pulse refer to the strength or weakness of the pulsation. The pulse is said to be hard when the vessel feels hard and incompressible. The soft pulse is the reverse of the hard one. By dicrotic pulse is meant that kind of pulsation which makes each beat seem double, and therefore it is generally called the double pulse.

The venous or jugular pulse is the pulsation so frequently observed in the jugular vein of cattle. It is particularly noticeable while they are ruminating—chewing the cud. It is not always associated with disease, but may be a symptom of some disease of the heart; in such cases the jugular pulse is continuous.

The location selected for feeling the pulse in cattle is where the submaxillary artery winds around the lower jaw bones, just at the lower edge of the flat muscle on the side of the cheek; or, if the cow is lying down, the metacarpal artery on the back part of the fore fetlock is very convenient for the purpose.

The Examination of the Heart.—Corresponding with the beats of the heart two sounds are emitted, which are of a definite type in healthy animals. The first is produced by the contraction of the heart and the flow of blood out of it; the second is caused by the rebound of blood in the aorta and the closure of the valves that prevent it from flowing backward into the heart, whence it came. The first sound is the longer and louder of the two, though of low pitch. The second sound is sharper and shorter, and is not always easy to hear in cattle. There is a brief interval between them.

To appreciate these sounds, the ear is placed against the left side of the chest, a little above the point where the elbow rests when the animal is standing in a natural position and about opposite the sixth rib. The heart sounds are both reduced in intensity when the animal is weak or when the heart is forced away from the chest wall by collections of fluid or by tubercular or other growths. Nonrhythmical heart sound is often caused by pericarditis or by disease of the valves. It may also be due to overfilling of the heart upon the right side, as occurs in severe congestion of the lungs and in some febrile diseases.

In pericarditis scraping, rubbing, or splashing sounds may be heard, entirely apart from the two normal sounds above described.

The impulse of the heart, as felt by placing the hand against the chest, is of some consequence in arriving at a conclusion in respect to disease of the heart; but it must be remembered that the impulse may be very much increased by diseases other than those of the heart, as, for example, inflammation of various organs, severe pains, etc. The impulse may also be increased (when disease does not exist) by work, exercise, fright, or any cause of excitement, or, in general, by anything that causes acceleration of the pulse.

The impulse of the heart may be felt and the sounds may be heard fairly well in lean cattle, but in fat ones it is difficult and often impossible to detect either impulse or sound with any degree of satisfaction.

Palpitation.—When the impulse of the heart is excessive—that is, when it beats more or less tumultuously—the familiar expression "palpitation of the heart" is applied; and by many it is called "thumps." The hand or ear placed against the chest easily detects the unnatural beating. In some cases it is so violent that the motion may be seen at a distance. Palpitation is but a symptom, and in many instances not connected with disease of the structure of the heart or its membranes. An animal badly frightened may have palpitation. When it comes on suddenly and soon passes away, it depends on some cause other than disease of the heart; but when it is gradually manifested, and becomes constant, although more pronounced at one time than another, heart disease may be suspected, especially if other symptoms of heart disease are present.

Injury to the Heart by Foreign Bodies.—Cattle are addicted to the habit of chewing and swallowing many objects not intended as articles of food. Every veterinarian of experience has met with instances to remind him of this, and it is well known to butchers. Among the great variety of things that have thus found their way into the stomachs of cattle the following have been noticed: Finger rings, knitting needles, old shoes, table knives, wood, pieces of leather, pieces of wire, buttons, hairpins, brushes, nails, coins, etc. The more sharply pointed objects sometimes penetrate the wall of the stomach, during which they may or may not cause enough irritation of the stomach to produce indigestion, gradually work their way through the diaphragm toward the heart, pierce the pericardium (bag inclosing the heart), wound the heart, and prove fatal to the animal. Cases are recorded in which the foreign body has actually worked its way into one of the cavities of the heart. However, instances are known in which the object took a different course, and finally worked its way toward the surface and was extracted from the wall of the chest. While it is possible that the object may pierce the wall at different parts of the alimentary canal, as it frequently does that of the rumen (paunch), it is thought that in the great majority of cases it passes through the wall of the reticulum (smaller honeycombed compartment, or second stomach) and is drawn toward the heart by the suction-like action of the chest. Post-mortem examinations have demonstrated the course it pursued, as adhesions and other results of the inflammation it caused were plainly to be seen. All manner of symptoms may precede those showing involvement of the heart, depending upon the location of the foreign body and the extent of inflammation caused by it. Severe indigestion may occur; stiffness and difficulty in moving about, due to the prods of the sharp body following muscular contraction; pain on pressure over the front, lower, and right sides of the abdomen;

coughing and difficult, quick breathing. In most cases the foreign body does not penetrate to the heart, nor even to the pericardium.

Symptoms.—The symptoms are as follows: The animal is dis-inclined to move actively, the step is restricted and cautious, sudden motion causes grunting, the attitude is constrained, the feet are drawn somewhat together, the back is arched, the face has an anxious expression. If the disease is of some days' standing, there is likely to be soft swelling (edema) beneath the neck, in the dewlap, and under the chest, between the fore legs. Breathing is short and difficult; it may clearly be painful. The pulse is rapid, 80 to 120 per minute. The muscles quiver as though the animal were cold. Rumination and appetite are depressed or checked. The dung is hard, and to void it appears to cause pain. These symptoms usually develop grad-ually, and, of course, they vary considerably in different animals, depending upon the size and location of the foreign body and the irritation caused by it.

As a matter of course, treatment in such cases is useless, but when it is possible to diagnose the case correctly the animal could be turned over to the butcher before the flesh becomes unfit for use; that is, before there is more than a little suppurtation and before there is fever. Knowing that cattle are prone to swallow such ob-jects, ordinary care may be exercised in keeping their surroundings as free of them as possible.

Pericarditis.—Inflammation of the pericardium (heart bag) is often associated with pneumonia and pleurisy, rheumatism, and other constitutional diseases, or with an injury. It also occurs as an inde-pendent affection, due to causes similar to those of other chest affec-tions, as exposure to cold or dampness and changes of the weather.

Symptoms.—It may be ushered in with a chill, followed by fe-ver, of more or less severity; the animal stands still and dull, with head hanging low, and anxiety expressed in its countenance. The pulse may be large, perhaps hard; there is also a venous pulse. The hand against the chest will feel the beating of the heart, which is often irregular, sometimes violent, and in other instances weak, de-pending in part upon the amount of fluid that has transuded into the pericardial sac. Legs are cold, the breathing quickened, and usu-ally abdominal; if the left side of the chest be pressed on or struck, the animal evinces pain. There may be spasms of the muscles in the region of the breast, neck, or hind legs. After a time, which varies in length, the legs may become swollen, and swelling may also appear under the chest and brisket.

In those animals in which the heart sounds may be heard some-what distinctly, the ear applied against the chest will detect a to-and-fro friction sound, corresponding to the beats of the heart. This sound is produced by the rubbing of the internal surface of the heart bag against the external surface of the heart. During the first stages of the inflammation these surfaces are dry, and the rubbing of one against the other during the contraction and relaxation of the heart produces this sound. The dry stage is followed by the exudation of fluid into the heart sac, and the friction is not heard until the fluid is absorbed sufficiently to allow the surfaces to come in contact again. But during the time the friction sound is lost a sound which has been called a churning noise may take its place.

The friction sound of pericarditis can not be mistaken for the friction sound of pleurisy if the examination is a careful one, because in the heart affection the sound is made in connection with the heart beats, while in the pleuritic affection the sound is synchronous with each respiration or breath of air taken in and expelled from the lungs.

Treatment.—When pericarditis is complicated with rheumatism or other diseases the latter must be treated as directed in the description of them. The animal must be kept in a quiet, comfortable place, where it will be free from excitement. Warm clothing should be applied to the body and the legs should be hand-rubbed until the circulation in them is re-established, and then snugly bandaged. The food should be nutritive and in moderate quantity. Bleeding should not be performed unless the case is in the hands of an expert.

At the beginning, give as a purgative Epsom salts—1 pound to an average-sized cow—dissolved in about a quart of warm water and administered as a drench. When there is much pain, 2 ounces of laudanum may be given, diluted with a pint of water, every three hours, until relief is given. Do not give the laudanum unless demanded by the severity of the pain, as it tends to constipation. Give one-half ounce of nitrate of potassium (saltpeter), dissolved in drinking water, four or five times a day. After the attack has abated, mustard mixed with water may be rubbed well over the left side of the chest to stimulate the absorption of the fluid contained within the pericardium. The other medicines may be discontinued and the following administered: Sulphate of iron, 2 ounces; powdered gentian, 6 ounces; mix and make eight powders. Give one powder every day at noon, mixed with food, if the animal will eat it, or shaken up with water in a bottle as a drench. Also the following: Iodid of potassium, 2 ounces; nitrate of potassium, 8 ounces; mix and make sixteen powders. Give one in drinking water or in drench every morning and evening. The last two prescriptions may be continued for several weeks if necessary.

If at any time during the attack much weakness is manifested, give the following drench every three hours: Spirits of nitrous ether, 3 ounces; rectified spirits, 4 ounces; water, 1 pint; mix and give as a drench.

In extreme cases tapping the pericardium with a trocar and canula to draw off the fluid is resorted to, but the operation requires exact anatomical knowledge.

After death from pericarditis there is always more or less fluid found in the pericardium; the surfaces are rough and covered with a yellow-colored exudate. There are also, in many cases, adhesions, to a greater or less extent, between the heart and pericardium.

Fatty Degeneration of the Heart.—This condition of the heart is met with in some cattle that are very fat, but it must be understood that the accumulation of fat around the heart is not referred to by this designation. In fatty degeneration the elements of the muscular tissue are replaced by fatty or oily granules. The muscle becomes weak, the heart contractions are insufficient and heart weakness is shown by general weakness, shortness of breath, and weak, rapid pulse.

Cyanosis.—Owing to the most prominent symptom, this condition is also called blue disease. It is seen occasionally in new-born calves. It is recognized by the blue color of the mucous membrane (easily seen by looking within the mouth and nostrils), the coldness of the surface of the body, and rapid, labored breathing. It is due to nonclosure of the foramen ovale, connecting the right with the left side of the heart, and the consequent mixing of the venous with the arterial blood. Calves so affected live but a short time.

Wounds of Arteries and Veins.—When a blood vessel is opened it may be told at a glance whether it is an artery or a vein by simply bearing in mind that bright-red blood comes from arteries and dark-red from veins. When a vein or a very small artery is severed the blood flows from the vessel in a continuous and even stream, but when one of the larger arteries is severed the blood comes from it in intermitting jets, or spurts, corresponding to the beats of the heart. It is well to call attention to the fact that the dark-red blood which flows or oozes from a wound soon becomes bright-red, because it gives up its carbonic-acid gas to the air, and absorbs oxygen gas from the air, which is exactly the change it undergoes in the capillaries of the lungs.

The general treatment of wounds will be found in another section; here it is only necessary to refer briefly to some of the most practical methods used to arrest hemorrhages, as instances occur where an animal may lose much strength from the loss of blood, or even bleed to death unless action is prompt.

Bleeding (Hemorrhage).—The severity of a hemorrhage depends upon the size of the vessel from which the blood escapes, though it may be stated that it is more serious when arteries are severed. If the wound in an artery is in the direction of its length, the blood escapes more freely than if the vessel is completely severed, because in the latter instance the severed ends retract, curl in, and may aid very much in arresting the flow. When the blood merely oozes from the wound, and even in cases where it flows in a small stream, the forming of the clot arrests the hemorrhage in a comparatively short time.

Slight hemorrhages may be checked by the continuous application to the wound of cold water, ice, or snow, as cold causes contraction of the small vessels. The water may be thrown on a wound from a hose, or dashed on it from the hand or a cup, or folds of cotton cloths may be held on the wound and kept wet. Ice or snow may be held against the wound, or they may be put in a bag and conveniently secured in position.

Hot water of an average temperature of 115° to 120° F. injected into the vagina or womb is often efficient in arresting hemorrhages from those organs. Tow, raw cotton, lint, or sponges may

Section of Tuberculous Lung of Cow. Dept. of Agr.

be forced into a wound and held or bound there with bandages. This is an excellent method for checking the flow of blood until the arrival of an expert. If the flow persists, these articles may be saturated with tincture of iron, but it is not advisable to use the tincture of iron if it can be avoided, as it is a caustic, and retards healing by causing a slough. The articles may be saturated with vinegar in cases of necessity, or tannic acid or alum dissolved in water may be used instead. The article (whichever is used) should be left in the wound sufficiently long to make sure that its removal will not be followed by a renewal of the hemorrhage. It must remain there one or two days in some instances.

An iron heated until it is white and then pressed on the bleeding vessel for three or four seconds is occasionally used. It should be at white heat and applied for a moment only, or else the charred tissue will come away with the iron and thus defeat the purpose of its application.

Compression may be applied in different ways, but only the most convenient will be mentioned. To many wounds bandages may easily be applied. The bandages may be made of linen, muslin, etc., sufficiently wide and long, according to the nature of the wound and the region to be bandaged. Bed sheets torn in strips the full length make excellent bandages for this purpose. Cotton batting, tow, or a piece of sponge may be placed on the wound and firmly bound there with the bandages.

In many instances ligating the vessel is necessary. A ligature is a piece of thread or string tied around the vessel. Ligating is almost entirely confined to arteries. Veins are not ligated unless very large (and even then only when other means are not available) on account of the danger of phlebitis, or inflammation of a vein. The ligature is tied around the end of the artery, but in some instances this is difficult, and it is necessary to include some of the adjacent tissue, although care should be taken that a nerve is not included. To apply a ligature, it is necessary to have artery forceps (tweezers or small pincers may suffice) by which to draw out the artery in order to tie the string around it. To grasp the vessel it may be necessary to sponge the blood from the wound so that the end will be exposed. In case the end of the bleeding artery has retracted, a sharp-pointed hook, called a tenaculum, is used to draw it out far enough to tie. The ligature should be drawn tightly, so that the middle and internal coats will be cut through.

Another method of checking hemorrhage is called torsion. It consists in catching the end of the bleeding vessel, drawing it out a little, and then twisting it around a few times with the forceps, which lacerates the internal coats so that a check is effected. This is very effectual in small vessels, and is to be preferred to ligatures, because it leaves no foreign body in the wound. A needle or pin may be stuck through the edges of a wound, and a string passed around between the free ends and the skin, or it may be passed around in the form of a figure 8, as is often done in the operation of bleeding from the jugular vein.

Inflammation of Veins (Phlebitis).—When bleeding is performed without proper care or with unclean fleam or lancet, inflammation of the vein may result, or it may be caused by the animal rubbing the wound against some object. When inflammation follows the operation, the coats of the vein become enlarged; so much so that the vessel may be felt hard and knotted beneath the skin, and when pressed on pain is evinced. A thin, watery discharge, tinged with blood, issues from the wound. When the pin is taken out it is found that the wound has not healed. The blood becomes coagulated in the vessel. In inflammation of the jugular the coagulation extends from the wound upward to the first large branch. Abscesses may form along the course of the vein. The inflammation is followed by obliteration of that part in which coagulation exists. This is of small import, as cattle have an accessory jugular vein which gradually enlarges and accommodates itself to the increased quantity of blood it must carry.

Treatment.—The treatment for inflammation of the vein is to clip the hair from along the course of the affected vessel and apply a blister, the cerate or cantharides. Abscesses should be opened as soon as they form, because there is a possibility of the pus getting into the circulation.

In the operation of bleeding the instruments should be clean and free from rust. If the skin is not sufficiently opened, or when closing the wound the skin is drawn out too much, blood may accumulate in the tissue, and if it does it should be removed by pressing absorbent cotton or a sponge on the part. Care should also be used in opening the vein, so that the instrument does not pass entirely through both sides of the vein and open the artery beneath it. (See Bleeding, or Blood-letting.)

DISEASES OF THE NERVOUS SYSTEM.

The nervous system is the distinguishing feature of animal life; without it there can be no intelligence, no instinct, no sensibility, no perception; in fact, existence would be nothing but vegetable life.

The senses—touch, taste, sight, hearing, smell—all depend on the nervous system. Motion depends on it. A muscle can not contract without receiving the stimulus from the nervous system. For example, if a nerve passing from a nerve center to a muscle is severed, the particular muscle that is supplied by the cut nerve is paralyzed.

The nervous system is often studied in two divisions—the cerebro-spinal division and the sympathetic division.

The cerebro-spinal division consists of the brain and spinal cord, nerves, and ganglia. The nerves of this division convey the impulses of motion and sensation, and supply all parts which are under the control of the will. For example, the voluntary muscular tissue includes all the muscles which act as the will directs. Another example, if anything comes in contact with any part of the skin, the impression is immediately perceived. All the special senses belong to this division.

The sympathetic division consists of nerves and ganglia. The muscular tissue, which acts independently of the will—as, for example, the stomach, intestines, womb, blood vessels, ducts, etc.—is called involuntary muscular tissue, and receives nervous stimulus from the sympathetic division.

The brain, spinal cord, and the ganglia are the central organs of the nervous system. The nerves conduct the nervous influence. The nerves terminate differently according to their function. The terminations are called end organs. The terminal end organs in the skin and other parts endowed with sensation receive the impressions, which are conveyed to the brain, where they are appreciated. They are so sensitive that the most gentle zephyr is perceived. They are so abundant that the point of the finest needle can not pierce the skin without coming in contact with them, and the sensation of pain is instantly conveyed to the brain. The terminal end organs of the nerves that supply the muscles are different, as they give the impulse which is conveyed by the motor nerves to the elements which constitute the muscle, and this impulse is the excitation which causes the muscle to contract. The terminal end organs of the special senses of taste, smell, etc., receive their special impressions, and their respective nerves carry the impressions to the brain.

There are two divisions of nerves, the afferent and efferent. The afferent nerves are those which convey the impression to the nerve centers. All the sensory nerves belong to this division. The efferent nerves are those which convey the nervous impulse outward from the nerve centers, and they are further classified according to the function of their respective centers. For example: Motor fibers carry the impulse from the nerve center to a muscle to cause contraction. Vaso-motor fibers carry the impulse to the muscular tissue in the blood vessels, which regulates their caliber. The secretory fibers convey the impulse to the cells of the glands and excite the activity of the gland, and its particular product is secreted or evolved, as, for instance, milk in the mammary gland. Inhibitory fibers control or inhibit the action of the organ to which they are distributed, as, for instance, the heart.

Nerve centers may be considered as a collection or group of nerve cells. Both the cerebro-spinal and the sympathetic divisions have nerve centers. The centers derive their special names from their functions. The brain is the great center of the nervous system, as it is the center of intelligence and perception. The centers of all the special senses, as well as the centers of various functions, are located in different parts of the brain. Nerve centers also exist in the spinal cord and in connection with the sympathetic system.

A nerve is a cord consisting of a certain number of fibers of nerve tissue, inclosed in a sheath of connective tissue. Nerves divide and subdivide, sending off branches, which ramify in all parts of the body, and, as they near their terminations, they contain but one or two fibers.

The brain and spinal cord are contained within a bony canal, which forms a protective covering for them. The spinal cord, or spinal marrow, lodged within the spinal canal, or hollow of the backbone, is continuous with the brain anteriorly, and terminates in a point in the sacrum (that part of the spinal column which immediately precedes the tail). The spinal cord gives off branches at each of the spaces between the segments of the backbone. These branches form nerve trunks which carry both sensory and motor impressions and impulses. The spinal cord is a grand nerve trunk to carry messages to or from the brain and to and from the reflex centers contained within itself.

The brain is contained within the cavity of the skull and is continuous with the spinal cord; there is nothing to mark the place where one leaves off and the other begins. The brain is the seat of reason and intelligence. Voluntary effort originates from the brain. Co-ordination, or harmony of movement, is controlled by the rear portion of the brain, known as the cerebellum.

The meninges are the membranes, three in number, which envelop the brain and spinal cord, and separate them from the bones which form the walls of the cranial cavity and spinal canal.

The sympathetic, also called the ganglionic, division of the nervous system consists of two chains of ganglia, reaching from the head to the tail, situated beneath the spinal column, one on either side. The presence of the ganglia or enlargements on the cords give them their chain-like appearance.

The sympathetic nerves are closely connected with the cerebrospinal nerves, but are not under the control of the will.

INFLAMMATION OF THE BRAIN AND ITS MEMBRANES (STAGGERS).

Inflammation of the brain is technically termed encephalitis and of its membranes cerebral-meningitis, but as both conditions usually occur together, and since it is practically impossible to distinguish one from the other by the symptoms shown by the diseased animal, they may as well be considered together here as varieties of the same disease. Staggers, coma, frenzy, etc., are terms that are sometimes applied to this disease in its different forms or stages.

Causes.—Severe blows on the head with a hard object, or the head coming violently in contact with the ground or other hard substance in a fall, may be followed by encephalitis. Irritation caused by tumors in the brain may produce inflammation. Food containing deleterious matters—for example, ergot and other fungi which contain a narcotic principle—is the most frequent cause of this affection, and hence it is often called grass staggers and stomach staggers. Highly nitrogenous foods are blamed for causing this disease. Parasites, mineral and narcotic poisons, hot weather, and severe exertion or excessive excitement may cause this condition. Inflammation of the brain may occur as a complication of some infectious disease or may follow some forms of indigestion. In many localities certain plants have the reputation of causing staggers.

Symptoms.—The symptoms vary much, but a careful observer will detect a trouble connected with the nervous system without much uncertainty. The first signs may be those of frenzy, but generally at the start the animal is dull and sleepy, with little or no inclination to move about; the head may be pressed against the wall or fence and the legs kept moving, as if the animal were endeavoring to walk through the obstruction; the body, especially the hind part, may be leaned against the side of the stall or stable, as if for support. The bowels are constipated; the urine, when passed, is small in quantity and darker in color than natural. There may be trembling and even spasms of muscles in different parts. In the dull stage the animal may breathe less frequently than is natural, and each breath may be accompanied with a snoring-like sound. The pulse may be large and less frequent than normal. If suddenly aroused from the drowsy state, the animal appears startled and stares wildly. When moving about it may stagger, the hind quarters swaying from side to side.

If delirium ensues, the cow is commonly said to be mad. She may bellow, stamp her feet, run about wildly, grate the teeth, froth at the mouth. If she is confined in the stable, she rears and plunges; the convulsions are so violent in many instances that it is really dangerous for one to attempt to render aid. The body may be covered with perspiration. She may fall; the muscles twitch and jerk; often the head is raised and then dashed against the ground until blood issues from the nose and mouth; the eyes may be bloodshot and sightless; the limbs stiff and outstretched, or they may be kicked about recklessly; the head may be drawn back and the tail drawn up; the urine may be squirted out in spurts; often the washer (membrane nictitans) is forced over the eye. When the convulsions cease they may be followed by a period of quiet unconsciousness (coma) which is more or less prolonged, when the animal may gradually regain consciousness, get up on its feet, and perhaps quietly partake of food, if there be any within reach, while at other times it arises with much difficulty and staggers blindly about the stall or field.

It must be remembered that all the foregoing symptoms are not always seen in the same case. In those cases usually designated sleepy staggers the general symptoms of drowsiness are presented, while in other cases the symptoms of frenzy cause the affection to be called mad staggers. In other cases there are symptoms of paralysis, swaying of the hind quarters, inability to rise, etc., and sometimes these symptoms of paralysis are the most striking manifestations and continue until death. Acute cases are accompanied by fever.

It is well to remark that when the disease follows injuries to the head the symptoms may not be manifested until two or three days (or longer) after the accident.

Treatment.—Recoveries are rare in spite of careful attention. To be of any service whatever the treatment must be prompt and begin with the disease. In the early stage when the pulse is large most cases will admit of bleeding. Eight or nine quarts of blood should be taken from the jugular vein. This should be followed immediately by a purgative, the following for a cow of average size: Epsom salts, 24 ounces; pulverized gamboge, one-half ounce; croton oil, 20 drops; warm water, 3 quarts; mix all together and give at once as a drench. About 2 quarts of warm water or warm soapsuds should be injected with a syringe into the rectum every three or four hours. It is best to keep the animal in a quiet, sheltered place, where it will be free from noise or other cause of excitement. All the cold water the animal will drink should be allowed, but food must be withheld, except bran slops occasionally in small quantities, or grass, if in season, which may be cut and carried fresh to the patient.

The skull must be examined and if sign of injury is found appropriate surgical treatment should be given.

During the convulsions all possible efforts should be made to prevent the animal injuring itself. The head should be held down on the ground and straw kept under it. Cold water may be continuously poured on the head, or bags filled with ice broken in small pieces may be applied to the head. Different authors recommend different remedies to allay the convulsions, but for two reasons it will be found extremely difficult to administer medicines during the convulsions: (1) While the animal is unconscious the power to swallow is lost, and therefore the medicine is more liable to go down the windpipe to the lungs than it is to go to the paunch; (2) The convulsions are often so violent that it would be utterly useless to attempt to drench the animal; and furthermore it must be borne in mind that during this stage the functions of digestion and absorption are suspended, and as a consequence the medicine (provided it finds its way to the paunch) is likely to remain there unabsorbed and therefore useless.

A blistering compound, composed of mustard, 1 ounce; pulverized cantharides, one-half ounce; hot water, 4 ounces, well mixed together, may be rubbed in over the loins, along the spine, and back of the head on each side of the neck. This is occasionally attended with beneficial effect, and especially so in those cases when paralysis is present.

If the purgative acts and the animal shows signs of improvement in the course of two or three days, 2 drams of iodid of potassium may be given every night and morning, dissolved in a half bucketful of drinking water, if the animal will drink it, or it may be dissolved in a half pint of water and given as a drench. Great care must be observed in regard to the food, which should be nutritive, but not coarse, and at first in small quantities, gradually increased as the patient improves. After some progress is made toward recovery 1½ drams of pulverized nux vomica may be given twice a day, added to the iodid of potassium drench. This should be administered so long as a staggering gait continues.

In those rare cases when recovery takes place it is only partial as a rule, as there is generally a sequel which remains, such as partial paralysis. However, this is but a slight drawback in cattle, because when it is seen to persist the medicine should be stopped and the animal fattened for butchering.

Postmortem examinations discover congestion of the brain and its membranes. In those cases which have exhibited much paralysis of the hind legs before death the cord may be congested in the lumbar regions (loins). When the disease has been caused by injury to the head, the congestion and extravasated blood may be found inside of the cavity in the location corresponding to the place where the injury was inflicted externally. In some cases pus is also discovered. It remains to be said that in all animals that have died from this affection the lungs are found very much congested. This may lead the superficial observer to suppose that the disease was a lung affection, but in fact it is only a natural consequence when death ensues from brain disease.

APOPLEXY.

That form of congestion of the brain known as parturient apoplexy, or parturient paresis, which is so frequently associated with the period of calving, is described in another part of this work. (See "Milk Fever.")

Cerebral apoplexy, not connected with parturition, is a rare disease among cattle. However, it may be due to degeneration and consequent rupture of a blood vessel in the brain.

CONCUSSION OF THE BRAIN.

Severe blows on the head, striking the head against some hard object while running, or falling on the head, may cause concussion of the brain. The injury may fracture bones of the cranium and produce compression of the brain.

EPILEPSY.

This affection is characterized by the occurrence of sudden convulsions. The animal may appear to be in a fair state of health usually, but at any time, in the stable or in the field, it may have a convulsion in which it will fall and lose consciousness. Epilepsy must not be confounded with vertigo—the fainting which is an effect of heart troubles.

The exact cause of epilepsy in the majority of cases is unknown. Post-mortem examinations in many instances have failed to discover any lesion in connection with the brain or nervous system; while in other instances disease of the brain has been found in the form of thickening of the membranes, abscesses, and tumors, and in some cases the affection has been manifested in connection with a diseased condition of the blood. The cause has also been traced to reflex irritation, due to teething, worms, and chronic indigestion.

Treatment.—When the affection is due to the last-named causes treatment may be successful if the cause is removed. If there are symptoms of worms or of indigestion, follow the general treatment advised for those troubles under their proper heads. If due to irritation caused by teething, the inflamed gums must be lanced. Examination of the mouth often develops the fact that one of the temporary teeth causes much irritation by remaining unshed, and thereby interfering with the growth of a permanent tooth. The offending tooth should be extracted. When the cause of epilepsy can not be discovered, it must be confessed that there is no prospect of a cure. However, some benefit may be expected from the occasional administration of a purgative dose of medicine. A pound of Epsom salts dissolved in a quart of warm water, for a cow of average size, may be given as a drench once or twice a month. In addition to the purgative, 4 drams of bromid of potassium, dissolved in the drinking water, three times a day, has proved very beneficial in some cases.

SUNSTROKE (PROSTRATION FROM HEAT).

Owing to the fact that cattle are seldom put to work at which they would have to undergo severe exertion, especially in collars, they are not frequently prostrated by the extreme heat of the summer months. When at pasture they select the coolest places in the shade of trees, in water, etc., when the heat becomes oppressive, and thereby avoid, as much as possible, the effects of it.

It does happen, however, that cattle that have been kept up for the purpose of fattening, when driven some distance in very hot weather, are sometimes prostrated, but it must be remembered that it is not really necessary for the animal to be exposed to the rays of the sun, as those confined in hot, close places may suffer. This often happens in shipping, when they are crowded together in cars.

Symptoms.—The premonitory signs are those of exhaustion—dullness, panting, frothing at the mouth, tongue hanging out, irregular gait, uneasiness, palpitation—when, if the circumstances which tend to the prostration are not mitigated, the animal staggers or sways from side to side, falls, struggles for a while, and then gradually becomes quiet, or the struggles may continue, with repeated but ineffectual efforts to regain a standing position. In serious cases the attack may be very sudden, unconsciousness occurring without continued or distressing premonitory symptoms.

Treatment.—At first when not very serious, removal to a quiet, sheltered place, with a few days on a reduced diet, is all that need be done. When the animal has fallen, apply cold water or ice to the head; rub the body and limbs with cloths or wisps of straw, and continue the rubbing for a considerable time. If the power of swallowing is not lost (which may be ascertained by pouring a little cold water into the mouth), give 3 drams of stronger liquor ammonia, diluted with a quart of cold water. Be very careful in drenching the animal when lying down. Repeat the drench in a half hour, and an hour after the first one has been given. Instead of the ammonia, a drench composed of 3 ounces of spirits of nitrous ether in a pint of water may be given, if more convenient, but the ammonia drench is preferable. If unconsciousness continues, so that a drench can not be administered, the same quantity of ammonia and water may be injected with a syringe into the rectum. The popular aqua ammonia, commonly called hartshorn, will do as well as the stronger liquor ammonia, but as it is weaker than the latter the dose for a cow is about 1½ ounces, which should be diluted with a quart of water before it is given to the animal, either as a drench or an enema. When ammonia can not be obtained a pint of whisky in a quart of water or an ounce of tincture of digitalis may be given.

As soon as the animal is able to rise it should be assisted and moved to the nearest shelter. All the cold water it will drink should be allowed. The ammonia or spirits of nitrous ether drench should be administered every three hours so long as there is much failure of strength. The diet should be limited for several days—bran slops and a little grass. When signs of returning strength are presented, 12 ounces of Epsom salts dissolved in a quart of warm water may be given in those cases which have been down and unconscious, but do not give it while much weakness remains, which may be for several days after the attack. The flesh of an animal that is suffering from heat stroke should not be prepared for use as food. On account of the fever with which the animal suffers, the flesh contains toxins that may render it poisonous to the consumer.

INJURIES TO THE SPINAL CORD.

The spinal cord is liable to concussion from blows and falls, and paralysis, to a greater or less extent, may be the result. Fracture, with displacement of the bones (vertebræ) which form the spinal column, by compressing the spinal cord, produces paralysis, which varies in its effect according to the part of the cord that is compressed. If the fracture is above the middle of the neck, death soon follows, as communication between the brain and diaphragm (the essential muscle of inspiration) is stopped. When the fracture is farther down in the neck, posterior to the origin of the phrenic nerve, the breathing continues, but there is paralysis in all parts posterior to the fracture, including the fore and hind legs. When the fracture is in the region of the loins the hind legs are paralyzed, but the fore legs are not. If the fracture is in the sacrum (the division of the spinal column between the loins and the tail), the tail alone is paralyzed.

As a matter of course, when the back is broken there is no remedy; the animal should be killed at once.

PARALYSIS.

Paralysis, or loss of motion in a part, may be due to a lesion of the brain, of the spinal cord, or of a nerve. It may also be caused by reflex irritation. When the paralysis affects both sides of the body, posterior to a point, it is further designated by the name paraplegia. When one side of the body (a lateral half) is paralyzed, the term hemiplegia is applied to the affection. When paralysis is caused by a lesion of a nerve, the paralysis is confined to the particular part supplied by the affected nerve.

As already pointed out, paralysis may be due to concussion of the spine, fracture of a bone of the spinal column with consequent compression of the spinal cord, concussion of the brain, or compression of the brain. An injury to one side of the brain may produce paralysis of the same side of the head, and of the opposite side of the body hemiplegia. Paralysis may occur in connection with parturient apoplexy, lead poisoning, ergotism, etc.

Rabies (*Hydrophobia*).—See discussion of this disease on pages 235-240.

LIGHTNING STROKE (ASPHYXIA ELECTRICA).

When an animal is struck by lightning the shock is instantaneously expended on the nervous system, and as a rule death occurs immediately, but when the shock is not fatal animation is suspended to a greater or less extent, as evidenced by prostration, unconsciousness, and paralysis.

Symptoms.—When not fatal, the symptoms vary much, according to the severity of the shock. The animal usually falls, as from an apoplectic attack, and, as a matter of course, the symptoms are such as are generally manifested in connection with concussion of the brain. The muscular system may be completely relaxed; the legs limber; the muscles flabby and soft to the touch, or there may be convulsions, spasms, and twitching of the muscles. The breathing is generally labored, irregular, or interrupted, and slower than normal.

In most instances the electrical fluid leaves its mark by singeing the hair, or by inflicting wounds, burns, or blisters. Sir B. Brodie tells a curious story of two bullocks, pied white and red, which were struck in different storms. In both cases the white hairs were consumed, while the red ones escaped.

Treatment.—So long as the beating of the heart is perceptible, the endeavor to resuscitate the animal should be continued. Dash cold water over the head and body; rub the body and legs; smartly whip the body with wet towels or switches. Mustard, mixed with water, should be well rubbed over the legs and back of the head on each side of the neck. Inject into the rectum 4 drams of stronger liquor ammonia, or 1½ ounces of hartshorn diluted with a quart of warm water. Cautiously hold an uncorked bottle of hartshorn to the nostrils, so that some of it is inhaled, but care should be taken that too much is not suddenly inhaled.

In desperate cases artificial respiration should be tried, as follows: With both hands spread out to cover a large surface, press on the abdomen (behind the ribs) and then on the chest (behind the shoulders), and continue in this manner, first on the abdomen and then on the chest in regular order, so that the chest and the abdomen are each pressed on alternately about twenty times a minute. The pressure should be slow and steady, so that the movement given by it to the walls of the chest and abdomen will resemble their motion in breathing. A hand bellows may be used as an aid to the foregoing method, as follows: Each time after the chest is pressed on the nozzle is inserted in the nostril and air slowly and gently forced in by the bellows.

When the animal revives sufficiently to be able to swallow, 4 drams of the stronger liquor ammonia, diluted with a quart of cold water, should be given as a drench, and the dose should be repeated in an hour. One and one-half ounces of ordinary hartshorn may be used instead of the stronger liquor ammonia, but, like the latter, it should be diluted with a quart or more of water, and even then care should be exercised in drenching.

In cases when the shock has not caused complete insensibility, recovery may be hastened by the ammonia and water drench, or 4 ounces of brandy diluted with a quart of water, or 8 ounces of whisky diluted with a quart of water. These doses may be given every three or four hours, if necessary. After recovery from the more serious symptoms, 2 drams of sulphate of quinine should be given twice a day until health is restored. If any paralysis remains, 1½ drams of pulverized nux vomica should be given twice a day with the quinine.

The foregoing treatment is also applicable when the electrical shock is given by telephone, electric car, or electric-light wires, etc. The wounds, burns, or blisters should be treated according to the antiseptic method of treating wounds.

TUMORS IN THE BRAIN, ETC.

Tumors of different kinds have been found within the cranial cavity, and in many cases there have been no well-marked symptoms exhibited during the life of the animal to lead one to suspect their existence. Cases are recorded where bony tumors have been found in the brain of cattle that died suddenly, but during life no signs of disease were manifested. Post-mortem examinations have discovered tubercles in the membranes of the brain. Abscesses, usually the result of inflammation of the brain, have been found in post-mortem. For the description of hydrocephalus, or dropsy of the brain, of calves, the reader is referred to the section on parturition. (See Water in the Head.)

Chorea, constant twitching and irregular spasmodic movements of the muscles, has been noticed in connection with, or as a sequel to, other affections, as, for example, parturient apoplexy.

Various diseases, the description of which will be found in other sections of this work, affect the nervous system to a greater or less extent—for example, ergotism, lead poisoning, uremia, parturient apoplexy, colic, and other affections associated with cramps, or spasms, etc. Disease of the ovaries or of the spinal cord, by reflex irritation, may cause estromania (see "Excess of Venereal Desire," page 153), constant desire for the bull.

THE URINARY ORGANS AND THEIR DISEASES.

These are not so prominent in cattle as in horses, yet when present they are of a similar kind. There is a stiff or straddling gait with the hind limbs and some difficulty in turning or in lying down and rising, the act drawing forth a groan. The frequent passage of urine in driblets, the continuous escape of the urine in drops, the sudden arrest of the flow when in full stream, the rhythmic contraction of the muscles under the anus without any flow resulting, the swelling of the sheath, the collection of hard, gritty masses on the hair surrounding the orifice of the sheath, the occurrence of dropsies in the limbs, under the chest or belly, or in either of these cavities, and finally the appearance of nervous stupor, may indicate serious disorder of the urinary organs. The condition of the urine passed may likewise lead to suspicion. It may be white, from crystallized carbonate of lime; brown, red, or even black, from the presence of blood or blood-coloring matter; yellow from biliary coloring matter; it may be frothy, from contained albumen; cloudy, from phosphates; glairy, from pus; or it may show gritty masses, from gravel. In many cases of urinary disorder in the ox, however, the symptoms are by no means prominent, and unless special examination is made of the loins, the bladder, and the urine the true nature of the malady may be overlooked.

DIURESIS (POLYURIA, DIABETES INSIPIDUS, EXCESSIVE SECRETION OF URINE).

A secretion of urine in excess of the normal amount may be looked on as disease, even if the result does not lead to immediate loss of condition. Cattle fed on distillery swill are striking examples of such excess caused by the enormous consumption of a liquid food, which nourishes and fattens in spite of the diuresis; but the condition is unwholesome, and cattle that have passed four or five months in a swill stable have fatty livers and kidneys, and never again do well on ordinary food. Diuresis may further occur from increase of blood pressure in the kidneys (diseases of the heart or lungs which hinder the onward passage of the blood, the eating of digitalis, English broom, the contraction of the blood vessels on the surface of the body in cold weather, etc.); also from acrid or diuretic plants taken with the food (dandelion, burdock, colchicum, digitalis, savin, resinous shoots, etc.); from excess of sugar in the food (beets, turnips, ripe sorghum); also from the use of frozen food (frosted turnip tops and other vegetables), and from the growths of certain molds in fodder (musty hay, mow-burnt hay, moldy oats, moldy bread, etc.). Finally, alkaline waters and alkaline incrustations on the soil may be active causes. In some of these cases the result is beneficial rather than injurious, as when cattle affected with gravel in the kidneys are entirely freed from this condition by a run at grass, or by an exclusive diet of roots or swill. In other cases, however, the health and condition suffer, and even inflammation of the kidneys may occur.

Treatment.—The treatment is mainly in the change of diet to a more solid aliment destitute of the special offensive ingredient. Boiled flaxseed is often the best diet or addition to the wholesome dry food, and, by the way of medicine, doses of 2 drams each of sulphate of iron and iodide of potassium may be given twice daily. In obstinate cases, 2 drams ergot of rye or of catechu may be added.

BLOODY URINE (RED WATER, MOOR-ILL, WOOD-ILL, HEMATURIA, HEMOGLOBINURIA).

This is a common affection among cattle in certain localities, above all on damp, undrained lands, and under a backward agriculture. It is simply bloody urine or hematuria when the blood is found in clots, or when under the microscope the blood globules can be detected as distinctly rounded, flattened disks. It is smoky urine—hemaglobinuria—when no such distinct clots nor blood disks can be found, but merely a general browning, reddening, or blackening of the urine by the presence of dissolved blood coloring matter. The bloody urine is the more direct result of structural disease of the kidneys or urinary passages (inflammation, stone, gravel, tumors hydatids, kidney worms, sprains of the loins), while the stained urine (hemaglobinuria) is usually the result of some general or more distant disorder in which the globules are destroyed in the circulating blood and the coloring matter dissolved in and diffused through the whole mass of the blood and of the urine secreted from it. As in the two forms blood and the elements of blood escape into the urine, albumen is always present, so that there is albuminuria with blood-coloring matter superadded. If due to stone or gravel, gritty particles are usually passed, and may be detected in the bottom of a dish in which the liquid is caught. If due to fracture or severe sprain of the loins, it is likely to be associated not only with some loss of control over the hind limbs and with staggering behind, but also with a more or less perfect paralysis of the tail. The blood-stained urine without red globules results from specific diseases—Texas fever, anthrax, spirillosis, and from eating irritant plants (broom, savin, mercury, hellebore, ranunculus, convolvulus, colchicum, oak shoots, ash, privet, hazel, hornbeam, and other astringent, acrid, or resinous plants, etc). The maybug or Spanish fly taken with the food or spread over a great extent of skin as a blister has a similar action. Frosted turnips or other roots will bring on the affection in some subjects. Among conditions which act by the direct destruction of the globules in the circulating blood may be named an excess of water in that fluid; the use of water from soils rich in decomposing vegetable matter and containing alkaline salts, particularly nitrites; and the presence in the water and food of the ptomaines of bacteria growth. Hence the prevalence of "red water" in marshy districts and on clayey and other impervious soils. Hence, too, the occurrence of bloody urine in the advanced stages of several contagious diseases. Some mineral poisons—such as iodin, arsenic, and phosphorus taken to excess— may cause hematuria, and finally the symptoms may be the mere result of a constitutional predisposition of the individual or family to bleeding. Exposure of the body to cold or wet will cause the affection in some predisposed subjects.

The specific symptom of bloody or smoky water is a very patent one. It may or may not be associated with fever, with the presence or absence of abdominal tenderness on pressure, with a very frothy state of the milk or even a reddish tinge, with or without marked paleness of the mucous membranes, and general weakness. When direct injury to the kidneys is the immediate cause of the disease the urine will be passed often, in small quantity at a time, and with much straining. When there is bloodlessness (a watery blood) from insufficient nourishment, fever is absent and the red water is at first the only symptom. When the active cause has been irritant plants, abdominal tenderness, colics, and other signs of bowel inflammations are marked features.

Treatment.—Treatment will vary according as the cause has been a direct irritant operating on a subject in vigorous health or a microbian poison acting on an animal deficient in blood and vigor. In the first form of red water a smart purgative (1 pound to 1½ pounds Glauber's salts) will clear away the irritants from the bowels and allay the coexistent high fever. It will also serve to divert to the bowels much of the irritant products already absorbed into the blood, and will thus protect the kidneys. In many such cases a liberal supply of wholesome, easily digestible food will be all the additional treatment required. In this connection demulcent food (boiled flaxseed, wheat bran) is especially good. If much blood has been lost, bitters (gentian, one-half ounce) and iron (sulphate of iron, 2 drams) should be given for a week.

For cases in which excess of diuretic plants has been taken, it may be well to replace the salts by 1 to 2 pints olive oil, adding 1 ounce laudanum and 2 drams gum camphor. Also to apply fomentations or a fresh sheepskin over the loins. Buttermilk or vinegar, one-half pint, or sulphuric acid, 60 drops in a pint of water, may also be employed at intervals as injections. In cases due to sprained or fractured loins, to inflamed kidneys, or to stone or gravel, the treatment will be as for the particular disease in question.

In hematuria from anemia (watery blood), whether from insufficient or badly adjusted rations or from the poisonous products of fermentations in impervious or marshy soils, the treatment must be essentially tonic and stimulating. Rich, abundant, and easily digestible food must be furnished. The different grains (oats, barley, wheat, bran, rye) and seeds (rape, linseed, cotton seed) are especially called for, and may be given either ground or boiled. As a bitter, sulphate of quinia, one-half dram, and tincture of muriate of iron, 2 drams, may be given in a pint of water thrice a day. In some cases 1 or 2 teaspoonfuls of oil of turpentine twice daily in milk will act favorably.

Prevention.—But in this anemic variety prevention is the great need. The drainage and cultivation of the dangerous soils is the main object. Until this can be accomplished young and newly purchased cattle, not yet inured to the poisons, must be kept from the dangerous fields and turned only on those which are already drained naturally or artificially. Further, they should have an abundant ration in which the local product of grass, hay, etc., is supplemented by grain or other seeds. Another point to be guarded against is the supply of water that has drained from marshes or impervious soils, rich in organic matter, as such is charged with nitrates, ptomaines, etc., which directly conduce to the disorder. Fence out from all such waters, and supply from living springs or deep wells only.

ALBUMEN IN THE URINE (ALBUMINURIA).

In bloody urine albumen is always present as an important constituent of the blood, and in congested and inflamed kidneys it is present as a part of the inflammatory exudate. Apart from these, albumen in the urine represents in different cases a variety of diseased conditions of the kidneys or of distant organs. Among the additional causes of albuminuria, may be named: (1) An excess of albumen in the blood (after easy calving with little loss of blood and before the secretion of milk has been established, or in cases of sudden suppression of the secretion of milk; (2) under increase of blood pressure (after deep drinking, after doses of digitalis or broom, after transfusion of blood from one animal to another, or in disease of the heart or lungs causing obstruction to the flow of blood from the veins); (3) after cutting (or disease) of the motor nerves of the vessels going to the kidneys, causing congestion of these organs; (4) violent exertion, hence long drives by road; the same happens with violent muscular spasms, as from strychnia poisoning, lockjaw, epilepsy, and convulsions; (5) in most fevers and extensive inflammations of important organs, like the lungs, or liver, the escape of the albumen being variously attributed to the high temperature of the body and disorder of the nerves, and to resulting congestion and disorder of the secreting cells of the kidneys; (6) in burns and some other congested states of the skin; (7) under the action of certain poisons (strong acids, phosphorus, arsenic, Spanish flies, carbolic acid, and those inducing bloody urine); (8) in certain conditions of weakness or congestion of the secreting cells of the kidneys, so that they allow this element of the blood to escape; (9) when the food is entirely wanting in common salt, albumen may appear in the urine temporarily after a full meal containing an excess of albumen. It can also be produced experimentally by puncturing the back part of the base of the brain (the floor of the fourth ventricle close to the point the injury to which causes sugary urine). In abscesses, tumors, or inflammation of the bladder, ureter, or urethra, the urine is albuminous.

It follows, therefore, that albumen in the urine does not indicate the existence of any one specific disease, and excepting when due to weakness or loss of function of the kidney cells, it must be looked on as an attendant on another disease, the true nature of which we must try to find out. These affections we must exclude one by one until we are left to assume the noninflammatory disorder of the secreting cells of the kidney. It is especially important to exclude inflammation of the kidney, and to do this may require a microscopic examination of the sediment of the urine and the demonstration of the entire absence of casts of the uriniferous tubes. (See "Nephritis.)

To detect albumen in the urine, the suspected and frothy liquid must be rendered sour by adding a few drops of nitric acid and then boiled in a test tube. If a solid precipitate forms, then add a few more drops of nitric acid, and if the liquid does not clear it up it is albumen. A precipitate thrown down by boiling and redissolved by nitric acid is probably phosphate of lime.

Treatment.—Treatment will usually be directed to the disease on which it is dependent. In the absence of any other recognizable disease, mucilaginous drinks of boiled flaxseed, slippery elm, or gum may be given, tannic acid one-half dram twice daily, and fomentations or even mustard poultices over the loins. When the disease is chronic and there is no attendant fever (elevation of temperature), tonics (hydrochloric acid, 6 drops in a pint of water; phosphate of iron, 2 drams, or sulphate of quinia, 2 drams, repeated twice daily) may be used. In all cases the patient should be kept carefully from cold and wet; a warm, dry shed, or in warm weather a dry, sunny yard or pasture, being especially desirable.

SUGAR IN URINE (DIABETES MELLITUS).

This is a frequent condition of the urine in parturition fever, but is practically unknown in cattle as a specific disease, associated with deranged liver or brain. As a mere attendant on another disease it will demand no special notice here.

INFLAMMATION OF THE KIDNEYS (NEPHRITIS).

This has been divided according as it affects the different parts of the kidneys, as: (1) Its fibrous covering (perinephritis); (2) the secreting tissue of its outer portion (parenchymatous); (3) the connective tissue (interstitial); (4) the lining membrane of its ducts (catarrhal); and (5) its pelvis or sac receiving the urine (pyelitis). It has also been distinguished according to the changes that take place in the kidney, especially as seen after death, according to the amount of albumen present in the urine, and according as the affection is acute or chronic. For the purposes of this work it will be convenient to consider these as one inflammatory disease, making a distinction merely between those that are acute and those that are chronic or of long standing.

The causes are in the main like those causing bloody urine, such as irritant and diuretic plants, Spanish flies applied as a blister or otherwise, exposure to cold and wet, the presence of stone or gravel in the kidneys, injuries to the back or loins, as by riding each other, the drinking of alkaline or selenitic water, the use of putrid, stagnant water, or of that containing bacteria and their products, the consumption of musty fodder, etc. (See Hematuria.)

The length of the loins in cattle predisposes these to mechanical injury, and in the lean and especially in the thin working ox the kidney is very liable to suffer. In the absence of an abundance of loose connective tissue and of fat, the kidneys lie in close contact with the muscles of the loins, and any injury to these may tend to put the kidney and its vessels on the stretch, or to cause its inflammation by direct extension of the disease from the injured muscle to the adjacent kidney. Thus, under unusually heavy draft, under slips and falls on slippery ground, under sudden unexpected drooping or twisting of the loins from missteps or from the feet sinking into holes, under the loading and jarring of the loins when animals ride each other in cases of heat, the kidneys are subject to injury and inflammation. A hard run, as when chased by a dog, may be the occasion of such an attack.

Inflammation of the kidneys may further be a form or an extension of a specific contagious disease, such as erysipelas, rinderpest, septicemia, or even of poisoning by the spores of fungi. Rivolta reports the case of a cow with spots of local congestion and blood staining in the kidney, the affected parts being loaded with bacteria. Unfortunately he neither cultivated the bacteria nor inoculated them, and thus the case stands without positive demonstration that these were the cause of disease.

The symptoms of nephritis are in certain cases very manifest, and in others so hidden that the existence of the affection can only be certainly recognized by a microscopic examination of the urine. In violent cases there is high fever, increase of the body temperature to 103° F. and upward; hurried breathing, with catching inspiration; accelerated pulse; dry, hot muzzle; burning of the roots of the horns

Cow Affected with Foot-and-Mouth Disease. B. A. I. 1902.

and ears, loss of appetite, suspended rumination, and indications of extreme sensitiveness in the loins. The patient stands with back arched and hind legs extended backward and outward, and passes water frequently, in driblets, of a high color and specific gravity, containing albumen and microscopic casts. When made to move, the patient does so with hesitation and groaning, especially if turned in a narrow circle; and when pinched on the flank, just beneath the lateral bony processes of the loins, especially on that side on which the disease predominates, it flinches and groans. If the examination is made with the oiled hand introduced through the last gut (rectum), the pressure upward on the kidneys gives rise to great pain and efforts to escape by moving away and by active contractions of the rectum for the expulsion of the hand. Sometimes there is a distinct swelling over the loins or quarter on one or both sides. In uncastrated males the testicle on the affected side is drawn up, or is alternately raised and dropped. In all there is a liability to tremors of the thigh on the side affected.

In some severe cases colicky pains are as violent as in the worst forms of indigestion and spasms of the bowels. The animal frequently shifts from one hind foot to the other, stamps, kicks at the belly, looks anxiously at its flank at frequent intervals, moans plaintively, lies down and quickly gets up again, grinds its teeth, twists its tail, and keeps the back habitually arched and rigid and the hind feet advanced under the belly. The bowels may be costive and the feces glistening with a coat of mucus, or they may be loose and irritable, and the paunch or even the bowels may become distended with gas (bloating) as the result of indigestion and fermentation. In some animals, male and female alike, the rigid arched condition of the back will give way to such undulating movements as are sometimes seen in the act of coition.

The disease does not always appear in its full severity; but for a day, or even two, there may be merely loss of appetite, impaired rumination, a disposition to remain lying down; yet when the patient is raised, it manifests suffering by anxiously looking at the flanks, shifting or stamping of the hind feet, shaking of the tail, and attempts to urinate, which are either fruitless or lead to the discharge of a small quantity of high-colored or perhaps bloody urine.

In chronic cases swelling of the legs or along the lower surface of chest or abdomen, or within these respective cavities, is a common symptom. So, also, stupor or coma, or even convulsions, may supervene from the poisonous action of urea and other waste or morbid products retained in the blood.

Treatment.—In the treatment of acute nephritis the first consideration is the removal of the cause. Acrid or diuretic plants in the food must be removed, and what of this kind is present in the stomach or bowels may be cleared away by a moderate dose of castor or olive oil; extensive surfaces of inflammation that have been blistered by Spanish flies must be washed clean with soapsuds; sprains of the back or loins must be treated by soothing fomentations or poultices, or by a fresh sheepskin with its fleshy side applied on the loins, and the patient must be kept in a narrow stall in which it can not turn even its head. The patient must be kept in a warm, dry building, so that the skin shall be kept active rather than the kidneys. Warm blanketing is equally important, or even mustard poultices over the loins will be useful. Blisters of Spanish flies, turpentine, or other agent which may be absorbed and irritate the kidneys must be avoided. The active fever may be checked by 15 drops tincture of aconite every four hours, or by one-third ounce acetanilid. If pain is very acute 1 ounce laudanum or 2 drams solid extract of belladonna will serve to relieve. When the severity of the disease has passed, a course of tonics (quinia, 2 drams, or gentian powder, 4 drams, daily) may be given. Diuretics, too, may be cautiously given at this advanced stage to relieve dropsy and give tone to the kidneys and general system (oil of turpentine, 2 teaspoonfuls; bicarbonate of soda, 1 teaspoonful, repeated twice a day). Pure water is essential, and it should not be given chilled; warm drinks are preferable.

In the chronic forms of kidney inflammation the same protection against cold and similar general treatment are demanded. Tonics, however, are important to improve the general health (phosphate of iron, 2 drams; powdered nux vomica, 20 grains; powdered gentian root, 4 drams, daily). In some instances the mineral acids (nitric acid, 60 drops, or nitro-muriatic acid, 60 drops, daily) may be employed with the bitters. Mustard applied to the loins in the form of a thin pulp made with water and covered for an hour with paper or other impervious envelope, or water hotter than the hand can bear, or cupping may be resorted to as a counterirritant. In cupping shave the loins, smear them with lard, then take a narrow-mouthed glass, expand the air within it by smearing its interior with a few drops of alcohol, setting it on fire and instantly pressing the mouth of the vessel to the oiled portion of the skin. As the air within the vessel cools it contracts, tending to form a partial vacuum, and the skin, charged with blood, is strongly drawn up within it. Several of these being applied at once a strong derivation from the affected kidneys is secured. In no case of inflamed or irritable kidney should Spanish flies or oil of turpentine be used upon the skin.

Parasites of the Kidney.—As the kidney is the usual channel by which the bacteria leave the system, this organ is liable to be implicated when microphytes exist in the blood, and congestions and blood extravasations are produced. In anthrax, Southern cattle fever (Texas fever), and other such affections bloody urine is the consequence. Of the larger parasites attacking the kidney may be specially named the cystic form of the echinococcus tapeworm of the dog, the cystic form of the unarmed or beef tapeworm of man, the diving bladderworm—the cystic form of the marginate tapeworm of the dog, and the giant strongyle—the largest of the roundworms. These give rise to general symptoms of kidney disease, but the true source of the trouble is only likely to be detected if the heads or hooklets of the tapeworm or the eggs of the roundworm are found on microscopic examination of the urine.

RETENTION OF URINE.

Inability to pass urine may come from any one of three conditions—first, spasm of the neck of the bladder; second, paralysis of the body of the bladder; third, obstruction of the channel of outlet by a stone (calculus) or other obstacle.

In spasm of the neck of the bladder the male animal may stand with the tail slightly raised and making rhythmical contractions of the muscle beneath the anus *(accelerator urinæ)*, but without passing a drop of liquid. In the female the hind legs are extended and widely parted, and the back is arched as if to urinate, but the effort is vain. If the oiled hand is introduced into the rectum or vagina in the early stages of the affection, the bladder may be felt beneath partially filled, but not overdistended with liquid, and its neck or mouth firm and rigid. In the more advanced stages of the affection the organ is felt as a great, tense, elastic bag, extending forward into the abdomen. In this condition the overdistended muscular coat of the bladder has lost its power of contraction, so that true paralysis has set in, the muscle closing the mouth of the sack alone retaining its contractile power.

In paralysis of the body of the bladder attention is rarely drawn to the urinary disorder until the bladder has been distended to full repletion and is almost ready to give way by rupture and to allow the escape of the contained liquid into the abdomen. Overdistention is the most common cause of the paralysis, yet it may occur from inflammation of the muscular wall of the bladder, or even from injury to the terminal part of the spinal marrow. In this last condition, however, the tail is likely to be powerless, and the neck of the bladder may also be paralyzed, so that the urine dribbles away continuously.

Causes.—Among the causes of spasm of the neck of the bladder may be named the lodgment of small stones or gravel, the feeding on irritant diuretics (see Bloody Urine, or Nephritis), the enforced retention of urine while at work or during a painful or difficult parturition. The irritation attendant on inflammation of the mucous membrane of the bladder may be a further cause of spasm of the neck, as may also be inflammation of the channel (urethra) back of the neck. Extensive applications of Spanish flies to the skin, the abuse of diuretics, and the occurrence of indigestion and spasms of the bowels are further causes. So long as spasmodic colic is unrelieved, retention of water from spasm of the neck of the bladder usually persists.

Treatment.—Treatment will depend largely on the cause. In indigestion the irritant contents of the bowels must be got rid of by laxatives and injections of warm water; Spanish-fly blisters must be washed from the surface; a prolonged and too active exertion must be intermitted. The spasm may be relaxed by injecting one-half ounce solid extract of belladonna in water into the rectum or by a solution of tobacco. Chloroform or ether may be given by inhalation, or chloral hydrate (1 ounce) may be given in water by the mouth. Fomentations of warm water may be made over the loins and between the thighs, and the oiled hand inserted into the rectum may press moderately on the anterior part of the bladder, which can be felt as an elastic fluctuating bag of an oval shape just beneath.

All other measures failing, the liquid must be drawn off through a tube (catheter). This is, however, exceedingly difficult, alike in male and female, and we can not expect an amateur to succeed in accomplishing it. In the cow the opening into the bladder is found in the median line of the floor of the generative entrance, about 4 inches in front of the external opening, but it is flanked on either side by a blind pouch, into which the catheter will pass, in ninety-nine cases out of a hundred, in the hands of any but the most skilled operator. In the bull or steer the penis, when retracted into its sheath, is bent upon itself like the letter S, just above the scrotum and testicles, and unless this bend is effaced by extending the organ forward out of its sheath it is quite impossible to pass a catheter beyond this point. When, however, the animal can be tempted by the presentation of a female to protrude the penis so that it can be seized and extended, or when it can be manipulated forward out of the sheath, it becomes possible to pass a catheter of small caliber (one-third inch or under) onward into the bladder. Youatt advised to lay open the sheath so as to reach and extend the penis, and others have advocated opening the urethra in the interval between the thighs or just beneath the anus, but such formidable operations are beyond the stock owner. The incision of the narrow urethra through the great thickness of muscular and erectile bleeding tissue just beneath the anus is especially an operation of extreme delicacy and difficulty. Drawing off the liquid through the tube of an aspirator is another possible resort for the professional man. The delicate needle of the aspirator is inserted in such cases through the floor of the vagina and upper wall of the bladder in the female, or through the floor of the rectum (last gut) and roof of the bladder in the male, or finally through the lower and back part of the abdominal wall, just in front of the bones of the pelvis (pubic bones), and thence through the lower and anterior part of the bladder near its blind anterior end. After relief has been obtained the administration of belladonna in 2-dram doses daily for several days will tend to prevent a recurrence of the retention.

When the body of the bladder has become benumbed or paralyzed by overdistention, we may seek to restore its tone by doses of one-half a dram of powdered nux vomica repeated daily, and by mustard plasters applied over the loins, on the back part of the belly inferiorly, or between the thighs. Small doses (2 drams) of balsam of copaiba are sometimes useful in imparting tone to the partly paralyzed organ.

INCONTINENCE OF URINE (PALSY OF THE NECK OF THE BLADDER).

This may occur from disease or injury to the posterior part of the spinal cord or from broken back, and in these cases the tail is likely to be paralyzed, and it may be also the hind limbs. In this case the urine dribbles away constantly, and the oiled hand in the vagina or rectum will feel the half-filled and flaccid bladder beneath and may easily empty it by pressure.

Treatment.—Treatment is only successful when the cause of the trouble can be remedied. After these (sprains of the back, etc.) have recovered, blisters (mustard) on the loins, the lower part of the abdomen, or between the thighs may be resorted to with success. Two drams daily of copaiba or of solid extract of belladonna or 2 grains Spanish flies may serve to restore the lost tone. These failing, the use of electric currents may still prove successful.

URINARY CALCULI (STONE, OR GRAVEL).

Stone, or gravel, consists in hard bodies mainly made up of the solid earthy constituents of the urine which have crystallized out of that liquid at some part of the urinary passage, and have remained as small particles (gravel), or have concreted into large masses (stone, calculus).

In looking for the immediate causes of urinary calculi we must accord a high place to all those conditions which determine the presence of excess of mucus, albumen, pus, blood, kidney casts, blood-coloring matter, etc., in the urine. A catarrhal inflammation of the pelvis of the kidney, of the ureter, or of the bladder, generating excess of mucus or pus; inflammation of the kidneys, causing the discharge into the urinary passages of blood, albumen, or hyaline casts; inflammation of the liver, lungs, or other distant organ, resulting in the escape of albumen in the urine; disorders of the liver or of the blood-forming functions, resulting in hematuria or hemoglobinuria; sprains or other injuries to the back, or disease of the spinal marrow, which cause the escape of blood with the urine; the presence in the bladder of a bacterian ferment, which determines the decomposition of the mucus and urea, the evolution of ammonia and the consequent destruction of the protecting cellular (epithelial) lining of the bladder, or the irritation caused by the presence of an already formed calculus, may produce the colloid or uncrystallizable body that proves so effective in the precipitation of stone or gravel. It has long been known that calculi will almost infallibly form around any foreign body introduced into the kidney or bladder, and I have seen a large calculous mass surrounding a splinter of an arrow that had penetrated and broken off in the body of a deer. The explanation is now satisfactory— the foreign body carries in with it bacteria, which acts as ferments upon the urine and mucus in addition to the mechanical injury caused by its presence. If such a body has been introduced through the solid tissues, there is, in addition, the presence of the blood and lymph derived from the wounded structures.

STONE IN THE KIDNEY (RENAL CALCULI).

In an animal leading the quiet, uneventful life of the ox, stones of large size may be present in the kidney without producing any disorder appreciable to the people about him. In cattle fattened on dry food in winter, on our magnesian limestone of New York, it is exceptional to find the substance of the kidney free from calculi about the size of a grain of wheat or less, and standing out as white objects in the general red of the cut surface of the organ. Similarly around the papillæ in the cup-like arms of the pelvis we find minute flattened or more or less rounded yellowish white concretions. Even the large concretions may prove apparently harmless. I have a calculus several ounces in weight which filled the entire pelvis of the kidney, which was found by accident in a fat carcass while being dressed. In work oxen, however, such concretions may give rise to symptoms of kidney disease, such as stiffness of the loins, shown especially in the acts of rising or turning, weakness of the hind parts when set to pull a heavy load, an irritability of the kidneys, shown by the frequent passage of urine in small quantity, tenderness of the loins, shown when they are pinched or lightly struck, and it may be the passage of blood or minute gritty masses with the urine. If the attack is severe, what is called renal colic (kidney colic) may be shown by frequent uneasy shifting of the hind limbs, shaking or twisting of the tail, looking round at the flanks, and lying down and rising again at short intervals without apparent cause. The frequent passage of urine, the bloody or gritty masses contained in it, and perhaps the hard, stony cylinders around the tufts of hair of the sheath, show that the source of the suffering is the urinary organs. In bad cases active inflammation of the kidneys may set in. (See Nephritis.)

URETERAL CALCULI.

These are small stones which have passed from the pelvis of the kidney into the canal (ureter) leading from the kidney to the bladder, but, being too large to pass on easily, have blocked that canal and forced the urine back upon the kidney. The result is the production of symptoms more violent than in renal calculi, though not varying, save in intensity, from those of renal colic. In case of complete and unrelieved obstruction, the secretion of the kidney on that side is entirely abolished, and it becomes the seat of passive congestion, and it may even be absorbed in greater part or as a whole, leaving only a fibrous sac containing fluid with a urinous odor. In small cattle, in which the oiled hand introduced into the last gut may reach the affected part, the distended ureter may be felt as a tense, elastic cord, extending forward from the point of obstruction on the lateral wall of the pelvis and beneath the loins toward the kidney. If relief is obtained by the onward passage of the stone a free flow of urine usually follows, in the midst of which may often be found gritty masses. If the outlets from both kidneys are similarly blocked, the animal becomes poisoned by the retention in the blood of the elements of the urine, and by their reabsorption after secretion.

Treatment of Renal and Ureteral Calculi.—Treatment is not very successful, as only the smallest calculi can pass through the ureter and enter the bladder, and even if they should do so they are liable to a progressive increase there, so that later they may cause the symptoms of stone in the bladder. Fortunately, ordinary dairy, growing, or fattening cattle rarely show evident symptoms of illness, and though they should do so they can usually be fattened and slaughtered before the health is seriously impaired. In work oxen the case is different, and acute symptoms may develop, but even then the animal may often be fitted for the butcher. When treatment is demanded it is primarily soothing and antispasmodic. Fomentations with warm water over the loins should be persisted in without intermission until relief has been secured. The soothing effect on the kidney will often relieve inflammation and irritation, should the stone be in that situation, while if in the ureter the warm fomentations will at once soothe irritation, relax spasm of the muscular coat of the canal, and favor an abundant secretion from the kidney, which, pressing on the obstructing stone, may slowly push it on into the bladder. Large doses of laudanum (2 ounces) or of solid extract of belladonna (2 drams) will not only soothe the pain but relax the spasm and favor the onward passage of the calculus. The animal should be encouraged to drink large quantities of cool water to favor the free secretion of a very watery urine, which will not only serve to obviate irritation and continued deposit caused by a highly concentrated urine, but will press the stone onward toward the bladder, and even in certain cases will tend to disintegrate it by solution of some of its elements, and thus to favor its crumbling and expulsion. This is a principle which must never be lost sight of in the treatment of calculi. The immersion of the stone in a liquid of a lower specific gravity than that in which it has formed and grown tends to dissolve out the more soluble of its component parts, and thus to destroy its density and cohesion at all points, and thereby to favor its complete disintegration and expulsion. This explains why cattle taken from a herd on our magnesian limestone in spring, after the long dry feeding of winter, usually furnish renal calculi, while cattle from the same herd in the fall, after a summer's run on a succulent pasture, are almost always free from concretions. The abundance of liquid taken in the green food and expelled through the kidneys and the low density or watery nature of the urine have so opened the texture and destroyed the density of the smaller stones and gravel that they have all been disintegrated and removed. This, too, is the main reason why benefit is derived from a prolonged stay at mineral springs by the human victims of gravel. If they had swallowed the same number of quarts of pure water at home and distributed it at suitable intervals over each day, they would have benefited largely without a visit to the springs.

It follows from what has been just said that a succulent diet, including a large amount of water (gruels, sloppy mashes, turnips, beets, potatoes, apples, pumpkins, ensilage, succulent grasses), is an important factor in the relief of the milder forms of stone and gravel.

Prevention.—Prevention of calculus especially demands this supply of water and watery rations on all soils and in all conditions in which there is a predisposition to this disease. It must also be sought by attempts to obviate all those conditions mentioned above as causative of the malady. Sometimes good rain water can be furnished in limestone districts, but putrid or bad smelling rain water is to be avoided as probably more injurious than that from the limestone. Unsuccessful attempts have been made to dissolve calculi by alkaline salts and mineral acids, respectively, but their failure as a remedy does not necessarily condemn them as preventives. One dram of caustic potash or of hydrochloric acid may be given daily in the drinking water. In diametrically opposite ways these attack and decompose the less soluble salts and form new ones which are more soluble and therefore little disposed to precipitate in the solid form. Both are beneficial as increasing the secretion of urine. In cases where the diet has been too highly charged with phosphates (wheat bran, etc.), these ailments must be restricted and water allowed ad libitum. Where the crystals passed with the urine are the sharp angular (octahedral) ones of oxalate of lime, then the breathing should be made more active by exercise, and any disease of the lungs subjected to appropriate treatment. If the crystals are triangular prisms of ammonia-magnesium phosphate or star-like forms with feathery rays, the indications are to withhold the food or water that abounds in magnesia and check the fermentation in the urine by attempts to destroy its bacteria. In the latter direction plenty of pure water, diuretics, and a daily dose of oil of turpentine in milk, or a dose thrice a day of a solution containing one-tenth grain each of biniodide of mercury and iodide of potassium would be indicated.

In considering the subject of prevention, it must never be forgotten that any disease of a distant organ which determines the passage from the blood into the urine of albumen or any other colloid (uncrystallizable) body is strongly provocative of calculus, and should, if possible, be corrected. Apart from cases due to geological formation, faulty feeding, and other causes, the grand preventive of calculus is a long summer's pasturage of succulent grasses, or in winter a diet of ensilage or other succulent food.

The calculi formed in part of silica demand special notice. This agent is secreted in the urine in the form of silicate of potash and is thrown down as insoluble silica when a stronger acid displaces it by combining with the potash to its exclusion. In cases of siliceous calculi, accordingly, the appropriate chemical prevention is caustic potash, which being present in the free state would attract to itself any free acid and leave the silica in its soluble condition as silicate of potash.

STONE IN THE BLADDER (VESICAL, OR URETHRAL CALCULUS).

Stone in the bladder may be of any size, but in the ox does not usually exceed half an inch in diameter. There may, however, be a number of small calculi; indeed, they are sometimes so small and numerous as to form a small pulpy magma by which the bladder is considerably distended.

Symptoms.—The symptoms of stone in the bladder may be absent until one of the masses escapes into the urethra, but when this occurs the escape of urine is prevented, or it is allowed to pass in drops or driblets only, and the effect of such obstruction becomes manifest. The point of obstruction is not always the same, but it is most frequently at the S-shaped curve of the penis, just above the testicles or scrotum. In cows and heifers the urethra is

DIRTY SEDIMENT IN BOTTOM OF BOTTLE OF
MILK. DEPT. OF AGR. 1909.

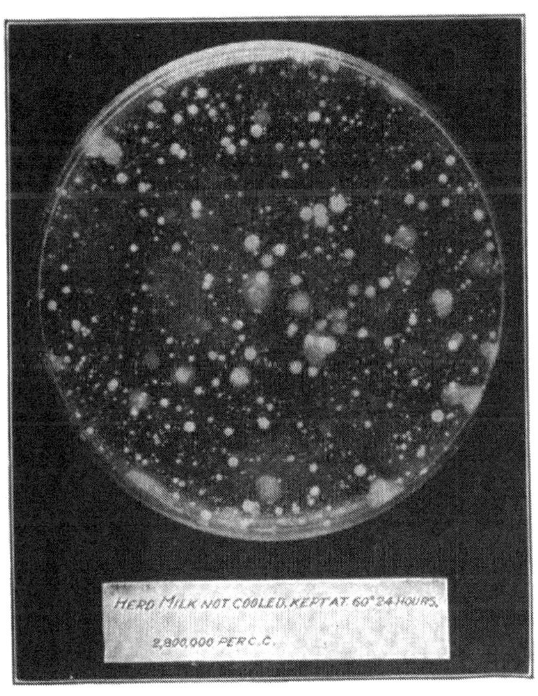

SHOWING BACTERIA IN MILK NOT COOLED BUT
KEPT AT 60 DEGREES FOR 24 HOURS.
NUMEROUS COLONIES; 2,800,000 IN A CUBIC
CENTIMETER. DEPT. OF AGR.

so short and becomes so widely dilated during the urination that the calculi easily escape in the flow of liquid and dangerous symptoms practically never appear.

Even in the male the signs of illness are at first very slight. A close observer may notice the cylinders of hard, earthy materials encircling the tufts of hair at the opening of the prepuce. It may further be observed that the stall remains dry and that the animal has not been seen to pass water when out of doors. The tail may at times be gently raised and contractions of the muscle (*accelerator urinae*) beneath the anus may take place in a rhythmical or pulsating manner. But as a rule no symptom is noticed for a couple of days, only the animal is lacking in his usual spirits. By this time the constantly accumulating urine has distended the bladder beyond its power of resistance and a rupture occurs, allowing the urine to escape into the cavity of the abdomen. Then dullness increases! the animal lies down most of his time; he becomes stupid and sometimes drowsy, with reddish brown congestion of the lining membrane of the eyelids; pressure on the abdomen causes pain, flinching, and perhaps groaning, and the lowest part of the belly fluctuates more and more as the escaping urine accumulates in greater and greater amount. If at this stage the oiled hand is introduced into the rectum (last gut), the animal flinches when pressure is made downward on the floor of the pelvis, and no round, distended bladder is felt. If the same examination is made prior to the rupture the rounded, tense, elastic bladder is felt extending forward into the abdomen, containing one or two gallons of liquid. There may be uneasy shifting of the hind limbs and twisting of the tail, also frequent lying down and rising, but these symptoms are exceptional.

When the obstruction is low down between the thighs (at the S-shaped flexure), the line of the pulsating urethra from the anus downward may be felt distended with liquid, and though it is seldom easy to distinguish the exact seat of the stone by the hard swelling of the urethra, yet there is usually tenderness at the point of obstruction, and from this it may be accurately located.

Treatment.—The treatment of stone in the bladder or urethra consists in the removal of the stone by incision and the use of forceps. When the stone has been arrested at the S-shaped flexure just above the scrotum, the patient being lean, the thickened tender part of the penis may be seized between the fingers and thumb of the left hand, while the calculus is exposed by a free incision with the knife held in the right. If there is no other obstruction between this point and the bladder, and if the latter has not yet ruptured, a flow of urine should take place from the opening. If there is no escape of liquid a catheter or sound, one-fourth of an inch in diameter, must be passed up through the canal (urethra) until it is arrested by the next stone, on which a similar incision should then be made to effect its extraction. In case the stone has been arrested in the portion of the urethra which is in front of the arch of the hip bone and inside the pelvis, it can only be reached by making an opening into the urethra beneath the anus and over the arch of the hip bone, and from this orifice exploring the urethra with fine forceps to the neck of the bladder or until the stone has been reached and extracted. The operation requires a very accurate knowledge of the parts, owing to the small size of the canal (urethra to be opened and the great thickness of erectile tissue to be cut through, while the free flow of blood is blinding to the operator. A staff should always be passed up through the urethra from the lower wound, if such has been made, or, in case of its absence, through the whole length of the penis, that organ having been drawn out of its sheath until the S-shaped curve has been effaced and the course of the canal rendered straight. Upon the end of this staff the incision can be made with far more confidence and certainty. The operation can only be undertaken by a skilled veterinary anatomist, but the hints given above may be valuable in showing the stock owner when he is being properly served in such a case.

In outlying districts, where no skilled operator can be had, a transverse incision may be made with a clean sharp knife through the root of the penis, just over the arch of the hip bone, when the urine will flow out in a full stream. The attendant bleeding may be ignored, or if profuse it may be checked by packing the wound firmly with cotton wool for some hours. The urine will continue to escape by the wound, and the ox should be fattened for the butcher.

The immediate relief is not to be looked upon as a permanent cure, as the calculi in the affected ox are usually numerous and later attacks are therefore to be looked for. Hence it is desirable to fatten and kill such cases after a successful operation. If a breeding animal is too valuable to be killed, he should be subjected to preventive measures, as laid down under Stone in the kidney.

It should be added that when the bladder is filled with a soft magma a catheter may be introduced through the whole length of the urethra, to be employed in pumping water into the bladder. This water is extracted through the same channel when it has been charged with the suspended solids by manipulations of the bladder with the oiled hand introduced through the rectum.

Calculi, or Gravel, in the Prepuce, or Sheath.—This is usually a collection of gravel, or a soft, putty-like material which causes a distinct swelling of the sheath and gives it a soft, doughy feeling when handled. It may be removed in part by oiled fingers introduced into the cavity, assisted by manipulation from without, or a tube may be inserted until the end extends behind the collection and water pumped in until the whole mass has been evacuated. Should even this fail of success the sheath may be slit open from the orifice back in the median line below until the offending matter can be reached and removed. In all such cases the interior of the sheath should be finally lubricated with sweet oil or vaseline. It is unnecessary to stitch up the wound made in the sheath. (See Inflammation of the Sheath).

LIST OF PUBLICATIONS ABRIDGED ABOVE.
Digestive System.
Special Report on Diseases of Cattle: U. S. Dept. Agr., Washington, D. C.
The Changes which take place in the Teeth of Cattle and Sheep with Age: Virginia Agr. Exp. Sta. Bulletin 11, Vol. IX. New Series.
Diseases of the Stomach and Bowels of Cattle: U. S. Dept. Agr., B. A. I. Circular 68, (revised).
An Aphthous Affection among Dairy Cows: Iowa Agr. Exp. Sta. Bulletin 14.
Respiratory System.
Special Report on Diseases of Cattle: U. S. Dept. Agr., Washington, D. C.
Pneumonia in Cattle: Kansas Agr. Exp. Sta. Press Bulletin 112.
Heart and Blood Vessels.
Special Report on Diseases of Cattle: U. S. Dept. Agr., Washington, D. C.
Nervous System.
Special Report on Diseases of Cattle: U. S. Dept. Agr., Washington, D. C.
A Nervous Disease of Cattle: Louisiana Agr. Exp. Sta. Bulletin 64, (2nd series).
The Supposed Relationship of White Snakeroot to Milksickness or Trembles: U. S. Dept. Agr., Bureau of Plant Industry Bulletin 121, Part 1.
Urinary Organs.
Special Report on Diseases of Cattle: U. S. Dept. Agr. Washington, D. C.
Founder in Horses and Red Water in Cattle: South Carolina Agr. Exp. Sta. Bulletin 26 (New Series.)

THE GENERATIVE ORGANS.

In reviewing this class of diseases, we have to note first, that they are almost exclusively restricted to breeding animals; and, second, that in keeping with the absolute difference of the organs in the male and female we find two essentially distinct lists of diseases affecting the two sexes.

EXCESS OF VENEREAL DESIRE (SATYRIASIS IN MALE, OR NYMPHOMANIA IN FEMALE).

This may occur in the male from too frequent sexual intercourse, or from injury and congestion of the base of the brain (vasodilator center in the medulla), or of the posterior end of the spinal cord, or it may be kept up by congestion or inflammation of the testicles or of the mucous membrane covering the penis. It may be manifested by a constant or frequent erection, by attempts at sexual connection, and sometimes by the discharge of semen without connection. In bad cases the feverishness and restlessness lead to loss of flesh, emaciation, and physical weakness.

It is, however, in the female especially that this morbid desire is most noticeable and injurious. It may be excited by the stimulating quality of the blood in cows fed to excess on highly nitrogenous food, as the seeds of the bean, pea, vetch, and tare, and as wheat bran, middlings, cotton seed gluten meal, etc., especially in the case of such as have no free exercise in the fields, and are subject to constant association with a vigorous young bull. A more frequent cause is the excitation or congestion of some part of the genital organs. Disease of the ovaries is pre-eminently the cause, and this may be by the formation of cysts (sacs containing liquid) or of solid tumors or degenerations, or, more commonly than all, the deposition of tubercle. Indeed, in case of tuberculosis attacking the abdominal organs of cows, the ovaries or the serous membranes that support and cover them (the broad ligaments of the womb) are peculiarly subject to attack and the animal has constant sexual excitement, incessantly riding or being ridden by other cattle, having no leisure to eat or chew the cud, but moving restlessly, wearing the flesh off its bones, and gradually wasting. In some localities these cows are known as "bullers," because they are nearly always disposed to take the bull, but they do not conceive, or, if they do, they are subject to early abortions. They are, therefore, useless alike for the dairy and for the feeder, unless the removal of the ovaries subdues the sexual excitement, when, in the absence of tuberculous disease elsewhere, they may be fattened for the butcher.

Among the other sources of irritation charged with causing nymphomania are tumors and cancers of the womb, rigid closure of the neck of the womb so that conception can not occur and the frequent services by the male stimulate the unsatisfied appetite, and inflammation, and a purulent discharge from the womb or vagina.

Treatment.—The treatment in each case will vary with the cause and is most satisfactory when that cause is a removable one. Overfeeding on richly nitrogenous food can be stopped, exercise in the open field secured, diseased ovaries may be removed, catarrhs of the womb and passages overcome by antiseptic astringent injections, and tumors of the womb may often be detached and extracted, the mouth of that organ having been first dilated by sponge tents or otherwise. The rubber dilator (impregnator) though sometimes helpful in the mare is rarely available for the cow, owing to the different condition of the mouth of the womb.

DIMINUTION OR LOSS OF VENEREAL DESIRE (ANAPHRODISIA).

This will occur in either sex from low condition and ill health. Long standing chronic diseases of important internal organs, leading to emaciation and weakness, or a prolonged semistarvation in winter may be sufficient cause. It is, however, much more common as the result of degeneration or extensive and destructive disease of the secreting organs (testicles, ovaries) which elaborate the male and female sexual products, respectively. Such diseases are, therefore, a common cause of sterility in both sexes. The old bull, fat and lazy, becomes sluggish and unreliable in serving, and finally gets to be useless for breeding purposes. This is not due to his weight and clumsiness alone, but largely to the fatty degeneration of his testicles and their excretory ducts, which prevents the due formation and maturation of the semen.

If he has been kept in extra high condition for exhibition in the show ring, this disqualification comes upon him sooner and becomes more irremediable.

Similarly the overfed, inactive cow, and above all the show cow, fails to come in heat at the usual intervals, shows little disposition to take the bull, and fails to conceive when served. Her trouble is the same in kind, namely, fatty degeneration of the ovaries and of their excretory ducts (Fallopian tubes), which prevents the formation or maturation of the ovum or, when it has formed, hinders its descent into the womb. Another common defect in such old fat cows is a rigid closure of the mouth of the womb, which prevents conception, even if the ovum reaches the interior of that organ and even if the semen is discharged into the vagina.

Preventive.—The true preventive of such conditions is to be found in a sound hygiene. The breeding animal should be of adult age, neither overfed nor underfed, but well fed and moderately exercised; in other words, the most vigorous health should be sought, not only that a strong race may be propagated, but that the whole herd, or nearly so, may breed with certainty.

In case of rigid closure of the mouth of the womb the only resort is dilatation. This is far more difficult and uncertain in the cow than in the mare. The neck of the womb is longer, is often tortuous in its course, and its walls so approximated to each other and so rigid that it may be all but impossible to follow it, and there is always danger of perforating its walls and opening into the cavity of the abdomen, or short of that of causing inflammation and a new rigid fibrous formation which, on healing, leaves matters worse than before. The opening must be carefully made with the finger, and when that has entered the womb further dilatation may be secured by inserting a sponge tent or by careful stretching with a mechanical dilator.

STERILITY FROM OTHER CAUSES.

The questions as to whether a bull is a sure stock getter and whether a cow is a breeder are so important that it would be wrong to pass over other prominent causes of sterility. Breeding at too early an age is a common source of increasing weakness of constitution which has obtained in certain breeds. Jerseys have especially been made the victims of this mistake, the object being to establish the highest milking powers in the smallest obtainable body which will demand the least material and outlay for its constant repair of waste. With success in this line there has been the counterbalancing disadvantage of impaired vigor, with too often lessened fertility as well as increased predisposition to disease. When the heifers of the race have for generation after generation been bred under a year old, the demand for the nourishment of the fetus is too great a drain on the immature animal, which accordingly remains small and stunted. As it fails to develop in size, so every organ fails to be nourished to perfection. Similarly with the immature bull put to too many cows; he fails to develop his full size, vigor, or stamina, and transfers his acquired weakness to his progeny. An increasing number of barren females and an increasing proclivity to abortions are the necessary results of both courses. When this early breeding has occurred accidentally it is well to dry up the dam just after calving, and to avoid having her served again until full grown.

Some highly fed and plethoric females seem to escape conception by the very intensity of the generative ardor. The frequent passage of urine, accompanied by contractions of the womb and vagina and a profuse secretion from their surfaces, leads to the expulsion of the semen after it has been lodged in the genital passages. This may be remedied somewhat by bleeding the cow shortly before putting to the bull, so as to diminish the richness and stimulating quality of the blood; or better by giving 1½ pounds of Epsom salts a day or two before she comes in heat, and subjecting her at the same time to a spare diet. Should the excessive ardor of the cow not be controllable in this way, she may be shut up for a day or two, until the heat is passing off, when under the lessened excitement the semen is more likely to be retained.

The various diseases of the ovaries, their tubes, the womb, the testicles and their excretory ducts, as referred to under "Excess of generative ardor," are causes of barrenness. In this connection it may be named that the discharges consequent on calving are fatal to the vitality of semen introduced before these have ceased to flow; hence service too soon after calving, or that of a cow which has had the womb or genital passages injured so as to keep up a muco-purulent flow until the animal comes in heat, is liable to fail of conception. Any such discharge should be first arrested by repeated injections as for leucorrhea, after which the male may be admitted.

Feeding on a very saccharine diet, which greatly favors the deposition of fat, seems to have an even more direct effect in preventing conception during such regimen. Among other causes of barrenness are all those that favor abortion, ergoted grasses, smutty wheat or corn, laxative or diuretic drinking water, and any improper or musty feed that causes indigestions, colics, and diseases of the urinary organs, notably gravel; also savin, rue, cantharides, and all other irritants of the bowels or kidneys.

Hermaphrodites are barren, of course, as their sexual organs are not distinctively either male or female. The heifer born as a twin is usually hermaphrodite and barren. But the animals of either sex in which development of the organs is arrested before they are fully matured remain as in the male or female prior to puberty, and are barren. Bulls with both testicles retained within the abdomen may go through the form of serving a cow, but the service is unfruitful; the spermatozoa are not fully elaborated. So I have examined a heifer with a properly formed but very small womb and an extremely narrow vagina and vulva, the walls of which were very muscular, that could never be made to conceive. A post-mortem examination would probably have disclosed an imperfectly formed ovary incapable of bringing ova to maturity.

A bull and cow that have been too closely inbred in the same line for generations may prove sexually incompatible and unable to generate together, though both are abundantly prolific when coupled with animals of other strains of blood.

Finally a bull may prove unable to get stock, not from any lack of sexual development, but from disease of other organs (back, loins, hind limbs), which renders him unable to mount with the energy requisite to the perfect service.

CONGESTION AND INFLAMMATION OF THE TESTICLES (ORCHITIS).

This usually results from blows or other direct injuries, but may be the result of excessive service or of the formation of some new growth (tumor) in the gland tissue. The bull moves stiffly, with straddling gait, and the right or left half of the scrotum in which the affected testicle lies is swollen, red, and tender, and the gland is drawn up within the sac and dropped down again at frequent intervals. It may be treated by rest; by 1½ pounds Epsom salts given in 4 quarts of water; by a restricted diet of some succulent food; by continued fomentations with warm water by means of sponges or rags sustained by a sling passed around the loins and back between the hind legs. The pain may be allayed by smearing with a solution of opium or of extract of belladonna. Should a soft point appear, indicating the formation of matter, it may be opened with a sharp lancet and the wound treated daily with a solution of a teaspoonful of carbolic acid in a half pint of water. Usually, however, when the inflammation has proceeded to this extent the gland will be ruined for purposes of procreation and must be cut out. (See "Castration").

INFLAMMATION OF THE SHEATH.

While this may occur in bulls from infection during copulation and from bruises, blows, and other mechanical injuries, the condition is more common in the ox in connection with the comparative inactivity of the parts. The sheath has a very small external opening, the mucous membrane of which is studded with sebaceous glands secreting a thick, unctuous matter of a strong, heavy odor. Behind this orifice is a distinct pouch, in which this unctuous matter is liable to accumulate when the penis is habitually drawn back. Moreover, the sheath has two muscles (protractors) which lengthen it passing into it from the region of the navel, and two (retractors) that shorten it passing into it from the lower surface of the pelvic bones above. The protractors keep the sheath stretched so that it habitually covers the penis, while the retractors shorten it up in the act of service, so that the penis can project to its full extent. In stud bulls the frequent protrusion of the erect and enlarged penis and the retraction and dilatation of the opening of the sheath serve to empty the pouch and prevent any accumulation of sebaceous matter or urine. In the ox, on the other hand, the undeveloped and inactive penis is usually drawn back so as to leave the anterior preputial pouch empty, so that the sebaceous matter has space to accumulate and is never expelled by the active retraction of the sheath and protrusion of the erect penis in service. Again, the ox rarely protrudes the tip of the penis in urination, the urine is discharged into the preputial pouch and lodges and decomposes there, so that there is a great liability to the precipitation of its earthy salts in the form of gravel. The decomposing ammoniacal urine, the gritty crystals precipitated from it, and the fetid, rancid, sebaceous matter set up inflammation in the delicate mucous membrane lining the passage. The membrane is thickened, reddened, rendered friable, and ultimately ulcerated, and the now narrowed sheath is blocked by the increasing mass of sebaceous and urinous material and the decomposing mucus and pus. The penis can no longer be protruded, the urine escapes in a small stream through the narrowing sheath, and finally the outlet is completely blocked and the urine distends the back part of the sheath. This will fluctuate on being handled, and soon the unhealthy inflammation extends on each side of it, causing a thick, doughy, tender swelling under the belly and between the thighs. The next step in the morbid course is overdistention of the bladder, with the occurrence of colicky pains, looking at the flanks, uneasy movements of the hind limbs, raising or twisting of the tail, pulsatory contractions of the urethra under the anus, and finally a false appearance of relief, which is caused by rupture of the bladder. Before this rupture takes place the distended bladder may press on the rectum and obstruct the passage of the bowel dejections. Two mistakes are therefore probable— first, that the bowels alone are to be relieved, and, second, that the trouble is obstruction of the urethra by a stone. Hence the need of examining the sheath and pushing the finger into its opening to see that there is no obstruction there, in all cases of retention of urine, overdistended bladder, or blocked rectum in the ox. The disease may be acute or chronic—the first by reason of acute adhesive inflammation blocking the outlet, the second by gradual thickening and ulceration of the sheath and blocking by the sebaceous and calculous accretions.

Treatment.—The treatment of this affection will depend on the stage. If recent and no instant danger of rupture of the bladder, the narrow opening of the sheath should be freely cut open in the median line below, and the sac emptied out with a finger or spoon, after which it should be thoroughly washed with tepid water. To make the cleansing more thorough a catheter or a small rubber tube may be inserted well back into the sheath, and water may be forced through it from a syringe or a funnel inserted into the other end of the tube and considerably elevated. A fountain syringe, which should be found in every house, answers admirably. The sheath may be daily washed out with tepid water, with a suds made with Castile soap, or with a weak solution of sulphate of zinc (one-half dram to a quart of water). If these attentions are impossible, most cases, after cleansing, will do well if merely driven through clean water up to the belly once a day.

In case the disease has progressed to absolute obstruction, with the bladder ready to rupture any moment, no time must be lost in

Portion of Steer's Hide, Showing the Texas Fever Tick (Boophilus Annultus) of the U. S. Natural Size.
Original. B. A. I. 1900.

opening into the urethra with a sharp knife over the bony arch under the anus, where the pulsations are seen in urinating. This incision is best made in the median line from above downward, but in the absence of a skillful operator a transverse incision with a sharp knife over the bone in the median line until the urine flows with a gush is better than to let the patient die. Considerable blood will be lost and the wound will heal tardily, but the ox will be preserved. Then the slitting and cleansing of the sheath can be done at leisure, as described above. If the bladder is ruptured, the case is hopeless.

INFLAMMATION OF THE SHEATH AND PENIS FROM BRUISING.

This also is an affection of work oxen, caused by the pressure and friction of the sling when the animals are held in the stocks for shoeing. This crushing of both sheath and penis for half an hour or more leads to the development, some hours later, of a hard, hot, and painful swelling, extending from the scrotum as far as the opening of the sheath. Fever sets in, with dry muzzle, red eyes, hard, full, rapid pulse, accelerated breathing, and elevated temperature. The ox stands obstinately with its hind legs drawn apart and urine falling drop by drop from the sheath. Appetite and rumination are suspended. In twenty-four hours there may be indications of advancing gangrene (mortification), the swelling becomes cold, soft, and doughy; it may even crack slightly from the presence of gas; a reddish brown fetid liquid oozes from the swelling, especially around the edges, and if the animal survives it is only with a great loss of substance of the sheath and penis.

Prevention.—The prevention of such an injury is easy. It is only necessary to see that the slings shall not press upon the posterior part of the abdomen. They must be kept in front of the sheath.

Treatment.—Treatment, to be effective, must be prompt and judicious. Put a strap around the patient with soft pads in contact with the affected parts, constantly soaked in cold water for at least twenty-four hours. A pound or two of Epsom salts in 4 quarts of hot water should also be given. The second day the parts may be washed with 1 quart of witch-hazel (extract), 2 drams sugar of lead, and 1 ounce laudanum, or the cold water irrigations may be continued if the active inflammation persists. In case the swelling continues hard and resistant, it may be pricked at the most prominent points to the depth of one-third of an inch with a lancet first dipped in dilute carbolic acid, and the whole surface should be washed frequently with chlorin water or other antiseptic.

When softening occurs in the center of a hard mass and fluctuation can be felt between two fingers pressed on different parts of such softening, it should be freely opened to let out the putrid pus, and the cavity should be syringed often with chlorin water.

In bad cases extensive sloughs of dead skin, of the whole wall of the sheath, and even of the penis, may take place, which will require careful antiseptic treatment. The soaking of the urine into the inflamed and softened tissue and the setting up of putrefactive action not only endanger great destruction of the tissues from putrid inflammation, but even threaten life itself from a general blood poisoning (septicemia). Every case should have skillful treatment to meet its various phases, but in the severe ones this is most urgently demanded.

INFLAMMATION OF THE URETHRA (GONORRHEA).

Like other males, the bull sometimes suffers from inflammation of the canal which conveys the urine through the penis, and forms a consequent whitish muco-purulent discharge. It may have originated in gravel, the excitement of too frequent service, infection from a cow with leucorrhea, or from extension of inflammation from the sheath Besides the oozing of the whitish liquid from the end of the penis and sheath, there is tenderness and pain when handled, and while there is no actual arrest of the urine, its flow is subject to frequent voluntary checks, as the scalding liquid irritates the tender surface.

Treatment.—If recognized before the discharge sets in, a dose of 1½ pounds of Epsom salts and local warm fomentations would be appropriate. After the onset of the whitish discharge a daily injection into the penis of a solution of 20 grains of permanganate of potash in a pint of water will be beneficial.

WARTS AND PAPILLARY GROWTHS ON THE PENIS.

These are not frequent in bull or ox. They may interfere with the protrusion of the organ from its sheath or with service, and always give rise to a bad smelling discharge.

Treatment.—They may be twisted off with the thumb and forefinger or cut off with a pair of scissors, and the seat burned with a pencil of lunar caustic. To get hold of the penis in the bull, bring him up to a cow. In the ox it will be necessary to push it out by manipulation through the sheath. In difficult cases the narrow opening of the sheath may be slit open.

WOUNDS OF THE PENIS.

The most common wounds are those sustained by blows of horns, sticks, etc. The blood vessels and sacs are ruptured to a greater or less extent and considerable swellings filled with coagulated blood and inflammatory products occur, leading to distortion of the organ, and it may be to the impossibility of protruding it.

Treatment.—A lotion of a dram of alum in a quart of water may be applied (injected into the sheath, if necessary), and a large sponge constantly irrigated by a stream of cold water may be kept applied by means of a surcingle to the outer side of the sheath. Incisions are rarely applicable to an organ of this kind, but in case of the existence of an extensive clot which is unlikely to be absorbed the lancet may be resorted to. If the injury leads to paralysis of the penis and hanging out of its sheath, it should be supported in a sling and astringents used freely until inflammation subsides. Then the restoration of power may be sought by a blister between the thighs, by the use of electricity, or by the careful use of nerve stimulants, such as strychnia (2 grains daily).

ULCERS ON THE PENIS.

Sores on the penis of the bull may result from gravel or sebaceous masses in the sheath or from having served a cow having leucorrhea.

Treatment.—These may be treated by frequent injections into the sheath of a lotion made with 1 dram of sugar of lead, 60 drops carbolic acid, and 1 quart water.

POLYPUS OF THE VAGINA OR UTERUS.

A polypus is a tumor growing from the mucous membrane, and often connected to it by a narrow neck. A definite cause can not always be assigned. If growing in the vagina, a polypus may project as a reddish, rounded tumor from the vulva, especially during the act of passing water. It can be distinguished from descent of the womb by the absence of the orifice of that cavity, which can be felt by the oiled hand beyond the tumor in the depth of the vagina. From a vaginal hernia caused by the protrusion of some abdominal organ enveloped by the relaxed wall of the vagina it may be distinguished by its persistence, its firm substance, and the impossibility of returning it into the abdomen by pressure. A hernia containing a portion of bowel gurgles when handled and can be completely effaced by pressure, the gut passing back into the abdomen.

A polypus in the womb is less easily recognized. At the time of calving it may be felt through the open mouth of the womb and recognized by the educated touch (it must be carefully distinguished from the mushroom-formed cotyledons, to which in ruminants the fetal membranes are attached). At other times, unless the womb is opened in the effort to expel it, the polypus can only be detected by examining the womb with the oiled hand introduced through the rectum.

Polypi may cause a muco-purulent discharge or they may only be suspected when they prove an obstacle to parturition. The best way to remove them is to put the cl ain of an ecraseur around the neck, or pedicle, of the tumor and tear it through; or the narrow neck may be torn through by the emasculator, or in an emergency it may be twisted through by rotating the tumor on its own axis. The removal of the tumor will allow calving to proceed; after which the sore may be treated by a daily injection of one-half dram of sulphate of zinc, 1 dram carbolic acid, and 1 quart milk-warm water.

PREGNANCY.

SIGNS OF PREGNANCY.

If a cow remains for three or four weeks after service without showing signs of heat (bulling), she is probably pregnant. There are very exceptional cases in which the well-fed cow will accept the bull weeks or months after actual conception, and others equally exceptional in which the well-thriven but unimpregnated female will refuse the male persistently, but these in no way invalidate the general rule.

The bull, no matter how vigorous or how ardent his sexual instinct, can not be made to pay any attention to a cow which is not in heat; hence indications of pregnancy can be had from both the male and female side. When she has conceived, the cow usually becomes more quiet and docile, and lays on flesh and fat more rapidly, especially during the first four months of gestation. The stimulus to digestion and nutrition created by the demands of the growing fetus, added to the quieter and more uneventful life, contributes to this result. Some feeders avail of this disposition to prepare heifers and cows speedily for the butcher.

The enlargement of the abdomen, and its droppings so that it bulges below and to each side, while it falls in at the flank, between the outer angle of the hip bone and the last rib, are significant features which, though they may be caused by abdominal tumor or dropsy, are usually marks of pregnancy. From the same increasing weight of the abdomen the spine in the region of the loins sinks so that the bones of the croup seem to rise, especially back toward the root of the tail. In the early stages of pregnancy the udder develops slowly, and toward its completion quite rapidly. For a long time there is merely a sense of greater fullness when handled; the wrinkles in the skin become shallower and are effaced, and the teats are materially enlarged. Beginning a few weeks after conception, this tends to a steady development, though slight alterations in the sense of successive growth and shrinkage are not uncommon. In milking cows this does not hold, as the milk usually tends to a steady diminution and the udder shrinks slowly until near the completion of the period, when it undergoes its sudden remarkable development, and yields at first a serous liquid and then the yellow colostrum, which coagulates when heated. As pregnancy advances the mucous membrane lining the vulva becomes swollen and of a darker bluish red hue, and the mucous secretion increases, becoming very abundant just before calving. When the feeding has not been altered or restricted, a steady diminution of the salts of lime excreted in the urine is an attendant on pregnancy, the lime being demanded for the growing body of the fetus.

After the fifth month the movements of the calf may often be observed in the right flank, nearly in front of the stifle, when the cow is drinking cold water. The sensation of cold on the side of the first stomach, which lies to the left and directly below the womb stimulates the calf to active movements, which are detected on the sudden jerking outward of the abdominal wall as if from blows delivered from within. In a loose pendent abdomen in the latter months of gestation the skin may often be seen pushed out at a sharp angle, irrespective of the period of drinking.

Another mode of examination through the flank is by touch. The palm of the hand is pressed strongly inward, about 8 inches in front of the stifle and a little below, several times in succession, and is then brought to rest with the pressure maintained. Presently there are felt distinct and characteristic movements of the fetus, which has been disturbed and roused to action. Another mode is to press the closed fist strongly inward in the same situation and hold it so, forming a deep indentation in the abdominal wall. Presently the knuckles are felt to be struck by a solid body, which is no other than the fetus that had been displaced to the left by the push of the hand, and now floats back in its liquid covering (amniotic fluid) downward and to the right.

Of all the modes of examination by touch, that done through the rectum gives the earliest satisfactory indications. The hand and arm well oiled are introduced, and the excrement having been removed if necessary, the palm of the hand is turned downward and the floor of the pelvis carefully examined. There will be felt in the median line the pear-shaped outline of the bladder, more or less full, rounded or tense, according to the quantity of urine it contains. Between this and the hand will be felt a soft, somewhat rounded tubular body, which divides in front into two smaller tubes or branches, extending to the right and left into the abdomen. This is the womb, which in its virgin, or unimpregnated, condition is of nearly uniform size from before backward, the main part or body being from 1½ to 2 inches across, and the two anterior branches or horns being individually little over an inch wide. Immediately after conception the body and one of the horns begin to enlarge, the vacant horn remaining disproportionately small, and the enlargement will be most marked at one point, where a solid rounded mass indicates the presence of the growing embryo. In case of twins, both horns are enlarged. At a more advanced stage, when the embryo begins to assume the form of the future animal, the rounded form gives place to a more or less irregular nodular mass, while later still the head, limbs, and body of the fetus may be distinctly made out. The chief source of fallacy is found in the very pendent abdomen of certain cows, into which in advanced gestation the fetus has dropped so low that it can not be felt by the hand in the rectum. The absence of the distinct outline of the vacant womb, however, and the clear indications obtained on external examination through the right flank will serve to prevent any mistake. The fetus may still be felt through the rectum if the abdomen is raised by a sheet passed from side to side beneath it.

Still another sign is the beating of the fetal heart, which may be heard in the latter half of pregnancy when the ear is pressed on the flank in front of the right stifle, or from that downward to the udder. The beats, which are best heard in the absence of rumbling are about 120 per minute, and easily distinguished from any bowel sounds by their perfect regularity.

DURATION OF PREGNANCY.

From extended statistics it is found that the average duration of pregnancy in the cow is two hundred and eighty-five days. A calf born at the two hundred and fortieth day may live, and a case is reported by Dietrichs of a calf born on the three hundred and thirty-fifth day, and another by the American Journal of Medical Science as born on the three hundred and thirty-sixth day. It is the general observation that in the majority of prolonged pregnancies the offspring is male. Lord Spencer found a preponderance of males between the two hundred and ninetieth and the three hundredth days, but strangely enough all born after the three hundredth day under his observation were females. It might be reasonably inferred that while the prevailing tendency is to carry the males overtime, yet that the smaller and comparatively much less developed female sometimes fails to stimulate the womb to contraction until very far beyond the regular date.

HYGIENE OF THE PREGNANT COW.

Among domestic animals considerations of hygiene must be made subservient to profit, and therefore the first consideration is not to secure the most robust health, but such a measure of vigor and stamina as is compatible with the most profitable utilization of the animal. The breeding cow must carry a calf every year, and this notwithstanding that she is at the same time suckling another large growing calf. The dairy cow must breed every year, and at the same time must furnish a generous flow of milk from nine to eleven months yearly. If her health is lowered thereby or her life shortened, the question of profit must still hold sway, and she must yield her place to another when disqualified. There are exceptions, of course, but this rule generally holds.

There are certain points, however, in which the interests of hygiene may be considered. The pregnant cow should have exercise, and as regards both exercise and food, nothing is better than a run on a smooth pasture. She should be withheld from all violent excitement, hunting with dogs, riding or being ridden by cows in heat, driving in herd rapidly through narrow gateways, causing to jump ditches or fences, subjecting to blows with the horns of pugnacious cattle, driving on icy or otherwise slippery ground, carrying in railroad cars, kicking by vicious attendants, and fastening or throwing down for operations. The diet should be good, not of a kind to fatten, but with a generous amount of nitrogenous constituents which will favor at once the yield of milk and the nourishment of the fetus. Aliments rich in lime and phosphates, like wheat bran, middlings, etc., can be used to advantage, as there is a constant drain of earthy salts for the building of the body of the calf, and thereby the danger of undue concentration of the urine is lessened.

Hard, innutritious, and indigestible aliments, musty grain or hay, partially ripened rye grass, millet, Hungarian grass, vetches, peas, or maize are objectionable, as they are liable to cause indigestion or even paralysis; and corn or hay affected by smut or ergot, or that has been spoiled by wet, overripened, and rendered fibrous and innutritious, are equally objectionable. The food should be in the main laxative, as costiveness and straining are liable to cause abortion. Roots and green food that have been frosted are objectionable, as being liable to cause indigestion, though in their fresh condition most wholesome and desirable. Ice-cold water should be avoided, as calculated to check the flow of milk, to derange digestion, and to cause abortion. A good temperature for the drink of the dairy cow is 55° F.

In the case of plethoric and heavy milking cows of mature age and in the prime of life, the hitherto liberal diet must be changed at the last week for the scantiest possible fare, and the bowels must be kept open by laxatives, if need be, if the owner would avoid milk fever. The pregnant cow should be kept away from the sight and odor of dead carcasses, from the smell of decomposing animal matter, and from stagnant and corrupting water. Her stall should not incline downward from shoulder to croup, lest the pressure of the abdominal organs should produce protrusion or abortion. She should be kept aloof from all causes of acute diseases, and all existing diseases should be remedied speedily and with as little excitement of the abdominal organs as possible. Strong purgatives and diuretics are to be especially avoided, unless it be in the very last days of gestation in very plethoric cows.

Finally, in the case of pure breeds, close association with animals of other breeds or crosses, or with animals of other colors, forms, or with defects, is to be carefully guarded against. The effects shown in the progeny may be exceptional, yet they are none the less sources of preventable loss.

PROTRUSION OF THE VAGINA (PROLAPSUS VAGINAE).

This is common during pregnancy from chronic relaxation of the vaginal walls and from lying in stalls that are lower behind than in front. The protrusion is of a rounded form and smooth, and if it embraces both sides of the canal it is double, with a passage between. It may sometimes be remedied by raising the hind part of the stall higher than the front part. This failing, a truss may be applied as for eversion of the womb, and worn until the period of calving approaches.

HERNIA (BREACH) OF THE UTERUS.

This occurs usually in advanced pregnancy from a gradual relaxation and distention of the lower wall of the abdomen in the region of the udder, so that the latter is displaced downward, and in the sac above and in front of it may be felt the form and movements of the fetus. In other cases the womb escapes through a great laceration of the abdominal muscles to one side of the udder, and the hernial mass extends down to one side of that organ. However unsightly, this often allows the animal to complete its pregnancy naturally, and a broad supporting bandage placed around the abdomen is about all that can be recommended. After calving it is best to fatten the cow.

CRAMPS OF THE HIND LIMBS.

The compression by the womb and fetus of the nerves passing through the pelvis sometimes causes cramp and inability to move the limb, but it disappears under friction and motion and is never seen after calving.

DROPSY OF THE HIND LIMBS AND BETWEEN THE THIGHS.

In the latter months of pregnancy the hind legs may swell beneath the hocks, or a soft swelling which pits on pressure with the finger appears from the vulva down between the thighs to the udder and in front. It is mainly due to the pressure of the enlarged womb on the blood vessels, is not dangerous, and disappears after calving.

DROPSY OF THE MEMBRANES OF THE FETUS (DROPSY OF THE WOMB).

The unimpregnated womb may be filled with a dropsical fluid, but the pregnant womb is more liable to become overdistended by an excess of fluid in the inner water bag in which the fetus floats. From an unhealthy state of this membrane or of the blood of the fetus (watery blood) this liquid may go on accumulating until the cow seems almost as broad as she is long. If the trouble has not originated in the ill health of the cow, the result is still to draw on her system, overtax her strength, and derange her digestion, so that the result may prove fatal to both mother and offspring. The natural resort is to draw off a portion of the fluid through a hollow needle passed through the neck of the womb or through its tense wall adjacent. This may be repeated several times, as demanded, to relieve the cow from the injurious distention.

PARALYSIS OF THE HIND PARTS.

In ill-fed, weak, unthrifty cows palsy of the hind limbs and tail may appear in the last weeks of pregnancy. The anus and rectum may participate in the palsy so far as to prevent defecation, and the rectum is more or less completely impacted. Something may be done for these cases by a warm, dry bed, an abundant diet fed warm, frictions with straw wisps or with a liniment of equal parts of oil of turpentine and sweet oil on the loins, croup, and limbs, by the daily use of ginger and gentian. The case becomes increasingly hopeful after calving, though some days may still elapse before the animal can support herself upon her limbs.

EXTRA-UTERINE GESTATION (FETUS DEVELOPING OUTSIDE THE WOMB).

These curious cases are rare and are usually divided into three types: (1) That in which the fetus is formed in or on the ovary (ovarian gestation); (2) that in which it is lodged in the Fallopian tube, or canal between the ovary and womb (tubal gestation); and (3) that in which it is lodged in the abdominal cavity and attached to one or more of its contents from which it draws its nourishment (abdominal gestation).

Symptoms.—The symptoms are those of pregnancy, which may be suddenly complicated by inflammation (peritonitis), owing to rupture of the sac containing the fetus; or at full term signs of calving appear, but no progress is made; an examination with the oiled hand in the vagina or rectum finds the womb empty and its mouth closed.

Treatment.—Little can be done in such cases.

PROLONGED RETENTION OF THE FETUS.

Even when the fetus has developed within the womb it may fail to be delivered at the proper time; labor pains have quickly subsided and the cow resumed her usual health. In such cases the calf dies, and its soft parts are gradually liquefied and absorbed,

A Cow in a Well Nourished Condition Affected with Advanced Tuberculosis of the Throat Lymph Glands. Year Book, 1908. (The Pressure of the Enlarged Glands Has Narrowed the Upper Air Passages so Much that the Least Exertion is Followed by Painful Breathing.)

A Tuberculous Bull Known to Pass Tubercle Bacilli with Ejecta from His Bowels. Year Book, 1908.

hile its bones remain for years in the womb inclosed in the remains of the fetal membranes. These may be expelled at any time
through the natural channels, or they may remain indefinitely
in the womb, not interfering with the general health, but preventing conception.

If the true condition of things is recognized at the time of the
subsidence of the labor pains, the mouth of the womb may be
dilated by the fingers, by the insertion of sponge tents, or by a
mechanical dilator the fetal membranes may be ruptured and the
calf extracted. After the removal of the calf and its membranes
the danger of putrid poisoning may be obviated by injecting an antiseptic solution.

ABORTION (SLINKING THE CALF).

Technically, abortion is the term used for the expulsion of the
off-spring before it can live out of the womb. Its expulsion after
it is capable of an independent existence is premature parturition.
In the cow this may be after seven and one-half months of pregnancy. Dairymen use the term abortion for the expulsion of the
product of conception at any time before the completion of the full
period of a normal pregnancy, and in this sense it will be employed
in this article.

Abortion in cows is either contagious or noncontagious. It
does not follow that the contagium is the sole cause in every case
in which it is present. We know that the organized germs of contagion vary much in potency at different times, and that the animal system also varies in susceptibility to their attack. The germ
may therefore be present in a herd without any manifest injury,
its disease-producing power having for the time abated consider-
bly, or the whole herd being in a condition of comparative insus-
ceptibility. At other times the same germ may have become so
virulent that almost all pregnant cows succumb to its force, or the
herd may have been subjected to other causes of abortion which,
though of themselves powerless to actually cause abortion, may
yet so predispose the animals that even the weaker germ will
operate with destructive effect. In dealing with this disease, therefore, it is the part of wisdom not to rest satisfied with the discovery
and removal of one specific cause, but rather to exert oneself to
find every existent cause and to secure a remedy by correcting all
the harmful conditions.

CAUSES OF NONCONTAGIOUS ABORTION.

As abortion most frequently occurs at those three-week intervals at which the cow would have been in heat if nonpregnant, we
may assume a predisposition at such times due to a periodicity in
the nervous system and functions. Poor condition is often a predisposing cause. This in its turn may result from poor or insufficient food, from the excessive drain upon the udder while bearing
the calf, from chronic wasting diseases, from worms, from dark,
damp, unhealthy buildings, etc. In some such cases the nourishment is so deficient that the fetus dies in the womb and is expelled

in consequence. Excessive loss of blood, attended as it usually is
by shock, becomes a direct cause of abortion.

Acute inflammations of important organs are notorious causes
of abortion, and in most contagious fevers it is a common result.
Affections of the chest which prevent due aeration of the blood
induce contractions of the womb, as shown experimentally by
Brown-Sequard. Pregnant women suffocated in smoke aborted in
many cases. (Retoul).

Chronic diseases of the abdominal organs are fertile sources
of abortion, especially those that cause bloating or diarrhea, or the
diseases of the ovaries, kidneys, or bladder.

Fatty degeneration of the heart, a common disease in old cows
of improved beef breeds, lessens the circulation in the placenta
(and fetus) and, arresting nutrition, may cause abortion.

Indigestions of all kinds are especially dangerous, as they are
usually associated with overdistention of the first stomach (paunch)
with gas. As this stomach lies directly beneath and to the left side
of the womb, any disorder, and above all an excessive distention of
that organ, presses on or affects the womb and its contents dangerously. It further causes contractions of the womb by preventing
aeration of the blood. Hence all that tends to indigestion is to be
carefully guarded against. Privation of water, which hinders
rumination and digestion; ice-cold water, which rouses the womb to
contraction and the calf to vigorous movement; green, succulent
grass, to which the cow has been unaccustomed; clover which has just
been wet with a slight shower; all green food, roots, potatoes, apples
pumpkins that are frozen or have been, or that are simply covered
with hoar frost; food that has been grown in wet seasons or that has
been badly harvested; growing corn, oats, etc., if the animal is unused to them; a too dry food or a too stimulating food (wheat
bran, pease, maize, and cotton seed) fed too lavishly may,
any one of them, induce abortion. The dry and stimulating food
last named bring on constipation with straining, and also elevated
temperature of the body, which, in itself, endangers the life of
the fetus.

Putrid, stagnant water is hurtful both to digestion and the fetus
and abortions in cows have been repeatedly traced to this source and
have ceased when pure water was supplied. Ergoted grasses have
long been known as a cause of widespread abortion in cows. It is
especially common in damp localities and cloudy seasons on meadows
shaded by trees and protected against the free sweep of the winds.
The same is to a large extent true of smut. Hence, wet years have
been often remarkable for the great prevalence of abortions. As
abortion is more prevalent in old dairying districts, the ergot may
not be the sole cause in this instance.

Both ergot and smut vary in potency according to the stage of
growth. Fodders harvested in wet seasons are always more or less
musty, and musty hay and grain have been long recognized as a
prolific cause of digestive, urinary, and cerebral disorders. Impactions and bloatings of the stomachs, excessive secretion of urine

(diuresis), and red-water are common results of such musty fodder, and we have already seen that such disorders of the digestive and urinary organs are very liable to affect the pregnant womb and induce abortion.

The riding of one another by cows is attended by such severe muscular exertion, jars, jolts, mental excitement, and gravitation of the womb and abdominal organs backward that it may easily cause abortion in a predisposed animal.

Keeping in stalls that slope too much behind (over 2 inches) acts in the same way, the compression due to lying and the gravitation backward proving more than a predisposed cow can safely bear.

Deep gutters behind the stalls, into which one or both hind limbs slip unexpectedly, strain the loins and jar the body and womb most injuriously. Slippery stalls in which the flooring boards are laid longitudinally in place of transversely, and on which no cleats or other device is adopted to give a firm foothold, are almost equally dangerous. Driving on icy ground or through a narrow doorway where the abdomen is liable to be jammed are other common causes. Offensive odors undoubtedly cause abortion. To understand this one must take into account the preternaturally acute sense of smell possessed by cattle. By this sense the bull instantly recognizes the pregnant cow and refrains from disturbing her, while man, with all his boasted skill and precise methods, finds it difficult to come to a just conclusion. The emanations from a cow in heat, however, will instantly draw the bull from a long distance. Carrion in the pasture fields or about slaughterhouses near by, the emanations from shallow graves, dead rats or chickens about the barns, and dead calves, the product of prior abortions, are often chargeable with the occurrence of abortions. Aborting cows often fail to expel the afterbirth, and if this remains hanging in a putrid condition it is most injurious to pregnant cows in the near vicinity. So with retained afterbirth in other cows after calving. That some cows kept in filthy stables or near-by slaughterhouses may become inured to the odors and escape the evil results is no disproof of the injurious effects so often seen in such cases.

The excitement, jarring, and jolting of a railroad journey will often cause abortion, especially as the cow nears the period of calving, and the terror or injury of railway or other accidents prove incomparably worse.

All irritant poisons cause abortions by the disorder and inflammation of the digestive organs, and if such agents act also on the kidneys or womb, the effect is materially enhanced. Powerful purgatives or diuretics should never be administered to the pregnant cow.

During pregnancy the contact of the expanding womb with the paunch, just beneath it, and its further intimate connection through nervous sympathy with the whole digestive system, leads to various functional disorders, and especially to a morbid craving for unnatural objects of food. In the cow this is shown in the chewing of bones, pieces of wood, iron bolts, articles of clothing, lumps of hardened paint, etc. An unsatisfied craving of this kind, producing constant excitement of the nervous system, will strongly conduce to abortion.   How much more so if the food is lacking in the mineral matter, and especially the phosphates necessary for the building up of the body of both dam and offspring, to say nothing of that drained off in every milking.   This state of things is present in many old dairy farms, from which the mineral matters of the surface soil have been sold off in the milk or cheese for generations and no return has been made in food or manure purchased.   Here is the craving of an imperative need, and if it is not supplied the health of the cow suffers and the life of the fetus may be sacrificed.

Among other causes of abortion must be named the death or the various illnesses of the fetus.   There is in addition a series of diseases of the mucous membrane of the womb, and of the fetal membranes which interfere with the supply of blood to the fetus or change its quality so that death is the natural result, followed by abortion.

CAUSE OF CONTAGIOUS ABORTION.

While any one of the above conditions may concur with the contagious principle in precipitating an epizootic of abortion, yet it is only by reason ofthe contagium that the disease can be indefinitely perpetuated and transferred from herd to herd.   When an aborting cow is placed in a herd that has hitherto been healthy, and shortly afterwards miscarriage becomes prevalent in that herd and continues year after year, in spite of the fact that all the other conditions of life in that herd remain the same as before, it is manifest that the result is due to contagion.   When a bull, living in a healthy herd, has been allowed to serve an aborting cow, or a cow from an aborting herd, and when the members of his own herd subsequently served by him abort in considerable numbers, contagion may be safely inferred. Mere living in the same pasture or building does not convey the infection.   Cows brought into the aborting herd in advanced pregnancy carry their calves to the full time.   But cows served by the infected bull, or that have had the infection conveyed by the tongue or tail of other animals, or by their own, or that have had the external genitals brought in contact with wall, fence, rubbing post, litter, or floor previously soiled by the infected animals, will be liable to suffer.   Galtier finds that the virus from the aborting cow causes abortions in the sow, ewe, goat, rabbit, and guinea pig, and that if it has been intensified by passing through either of the two last-named animals it will affect also the mare, bitch, and cat.

It does not appear that it is always the same organism which causes contagious abortion.   In France, Nocard found in the aborting membranes and the mucous membrane cocci, or globular bodies, singly or in chains, and a very delicate rod-shaped organism by which the disease was propagated and which survived in the womb through the interval between successive pregnancies.   The Scottish commission found as many as five separate kinds of bacteria.   Bang, in Denmark, found a very delicate rod-shaped organism showing its most active growth at two different depths in nutrient gelatin, and which produced abortion in twenty-one days when inoculated on the susceptible pregnant cow.   In America, Chester, of Delaware, and

Moore, of New York, constantly found organisms differing somewhat in the two States, but evidently of the same group with the colon germ (*Bacillus coli communis*). These were never found in the healthy pregnant womb, but in the cow that had aborted they continued to live in that organ for many months after the loss of the fetus.

We may reasonably conclude that any micro-organism which can live in or on the lining membrane of the womb producing a catarrhal inflammation, and which can be transferred from animal to animal without losing its vitality or potency, is of necessity a cause of contagious abortion. As viewed, therefore, from the particular germ that may be present, we must recognize not one form only of contagious abortion, but several, each due to its own infecting germ, and each differing from others in minor particulars, like duration of incubation, infection of the general system, and the like. In Europe the germs discovered seem to affect the general system much more than do those found in America. Bang's germ caused abortion in twenty-one days; the New York germ, inoculated at service, often fails to cause abortion before the fifth or seventh month.

Symptoms of Abortion.—As occurring during the first two or three months of gestation, symptoms may escape detection, and unless the aborted product is seen the fact of abortion may escape notice. Some soiling of the tail with mucus, blood, and the waters may be observed or the udder may show extra firmness, and in the virgin heifer or dry cow the presence of a few drops of milk may be suggestive, or the fetus and its membranes may be found in the gutter or elsewhere as a mere clot of blood or as a membranous ball in which the forming body of the fetus is found. In water the villi of the outer membrane (chorion) float out, giving it a characteristically shaggy appearance.

In advanced pregnancy abortion is largely the counterpart of parturition, so that a special description is superfluous. The important thing is to distinguish the early symptoms from those of other diseases, so that the tendency may be arrested and the animal carried to full time if possible. A cow is dull, sluggish, separate from the herd, chewing the cud languidly, or there may be frequent lying down and rising, uneasy movements of the hind feet or of the tail, and slightly accelerated pulse and breathing, and dry muzzle. The important thing is not to confound it with digestive or urinary disorder, but in a pregnant cow to examine at once for any increase of mucus in the vagina, or for blood or liquid there or on the root of the tail; for any enlargement, firmness, or tenderness of the udder; or in dry cows examine for milk; and above all for any slight straining suggestive of labor pains.

In many cases the membranes are discharged with the fetus; in others, in advanced pregnancy, they fail to come away, and remain hanging from the vulva, putrefying and falling piecemeal, finally resulting in a fetid discharge from the womb. According to the size of the herd, contagious abortions will follow one another at intervals of one to four or more weeks, in the order of their infection or of the recurrence of the period of activity of the womb which corresponds to the occurrence of heat.

Prevention.—Weakness and bloodlessness are to be obviated by generous feeding, and especially in aliments (wheat bran, rape cake, cotton seed, oats, barley, beans, pease, etc.), rich in earthy salts, which will also serve to correct the morbid appetite. This will also regenerate the exhausted soil if the manure is returned to it. In the same way the application of ground bones or phosphates will correct the evil, acting in this case through the soil first and raising better food for the stock. The ravages of worms are to be obviated by avoiding infested pastures, ponds, streams, shallow wells, or those receiving any surface leakage from land where stock go, and by feeding salt at will, as this agent is destructive to most young worms.

The tendency to urinary calculi in winter is avoided by a succulent diet (ensilage, steamed food, roots, pumpkins, apples, potatoes, slops), and by the avoidance of the special causes named under "Gravel." Furnishing water inside the barn in winter in place of driving once a day to take their fill of ice cold water will obviate a common evil. Putrid and stagnant waters are to be avoided. Sudden changes of food are always reprehensible, but much more so in the pregnant animal. Let the change be gradual. Carefully avoid the use of spoiled or unwholesome food.

In case of prevalence of ergot in a pasture it should be kept eaten down or cut down with a mower so that no portion runs to seed. In case of a meadow the grass must be cut early before the seeds have filled. The most dangerous time appears to be between the formation of the milky seed and the full ripening. Yet the ergot is larger in proportion to the ripeness, so that the loss of potency is made up in quantity. The ripe seed and ergot may be removed by thrashing and the hay safely fed. It may also be noted that both ergot and smut may be safely fed in moderate quantity, provided it is used with succulent food (ensilage, roots, etc.), or with free access to water, and salt is an excellent accessory as encouraging the animal to drink. Both ergot and smut are most injurious in winter, when the water supply is frozen up or accessible only at long intervals. The ergoted seed when thrashed out can not be safely sown, but if first boiled it may be fed in small amount or turned into manure. The growth of both ergot and smut may be to a large extent prevented by the time-honored Scotch practice of sprinkling the seed with a saturated solution of sulphate of copper before sowing.

Fields badly affected with ergot or smut may be practically renewed by plowing up and cultivating for a series of years under crops (turnips, beets, potatoes, buckwheat, etc.) which do not harbor the fungus and which require much cultivation and exposure of the soil. Drainage and the removal of all unnecessary barriers to the free action of sunshine and wind are important provisions.

Other precautions concerning separation from cows in heat—a proper construction of stalls, the avoidance of carrion and other offensive odors, protection from all kinds of mechanical injuries, including overdriving and carrying by rail in advanced pregnancy, the exclusion of all irritants or strong purgatives and diuretics from food or medicine, and the guarding against all causes of indigestion and bloating—have been sufficiently indicated under "Causes." For protection of the womb and fetus against the various causes of disease, available methods are not so evident. For cows that have aborted in the last pregnancy, chlorate of potash, 3 drams daily before the recurrence of the expected abortion, has been held to be useful.

TREATMENT OF NONCONTAGIOUS ABORTION.

Although the first symptoms of abortion have appeared, it does not follow that it will go on to completion. So long as the fetus has not perished, if the waters have not been discharged, nor the water bags presented, attempts should be made to check its progress. Every appreciable and removable cause should be done away with, the cow should be placed in a quiet stall alone, and agents given to check the excitement of the labor pains. Laudanum in doses of 1 ounce for a small cow or 2 ounces for a large one should be promptly administered and repeated in three or four hours, should the labor pains recur. This may be kept up for days or even weeks if necessary, though that is rarely required, as the trouble either subsides or abortion occurs. If the laudanum seems to lack permanency of action, use bromid of potassium, or, better, extract of *Viburnum prunifolium* (40 grains), at intervals of two or three hours until five or six doses have been given.

PREVENTION AND TREATMENT OF CONTAGIOUS ABORTION.

So far as this differs from the treatment of sporadic abortion, it consists in separation and the free use of germicides or disinfectants.

(1) Separate all aborting cows in isolated building, yard, and pasture, allowing no other cows to have access even to their manure, liquid or solid. Not even breeding ewes, goats, sows, rabbits, or mares should be allowed to go from the isolated to the noninfected premises. Separate attendants and utensils are desirable.

(2) Scrape and wash the back part of the stall and gutter and water it with a solution of 5 ounces sulphate of copper (bluestone) in 1 gallon pure water. Repeat this cleaning and watering at least once a week. This should in all cases be applied to every stall where an aborting cow has stood and to those adjacent. To treat the whole in the same way would be even better, as it is impossible to say how many of the cows harbor the germ. This is the more needful as that in one to three years, if the aborting cow is kept on, she becomes insusceptible and carries her calf to full time. A cow may therefore be infecting to others though she herself no longer aborts.

(3) Dissolve 1 dram corrosive sublimate, 1 ounce each of alcohol and glycerin, and shake this up in a gallon of water, to use as an injection into the vagina and a wash for the parts about the vulva and root of the tail. Being very poisonous, it should be kept in a wooden barrel out of the way of animals or children. Every morning the vulva, anus, back of the hips, and root of the tail should be

sponged with this liquid, and this is best applied to the whole herd. A 1 per cent solution of carbolic acid is a good substitute.

(4)   When any case of abortion has occurred the fetal membranes must be removed by the hand without delay, and, together with the fetus, destroyed by burning or boiling, or buried deeply, and the stall should be cleansed and watered freely with the copper solution.   Then the womb should be washed out with 1½ gallons of the corrosive sublimate solution injected through a rubber tube introduced to the depth of the womb and with a funnel in its outer elevated end.   This should be repeated daily for a week.   In the case of the other non-pregnant cows of the herd one injection of the same kind should be made into the vagina, after which they need only have their external parts and tail washed with the solution daily.

(5)   Do not breed aborting cows for two or three months, then use a separate bull, injecting his sheath and washing his belly before and after each service with the carbolic-acid solution.   Exclude all outside cows from service by the regular herd sire.

As a certain number of the cows will harbor the germ in the womb when treatment is started, it is not to be expected that abortions will cease at once, but by keeping up the treatment the trouble may be got rid of in the following year.   As an aborting cow is usually of little use for the dairy, it is best to separate and fatten her and apply treatment to those that remain.   In this, as in other delicate manipulations, the stock owner will consult his own interest by employing an accomplished veterinarian and avoiding such as have not had the privileges of a thorough professional education. In addition to the above, the removal of all manure and contaminated litter and the sprinkling of the surface with the sulphate of copper solution is called for.   Drains should no less be thoroughly rinsed and disinfected.   Milking stools and other implements may be treated in the same way, or with carbolic acid or boiling water.   Great care should be taken to guard against bull or cows from an aborting herd or district; streams even may be suspected if there is an aborting herd near by and higher up on that stream.   Cows sent to bull from an aborting herd are to be positively denied, and workmen that have attended on such a herd should be required to wash and disinfect their clothes and persons.

NOTE.—It is impossible to lay too much stress on the importance of protecting a sound herd against contagious abortion rather than of treating animals already diseased.   This consists principally in purchasing animals from clean herds only, in isolating all new purchases and in not breeding to them until they have been proved free from infection, or in disinfecting the genitals of all newly acquired animals for at least a week.

In cases where it is desired to treat pregnant cows to prevent them from aborting, hypodermic injections of 2 drams of a 2 per cent solution of carbolic acid every two weeks until eight injections have been given, may be tried, but too much success should not be expected from this treatment.   The most suitable place for the injection is on

A Typical Holstein-Friesian Cow.   Ann. Rpt. Soc. Agr. N. S. 1908.

Holstein-Friesian Bull.   Nova Scotia; Many Times a Winner of Championships.
Ann. Rpt. Soc. Agr. N. S. 1908.

the side of the neck. Range cattle may be more readily treated by the use of medicated salt placed in troughs accessible to the animals. This salt is easily prepared by pouring 4 ounces of liquefied crude carbolic acid upon 12 quarts of ordinary barrel salt, after which they are thoroughly mixed.

CALVING (PARTURITION).

SYMPTOMS OF CALVING.

In the cow the premonitions of calving are the enlargement of the udder, which becomes firm and resistant to the touch, with more or less swelling in front, and yields a serous milky fluid; the enlargement and swelling of the vulva, which discharges an abundant stringy mucus; the drooping of the belly, and the falling in of the muscles at each side of the root of the tail, so as to leave deep hollows. When this last symptom is seen calving may be counted on in twenty-four hours or in two or three days. When the act is imminent, the cow becomes uneasy, moves restlessly, leaves off eating, in the field leaves the herd, lies down and rises again as if in pain, shifts upon her hind feet, moves the tail, and may bellow or moan. When labor pains come on the back is arched, the croup drooped, the belly is drawn up, and straining is more or less violent and continuous. Meanwhile blood may have appeared on the vulva and tail, and soon the clear water bags protrude between the lips of the vulva. They increase rapidly, hanging down toward the hocks, and the fore or hind feet can be detected within them. With the rupture of the bags and escape of the waters the womb contracts on the solid angular body of the fetus and is at once stimulated to more violent contractions, so that the work proceeds with redoubled energy to the complete expulsion. This is the reason why it is wrong to rupture the water bags if the presentation is normal, as they furnish a soft, uniform pressure for the preliminary dilation of the mouth of the womb and passages, in anticipation of the severe strain put upon them as the solid body of the calf passes.

The cow often calves standing, in which case the navel string is broken as the calf falls to the ground. If, however, she is recumbent, this cord is torn through as she rises up. The afterpains come on three or four hours later and expel the membranes, which should never be left longer than twenty-four hours.

NATURAL PRESENTATION.

When there is but one calf the natural presentation is that of the fore feet with the front of the hoofs and knees turned upward toward the tail of the dam and the nose lying between the knees. If there are twins the natural position of the second is that of the hind feet, the heels and hocks turned upward toward the cow's tail. In both of these natural positions the curvature of the body of the calf —the back arched upward—is the same with the curvature of the passages, which descend anteriorly into the womb, ascend over the brim of the pelvis, and descend again toward the external opening (vulva). Any presentation differing from the above is abnormal.

OBSTACLES TO PARTURITION.

With a well-formed cow and calf and a natural presentation as above, calving is usually prompt and easy. Obstacles may, however, come from failure of the mouth of the womb to dilate; from twisting of the neck of the womb; from tumors in the vagina; from dropsy in the womb or abdomen; from over distension of the rectum or bladder; from undue narrowing of the passages; from excess of fat in the walls of the pelvis; from the disturbance of a nervous cow by noises; from stone or urine in the bladder; from wrong presentation of the calf, its back being turned downward or to one side in place of upward toward the spine of the dam; from the bending backward into the body of the womb of one or more limbs or of the head; from presentation of the back, shoulder, or croup, all four limbs being turned back; from presentation of all four feet at once; from obstruction caused by an extra head or extra limbs, or double body on the part of the offspring, from dropsy or other disease of the calf; from excessive or imperfect development of the calf; from the impaction of twins at the same time into the passages; or it may be at times from the mere excessive volume of the fetus.

GENERAL MAXIMS FOR THE ASSISTANT CONCERNING DIFFICULT PARTURITION.

Do Not Interfere Too Soon.—After labor pains set in, give a reasonable time for the water bags to protrude and burst spontaneously, and only interfere when delay suggests some mechanical obstruction. If there is no mechanical obstruction, let the calf be expelled slowly by the unaided efforts of the cow. Bruises and lacerations of the passages and flooding from the uncontracted womb may come from the too speedy extraction of the calf. When assistance is necessary, the operator should dress in a thick flannel shirt from which the sleeves have been cut off clear up to the shoulders. This avoids danger of exposure, and yet leaves the whole arm free and untrammeled. Before inserting the hand, it and the arm should be smeared with oil, lard, or vaseline, care being taken that the oil or lard is fresh, neither salted nor rancid, and that it has been purified by boiling or rendered antiseptic by the addition of a teaspoonful of carbolic acid to the pound.

This is a valuable precaution against infecting the cow by introducing putrid ferments into the passages, and against poisoning of the arm by decomposing discharges in case the calving is unduly protracted. When labor pains have lasted some time without any signs of the water bags, the dropping in at the sides of the rump, and the other preparations for calving being accomplished, the hand should be introduced to examine. When the water bags have burst and neither feet nor head appear for some time, examination should be made. When one fore foot only and the head appears, or both fore feet without the head, or the head without the fore feet, examine. If one hind foot appears without the other, make examination. The presenting limb or head should be secured by a rope with a running noose, so that it may not pass back into the womb and get lost during the subsequent manipulations, but may be retained in the vagina or brought up again easily. In searching for a missing member, it is usually better to turn the head of the cow down hill, so that the gravitation of the fetus and abdominal organs forward into the belly of the cow may give more room in which to bring up the missing limb or head. If the cow is lying down turn her on the side opposite to that on which the limb is missing, so that there may be more room for bringing the latter up. Even if a missing limb is reached it is vain to attempt to bring it up during a labor pain. Wait until the pain has ceased, and attempt to straighten out the limb before the next pain comes on. If the pains are violent and continuous, they may be checked by pinching the back or by putting a tight surcingle round the body in front of the udder. These failing, 1 ounce or 1½ ounces of chloral hydrate in a quart of water may be given to check the pains. If the passages have dried up or lost their natural lubricating liquid, smear the interior of the passages and womb, and the surface of the calf so far as it can be reached, with pure fresh lard; or pure sweet oil may be run into the womb through a rubber tube (fountain syringe). In dragging upon the fetus apply strong traction only while the mother is straining, and drag downward toward the hocks as well as backward. The natural curvature of both fetus and passages is thus followed, and the extraction rendered easier.

DISEASES FOLLOWING CALVING.
FLOODING (BLEEDING FROM THE WOMB).

Though not so common in the cow as in the human female, flooding is sufficiently frequent to demand attention. It may depend on a too rapid calving, and a consequent failure of the womb to contract when the calf has been removed. Other causes are laceration of the cotyledons of the womb, and the unnatural adhesion of the membranes to the womb, which bleeds when the two are torn apart. Finally, eversion of the womb (casting the withers) is an occasional cause of flooding. The trouble is only too evident when the blood flows from the external passages in drops or in a fine stream. But when it is retained in the cavity of the womb it may remain unsuspected until it has rendered the animal almost bloodless. The symptoms in such a case are paleness of the eyes, nose, mouth, and of the lips of the vulva, a weak, rapid pulse, violent and perhaps loud beating of the heart (palpitations), sunken, staring eyes, coldness of the skin, ears, horns, and limbs, perspiration, weakness in standing, staggering gait, and finally inability to rise, and death in convulsions. If these symptoms are seen, the oiled hand should be introduced into the womb, which will be found open and flaccid and containing large blood clots.

Treatment.—Treatment consists in the removal of the fetal membranes and blood clots from the womb (which will not contract while they are present), the dashing of cold water on the loins, right flank, and vulva, and if these measures fail the injection of cold water into the womb through a rubber tube furnished with a funnel. In obstinate cases a good-sized sponge soaked in tincture of muriate of iron should be introduced into the womb and firmly squeezed, so as to bring the iron in contact with the bleeding surface. This is at once an astringent and a coagulant for the blood, besides stimulating the womb to contraction. In the absence of this agent astringents (solution of copperas, alum, tannic acid, or acetate of lead) may be thrown into the womb, and one-half dram doses of acetate of lead may be given by the mouth, or 1 ounce powdered ergot of rye may be given in gruel. When nothing else is at hand, an injection of oil of turpentine will sometimes promptly check the bleeding.

EVERSION OF THE WOMB (CASTING THE WITHERS).

Like flooding, this is the result of failure of the womb to contract after calving. If that organ contracts naturally, the afterbirth is expelled, the internal cavity of the womb is nearly closed, and the mouth of the organ becomes so narrow that the hand can not be forced through, much less the whole mass of the matrix. When, however, it fails to contract, the closed end of one of the horns may fall into its open internal cavity, and under the compression of the adjacent intestines, and the straining and contraction of the abdominal walls, it is forced farther and farther, until the whole organ is turned outside in, slides back through the vagina, and hangs from the vulva. The womb can be instantly distinguished from the protruding vagina or bladder by the presence over its whole surface of fifty to one hundred mushroom-like bodies (cotyledons), each 2 to 3 inches in diameter, and attached by a narrow neck. When fully everted, it is further recognizable by a large, undivided body hanging from the vulva, and two horns or divisions which hang down toward the hocks. In the imperfect eversions the body of the womb may be present with two depressions leading into the two horns. In the cases of some standing the organ has become inflamed and gorged with blood until it is as large as a bushel basket, and its surface has a dark-red, blood-like hue, and tears and bleeds on the slightest touch. Still later lacerations, raw sores, and even gangrene are shown in the mass. At the moment of protrusion the general health is not altered, but soon the inflammation and fever with the violent and continued straining induce exhaustion, and the cow lies down, making no attempt to rise.

Treatment.—Treatment will vary somewhat, according to the degree of the eversion. In partial eversion, with the womb protruding only slightly from the vulva and the cow standing, let an assistant pinch the back to prevent straining while the operator pushes his closed fist into the center of the mass and carries it back through the vagina, assisting in returning the surrounding parts by the other hand. In more complete eversion, but with the womb as yet of its natural bulk and consistency, and the cow standing, straining being checked by pinching the back, a sheet is held by two men so as to sustain the everted womb and raise it to the level of the vulva. It is now sponged clean with cold water, the cold being useful in driving out the blood and reducing the bulk, and finally it may be sponged over with laudanum or with a weak solution of carbolic acid (1 dram to 1 quart water).

The closed fist may now be planted in the rounded end of the largest horn and pushed on so as to turn it back within itself and carry it on through the vagina, the other hand being used meanwhile to assist in the inversion and in pushing the different masses in succession within the lips of the vulva. In case of failure, resort should be had at once to a plan which I have successfully followed for many years. Take a long linen or cotton bandage, 5 or 6 inches wide, and wind it around the protruding womb as tightly as it can be drawn, beginning at the free end and gradually covering the entire mass up to the vulva. By this means the greater part of the blood will be forced out of the organ and its bulk greatly reduced, so that its reduction is much facilitated. An additional advantage is found in the protection given to the womb by its investing bandage while it is being pushed forward into the vagina and abdomen. In manipulating the exposed womb there is always danger of laceration, but when the organ is covered with a sheet it is next to impossible to tear it. The subsequent manipulation is as in the other case, by pushing the blind end forward within itself with the closed fist and carrying this on through the vagina into the abdomen with the constant assistance of the other hand. It will often be found convenient to use the edge of the left hand to push the outer part of the protruding mass inside the lips of the vulva, while the right hand and arm are carrying the central portions forward through the vagina. An intelligent assistant, pushing with the palms of both hands on the outer portion of the mass, will also afford material assistance. As the womb is turned within itself the wrapping bandage will gradually loosen, but once the great mass has entered the passages it is easy to compel the rest to follow, and the compression by the bandage is no longer so important. When the womb is fully replaced the bandage is left in its interior in a series of loose folds, and can be easily withdrawn. It is well to move the hand from side to side to insure that the two horns of the womb are fully extended and on about the same level before withdrawing the arm and applying a truss.

When the womb has been long everted and is gorged with blood, inflamed, and friable there is often the additional disadvantage that the animal is unable or unwilling to rise. When lying down the straining can not be controlled so effectually, and the compression of the belly is so great as to prove a serious obstacle to reduction, even in the absence of straining. The straining may be checked by 2 or 3 ounces of laudanum or 2 ounces of chloral hydrate, or by inhalation of chloroform to insensibility, and then by raising the hind parts on straw bundles the gravitation of the abdominal organs forward may be made to lessen the resistance. If success can not be had in this way, the cow may be further turned on her back, and if return is still impossible, the hind limbs may be tied together and drawn up to a beam overhead by the aid of a pulley. In this position, in place of the pressure backward of the bowels proving a hindrance, their gravitation forward proves a most material help to reduction. In seeking to return the womb the sponging with ice-cold water, the raising on a sheet, and the wrapping in a tight bandage should be resorted to. Another method which is especially commendable in these inflamed conditions of the womb is to bring a piece of linen sheet, 30 by 36 inches, under the womb, with its anterior border close up to the vulva, then turn the posterior border upward and forward over the organ, and cross the two ends over this and over each other above. The ends of the sheet are steadily drawn, so as to tighten its hold on the womb, which is thus held on the level of the vulva or above, and cold water is constantly poured upon the mass. The reduction is further sought by compression of the mass with the palms applied outside the sheet. Fifteen or twenty minutes are usually sufficient to cause the return of the womb, provided straining is prevented by pinching of the back or otherwise.

In old and aggravated cases, with the womb torn, bruised, or even gangrenous, the only resort is to amputate the entire mass. This is done by tying a strong waxed cord around the protruding mass close up to the vulva, winding the cord around pieces of wood, so as to draw it as tightly as possible, cutting off the organ below this ligature, tying a thread on any artery that may still bleed, and returning the stump well into the vagina.

Retention of the returned womb is the next point, and this is most easily accomplished by a rope truss. Take two ropes, each about 18 feet long and an inch in thickness. Double each rope at its middle, and lay the one above the other at the bend so as to form an ovoid of about 8 inches in its long diameter. Twist each end of the one rope twice around the other, so that this ovoid will remain when they are drawn tight. Tie a strap or rope around the back part of the neck and a surcingle around the body. Place the rope truss on the animal so that the ovoid ring shall surround the vulva, the two ascending ropes on the right and left of the tail and the two descending ones down inside the thighs on the right and left of the udder. These descending ropes are carried forward on the sides of the body and tied to the surcingle and to the neck collar. The ascending ropes proceed forward on the middle of the back, twisting over each other, and are tied to the surcingle and collar. The upper and lower ropes are drawn so tightly that the rope ring is made to press firmly all around the vulva without risk of displacement. This should be worn for several days, until the womb shall have closed and all risk of further eversion is at an end. Variations of this device are found in the use of a narrow triangle of iron applied around the vulva and fixed by a similar arrangement of ropes, surcingle, and collar, a common crupper similarly held around the vulva, stitches through the vulva, and wires inserted through the skin on the two hips, so that they will cross behind the vulva; also pessaries of various kinds inserted in the vagina. None of these, however, presents any advantage over the simple and comparatively painless rope truss described above. Such additional precautions as keeping the cow in a stall higher behind than in front, and seeing that the diet is slightly laxative and non-stimulating may be named. If straining is persistent, ounce doses of laudanum may be employed twice a day, and the same may be injected into the vagina.

If the womb has been cut off, injections of a solution of a teaspoonful of carbolic acid in a quart of water should be employed daily, or more frequently, until the discharge ceases.

EVERSION OF THE BLADDER.

A genuine eversion of the bladder is almost unknown in the cow, owing to the extreme narrowness of its mouth. The protrusion of the bladder, however, through a laceration in the floor of the vagina sustained in calving, and its subsequent protrusion through the vulva, is sometimes met with. In this case the protruding bladder contains urine, which can never be the case in a real eversion, in which the inner surface of the bladder and the openings of the ureters are both exposed outside the vulva. The presence of a bag containing water, which is connected with the floor of the vagina, will serve to identify this condition. If the position of the bladder in the vulva renders it impracticable to pass a catheter to draw off the urine, pierce the organ with the nozzle of a hypodermic syringe, or even a very small trocar and canula, and draw off the water, when it will be found an easy matter to return the bladder to its place. The rent in the vagina can be stitched up, but as there would be risk in any subsequent calving it is best to prepare the cow for the butcher.

RUPTURE OF THE BLADDER.

This has been known to occur in protracted parturition when the fetus finally passed while the bladder was full. The symptoms are those of complete suppression of urine and tenderness of the abdomen, with a steady accumulation of liquid and fluctuation on handling its lower part. If the hand is introduced into the vagina it is felt to be hot and tender, and perhaps slightly swollen along its floor. As a final test, if the lower fluctuating part of the abdomen is punctured with a hypodermic needle, a straw-colored liquid of an urinous odor flows out. The condition has been considered as past hope. The only chance for recovery would be in opening the abdomen, evacuating the liquid, and stitching up the rent in the bladder, but at such a season and with inflammation already started there would be little to hope for.

RUPTURE OF THE WOMB.

When the womb has been rendered friable by disease this may occur in the course of the labor, but much more frequently it occurs from violence sustained in attempting assistance in difficult parturition. It is also liable to occur during eversion of the organ through efforts to replace it.

If it happens while the calf is still in the womb, it will usually bleed freely and continuously until the fetus has been extracted, so that the womb can contract on itself and expel its excess of blood. Another danger is that in case of a large rent the calf may escape into the cavity of the abdomen and parturition become impossible. Still another danger is that of the introduction of septic germs and the setting up of a fatal inflammation of the lining membrane of the belly (peritoneum). Still another is the escape of the small intestine through the rent and on through the vagina and vulva, so as to protrude externally and receive perhaps fatal injuries. In case of rupture before calving, that act should be completed as rapidly and carefully as possible, the fetal membranes removed and the contracttion of the womb sought by dashing cold water on the loins, the right flank, or the vulva. If the calf has escaped into the abdomen and can not be brought through the natural channels it may be permissible to fix the animal and extract it through the side, as in the Cæsarian section. If the laceration has happened during eversion of the womb it is usually less redoubtable, because the womb contracts more readily under the stimulus of the cold air so recently applied. In case the abdomen has been laid open it is well to stitch up the rent, but if not it should be left to nature, and will often heal satisfactorily, the cow even breeding successfully in after years.

LACERATIONS AND RUPTURES OF THE VAGINA.

Rupture of the floor of the vagina has been already referred to as allowing the protrusion of the bladder. Laceration of the roof of this passage is also met with as the result of deviations of the hind limbs and feet upward when the calf lies on its back. In some such cases the opening passes clear into the rectum, or the foot may even pass out through the anus, so that that opening and the vulva are laid open into one.

Simple superficial lacerations of the vaginal walls are not usually serious, and heal readily unless septic inflammation sets in, in which case the cow is likely to perish. They may be treated with soothing and antiseptic injections, such as carbolic acid, 1 dram; water, 1 quart.

The more serious injuries depend on the complications. Rupture of the anterior part of the canal, close to the mouth of the womb, may lead to the introduction of infecting germs into the cavity of the abdomen, or protrusion of the bowel through the rent and externally, either of which is likely to prove fatal. If both these conditions are escaped the womb may heal spontaneously. Rupture into the bladder may lead to nothing worse than a constant dribbling of urine from the vulva. The cow should be fattened if she survives. Rupture into the rectum will entail a constant escape of feces through the vulva, and, of course, the same condition exists when the anus as well has been torn open. I have successfully sewed up an opening of this kind in the mare, but in the cow it is probably better to prepare for the butcher.

CLOTS OF BLOOD IN THE WALLS OF THE VAGINA.

During calving the vagina may be bruised so as to cause escape of blood beneath the mucous membrane and its coagulation into large bulging clots. The vulva may appear swollen, and on separating its lips the mucous membrane of the vagina is seen to be raised into irregular rounded swellings of a dark-blue or black color, and which pit on pressure of the finger. If the accumulation of blood is not extensive it may be reabsorbed, but if abundant it may lead to irritation and dangerous inflammation, and should be incised with a lancet and the clots cleared out. The wounds may then be sponged twice a day with a lotion made with 1 dram sulphate of zinc, 1 dram carbolic acid, and 1 quart water.

RETAINED AFTERBIRTH.

The cow, of all our domestic animals, is especially subject to this accident. This may be partly accounted for by the firm connections established through the fifty to one hundred cotyledons in which the fetal membranes dovetail with the follicles of the womb. It is also most liable to occur after abortion, in which preparation has not been made by fatty degeneration for the severance of these close connections. In the occurrence of inflammation, causing the formation of new tissue between the membranes and the womb, we find the occasion of unnaturally firm adhesions which prevent the spontaneous detachment of the membranes. Again, in low conditions of health and an imperfect power of contraction we find a potent cause of retention, the general debility showing particularly in the indisposition of the womb to contract, after calving, with sufficient energy to expel the afterbirth. Hence we find the condition common with insufficient or innutritious food, and in years or localities in which the fodder has suffered from weather. Ergoted, smutty, or musty fodder, by causing abortion, is a frequent cause of retention. Old cows are more subject than young ones, probably because of diminishing vigor. A temporary retention is sometimes due to a too rapid closure of the neck of the womb after calving, causing strangulation and imprisonment of the membranes. Conditions favoring this are the drinking of cold (iced) water, the eating of cold food (frosted roots), and (through sympathy between udder and womb) a too prompt sucking by the calf or milking by the attendant.

Symptoms.—The symptoms of retention of the afterbirth are usually only too evident, as the membranes hang from the vulva and rot away gradually, causing the most offensive odor throughout the building. When retained within the womb by the closure of its mouth and similarly in cases in which the protruded part has rotted off, the decomposition continues and the fetid products escaping by the vulva appear in offensively smelling pools on the floor, and mat together tho hairs near the root of the tail. The septic materials retained in the womb cause inflammation of its lining membrane, and this, together with the absorption into the blood of the products of putrefaction, leads to ill health, emaciation, and drying up of the milk.

Treatment.—Treatment will vary according to the conditions. When the cow is in low condition or when retention is connected with drinking iced water or eating frozen food, hot drinks and hot mashes of wheat bran or other aliment may be all sufficient. If, along with the above conditions, the bowels are somewhat confined, an ounce of ground ginger, or half an ounce of black pepper, given with a quart of sweet oil, or 1½ pounds of Glauber's salts, the latter in at least 4 quarts of warm water, will often prove effectual. A bottle or two of flaxseed tea, made by prolonged boiling, should also be given at frequent intervals. Other stimulants, like rue, savin, laurel, and carminitives like anise, cumin, and coriander are preferred by some, but with very questionable reason, the more so that the first three are not without danger. Ergot of rye, 1 ounce, or extract of the same, 1 dram, may be resorted to to induce contraction of the womb. The mechanical extraction of the membranes is, however, often called for; of this there are several methods. The simplest is to hang a weight of 1 or 2 pounds to the hanging portion, and allow this, by its constant dragging and by its jerking effect when the cow moves, to pull the membranes from their attachments and to stimulate the womb to expulsive contractions. But in the neglected cases, when the dependant mass is already badly decomposed, it is liable to tear across under the added weight, leaving a portion of the offensive material imprisoned in the womb. Again, this uncontrolled dragging upon a relaxed womb will (in exceptional cases only, it is true) cause it to become everted and to protrude in this condition from the vulva.

A second resort is to seize the dependant part of the afterbirth between two sticks, and roll it up on these until they lie against the vulva; then, by careful traction, accompanied by slight jerking movements from side to side, the womb is stimulated to expulsive contractions and the afterbirth is wound up more and more on the sticks until finally its last connections with the womb are severed and the remainder is expelled suddenly en masse. It is quite evident that neglected cases with putrid membranes are poor subjects for this method, as the afterbirth is liable to tear across, leaving a mass in the womb. During the progress of the work any indication of tearing is the signal to stop and proceed with greater caution or altogether abandon the attempt in this way.

The third method (that with the skilled hand) is the most promptly and certainly successful. For this the operator had best strip and dress as for a parturition case. Again, the operation should be undertaken within twenty-four hours after calving, since later the mouth of the womb may be so closed that it becomes difficult to introduce the hand. The operator should smear his arms with carbolized lard or vaseline to protect them against infection, and particularly in delayed cases with putrid membranes. An assistant holds the tail to one side while the operator seizes the hanging afterbirth with the left hand, while he introduces the right along the right side of the vagina and womb, letting the membranes slide through his palm until he reaches the first cotyledon to which they remain adherent. In case no such connection is within reach, gentle traction is made on the membranes with the left hand until the deeper parts of the womb are brought within reach and the attachments to the cotyledons can be reached. Then the soft projection of the membrane, which is attached to the firm fungus-shaped cotyledon on the inner surface of the womb, is seized by the little finger, and the other fingers and thumb are closed on it so as to tear it out from its connections. To explain this it is only necessary to say that the projection from the membrane is covered by soft conical processes, which are received into cavities of a corresponding size on the summit of the firm mushroom-shaped cotyledon growing from the inner surface of the womb. To draw upon the former, therefore, is to extract its soft villous processes from within the follicles or cavities of the other. If it is at times difficult to start this extraction it may be necessary to get the finger nail inserted between the two, and once started the finger may be pushed on, lifting all the villi in turn out of their cavities. This process of separating the cotyledons must be carefully conducted, one after another, until the last has been detached and the afterbirth comes freely out of the passages. I have never found any evil result from the removal of the whole mass at one operation, but Shaack mentions the eversion of the womb as the possible result of the necessary traction, and in cases in which those in the most distant part of the horn of the womb can not be easily reached, he advises to attach a cord to the membranes inside the vulva, letting it hang out behind, and to cut off the membranes below the cord. Then, after two or three days' delay, he extracts the remainder, now softened and easily detached. If carefully conducted, so as not to tear the cotyledons of the womb, the operation is eminently successful; the cow suffers little, and the straining roused by the manipulations soon subsides. Keeping in a quiet, dark place, or driving a short distance at a walking pace, will serve to quiet these. When the membranes have been withdrawn, the hand, half closed, may be used to draw out of the womb the offensive liquid that has collected. If the case is a neglected one, and the discharge is very offensive, the womb must be injected as for leucorrhea.

INFLAMMATION OF THE VAGINA (VAGINITIS).

This may occur independently of inflammation of the womb, and usually as the result of bruises, lacerations, or other injuries sustained during calving. It will be shown by swelling of the lips of the vulva, which, together with their lining membrane, become of a dark-red or leaden hue, and the mucous discharge increases and becomes whitish or purulent, and it may be fetid. Slight cases recover spontaneously, or under warm fomentations or mild astringent injections (a teaspoonful of carbolic acid in a quart of water), but severe cases may go on to the formation of large sores (ulcers), or considerable portions of the mucous membrane may die and slough off. Baumeister records two cases of diphtheritic vaginitis, the second case in a cow four weeks calved, contracted from the first in a newly calved cow. Both proved fatal, with formation of false membranes as far as the interior of the womb. In all severe cases the antiseptic injections must be applied most assiduously. The carbolic acid may be increased to one-half ounce to a quart, or chlorine water, or peroxide of hydrogen solution may be injected at least three times a day. Hyposulphite of soda, 1 ounce to a quart of water, is an excellent application, and the same amount may be given by the mouth.

LEUCORRHEA (MUCOPURULENT DISCHARGE FROM THE PASSAGES).

This is due to a continued or chronic inflammation of the womb, or the vagina, or both. It usually results from injuries sustained in calving, or from irritation by putrid matters in connection with retained afterbirth, or from the use of some object in the vagina (pessary) to prevent eversion of the womb. Exposure to cold or other cause of disturbance of the health may affect an organ so susceptible as this at the time of parturition so as to cause inflammation.

Symptoms.—The main symptom is the glairy white discharge flowing constantly or intermittently (when the cow lies down), soiling the tail and matting its hairs and those of the vulva. When the lips of the vulva are drawn apart the mucous membrane is seen to be red, with minute elevations, or pale and smooth. The health may not suffer at first, but if the discharge continues and is putrid the health fails, the milk shrinks, and flesh is lost. If the womb is involved the hand introduced into the vagina may detect the mouth of the womb slightly open and the liquid collected within its cavity. Examination with the oiled hand in the rectum may detect the outline of the womb beneath, somewhat enlarged, and fluctuating under the touch from contained fluid. In some cases heat is more frequent or intense than natural, but the animal rarely conceives when served, and, if she does, is likely to abort.

Treatment.—Treatment with the injections advised for vaginitis is successful in mild or recent cases. In obstinate ones stronger solutions may be used after the womb has been washed out by a stream of tepid water until it comes clear. A rubber tube is inserted into the womb, a funnel placed in its raised end, and the water, and afterwards the solution, poured slowly through this. If the neck of the womb is so close that the liquid can not escape, a second tube may be inserted to drain it off. As injections may be used chlorid of zinc, one-half dram to the quart of water, or sulphate of iron, 1 dram to the quart. Three drams of sulphate of iron and one-half ounce ground ginger may also be given in the food daily.

INFLAMMATION OF THE WOMB (METRITIS, INFLAMMATION OF WOMB AND ABDOMEN, OR METROPERITONITIS).

Inflammation of the womb may be slight or violent, simple or associated with putrefaction of its liquid contents and general poisoning, or it may extend so that the inflammation affects the lining membrane of the whole abdominal cavity. In the last two cases the malady is a very grave one.

Causes.—The causes are largely the same as those causing inflammation of the vagina. Greater importance must, however, be attached to exposure to cold and wet and septic infection.

Symptoms.—The symptoms appear two or three days after calving, when the cow may be seen to shiver, or the hair stands erect, especially along the spine, and the horns, ears, and limbs are cold. The temperature in the rectum is elevated by one or two degrees, the pulse is small, hard, and rapid (70 to 100), appetite is lost, rumination ceases, and the milk shrinks in quantity or is entirely arrested, and the breathing is hurried. The hind limbs may shift uneasily, the tail be twisted, the head and eyes turn to the right flank, and the teeth are ground. With the flush of heat to the horns and other extremities, there is redness of the eyes, nose, and mouth, and usually a dark redness about the vulva. Pressure on the right flank gives manifest pain, causing moaning or grunting, and the hind limbs are moved stiffly, extremely so if the general lining of the abdomen is involved. In severe cases the cow lies down and can not be made to rise. There is usually marked thirst, the bowels are costive, and dung is passed with pain and effort. The hand inserted into the vagina perceives the increased heat, and when the neck of the womb is touched the cow winces with pain. Examination through the rectum detects enlargement and tenderness of the womb. The discharge from the vulva is at first watery, but becomes thick, yellow, and finally red or brown, with a heavy or fetid color. Some cases recover speedily and may be almost well in a couple of days; a large proportion perish within two days of the attack, and some merge into the chronic form, terminating in leucorrhea. In the worst cases there is local septic infection and ulceration, or even gangrene of the parts, or there is general septicemia, or the inflammation involving the veins of the womb causes coagulation of the blood contained in them, and the washing out of the clots to the right heart and lungs leads to blocking of the vessels in the latter and complicating pneumonia. Inflammations of the womb and passages after calving are always liable to these complications, and consequently to a fatal issue. Franck records three instances of rapidly fatal metritis in cows, all of which had been poisoned from an adjacent cow with retained and putrid afterbirth. Others have had similar cases.

Treatment.—Treatment in the slight cases of simple inflammation does not differ much from that adopted for vaginitis, only care must be taken that the astringent and antiseptic injections are made to penetrate into the womb. After having washed out the womb a solution of chloride of lime or permanganate of potash (one-half ounce to 1 quart of water), with an ounce each of glycerin and laudanum to render it more soothing, will often answer every purpose. It is usually desirable to open the bowels with 1½ pounds Glauber's salts and 1 ounce ginger in 4 quarts of warm water and to apply fomentations of warm water or even mustard poultices or turpentine to the right flank.

In the violent attacks with high temperature and much prostration, besides the salts agents must be given to lower the temperature and counteract the septic poisoning. Salicylate of soda one-half ounce, or quinia 2 drams, repeated every four hours, will help in both ways, or ounce doses of hyposulphite of soda or dram doses of carbolic acid may be given at equal intervals until six doses have been taken. Tincture of aconite has often been used in 20-drop doses every six hours. If the temperature rises to 106° or 107° F., it must be met by the direct application of cold or iced water to the surface. The animal may be covered with wet sheets and cold water poured on these at intervals until the temperature in the rectum is lowered to 102° F. In summer the cow may be allowed to dry spontaneously, while in winter it should be rubbed dry and blanketed. Even in the absence of high temperature much good may be obtained from the soothing influence of a wet sheet covering the loins and flanks and well covered at all points by a dry one. This may be followed next day by a free application of mustard and oil of turpentine. When the animal shows extreme prostration alcohol (1 pint) or carbonate of ammonia (1 ounce) may be given to tide over the danger, but such cases usually perish.

In this disease, even more than in difficult and protracted parturition or retained placenta, the attendants must carefully guard against the infection of their hands and arms from the diseased parts. The hand and arm before entering the passage should always be well smeared with lard impregnated with carbolic acid.

MILK FEVER (PARTURITION FEVER, PARTURIENT APOPLEXY, OR PARTURIENT COLLAPSE).

The common name for this malady—milk fever—is an erroneous and misleading one, as in reality fever is usually absent; instead, there is generally an actual reduction in body temperature. A far better and more distinctive term and one that describes the actual condition much more precisely is parturient paresis. The disease has also several other names in various parts of the country, such as calving fever, parturition fever, parturient apoplexy, parturient collapse, puerperal fever, vitulary fever, and dropping after calving.

Description of Disease.—Milk fever is a disease of well-nourished, plethoric, heavy-milking cows; it occurs during the most active period of life (fourth to sixth calf), and is characterized by its sudden onset, and the complete paralysis of the animal with loss of sensation, and by following closely the act of calving, or parturition, terminating in a short time in recovery or death. One attack predisposes the animal to a recurrence of the trouble. While this disease may occur at any time during the whole year, it is seen principally during the warm summer season. The affection is almost entirely confined to the cow, although a few cases have been reported in the sow and goat. Sheep are entirely free from the disease.

Predisposition and Cause.—There are few diseases among our domesticated animals regarding the exact cause of which more widely different theories have been advanced than that of milk fever. The causes may properly be divided into two kinds—predisposing and direct. Experience shows one of the most prominent predisposing causes to be the great activity of the milk-secreting structure, namely, the udder. This organ is most active after the fourth, fifth, and sixth parturition, and this is the time of life when the vast majority of cases occur. The disease is almost unknown in heifers with the first calf and decreases in frequency steadily after the most active milking period is past. It is rarely, if ever, met with in pure beef breeds, such as the Shorthorn, Angus, and Hereford, while its main inroads are made into the heavy-milking breeds, such as the Holstein, Jersey, and Guernsey. Another factor that is probably of equal importance with the activity of the udder in producing the disease is the existence of a plethoric condition of the system, the result of excessive feeding and lack of exercise before calving. In heavy-milking cows all the food eaten in excess of that required to make up for the normal waste of the system is turned into milk and not used for the laying on of flesh or fat. Fleshiness is therefore an unnatural condition in these animals, and the period during which they are "dry" is usually very short; indeed, many of these cows continue to secrete milk right up to the time of calving. In those cases where the animals go dry the excess of nutriment in the food has no avenue of escape and immediately becomes stored up in the glands and in the blood, throwing the system into a high state of plethora. Now, at the time of calving all the blood which has been supplying the fetus is suddenly thrown back on the circulation, and if the udder does not begin active secretion very promptly plethora becomes extreme. The blood plasma under these conditions is very rich and dense, containing a large percentage of albumen and glycogen, and causing a shrinkage in size of the blood cells. This condition is invariably seen when the blood of milk-fever patients is examined under the microscope.

Fatness of the animal has been ascribed an important place among the causes of milk fever. This, however, in itself is probably not a predisposing cause. The beef breeds (Angus and Shorthorn) are usually in far better condition at the time of calving than the milking breeds (Jersey and Holstein), and yet milk fever is a rarity in the former. At the same time it must be understood that a fat Jersey is more predisposed than one poor in flesh. In the fat Jersey the system is already loaded with an excess of nutriment, and, at the time of calving, extreme plethora is more readily produced than in the thin animal where the excess of nutritive elements could be more readily used and stored in the depleted muscular and glandular structures of the body. Fatness is therefore only of importance in the production of the disease in so far as it tends to increase glandular activity, particularly of the udder, and because of the higher state of plethora of the fat animal.

Symptoms.—This disease in its typical and most common form is comparatively easy to diagnose and one which almost every dairyman knows immediately before the arrival of the veterinarian. It usually comes on within two days after the birth of the calf and is practically never seen after the second week. In isolated instances it has been observed a few days before calving. At the commencement of the attack there is usually excitement; the cow is restless, treads with the hind feet, switches the tail, stares anxiously around the stall or walks about uneasily. She may bellow occasionally, show slight colicky symptoms, and make ineffectual attempts at relieving the bowels. These symptoms are rarely recognized by the owner, but they are followed within a few hours by beginning paralysis, indicated by a staggering gait, especially in the hind legs, and by weakening of the knees and fetlocks in front. The patient now becomes quieter, the gait more staggering and weak, and finally the animal goes down and is unable to rise. The paralysis by this time is general, the calf is unnoticed, and the cow lies perfectly quiet with the eyes partly closed and staring and showing a complete absence of winking when the eyeball is touched. She is absolutely unheedful of her surroundings and flies may alight with impunity on all parts of the body without causing the slightest movement to dislodge them. While down the patient assumes a very characteristic position, which is of great aid in diagnosis. The head is turned around to the side (usually the left) and rests on the chest, causing a peculiar arching of the neck. If the head is drawn out straight, it immediately flops around to the side again when the force is removed. The body usually rests slightly to one side, with the hind legs extended forward and outward and the fore legs doubled up in their normal position. There is paralysis of the muscles of the throat, so that swallowing is impossible, and in case drenching is attempted there is great danger of the fluids going into the lungs and setting up traumatic pneumonia. Paralysis of the rectum and bladder is also complete and the movement of the intestines is so suppressed that purgatives are frequently powerless to reestablish it. Fermentation in the paunch with consequent bloating is sometimes seen, particularly when the patient is allowed to be stretched out on her side. The secretion of milk is diminished and may be suspended entirely. Sugar is voided in the urine, depending in quantity on the severity of the attack. The pulse is weak and at times hardly perceptible to the finger, averaging from 50 to 70 beats per minute. Later in the disease, however, and especially in those cases with unfavorable terminations, it may reach 100 per minute. There is seldom noticed a rise of temperature. Sometimes at the commencement of the attack the temperature may reach 103° F., but there is a steady decrease to as low as 95° F. as the disease progresses. The temperature rapidly rises again as improvement is manifested. Convalescence occurs rapidly, and on the day following the onset of the disease, and in some cases even within a few hours, the animal may be up eating and drinking in a normal manner. Sometimes, however, a slight paralysis of the hind quarters persists, and may remain for a week or even longer, indicating that some structural change must have occurred in the nerve centers. In fatal cases the animal may remain perfectly quiet and die in a comatose condition from complete paralysis of the nervous system, but more frequently there is some agitation and excitement prior to death with tossing about of the head. Death, like recovery, usually occurs in from eighteen to seventy-two hours after the onset of the malady.

Treatment.—In the administration of medicine by the mouth, and especially drenches, great care should be taken to prevent the fluids from getting into the larynx and from there into the lungs where they will set up traumatic pneumonia, which is almost invariably fatal. In case the throat is not paralyzed the drench may prove of value and should be given slowly and immediately stopped at the first sign of uneasiness or coughing on the part of the animal. While the patient lies on the side she must raise the weight of her body at each inspiration, which is very exhausting, and hypostatic congestion of the dependent lung is greatly favored. Consequently it is of importance that the cow should be kept propped up on the breastbone by means of bags of chaff or straw placed against her side. In the way of medicinal treatment purgatives may be given in the first stage of the disease when the animal can swallow, with the precautions above mentioned. One pound of Epsom salts and 2 ounces of creolin dissolved in a pint of water will prove beneficial. The creolin is added for its antiseptic action to prevent fermentation in the paunch with the consequent danger of the eructation of foods and

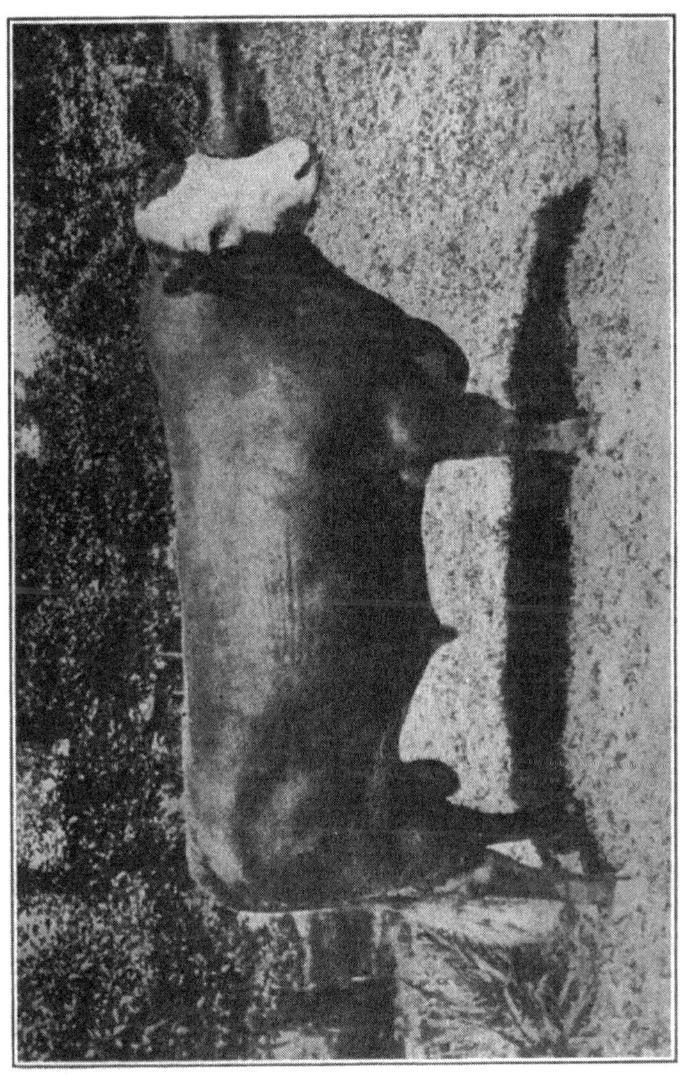

Polled Hereford Bull. Dept. of Agr.

their subsequent passage into the windpipe. Ammonium carbonate in 2-dram doses dissolved in 2 ounces of water will be found to act equally as well as the creolin in this respect. Epsom salts is rather slow in its action, and an injection under the skin with a hypodermic syringe of 1½ to 2 grains of eserine sulphate, when obtainable, will be found quicker and more efficacious. The rectum should be emptied and injections of 1 to 2 gallons of warm water given to stimulate intestinal movements. However, the normal movement of the bowels, once lost, is exceedingly hard to reestablish, and sometimes all efforts in that direction fail. The urine should be drawn with a catheter or by pressure on the bladder with the hand in the rectum, as the bladder is paralyzed and unable to empty itself.

The feeble pulse and subnormal temperature call for the administration of stimulants. Injections under the skin of 1 dram of the following solution every three hours are probably the most efficacious: 80 grains of caffein, 60 grains of sodium salicylate, and 4 drams of water. Similar injections of 1 grain of strychnia sulphate three times daily will also be found very beneficial, although numerous other drugs may be recommended, as spirits of camphor, veratrin, tincture of digitalis, alcohol, etc. In case the animal is very excitable the head should be restrained in such a manner as to prevent injury, and, in case the violence becomes excessive, 1½ ounces of chloral dissolved in a quart of water may be injected into the rectum, or 5 grains of morphine sulphate under the skin.

The Air Treatment.—Of all known methods of treating milk fever, the injection of sterile atmospheric air into the udder is by far the most simple and practicable as well as the most efficacious and harmless one at our disposal, and only occasionally requires that medicinal treatment be given.

The method of injecting filtered air into the udder is easy of manipulation, requires but little time, and is readily accomplished by means of a milk-fever apparatus. It consists of a metal cylinder with milled screw-caps on either end. Cap may be removed in order to place sterile absorbent cotton within the chamber. To this cap the rubber bellows are connected by 9 inches or rubber tubing. Cap is to be removed together with the attached 18 inches of rubber hose, at the free end of which is the self-retaining milking tube, for the purpose of disinfection before treating each case. The pulling on or off of the tubing on the nozzles of the milled caps is thus rendered unnecessary. Within the metal cylinder is a wire net, which prevents the obstruction of the outlet of the chamber by holding back the sterile cotton, and also permits of the unscrewing of the lower cap and the disinfection of this portion of the apparatus, including the milking tube, without contaminating the packing. Absorbent cotton impregnated with carbolic acid (carbolized cotton) or other suitable disinfectant can be purchased from the drug trade in most localities, and is better, though slightly more expensive, than the plain cotton.

Previous to making the air injection, the hands of the operator should be thoroughly cleansed and the udder should receive the same careful antiseptic treatment as has been recommended in discussing the injection of potassium iodide. Soap and water should be applied to the teats and udder, after which they should be carefully disinfected with a 5 per cent solution of carbolic acid (3 tablespoonfuls of pure carbolic acid to 1 quart of water). A clean towel should then be placed under the udder to prevent the teats from coming in contact with dirt or filth of any kind. The milking tube, before it is placed in the teat, should have been perfectly sterilized by boiling for fifteen minutes, with the lower hose and cap of the cylinder attached, and the apparatus should be wrapped in a clean towel, without touching the milking tube, to prevent contamination before use. If the apparatus has been subjected to this treatment shortly before and it is desired to disinfect only the milking tube, the latter may be placed in a 5 per cent solution of carbolic acid for five minutes. It is then carefully inserted into the milk duct of the teat without emptying the udder of milk. Air is now pumped from the bulb into the reservoir, consequently a continuous flow of air is forced through the filtering chamber and into the udder. Slight massage or kneading of the udder will cause the innermost recesses of the milk tubules to become distended with the injected air. After one-quarter of the udder is well distended the milking tube is removed, care being taken to prevent the outflow of air by having an assistant tie a broad piece of tape about the teat at the time the milking tube is withdrawn. The same treatment is repeated with the other three teats until the udder is satisfactorily distended. In case the air becomes absorbed and no improvement is noted within five hours, a repetition of this treatment should be made under the same antiseptic precautions as at first. The tape should be removed from the teats two or three hours after the cow gets on her feet, the constricting muscles at the tip of the teats being now depended on for retaining the air. In this manner the air may be left in the udder for twenty-four hours, and when recovery is assured, it should be gradually milked out. It is needless to say that the calf should not be permitted to suck during this period.

Inflammation of the udder (caked bag) is avoided if the milking tube is thoroughly disinfected before each application, and if the cow's teats and bag and the hands of the operator have been properly cleansed. If the apparatus is kept in its case free from dust and dirt, the absorbent or medicated cotton in the metal cylinder will efficiently filter enough air to distend the udders of six cows. After this number has been treated it is advisable to replace the old cotton with a fresh sterile supply, which should be placed loosely in the cylinder.

While this method of treating milk fever is a comparatively easy one for a farmer or dairyman to adopt, he can not expect to have the same successful results as those obtained by a skilled veterinarian, and it is therefore advisable that the services of such a veterinarian should always be obtained in those districts where it is possible. In many cases it will be found that the injection of air into the udder will be sufficient to combat the disease without any other treatment, but it is always advisable to study the symptoms of each individual case and administer in a rational manner the indicated medicines.

Prevention.—Until recently most stringent measures were resorted to by every careful dairyman to prevent the development of the disease in his herd. However, since the treatment of the present day has so greatly reduced, and even in some cases obliterated, the mortality, prevention is no longer such an important problem and therefore preventive measures which have a severe and lasting effect upon the animals should be abandoned from an economic standpoint. It has long been advocated to starve all suspected animals for two weeks prior to the birth of the calf. It is frequently noted that this has an injurious effect on the milk flow of the animal, from which it may require several weeks for her to recover and gain her normal output of milk. This measure is no longer considered advisable, as it is better to have cows attacked with the disease once in a while (the mortality being less than 5 per cent) than to decrease the flow from every heavy-milking cow for one to three weeks after she comes fresh by starving her before calving.

A method which is not quite so sure of reducing the plethoric condition of the cow, but which nevertheless proves very efficient and is without the slightest permanent injurious effect, is the administration of 1 to 1½ pounds of Epsom salts two or three days prior to calving. In case this has been neglected and a well-nourished, heavy-milking cow has passed through an easy nonexhausting calf birth, the administration of the salts after the labor is over should by no means be neglected. Bloodletting has also been advocated, but there is always the danger of exciting the blood-making organs to excessive activity, thus largely neutralizing the effect. It should therefore be resorted to only when the cow is extremely fat, is a heavy milker, and has had one or more previous attacks. The blood should be drawn from the jugular vein until the pulse softens perceptibly, 1½ pints for every 100 pounds of the animal's body weight being about the right amount.

Another very good preventive measure, and one easily carried out, though frequently overlooked, is to give the cow plenty of exercise up to the time of calving. Many animals are allowed to run continuously on pastures from the time they go dry until a week or two before calving, when they are transferred to the stable without any subsequent exercise. This is very conducive to the enriching of the blood and the development of the disease.

The most recent preventive treatment suggested is in line with the favorable results obtained by the injection of air into the udder. It consists in allowing the susceptible cow to retain in the udder for 24 hours after calving all the milk except the small quantity required by the calf, which should be taken if possible from each quarter.

PALSY AFTER CALVING (DROPPING AFTER CALVING).

This consists in a more or less complete loss of control of the hind limbs occurring after calving, and due either to low condition, weakness, and exposure to cold or to injurious compression of the nerves of the hind limbs by a large calf passing through the pelvis. Its symptoms do not differ from those of palsy of the hind limbs, occurring at other times, and it may be treated in the same way, excepting so far as bruises of the vagina may demand special soothing treatment.

CONGESTION OF THE UDDER (GARGET).

In heavy milkers, before and just after calving, it is the rule that the mammary gland is enlarged, hot, tense and tender, and that a slight exudation or pasty swelling extends forward from the gland on the lower surface of the abdomen. This physiological congestion is looked upon as a matter of course, and disappears in two or three days when the secretion of milk has been fully established. This breaking up of the bag may be greatly hastened by the sucking of a hungry calf and the kneading it gives the udder with its nose, by stripping the glands clean thrice daily, and by active rubbing at each milking with the palm of the hand, with or without lard, or, better, with camphorated ointment.

The congestion may be at times aggravated by standing in a draft of cold air or by neglect to milk for an entire day or more (overstocking, hefting) with the view of making a great show of udder for purposes of sale. In such cases the surface of the bag pits on pressure, and the milk has a reddish tinge or even streaks of blood, or it is partially or fully clotted and is drawn with difficulty, mixed, it may be, with a yellowish serum (whey) which has separated from the casein. This should be treated like the above, though it may sometimes demand fomentations with warm water to ward off inflammation, and it may be a week before the natural condition of the gland is restored.

INFLAMMATION OF THE UDDER (SIMPLE MAMMITIS).

Congestion may merge into active inflammation, or it may arise direct, in connection with exposure to cold or wet, with standing in a cold draft, with blows on the udder with clubs, stones, horns, or feet, with injury from a sharp or cold stone, or the projecting edge of a board or end of a nail in the floor, with sudden and extreme changes of weather, with overfeeding on rich albuminous food like cotton seed, beans, or pease, with indigestions, with sores on the teats, or with insufficient stripping of the udder in milking. In the period of full milk the organ is so susceptible that any serious disturbance of the general health is liable to fall upon the udder.

Symptoms.—The symptoms and mode of onset vary in different cases. When following exposure there is usually a violent shivering fit, with cold horns, ears, tail and limbs, and general erection of the hair. This is succeeded by a flush of heat (reaction) in which the horns, ears, and limbs become unnaturally warm and the gland swells up and becomes firm and solid in one, two, three, or all four quarters. There is hot, dry muzzle, elevated temperature, full, accelerated pulse, and excited breathing, impaired or suspended appetite, and rumination with more or less costiveness, suppression of urine, and a lessened yield of milk, which may be entirely suppressed in the affected quarter.

In other cases the shivering escapes notice, the general disorder of the system is little marked or comes on late, and the first observed sign of illness is the firm swelling heat, and tenderness of the bag. As the inflammation increases and extends, the hot, tender udder causes the animal to straddle with its hind limbs, and when walking to halt on the limb on that side. If the cow lies down it is on the unaffected side. With the increase in intensity and the extension of the inflammation the general fever manifests itself more prominently. In some instances the connective tissue beneath the skin and between the lobules of the gland is affected, and then the swelling is uniformly rounded and of nearly the same consistency, pitting everywhere on pressure. In other cases it primarily attacks the secreting tissue of the gland, and then the swelling is more localized and appears as hard, nodular masses in the interior of the gland. This last is the usual form of inflammation occurring from infection entering by the teats.

In all cases, but especially in the last-named form, the milk is suppressed and replaced by a watery fluid colored with blood (sometimes deeply) and mingled with masses of clotted casein. Later it becomes white and purulent, and in many cases of an offensive odor.

The course of the disease is sometimes so rapid and at others so slow that no definite rule can be laid down. In two or three days, or from that to the end of the week, the bag may soften, lose its heat and tenderness, and subside into the healthy condition, even resuming the secretion of milk. The longer the inflammatory hardness continues the greater the probability that its complete restoration will not be effected. When a portion of the gland fails to be restored in this way, and has its secretion arrested, it usually shrinks to a smaller size. More commonly a greater amount of the inflammatory product remains in the gland and develops into a solid fibrous mass, causing permanent hardening (induration). In other cases, in place of the product of inflammation developing a fibrous mass, it softens and breaks down into the white creamy liquid pus (abscess). This abscess may make its way to the surface and escape externally, or it may burst into a milk duct and discharge through the teat. It may break into both and establish a channel for the escape of milk (fistula). In the worst types of the disease gangrene may ensue, a quarter or half or even the whole udder, losing its vitality, and sloughing off if the cow can bear up against the depressing influence. These gangrenous cases are probably always the result of infection and sometimes run a very rapidly fatal course. I recall one to which I was called as soon as the owner noticed it, yet I found one quarter dark blue, cold, and showing a tendency to the formation of blebs containing a bloody secretion. The cow, which had waded through a depth of semiliquid manure to reach her stall, died within twenty-four hours.

Treatment.—Treatment will vary with the type and the stage of the disease. If the case is seen in the shivering fit, every effort should be made to cut that short, as the inflammation may be thereby greatly moderated, if not checked. Copious drinks of warm water thrown in from horn or bottle; equally copious warm injections; the application of heat in some form to the surface of the body (by a rug wrung out of hot water; by hanging over the back and loins bags loosely filled with bran, sand, salt, chaff, or other agent previously heated in a stove; by the use of a flatiron or the warming of the surface by a hot-air bath), or by active friction with straw wisps by two or more persons; the administration of a pint of strong alcoholic liquor, or of 1 ounce of ground ginger, may serve to cut short the attack. After half an hour's sweat rub dry and cover with a dry blanket.

If, on the other hand, there is little or no fever, and only a slight inflammation, rub well with camphorated ointment or a weak iodine ointment, and milk three, four, or six times a day, rubbing the bag thoroughly each time. Milking must be done with great gentleness, squeezing the teat in place of pulling and stripping it, and if this causes too much pain, the teat tube or the spring teat dilator may be employed. Antiseptic injections of the teats and udder are often useful, and iodoform in water has been especially recommended. It may be replaced by one of the injections advised for parturition fever, used with the same careful precautions.

In cases in which the fever has set in and the inflammation is more advanced, a dose of laxative medicine is desirable (Epsom salts, 1 to 2 pounds; ginger, 1 ounce), which may be followed, after the purging has ceased, by daily doses of saltpeter, 1 ounce. Many rely on cooling and astringent applications to the inflamed quarter (vinegar, sugar-of-lead lotion, cold water, ice, etc.), but a safer and better resort is continued fomentation with warm water. A bucket of warm water, replenished as it cools, may be set beneath the udder, and two persons can raise a rug out of this and hold it against the udder, dipping it anew whenever the heat is somewhat lost. Or a sheet may be passed around the body, with four holes cut for the teats and soft rags packed between it and the udder, and kept warm by pouring on water as warm as the hands can bear every ten or fifteen minutes. When this has been kept up for an hour or two the bag may be dried, well rubbed with soap, and left thus with a soapy coating. If the pain is great, extract of belladonna may be applied along with the soap, and a dry suspensory bandage with holes for the teats may be applied. Strong mercurial ointment is very useful in relieving pain and softening the bag. This is especially valuable when the disease is protracted and induration threatens. It may be mixed with an equal amount of soap and half the amount of extract of belladonna. In cases of threatened induration excellent results are sometimes obtained from a weak induction current of electricity sent through the gland daily for ten minutes.

If *abscess* threatens it may be favored by fomentation and opened as soon as fluctuation from finger to finger shows the formation of matter at a point formerly hard. The wound may bleed freely, and there is a risk of opening a milk duct, yet relief will be secured, and a dressing twice daily with a lotion of carbolic acid, 1 part, water, 20 parts, and glycerin, 1 part, will suffice to keep the wound clean and healthy.

Gangrene of the affected part is often fatal. It demands antiseptics (chlorid of zinc, 1 dram to 1 quart water) applied frequently to the part, or, if the case can not be attended, smear the affected quarter with melted Venice turpentine, or even wood tar. Antiseptic tonics (tincture of muriate of iron, 4 drams) may also be given four times daily in a quart of water.

CONTAGIOUS MAMMITIS (CONTAGIOUS INFLAMMATION OF THE UDDER).

As stated in the last article, that form of inflammation of the udder which attacks the gland ducts and follicles, causing deepseated, hard, nodular swellings, is often contagious. .

The most common cause of contagious mammitis in cattle is a spherical bacterium in chain form (*Streptococcus*). (Moore, Ward.) Contagious mammatis is not a single affection, but a group of diseases which have this in common, that they attack the udder.

Prevention.—Prevention is to be especially sought in all such cases. In purchasing new cows see that they come from a herd where the teats and udder are sound. If a new cow with unknown antecedents comes from a public market, let her be milked for a week by a person who does not milk any other cows. Keep her in a separate stall from others, so that there may be no infection from litter or flooring. Wash the udder with soap and water, and wet with a solution of two teaspoonfuls carbolic acid in a pint of water before letting the regular milker of the other cows take her. If any cow in the herd shows the indurated end of the teat or the inflammation and nodula tender character of the gland, separate her at once and give her a separate milker. If another cow is to be put into the stall she occupied, first clean and scrape it, and wet it with a strong solution of bluestone, 5 ounces in a gallon of water. The milk may be drawn off with a teat tube, or spring teat dilator, and the milk ducts injected frequently with a solution of peroxide of hydrogen or iodoform. I have had little success in checking the upward progress of the disease through the teat with carbolic acid or boracic acid solutions. Used on the outside of the other teats, however, these may serve to prevent them from becoming infected. In the absence of peroxide of hydrogen the affected teat may be injected with a solution of 1 grain corrosive sublimate in a pint of water, and the same may be used on the other teats, provided it is washed off every time before milking.

As additional precautions, no cow with a retained afterbirth or unhealthy discharge from the womb should be left with the other cows. Such cows doubtless infect their own udders and those of the cows next them by lashing with their soiled tail. If milkers handle retained afterbirth or vaginal discharge, or unhealthy wounds, or assist in a difficult and protracted parturition, they should wash the hands and arms thoroughly with soap and warm water and then rub them with the corrosive sublimate solution, or if not, at least with one of carbolic acid. Clothes stained with such offensive products should be washed.

The general treatment of contagious mammitis does not differ from that of the simple form, except that antiseptics should be given by the mouth as well as applied locally (hyposulphite of soda, one-half ounce daily).

COWPOX.

This is another form of contagious inflammation of the udder which does not spread readily from animal to animal except by the hands of the milker. It is held to occur spontaneously in the cow, but this is altogether improbable, and so-called spontaneous cases are rather to be looked on as instances in which the germs have been preserved dry in the buildings or introduced in some unknown manner. It is not uncommon in the horse, attacking the heels, the lips, or some other inoculated part of the body, and is then easily transferred to the cow, if the same man grooms and dresses the horse and milks the cow. It may also appear in the cow by infection, more or less direct, from a person who has been successfully vaccinated. Many believe that it is only a form of the smallpox of man modified by passing through the system of cow or horse. It is, however, unreasonable to suppose that this alleged modified smallpox could have been transmitted from child to child (the most susceptible of the human race) for ninety years, under all possible conditions, without once reverting to its original type of smallpox. Chauveau's experiments on both cattle and horses with the virus of smallpox and its inoculation back on the human subject go far to show that in the climate of western Europe, at least, no such transformation takes place. Smallpox remains smallpox and cowpox, cowpox. Again, smallpox is communicable to a person who visits the patient in his room but avoids touching him, while cowpox is never thus transferred through the air unless deliberately diffused in the form of spray. The demonstration of a protozoan germ in smallpox implies a similar microbe in cowpox.

The disease in the cow is ushered in by a slight fever, which, however, is usually overlooked, and the first sign is tenderness of the teats. Examined, these may be redder and hotter than normal, and at the end of two days there appear little nodules, like small peas, of a pale-red color, and increasing so that they may measure three-fourths of an inch to 1 inch in diameter by the seventh day. The yield of milk diminishes, and when heated it coagulates slightly. From the seventh to the tenth day the eruption forms into a blister with a depression in the center and raised margins, and from which the whole of the liquid can not be drawn out by a single puncture. The blister, in other words, is chambered, and each chamber must be opened to evacuate the whole of the contents. If the pock forms on a surface where there is thick hair, it does not rise as a blister, but oozes out a straw-colored fluid which concretes on the hairs in an amber-colored mass. In one or two days after the pock is full it becomes yellow from contained pus, and then dries into a brownish yellow scab, which finally falls, leaving one or more distinct pits in the skin. Upon the teats, however, this regular course is rarely seen; the vesicles are burst by the hands of the milker as soon as liquid is formed, and as they continue to suffer at each milking they form raw, angry sores, scabbing more or less at intervals, but slow to undergo healing.

The only treatment required is to heal the sores; and as milking is the main cause of their persistence, that must be done as gently as possible, or even with the teat tube or dilator. It is essential to check the propagation of the germ, and for this purpose the sore teats may be washed frequently with a solution of half an ounce hyposulphite of soda in a pint of water. This will usually check the inflammation and cut short the malady.

SUPPRESSION OF MILK.

The absence of milk in the udder may result from ill health, debility, emaciation, chronic diseases of the bag, wasting of the gland from previous disease, or insufficient food, but sometimes it will occur suddenly without any appreciable cause. The treatment will consist in removing the cause of the disease, feeding well on rich albuminoid food made into warm mashes, and giving ounce doses of aromatic carminatives, like anise-seed, fennel-seed, etc. Rubbing and stripping the udder are useful; and the application of oil of lavender or of turpentine, or even a blister of Spanish flies, will sometimes succeed.

BLOODY MILK.

Blood may escape with the milk when the udder has been injured by blows, also when it is congested or inflamed, when the circulation through it has been suddenly increased by richer and more abundant food, or when the cow is under the excitement of heat. The milk frothing up and assuming a pink tinge is often the first sign of red-water, and it may result from eating acrid or irritant plants, like the Ranunculaceæ, resinous plants, etc. Deposits of tubercle or tumors in the udder, or induration of the gland, may be efficient causes, tho irritation caused by milking contributing to draw the blood. Finally, there may be a reddish tinge or sediment when madder or logwood has been eaten.

In milk which becomes red after it is drawn it may be due to the presence in it of the *micrococcus prodigiosus*. This also grows on bread, and is the explanation of the supposed miracle of the "bleeding host."

The treatment will vary with the cause. In congested glands give 1 pound of Epsom salts and daily thereafter one-half ounce saltpeter, with a dram of chlorate of potash; bathe the bag with hot or cold water, and rub with camphorated lard. If the food is too rich or abundant it must be reduced. If from acrid plants these must be removed from pasture or fodder. Induration of the udder may be met by rubbing with a combination of iodin ointment 1 part, soft soap 2 parts; or mercurial ointment and soap may be used. Careful milking is imperative.

BLUE MILK.

Watery milk is blue, but the presence of a germ (*Bacillus cyanogenes*) causes a distinct blue shade even in rich milk and cream. It may reach the milk after it has been drawn, or it may find its way into the opening of the milk ducts and enter the milk as it is drawn. In the latter case, frequent milking and the injection into the teats of a solution of 2 drams of hyposulphite of soda in a pint of water will serve to destroy them.

STRINGY MILK.

This may be caused by fungi developing in the liquid, and that the spores are present in the system of the cow may be safely inferred from the fact that in a large herd two or three cows only will yield such milk at a time, and that after a run of ten days or a fortnight they will recover and others will be attacked. I have found that such affected cows had the temperature raised one or two degrees above the others. Like most other fungi this does not grow out into filaments within the body of the cow, but in five or six hours after milking the surface layers are found to be one dense network of filaments. If a needle is dipped in this and lifted, the liquid is drawn out into a long thread. In one case which I investigated near Ithaca, N. Y., the contamination was manifestly due to a spring which oozed out of a bank of black muck soil and stood in pools mixed with the dejections of animals. Inoculation of pure milk with the water as it flowed out of this bank developed in it the fungus and the stringy characters. By fencing in this spring and giving the affected cows each 2 drams bisulphite of soda daily, the trouble was arrested promptly and permanently.

BITTER MILK.

Abnormal flavors in milk and milk products may be due to a number of causes. It is well known that certain weeds eaten by cows impart a characteristic flavor to the milk. Garlic or wild onion is a very noticeable example. The Alabama Station succeeded in removing the taste of bitterweed from cream (but not from milk) by mixing the cream with two or more times it volume of warm water and then separating again with a centrifugal separator. Proper attention to the feeding of cows will, of course, prevent trouble of this kind.

In 1890 H. W. Conn, of the Connecticut Storrs Experiment Station, isolated a species of bacteria from a sample of bitter cream and showed experimentally that the organism was the cause of the trouble. Several other investigators have also shown that bacteria may be the cause of bitterness in milk. A bulletin of the Ontario Agricultural College and Experimental Farm, by F. C. Harrison, publishes some interesting observations on bitter milk. In this case, however, the bitter flavor was caused by a form of yeast rather than by bacteria. Numerous cheese factories in Ontario were annoyed by the development of a bitter flavor in milk and curd. From a sample of such curd a yeast-like micro-organism designated *Torula amara*, or bitter torula, was isolated. This yeast, when separated from all other micro-organisms and added to milk which had been rendered sterile by heat, produced the characteristic bitter flavor. Cultures of the torula were added to milk, and the cheese and butter manufactured from it also possessed the bitter taste. In the investigations at one factory the torula was not found in milk drawn into sterile dishes nor in the air of the stable, but was found regularly in mixed milk, cheese, whey, can washings, and also on the leaves of certain trees under which milk cans were habitually kept.

In preventing such troubles as bitter milk, proper care of the milk is essential. Milk cans and all other utensils should be thoroughly washed and sterilized by heat, the milking should be done under the most favorable conditions for lessening contamination, the milk should be cooled promptly, and guarded as carefully as possible from all known sources of infection.

CHAPPED TEATS.

These may be caused by anything which irritates them. The powerful sucking of the calf, the sudden chilling of the teat in winter after the calf has just let it go or after the completion of milking with a wet hand; contact with cold water, or stagnant putrid water, or with filth or irritants when lying down; slight congestions of the skin in connection with overstocking, and, indeed, any source of local irritation may cause chapping. This may be slight or extend into great gaping sores and induce retention of milk or even mammitis. Soothing applications of vaseline, or a combination of equal parts of spermaceti and oil of sweet almonds may be applied. If healing is tardy, add 10 grains balsam of Peru to the ounce of ointment. If the irritation is very great, wash first with a solution of 1 dram sugar of lead in 1 pint of water, and then apply benzoated oxide of zinc ointment.

WARTS ON THE TEATS.

These are often very troublesome, yet they may be greatly benefited or entirely removed by smearing them thickly after each milking with pure olive oil. If they persist they may be cut off with a sharp pair of scissors and the sore touched with a stick of lunar caustic. They may now be oiled and the caustic repeated as demanded to prevent their renewed growth.

Scabby teats may be smeared with vaseline containing enough carbolic acid to give it an odor.

TEAT BLOCKED BY CONCRETION OF CASEIN.

Under unhealthy conditions of the gland or milk ducts, clots of casein form, and these, pressed clear of most of their liquid and rolled into rounded masses, may block the passage. They can be moved up and down by manipulation of the teat, and if they can not be pressed out they may be extracted by using the spring teat dilator, being held surrounded by its three limbs. Before extraction is attempted an ounce of almond oil, previously boiled, should be injected into the teat.

TEAT BLOCKED BY CALCULUS.

When the calcareous matter of the milk has been precipitated in the form of a smooth, rounded stone, a rough conglomerated concretion, or a fine, sand-like débris, it may cause obstruction and irritation. These bodies are felt to be much harder than those formed by casein, and the milk usually contains gritty particles. Extraction may be attempted by simple milking in the case of the finely divided gritty matter, or with the spring dilator in the case of the larger masses. Should this fail the teat may be laid open with the knife and sewed up again or closed with collodion, but such an operation is best deferred until the cow is dry.

TEAT BLOCKED BY A WARTY OR OTHER GROWTH INSIDE.

In this case the obstruction may be near the orifice of the teat or higher up, and the solid mass is not movable up and down with the same freedom as are concretions and calculi. The movement is limited by the elasticity of the inner membrane of the teat from which it grows, and is somewhat freer in certain cases because the growth has become loose and hangs by a narrow neck. In the case of the looser growths they may be snared by a fine spring wire passed as a loop through a fine tube (like a teat tube open at each end), and introduced into the teat. When this can not be done, the only resort is to cut in and excise it while the cow is dry.

THICKENING OF THE MUCOUS MEMBRANE AND CLOSURE OF THE MILK DUCT.

As a result of inflammation extending from without inward, a gradual narrowing of the milk duct may occur from thickening and narrowing of its lining membrane. This may be limited to a small area near the lower end, or it may extend through the whole length of the teat. The stream of milk becomes finer and finer until it finally ceases altogether, and a firm cord is felt running through the teat. If the constriction is only at the outlet, the teat may be seized and distended by pressing the milk down into it from above, and an incision may be made with a sharp penknife in two directions at right angles to each other and directly in the original opening. The knife should be first cleansed in boiling water. The opening may be kept from closing by a dumb-bell shaped bougie of gutta-percha or by the spring dilator. If the obstruction is more extended it may be perforated by Luthi's perforating sound. This is a steel wire with a ring at one end, and at the other is screwed on to the wire a conical cap with sharp cutting edges at the base, which scrapes away the thickened masses of cells as it is drawn back. This may be passed again and again to sufficiently enlarge the passage, and then the passage may be kept open by wearing a long dumb-bell bougie, a thick piece of carbolized catgut, or a spring dilator. If the passage can not be sufficiently opened with the sound it may be incised by the hidden bistoury. This is a knife lying alongside a flattened protector with smooth rounded edges, but which can be projected to any required distance by a lever on the handle. The incisions are made in four directions and as deep as may be necessary, and the walls can then be held apart by the spring dilator until they heal. In case the constriction and thickening of the canal extend the whole length of the teat, it is practically beyond remedy, as the gland is usually involved so as to render it useless.

CLOSURE OF THE MILK DUCT BY A MEMBRANE.

In this form the duct of the teat is closed by the constriction of its lining membrane at one point, usually without thickening. The closure usually takes place while the cow is dry; otherwise its prog ress is gradual, and for a time the milk may still be pressed through slowly. In such a case, if left at rest, the lower part of the teat fills up and the milk flows in a full stream at the first pressure, but after this it will not fill up again without sufficient time for it to filter through. This is to be cut open by the hidden bistoury, which may be first passed through the opening of the membrane, if such exists. If not it may be bored through, or it may be pressed up against the membrane at one side of the teat and opened toward the center, so as to cut its way through. Incisions should be made in at least two opposite directions, and the edges may be then held apart by wearing the spring dilator until healing has been completed.

In all cases of operations on the teats the instruments must be thoroughly disinfected with hot water, or by dipping in carbolic acid and then in water that has been boiled.

OPENING IN THE SIDE OF THE TEAT (MILK FISTULA).

This may occur from wounds penetrating the milk duct and failing to close, or it may be congenital, and then very often it leads to a distinct milk duct and an independent portion of the gland. In the first form it is only necessary to dissect away the skin leading into the opening for some distance down, to close the orifice with stitches, and to cover the whole with collodion. A teat tube or spring dilator may be worn to drain off the milk and prevent distention and reopening of the orifice. In case of an independent milk duct and gland one or two courses may be selected—to open the one duct into the other by incision and then close the offending opening, or to inject the superfluous gland through its duct with a caustic solution, so as to destroy its secreting power. In both cases it is desirable to wait until the cow goes dry.

DISEASES OF YOUNG CALVES.

SUSPENDED BREATHING.

The moment the circulation through the navel string is stopped the blood of the calf begins to get overcharged with carbon dioxid (CO_2), and unless breathing is speedily established death promptly follows. Fortunately the desire to breathe, roused by the circulation of the venous blood and the reflex action from the wet and chilling skin, usually at once starts the contractions of the diaphragm and life is insured. Among the obstacles to breathing may be named suffocation before or during birth from compression of the navel cord and the arrest of its circulation; the detachment of the fetal membranes from the womb before the calf is born; a too free communication between the two auricles of the heart (foramen ovale) by which the nonaerated blood has mixed too abundantly with the aerated and induced debility and profound weakness; a condition of ill health and debility of the calf as a result of semistarvation, overwork, or disease of the cow; fainting in such debilitated calf when calving has been difficult and prolonged; the birth of the calf with its head enveloped in the fetal membranes, so that it has been unable to breathe, and the presence of tenacious phlegm in the mouth and nose, acting in the same manner.

Besides the importance of proper care and feeding of the cow as a preventive measure, attention should be given at once to relieve the newborn calf of its investing membrane and of any mucus that has collected in mouth or nostrils. Wiping out the nose deeply with a finger or feather excites to sneezing, hence to breathing. Blowing into the nose has a similar effect. Sucking the nostril through a tube applied to it is even more effective. Slapping the chest with the palm of the hand or with a towel dipped in cold water, compression and relaxation alternately of the walls of the chest, may start the action, and ammonia or even tobacco smoke blown into the nose may suffice. Every second is precious, however, and if possible the lungs should be dilated by forcibly introducing air from a bellows or from the human lungs. As the air is blown in through bellows or a tube the upper end of the windpipe must be pressed back against the gullet, as otherwise the air will go to the stomach. In a large dairy a piece of elastic tubing one-third of an inch in bore should be kept at hand for sucking and blowing in such cases.

BLEEDING FROM THE NAVEL.

This may occur in two conditions—when the cord is cut off too close to the navel and left untied and when it tears off at the navel. It may also bleed when torn across naturally, if it is sucked by the dam or another calf. In an animal with little plasticity to its blood it will flow under almost any circumstances. Where any cord is left it is always safe to tie it, and it is only when it is swollen and may possibly contain a loop of the bowel that there is danger in doing so. By pressing upward any bulk contents such danger is avoided. If torn or cut too close to be tied the bleeding may be checked by applying alum, copperas, or for a fraction of a second the end of an iron rod at a dull-red heat. If much blood has been lost it may be requisite to transfuse several ounces of blood or of a weak common-salt solution into the open umbilical vein.

URINE DISCHARGED THROUGH THE NAVEL (PERSISTENT URACHUS).

Before birth the urine passes from the bladder by a special tube through the navel and navel string into the outer water bag (allantois). This closes at birth, and the tube shrinks into a fine cord up to the bladder. It is only in the bull calf that it is likely to remain open, doubtless because of the long, narrow channel through which the urine must otherwise escape. The urethra, too, is sometimes abnormally narrow, or even closed, in the male. If part of the cord remains tie it and allow the whole to wither up naturally. If the cord has been removed and the tube (urachus) protrudes, discharging the urine, that alone must be tied. If there is nothing pendent the urachus must be seized, covered by the skin, and, a curved needle being passed through the skin and above the duct, it may be tied along with this skin. A blister of Spanish flies, causing swelling of the skin, will often close the orifice. So with the hot iron. If the urethra of the male is impervious it can rarely be remedied.

INFLAMMATION OF THE URACHUS (NAVEL URINE DUCT).

This may originate in direct mechanical injury to the navel in calving, or shortly after, with or without the lodgment of irritant and septic matter on its lacerated or cut end. The mere contact with healthy urine, hitherto harmless, can now be looked on as becoming suddenly irritating. The affection is usually marked by the presence of redness and swelling at the posterior part of the navel and the escape of urine and a few drops of whitish serous pus from the orifice of the urachus. In those cases in which urine is not discharged a tender swelling, like a thick cord extending upward and backward from the navel into the abdomen, may be identified. The navel enlargement may be considerable, but it is solid, does not gurgle on handling, and can not be done away with by pressing it back into the abdomen, as in a case of hernia.

In cases at first closed the pus may burst out later, coming from the back part of the navel and the swelling extending backward. In other cases whitish pus may pass with the urine by the ordinary channel, showing that it has opened back into the bladder. In other cases the umbilical veins become involved, in which case the swelling extends forward as well as backward. Thus the disease may result in destructive disorders of the liver, lungs, and, above all, of the joints.

The disease may usually be warded off or rendered simple and comparatively harmless by applying antiseptics to the navel string at birth (carbolic acid 1 part, water and glycerin 5 parts each, or wood tar). Later, antiseptics may be freely used (hyposulphite of soda 4 drams, water 1 quart) as an application to the surface and as an injection into the urachus, or even into the bladder if the two still communicate. If they no longer communicate, a stronger injection may be used (tincture of perchlorid of iron 60 drops, alcohol 1 ounce). Several weeks will be required for complete recovery.

ABSCESS OF THE NAVEL.

As the result of irritation at calving or by the withered cord, or by licking with the rough tongue of the cow, inflammation may attack the loose connective tissue of the navel to the exclusion of the urachus and veins, and go on to the formation of matter. In this case a firm swelling appears as large as the fist, which softens in the center and may finally burst and discharge. The opening, however, is usually small and may close prematurely, so that abscess after abscess is formed. It is distinguished from hernia by the fact that it can not be returned into the abdomen, and from inflammations of the veins and urachus by the absence of swellings forward and backward along the lines of these canals.

Treatment.—Treatment consists in an early opening of the abscess by a free incision and the injection twice a day of an astringent antiseptic (chlorid of zinc one-half dram, water 1 pint).

INFLAMMATION OF THE NAVEL VEINS (UMBILICAL PHLEBITIS).

In this affection of the navel the inflammation may start directly from mechanical injury, as in either of the two forms just described, but on this are inoculated infective microbes, derived from a retained and putrefying afterbirth, an abortion, a metritis, a fetid discharge from the womb, an unhealthy open sore, a case of erysipelas, from overcrowding, from filthy floor or bedding, or from an offensive accumulation of manure, solid or liquid. As the microbes vary in different cases, given outbreaks will differ materially in their nature. One is erysipelatoid; another purulent infection with the tendency to secondary abscesses in the joints, liver, lungs, etc.; another is due to a septic germ and is associated with fetid discharge from the navel and general putrid blood poisoning. In estimating the causes of the disease we must not omit debility of the calf when the mother has been underfed or badly housed or when either she or the fetus has been diseased.

Symptoms.—The symptoms will vary. With the chain-form germs (streptococci) the navel becomes intensely red, with a very firm, painful swelling, ending abruptly at the edges in sound skin and extending forward along the umbilical veins.

Diarrhea is a common symptom, and death ensues early, the blood after death being found unclotted.

Complicated cases are common, and in all alike the umbilical veins usually remain open and can be explored by a probe passed at first upward and then forward toward the liver.

Prevention is sought by applying a lotion of carbolic acid or iodine solution to the navel string at birth, or it may be smeared with common wood tar, which is at once antiseptic and a protective covering against germs. In the absence of either a strong decoction of tea of oak bark may be used.

Local Treatment consists in the application of antiseptics to the surface and their injection into the vein. As a lotion use carbolic acid, 1 ounce in a quart of strong decoction of oak bark, or salicylic acid or salol may be sprinkled on the surface. The interior of the vein should be swabbed out with a probe wrapped around with cotton wool and dipped in boracic or salicylic acid.

If complications have extended to the liver or other internal organs, or the joints, other treatment will be demanded. In acute cases of general infection an early fatal result is to be expected.

PYEMIC AND SEPTICEMIC INFLAMMATION OF JOINTS IN CALVES
(JOINT-ILL).

This disease, also called joint-evil, is not infrequent among young animals, especially calves and foals, and occurs within six weeks after birth. The disease is localized in the joints, but the infection may reach the liver or other viscera, causing small areas of necrosis. One or more joints may be involved, a condition manifested by local painful swellings. The animal is stiff and lame and lies down most of the time, showing fever, inappetence, and accelerated respiration. The joint cavity is filled with pus, which finally causes ulceration of the cartilage and even necrosis of the adjoin-

Shorthorn Cow. Dept. of Agr.

Devon Cow. Dept. of Agr.

ing bone. In the purulent material of the joint *B. necrophorus* has been found by Mettam and others, who claim that the disease starts in such cases by infection of the umbilicus with the necrosis bacilli. Of course, it is not to be presumed that all cases of joint-ill are caused by this organism, since it has been proved definitely that the pus-producing cocci and the bacillus of white scour may enter the unhealed umbilicus and be carried by the umbilical vein to the liver, where they are thrown into the circulation to become localized in one or more joints. But the very fact that this does not occur in the latter cases presupposes the probability of the same occurrence with *B. necrophorus.*

Symptoms.—The symptoms are swelling of one or more joints, which are very hot and tender. The calf is stiff and lame, lies down constantly, and cares not to suck. There is very high fever and accelerated breathing and pulse, and there is swelling and purulent discharge (often fetid) from the navel. There may be added symptoms of disease of the liver, lungs, heart, or bowels, on which we need not here delay. The important point is to determine the condition of the navel in all such cases of diseased and swollen joints beginning in the first month of life, and in all cases of general stiffness, for besides the diseases of the internal organs there may be abscesses formed among the muscles of the trunk, though the joints appear sound. Cases of this kind, if they do not speedily die, tend to become emaciated and perish later in a state of weakness and exhaustion.

Prevention.—Prevention must begin with the purity of the buildings and the navel, as noted in the last article.

Treatment.—Treatment is in the main antiseptic. The slighter forms may be painted daily with tincture of iodin; or an ointment of biniodid of mercury (1 dram) and lard (2 ounces) may be rubbed on the affected joints daily until they are blistered. In case of swellings containing matter this may be drawn off through the nozzle of a hypodermic syringe and the following solution injected: Compound tincture of iodine, 1 dram; distilled (or boiled) water, 2 ounces. Internally the calf may take 5 grains quinia twice daily and 15 grains hyposulphite of soda, or 20 grains salicylate of soda three times a day.

UMBILICAL HERNIA (BREACH AT THE NAVEL).

This may exist at birth from imperfect closure of the muscles around the opening; it may even extend backward for a distance, from the two sides failing to come together. Apart from this, the trouble rarely appears after the calf has been some time on solid food, as the paunch then extends down to the right immediately over the navel, and thus forms an internal pad, preventing the protrusion of intestine.

Symptoms.—The symptoms of umbilical hernia are a soft swelling at the navel, with contents that usually gurgle on handling, and can be entirely returned into the abdomen by pressure. The diseases of the navel hitherto considered have not gurgling contents, and can not be completely returned into the abdomen. The only exception in the case of the hernia is when the walls of the sac have become greatly thickened; these will, of course, remain as a swelling after the bowel has been returned; and when the protruding bowel has contracted permanent adhesions to the sac it is impossible to return it fully without first severing that connection.

Treatment.—Treatment is not always necessary. A small hernia, like an egg in a new-born calf, will usually recover of itself as the animal changes its diet to solid food and has the paunch fully developed as an internal pad.

In other cases apply a leather pad of 8 inches square attached around the body by two elastic bands connected with its four corners, and an elastic band passing from its front border to a collar encircling the neck, and two other elastic bands from the neck collar along the two sides of the body to the two bands passing up over the back.

For small hernias nitric acid may be used to destroy the skin and cause such swelling as to close the orifice before the skin is separated. For a mass like a large goose egg one-half ounce of the acid may be rubbed in for three minutes. No more must be applied for fifteen days. For large masses this is inapplicable, and with too much loss of skin the orifice may fail to close and the bowels may escape.

The application of a clamp like those used in castration is a most effective method, but great care must be taken to see that all the contents of the sac are returned so that none may be inclosed in the clamp.

Another most effective resort is to make a saturated solution of common salt, filter and boil it, and when cool inject under the skin (not into the sac) on each side of the hernia a dram of the fluid. A bandage may then be put around the body. In ten hours an enormous swelling will have taken place, pressing back the bowel into the abdomen. When this subsides the wound will have closed.

DROPSY OF THE NAVEL.

A sac formed at the navel, by contained liquid accumulated by reason of sucking by other calves, is unsightly and sometimes injurious. After making sure that it is simply a dropsical collection it may be deeply punctured at various points with a large-sized lancet or knife, fomented with hot water, and then daily treated with a strong decoction of white-oak bark.

THE BLUE DISEASE (CYANOSIS).

This appearing in the calf at birth is due to the orifice between the two auricles of the heart (foramen ovale) remaining too open, allowing the nonaerated (venous) blood to mix with the aerated (arterial) blood, and it is beyond the reach of treatment. It is recognized by the blueness of the eyes, nose, mouth, and other mucous membranes, the coldness of the surface, and the extreme sensitiveness to cold.

CALF DIPHTHERIA (NECROTIC STOMATIS). SEE INFECTIOUS DISEASES.

Constipation.—At birth the bowels of the calf contain the meconium, a tenacious, gluey, brownish yellow material largely derived from the liver, which must be expelled before they can start their functions normally. The first milk of the cow (colostrum, beestings), rich in albumen and salts, is nature's laxative to expel this now offensive material and should never be withheld from the calf. If, for lack of this, from the dry feeding of the cow, or from any other cause, the calf is costive, straining violently without passage, lying down and rising as in colic, and failing in appetite, no time should be lost in giving relief by an ounce dose of castor oil, assisting its action by injections of soapsuds or oil. Whatever meconium is within reach of the finger should be carefully removed. It is also important to give the cow a sloppy, laxative diet.

Indigestion.—This may occur from many different causes, as costiveness; a too liberal supply of milk; milk too rich; the furnishing of the milk of a cow long after calving to a very young calf; allowing a calf to suck the first milk of a cow that has been hunted, driven by road, shipped by rail, or otherwise violently excited; allowing the calf too long time between meals, so that impelled by hunger it quickly overloads and clogs the stomach; feeding from the pail milk that has been held over in unwashed (unscalded) buckets, so that it is fermented and spoiled; feeding the milk of cows kept on unwholesome food; keeping the calves in cold, damp, dark, filthy, or bad-smelling pens; feeding the calves on artificial mixtures containing too much starchy matter; or overfeeding the calves on artificial food that may be appropriate enough in smaller amount. The licking of hair from themselves or others and its formation into balls in the stomach will cause obstinate indigestion in the calf.

Symptoms.—The symptoms are dullness, indisposition to move, uneasiness, eructations of gas from the stomach, sour breath, entire loss of appetite, lying down and rising as if in pain, fullness of the abdomen, which gives out a drumlike sound when tapped with the fingers. The costiveness may be marked at first, but soon it gives place to diarrhea, by which the offensive matters may be carried off and health restored. In other cases it becomes aggravated, merges into inflammation of the bowels, fever sets in, and the calf gradually sinks.

Prevention.—Prevention consists in avoiding the causes above enumerated or any others that may be detected.

Treatment.—Treatment consists in first clearing away the irritant present in the bowels. For this purpose 1 or 2 ounces of castor oil with 20 drops of laudanum may be given, and if the sour eructations are marked a tablespoonful of limewater or one-fourth ounce calcined magnesia may be given and repeated two or three times a day. If the disorder continues after the removal of the irritant, a large tablespoonful of rennet, or 30 grains of pepsin, may be given at each meal along with a teaspoonful of tincture of gentian. Any return of constipation must be treated by injections of warm water and soap, while the persistence of diarrhea must be met as advised under the article following this. In case of the formation of loose hair balls inclosing milk undergoing putrid fermentation temporary benefit may be obtained by giving a tablespoonful of vegetable charcoal three or four times a day, but the only real remedy for these is to cut open the paunch and extract them. At this early age they may be found in the third or even the fourth stomach; in the adult they are confined to the first two, and are comparatively harmless.

DIARRHEA (SCOURING) IN CALVES (SIMPLE AND CONTAGIOUS).

As stated in the last article, scouring is a common result of indigestion, and at first may be nothing more than an attempt of nature to relieve the stomach and bowels of offensive and irritating contents. As the indigestion persists, however, the fermentations going on in the undigested masses become steadily more complex and active, and what was at first the mere result of irritation or suspended digestion comes to be a genuine contagious disease, in which the organized ferments (bacteria) propagate the affection from animal to animal and from herd to herd. More than once I have seen such epizootic diarrhea start on the headwaters of a creek, and, traveling along that stream, follow the watershed and attack the herds supplied with water from the contaminated channel. In the same way the disease, once started in a cow stable, is liable to persist for years, or until the building has been thoroughly cleansed and disinfected. It may be carried into a healthy stable by the introduction of a cow brought from an infected stable when she is closely approaching calving. Another method of its introduction is by the purchase of a calf from a herd where the infection exists.

In enumerating the other causes of this disease we may refer to those noted above as inducing indigestion. As a primary consideration, any condition which lowers the vitality or vigor of the calf must be accorded a prominent place among factors which, apart from contagion, contribute to start the disease *de novo*. Other things being equal, the strong, vigorous races are the least predisposed to the malady, and in this respect the compact form, the healthy coat, the clear eye, and the bold, active carriage are desirable. Even the color of the hair is not unimportant, as in the same herd I have found a far greater number of victims among the light colors (light yellow, light brown) than among those of a darker tint. This constitutional predisposition to indigestion and diarrhea is sometimes fostered by too close breeding, without taking due account of the maintenance of a robust constitution, and hence animals that are very much inbred need to be especially observed and cared for unless their inherent vigor has been thoroughly attested.

The surroundings of the calf are powerful influences. Calves kept indoors suffer to a greater extent than those running in the open air and having the invigorating influences of sunshine, pure air, and exercise; but close, crowded, filthy, bad-smelling buildings are especially causative of the complaint. The condition of the nursing cow and her milk is another potent cause of trouble.

Symptoms.—The symptoms of diarrhea may appear so promptly after birth as to lead to the idea that the cause already existed in the body of the calf, and it usually shows itself before the end of the second week. It may be preceded by constipation, as in retained meconium, or by fetid eructations and colicky pains, as in acute indigestion. The tail is stained by the liquid dejections, which are at first simply soft and mixed with mucus with a sour odor, accompanied by a peculiar and characteristic fetor (suggesting rotten cheese), which continually grows worse. The amount of water and mucus steadily increases, the normal predominance of fatty matters becoming modified by the presence of a considerable amount of undigested casein, which is not present in the healthy feces, and in acute cases death may result in one or two days from the combined drain on the system and the poisoning by the absorbed products of the decomposition in the stomach and bowels. When the case is prolonged the passages, at first five or six per day, increase to fifteen or twenty, and pass with more and more straining, so that they are projected from the animal in a liquid stream. The color of the feces, at first yellow, becomes a lighter grayish yellow or a dirty white (hence the name white scour), and the fetor becomes intolerable.

At first the calf retains its appetite, but as the severity of the disease increases, the animal shows less and less disposition to suck, and has lost all vivacity, lying dull and listless, and, when raised, walking weakly and unsteadily. Flesh is lost rapidly, the hair stands erect, the skin gets dry and scurfy, the nose is dry and hot, or this condition alternates with a moist and cool one. By this time the mouth and skin, as well as the breath and dung, exhale the peculiar penetrating, sour, offensive odor, and the poor calf has become an object of disgust to all that approach it. At first, and unless inflammation of the stomach and bowels supervene (and unless the affection has started in indigestion and colic), the belly is not bloated or painful on pressure, symptoms of acute colicky pains are absent, and the bowels do not rumble, neither are bubbles of gas mingled with the feces. The irritant products of the intestinal fermentations may, however, irritate and excoriate the skin around the anus, which becomes red, raw, and broken out in sores for some distance. Similarly, the rectum, exposed by reason of the relaxed condition of the anus, or temporarily in straining to pass the liquid dejection, is of a more or less deep red, and it may be ulcerated. Fever, with rapid pulse and increased breathing and temperature, usually comes on with the very fetid character of the feces and is more pronounced as the bowels become inflamed, the abdomen sore to the touch and tucked up, and the feces more watery, and even mixed with blood.

Prevention.—The prevention of these cases is the prevention of constipation and indigestion, with all their varied causes as above enumerated, the selection of a strong, vigorous stock, and, above all, the combating of contagion, especially in the separation of the sick from the healthy, and in the thorough purification and disinfection of the buildings. The cleansing and sweetening of all drains, the removal of dung heaps, and the washing and scraping of floors and walls, followed by a liberal application of chlorid of lime (bleaching powder), 4 ounces to the gallon, are indicated. Great care must be exercised in the feeding of the cow to have sound and wholesome food and water, so apportioned as to make the milk neither too rich nor too poor, and to her health, so that the calf may be saved from the evil consequences of poisonous principles that may be produced in the body of the cow. The calves should be carefully kept apart from all calving cows and their discharges. Similarly, each calf must have special attention to see that its nurse gives milk which agrees with it, and that this is furnished at suitable times. If allowed to suck, it should either be left with the cow or it may be fed three times a day. If it becomes hungry twice a day it is more likely to overload and derange the stomach, and if left too long hungry it is tempted to take in unsuitable and unwholesome food, for which its stomach is as yet unprepared. So, if fed from the pail, it is safer to do so three times daily than twice. The utmost cleanliness of feeding dishes should be secured and the feeder must be ever on the alert to prevent the strong and hungry from drinking the milk of the weaker in addition to their own. In case the cow nurse has been subjected to any great excitement by reason of travel, hunting, or carrying, the first milk she yields thereafter should be used for some other purpose and only the second allowed to the calf. Indeed, one and all of the conditions above indicated as causes should be judiciously guarded against.

Treatment.—Treatment will vary according to the nature and stage of the disease. When the disease is not widespread, but isolated cases only occur, it may be assumed to be a simple diarrhea and is easily dealt with. The first object is to remove the irritant matter from stomach and bowels, and for this 1 or 2 ounces of castor oil may be given, according to the size of the calf. Reduce the milk by one-half or two-thirds. If the stools smell particularly sour, it may be replaced by 1 ounce calcined magnesia, and in any case a tablespoonful or two of limewater must be given with each meal. Great harm is often done by giving opium and astringents at the outset. These merely serve to bind up the bowels and retain the irritant source of the trouble.

If the outbreak is general and evidently the result of contagion, the first consideration is to remove all sources of such contamination. Test the milk of the cow with blue litmus paper, and, if it reddens, reject the milk of that cow until by sound, dry feeding, with perhaps a course of hyposulphite of soda and gentian root, her milk shall have been made alkaline. The castor oil or magnesia will still be demanded to clear away the (now infecting) irritants, but they should be combined with antiseptics, and, while the limewater and the carminative mixture may still be used, a most valuable addition will be found in the following: Calomel, 10 grains; prepared chalk, 1 ounce; creosote, 1 teaspoonful; mix, divide into ten parts, and give one four times a day. Or the following may be given four times a day: One dram Dover's powder, 6 grains powdered ipecacuanha; mix, divide into ten equal parts. Injections of solutions of gum arabic are often useful, and if the anus is red and excoriated, one-half dram of copperas may be added to each pint of the gummy solution. All the milk given must be boiled, and if that does not agree, eggs made into an emulsion with barley water may be substituted. Small doses (tablespoonful) of port wine are often useful from the first, and as the feces lose their watery character and become more consistent, tincture of gentian in doses of 2 teaspoonfuls may be given three or four times a day. Counter-irritants, such as mustard, ammonia, or oil of turpentine, may be rubbed on the abdomen when that becomes tender to the touch.

[A treatment that is most excellent for this trouble consists in giving one teaspoonful of a mixture of one-half ounce of Formalin in fifteen and one-half ounces of water in each pint of milk fed to the calf.]

ACUTE CONTAGIOUS SCOURING IN THE NEWBORN.

The most violent and deadly form of diarrhea in the newborn calf deserves a special mention. This may appear immediately after birth, and shows itself almost invariably within the first or second day. The most intense symptoms of white scour are complicated by great dullness, weakness, and prostration, sunken eyes, retracted belly, short, hurried breathing, and very low temperature, the calf lying on its side, with the head resting on the ground, lethargic and unconscious or regardless of all around it. The bowel discharges are profuse, yellowish white, and very offensive. As a rule, death ensues within twenty-four to thirty-six hours.

A marked characteristic of this form of illness is that it attacks almost every calf born in the herd, or in the building, rather, and if the calf escapes an attack in the first two or three days of its life it usually survives. Those that recover from an attack, however, are liable to suffer from an infective inflammation of the lungs one or two weeks later. The infection clings to a stable for years, rendering it impossible in many cases to preserve and raise the calves. It has frequently coincided with abortions and failures to conceive in the same herd, so that it has been thought that the same infective germ produces one type of abortion. On the other hand, the removal of the calving cow from the herd to calve in a separate building, hitherto unused and therefore uninfected, usually secures the escape and survival of the offspring.

Prevention.—The disease is so certainly and speedily fatal that it is hopeless to expect recovery, and therefore prevention is the rational resort.

When a herd is small, the removal of the dam to a clean, unused stable a few days before calving and her retention there for a week usually succeeds. But it is in the large herd that the disease is mainly to be dreaded, and in this it is impossible to furnish new and pure stables for each successive group of two or three calving cows. The thorough disinfection of the general stable ought to succeed; yet I have seen the cleanest and purest stable repeatedly disinfected with corrosive sublimate without stopping the malady. It would appear as if the germ lodged on the surface or in the bowels of the cow and tided the infection over the period of stable disinfection. But though insufficient themselves, the supply of separate calving boxes and the frequent thorough cleaning and disinfection of both these and the stables should not be neglected. The most important measure, however, is the disinfection of the navel.

The cow should be furnished with abundance of dry, clean bedding, sprinkled with a solution of carbolic acid. As soon as calving sets in, the tail and hips, anus and vulva, should be sponged with a carbolic-acid solution (one-half ounce to the quart), and the vagina injected with a weaker solution (2 drams to the quart). Fresh carbolized bedding should be constantly supplied, so that the calf shall be dropped on that and not on soaked litter nor manure. The navel string should be at once tied with a cord that has been taken from a strong solution of carbolic acid. The stump of the cord and the adjacent skin should then be washed with the following solution: Iodin, one-half dram; iodid of potassium, one-half dram; water, 1 quart. When dry, it may be covered with a coating of collodion or tar, each containing 1 per cent of iodin.

Whenever a calf shows any signs of scouring, it should be instantly removed to another pen and building, and the vacated one should be thoroughly cleaned and disinfected. Different attendants should take care of the sound calves and the infected ones, and all utensils, litter, etc., kept scrupulously apart.

After one week the healthy calves may usually be safely herded together or they may be safely placed in the cow stable.

OTHER AILMENTS OF THE CALF.

Among these may be named several congenital imperfections, such as imperforate anus, vulva, or prepuce, which are to be recognized by the inability to pass dung or urine, in spite of straining, and the formation of swellings in the anus, vulva, or sheath. Each must be carefully incised with the knife, taking care not to injure the muscles which circumscribe the respective openings. Also tongue-tie, in which the thin flaccid mucous membrane passing from the median line of the lower surface of the tongue binds the latter too closely to the floor of the mouth and renders the tongue unfit for gathering in the food in after life. This must be cut with knife or scissors, so as to give the tongue a reasonable amount of liberty.

Aphtha, or *Thrush,* is another trouble of the sucking calf, showing itself as a white, curdy elevation on the tongue, lips, cheeks, or gums, and when detached leaving a raw, red, angry surface. It is due to the growth of a vegetable parasite long recognized as the *Oidium albicans (Saccharomyces albicans).* It is easily removed by rubbing with powdered borax, but inasmuch as other colonies are likely to start either in the mouth or lower down in the pharynx, gullet, or stomach, it is well to give a dose of one-half dram of hyposulphite of soda in water day by day for several days.

Rickets is not a common disease in calves, and comes on, if at all, later than those we have been considering. It consists in softening and friability of the bones from a deficiency of lime salts, and appears to be mainly connected with an inherited weakness of constitution, unsuitable feeding, cold, close, damp buildings, microbian infection, and other conditions inimical to health. The prevention and treatment of rickets consists essentially in the improvement of the digestion and general health; hence sunshine, open air, exercise, nourishing food and tonics are indicated.

LIST OF PUBLICATIONS ABRIDGED ABOVE.

Abortion in Cattle: North Dakota Agr. Exp. Sta. Bulletin 54.

Contagious Abortion in Montana: Montana Agr. Exp. Sta. Bulletin 49.

Infectious Abortion in Cows: Virginia Agr. Exp. Sta. Bulletins 13 and 2 Vol. I (New Series).

Contagious Abortion in Cattle: Arizona Agr. Exp. Sta. Bulletins 57 and 65.

The Prevalence, Cause and Treatment of Abortion, Milk Fever and Garget: New Jersey Agr. Exp. Sta. Bulletin 127.

The Review of Prof. Bang's Work With Contagious Abortion: Michigan Agr. Exp. Sta. Special Bulletin 13.

Contagious Abortion of Cows: Illinois Agr. Exp. Sta. Bulletin 152.

Common Ailments of Breeding Cattle: Georgia Agr. Exp. Sta. Bulletin 60.

Abortion or Slinking of the Calf: Bureau of Animal Industry, U. S. Dept. Agr. Circular 67.

Milk Fever, Its Causes, Symptoms and Successful Treatment: Virginia Agr. Exp. Sta. Bulletin 158.

Milk Fever: Mississippi Agr. Exp. Sta. Bulletin 71.

Milk Fever: New Jersey Agr. Exp. Sta. Bulletin 127.

Milk Fever, Its Prevention and Successful Treatment: South Carolina Agr. Exp. Sta. Bulletin 139.

Parturient Paralysis and the Schmidt Treatment: Iowa Agr. Exp. Sta. Bulletin 58.

Parturient Apoplexy: Indiana Agr. Exp. Sta. Bulletins 17 and 62.

Milk Fever, Its Simple and Successful Treatment: Farmer's Bulletin, U. S. Dept. Agr. 206.

Scours in New-Born Calves: North Dakota Agr. Exp. Sta. Bulletin 54.

Calf Scours:—A New Method of Treatment: South Carolina Agr. Exp. Sta. Bulletin 122.

Special Report on the Diseases of Cattle: Bureau of Animal Industry, U. S. Dept. Agr., Washington, D. C.

INFECTIOUS DISEASES OF CATTLE.

The importance to the farmer and stock raiser of a general knowledge of the nature of infectious diseases need not be insisted on, as it must be evident to all who have charge of farm animals. The growing facilities for intercourse between one section of a country and another, and between different countries, cause a wide distribution of the infectious diseases once restricted to a definite locality. Not only the animals themselves, but the cars, vessels, or other conveyances in which they are carried may become agents for the dissemination of disease. The growing tendency of specialization in agriculture, which leads to the maintenance of large herds of cattle, sheep, and hogs, makes infectious diseases more common and more dangerous. Fresh animals are being continually introduced which may be the carriers of disease from other herds, and when disease is once brought into a large herd the losses become very high, because it is difficult, if not impossible, to check it after it has once obtained a foothold.

These considerations make it plain that only by the most careful supervision by intelligent men who understand the nature of infectious diseases and their causes in a general way can these be kept away. We must likewise consider how incomplete our knowledge concerning many diseases is, and probably will be for some time to come. The suggestions and recommendations offered by investigators may, therefore, not always be correct, and may require frequent modification as our information grows more comprehensive and exact.

An infectious disease may be defined as any malady caused by the introduction into the body of minute organisms of a vegetable or animal nature which have the power of indefinite multiplication and of setting free certain peculiar poisons which are chiefly responsible for the morbid changes.

This definition might include diseases due to certain animal parasites, such as trichinæ, for example, which multiply in the digestive tract, but whose progeny is limited to a single generation, By common consent the term infectious is restricted to those diseases caused by the invasion and multiplication of certain very minute unicellular organisms included under the general classes of bacteria and protozoa. Nearly all the diseases of cattle for which a definite cause has been traced are due to bacteria. Among these are tuberculosis, anthrax, blackleg, and tetanus (or lockjaw). Some diseases, such as Texas fever and nagana, are traceable to protozoa, while others, like actinomycosis and aspergillosis, are caused by fungi. Those diseases of which the cause is unknown or imperfectly worked out are pleuro-pneumonia, rinderpest, foot-and-mouth disease, rabies, cowpox, malignant catarrh, and dysentery.

Bacteria may be defined as very minute, unicellular organisms of a plant-like character. They multiply in two ways. The bacterium elongates and then divides in the middle to form 2 daughter cells. These go through the same process at once, and thus 4 cells are produced. The division of these leads to 8, the division of 8 to 16, and so on indefinitely. The rapidity with which this multiplication takes place depends upon the nature of the bacterium. The bacillus of tuberculosis multiplies very slowly, while that of anthrax multiplies with great rapidity, provided both are in the most favorable condition. Another mode of reproduction, limited to certain classes of bacteria, consists in the formation of a spore within the body of the bacterium. Spore formation usually takes place when the conditions pertaining to the growth of the bacteria become unfavorable. The spores are much more resistant to destructive agents than the bacteria which produced them. The anthrax spore may live several years in a dried state, but the anthrax bacillus perishes in a few days under like conditions. This matter will be referred to again when we come to discuss the subject of disinfection.

Of the protozoa which cause disease very little is at present known. These parasites have a more complex life history than bacteria; and their thorough investigation is at present hampered with great difficulties.

The differences in the symptoms and lesions of the various infectious diseases are due to differences in the respective organisms causing them. Similarly the great differences observed in the sources from which animals become infected and the manner in which infection takes place are due to differences in the life history of these minute organisms. Much discussion has taken place of late years concerning the precise meaning of the words infection and contagion. But these words are now wholly inadequate to express the complex processes of infection, and it may be said that each species of bacterium or protozoon has its own peculiar way of invading the animal body, differing more or less from all the rest. There are, however, a few broad distinctions which may be expressed with the help of these old terms. Infection, as laid down above, refers at present in a comprehensive way to all micro-organisms capable of setting up disease in the body. Some micro-organisms are transmitted directly from one animal to another, and the diseases produced may be called contagious. Among these are included pleuro-pneumonia, rinderpest, foot-and-mouth disease, rabies, cow-pox, and tuberculosis. Again, certain organisms are perhaps never transmitted from one animal to another, but may come from the soil. Among these are tetanus, blackleg, anthrax to a large extent, and perhaps actinomycosis in part. These diseases, according to some authorities, may be called miasmatic. There is a third class of infectious diseases of which the specific bacteria are transmitted from one animal to another, as with the contagious diseases, but the bacteria may, under certain favorable conditions, find enough food in the soil and the surroundings of animals to multiply to some extent after they have left the sick and before they gain entrance into a healthy animal.

This general classification is subject to change if we take into consideration other characteristics. Thus tuberculosis would not by many be considered contagious in the sense that foot-and-mouth disease is, because of the insidious beginning and slow course of the disease. Yet the bacillus must come from pre-existing disease in either case. The disease of rabies, or hydrophobia, is not contagious in the sense that rinderpest is, because the virus of rabies must be inoculated into a wound before it can take effect. Yet in both cases the virus passes without modification from one animal to another, though in different ways.

Again, all the diseases under the second group, which seem to come from the soil and from pastures, are in one sense contagious in that the virus may be taken from a sick animal and inoculated directly into a healthy animal with positive result. Other illustrations may be cited which show that these old terms are not in themselves satisfactory. There are so many conditions which enter into the process of infection that no single classification will give a sufficiently correct or comprehensive idea of it. These statements will be easily understood if the different infectious diseases in the following pages be studied with reference to the way or ways in which each disease may be contracted. Enough has been said, therefore, to show that, if we wish to make ourselves acquainted with the dangers of any given disease, we must study that disease and not rely upon any single word to tell the whole story.

Infectious diseases have, as a general rule, a period of incubation, which comprises the time elapsing between the exposure to the infection and the actual appearance of the disease. This period varies with the malady. The most common symptom of this class of diseases is fever. The severity of the fever is measured by the temperature of the animal and this is readily and accurately ascertainable by the clinical thermometer. The other symptoms are variable and depend upon the particular organ or organs most implicated. Loss of appetite, cessation of rumination and milk secretion, and general dullness are symptoms quite invariably present in most infectious diseases.

During the course of infectious diseases secondary diseases or complications may arise which are largely due to bacteria other than those producing the original malady. These complications are often so severe as to become fatal. In general it may be stated that they are due to filthy surroundings, and hence cleanliness may become an important aid to recovery.

The treatment of infectious diseases is given under each malady so far as this is allowable or advisable. These diseases are not, as a rule, amenable to treatment. When the symptoms have once appeared the disease is apt to run its course in spite of treatment, and, if it is one from which animals usually recover, all that can be done is to put them into the most favorable surroundings. Many infectious diseases lead sooner or later to death, and treatment is useless so far as the sick are concerned, and it may be worse than useless for those not yet infected. All animals suffering with infectious diseases are a menace to all others more or less directly. They represent for the time being manufactories of disease germs, and they are giving them off more or less abundantly during the period of disease. They may infect others directly or they may scatter the virus about, and the surroundings may become a future source of infection for healthy animals. This leads us to the subject of prevention as the most important of all which claim our attention. In this place only a few general remarks will suffice to bring the subject before the reader.

The most important thing is to keep disease away from a herd or farm. To do this all sick or suspicious animals should be avoided. A grave form of disease may be introduced by apparently mild or trivial cases brought in from without. It is generally conceded that continual change and movement of animals are the most potent means by which infectious diseases are disseminated.

With some cattle diseases, such as anthrax, rinderpest, and pleuro-pneumonia, preventive inoculation is resorted to in some countries. This may be desirable when certain diseases have become stationary in any locality, so that eradication is impossible. It should not be practiced in territories where a given disease may still be extirpated by ordinary precautions. Preventive inoculation is applicable to only a few maladies and therefore its aid in the control of diseases is a limited one.

When an infectious disease has gained foothold in a herd the course to be pursued in getting rid of it will depend upon the nature of the malady. A good rule is to kill diseased animals, especially when the disease is likely to run a chronic course, as in tuberculosis. The next important step is to separate the well from the sick by placing the former on fresh ground. This is rarely possible; hence the destruction or removal of the sick, with thorough disinfection of the infected locality, is the next thing to be done. As to the disinfectants to be used, special directions are given under the various diseases. [See pages 32-45.]

CONTAGIOUS PLEURO-PNEUMONIA.

This disease has been eradicated from the United States, and it is not probable that it will ever be seen in this country again.

FOOT-AND-MOUTH DISEASE.

This disease is also known as epizootic aphtha, aphthous fever, infectious aphtha, eczema epizootica, and may be defined as an acute, highly contagious fever of a specific nature, characterized by the eruption of vesicles, or blisters, in the mouth, around the coronets of the feet, and between the toes. Every appearance of foot-and-mouth disease upon American soil has been quickly followed by the total suppression of the disease.

BLOOD POISONING (SEPTICEMIA AND PYEMIA).

These two names are applied to diseased conditions which are so nearly alike in their symptoms that it is sometimes difficult to distinguish the one from the other. Indeed, the name pyosepticemia, or septicopyemia, is often applied where it is impossible to make a distinction between septicemia and pyemia or where each is equally responsible for the diseased condition. The name septicemia is derived from two Greek words meaning poison and blood, and signifies that the germ lives in the blood, hence the use of the term blood poisoning for this disease. Pyemia is likewise derived from two Greek words, meaning "pus" and "blood," and is that form of septicemia caused by pus-producing organisms and characterized by secondary abscesses.

Causes.—Neither of these diseases is brought about, strictly speaking, by any specific organism, hence neither can be looked upon as a specific disease. The organisms most frequently found in cases of septicemia are, on the whole, the same as those of pyemia, and may be either pus cocci, the bacillus coli, or other pus-producing organisms. These organisms are often found as secondary invaders in other diseases, such as advanced cases of tuberculosis, in which cases they are responsible for the formation of pus.

Aside from the causative organism, or, in other words, the active cause, there are many secondary causes. The most important of these in pyemia is a break in continuity of the protective covering, as a wound, which affords an entrance into the tissues for the organisms. Among the different varieties of wounds may be mentioned cuts, bruises, punctures, burns, chemical or frozen wounds, and compound fractures of bones. Injuries received during parturition, stoppage of the milk ducts, and infection of the umbilicus in the newly born are also frequent causes of pyemia. Septicemia usually follows surgical wounds, local suppuration, enteritis, bronchitis—in fact, wherever there is a local lesion of any kind permitting germs to enter the blood. Septicemia was formerly applied to designate the condition in which the organisms were localized, but in which their toxins were diffused in the blood. Pyemia was made to represent that condition where the organisms were localized, but in which the pus was transported by the blood. These terms now are applied to conditions in which both the organisms and their toxins, or the pus, are present in the blood. The term septicemia is indicated where intoxication is the more pronounced symptom and pyemia where pus formation and metastatic or secondary abscess formation are observed.

Symptoms.—The symptoms of both diseases include primarily a high fever (104° to 107° F.). Coupled with this there is disinclination to move, the animal is depressed and not cognizant of its surroundings. The pulse is rapid, small, and feeble, respiration increased, mucous membrane injected, swollen, and of a yellowish tinge. Appetite is lost and death follows in the case of septicemia in from two to four days. In pyemia the symptoms come on more slowly and are not so intense as in septicemia, while the course of the disease is longer, lasting from six days to four weeks. The mortality is not so great as in septicemia, but the period of convalescence is always long.

Lesions.—Septicemia is characterized by the destructive changes in the blood, which is chocolate color, noncoagulable, and swarms with bacteria. The lining membranes of the heart are studded with red spots, often running together to form a large hemorrhagic area. The lungs, liver, and kidneys may also show these hemorrhages. The spleen is enlarged and full of black blood. The cadaver decomposes very rapidly and in some cases forms great quantities of fetid gas. In pyemia, in addition to these lesions, there are abscesses formed in the various organs throughout the body. If the disease develops slowly a postmortem shows these abscesses to be the chief alterations. The pus content is usually greenish, stained with blood, and contains strings of fibrous tissue and necrosed matter.

Treatment.—Treatment is almost futile in advanced cases of either disease. Septicemia is usually fatal and pyemia frequently so. Prevention, and the immediate treatment of local infections, are the surest means of combating these diseases. For local treatment of wounds the usual antiseptics are indicated, such as 5 per cent creolin, or carbolic acid, or one one-thousandth bichloride of mercury solution. For pyemia, where the abscesses are near the skin, open them and treat antiseptically by injecting any of the previous mentioned germicides. General and heart stimulants are indicated, such as a drench containing digitalis 2 drams and alcohol 2 ounces. Quinine and calomel in repeated small doses of one-half dram each three times a day are sometimes beneficial. Camphor in the form of oil of camphor (camphor dissolved in 10 parts of sweet oil) is a good stimulant and has some antiseptic properties, which makes it a valuable drug in combating these diseases when given in doses of 2 drams three times daily.

HEMORRHAGIC SEPTICEMIA.

Hemorrhagic septicemia is a name applied to a highly fatal, infectious disease existing in various species of domestic and wild animals, due to a micro-organism having definite biological characters and possessing the properties of producing clearly defined and characteristic lesions.

This casual agent, *Bacterium bovisepticum,* belongs to the same group of cocco-bacilli as those causing chicken cholera, swine plague, and rabit septicemia, and may be described as an ovoid, nonmotile, polar staining bacterium with rounded ends 1/38,000 of an inch wide by 1/20,000 of an inch long, sometimes seen in pairs and sometimes in chains.

Various names have been applied to this disease, and though the causative agent and the distinctive lesions are well known it is more than likely that the affection is seldom recognized. It was described by Bollinger in 1878, and named Wild und Rinderseuche, from its having affected deer, wild boars, cattle, and horses in an epizootic which swept over Germany at that time. However, before this several epizootics of what was evidently the same disease had been well described, notably that which occurred in England in 1854. Since then it has occurred in epizootic and enzootic forms in many sections of Europe, Asia, Africa, and America. In this country the disease has been observed in Texas, Tennessee, New York, Minnesota, Pennsylvania, District of Columbia, South Dakota, and Wisconsin. Other names given to it are game and cattle disease, buffalo disease, barbone, pasteurellosis bovina, ghotwa, and infectious pneumoenteritis.

In earlier times it was evidently confounded with gloss anthrax, and even now it is probably mistaken in a great many instances for anthrax, blackleg, cornstalk disease, and cerebro-spinal meningitis.

The disease is essentially a septicemia, or blood poisoning, and the microbic invasion occurs from inoculation probably either through abrasions of the skin or by injury to the mucous membranes from coarse fodder, etc. Moore and Smith have found bacteria belonging to this group in the mouths and nasal cavities of healthy animals, including cattle; but these organisms proved to be nonpathogenic. As is well known, however, many pathogenic germs at times exist in a saprophytic state, and it is not hard to conceive how a microbe may cease such existence and assume parasitic or pathogenic properties when the surroundings are eminently favorable. This may be a connecting link in the etiology of sporadic outbreaks of the disease where every other hypothesis as to its genesis seems untenable. The disease seems to occur most frequently in swampy or mucky localities or in pastures receiving the overflow from infected fields. It is said to occur usually in the spring of the year, when the melting snows and rains bring to the surface the subterranean waters from rich soils containing nitrogenous materials in which the bacteria have been existing. In a great many instances there does not seem to be any plausible explanation for an outbreak of the disease and one can only surmise as to its origin.

Symptoms.—Three forms of the disease are recognized, based upon the distribution of the lesions—the superficial, or cutaneous, the pectoral, or thoracic, and the intestinal form. The latter is a usual accompaniment of the other two, and may be mild or severe. Naturally, the symptoms vary according to the violence of the attack and to the particular form of disease with which the animal is affected. In the superficial, or cutaneous, form the presence of a swollen tongue, throat, and dewlap, or even of the lower portion of the legs, gives us a clew to the trouble. An entire loss of appetite occurs, and in milch cows there is a diminution of the milk secretion. The temperature may be only slightly elevated, but it is usually very high. Salivation is set up due to the inflammation of the mouth and pharynx. Unsuccessful efforts at eating and swallowing are made. There may be difficulty in breathing, depending on the amount of involvement of the larynx, trachea, bronchi, or lungs. There may be a blood-stained discharge from the nostrils, and the mucous membrane of the same will often show symptoms as hemorrhages. The pulmonary form shows the same symptoms as croupous pneumonia with a frequent suffocative cough and oppressed breathing, or dyspnea. When the intestines are involved the patient strains to defecate, and passes shreds of intestinal mucus along with blood-stained feces. The urine may also be tinged with blood. Finally a severe diarrhea takes place, the animal becomes correspondingly weak, and death takes place in twenty-four to thirty-six hours. Cases may die in as short a period as six to eight hours, while in the pectoral form of the disease the animal may linger six or eight days. Cases have been reported which became chronic and in which death did not take place for a month or more. In some of the cases running an acute course, symptoms of toxemia are present; there is a lack of sensation of the skin, staggering gait, trembling, eyes fixed, neck at times bent to one side, and the eyes showing a wild expression. At times the animals appear as if in pain and look around at the flanks. In the pectoral form they may stand with the fore legs wide apart in evident effort to breathe more freely. Sometimes there is a champing of the jaws and a very free flow of glairy saliva dropping from the mouth. The prognosis is decidedly unfavorable and 80 to 90 per cent of the cases result fatally.

Burial of Carcasses of Cattle. B. A. I. 1902.

Lesions.—The characteristic lesions of hemorrhagic septicemia consist of hemorrhagic areas in the subcutaneous, subserous, and muscular tissues, the lymph glands, and the viscera; in fact, they are distributed more or less widely throughout the body and vary in size from a mere speck to the diameter of a half dollar or even larger. The superficial form presents itself first as a doughy tumefaction of the skin about the region of the throat, neck, dewlap, or legs, and which pits on pressure. This tumefaction consists essentially of a sero-gelatinous exudate into the subcutaneous and intermuscular tissues.

Bloody extravasations may take place in subcutaneous tissues in various localities, but they are usually seen about the lower portion of the neck. The mucous membranes and submucous tissues of the mouth, tongue, pharynx, and larynx become involved in the process and are greatly thickened, inflamed, and infiltrated with serum. The mucous membrane becomes reddish purple, and that of the nostrils may in addition show hemorrhagic spots on its surface. The lymphatic glands in this region are also swollen and infiltrated with bloody serum. The salivary glands are pale and dry. The pectoral type, though at times existing alone, may coexist with the cutaneous form. The inflammatory edema of the mouth extends to the mucous membrane of the trachea and bronchi, producing an extensive thickening and a yellowish infiltration. The lung shows interstitial thickening, due to the outpouring of serum into its meshes. It may become pneumonic.

The diaphragm, heart sac, and heart walls show numerous hemorrhagic points and larger bloody extravasations. Sometimes there is a serous pleurisy, with more or less fibrinous exudate. In the intestinal form the submucous and subperitoneal tissues show alterations from a few hemorrhagic spots to large bloody suffusions, or even gelatinous infiltrations. This latter is seen about the region of the pancreas and in the folds of the mesentery. There is a severe hemorrhagic inflammation of the intestines and a staining of the intestinal contents with blood. The muscular system throughout shows hemorrhagic areas. The abdominal viscera, liver, spleen, and kidneys often present hemorrhagic lesions.

Differential Diagnosis.—Anthrax, which presents superficial swellings, like hemorrhagic septicemia, may be distinguished from that affection on postmortem examination by the enlargement and engorgement of the spleen, the contents of which are soft and tarry. The blood of anthrax animals is very dark, and does not become light red on exposure to air, nor does it coagulate, while in hemorrhagic septicemia the blood is normal in appearance and coagulates. The detection of the anthrax bacillus in the blood would be final.

In blackleg the animals affected are usually under 2 years of age. The swellings are quite evident, and usually occur on the legs, above the knees or hocks, and are distended with gas, which crackles, or crepitates, when pressed upon. If one of these tumors be opened, a bloody serum will exude, and the contained gas gives off the odor of rancid butter. The internal hemorrhages are not general, although they may occur. A microscopic examination of the juices from the tumefaction will show the blackleg bacillus.

In cerebro-spinal meningitis the causative agent is unknown, but probably exists in the food. It may occur in any locality and at any season of the year. There are no local swellings, and cattle are not frequently affected.

Cornstalk disease may be differentiated from this affection from the fact that it always occurs after the cattle are turned into a cornstalk field, by its sudden onset, the absence of any characteristic symptoms or postmortem lesions, and the failure to find the causative agent in the blood.

In making a postmortem examination of animals affected with hemorrhagic septicemia, it would be well to examine the articular surfaces of the long bones, as it has been reported that they are frequently ulcerated. This should apply especially to those cases that have shown lameness.

Treatment.—Treatment is absolutely useless, so far as we know at present, and for all practical purposes prophylaxis alone should be relied upon. The same sanitary precautions, such as isolation, disinfection, and burial or burning of all dead carcasses, should be observed as for anthrax and other highly infectious diseases. Separate the apparently well animals from the sick by placing them in a separate, noninfected lot. Leave them here for a few days, and if any new cases develop change the well ones again. Thoroughly disinfect all the premises, barns, stalls, litter, and stable utensils.

VESICULAR ERUPTION OF THE GENITAL ORGANS.

This contagious disease is called coital exanthema or vesicular exanthema, and is more or less prevalent on the Continent. It has also been observed in the breeding districts of the United States. It is the subject of legislation in Germany, and governmental statistics are published annually concerning its distribution in the Empire. According to the reports from Hungary, 492 head of cattle were attacked during 1898, 587 in 1899, and 207 in 1900.

A similar or perhaps identical disease of horses has the same distribution and is transmissible from horses to cattle and vice versa.

The disease may be defined as a highly contagious eruption situated upon the external genital organs of both sexes and accompanied with little or no general disturbance of health. The contagion, the nature of which remains still unknown, is transmitted mainly during copulation. The bull may have the disease and convey it to all the cows with which he comes in contact; or he may become infected by one cow, and, although not showing the disease, he may transmit it for several days after to all other cows during copulation. Simple contact between one cow and another may convey the disease, or the sponges used in cleaning the diseased may carry the virus to the healthy. It has also been conveyed to healthy cows by these animals lying with their hind quarters against infected wooden troughs.

Symptoms.—The period elapsing between the infection and the appearance of symptoms is somewhat variable. It is usually given as three to six days. It may be briefer or much longer. In cows the mucous membrane of the vagina and the vulva become swollen, inflamed, very tender, and covered with dark-red spots. The secretion is very abundant and consists at first largely of serum and mucus resembling the white of an egg. Small vesicles then appear, which rapidly burst and are converted into excoriations or deeper ulcerations. The secretion becomes more purulent and is apt to dry in crusts about the root of the tail. The eruption is accompanied with much itching and difficulty in urinating. The walk may be stiff and awkward. In bulls the eruption is situated on the prepuce and the end of the penis, and consists of pimples, vesicles, and ulcers, as in cows. It is accompanied by a little purulent discharge from the prepuce, itching, and difficulty in urinating. In severe cases the inflammation and swelling may extend backward to the scrotum and forward upon the abdomen.

The disease lasts from one to four weeks and always terminates in recovery. The acute stage lasts only four or five days, while the complete healing of the inflammation is slow. The eruption is usually accompanied by very little general disturbance. If the pain and irritation are severe, there may be some slight loss of appetite and diminished milk secretion in cows. The disease rarely causes abortion. Chronic catarrh of the vagina and permanent sterility frequently follow as sequelæ.

Treatment need not be resorted to excepting in severe cases. The secretion and exudation should be washed off and a mild antiseptic applied, such as a 1 per cent solution of carbolic acid (1 ounce to 3 quarts of water) or 2 per cent solution of lysol or creolin in water. Care must be taken not to carry the disease from the sick to the well by sponges, etc., which have come in contact with the affected organs. These should be destroyed. To prevent the spread of the disease the infected animals should be kept isolated until they have recovered.

RABIES OF CATTLE.

Rabies is a disease pre-eminently affecting the canine race, although all warm-blooded animals, including man, are susceptible to the malady, which is always communicated through bites from a preceding case. It has required many years of patient scientific research to lead the ablest investigators to a clear comprehension of the cause, nature, and characteristics of this affection. It was known and described several centuries prior to the beginning of the Christian era, and from the earliest dawn of history the disease has been feared and dreaded. Its terrible manifestations have always been surrounded with an atmosphere of awe and mystery, and it is not surprising that myths, fallacies, and misconceptions in regard to it have been common and widely accepted. As the investigations by which we have come to a tolerably clear understanding of the facts concerning rabies have been comparatively recent and have appeared for the most part in scientific periodicals, fallacies in regard to the disease continue to have a strong hold upon the public mind. For instance, it is still a widely prevalent belief that if persons or animals are bitten by a dog they are liable to become rabid if the dog should contract the disease at any future time. There is no foundation for this impression, and it would be a great comfort to many people who are now and then bitten by animals if the fallacy of this idea were appreciated. All experience, both scientific and practical, goes to show that rabies is transmitted only by animals that are actually diseased at the time the bite is inflicted. Rabies is an infectious disease involving the nervous system and characterized by extreme excitability and other nervous disorders and always terminating in death. The contagion of this disease has never been isolated, but the fact that it is caused by a specific organism principally found in the nervous system is indisputable. For instance, if an emulsion of the brain of a rabid animal is filtered through a germ-proof filter, the filtrate will be harmless. This fact indicates that the infectious principle is not in solution, but is an organism withheld from the filtrate by the filter. This contagion can only be propagated in the body of an animal. It is transmitted naturally from one animal to another solely by bites, and the old idea of spontaneous appearance of the disease is absolutely fallacious. It may be produced artificially by inoculating susceptible animals with an emulsion of the brain or spinal cord, as well as the saliva, milk, and other secretions of the affected animal. The blood, on the contrary, seems to be free from the infectious principle. The saliva contains the virus, which, under natural conditions, is introduced into or under the skin on the tooth of the rabid animal. The disease is widespread, being found in many countries of Europe, Asia and Africa and in certain sections of the United States.

Owing to the rigid quarantine regulations enforced against dogs imported into Australia, that country remains absolutely free from the disease. Following the canine race, cattle seem to be the most frequently affected, probably because rabid dogs, next to their morbid desire to attack other members of their own race, have a better opportunity to bite grazing cattle than any other species of animal. The relative frequency of rabies in these two species of animal is indicated by the carefully compiled statistics of the German Empire, which show that 904 dogs and 223 cows died of rabies in 1898, while in 1899 there were 911 cases in dogs and 171 in cattle. The latter received bites most frequently on the hind legs and in the hips and about the lower jaw. These places are most accessible to dogs, owing to the habit of cattle to drive their tormentors away by lowering their heads and using their horns. Every animal bitten does not necessarily develop the disease, but the percentage of fatalities has been variously estimated and averages from 25 to 30 per cent of the bitten cattle. This, however, depends on the location and size of the wound, as well as the amount of hemorrhage produced, and various other conditions. In general, the nearer the bite is located to the central nervous system and the deeper the wound inflicted, the greater the danger of a fatal result. In cases where the hemorrhage resulting from the bite is profuse, there is a possibility that the virus will be washed out of the wound and thus obviate the danger of subsequent appearance of the disease.

The virus after being deposited in the wound remains latent for an extremely variable period of time, which also depends on the size and depth of the wound as well as its location and the amount of the virulent saliva introduced. Experiments have proved that the virus follows the course of the nerves to the spinal cord and along the latter to the brain before the symptoms appear. Gerlach having collected the statistics from 133 cases has found this time, known as the period of incubation, to vary from fourteen to two hundred and eighty-five days. The great majority of cases, however, contract the disease in one to three months after the bite has been inflicted.

Symptoms.—As in dogs, both furious and dumb rabies are met with, the former being more common in cattle. However, a sharp line of distinction can not be drawn between these two forms of the disease, as the furious form usually merges into the dumb, due to the paralysis which always appears prior to death. The typical cases of dumb rabies are those where the paralysis appears at the beginning of the attack and remains until the death of the animal. The disease first manifests itself by a loss of appetite and rumination and stopping of the secretion of milk, great restlessness, anxiety, manifestation of fear, and change in the disposition of the animal. This preliminary stage is followed in a day or two by the stage of excitation, or madness, which is indicated by increasing restlessness, loud roaring at times with a peculiar change in the sound of the voice, violent butting with the horns and pawing the ground with the feet, with an insane tendency to attack other animals, although the desire to bite is not so marked in cattle as in the canine race. A constant symptom is the increased secretion of saliva with a consequent frothing at the mouth, or the secretion may hang from the lips in long strings. Constipation is marked, and there is manifested a continual, although unsuccessful, desire to defecate. Spasms of the muscles in different parts of the body are also seen at intervals. About the fourth day the animal usually becomes quieter and the walk is stiff, unsteady, and swaying, showing that the final paralysis is coming on. This is called the paralytic stage. The loss of flesh is extremely rapid, and even during the short course of the disease the animal becomes exceedingly emaciated. The temperature is never elevated, it usually remaining about normal or even subnormal. Finally, there is complete paralysis of the hind quarters, the animal being unable to rise, and but for irregular convulsive movements lies in a comatose condition, and dies usually from the fourth to the sixth day after the appearance of the first symptom.

TRANSMISSION OF THE DISEASE BY MILK AND MEAT.

While the virus of rabies is most frequently found in the central nervous system and the salivary glands, it may also be found in other glands and secretions, including the mammary glands and the milk. That rabies may at times be excreted with the milk has been proved by Nocard, Perroncito, Bardach, and the writer. In these latter experiments the milk of a rabid bitch having a litter of puppies was inoculated intramuscularly into rabbits and guinea pigs, and produced typical rabies; but the puppies, removed from the mother when the first symptoms developed, were kept under observation for 18 months without developing the disease. The reason for these negative results in the puppies may be explained (1) by not having been bitten by the mother before she was removed, and (2) the absence of any abrasion in the alimentary tract through which the virus could have entered the circulation.

It is a generally accepted fact that rabies can not be transmitted to normal animals through food containing the virus of the disease unless lesions are present in the alimentary canal; but the conclusion that there is no danger to the consumer from the meat or milk of animals that are rabid is not tenable, since abrasions of the lips, mouth, and pharynx are all too frequent to permit of such risks. These products must therefore be considered as dangerous to health.

One case is on record where a baby in Cuba developed rabies from nursing its mother while the latter was in the early stages of hydrophobia. In this case, however, the virus in the milk may have entered the circulation through abrasions of the gums during teething. Similar cases have been reported in veterinary practice where the virus of rabies was observed to have been passed to the offspring through the mother's milk, but in these cases it is impossible to eliminate an obscure bite from the bitch or lesions of the gums during this early age. While it is not probable that cattle would be milked after the symptoms of rabies developed, it is nevertheless important to realize the danger of using such milk and the necessity for preventing calves from sucking such diseased cows.

All attempts to convey the disease to healthy dogs by feeding them upon meat from infected animals have given negative results. Nevertheless the meat of rabid animals must be considered as unfit for food, and the meat-inspection regulations enforced by the various countries having such inspection provide for the total condemnation of the carcasses of these animals.

Infection has occurred in man from making autopsies on rabid dogs, and it is likewise possible to result if inoculation occurs while handling the meat of rabid cattle, hogs, or sheep. Ostertag reports the case of a veterinary student at Copenhagen who infected a wound on his finger while making an autopsy on a dog dead of rabies and died of the disease. Another somewhat similar case occurred in a veterinary student at Dresden in consequence of an injury received while holding a post-mortem on a rabid dog.

Wyrsykowski, in an attempt to discover the reason for the fact that no illness followed the eating of the meat and even the brain of rabid animals, tested the action of the gastric juice upon infectious material in vitro. Twenty-one rabbits were inoculated with this artificially digested virus, but not one animal contracted the disease, while all the 17 check rabbits which were inoculated with undigested rabies virus developed the disease and died. It is evident, therefore, that the gastric juice has a pronounced deleterious effect upon the virus of rabies.

Anatomy.—If the animals which have succumbed to rabies be examined postmortem, very slight evidence of disease will be found in any of the organs, and, indeed, the absence of any specific lesions may be considered as characteristic. The blood is dark and imperfectly coagulated. The throat is frequently reddened, and there may be small spots of extravasated blood in the intestines. The stomachs are usually empty. In the spleen there may be hemorrhage enlargements (infarcts). The cadavers rapidly undergo decomposition.

Differential Diagnosis.—It is not an easy matter to decide definitely that a given animal has rabies, since the symptoms given above belong in part to a variety of other diseases, among which may be mentioned the excitement seen in young animals following close confinement, certain vegetable and mineral poisons, acute enteritis, and alterations of the central nervous system in cattle, the most common of which is tuberculosis of the brain and its covering membranes. However, the postmortem lesions should assist in making correct diagnosis. Tetanus may readily be differentiated from rabies by the persistence of muscular cramps, especially of the face and abdomen, which cause these muscles to become set and as hard as wood. In tetanus there is also an absence of a depraved appetite or of a wilful propensity to hurt other animals or to damage the surroundings. The cow remains quiet and the general muscular contraction gives the animal a rigid appearance. There is an absence of paralysis which marks the advanced stage of rabies. The dumb form of rabies in dogs is characterized by the paralysis and pendency of the lower jaw, while in tetanus the jaws are locked. This locking of the jaws in cattle renders the animal incapable of bellowing as in rabies. Finally, tetanus may be distinguished from rabies by the fact that the central nervous system does not contain the infectious principle, while in rabies the inoculation of test rabbits with the brain or cord of a rabid animal will produce the disease with characteristic symptoms after an interval of fifteen to twenty days. This period of incubation is much longer than in teta ius, since the inoculation of rabbits with tetanus cultures invariably results in death after a short period and usually within three days. The positive evidence that a rabid dog has been near cattle would greatly assist in making a decision in doubtful cases. The disease in dogs is pretty well recognized by most people, but in case a suspected dog is killed it is desirable to open the animal and examine the contents of the stomach. While food is absent, a variety of odd things may be present which the abnormally changed appetite of the rabid dog has induced it to swallow. Among such things may be straws, sticks, glass, rags, earth pieces of leather, and whatever the animal may have encountered small enough to be swallowed. This miscellaneous collection in the stomach of dogs, together with absence of food, is regarded by authorities as a very valuable sign, and may be made use of by laymen in case of doubt. In important cases, however, the head of the dog, cow, or other suspected animal should be removed and sent to the nearest biological laboratory, where a positive diagnosis can be made within thirty-six hours by the histological examination of the plexiform nerve ganglia, and within two or three weeks by the intra-cerebral inoculation of rabbits with an emulsion of the brain of the suspected animal.

Treatment.—This is useless after the first appearance of symptoms. When, however, a wound inflicted by a rabid animal can be discovered, it should be immediately cauterized or even completely extirpated, care being taken to cut entirely around the wound in the healthy tissues. For cauterizing the wound, fuming nitric acid, the hot iron, and 10 per cent solution of zinc chloride are the most efficacious. To afford an absolute protection, this should be done within a few moments after the bite has been inflicted, although even as late as a few hours it has been known to thwart the development of the disease.

Pasteur has originated and perfected a system of preventive inoculation against this disease which has greatly reduced the mortality in human subjects. Its application to animals, however, is more difficult, requiring considerable time and expense, and is therefore only economically applicable in cases where very valuable animals are bitten by dogs known to be mad. Sanitary regulations which seek to control effectively the disease by exterminating it among dogs are most likely to prove successful. The measures which are adopted to this end can not be discussed in this place, but it is a striking fact that where the muzzling of all dogs has been rigidly enforced, as in England and in certain German districts, the disease has been practically stamped out.

TUBERCULOSIS.

Tuberculosis is a widespread disease affecting animals and also man. Human beings and cattle are its chief victims, but there is no kind of animal that will not take it. Hogs and chickens are quite often affected; horses, sheep, and goats but seldom, while cattle are the most susceptible of all animals.

Nature of the Disease.—Tuberculosis is contagious, or catching. It spreads from cow to cow in a herd until most of them are affected. This may not attract much notice from the owner, as the disease is slow to develop and a cow may be affected with it for several months and sometimes years before any signs of ill health are to be seen.

This slow development is the chief reason for the great loss it causes to the farmer. He does not suspect its presence in his herd until perhaps a large number are diseased. If the disease developed rapidly and caused death in a few days, the owner would soon take steps to check its progress and protect the rest of his herd. Tuberculosis is slow and hidden in its course and thus arouses no suspicion until great damage is done.

History.—Where did tuberculosis come from? We do not know. History records it from the earliest times. Over a century ago its contagious nature was suspected and many facts were recorded to prove that it must be catching. Doctors differed about it and for a long time the question was hotly disputed. Finally it was settled by

Dr. Robert Koch, a distinguished German physician, who discovered the germ of the disease in the year 1882, and named it *Bacillus tuberculosis*. He proved by experiment that the disease is produced by these germs and without them the disease can not be produced. It is now universally admitted that tuberculosis is a contagious disease and may be transmitted from animal to man.

In America the disease was introduced with early importations of cattle and has been with us ever since. Modern methods of transportation by rail and water have spread the disease from one end of the continent to the other. No part of the country is entirely free from it, but it is more prevalent near the great centers of population than in the remoter parts.

Importance.—The importance of the disease must be estimated from two points of view, first, the loss it entails upon the cattle owner, and second, the danger of communication to human beings.

Consider first its effect upon the pocket of the owner of cattle, whether farmer, breeder, or dairyman. A serious percentage of the dairy cows of the continent are affected, and the disease is found in even a larger percentage of dairy herds. The disease is commoner in some regions than in others.

It is no uncommon thing to find as many as 70 or 80 per cent of the cows in a herd diseased. These animals will be in various stages of the disease, some recently infected showing no sign of ill health, others badly diseased, but outwardly appearing healthy, while a few are evidently breaking down and wasting away.

The loss to the owner is evident when a cow dies of the disease, or when an apparently healthy cow is slaughtered for beef and found so badly affected as to be unfit for food. The calves in such a herd do not long remain healthy. They catch the disease before they are many months old and are a source of loss instead of gain.

Although the disease is most frequently found in herds that are more or less closely confined, such as dairy herds and purebred cattle, other herds are by no means free from it. Even range cattle are sometimes affected, and the infection spreads in spite of the open-air life of the cattle.

Tuberculosis is common among hogs. The public abattoirs report that a serious percentage of all hogs inspected is found to be tuberculous. The aggregate of these losses among cattle and hogs is enormous, amounting to millions of dollars every year, besides materially decreasing the food supply of the country.

Turning to the other aspect of the case, the danger of infection of human beings with tuberculosis from cattle, we have only to consider a few facts to realize its vital importance to every community.

Milk is the staple food of infants and young children and is usually taken in the raw state. If this milk is from a tuberculous cow, it may contain millions of living tubercle germs. Young children fed on such milk often contract the disease, and it is a frequent cause of death among them.

Meat from tuberculous cattle is not so likely to convey the infection, for several reasons. It does not so frequently contain the germs, cooking destroys those that may be present, and, lastly, meat is not consumed by very young children.

Symptoms.—Before describing the symptoms or signs by which tuberculosis is recognized or suspected in a living animal it is well to state that there is no symptom that can be relied on with certainty. Any of the symptoms may sometimes be caused by some other disease, and not one of them is characteristic of tuberculosis alone.

Many of the symptoms that are relied on by the human physician in reaching his opinion are not available in examining cattle. The thickness of the skin and chest wall, for instance, makes it difficult to detect a diseased condition of their lungs by listening to the sounds made in breathing, whereas this is comparatively easy in human beings.

It must also be clearly remembered that cattle may be very badly diseased and yet show no symptoms of ill health. They may be fat and sleek, looking the picture of health, while their lungs and other organs are full of tubercles. Such cases can only be detected by the tuberculin test.

As tuberculosis may attack almost any organ of the body, we may have in each case the symptoms connected with the part affected as well as those affecting the general state of the body as a whole. We will take up in detail each of the more important symptoms suggestive of the disease:

Unthriftiness.—The animal is not doing as well as it should for the care and feed it is getting. Its coat is rough and its skin has lost its suppleness and feels harsh and thick.

Loss of Flesh.—Along with the unthriftiness is noticed a gradual loss of flesh; the animal gets thinner from week to week. It appears to be pining away, and such cows have been known to dairymen for a long time under the name of piners or wasters. After a time they are reduced almost to skin and bone.

Cough.—This symptom is only present when the disease is attacking the lungs or some part of the breathing organs. It is not a loud, sonorous cough, but rather a subdued and infrequent one, and may be heard only at such times as when the stable is first opened in the morning or when the animal is driven. At a later stage of the disease it may be heard at any time of the day. Cows do not usually appear to cough up anything. This is because they do not spit. Most of the material coughed up from the lungs is swallowed, but many tuberculosis germs escape from the mouth in the form of spray or are discharged from the nose.

Enlarged Glands.—Enlargements in the region of the throat, especially when they cause difficulty in breathing, are very apt to be due to tuberculosis.

Loss of Appetite.—This symptom is not seen until the later stages of the disease, when the animal is evidently wasting.

Bloating.—Sometimes the diseased glands in the chest prevent the usual passage of gas from the paunch to the mouth by pressing on the gullet. In this case the cow suffers from bloating, and the paunch is often greatly distended with gas.   This, however, is not a very frequent symptom.

Diarrhea.—Looseness of the bowels or scouring is seen in cattle affected with the disease in the bowels.   This kind of scouring can not be cured by any known treatment.

Hard Lumps on the Udder.—When tuberculosis attacks the udder no change can be detected at first, but after a time hard lumps can be felt in some parts of the organ after it is milked out.   Milk from such an udder must not be used, as it is almost certain to be teeming with germs of the disease.

Post-mortem Appearances.—When the carcass of a cow affected with tuberculosis is opened the disease may be found in any part of the body.   Lumps (tubercles) may be present in the substance of an organ such as the lung or liver, or they may be growing on the surface.   These lumps may be so small as to be scarcely noticeable, or they may be as large as the closed fist, or even larger.   If one of the lumps is cut open, the inside is yellowish and grits on the knife like sand, or else is of a cheesy nature, soft and creamy, or hard and dry.

The lung is a favorite place for tubercles, and should always be examined.   Lymph glands are often the seat of tuberculous changes.   When healthy a lymph gland is a little rounded body not much larger than a good-sized bean, the largest only the size of one's thumb.   They are found all through the body, and when healthy are so small as to attract very little attention.   Tuberculosis may cause them to grow to an enormous size, sometimes as large as a child's head.   In this condition they are similar to the tuberculous lumps already described.   Those lying between the lungs and in the throat are the most frequently affected.

Tubercles may be found in any part of the body—glands, lungs, liver, bowels, kidneys, womb, udder, and even bones.   The muscles and skin are seldom affected.

The Tubercle Bacillus.—The germ of the disease, the tubercle bacillus, is a tiny, slender, rod-shaped body.   Several thousands of them placed end to end would be needed to measure an inch, so that they are quite invisible to the naked eye.   A powerful microscope is needed to see them.

Once the bacillus has gained lodgment inside the body of an animal, it begins to grow and multiply.   It gets longer, and when full grown divides crosswise, making two out of one.   Each of these goes through the same process, the two become four, the four eight, the eight sixteen, and so on indefinitely.

This multiplication takes place quite rapidly when conditions are favorable, a few hours only being required for the birth of each generation.   Nature, however, does not permit this process to continue long without offering some resistance.   The forces of the body are aroused to action and a battle begins between the tissues of the body and the army of the invaders.

The first line of defense is composed of the white cells of the blood, which hurry to the scene of action and endeavor to destroy the invaders by eating them up.   Sometimes they are successful and the bacilli are destroyed, the infection checked. Often they fail in their object and are themselves destroyed and the multiplication of the germs continues.

The second line of defense is formed by the cells of the tissue invaded by the germs. These cells arrange themselves in a circle around the germs and try to form a living wall between them and the rest of the body. This barrier gradually becomes thicker and thicker and forms a little hard lump or tubercle from which the disease gets its name. If this wall is complete and successfully imprisons the bacilli, these gradually die and the disease in that particular spot is arrested.

Frequently, however, both these safeguards are overcome. The germs break through the barriers and are carried in the blood stream or lymph channels to other parts of the body. New points of attack are selected and the process begins again but with less chance on the side of the animal. As the tubercles increase in number the power of the body to grapple with them becomes less and less, and gradually the animal falls a prey to the disease.

The tubercle bacillus does not multiply outside the body of an animal. It can live for a long time in favorable surroundings, such as dark and dirty stables. Sunlight soon destroys it. Freezing does not hurt it, but it can only stand a moderate amount of heat. Exposure to 149° F. for 20 minutes kills it. Protected by a layer of dried mucus, such as is coughed up from the lungs, it withstands drying, light, and ordinary disinfectants, but is readily killed by steam or boiling water.

How the Disease Spreads.—Sooner or later the tuberculous cow begins to give off the germs of the disease. The germs escape by the mouth and nose, the bowels, in the milk, and in discharges from the genital organs. When the germs are being given off in any of these ways, the disease is known as open tuberculosis.

Germs discharged from the mouth and nose are coughed up from the lungs and are sprayed over the food in front of the cow or are carried in the air for a time until they fall to the ground. Cows in adjoining stalls may take in these germs in the air they breathe or in the food they eat and so contract the disease.

Germs discharged from the bowels are mixed with the manure, and may infect cattle and hogs that are allowed to pick over the dung heap. The practice of having hogs and cattle together in the same yard is sure to result in the infection of the hogs if any of the cattle are affected. The germs in the manure come from matter that is coughed up and swallowed, and in some cases from tuberculosis in the bowels themselves. Manure containing tubercle germs may easily infect the milk. Particles of dried manure may fall into the milk pail from the skin of a dirty cow or be accidentally flicked off from the tail and fall into the milk. Straining the milk afterwards only removes the larger particles. The smaller ones, including the germs, remain in the milk.

When the udder is tuberculous the milk contains the germs in vast numbers. Such milk may look and taste perfectly good, but readily transmits the disease to young animals. It is very dangerous to children. Hogs and calves are very readily infected by it.

How a Herd Is Infected.—Tuberculosis may be introduced into a healthy herd in a number of ways.

1. By the purchase of a bull or other animal that is infected with the disease. This animal may be apparently healthy at the time of purchase, but if it contains the germs, the disease may develop and spread to other cattle. New animals should only be bought from a herd that is known to be healthy.

2. By feeding calves with milk, buttermilk, or whey that has come from tuberculous cows. A farmer may have a healthy herd, but if he brings home skim milk from a creamery and feeds it to his calves he may give them the disease. Such milk should be rendered safe by boiling or pasteurizing it.

3. By showing cattle at fairs and exhibitions where no proper care is taken to keep out diseased stock or to disinfect the stables.

4. By shipping animals in cars that have not been disinfected, as these may have recently carried diseased cattle.

5. By allowing cattle to graze with diseased ones, or to come in contact with them over fences.

The Tuberculin Test.—Tuberculosis develops so slowly that in many cases it is months and sometimes years before any symptoms are shown. During this period the infected animals can not be distinguished from the healthy in any ordinary way. There is a test, however, which does no harm to the healthy yet detects the diseased practically without fail. This is known as the tuberculin test, because the substance used in making it is called tuberculin.

What Is Tuberculin?—Tuberculin is a fluid containing the products of the tubercle germ without the germs themselves. As it contains no living germs, it can not convey the disease. Great skill is required in its preparation. A special fluid (or culture medium) is prepared and the tubercle bacilli planted in it, great care being taken to keep all other germs out. The fluid is then placed in a special kind of incubator and kept at the temperature of the animal body. Under these conditions the germs grow and multiply. Gradually the fluid becomes filled with the products of the germs. When the right point is reached the fluid is heated sufficiently to kill the germs, which are then strained out. The remaining fluid is tuberculin.

Tuberculin does not harm healthy cattle, even in large doses, but on diseased animals it produces a marked effect. This is shown by a feverish attack which comes on about 8 to 12 hours after the tuberculin is administered, lasts a few hours, and then subsides. This temporary fever is called the reaction, and animals which show it are called reactors. The value of the test lies in the fact that diseased animals react, while healthy ones do not.

Reliability of the Test.—The tuberculin test in the hands of a competent and experienced man is much more accurate than any other method of detecting tuberculosis. The records of large numbers of tests made by Government officials show that with certain precautions it is accurate in 98 per cent of the reactions obtained. This gives a margin of a possible 2 per cent of error, and this small number may be still further lessened by care in making the test. For practical purposes any animal that reacts must be considered tuberculous.

Limitations of the Test.—The test should not be applied to cows that have just calved or are about to calve, as the temperature at this time is apt to vary considerably from the normal. For this same reason it should not be applied to any animal that is in a feverish condition from any cause.

The test fails to detect the presence of the disease in the animal that is very recently infected. The disease has to make a little progress before the test reveals its presence, and in the beginning of each case there is a period between the entrance of the germs into the body and the time when they have multiplied sufficiently for the test to reveal their presence. This is called the period of incubation and lasts from ten days to two months.

When the disease is far advanced and the animal is wasting, the test sometimes fails to detect it. This is not of much practical importance, as such cases can generally be recognized without the aid of tuberculin.

Protective Inoculation.—For some years efforts have been made to discover a method of rendering cattle immune to the disease in such a way as men are protected from smallpox by vaccination. Up to the present these efforts have been only partially successful, and until the methods in use have been perfected by further investigations they can not be recommended as of practical use in the suppression of the disease.

Suppression of the Disease.—The first step in getting rid of the disease is to find out how many of the herd are affected by it. This is done by applying the tuberculin test. This will show a larger or smaller number of the herd to be affected, and the proper course to pursue will depend largely upon the proportion of the reactors in it.

Suppose that only a few cattle react, say 15 out of 100, or in that proportion. In this case the reactors are first carefully examined, and if any of them show symptoms of the disease by coughing, loss of condition, or any other of the signs by which the disease is recognized without the test, such animals should be slaughtered.

The other reactors should then be entirely separated from the healthy cattle. If possible they should be put in a separate building, but if this can not be done a tight partition should be built between the diseased and the healthy cattle and separate ventilation provided. The person who attends to the reactors should not go near the healthy animals, as he may carry the infection to them on his hands, clothes, or boots. For the same reason the feeding and watering must be done with separate utensils.

When at pasture the reactors must not be put into a field where they can reach across a fence to healthy cattle. Whenever a calf is born among the reactors it should be immediately separated from its mother and brought up by hand or on a healthy cow. The calf is usually born healthy, but would soon catch the disease from its mother if allowed to remain with her,

The milk of reacting cows may be used if it is first boiled or heated to a point sufficient to kill the germs. This heating to a point less than boiling is called pasteurizing, and is safe provided all the milk reaches the required degree of heat and is kept there sufficiently long. For this it is necessary to keep the milk for 20 minutes at 149° F. or for 5 minutes at 176° F.

This system of dealing with tuberculosis in a herd was planned by Prof. Bang, of Denmark, and has been very successfully followed in that country for some years. It has the advantage of allowing the reactors to be made use of while a sound herd is being built up. Under this system the sound herd increases in numbers as healthy calves are added to it, while the diseased herd becomes smaller as the reactors die off or are killed as open cases of tuberculosis. Finally a point is reached where only a very few reactors remain, and the owner will then find it to his interest to kill them rather than have the trouble of keeping them isolated.

Some time is required for the successful carrying out of the Bang system, and the owner must be prepared to follow it steadily and faithfully for the whole time that is needed, which may be several years. During this time the healthy herd must be tested every six months and any reactors removed to the diseased herd. At the same time a sharp lookout must be kept for animals showing definite symptoms of the disease. These should be destroyed promptly, as they are the most dangerous source of infection.

Dealing With a Badly Infected Herd.—Where the test shows more than half the number diseased, a somewhat different plan is required than the Bang system. This herd is so badly affected that the non-reactors can not safely be considered healthy. Many of them are sure to have been infected with the disease quite recently, so that the test fails to detect it. These will react at the next test, and in the meantime may develop the disease so rapidly as to infect others. This will repeat the difficulty occurring at the first test, and it would be a long and tedious process of weeding before even a small but perfectly healthy herd could be established.

For these reasons it is better to treat such a herd as if it were entirely diseased and to begin with the newborn calves to build up a healthy herd. The method from this point is exactly the same as the Bang system, except that as there are no healthy cows to act as foster mothers the calves must be raised on pasteurized milk. At 6 months old the calves are tested and reactors are transferred to the other herd. This plan was devised by a German veterinary surgeon named Ostertag, and is known as the Ostertag system. It is very successful when carefully carried out.

While getting rid of the disease by whatever system may be adopted, an animal should never be bought for the healthy herd unless known to be healthy. The tuberculin test should be applied, and if possible the animal should be selected from a herd that is known to be free from tuberculosis. New purchases should be isolated or kept apart from the healthy herd, and if possible from each other for at least three months, when they should be retested to make sure they are healthy before putting them with other cattle.

Sanitation.—Dark, dirty, crowded stables are favorable to tuberculosis. Under these conditions the disease spreads rapidly and is only kept out with difficulty. Clean, airy, well-lighted stables, on the other hand, are unfavorable to the development of the disease. If brought into such a stable it does not spread so rapidly and is not so difficult to get rid of as in the first case. A well-built, sanitary stable need not be made of expensive material or of elaborate design, but should have plenty of light, air, and drainage.

Light is very important. Direct sunlight is a great destroyer of germ life. Tubercle bacilli soon die if exposed to sunlight. It is a disinfectant, always ready to work without cost. Sunlight is also necessary to the health of animals. Men deprived of it for any length of time, as prisoners in jail, become pale and lose the appearance of health. Cattle that are constantly confined in dark stables become lowered in vitality and are ready to catch any disease with which they come in contact. For these reasons the cow stables should have plenty of windows, on two or more sides, if possible, so that the sunlight can reach every part of the interior some part of the day.

Pure air is also very important. In badly ventilated stables the air is breathed over and over again until it becomes more or less poisonous. Animals kept in such conditions become gradually reduced in vitality. This change may not be noticeable to the observer, but becomes apparent if the animal is exposed to disease. It easily contracts disease and does not recover from it readily.

Stables should therefore have plenty of air space for each animal. This requires the ceiling to be high, the stalls roomy, and the passages wide. In addition to this ample air space some way of changing the air in a stable must be provided. This is done by means of suitable openings in the walls and roof and comprises the system of ventilation.

Ventilation to be successful must provide for two things—first, the removal of the foul air from the inside, and, second, the bringing in of fresh air from outside the building. No system is good that fails to accomplish these objects without causing unnecessary drafts.

The usual way is to bring in fresh air through open windows, and in cold weather through ventilating shafts, which may be concealed in the walls or beneath the floor. The foul air is removed by open windows and by ventilating shafts from the ceiling to the roof, where they are usually protected by a hood. When both inlets and outlets are proportioned to the size of the building there should be a constant circulation of air and no sensation of closeness should be perceptible in the stable.

Drainage removes the liquid refuse from the stable by suitable gutters and drains. It can not do this unless the floor is water-tight, and concrete flooring is therefore recommended. Urine leaking through cracks in the floor until the soil beneath is saturated is a frequent source of foul odors and unhealthy stables.

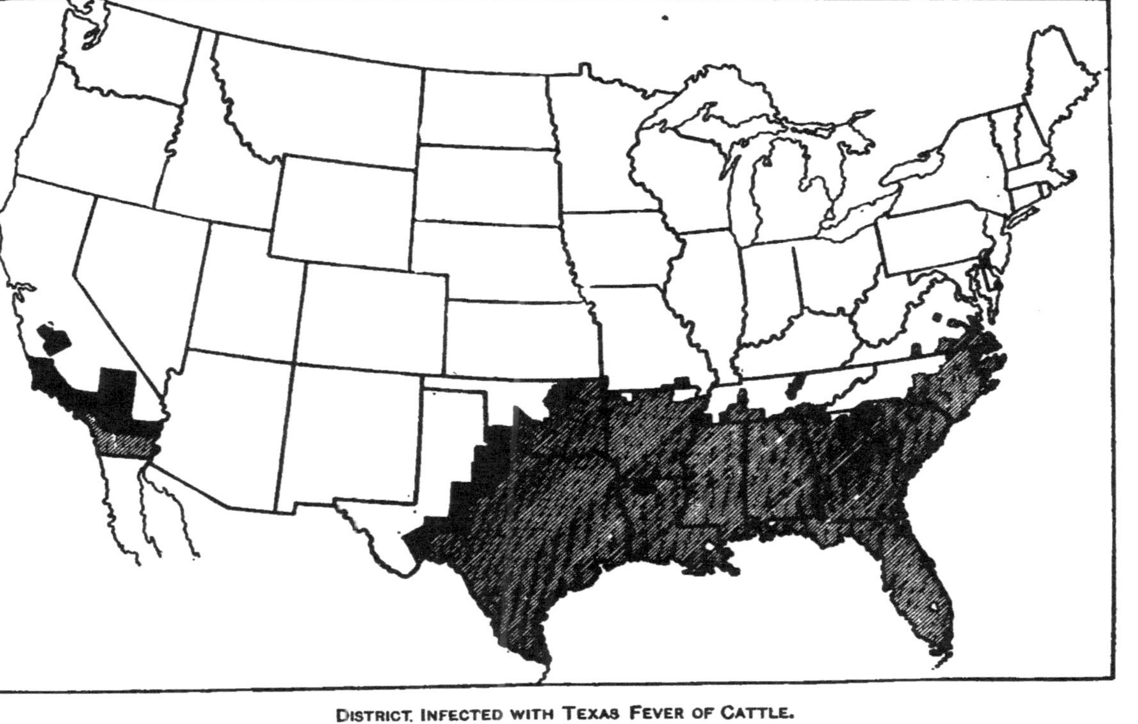

DISTRICT. INFECTED WITH TEXAS FEVER OF CATTLE.

Shaded and solid black portions show area quarantined. Cattle may be shipped interstate from the shaded area only for immediate slaughter. In the solid black area the infection is slight, and cattle officially inspected and found free from infection may be shipped interstate therefrom for purposes other than immediate slaughter. The quarantined area is subject to change at any time.

Cleanliness.—Since the manure of tuberculous cattle often contains living tubercle germs in vast numbers, the importance of keeping it well cleaned out of the stable is readily seen. Such manure is not only dangerous to other cattle in the stable, but may be the means of conveying the disease to children. Often cows are seen with their flanks incrusted with dry dung. Parts often break off while the cow is milked, and some of it is likely to fall into the milk pail. The larger lumps are strained out, but the smaller particles remain, and also the tubercle germs, which are small enough to pass through any strainer. These stay in the milk and make it a fruitful cause of the disease in the young.

Stables should be cleaned out often and the manure put where it can not be picked over by hogs or cattle. These animals are easily infected in that way. Cleanliness also includes keeping the walls and ceilings free from dirt, dust, and cobwebs. These are all good resting places for disease germs.

Whitewashing the interior of the stable at least twice a year is a great aid to cleanliness, and also has a distinct effect in destroying disease germs. In many municipalities dairy stables are required to be whitewashed at regular intervals, and it is a practice that should be universal.

VACCINATION OF CATTLE AGAINST TUBERCULOSIS.

The heavy annual losses which are caused by the ravages of tuberculosis among domesticated animals have been appreciated by the inhabitants of infected countries for many years. Owing to this realization of the extent of the havoc wrought by this insidious disease, earnest thought and study have been devoted by scientific forces in all civilized countries to the question of its eradication.

It was known from the first that the fight against tuberculosis among cattle would be a prolonged one because of the hidden manner in which the disease makes its attack, but when the suggestion was made that cattle might be safely and completely immunized against the disease the advantages which might arise from this method of procedure became at once apparent. It is obvious that if the young animals of an infected herd or locality can be thoroughly protected from tubercular infection the root of the matter has been reached, and it is then only a question of time when all the remaining animals can be disposed of and the premises can be cleaned and disinfected and kept free from tuberculosis.

An appreciation of the advantages accruing from immunization in our tuberculous herds led the Bureau of Animal Industry to inaugurate the tests here recorded. It was clearly seen that it was most desirable to devise some method whereby cattle could be immunized rapidly and without danger to themselves or their attendants. Therefore a number of the most promising methods of applying the immunizing agent have been tried, and while none of them have proved perfect, some have been more or less efficacious in enhancing the powers of resistance of the animals treated.

REVIEW OF RECENT LITERATURE.

At the Ninth International Congress of Veterinary Medicine, held at The Hague in September, 1909, the subject of immunization against tuberculosis received most interested attention, and the papers which dealt with this question were actively discussed. Among the opinions which were expressed during this discussion we quote from Dr. A. Eber, of Leipsic; Dr. J. F. Heymanns, of Ghent; Dr. Klimmer, of Dresden; Dr. Vallée, of Alfort; and Dr. Arloing, of Lyon.

Dr. Eber stated that the following conclusions had been reached by him after careful study of the entire question and after observing the results of numerous preventive inoculations:

The receptivity of young cattle to experimental infection by virulent tubercle bacilli may be materially diminished by previous inoculation with the Koch bacillus, even of varied origin and virulence. The immunity thus conferred is not absolute. The immunized cattle will succumb from the effects of a sufficiently heavy dose of tuberculous virus.

The increase of resistance is not complete for some time (at least three months) after inoculation, and has entirely disappeared at the end of the first or second year. The degree and duration of the experimental immunity are influenced by the individual resistance, and up to a certain point by the quality of the vaccine used.

No experimental method permits one to foresee the manner in which the vaccinated animals will comport themselves toward natural or enzootic contagion. Practice alone must decide the value of immunization in the struggle against bovine tuberculosis. Tuberculin does not positively disclose the existence of tuberculous centers upon animals previously treated by injections of living tubercle bacilli. Science has not yet granted us a method of inoculation which permits effective struggle against tuberculosis in regions seriously infected.

The new researches simply shed a light upon preventive inoculation when combined with other prophylactic measures (killing animals affected with open tuberculosis, raising the calves on sterilized milk, plowing pastures) during the struggle against tuberculosis.

In practice one prefers methods of immunization which permit annual reinoculation. Nevertheless, more exact researches must be instituted for the purpose of determining if annual preventive inoculation is sufficient in every case to confer satisfactory immunity.

It is of great importance for the future to study further the influence of the mode of inoculation (intravenous, subcutaneous, digestive) upon the quality and duration of the immunity acquired, keeping constantly in mind at the same time the various doors of entrance of natural infection (digestive or respiratory).

Dr. Heymanns limited his report to a discussion of the method which he discovered, and which consists in inserting into the animal vaccinated the unattenuated tubercle bacilli inclosed within a dialyzing membrane.

Healthy animals thus vaccinated offer greater resistance to infection, whether by inoculation or stabling, than the checks. Although the duration and the degree of immunity are limited, the results obtained during four years upon more than 10,000 subjects have been most encouraging.

In practicing annually tuberculination and vaccination of all the cattle in contaminated stables without separating the tuberculous from the nontuberculous and without heating the milk, 86 per cent of the tuberculous centers have been practically wiped out after three or four years without the appearance of any serious trouble during the experiment. Upon stables more seriously contaminated Heymanns recognizes the fact that simple vaccination and tuberculination are ineffective, because the healthy cattle reinfect themselves in proportion to the intensity of the contagion. Upon such farms, in addition to vaccination, appropriate prophylaxis must be imposed.

The tuberculous cattle vaccinated and tested with tuberculin annually react less and less to the tuberculin, and by the third application of the tuberculin test 50 to 60 per cent of them fail to show any thermic elevation whatever.

The results of more than 1,000 autopsies upon vaccinated cattle indicate that in general healthy cattle that have been vaccinated have remained immune to tuberculosis and that the tuberculous animals, having ceased to react to tuberculin, present an arrested tuberculosis, even a regression, but the total absence of tuberculous lesions is exceptional.

In conclusion, Heymanns states that his antituberculous vaccination is a method practical and efficacious and, taken together with prophylactic measures, forms a valuable base in the struggle against tuberculosis, permitting one to struggle victoriously against this foe of our stables and this danger of infection to man.

Dr. Klimmer has examined the following methods of vaccination: First, the bovo-vaccination of Von Behring; second, the vaccination with tauruman of Koch and Schutz; third, the method of Heymanns; and fourth, the method of Klimmer.

The method of Klimmer consists in vaccinating with attenuated human tubercle bacilli. The nontuberculous animals are vaccinated twice during the first year, and those that are tuberculous are vaccinated every three months. The following year all the animals are vaccinated but once.

The preventive methods of Von Behring and of Koch and Schutz have proven practically inefficient. The reason is found in the short duration of the immunity which they produce and in the impossibility, while following sanitary regulations, of revaccinating either with bovo-vaccine or the tauruman. Klimmer claims that it is not possible at this date to estimate the curative value of the method devised by Heymanns.

The method of Klimmer has not yet been sufficiently tested. Nevertheless, out of 43 vaccinated animals which had been exposed, some of them during many years, to natural tuberculous contagion, not a single one had developed tuberculosis up to the time of his report. Tuberculous young cattle have been vaccinated and from one to three years later have been killed, when autopsy has shown that the progress of the disease has been arrested, the tuberculous centers have become encapsulated and frequently calcified, and that there has been no formation of new tuberculous centers.

Dr. Vallée believes that we must recognize that, in spite of the enormous benefits realized on all sides, none of the proposed methods of vaccination has yet furnished definite results. He states:

1. Nevertheless, the inoculation of cattle by any method with virulent human tubercle bacilli confers an appreciable resistance against various methods of experimental infection and also against natural contagion.

2. The resistance conferred is directly proportional to the quantity and virulence of the bacilli injected, but however great their value, the immunity conferred by them does not persist longer than 12 to 18 months.

3. The introduction of living bacilli as a vaccine contaminates the entire organism. This peculiarity necessitates a special guard over the animals immunized, should they be sent to slaughter during the six months which follow the last vaccination.

4. Whatever the mode chosen for introducing the vaccine, the resistance conferred is insufficient to assure the complete resorption of the bacilli inoculated for prolonging immunity.

5. The resistance to infection by the digestive tube of the animal vaccinated by that method is incomparably superior to that acquired by animals by the intravenous method, because it permits the organism to obtain complete resorption of the virulent material inoculated. Considering the frequency of infection through the digestive canal in cattle, the application of vaccinating material through the mouth appears preferable to every other method.

6. Vaccination by the digestive method can not be made entirely free from danger of infection if one uses virulent bacilli of the bovine type. The use of bacilli of the human type of slight virulence is, therefore, preferable, as these furnish results comparatively equal to those of the bovine type.

7. Vaccination by way of the mouth is not easily obtained except upon very young subjects.

8. Vaccination by way of the mouth does not place the animals entirely beyond danger of infection with tuberculosis. It permits them to resist for more than a year contact with cattle which present open lesions of tuberculosis and, following this, present no lesions beyond insignificant tubercular nodules in the various glands. On this account it merits systematic study and further practical application.

9. The resistance conferred by subcutaneous methods is inferior to that obtained by way of the circulation.

10. Vaccination by the use of killed bacilli has given results inferior to those obtained with living and virulent organisms.

11. No definite conclusion can yet be actually formulated in regard to the various methods of immunization under discussion, but their systematic application will permit a determination of their real practical value.

The method of immunization proposed by Arloing does not exactly resemble any of the other systems which are at present in use.

Most of these latter methods depend on the employment of attenuated tubercle bacilli, but the vaccines employed by Arloing are not composed of bacilli modified specially in any case either by heat or antiseptics or by a passage through the organisms of cold-blooded or other animals. On the contrary, his vaccine contains living bacilli of bovine origin profoundly modified in their tubercle-producing power by a long series of cultures in the depth of glycerinated bouillon. The modifications which they have taken on are henceforth fixed and of such a kind that these bacilli form races indefinitely transmissible. These races, comparable to the antianthrax vaccines of Pasteur, can no longer cause tuberculosis of the viscera and glands under the conditions where they are recommended to be employed. Being without danger to the monkey, Arloing considers that they are also without danger to man. By their characters these vaccines are somewhat similar to the virulent vaccines of Prof. Klimmer, of Dresden. They can not cause any fatal infection in the ox, which is contrary to the bovovaccine of Von Behring and the tauruman of Koch and Schütz, since these may be fatal to from 7 to 8 out of every 1,000 subjects vaccinated.

Arloing concludes by stating that the phase of experimental researches in tuberculosis vaccination is not closed, and it is to be hoped that by perseverance in laboratory studies the methods will be perfected, and we will know better the conditions which follow and those which guarantee success. But such as they are to-day, it would be negligent not to profit by the results acquired to try and restrain the ravages of bovine tuberculosis by associating vaccination with ordinary prophylactic measures, as one does for other contagious maladies.

As a result of these various papers and the discussions which they elicited, the following resolutions were adopted by the Ninth International Congress held at The Hague in 1909:

1. At the present time there is no vaccination which in itself is sufficient to combat in an efficient manner bovine tuberculosis in heavily infected herds.

2. In how far it is possible to bring about a more successful issue of the difficult struggle against bovine tuberculosis by a combination of vaccination with prophylactic and hygienic measures must be demonstrated by new practical experiments.

3. The congress urgently requests the Governments to grant the means for extensive experiments to examine the methods of vaccination against bovine tuberculosis under the different conditions of agricultural practice.

THE BUREAU EXPERIMENTS.

Probably no methods for the immunization of cattle against tuberculosis have been more widely discussed or have given better results than those known as Pearson's and Von Behring's. The two are practically alike, and consist of the intravenous injection of living cultures of human tubercle bacilli of a virulence too low to cause a progressive tuberculosis in cattle. The tubercle bacilli are grown in artificial cultures, and in a very finely subdivided condition, suspended in fluid in definitely known quantities, are injected into a vein of the animal to be protected. The methods of bovo-vaccination of Pearson and Von Behring were both tested, with what results will follow later.

In addition to studying these methods, attempts were made to cause immunity by subcutaneous injections of tubercle bacilli of different degrees of virulence as well as by the transfusion of blood from artificially immunized to susceptible animals.

Finally, a test was made of what is known as Heymanns's capsule method of protective treatment, for the efficiency of which the discoverer, after applying it to a large number of animals in his own country, makes very strong claims.

TEST ACCORDING TO VON BEHRING'S METHOD.

On June 2, 1906, the first nine calves and on June 12 the tenth calf in the following list were given each an intrajugular injection of 3 cubic centimeters of a suspension of tubercle bacilli of the human type. The tubercle bacilli used to make the suspension were from what was known as Case 30 and each cubic centimeter of the suspension was equal to 0.0013 gram of tubercle bacilli:

Bull calf No. 427, about 2 to $2\frac{1}{2}$ months old; bull calf No. 429, about 2 to $2\frac{1}{2}$ months old; bull calf No. 431, about 2 to $2\frac{1}{2}$ months old; heifer calf No. 432, about $2\frac{1}{2}$ to 3 months old; heifer calf No. 435, about 2 to $2\frac{1}{2}$ months old; heifer calf No. 436, about 2 to $2\frac{1}{2}$ months old; bull calf No. 438, about 2 to $2\frac{1}{2}$ months old; bull calf No. 439, about $2\frac{1}{2}$ to 3 months old; bull calf No. 441, about 2 to $2\frac{1}{2}$ months old; bull calf No. 444, about 3 to $3\frac{1}{2}$ months old.

The ages of the calves as above given refer to the date on which the injections were made. With the exception of a subsequent brief elevation of temperature and the development of a small tumor in the skin over the jugular at the point of injection in several of the calves, the injections were followed by no marked adverse conditions.

On September 7, 1906, each of the 10 calves was given a second intrajugular injection of tubercle bacilli prepared from culture Case 30. The suspension used for the second injection, of which the dose was 3 c. c., represented 0.02 gram of tubercle bacilli per cubic centimeter.

The second injection was followed by a more marked elevation of temperature than the first, which may, in part at least, be attributed to the mechanically irritant action of the injected tubercle bacilli in the fine pulmonary capillaries.

Of the 10 calves, 1 (No. 444) was killed and examined post-mortem without being exposed to tuberculosis to determine what changes had been caused by the injections of tubercle bacilli it had received. The remaining 9 were exposed to a tuberculous environment, as follows:

Nos. 427 and 432, October 30, 1906; Nos. 429 and 435, February 27, 1907; Nos. 431 and 436, April 25, 1907; Nos. 438 and 441, July 25, 1907; No. 439, November 8, 1907.

Control animals were added at the time of each exposure, but as a matter of convenience the controls will be treated separately, as such treatment will facilitate a better comparison between the several protective methods against tuberculosis that were tested.

The tuberculous environment to which the animals used in these experiments were exposed was a large cow stable with an adjacent cow yard. In this stable and yard the infection was provided by a number of cattle affected with advanced tuberculosis, of which it was definitely known that they were freely expelling tubercle bacilli. In the yard into which the cattle were turned daily for from 2 to 8 hours, depending upon the state of the weather, all the cattle treated, checks and diseased, were allowed to mingle as they chose; in the stable the cattle were made to occupy stalls in such rotation that the exposure of the different individuals was equalized as much as possible.

The dates on which the 10 calves were killed and a short memorandum of the lesions found on autopsy follow:

No. 444, treated but not exposed reacted to tuberculin October 17, 1907 (13 months after last bovo-vaccination injection). Killed November 7, 1907. No lesions found, but firm pulmonary adhesions and one small glistening nodule, 3 mm. in diameter, in the lung. No tubercle bacilli on microscopic examination or animal inoculation were found in the minute glistening nodule, which may have been a small healed tubercle caused by bacilli from one of the intravenous injections.

No. 427, killed April 23, 1908, after having been exposed to a tuberculous environment for about 18 months. No lesions of tuberculosis.

No. 432, killed March 9, 1909, after having been exposed to a tuberculous environment over 2 years. No lesions of tuberculosis.

No. 429, killed July 16, 1909, after having been exposed to a tuberculous environment over 2 years. No lesions of tuberculosis.

No. 435, killed April 10, 1909, after having been exposed to a tuberculous environment over 2 years. One post-pharyngeal gland twice the normal size and almost entirely tuberculous. No other lesions.

No. 431, killed March 25, 1909, after having been in a tuberculous environment almost 2 years. Mediastinal glands contained a number of minute necrotic foci which failed to show the presence of tubercle bacilli on microscopic examination and guinea-pig inoculation. Lungs contained a number of minute areas which had the appearance of healing tubercles; no bacilli found in these areas.

No. 436, killed March 29, 1909, after having been in a tuberculous environment almost 2 years. No lesions of tuberculosis.

No. 438, killed April 10, 1909, after having been in a tuberculous environment over 2 years. No lesions of tuberculosis.

No. 441, killed April 9, 1909, after having been in a tuberculous environment over 2 years. Autopsy showed minute lesions in the azygos lobe of lung and a small focus 3 mm. in diameter in the right prescapular gland, no tubercle bacilli found in the lung lesions. The prescapular lesions showed tubercle bacilli on microscopic examination and guinea-pig inoculation.

No. 439, killed March 29, 1909, after having been exposed about 16 months to a tuberculous environment. Tubercles in the posterior mediastinal glands, which on guinea-pig inoculation caused generalized tuberculosis.

TEST ACCORDING TO PEARSON'S METHOD.

On June 2, 1906, the first 9 calves, and on June 12, the tenth calf in the following list were given each an intrajugular injection of 3 c. c. of a suspension of tubercle bacilli of the human type. The tubercle culture used to make the suspension was "Case 32," and each cubic centimeter of the suspension was equal to 0.0013 gram of tubercle bacilli.

Heifer calf No. 412, about 4 months old; heifer calf No. 413, about 3 months old; bull calf No. 425, about 2½ to 3 months old; bull calf No. 426, about 2½ to 3 months old; bull calf No. 428, about 2½ to 3 months old; heifer calf No. 430, about 2½ to 3 months old; bull calf No. 433, about 2½ to 3 months old; bull calf No. 440, about 2½ to 3 months old; heifer calf No. 442, about 2½ to 3 months old; heifer calf No. 445, about 3 months old.

The ages of the calves as given above refer to the date on which the injections were made. On July 18, 1906, the 10 calves were given a second intrajugular injection of a suspension of tubercle bacilli in all respects relative to dose and strength similar to the first injection.

On September 11, 1906, the calves received a third intrajugular injection of a suspension of tubercle bacilli. The third dose, like the other two, was 3 c. c., but the suspension was stronger, 1 c. c. being equal to 0.002 gram of tubercle bacilli.

With the exception of some elevation in temperature, most marked after the third injection, the calves showed no pronounced symptoms as the result of the injections. Of the 10 calves, 1 (No. 445) was killed and examined post-mortem without being exposed to tuberculosis, to determine what lesions, if any, had been caused by the three injections of tubercle bacilli. The remaining 9 calves were exposed to a tuberculous environment, as follows:

Nos. 412 and 425, October 30, 1906; Nos. 413 and 426, February 21, 1907; Nos. 428 and 430, April 25, 1907; No. 440, November 8, 1907.

Control animals were added at the time of each exposure. The character of the tuberculous environment has already been described.

The dates on which the 10 calves were killed and a short memorandum of the lesions found on autopsy follow:

No. 445, treated but not exposed, reacted to tuberculin October 17, 1907 (about 13 months after last bovo-vaccination injection), killed November 7, 1907. No lesions of disease.

No. 412, killed April 23, 1908, after having been exposed to a tuberculous environment about 18 months. No lesions of disease.

No 425, died December 18, 1906, after having been exposed to a tuberculous environment about 6 weeks. Cause of death, inflammation of the intestines. No lesions of tuberculosis.

No. 413, killed August 9, 1909, after having been exposed to a tuberculous environment over 2 years. No lesions of disease.

No. 426, killed April 1, 1909, after having been in a tuberculous environment over 2 years. Lungs were found to contain a few very minute tubercles.

No. 428, killed March 29, 1909, after having been in a tuberculous environment nearly 2 years. No lesions of tuberculosis.

No. 430, killed March 22, 1909, after having been in a tuberculous environment nearly 2 years. The pleura and mediastinal glands show minute lesions closely resembling tuberculosis, but no tubercle bacilli could be found in these lesions by microscopic examination or guinea-pig inoculation.

No. 433, killed July 16, 1909, after having been exposed to a tuberculous environment about 2 years. No lesions of tuberculosis.

No. 442, killed July 16, 1909, after having been exposed to a tuberculous environment about 18 months. No lesions of tuberculosis.

No 440, killed April 10, 1909, after having been exposed to a tuberculous environment nearly 18 months. No lesions of tuberculosis.

VACCINATION BY SUBCUTANEOUS INJECTION.

Injections into the End of the Tail.—As the earlier investigations of the Bureau of Animal Industry on the subject of protective inoculations against tuberculosis had given results indicating that the degree of immunity conferred by the injection of living tubercle bacilli into the bodies of cattle depended rather upon the virulence of the injected bacilli than upon the method of injection or the number of injections, a series of tests was made relative to the effects from injecting cattle with quite virulent tubercle bacilli into a portion of the body (the end of the tail) from which the infection, with its strong tendency to become localized, would have to move some distance before it could reach its favorite location in the body. The end of the tail also offered the advantage that the character and process of the inoculation disease could be watched and that treatment, surgical if necessary, could be applied.

On June 20, 1906, the following 4 calves received each a subcutaneous injection, immediately above the brush at the end of the tail, of 3 c. c. of a suspension of bovine tubercle bacilli. The tubercle culture used was "Bovine III," and each 3 c. c. of the suspension was equal to 0.01 gram of tubercle bacilli.

Heifer calf No. 447, about 3 months old; Heifer calf No. 448, about 3 months old; Bull calf No. 450, about 3 months old; Bull calf No. 451, about 2½ months old.

The tuberculous disease caused in the tails of the animals varied considerably. In one case, No. 447, it was necessary to amputate the tail. The four animals were exposed to a tuberculous environment beginning some time after the protective injections had been made. Later on, when they were killed and examined post-mortem, all with the exception of No. 450 were found to have tuberculous lesions directly traceable to the tubercle bacilli injected into the ends of their tails, proving definitely that the strain of tubercle bacillus used was too virulent for the injection of calves in any manner.

Calf No. 450, after remaining in a tuberculous environment for several years, was found on autopsy to be in excellent condition and entirely free from lesions of tuberculosis.

On June 20, 1906, the following 5 calves received each a subcutaneous injection, immediately above the brush at the end of the tail, of 3 c. c. of a suspension of a virulent human tubercle bacilli. The tubercle culture used was "Boy V," and each cubic centimeter of the suspension represented 0.01 gram of tubercle bacilli.

Heifer calf No. 449, about 3½ months old; Bull calf No. 452, about 2½ months old; Bull calf No. 453, about 2½ months old; Bull calf No. 454, about 3 months old; Heifer calf No. 455, about 3 months old.

With the exception of a slight swelling at the seat of injection which gradually subsided, the treatment received by the calves caused no visible lesions. Some time after the protective injections were made the calves were exposed to a tuberculous environment and later on they were killed and examined post-mortem.

Calves 449 and 453 showed no lesions of tuberculosis as result of either the protective injections or the exposure. Calves 452 and 454 each showed a small tuberculous abscess at the seat of inoculation in the tail and small tuberculous foci in the coccygeal lymph glands (the lymph glands located near the root of the tail), and no lesions as a result of the exposure to tuberculosis after the protective injections had been made. Calf 455 was found on autopsy to have tuberculous lesions in the coccygeal and pharyngeal glands, or, in other words, to have contracted tuberculosis both from the protective injection and the subsequent exposure.

All the tuberculous lesions found were small, but calves 452, 454, and 455 show conclusively that the strain of tubercle bacillus injected was too virulent to be used for immunizing purposes. Calves 449, 452, 453, 454 indicate that even a subcutaneous injection of tubercle bacilli can protect against subsequent exposure in a tuberculous environment, and No. 455 shows that a tuberculous process induced by inoculation does not necessarily, in all instances, protect against fresh infection from without, and this is one of the most important facts with which we have to deal in the question of bovo-vaccination.

On November 14, 1906, the following cattle received each subcutaneous injection, immediately above the brush at the end of the tail, of 3 c. c. of a suspension of bovine tubercle bacilli. The tubercle culture used was "Bovine III," and each cubic centimeter of suspension was equal to 0.01 gram of tubercle bacilli.

Heifer No. 406, about 18 months old; Heifer No. 386, about 16 months old; Cow No. 336, about 3 years old; Cow No. 215, about 6 years old.

One of the above animals (cow No. 336) died about four months after injection without additional exposure to tuberculosis. The cause of death was inflammation of the intestines, but she showed a well-marked tuberculous lesion in her tail at the seat of injection and tuberculous lesions in four mediastinal glands. All other parts of her body were free from tuberculosis.

Heifers 406 and 386 and cow 215 were killed after having been exposed to a tuberculous environment for quite a long time, and showed tuberculous lesions which might have been caused in part by the exposure, and which were certainly caused in part by the injection of tubercle bacilli.

Injection Under the Skin of the Neck.—On June 21, 1906, the following 5 calves were each injected with 3 c. c. of a suspension of virulent human tubercle bacilli. The dose in each case was divided into two parts, and one part was introduced under the skin on the right side of the neck and the other part under the skin on the left side of the neck. Each 3 c. c. of the suspension injected represented 0.01 gram of tubercle bacilli.

Bull calf No. 456, about 2½ months old; Bull calf No. 457, about 3 months old; Bull calf No. 458, about 2½ months old; Heifer calf No. 459, about 2½ months old; Heifer calf No. 462, about 2½ months old.

Calves 458 and 462 died in about two months as a result of tuberculosis caused by the injection of tubercle bacilli. The remaining three animals were exposed to a tuberculous environment for some time and were subsequently killed and examined post-mortem. All showed extensive lesions of tuberculosis, no doubt almost entirely due to the injection of tubercle bacilli, showing that either this method of treatment was too severe or that the culture of tubercle bacilli used was too virulent.

In addition to the foregoing subcutaneous injection, 10 calves, Nos. 440, 460, 463, 464, 465, 466, 469, 470, 473, and 474, were each given two successive injections of virulent tubercle bacilli, with an interval between the two injections. These calves all contracted tuberculosis from the treatment received, and simply emphasized that subcutaneous injections, no matter what part of the body is used as the seat of injection, are dangerous when the bacilli injected have a true virulence for cattle. In a later and fuller report on this work it is expected that the lesions caused by the various injections may be given and discussed in detail.

Among the subcutaneous injections only those made into the ends of the tails of calves 449, 452, 453, 454, and 455 with virulent human cultures hold out any encouragement that a subcutaneous method of protective inoculations against tuberculosis can be developed. The results with these animals, however, are quite encouraging and indicate the advisability of making tests of successive injections into the tails of cattle, beginning with fairly virulent cultures.

CHECKS OR CONTROL ANIMALS.

The following 11 untreated cattle, which were similar in age, size, and condition to those given intravenous protective treatment according to the methods of Pearson and Von Behring, were exposed for the same length of time to the same tuberculous environment to which the treated or protected animals were exposed. For the sake of brevity only a sufficient account of these animals will be given now to show that the environment contained the necessary amount of virulent, infectious material to cause tuberculosis of most cattle exposed in it.

Heifer No. 471 contracted tuberculosis of the mediastinal and mesenteric glands.

Heifer No. 472 contracted tuberculosis of one post-pharyngeal gland.

Heifer No. 475 contracted tuberculosis of the mediastinal glands.

Heifer No. 526 contracted tuberculosis of the mediastinal glands.

Steer No. 530 contracted tuberculosis of the lung and mediastinal glands.

Steer No. 531 remained healthy.

Heifer No. 539 contracted tuberculosis of one post-pharyngeal gland.

Heifer No. 540 contracted generalized tuberculosis.

Heifer No. 570 contracted tuberculosis of the mediastinal glands.

Bull No. 573 contracted tuberculosis of the lung and mediastinal glands.

Cow No. 579 remained healthy.

Of course it is to be understood that these cattle were carefully tested with tuberculin and found to be free from tuberculosis before they were exposed as control animals in the experiment. It is desired to avoid all detail not to some extent essential for a general statement in the present report.

In addition to the check or control cattle specially related to the tests of the Pearson and Von Behring methods of bovo-vaccination, three other check animals were also introduced into the same tuberculous environment, which was in all instances used as the means to test the amount of immunity acquired by the treated animals in these series of experiments. The three additional animals were Nos. 477, 484, and 549, and all three contracted tuberculosis as the result of the exposure.

There was thus a total of 14 checks or controls, of which 12 became infected with tuberculosis, thus showing that the character of the exposure to which the treated cattle were subjected was quite severe. The time at which the various control animals were introduced into the tuberculous environment and the length of time they were permitted to remain in it were carefully planned in connection with the exposure of the treated animals, so that any failure among the latter to become infected could be properly valued through a comparison of the treated with the control animals.

One statement which has an important bearing on the intravenous methods of producing resistance against tuberculosis must be added here. All our cattle treated with intravenous injections of tubercle bacilli showed, on careful post-mortem examination, some pulmonary lesions, such as thickening of the pulmonary connective tissue, adhesions between the lobes of the lungs and of the lungs to the chest wall and diaphragm, to be sure only very slight in most instances, but which could be accounted for in no other way than as remnants of the disturbance caused by the injected bacilli. This alone constitutes a condition which should receive further attention before a system of bovo-vaccination requiring the intravenous injection of living cultures of tubercle bacilli is practiced on a wholesale scale, and, in conjunction with what we know about the retention of tubercle bacilli in the tissues after injection and the uncertainty about the manner and state in which they leave the body, should teach us to proceed cautiously in the adoption of protective methods, notwithstanding the fact that the results obtained prove conclusively that actual, strong resistance to tuberculosis can be established by using them.

COMPARISON OF THE FOREGOING METHODS.

From the brief accounts that have been given we see that 3 of the 9 cattle treated according to the method of Von Behring and afterwards exposed contracted tuberculosis, that 1 of the 9 cattle treated by the method of Pearson and afterwards exposed contracted tuberculosis, and that of 14 checks or untreated control animals 12 became infected on exposure.

Of the 8 animals that received injections of bovine tubercle culture subcutaneously into the ends of their tails (4 old and 4 young animals), all but 1 young animal contracted disease as the result of the injections. The one that escaped disease from the injection also resisted tuberculosis on exposure.

Of the 5 cattle that received human culture injections into the ends of their tails, 2 became immune without inoculation disease, 2 were immune but had slight inoculation disease, and 1 had both inoculation and exposure disease. The injection of tubercle cultures under the skin of the neck of animals caused them all to contract tuberculosis. The several methods may be compared as follows:

Von Behring cattle, 66 2-3 per cent successfully protected for a period approximating 2 years.

Pearson cattle, 88 8-10 per cent successfully protected for a period approximating 2 years.

Bovine cultures, tail, protected 12½ per cent.

Human cultures, tail, protected 40 per cent.*

Injections under skin protected 0 per cent.

The above percentages can best be valued by comparing them

---

*It should be borne in mind that the human cultures injected in the tail actually protected 80 per cent. of the cattle treated against the infection in the environment to which they were exposed.

with the check or control animals, among 14 of which only 2, or 14 2-7 per cent, escaped.

If the only question to be considered in connection with bovo-vaccination was the protection of cattle against tuberculosis, the foregoing results would give us excellent reasons to be very cheerful. Lately, however, studies made by various investigators on the elimination of tubercle bacilli, after injection, from the bodies of animals teach us to be very careful about adopting methods of immunization for purely economic purposes that may be dangerous for those who afterwards use the products of the treated animals.

The work of the Bureau of Animal Industry in the past has also demonstrated that tubercle bacilli injected into the circulation or under the skin of cattle may remain incorporated in their tissues for long periods of time, with only a gradual or very slow loss of virulence. These are important factors that must not discourage further work to build on the knowledge we have gained, but which must be kept in mind and be permitted to have their due influence on our subsequent investigations.

Very careful autopsies of cattle treated by intravenous inoculation of tubercle bacilli according to the methods of Von Behring and Pearson show that the more or less attenuated tubercle bacilli that engender immunity against tuberculosis rarely leave the treated subjects wholly free from lesions that can be accounted for in any other way than as due to the pathogenic activity within the animal's body of the injected bacilli.

TEST OF THE HEYMANNS METHOD OF BOVO-VACCINATION.

A protective treatment for cattle against tuberculosis, named the Heymanns method after its inventor, has received considerable attention during the last few years. The technique of this method was demonstrated in America by Prof. Heymanns himself during the meeting of the International Congress on Tuberculosis at Washington in 1908, and the efficiency of the method has been carefully tested by the Bureau of Animal Industry with cattle and hogs.

Heymanns's method, briefly, is the introduction of virulent bovine tubercle bacilli, enveloped in a closed sack of vegetable fiber, which in turn is inclosed in a gelatin capsule, under the skin of the animal to be protected. The supposition is that the vegetable sack will confine the tubercle bacilli at the seat of inoculation and that the treated animal will be immunized by protective fluids that form within the closed vegetable sack and pass outward from it, into the animal's system generally, by an osmotic process. The closed sack of vegetable material in combination with the gelatin capsule is commonly known as the Heymanns capsule.

In the fall of 1908, 12 cattle and 10 hogs were inoculated with Heymanns's capsules. The animals were divided into three groups, and one group of hogs and cattle were exposed immediately after treatment to a tuberculous environment, a second about 2 months later, and a third about 2 months after the second. With each group of hogs a similar number of untreated hogs were exposed as checks. As the cattle and hogs were exposed in the same tuberculosis environment in which the degree of immunity acquired by all the other bovo-vaccinated animals discussed in this paper was tested, no checks were really necessary for the Heymanns treated cattle. The checks on the other experiments were serviceable for this one also, but, nevertheless, 4 additional cattle as special checks on the value of the Heymanns method were added to the already large number used to prove the character of the tuberculous environment to which exposure was made.

Among the Heymanns treated hogs 1 contracted generalized tuberculosis from the treatment and 1 died prematurely as the result of an injury. When the remaining 8 hogs with their 10 checks were killed, after an exposure to natural infection varying from 8 months to a year, all the principals and checks were found to be affected with tuberculosis, not one of either lot having escaped the disease; and the lesions in the treated animals were in no respect different from those found in the checks. Hence it is very clear that Heymanns's method is absolutely worthless for hogs.

Among the 12 cattle treated 1 died prematurely, and the remaining 11, when they were killed and examined post-mortem, all showed lesions of tuberculosis, and the lesions were very similar to the tuberculous lesions found in the 4 cattle that served as special checks on the Heymanns capsule cattle. One of the treated animals showed tuberculosis directly traceable to the capsule with which it was inoculated for protection. Hence, as with the hogs, the only conclusion that can be drawn with the cattle is that Heymanns's capsule method of bovo-vaccination is inefficient.

In order to test the claims made by Prof. Heymanns that the vegetable sack in which he incloses the tubercle bacilli used in his method of bovo-vaccination would not permit the passage of bacteria, a number of sheep were inoculated with anthrax bacilli inclosed in Heymanns's capsules. The sheep rapidly contracted and succumbed to anthrax, and the anthrax bacilli (which are larger, of course, than tubercle bacilli) were proven to have escaped through the walls of the capsules and to have gotten into the blood circulation. Blood examined from the tips of the ears of the sheep showed numerous anthrax bacilli. We may conclude from this that the fact that tubercle bacilli under the skin in Heymanns's capsules are frequently restrained at the point of inoculation depends upon other conditions than the inability of the germs to pass through the walls of the vegetable sack in which they are enveloped.

BLOOD TRANSFUSIONS.

It may be of interest to add a short note that blood transfusions from highly immunized cattle into tuberculous cattle for curative purposes and into healthy cattle in order to make them resistant to tuberculosis have been tested on a small scale. The idea that such transfusions may give good results originated with Dr. George W. Crile, of Cleveland, Ohio, who personally made the various transfusions required in the experiment.

The blood for the transfusions was supplied by cattle that had been immunized by the methods of Pearson and Von Behring and that had resisted infection after a long-continued exposure to the tuberculous environment previously described, in which about 86 per cent of all exposed, untreated, or check cattle contracted tuberculosis.

As far as the very small number of cattle used justifies drawing conclusions, the blood-transfusion experiments gave wholly negative results and hold out no encouragement as being a means by which tuberculosis can be treated or the resistance to infection strengthened. The treated animals may have been too far advanced in the disease to derive benefit from any form of treatment, but the animals which received blood to immunize them apparently were as susceptible to infection as those that had received no treatment.

GENERAL CONCLUSIONS.

The only conclusion to which we are entitled from this work and from careful study of the writings of others on the subject of protective inoculation against tuberculosis may be stated as follows: Though results have been obtained which are very encouraging to the investigator and which prompt him to strive onward with renewed vigor and hope, no system of bovo-vaccination has reached a stage at the present time that justifies its use in common practice.

TUBERCULOSIS, ITS CAUSE, ITS EFFECT AND MODE OF DISTRIBUTION.

What is Tuberculosis? A transmissable disease caused by a specific kind of bacteria. A transmissible disease is one produced by a living organism which enters the body of an animal and grows therein, producing harmful changes, which may or may not cause the death of the animal. The organisms leave the body of the diseased animal in various ways and enter the body of a second, healthy animal. Thus, each case of a transmissible disease must come from a pre-existing case of the same disease. Sometimes the connection between the different cases is easily traced, at other times not.

What Other Names are Applied to Tuberculosis? Consumption and phthisis are terms used to designate tuberculosis of the lungs in man. By scrofula was formerly meant tuberculosis of the glands of the neck. Lupus is tuberculosis of the skin, and cold abscesses and hip-joint disease are likely to be tuberculosis of the bones. Grapes and pearl disease are names often applied by the butcher to certain types of the disease in cattle.

What Animals Have Tuberculosis? All warm blooded and some cold blooded animals. In man it is the most important of all transmissible diseases, which include such diseases as typhoid fever, diptheria, scarlet fever, small pox, measles, mumps, etc. In the northern portion of this country it is the most important disease of cattle. Of the domestic animals, cattle, hogs and fowls are most often affected, sheep, horses, dogs and cats but rarely. Most of the wild animals in captivity die of tuberculosis.

GRADE HOLSTEIN. NOTE MILK VEINS AND SHAPELY UDDER. DEPT. OF AGR.

Where is Tuberculosis Found? It is world-wide in man and practically so in cattle. The native cattle in different countries were originally free from it, but the introduction of the improved breeds of cattle from northwestern Europe to all parts of the globe, resulted in the spread of the germs of tuberculosis.

What Determines the Distribution of Tuberculosis? The germs are carried in the bodies of the diseased animals. If such animals are brought into a herd, the disease spreads from these to the healthy animals. Thus, the custom of buying and selling stock, especially of the improved types, is one of the most potent means of spreading the disease from herd to herd. Where milk is produced mainly for city use, the custom of disposing of milch cows when they dry off and of replacing them with fresh milkers is conducive to the introduction and rapid spread of the disease in the herd. A large herd is more often affected than a small one, because the opportunity for introducing a diseased animal into the herd is dependent on the number of animals purchased. If 50 animals are purchased from 25 different herds in the older dairy regions of the state, some tubercular animals are almost certain to be found among them. One tuberculous animal is *enough to start the disease in a healthy herd.*

Is One Breed of Cattle More Susceptible to Tuberculosis Than Another? Cattle of any breed, beef or dairy, acquire tuberculosis easily and quickly, when once brought in contact with diseased animals giving off tubercle bacilli. The reasons why more dairy than beef cattle have been found to be affected is because of the much greater interchange; the longer period for which they are retained; and the closer confinement to which they are subjected.

What Parts of the Body may be Affected by Tuberculosis? Any part of the body may be affected, but in each kind of animal there are certain parts in which the disease is most likely to occur in case it is present at all.

What Parts of the Body are most Often Affected by Tuberculosis? In man the lungs are most frequently involved. In cattle the parts most frequently affected are:

1. The lymphatic glands at the base of the skull, the *pharyngeal glands,* which can be readily recognized when the head is removed by the butcher. These glands will be found on either side of the wind pipe and gullet close to the joint between the head and the first vertebra. 2. The lymphatic glands on the wind pipe between the lungs, the *bronchial and mediastinal glands.* 3. The lungs. 4. The liver. 5. The spleen (milt). 6. The lymphatic glands of the intestine, *the mesenteric glands,* and the membranes of the abdominal cavity.

In hogs the lymphatic glands of the neck are most frequently affected, as are also the lungs and associated lymphatic glands, the liver, the spleen, and the lymphatic glands of the intestines.

What Other Parts of the Body May Be Affected? The lymphatic glands in all parts of the body may be diseased, even those situated in the muscles. The brain and spinal cord are sometimes affected as are the bones, joints and skin. Tuberculosis is also found in the reproductive organs. The udder is affected in about two per cent of tubercular animals. The disease may be located in parts of the body not usually examined, and it may be present in any part; hence, it is very difficult and often impossible to say from an ordinary post-mortem examination that an animal that has reacted to tuberculin is actually free from the disease and that the tuberculin test is in error. The tissue can sometimes be shown to be tubercular by microscopical examination when no signs are visible to the naked eye.

What is the Appearance of the Diseased Organs? The word consumption is often applied to tuberculosis and thus many have been led to believe that tubercular organs are shriveled or shrunken in size, i. e., consumed by disease. On the contrary, a tubercular organ, especially in domestic animals, is usually larger, often several times larger, than normal. The lymph glands especially, become enormously enlarged, and if such enlarged glands are in the neck, may often cause difficulty in breathing, due to the pressure on the wind pipe. The lungs frequently may be much enlarged, often weighing several times as much as healthy organs. Hard bunches or swellings, are usually present in the diseased organs, and are the cause of the enormous increase in size so often noted.

What Gives the Disease the Name Tuberculosis? The name is derived from the characteristic bunches or swellings known as tubercles which are invariably found in diseased animals. These tubercles are at first microscopic in size, but due to growth and by fusion of two or more, they may often become several inches in diameter. On the membranes of the body cavities they sometimes appear as pearl-gray nodules, thus giving rise to the name pearl disease. The tubercles attached to these membranes often look like clusters of small grapes. This has caused the term grapes to be sometimes applied to such an appearance. A tuberculous liver generally shows bright yellow spots on the surface and upon cutting tubercular abscesses are revealed.

What is the Internal Appearance of the Tubercles? The smaller tubercles when cut show a uniform, gray color. As they increase in size, a small, yellow mass which slowly enlarges is developed in the center. The larger tubercles are often filled with creamy, yellow pus. Again they may be hard and gritty, due to the deposition of lime salts. This condition is known as calcification. When the blade of a knife is drawn across the cut surface a scratching sound is heard. The appearance is that of yellow, granular material, which often reminds one of corn meal. The large cavities filled with pus are usually called tubercular abscesses. They are found in the lungs, liver and lymphatic glands. The material within the tubercle contains the tubercle bacilli.

How Does the Tuberculous Udder Appear? The healthy udder is uniformly soft, while the tuberculous udder contains the hard tubercles, which, when near the surface or when large, can be felt. As the disease progresses, the infected quarter (for the disease is generally confined to one quarter), becomes enlarged and hard. There is, however, no fever nor pain and the swelling does not disappear, as in the case of garget (inflammation of the udder), but continues to grow more pronounced. The milk is usually normal in appearance and composition but in severe cases may become watery.

How Should a Carcass Be Examined for Tuberculosis? The general appearance of the different parts of the body to be examined should be carefully noted; they should be carefully felt for tubercles, and if any suspicious places are discovered the organ should be cut. Unless one has had some experience in such examinations it is advisable to cut the various glands and organs, even though no suspicious places are found.

The head should be severed as usual and the glands of the throat (*pharyngeal*), removed and examined for enlargements. Cut each gland into several slices and note the presence of any yellowish or greyish-yellow areas. A healthy gland is light gray or pinkish in color throughout, or in old animals, is often dark, or almost black, from pigment. Remove the udder, examine carefully for bunches (tubercles); also examine the lymph glands just above the hind quarters of the udder.

Open the abdominal cavity. Examine the liver, spleen and kidneys, first noting their general appearance. If any yellowish areas are found, cut through at this point. Note whether the membranes covering the stomach, etc., (the omentum or caul) are smooth and thin, or studded with nodules or tubercles.

The intestines proper should be examined, altogether the disease is rarely found on the gut wall itself. The disease is much more likely to be found in the mesenteric lymph glands which run parallel to the intestines several inches from the same, in the membrane that holds the intestines in place. Examine the uterus and the walls of the abdominal cavity which should be perfectly smooth.

Open the lung cavity, remove the lungs, together with the gullet, wind pipe and heart entire. Healthy lung tissue is uniformly soft and pink in color. Remove the glands on the wind-pipe and gullet and especially those at the forks of the wind-pipe, and note whether they are enlarged or not. Cut open in order to discover small tubercles.

If the animal is tubercular, evidences will usually be found in the parts of the body mentioned, but its non-detection in these parts is not absolutely positive evidence of the absence of the disease in the animal, for in the earlier stages nodules of small size may be readily overlooked.

What Diseases May Be Mistaken for Tuberculosis? In the case of lumpy jaw (actinomycosis) nodules may be formed in the lungs and udder that closely resemble those of tuberculosis. In sheep the wall of the intestines may show a nodular condition, known as nodular disease or knotty gut, caused by a minute, animal parasite that burrows its way into the wall of the intestine.

How Do the Tubercle Bacilli Leave the Body of the Diseased Animal? In a number of ways, depending upon the location of the tubercular nodules. These masses gradually undergo softening and finally break, discharging their contents into the air passages of the lungs and into the milk ducts. The bacteria may thus be thrown off the body in the material coughed up from the lungs, which is, in part, expelled from the mouth, but the larger part is swallowed and the bacteria leave the body in the manure. They are also thrown off in the milk, and in the discharges from the uterus and in the urine.

How Do the Bacteria Enter the Body of a Healthy Animal? The manure of tuberculous cows gradually undergoes drying and is finally broken into small particles which find their way into the air and are thus breathed in by other cattle. This inhaled dust lodges in the nasal passages and throat, and the tubercle bacilli pass into the glands of the neck and into the lungs. Some of the tubercle organisms are swallowed and finding their way through the intestinal wall, pass into the lymph glands and thus are introduced into the circulation.

Where infected milk is fed to cattle and hogs, the tubercle bacilli penetrate the walls of the throat and intestine and are deposited in the lymph glands and lungs; hence, these parts are frequently diseased. Tuberculous material ejected from the mouth in coughing or drooling is spread in the manger, which surface may be licked by another animal. This direct means of infection is now believed to be a most important way of spreading tuberculosis, possibly more so than dust. Hogs running after tuberculous cattle in feeding lots become infected from the manure.

What Is Open Tuberculosis? When the disease is present in organs that open to the exterior of the body such as the lungs, kidneys, uterus, and udder.

What Is Closed Tuberculosis? When the disease is present in parts of the body that have no exterior opening. An animal with closed tuberculosis is not a source of danger to man or other animals since no tubercle bacilli can leave the body. An animal with open tuberculosis is a constant source of danger because the organisms are given off more or less constantly.

Does Closed Tuberculosis Change to Open? Almost always the disease spreads from the lymph glands to lungs, etc., and then the animal becomes an active means of spreading tubercle bacilli. No one can tell when this may occur, so every tubercular animal must be looked upon as a source of infection and should be removed from the herd.

Is Tuberculous Inherited? But rarely, only when the reproductive organs are diseased. Ordinarily, the disease is contracted subsequent to birth.

How Is the Disease Introduced Into the Herd? 1. By the purchase of diseased animals. 2. By feeding mixed factory by-products, such as raw, creamery skim milk and whey. 3. By direct contact with an affected animal.

What Favors Its Spread in the Herd? The rate of spread in the herd is dependent on the number of tubercular animals and the number of tubercle bacilli ejected by them. One diseased animal often suffices to infect the healthy part of the herd, but with a larger number of diseased animals in a herd the spread is more rapid. The condition of the herd as to general health, exerts an influence on the rate of spread of tuberculosis. Good and abundant feed, proper ventilation and sunlight are conducive to health and retard the spread of the disease in a herd. But tuberculosis may, nevertheless, spread rapidly amongst cattle that are kept continually out of doors. No conditions, however sanitary, will save a herd constantly exposed to infection from animals giving off tubercle bacilli.

Can Healthy Cattle Become Tubercular If Kept in Unsanitary Stables? Tuberculosis of cattle cannot develop without two necessary conditions: First, a susceptible host, the cow; Second, the tubercle bacillus. Both factors are absolutely essential to the occurrence of the disease. Bad sanitary conditions favor the spread of tuberculosis, but *never* cause this disease.

Can the Tubercle Organism Occur and Develop Outside of the Body of the Animal? Owing to the fact that the tubercle bacillus is a parasitic organism, living upon the body juices, and at the temperature of warm blooded animals, it cannot multiply and develop under conditions such as occur in nature, outside of the bodies of animals and men, but it is capable of remaining alive for an unknown time, depending upon conditions, such as moisture, light, etc.

Does a Tubercular Animal Show Physical Signs of the Disease? It is often thought that a tubercular animal should show physical signs of illness and that the disease should be detected by a careful examination. Such is not the case; even the most experienced and careful veterinarian cannot be certain by a physical examination whether an animal is tubercular or not. This is especially true when the disease is not widely distributed in the body, but even when the lungs and other internal organs are badly affected, it cannot usually be detected by a physical examination of the living animal. If the lymphatic glands that can be felt from the surface of the body are enlarged, or if the animal is so diseased that the normal functions of the body are disturbed, the disease can be detected by physical examination.

A badly diseased animal loses flesh, the coat becomes rough, the eyes dull and staring, and there is a general appearance of lack of vitality. Since in this stage the lungs are almost certain to be involved, the animal may cough, especially after exercising.

No reliance, however, can be placed on the occurence of physical symptoms, (1) because there are many other troubles that produce the same symptoms, and (2) because in the beginning stages, and often in the more advanced stages, no symptoms whatever appear. The animal may be apparently in perfect health and have a good flow of milk, and yet be a constant source of danger, because the tubercle organisms are being thrown off from the body, in the sputum, manure and milk.

Is It Wise to Introduce an Unsound or Unhealthy Cow Into Your Herd? Any farmer about to purchase a horse examines it for soundness because he knows an unsound horse will be of doubtful value to him. Yet spavin, ringbone, heaves, cribbing, and balking are not directly transmissible troubles. Tuberculosis, an unsoundness of cattle and hogs, is transmissible to other animals; hence every tubercular cow is likely to cause the farmer more loss than ten spavined horses because:

1. Tuberculosis causes the death of a certain number of animals after it has become established in a herd. 2. Tuberculosis causes a waste of food when it is fed to animals that cannot give an adequate return. 3. Tuberculosis causes heavy loss through the infection of other animals. 4. Tuberculosis reduces the productive and market value of cows. As soon as an animal shows physical evidence of the disease, it has no market value. 5. Tuberculosis destroys the good reputation of a herd, rendering it difficult to sell animals and often hard to dispose of their products. Especially is this true in pure-bred herds.

It is estimated by the Federal authorities that tuberculosis of cattle and hogs causes an annual loss of $23,000,000 in the United States.

What Per Cent of Domestic Animals Have Tuberculosis? It varies widely in different countries and in different parts of the same country. From July, 1908, to July, 1910, over 90,000 animals, largely milch cows, were examined for tuberculosis in Wisconsin and about five per cent were found to be diseased. The tests in earlier years revealed a much greater per cent of tubercular animals. It is believed that the spread of the disease is being constantly checked through the agency of a number of factors. One of the most important is the realization by many farmers of the economic importance of the disease, which has led them to eliminate the diseased animals from their herds and to maintain healthy herds. In some other states a much greater per cent of tubercular cattle is found, since no active measures are taken to educate the farmer concerning the importance of tuberculosis, and hence no adequate efforts have been made to prevent the introduction of diseased animals into the herds.

What Is the Sanitary Significance of Tuberculosis of Cattle and Hogs? It has been shown beyond all doubt that tubercle bacilli from cattle are able to cause the disease in human beings. If infected foods, such as meat and milk, are consumed in a raw state there is opportunity for infection. It is not believed that adults acquire tuberculosis easily from the use of such food, but with children the case seems to be far different. From the data collected within the last 10 years, it seems probable that about 20 per cent of tuberculosis in children, i. e., those under 16 years of age, is due to organisms coming from cattle.

There is little danger from meat as tuberculosis does not usually affect the muscles, and besides the heating to which meat is subjected in cooking is sufficient to destroy the tubercle bacillus. The danger from milk is far greater, since it is usually consumed as raw milk, and since it is the food most frequently infected, and forms the chief food of children.

How Does Milk Become Infected With Tubercle Bacilli? As has been shown, the organisms leave the body of the diseased animal in a number of ways and may be introduced directly or indirectly, into milk. Tubercles in the udder may discharge their contents directly into the milk ducts, and thus the milk is contaminated before withdrawal from the udder. Proof exists that milk may be infected before withdrawal even though no tuberculosis can be demonstrated in the udder.

The tubercles in the lungs discharge their contents into the air passages, and the infectious material is coughed up. A small portion is discharged from the mouth during the act of coughing, but the larger part is swallowed; the tubercle bacilli pass uninjured through the stomachs and intestines of the animals and are eliminated in the manure. After being drawn, the milk may become contaminated by the introduction of manure and dust from the coat of the cow during the milking. The more clean the method of production of milk, the less important becomes this source of its infection. Milk may also become infected from healthy cows in a tuberculous herd, if the coat of the healthy animal becomes soiled with infected manure.

How Frequently Does Milk Contain Tubercle Bacilli?—This varies so widely that it is difficult to answer this question. In those parts of the country in which a considerable portion of the milch cows are tubercular, the mixed milk coming from a number of herds is certain to contain tubercle bacilli almost constantly in greater or less numbers. In the case of single herds, the opportunity for infection of milk depends upon the presence or absence of the disease and upon the number of diseased animals in the herd. If a cow has tuberculosis the milk may contain tubercle bacilli. In order to be certain that the milk does not contain them, the cows must be *free* from the disease.

Is Milk an Important Means of Spreading Tuberculosis? It is probably second in importance to the transfer of animals. It has been shown that calves and hogs acquire tuberculosis easily when fed on infected milk. Hogs, especially, are most easily infected through the food, a single feeding of infected milk being often sufficient to cause the disease.

How Can the Spread of Tuberculosis by Milk and Other Dairy Products Be Prevented?—The patron of a cheese factory or whole milk creamery carries to his calves and hogs a mixture of the milk and whey from all of the other patrons, some of whom may have badly diseased herds. It is important that these by-products be treated so as to destroy any tubercle organisms they may contain. This can be done by heating the skim milk and whey. Such a process is compulsory in Denmark. Minnesota and Iowa also have laws requiring these by-products to be heated. The heating of skim milk and whey can be done with inexpensive apparatus. Most frequently it is accomplished by the injection of steam. In those states requiring the treatment of these by-products, the laws provide that they shall be heated to 176 degrees F., since at this temperature milk and whey undergo a change that can be readily detected by the inspector, whose duty it is to determine whether the law is being obeyed.

A lower temperature will, however, destroy tubercle bacilli. If skim milk or whey is heated to 155 degrees F. and allowed to cool slowly all tubercle bacilli will be killed. If it is desired to have buttermilk free from such disease bacteria, the cream must be pasturized before churning. Heating the buttermilk causes the curd to settle and makes the buttermilk difficult to handle.

The heating of whey and skim milk is desirable since it insures the return of these products in a sweet condition to the farm. Such material has a higher feeding value than sour fermented by-products. The treatment has also been found to be of great service in improving the quality of the milk, since the cans do not become contaminated with harmful bacteria which may find their way into the milk supply when the cans are poorly washed. The process of heating whey is being rapidly introduced in Canada for the purpose of improving the quality of milk.

The use of the farm separator also overcomes the danger of introducing tuberculosis from factory by-products, as in this way the milk of the home herd alone is fed. The creamery separator slime should never be used as feed. It should be burned.

Why Does the Farmer so Frequently Fail to Appreciate the Danger From Tuberculosis?—Every farmer is afraid of hog cholera because it quickly causes large losses. It appears, destroys the majority of the herd, and disappears. Tuberculosis causes greater loss, but attracts little attention, because it develops slowly in the animal, and may require years to produce death. The animals decline so slowly that it seems as though some inevitable, unpreventable trouble were present. So human tuberculosis used to be considered. Now, however, it is looked upon as preventable and curable.

How Can Tuberculosis Be Detected?—A physical examination of a tubercular animal fails to reveal any characteristic symptoms that permit of the detection of the disease except in the later stages and the only way in which the presence of tuberculosis can be detected with certainty in all stages in the living animal is by the tuberculin test.

THE TUBERCULIN TEST, ITS MODE OF APPLICATION AND INTERPRETATION.

What is the Tuberculin Test?—If a tuberculous cow has a small quantity of tuberculin introduced beneath the skin, a temporary fever will result, which can be detected by taking the temperature of the animal; a healthy animal shows no such fever.

What Is Tuberculin?—The tubercle bacillus is grown in beef broth containing glycerine. After the maximum growth has taken place, the entire mass of broth and growth is heated to 212 degrees F. for 5 to 6 hours. This kills the bacteria and serves to extract the contents of their cells. The dead cells are removed by filtration and the liquid evaporated to one-tenth of its original volume. To preserve it, carbolic acid is added and it is then diluted for use. *It is impossible for the tuberculin to contain any living tubercle bacilli.*

Does the Use of Tuberculin Injure Animals?—Tuberculin has no ill effect, whatever, on healthy animals, and no harmful effect on tuberculous animals. It does not, in the amounts used in testing, have any effect on the progress of the disease in the animal, nor can it in any way produce the disease. With many of our best herds it has been used regularly for 10 to 15 years with absolutely no injurious effects. The statements that the test causes abortion or other ailments are without foundation. The flow of milk is not changed to an appreciable extent, even in the case of tubercular animals.

How Is the Tuberculin Test Made?—The application of the test may be divided into three parts: 1. The determination of the normal temperature of such animal; 2. The injection of tuberculin; 3. The determination of whether a fever has resulted.

The Initial Temperature of Two Cows, With Rate of Pulse and Number of Respirations Per Minute.

Hour	Cow No. 1			Cow No. 2		
	Temperature	Pulse	Respiration	Temperature	Pulse	Respiration
9 A. M.	99.8	48	18	98.6	48	15
10 A. M.	99.5	66	19	98.6	60	15
11 A. M.	99.0	60	15	99.0	60	15
12 noon	100.8	54	15	99.4	54	15
1 P. M.	101.4	54	15	100.0	54	18
2 P. M.	101.6	48	15	100.2	54	18
3 P. M.	102.0	60	24	100.4	72	24
4 P. M.	103.0	66	24	102.7	72	24
5 P. M.	103.3	66	24	102.8	72	27
6 P. M.	103.1	57	18	103.0	60	27
7 P. M.	102.2	60	20	102.4	60	24
8 P. M.	103.0	56	16	102.0	60	24
9 P. M.	103.1	52	24	102.2	50	24
10 P. M.	102.5	60	20	102.0	50	18
11 P. M.	102.5	60	20	102.0	60	20
12 midnight	102.4	56	18	101.6	54	20
1 A. M.	101.8	60	20	101.4	58	24
2 A. M.	102.0	64	18	102.2	58	18
3 A. M.	102.0	60	18	101.6	58	18
4 A. M.	102.2	54	24	101.5	60	24
5 A. M.	101.6	56	24	102.0	60	18
6 A. M.	101.8	60	18	102.2	60	20
8 A. M.	102.5	56	16	103.2	60	18

Why Is It Necessary to Determine the Normal Temperature?—The temperature of cattle, unlike that of man, varies widely, not only in different animals, but in the same animal at different times.

The temperature of a cow is usually between 101-102 degrees F.; that of calves and of fat stock somewhat higher, while old cows and those low in vitality usually show somewhat lower temperatures. The following table will give an idea of the variations in temperature that may be noted in the same animal. There is also included the pulse rate and number of respirations per minute.

How Is the Temperature Taken?—The temperature is taken by means of a clinical or fever thermometer, which is inserted in the rectum. In the fever thermometer, the mercury remains at the highest point reached until it is shaken down. It is important that the thermometer be accurate; the better grades are generally sold with a certificate showing their relative accuracy. The quickness with which a proper reading can be secured varies considerably, depending upon the volume and shape of the bulb of the thermometer, as well as the thickness of the glass walls. The one-minute thermometer, i. e., those registering in that time, are too fragile for general use in testing cattle. The two-minute veterinary thermometer is preferable. It may be used with or without an open metal case. The case protects the thermometer, but causes it to act more slowly and makes it more difficult to read. Since the thermometer cannot be read like an ordinary air thermometer, it is essential that one receive personal instruction in the manipulation, use and reading of the fever thermometer.

How Are the Thermometers Used?—It is important that before insertion in the animal, each thermometer is shaken down so that the mercury stands *below* 98 degrees F. Smear a little vaseline on the bulb to render insertion easier, then insert the thermometer to its full length in the rectum. It is important that some way be provided to fasten the thermometer to the animal so that it shall not be lost or broken when excreta is passed. The bull dog clamp may be snapped onto the long hairs at the root of the tail. The thermometer should be allowed to remain in the animal at least *three* minutes. Remove, read, and record the reading. Shake down, noting the thermometer to see that it records lower than 98 degrees F. If a person is provided with a number of thermometers (3 to 6), temperatures can be taken in a number of animals at once. Exposure in the animal for longer than a three-minute period does not affect the accuracy of results.

Some animals object to the insertion of the thermometer, especially those not used to being handled. If the helper will scratch them with a curry comb, no difficulty will usually be had.

How Many Temperatures Should Be Taken in Order to Determine the Normal Temperature?—At least three and preferably four temperatures should be taken at intervals of two or three hours; for example, at 12, 2, 4, and 6 o'clock. Each animal should be marked so there will be no danger of confusion. This can be done by placing a gummed label on the hair near the hips.

How Is the Tuberculin Injected?—By means of a hypodermic syringe, the tuberculin is injected beneath the skin, the most convenient place for injection being just back or in front of the shoulders. This places the operator out of danger of being kicked. The injection may be made on the side toward the operator, or on the opposite side by reaching over the back of the animal. The skin is lifted up with one hand and the needle thrust through at right angles but parallel to the side of the animal so that the contents of the syringe may be discharged underneath the skin, but not into the muscles.

The syringe should be graduated in cubic centimeters. It should be provided with a "stop" so that a definite amount of tuberculin and no more can be easily injected. The needles should slip onto the barrel of the syringe, rather than screw on. This enables the operator to insert the needle before it is attached to the syringe and thus decreases the danger of breaking the needle if the animal moves. The needles should be kept sharp by whetting on an oil stone in order that they may be inserted easily. Before use the syringe should be disinfected or sterilized, so that infection with harmful bacteria at the point of inoculation may not take place. If the washer on the plunger is rubber, the syringe may be placed in cold water, which is then heated to the boiling point. If the washer is leather, the syringe must not be heated, but may be disinfected by placing in a five per cent solution of carbolic acid for a number of hours. Use glycerine, rather than vaseline, on the plunger to make it slide easily. The syringe may be filled directly from the bottle through the needle.

In order to prevent infection at the point of inoculation, the point at which the injection is to be made should be saturated with a five per cent solution of carbolic acid.

What Is a Proper Dose of Tuberculin?—The tuberculin furnished by the state is of such concentration that 2 cc. should be used for an ordinary sized animal, 900 to 1100 pounds. Proportionally larger or smaller amounts should be used for heavy or light animals. Bulls weighing 1500 to 2000 pounds should receive 3 to 4 cc., young animals 400 to 600 pounds, 1 cc., etc.

When Is the Tuberculin to Be Injected?—The injection should be made at such a time that the temperature can again be taken eight hours later. From 8 to 10 p. m. is the most convenient time, as it is then possible to begin the second series of temperature readings in the morning.

How Many Temperatures Should Be Taken After Injection?— Begin at the eighth hour after injection and continue at two hour intervals until at least the eighteenth hour after injection. With all animals that show a fever the temperatures should be taken until it begins to fall in a decided manner.

How Should the Animals Be Cared for During the Test?—As far as possible they should be handled in the regular manner used on the particular farm. Cattle not fed or watered at accustomed times may become nervous, and the temperature will rise. If the daily routine is not such as will enable the test to be made conveniently, change a week or ten days before the test is to be made, so that the cattle may become accustomed to it. During the test the cattle must be kept in the barn for about 24 hours.

Attention must be paid to the watering during the test, especially while the temperatures are being taken after injection. If an animal drinks a large amount of *cold* water, the temperature will be lowered. It is possible to have fever produced by the tuberculin, and due to the drinking of a large amount of cold water, the temperature so lowered that the fever will not be detected. This may lead to incorrectness in interpreting the temperatures and a cow may be passed as healthy, when in reality she is diseased. If the water can be warmed, it can be given in any amount. If cold water must be used and the animals are generally watered during the morning, when temperatures are being taken, a pailful may be given to each animal at periods of an hour or so; preferably immediately after a reading has been taken. The small quantity will not affect the temperature. Care should also be taken that none of the preliminary temperatures are lowered by the watering.

What Animals Should Not Be Tested?—The temperatures before injection not only serve to show the normal temperatures of each animal, but whether any have a fever, due to some cause or other. Such animals should not be injected because it cannot be told with certainty whether the fever on the second day is due to the same cause or to the tuberculin. As a rule, the following animals should not be tested:

1. Those soon to calve. 2. Those that have just calved, especially when the afterbirth was not discharged in a normal manner. 3. Animals in heat. 4. Animals suffering from garget (mammitis), or inflammation in other parts of the body. 5. Animals that have aborted within a short time. 6. Those that show a single temperature before inoculation of 103.5 degrees F. or above. Calves and fat stock may have a normal temperature of 103 to 103.5 and may be tested if all of the temperatures are uniformly high. It is not considered wise to test calves under three months old.

If it is desirable that the animals in the classes just enumerated be tested with the remainder of the herd, it may be done, but if any show a reaction, it is usually advisable to hold them for a retest. If no reaction occurs, the test is as reliable in the case of such animals as in any. Animals with an abnormal temperature should not be tested under any condition.

When Is the Best Time to Test?—The most convenient time to test the herd is while the cattle are in the stable, shortly after they are put up for the fall, or in the spring. It can be done at any time during the winter, but not so conveniently in very cold weather.

During the summer the cattle must be taken out of the pasture and kept in the stable. This causes them to become uneasy. During very hot weather, the temperature of the cattle may be high and may lead to errors. If it is necessary to test during the summer, it can be done, but the work can be done more satisfactorily during the fall and winter.

How Are the Temperatures Interpreted?—The average of the temperatures before injection is determined and if the highest temperature after the injection is 2 degrees F. or more above the average normal, the animal is generally regarded as having given a positive reaction.

Usually the rise in temperature of a tubercular animal is much greater—4 to 6 degrees F.—and there is no question as to the result. When the rise is close to 2 degrees F. and the temperature not above 104 at any time, the reaction is classed as doubtful. In all cases, and especially in the doubtful ones, the interpretation of the record should be made by an experienced person, who should be furnished with all the information possible, concerning the condition of the animals, the age, whether raised or purchased, whether from a healthy or diseased herd, the number of reacting animals in the herd tested, whether tested previously or not, etc.

The positive, tuberculin reaction generally shows a regular rise, the temperature remaining at the highest point for only a short time, then falling gradually to the normal. The decline is usually more rapid than the rise, although exceptions are noted. The character of the curve should also be taken into consideration. A widely fluctuating temperature, say a high, then low and later a high temperature, is not a characteristic curve and should be classed as doubtful rather than as a positive reaction.

Are Any Other Changes to Be Noted in a Reacting Animal Other Than the Rise in Temperature?—Some of the reacting animals show the effects of the tuberculin by shivering, staring coat, refusal to eat, etc. In some cases these symptoms are very noticeable, in others they do not appear at all. In the case of nonreacting animals, no such symptoms are ever noted. There is also frequently to be noted at the point of injection, a slight swelling in the case of reacting animals, but usually this is so slight that it is not noticeable.

Are There Other Ways of Testing Cattle for Tuberculosis Other Than by the Detection of a Fever After Subcutaneous Inoculation? —A number of other tests have been tried, but none have been found nearly so reliable as the subcutaneous, the method above described. Tuberculin especially prepared, has been placed in the eye, or rubbed on a small area of the skin after it has been scratched, or injected into, not beneath, the skin. In the case of many tuberculous animals, a more or less marked inflammation of the eye or skin at the point of application results.

What Should Be Done With the Animals That Give Doubtful Reactions?—They should be retested, but this should not be done for at least 60 days, as a tuberculous animal will not react to a second dose of tuberculin injected soon after the first. Time must be given for the original tuberculin to be eliminated from the system. When retested, a *triple* dose should be given.

Is the Test Always Correct?—Not absolutely so, for a number of reasons. When applied with judgment and care, it is correct in at least 95 per cent of the cases.

To What Are Errors Due?—If cattle are tested that come in the classes mentioned as those that should not be tested, a fever may be noted that is not the result of the tuberculin, or if the cattle are excited, and nervous, a false reaction may be obtained. In this way healthy cows may be wrongly adjudged tubercular. Other cases classed as errors are due to the incomplete post-mortem examination of the animal. The disease may be located in some part of the body not usually examined, such as the brain, bone marrow, glands of the muscles, etc. It is usually impossible to make a thorough examination of the entire carcass especially where the examination must be hurried and superficial as that done by regular meat inspectors whose duty it is not to determine whether the animal is actually diseased or not, but whether the meat should be condemned as unwholesome for food.

Do All Tubercular Animals React to the Test?—Animals in which the disease is far advanced and in which much diseased tissue exists do not always react to a normal dose of tuberculin. Such animals, however, usually show physical signs of the disease. Animals in which the disease is still in the period of incubation do not react. By the period of incubation is meant the time after infection has occurred, but before the disease has become established in the body. In tuberculosis this period may be several months in length.

Animals in which the disease has ceased to progress may not react. Such an animal may react once, but may not react for a number of subsequent tests and may then again react, because the disease has been active, then dormant, and again become active.

Do Cattle Recover From Tuberculosis?—Some animals react once, but not on subsequent tests. If failure to react depends upon the disease becoming dormant, such a condition might be taken to indicate recovery, but so little is known concerning this condition, that it is not advisable to take possible recovery into account in the handling of tubercular animals.

Does the Tuberculin Test Tell Anything Concerning the Extent of the Disease in the Animal?—Nothing whatever. An animal with a single diseased gland will give as marked a reaction as one badly diseased.

THE CONTROL OF TUBERCULOSIS.

How Can a Diseased Herd Be Freed From Tuberculosis?—Test the whole herd. Remove all reacting animals. Retest all suspicious animals in three months, and the entire herd again in one year and *annually* thereafter. Disinfect the stable.

How Can a Herd Be Kept Free From Tuberculosis?—Test annually or at least every two years, and retest all suspicious cases in three months. Test every animal introduced into the herd at the time of purchase, and again in three months. Use a farm separator or feed only skim milk and whey that have been heated.

Is the Above Plan Certain to Prove a Successful One?—No, because an animal in the period of incubation may be purchased, she may not react at the first or second test, and yet may before the next test, 9 to 12 months later, serve to infect other cows.

How Can the Owner Be Perfectly Certain Not to Introduce Tuberculosis Into the Herd?—Buying animals only from herds known *absolutely* to be *free* from tuberculosis,

How Can a Barn Be Disinfected?—The stable should receive a thorough cleaning. Remove all litter and loose wood work, such as box mangers; scrape walls and floors to remove *all* accumulations of dried manure and dust. This can best be done after moistening with a 1 to 1000 solution of corrosive sublimate (one-half ounce to 4 gallons of water). Keep the solution in wooden vessels and remember that it is a strong poison for animals. This solution serves to prevent dust during the cleaning. The removal of litter and dust removes most of the tubercle bacilli from the stable and allows the disinfectant to come in contact with the remainder. Tubercle bacilli in dried manure cannot be killed easily by any disinfectant. Do not place the material removed in the barn yard where cows have access to it, but burn or otherwise dispose of it.

Provide abundant light, 4 sq. ft. of glass per animal, and some means of ventilation for the stable. Cows in light, well-ventilated stables are healthier and less likely to acquire tuberculosis than those kept under less sanitary conditions.

Whitewash the stable. Prepare whitewash as follows: To each 100 parts of *fresh* lime add 60 parts of water; the result should be a dry powder. Sift the slaked lime and add water at the rate of 4 quarts of water to one of lime if the wash is to be applied with a brush. It is preferable to apply it with a spray pump, since by this method it can be forced into every crack. For this purpose the solution must be thinner than where applied with a brush. Whitewash the barn at intervals of six months, or at least once a year.

Can a Healthy Herd Be Raised From a Tuberculous Herd?— Since the calves from tuberculous cows are quite certain to be free from the disease when dropped, a healthy herd can be raised from a diseased foundation by removing the calves from their dams as soon as born (it is usually wise to allow them to suck once or twice), and feeding them on the milk of healthy cows or on the pasteurized milk of the reacting cows. The calves are not to be kept in the same stable, yards, or pastures; in short, no communication of the healthy calves must be allowed with the diseased cows.

COWPOX (VARIOLA).

Variola of cattle, commonly known as cowpox, is a contagious disease of cattle which manifests its presence through an elevation of temperature, a shrinkage in milk production, and by the appearance of characteristic pustular eruptions, especially upon the teats and udders of dairy cows. Although this is a contagious disease strictly speaking, it is so universally harmless and benign in its course that it is robbed of the terrors which usually accompany all spreading diseases, and is allowed to enter a herd of cattle, run its course, and disappear without exciting any particular notice. The disease is quite common in this country, especially in the eastern States.

The contagion of cowpox does not travel through the air from animal to animal, but is only transmitted by actual contact of the contagious principle with the skin of some susceptible animal. It may be carried in this manner, not alone from cattle to cattle, but horses, sheep, goats, and man may readily contract the disease whenever suitable conditions attend their inoculation.

An identical disease frequently appears upon horses, attacking their heels, and thence extending upward along the leg, producing, as it progresses, inflammation and swelling of the skin, followed later by pustules, which soon rupture, discharging a sticky, disagreeable secretion. Other parts of the body are frequently affected in like manner, especially in the region of the head, where the eruptions may appear upon lips and nostrils, or upon the mucous surfaces of the nasal cavities, mouth, or eyes.

Variola of the horse is readily transmitted to cattle, if both are cared for by the same attendant, and, conversely, variola of cattle may be carried from the cow to the horse on the hands of a person who has been milking a cow affected with the disease.

The method of vaccination with material derived from the eruptions of cowpox as a safeguard against the ravages of smallpox in members of the human family is well known. The immunity which such vaccination confers upon the human subject has led many writers to assert that cowpox is simply a modified form of smallpox, whose harmless attack upon the human system is due to a certain attenuation derived during its passage through the system of the cow or horse. The result of numerous experiments, which have been carried out for the purpose of determining the relationship existing between variola of the human and bovine families, seems to show, however, that although possessing many similar characteristics, they are nevertheless distinct, and that in spite of repeated inoculations from cattle to man, and vice versa, no transformation in the real character of the disease ever takes place.

Symptoms.—The disease appears in four to seven days after natural infection, or may evince itself in two or three days as the result of artificial inoculation. Young milch cows are most susceptible to an attack, but older cows, bulls, or young cattle are by no means immune. The attack causes a slight rise in temperature, which is soon followed by the appearance of reddened, inflamed areas, principally upon the teats and udder, and at times on the abdominal skin or the skin of the inner surface of the thighs. In a few cases the skin of the throat and jaws has been found similarly involved. If the affected parts are examined on the second day after the establishment of the inflammation numerous pale red nodules will be found, which gradually expand until they reach a diameter of one-half inch or even larger within a few days. At this period the tops of the nodules become transformed into vesicles which are depressed in the center and contain a pale serous fluid. They usually reach their maturity by the tenth day of the course of the disease and are then the size of a bean. From this time the contents of the vesicles become purulent, which requires about three days, when the typical pox pustule is present, consisting of a swelling with broad, reddened base, within which is an elevated, conical abscess varying from the size of a pea to that of a hazelnut.

HOLSTEIN COW OF GOOD TYPE AND VIGOR. DEPT. OF AGR.

The course of the disease after the full maturity of the pustule is rapid where outside interference has not caused a premature rupture of the small abscess at the apex of the swelling. The pustules gradually become darker colored and dryer until nothing remains but a thick scab, which at last falls off, leaving only a slight whitish scar behind. The total duration of the disease covers some twenty days in each animal, and, owing to the slow spread of the infection from animal to animal, many weeks may elapse before a stable can be fully freed from it. The fallen scabs and crusts may retain their contagious properties for several days when mixed with litter and bedding upon the floor of the stable, and during this period they are at any time capable of producing new outbreaks should fresh cattle be brought into the stalls and thus come into actual contact with them. Again, the pustules may appear, one after another, on a single animal in which case the duration of the disease is materially lengthened.

Treatment.—In herds of cattle that regularly receive careful handling, no special treatment will be found necessary beyond the application of softening and disinfecting agents to such vesicles upon the teats as may have become ruptured by the hands of the milker. Carbolized vaseline or iodoform ointment will be found well suited to this work. In more persistent cases it may be found desirable to use a milking tube in order to prevent the repeated opening of the pustules during the operation of milking. Washing the sores twice daily with a weak solution of zinc chloride (2½ per cent solution) has been found to assist in checking the inflammation and to cleanse and heal the parts by its germicidal action. When the udder is hard, swollen, and painful, support it by a bandage and foment frequently with hot water. If calves are allowed to suckle the cows the pustules become confluent, and the ulcerations may extend up into the teat, causing garget and ruining the whole quarter of the udder.

As young cows are most susceptible to variola, the milker must exercise constant patience with these affected animals so long as their teats or udders are sore and tender, else the patient may contract vicious habits while resisting painful handling. The flow of milk is usually lessened as soon as the fever becomes established, but returns to normal with the return of perfect health.

The practice of thorough cleanliness in handling or milking affected cattle may, in many instances, prevent the dissemination of the trouble among the healthy portion of the herd, but even the greatest care may prove insufficient to check the spread until it has attacked each animal of the herd in turn.

ACTINOMYCOSIS, OR LUMPY JAW.

Cause of the Disease.—Actinomycosis, also known as lumpy jaw, big jaw, wooden tongue, etc., is a chronic infectious disease characterized by the formation of peculiar tumors in various regions of the body, more particularly the head, and due to the specific action of a certain fungus (actinomyces). This fungus is an organism which occurs in the tissues in the form of rosettes, and it has therefore been termed the ray fungus. The disease is not directly transmitted from one animal to another, but it seems apparent that the fungus is conveyed into the tissues by various foodstuffs through slight wounds of the mucous membrane of the mouth, decayed teeth, or during the shedding of milk teeth. The ray fungus is found in nature vegetated on grasses, on the awns of barley, the spears of oats, and on other grains. Quantities of the fungi have been found between vegetable fibers of barley which had penetrated the gums of cattle and on the awns of grain embedded in the tongues of cows.

The tumors and abscesses wherever they may be situated are all found to be the same in origin by the presence of the actinomyces fungus. When they are incised, a very close scrutiny with the naked eye, or at most a hand lens, will reveal the presence of minute grains which vary from a pale-yellow to a sulphur-yellow color. They may be very abundant or so few as to be overlooked. They are embedded in the soft tissues composing the tumor or in the pus of the abscess. With a needle they are easily lifted out from the tissue, and then they appear as roundish masses about one-half millimeter (1/50 inch) in diameter.

These are the bodies whose presence causes sufficient irritation in the tissues into which they find their way to set up inflammatory growths. These growths increase as the fungus continues to multiply until they reach enormous dimensions, if the affected animal is permitted to live long enough. The true nature of this parasite is not yet definitely settled, although many excellent observers have occupied themselves with it. According to earlier observers it is a true fungus. Later ones are inclined to place it among the higher bacteria. Further investigations will be necessary to clear up this subject.

Whatever be the situation of the disease caused by actinomyces, its nature is fundamentally the same and peculiar to the fungus. The pathological details which make this statement clear can not be entered upon in this place, nor would they be of any practical value to the farmer. We will simply dwell upon a few obvious characters.

The consistency of the tumor varies in different situations according to the quantity of fibrous or connective tissue present. When very little of this is present the tumor is of a very soft consistency. As the quantity of connective tissue is increased the tumor is firmer and of a more honeycombed appearance. The individual actinomyces colonies are lodged in the spaces or interstices formed by the meshwork of the connective tissue. There they are surrounded by a mantle of cellular elements which fill up the spaces. By scraping the cut surface of such a tumor these cell masses inclosing the fungi come away, and the latter may be seen as pale-yellow or sulphur-yellow specks, as described above.

Location and Description.—In cattle the disease process may be located both externally, where it is readily detected, and in internal organs. Its preferred seat is on the bones of the lower and upper jaw, in the parotid salivary gland in the angle of the jaw, and in the region of the throat. It may also appear under the skin in different parts of the body. Internally it may attack the tongue and appear in the form of a tumor in the mouth, pharynx, and larynx. It may cause extensive disease of the lungs, more rarely of the digestive tract.

It appears, furthermore, that in certain districts or countries the disease seems to attack, by preference, certain parts. Thus in England actinomycosis of the tongue is most prevalent. In Denmark the soft parts of the head are most prone to disease, while in Russia the lips are the usual seat. In certain parts of Germany actinomycotic tumors of the throat (pharynx), in others disease of the jawbones, is most frequently encountered.

When the disease attacks the soft parts of the head a rather firm swelling appears, in which are formed one or more smaller projecting tumors, varying from the size of a nut to that of an egg. These push their way outward and finally break through the skin as small, reddish, funguslike bodies covered with thin sloughs. Or the original swelling, in place of enlarging in the manner described, may become transformed into an abscess which finally bursts to discharge creamy pus. The abscess cavity, however, does not disappear, but is soon filled with funguslike growths which force their way outward through the opening.

When the tumors are situated within the cavity of the pharynx they have broken through from some gland, perhaps beneath the mucous membrane, where the disease first appeared, and hang or project into the cavity of the pharynx either as pendulous masses with a slender stem or as tumors with a broad base. Their position may be such as to interfere with swallowing and with breathing. In either case serious symptoms will soon appear.

The invasion of the bones of the jaws by actinomycosis must be regarded as one of the most serious forms of the disease. It may start in the marrow of the bone and by a slow extension gradually cause it to become thickened and porous. The growth may continue outward, and after working its way through muscle and skin finally break through and appear externally as stinking fungoid growths. The growth may at the same time work its way inward and appear in the mouth. The disease may also begin in the periosteum, or covering of the bone, and destroy the bone from without inward. When the tongue is affected the animal finds it difficult to eat, the tongue is hard, inflexible, and swollen painfully, and in the advanced cases hangs from the mouth with abundant salivation, thus meriting the term wooden tongue applied to this condition.

Actinomycosis of the lungs is occasionaly observed, and it is not improbable that it has been mistaken at times for tuberculosis. The actinomyces grains are, however, easily observed if the diseased tissue be carefully examined. The changes in the lungs as they appear to the naked eye vary considerably from case to case. Thus, in one animal the lungs were affected as in ordinary broncho-pneumonia as to the location, extent, and appearance of the disease process. The affected lobes had a dark-red flesh appearance, with yellowish areas sprinkled in here and there. These latter areas were the seat of multiplication of the actinomyces fungus. In another case, of which only a small portion of the lungs was sent to the laboratory, these were completely transformed into a uniformly grayish mass, very soft, and pulpy to the touch, and appearing like very soft and moist dough. The actinomyces grains were exceedingly abundant in this tissue, and appeared when the tissue was incised as minute sulphur-yellow grains, densely sprinkled through the tissue, which readily came away and adhered to the knife blade. In still another case a portion of the lung tissue was converted into large, soft masses from 1 to 3 inches in diameter, each partly inclosed in very dense connective tissue. These soft, grayish-yellow masses likewise resembled moist dough in their consistency, and the actinomyces grains, though neither very distinct nor at all abundant, were easily fished out and identified as such. A portion of this growth, which was as large as a child's head, was converted into an abscess filled with creamy semiliquid pus.

This case differed from the preceding in that all appearance of lung tissue had disappeared from the diseased mass. Only on the exterior could the lung tissue be recognized, although even there it had been largely converted into very dense, whitish, connective tissue inclosing the fungoid growth. In the other case the external form of the lung and the shape and outline of the lobules were preserved, but the lung tissue itself was not recognizable as such. In the case first mentioned the changes were still less marked, and actinomycosis would not have been suspected by a simple inspection. These few illustrations suffice to show that actinomycosis of the lungs may appear under quite different forms, and that the nature of the disease can be accurately determined only by finding the fungus itself. Rarely actinomycosis attacks the body externally in places other than the head and neck. Crookshank describes the case of a bull in which the flank was attacked and subsequently the scrotum became diseased. A large portion of the skin of the flank was destroyed and covered with a leathery crust. When this was pulled away the pus beneath it showed the actinomyces grains to the naked eye.

Actinomycosis may also involve the udder, the spermatic cord of castrated animals, vagina, and, when it becomes generalized, the brain, liver, spleen, and muscular tissue.

Actinomycosis may in some cases be confounded with tuberculosis. The diagnosis does not offer any difficulties, since the presence of the actinomyces fungus at once removes any existing doubts. As has already been intimated, these grains, simulating sulphur balls, are visible to the naked eye, and their nature is readily determined with the aid of a microscope.

The course of the disease is quite slow. As the tumors grow they may interfere with the natural functions of the body. According to their situation, mastication, rumination, or breathing may be interfered with, and in this way the animal may become emaciated. Actinomycosis of the jawbones leads to the destruction of the teeth and impedes the movements necessary to chewing the food. Similarly, when the disease attacks the soft parts of the head obstructions may arise in the mouth by an inward growth of the tumor. If tumors exist in the pharynx they may partially obstruct the movements necessary to breathing, or close the air passages and cause partial suffocation.   Actinomycosis of the tongue, in interfering with the many and varied movements of this important organ, is also a serious matter.   There is no reason to suppose that the localized disease interferes with the general health in any other way than indirectly until internal organs, such as the lungs, become involved.

A very small proportion of the cases may recover spontaneously, the tumors being encysted or undergoing calcification.   In most cases the disease yields readily to proper treatment, and about 75 per cent of the affected animals may be cured.

Prevention.—The question as to how and where animals take this disease is one concerning which we are still in the stage of conjecture, because we possess as yet very little information concerning the life history of the actinomyces itself.   The quite unanimous view of all observers is that animals become infected from the food.   The fungus is lodged upon the plants and in some way enters the tissues of the head, the lungs, and the digestive tract, where it sets up its peculiar activity.   It is likewise generally believed that the fungus is, as it were, inoculated into the affected part.   This inoculation is performed by the sharp and pointed parts of plants which penetrate the mucous membrane and carry with them the fungus.   The disease is therefore inoculable rather than contagious.   The mere presence of the diseased animal will not give rise to disease in healthy animals unless the actinomyces grains pass directly from the diseased into some wound or abrasion of the healthy or else drop upon the food which is consumed by the healthy.   Not only are these views deducible from clinical observation, but they have been proved by the positive inoculation of calves and smaller animals with actinomyces. The danger, therefore, of the presence of actinomyces for healthy animals is a limited one.   Nevertheless an animal affected with this disease should not be allowed to go at large or run with other animals. If the fungus is being scattered by discharging growths we certainly can not state at this stage of our knowledge that other animals may not be infected by such distribution, and we must assume, until more positive information is at hand, that this actually occurs.

It is, however, the opinion of the majority of authorities that when actinomycosis appears among a large number of animals they all contract it in the same way from the food.   Much speculation has therefore arisen whether any particular plant or group of plants is the source of the infection and whether any special condition of the soil favors it.   Very little positive information is at hand on these questions.   It would be very desirable for those who live in localities where this disease is prevalent to make statistical and other observations on the occurrence of the disease with reference to the season of the year, the kind of food, the nature of the soil (whether swampy or dry, recently reclaimed or cultivated for a long time) upon which the animals are pastured or upon which the food is grown.

It is highly probable that such investigations will lead to an understanding of the source of the fungus and the means of checking the spread of the disease itself.   Veterinarian Jensen, of Denmark, made some observations upon an extensive outbreak of actinomycosis a number of years ago, which led him to infer that the animals were inoculated by eating barley straw harvested from pieces of ground just reclaimed from the sea. While the animals remained unaffected as long as they pastured on this ground or ate the hay obtained from it, they became diseased after eating the straw of cereals from the same territory. Others have found that cattle grazing upon low pastures along the banks of streams and subject to inundations are more prone to the disease. It has also been observed that food gathered from such grounds may give rise to the disease even after prolonged drying. Actinomycosis is not infrequent in southwestern cattle and is generally supposed to be the result of eating the prickly fruit of the cactus plant, causing wounds of the mucous membrane and subsequent infection with the parasite. Much additional information of a similar kind must be forthcoming before the source and manner of infection in this disease and its dependence upon external conditions will be known. It is not at all improbable that these may vary considerably from place to place.

Treatment.—Until recently treatment has been almost entirely surgical. When the tumors are external and attached to soft parts only, an early removal may lead to recovery. This, of course, can only be undertaken by a trained veterinarian, especially as the various parts of the head and neck contain important vessels, nerves, and ducts which should be injured as little as possible in any operation. Unless the tumor is completely removed it will reappear. Disease of the jawbones is at best a very serious matter, and treatment is likely to be of no avail.

The iodide of potassium is given in doses of 1½ to 2½ drams once a day, dissolved in water, and administered as a drench. The dose should vary somewhat with the size of the animal and with the effects that are produced. If the dose is sufficiently large there appear signs of iodism in the course of a week or ten days. The skin becomes scurfy, there is a weeping from the eyes, catarrh of the nose, and loss of appetite. When these symptoms appear the medicine may be suspended for a few days and afterwards resumed in the same dose. The cure requires from three to six weeks' treatment. Some animals do not improve under treatment with iodide of potassium, and these are generally the ones which show no signs of iodism.

If there is no sign of improvement after the animals have been treated four or five weeks, and the medicine has been given in as large doses as appear desirable, it is an indication that the particular animal is not susceptible to the curative effects of the drug, and the treatment may therefore be abandoned.

It is not, however, advisable to administer iodide of potassium to milch cows, as it will considerably reduce the milk secretion or stop it altogether. Furthermore, a great part of the drug is excreted through the milk, making the milk unfit for use. It should not be given to animals in advanced pregnancy, as there is danger of producing abortion.

The best results are obtained by pushing the drug until you see its effect. The many tests to which this treatment has been subjected have proved with few exceptions its specific curative value. In addition to this the tumor should be painted externally with the tincture of iodine or Lugol's solution, or one of these solutions should be injected subcutaneously into the tumor.

M. Godbille has given as much as 4 drams of potassium iodide in one day to a steer, decreasing the dose one-fourth dram each day until the dose was 1¼ drams, which was maintained until the twelfth day of treatment, when the steer appeared entirely cured.

M. Nocard gave the first day 1½ drams in one dose to a cow; the second and succeeding days a dose of 1 dram in the morning and evening, in each case before feeding. This treatment was continued for ten days, when the animal was cured.

ACTINOMYCOSIS AND THE PUBLIC HEALTH.

The interest which is shown concerning this cattle disease is largely due to the fact that the same disease attacks human beings. Its slow progress, its tendency to remain restricted to certain localities, and the absence of any directly contagious properties have thus far not aroused any anxiety in other countries as to its influence on the cattle industry, not even to the point of placing it among the infectious diseases of which statistics are annually published. Its possible bearing on public health has, however, given this disease a place in the public mind which it hardly deserves.

It has already been stated that the actinomyces fungus found in human disease is considered by authorities the same as that occurring in bovine affections. It is therefore of interest to conclude this article with a brief discussion of the disease in man and its relation to actinomycosis in cattle.

In man the location of the disease process corresponds fairly well with that in cattle. The majority of cases which have been reported in different parts of the world—and they are now quite numerous—indicate disease of the face. The skin, tongue, or the jawbones may become affected, and by a very slow process it may extend downward upon the neck and even into the cavity of the chest. In many cases the teeth have been found in a state of more or less advanced decay and ulceration. In a few cases disease of the lungs was observed without coexisting disease of the bones or soft parts of the head. In such cases the fungus must have been inhaled. The disease of the lungs after a time extends upon the chest wall. Here it may corrode the ribs and work its way through the muscles and the skin. An abscess is thus formed, discharging pus containing actinomyces grains. Disease of the digestive organs caused by this fungus has also been observed in a few instances.

Granting the identity of the disease in man and cattle, the question has been raised whether cattle are responsible for the disease in man. Any transmission of the infectious agent may be conceived of as taking place during the life of the animal and after slaughter from the meat. That human beings have contracted actinomycosis by coming in contact with diseased cattle is not shown by the cases that have hitherto been reported, for the occupations of most of the patients did not bring them into any relation whatever with cattle.

While the possibility of such direct transmission is not denied, never theless it must be considered extremely rare.   Practically the sam position is maintained at present by most authorities as regards th transmission of the disease to man by eating meat.   Israel, who ha studied this question carefully, found the disease in Jews who neve ate pork* and who likewise were protected by the rigorous meat in spection practiced by their sect from bovine actinomycosis.   Furthe more, it must be borne in mind that actinomycosis is a local diseas causing great destruction of tissue where the fungus multiplies, bu very rarely becoming generally disseminated over the body from th original disease focus.   The fungus is only found in places where th disease process is manifest to the eye or becomes so in a very shor time after the lodgment of the fungus.   Only the greatest negligenc would allow the actually diseased parts to be sold and consumed Finally, this parasite, like all others, would be destroyed in the proc ess of cooking.   The majority of authorities thus do not believ that actinomycosis in man is directly traceable to the disease in an mals, but are of the opinion that both man and animals are infecte from a third source.   This source has already been discussed abov How far these views may be modified by further and more telling in vestigations of the parasitic fungus itself no one can predict.   Ther are still wide gaps in our knowledge, and the above presentation sim ply summarizes the prevailing views,to which there are,of course,dis senters.   An attempt to give the views of both sides on this question would necessitate the summarizing and impartial discussion of all th experiments thus far made—a task entirely beyond the scope of th present work.

Whether an animal affected with actinomycosis should be use for human food after all diseased organs and tissues have been thor oughly removed is a question the answer to which depends on variety of circumstances.   Among these may be mentioned the thor oughness of the meat inspection itself, which allows no really disease animal to pass muster, the extent of the disease, and the general con dition of the animal affected.

Whether an animal affected with actinomyces should be use for human food after all diseased organs and tissues have been thor oughly removed depends upon the extent of the disease and the gen eral condition of the animal affected.   If the carcass is in a well-nour ished condition and there is no evidence upon post-mortem examina tion that the disease has extended from a primary area of infectio in the head, the carcass may be passed, but the head, including th tongue, should be condemned.   If the carcass is in a well-nourishe condition and the disease has extended beyond the primary area o. infection, the carcass may be passed after destroying the affecte parts, provided the lesions are slight, calcified, or encapsulated, an are confined to a single body cavity in addition to the original seat o infection.   When, however, the general health of the animal is af fected, or when there are more extensive areas or a larger number o

---

*Hogs are subject to actinomycosis.

Red Polled Bull. Dept. of Agr.

rhorn Bull; "Polikao" at Seven Years of Age. Champion at Rural Soci-
' Show in 1905. Weight when Photographed 2,700 Pounds. Dept. of Agr.

centers of disease scattered throughout the body than above described, the carcass should be condemned as unfit for human food.

ANTHRAX.

Anthrax, or charbon, may be defined as an infectious disease which is caused by specific bacteria, known as anthrax bacilli, and which is more or less restricted by conditions of soil and moisture to definite geographical localities. While it is chiefly limited to cattle and sheep, it may be transmitted to goats, horses, cats, and certain kinds of game. Smaller animals, such as mice, rabbits, and guinea pigs, speedily succumb to inoculation. Dogs and hogs are slightly susceptible, while fowls are practically immune. The variety of domesticated animals which it may attack renders it one of the most dreaded scourges of animal life. It may even attack man. Of this more will be stated farther on.

Cause.—The cause of anthrax is a microscopic organism known as the anthrax bacillus. In form it is cylindrical or rod-like, measuring 1/5,000 to 1/2,500 inch in length and 1/25,000 inch in diameter. Like all bacteria, these rod-like bodies have the power of indefinite multiplication, and in the body of infected animals they produce death by rapidly increasing in numbers and producing substances which poison the body. In the blood they multiply in number by becoming elongated and then dividing into two, each new organism continuing the same process indefinitely. Outside of the body, however, they multiply in a different way when under conditions unfavorable to growth. Oval bodies, which are called spores, appear within the rods, and remain alive and capable of germination after years of drying. They also resist heat to a remarkable degree, so that boiling water is necessary to destroy them. The bacilli themselves, on the other hand, show only very little resistance to heat and drying. It has long been known that the anthrax virus thrives best under certain conditions of the soil and on territories subject to floods and inundations. The particular kinds of soil upon which the disease is observed are black, loose, warm, humous soils, also those containing lime, marl, and clay, finally peaty, swampy soils resting upon strata which hold the water, or, in other words, are impervious. Hence fields containing stagnant pools may be the source of infection. The infection may be limited to certain farms, or even to restricted areas on such farms. Even the Alps, over 3,000 feet above sea level, where such conditions prevail in secluded valleys, anthrax persists among herds.

Aside from these limitations to specific conditions of the soil, anthrax is a disease of world-wide distribution. It exists in most countries of Europe, in Asia, Africa, Australia, and in our own country in the lower Missippi Valley, the Gulf States, and in some of the Eastern and Western States. It seems to be gradually spreading in this country and occurs in new districts every year.

Meteorological conditions also have an important share in determining the severity of the disease. On those tracts subject to inundations in spring a very hot, dry summer is apt to cause a severe outbreak. The relation which the bacillus bears to these conditions is not positively known. It may be that during and immediately after inundations or in stagnant water the bacilli find enough nourishment in the water here and there to multiply and produce an abundant crop of spores, which are subsequently carried, in a dry condition, by the winds during the period of drought and disseminated over the vegetation. Animals feeding upon this vegetation may contract the disease if the spores germinate in the body.

Another source of the virus, and one regarded by many authorities as perhaps the most important, is the body of an animal which has died of anthrax. It will be remembered that in such bodies the anthrax bacilli are present in enormous numbers, and wherever blood or other body fluids are exposed to the air on the surface of the carcass there the formation of spores will go on in the warm season of the year with great rapidity. It will thus be readily understood how this disease may become stationary in a given locality and appear year after year and even grow in severity if the carcasses of animals which have succumbed to it are not properly disposed of. These should be buried deeply, so that spore formation may be prevented and no animal have access to them. By exercising this precaution the disease will not be disseminated by flies and other insect pests.

We have thus two agents at work in maintaining the disease in any locality—the soil and meteorological conditions and the carcasses of animals that have died of the disease. Besides these dangers, which are of immediate consequence to cattle on pastures, the virus may be carried from place to place in hides, hair, wool, hoofs, and horns, and it may be stored in the hay or other fodder from the infected fields and cause an outbreak among stabled animals feeding upon it in winter. In this manner the affection has been introduced into far distant localities.

How Cattle Are Infected.—We have seen above that the spores of the anthrax bacilli, which correspond in their functions to the seeds of higher plants, and which are the elements that resist the unfavorable conditions in the soil, air, and water longest, are the chief agents of infection. They may be taken into the body with the food and produce disease which begins in the intestinal tract; or they may come in contact with scratches, bites, or other wounds of the skin, the mouth, and tongue, and produce in these situations swellings or carbuncles. From such swellings the bacilli penetrate into the blood and produce a general disease.

It has likewise been claimed that the disease may be transmitted by various kinds of insects which carry the bacilli from the sick and inoculate the healthy as they pierce the skin. When infection of the blood takes place from the intestines the carbuncles may be absent. It has already been stated that since the anthrax spores live for several years, the disease may be contracted in winter from food gathered on permanently infected fields.

The disease may appear sporadically, i. e., only one or several animals may be infected while the rest of the herd remain well, or it may appear as an epizoötic attacking a large number at about the same time.

Symptoms.—The symptoms in cattle vary considerably, according as the disease begins in the skin, in the lungs, or in the intestines. They depend also on the severity of the attack. Thus we may have what is called *anthrax peracutus* or apoplectiform, when the animal dies very suddenly as if from apoplexy. Such cases usually occur in the beginning of an outbreak. The animal, without having shown any signs of disease, suddenly drops down in the pasture and dies in convulsions, or an animal apparently well at night is found dead in the morning.

The second type *(anthrax acutus)*, without any external swellings, is the one most commonly observed in cattle. The disease begins with a high fever. The temperature may reach 106° to 107° F. The pulse beats from 80 to 100 per minute. Feeding and rumination are suspended. Chills and muscular tremors may appear and the skin shows uneven temperature. The ears and base of the horns are cold, the coat staring. The animals are dull and stupid and manifest great weakness.

To these symptoms others are added in the course of the disease. The dullness may give way to great uneasiness, champing of the jaws, spasms of the limbs, kicking and pawing the ground. The breathing may become labored. The nostrils then dilate, the mouth is open, the head raised, and all muscles of the chest are strained during breathing, while the visible mucous membranes (nose, mouth, rectum, and vagina) become bluish. If the disease has started in the bowels, there is much pain, as shown by the moaning of the animal; the discharges, at first firm, become softer and covered with serum, mucus, and blood.

As the disease approaches the fatal termination the weakness of the animal increases. It leans against supports or lies down. Blood vessels may rupture and give rise to spots of blood on the various mucous membranes and bloody discharges from nose, mouth, rectum, and vagina. The urine not infrequently contains blood (red-water). Death ensues within one or two days.

A third type of the disease *(anthrax subacutus)* includes those cases in which the disease is more prolonged. It may last from three to seven days and terminate fatally or end in recovery. In this type, which is rarely observed, the symptoms are practically as described in the acute form, only less marked.

In connection with these types of intestinal anthrax, swellings may appear under the skin in different parts of the body, or the disease may start from such a swelling, caused by the inoculation of anthrax spores in one of the several different ways already described. If the disease begins in the skin it agrees in general with the subacute form in prolonged duration, and it may occasionally terminate in recovery if the swellings are thoroughly incised and treated.

Lesions.—These swellings appear as edemas and carbuncles. The former are doughy tumors of a more or less flattish form passing gradually into the surrounding healthy tissue. They are situated as a rule beneath the skin in the fatty layer, and the skin itself is at first of healthy appearance, so that they are often overlooked, especially when covered with a good coat of hair. When they are cut open they are found to consist of a peculiar jelly-like mass of a yellowish color and more or less stained by blood. The carbuncles are firm, hot, tender swellings, which later become cool and painless and undergo mortification. The edemas and carbuncles may also appear in the mouth, pharynx, larynx, in the tongue, and in the rectum.

The bodies of cattle which have died of anthrax soon lose their rigidity and become bloated, because decomposition sets in very rapidly. From the mouth, nose, and anus blood-stained fluid flows in small quantities. When such carcasses are opened and examined, it will be found that nearly all organs are sprinkled with spots of blood or extravasations of various sizes. The spleen is enlarged from two to five times, the pulp blackish and soft and occasionally disintegrated. The blood is of tarry consistency, not firmly coagulated, and blackish in color. In the abdomen, the thoracic cavity, and in the pericardium, or bag surrounding the heart, more or less blood-stained fluid is present. In addition to these characteristic signs, the carbuncles and swellings under the skin, already described, will aid in determining the true nature of the disease. The most reliable method of diagnosis is the examination of the blood and tissues for anthrax bacilli. This requires a trained bacteriologist. The fatal cases of anthrax number 70 to 90 per cent, and are usually more numerous at the first outbreak of the disease.

Differential Diagnosis.—The diagnosis from blackleg may be made by noting the subcutaneous swellings which appear upon the patient. Those of blackleg are found to crackle under pressure with the finger, owing to the presence of gas within the tissues, while the tumors of anthrax, being due to the presence of serum, are entirely free from this quality and have a somewhat doughy consistence. The tumors of blackleg usually locate on the shoulder or thigh and are not found so frequently about the neck and side of the body as are the swellings of anthrax. The blood of animals dead of blackleg is normal, and the spleen does not appear swollen or darkened, as in animals affected with anthrax. The chief differences between anthrax and Texas fever are that the course of the former is more acute and the blood of the animal is dark and of a tar-like consistence, while in the case of Texas fever it will be found thinner than normal. The presence of Texas fever ticks on the cattle would also lead one to suspect Texas fever in regions where cattle are not immune from this disease.

Treatment.—This is as a rule ineffectual and useless, excepting perhaps in cases which originate from external wounds. The swellings should be opened freely by long incisions with a sharp knife and washed several times daily with carbolic acid solution (1 ounce to a quart of water). Care should be taken to disinfect thoroughly any fluid discharges that may follow such incision. When suppuration has set in, the treatment recommended in the chapter on wounds should be carried out.

Prevention.—Since treatment is of little or no avail in this disease, prevention is the most important subject demanding consideration. The various means to be suggested may be brought under two heads: (1) The surroundings of the animal, and (2) protective inoculation.

(1) What has already been stated in the foregoing pages on those conditions of the pastures which are favorable to anthrax will suggest to most minds, after a little thought, some of the preventive measures which may be of service in reducing losses in anthrax localities. All that conduces to a better state of the soil should be attempted. The State or Nation should do its share in preventing frequent inundations, by appropriate engineering. If pools of stagnant water exist on the pastures, or if any particular portions are known by experience to give rise to anthrax, they should be fenced off. Efforts should likewise be made toward the proper draining of swampy lands frequented by cattle. Sometimes it has been found desirable to abandon for a season any infected and dangerous pastures. This remedy can not be carried out by most farmers, and it is liable to extend the infected territory. In some instances withdrawal of cattle from pastures entirely and feeding them in stables is said to have reduced the losses.

It is of the utmost importance that carcasses of animals which have died of anthrax should be properly disposed of, since every portion of such animal contains the bacilli, ready to form spores when exposed to the air. Perhaps the simplest means is to bury the carcasses deep, where they can not be exposed by dogs or wild animals. It may be necessary to bury them on the pasture, but it is better to remove them to places not frequented by susceptible animals and to a point where drainage from the graves can not infect any water supply.

If they are moved some distance it must be borne in mind that the ground and all objects which have come in contact with the carcass should be disinfected. This is best accomplished with chlorid of lime. For washing utensils, etc., a 5 per cent solution may be prepared by adding 3 ounces to 2 quarts of water. This should be prepared fresh from the powder, and it is but little trouble to have a small tin measure of known capacity to dip out the powder, to be added to the water whenever necessary. The carcass and the ground should be sprinkled with powdered chlorid, or, if this be not at hand, an abundance of ordinary unslaked lime should be used in its place.

The removal of carcasses to rendering establishments is always fraught with danger, unless those who handle them are thoroughly aware of the danger of scattering the virus by careless handling in wagons which are not tight. As a rule, the persons in charge of such transfer have no training for this important work, so that deep burial is to be preferred. Burning large carcasses is not always feasible. It is, however, the most certain means of destroying infectious material of any kind, and should be resorted to whenever practicable and economical. All carcasses, whether buried, rendered, or burned, should be disposed of without being opened. When stables have become infected they should be thoroughly cleaned out, and the solution of chloride of lime freely applied on floors and woodwork. The feed should be carefully protected from contamination with the manure or other discharges from the sick.

(2) *Preventive Inoculation.*—One of the most important discoveries in connection with this disease was made by Louis Pasteur in 1881, and consisted in the new principle of producing immunity by the inoculation of weakened cultures of the bacillus causing the disease. This method has been quite extensively adopted in France, and to some extent in other European countries, and in the United States. The fluid used for inoculation consists of bouillon in which modified anthrax bacilli have multiplied and are present in large numbers. The bacilli have been modified by heat so that they have lost to a certain degree their original virulence. Two vaccines are prepared. The first or weaker for the first inoculation is obtained by subjecting the bacilli to the attenuating effects of heat for a longer period of time than is the case with the second or stronger vaccine for a second inoculation some twelve days later.

These vaccines have been used for cattle and sheep. Their power to prevent a subsequent attack of anthrax has been the subject of controversy ever since their use began. The French claim that the vaccines are successful in protecting cattle and sheep and that the losses from anthrax in France have been much reduced by their persistent application. According to other observers there are several difficulties inherent in the practical application of anthrax vaccination. Among these may be mentioned the variable degree of attenuation of different tubes of the vaccine and the varying susceptibility of the animals to be inoculated. Nevertheless, the use of this vaccine is increasing and has reduced the mortality in the affected districts from an average of 10 per cent with sheep to less than 1 per cent, and from 5 per cent with cattle to less than one-half of 1 per cent.

It is very important to call attention to the possibility of distributing anthrax by this method of protective inoculation, since the bacilli themselves are present in the culture liquid. It is true that they have been modified and weakened by the process adopted by Pasteur, but it is not impossible that such modified virus may regain its original virulence after it has been scattered broadcast by the inoculation of large herds. No vaccination should therefore be permitted in localities free from anthrax. It is also obviously unsafe to have such vaccine injected by a layman; instead, it should be handled only by a competent veterinarian.

Anthrax is an entirely different disease from blackleg, and therefore blackleg vaccine does not act as a preventive against anthrax.

ANTHRAX IN MAN (MALIGNANT PUSTULE, OR CARBUNCLE).

Anthrax may be transmitted to a man in handling the carcasses and hides of animals which have succumbed to the disease. The infection usually takes place through some abrasion or slight wound of the skin into which the anthrax spores, or bacilli, find their way. The point of inoculation appears at first as a dark point or patch, compared by some writers to the sting of a flea. After a few hours this is changed into a reddened pimple, which bears on its summit, usually around a hair, a yellowish blister, or vesicle, which later on becomes red or bluish in color. The burning sensation in this stage is very great. Later on, this pimple enlarges, its center becomes dry, gangrenous, and is surrounded by an elevated discolored swelling. The center becomes drier and more leather-like, and sinks in as the whole increases in size. The skin around this swelling, or carbuncle, is stained yellow or bluish, and is not infrequently swollen and doughy to the touch. The carbuncle itself rarely grows larger than a pea or a small nut, and is but slightly painful.

Anthrax swellings, or edemas, already described as occurring in cattle, may also be found in man, and they are at times so extensive as to produce distortion in the appearance of the part of the body on which they are located. The color of the skin over these swellings varies according to the situation and thickness of the skin and the stage of the disease, and may be white, red, bluish, or blackish.

As these carbuncles and swellings may lead, sooner or later, to an infection of the entire body, and thus be fatal, surgical assistance should at once be called if there is well-grounded suspicion that any swellings resembling those described above have been due to inoculation with anthrax virus. Inasmuch as physicians differ as to treatment of such accidents in man, it would be out of place to make any suggestions in this connection.

To show that the transmission of anthrax to man is not so very uncommon, we take the following figures from the report of the German Government for 1890: One hundred and eleven cases were brought to the notice of the authorities, of which 11 terminated fatally. The largest number of inoculations were due to the slaughtering, opening, and skinning of animals affected with anthrax. Hence the butchers suffered most extensively. Of the 111 thus affected, 36 belonged to this craft.

In addition to anthrax of the skin (known as malignant pustule), human beings are subject, though very rarely, to the disease of the lungs and the digestive organs. In the former case the spores are inhaled by workmen in establishments in which wool, hides, and rags are worked over, and it is therefore known as wool-sorter's disease. In the latter case the disease is contracted by eating the flesh of diseased animals which has not been thoroughly cooked. These forms of the disease are more fatal than those in which the disease starts from the skin.

BLACKLEG.

Blackleg, blackquarter, quarter-ill, symptomatic anthrax, *charbon symptomatique* of the French, *Rauschbrand* of the Germans, is a rapidly fatal infectious disease of young cattle, associated with external swellings which emit a crackling sound when handled. This disease was formerly regarded identical with anthrax, but investigations carried out by various scientists in recent times have definitely proved the entire dissimilarity of the two affections, both from a clinical and causal standpoint. The disease is produced by a specific bacillus, readily distinguishable from that causing anthrax. Cattle between 6 months and 2 years of age are the most susceptible. Sucking calves under 6 months are rarely attacked, nor are they as susceptible to inoculation as older animals. Cattle over 2 years of age may become affected, but such cases are infrequent. Sheep and goats may also contract this disease, but man, horses, hogs, dogs, cats, and fowls appear to be immune.

Like anthrax, blackbleg is more or less restricted to definite localities. There are certain pastures upon which the disease regularly appears in the summer and fall of the year. As to any peculiarities of the soil nothing is definitely known. Some authors are inclined to regard moist, undrained, and swampy pastures favorable to this disease, but these theories will hardly hold, as it is found in all kinds of soils, in all altitudes, at all seasons of the year, and under various climatic conditions. It occurs in this country from the Atlantic to the Pacific and from Mexico to Canada, but it is more prevalent in Western and Southwestern States. Cattle in Cuba and Australia also suffer.

The cause of the disease is a bacillus resembling in some minor respects the anthrax bacillus and differing but little from it in size. It also possesses the power of forming within itself a spore. What has already been stated concerning the significance of the spore of the anthrax bacillus applies equally well to these bodies. They resist destructive agents for a considerable length of time, and may still produce disease when inoculated after several years of drying. This fact may account for the occasional appearance of blackleg in stables. In order to meet the requirements for the development of the spores, which only takes place in the absence of the atmosphere, it is necessary that the wound be very small and deep enough to penetrate the subcutaneous tissue.

Several observers have found this organism in the mud of swamps. By placing a little of this mud under the skin the disease has been called forth.

Since the disease may be produced by placing under the skin material containing the specific bacilli and spores, it has been assumed that cattle contract the disease through wounds, principally of the skin, or very rarely of the mouth, tongue, and throat. Slight wounds into which the virus may find access may be caused by barbed wire, stubbles, thorns, briers, grass burs, and sharp or pointed parts of food.

Pure Bred Jersey.   Foundation Cow for Jersey Herd at College Farm.   Dept. of Agr.

The symptoms of blackleg may be either of a general or a local nature, though more frequently of the latter. The general symptoms are very much like those belonging to other acute infectious or bacterial diseases. They begin from one to three days after the infection has taken place with loss of appetite and of rumination, with dullness and debility, and a high fever. The temperature may rise to 107° F. To these may be added lameness or stiffness of one or more limbs, due to the tumor or swelling quite invariably accompanying the disease. After a period of disease lasting from one to three days the affected animal almost always succumbs. Death is preceded by increasing weakness, difficult breathing, and occasional attacks of violent convulsions.

The most important characteristic of this disease is the appearance of a tumor or swelling under the skin of the affected animal a few hours after the setting in of the constitutional symptoms described above. In some cases it may appear first. This tumor may be located on the thighs (hence blackleg, blackquarter), the neck, the shoulder, the breast, the flanks, or the rump; never below the carpal (or knee) and the hock joint. It more rarely appears in the throat and at the base of the tongue. The tumor, at first small and painful, spreads very rapidly both in depth and extent. When it is stroked or handled a peculiar crackling sound is heard under the skin. This is due to a collection of gas formed by the bacilli as they multiply. At this stage the skin becomes dry, parchment-like, and cool to the touch in the center of the tumor. If the swelling is cut into, a frothy, dark-red, rather disagreeably smelling fluid is discharged. The animal manifests little or no pain during the operation.

As it is frequently desirable to know whether the disease is anthrax or blackleg, a few of the most obvious post-mortem changes may here be cited. The characteristic tumor with its crackling sound when stroked has already been described. If after the death of the animal it be more thoroughly examined, it will be noted that the tissue under the skin is infiltrated with blood and yellowish, jelly-like material and gas bubbles. The muscular tissue beneath the swelling may be brownish or black, shading into dark red. It is soft and easily torn and broken up. The muscle tissue is distended with numerous smaller or larger gas-filled cavities, often to such an extent as to produce a resemblance to lung tissue. Upon incision it does not collapse perceptibly, as the gas cavities are not connected with each other.

In the abdomen and the thorax blood-stained fluid is not infrequently found, together with blood-staining of the lining membrane of these cavities. Blood spots (or ecchymoses) are also found on the heart and lungs. The liver is congested, but the spleen is always normal.

Differential Diagnosis.—Among the features of this disease which distinguish it from anthrax may be mentioned the unchanged spleen and the ready clotting of the blood. It will be remembered that in anthrax the spleen (milt) is very much enlarged, the blood tarry, coagulating feebly. The anthrax carbuncles and swellings differ from the blackleg swellings in not containing gas, in being hard and solid, and in causing death less rapidly.

It is difficult to distinguish between the swellings of blackleg and malignant edema, since they resemble each other very closely and both are distended with gas. Malignant edema, however, generally starts from a wound of considerable size; it usually follows surgical operations, and does not result from the small abrasions and pricks to which animals are subjected in pastures. Inoculation experiments of guinea pigs, rabbits, and chickens will also disclose the differences between the above three diseases, since all of these species are killed by the germ of malignant edema, only the first two species by the anthrax bacillus, while the guinea pigs alone will succumb to the blackleg infection. Hemorrhagic septicemia may be differentiated from blackleg by its affecting cattle of all ages, by the location of the swelling usually about the region of the throat, neck, and dewlap, by the soft, doughy character of these swellings without the presence of gas bubbles, and finally by the characteristic hemorrhages widely distributed throughout the body. Other means of diagnosis, which have reference to the specific bacilli, to the inoculable character of the virus upon small animals, and which are of decisive and final importance, can be utilized only by the trained bacteriologist and veterinarian.

Treatment.—In this disease remedies have thus far proved unavailing. Some writers recommend the use of certain drugs, which seem to have been beneficial in a few cases, but a thorough trial has shown them to be valueless. Others advise that the swelling be opened by deep and long incisions and a strong disinfectant, such as a 5 per cent solution of carbolic acid, applied to the exposed parts, but this procedure can not be too strongly condemned. Since nearly all those attacked die in spite of every kind of treatment, and in view of the fact that the germs of the disease are scattered over the stables or pastures when these tumors are opened, thus becoming a source of danger to other cattle, it is obvious that such measures do more harm than good and should be put aside as dangerous. Bleeding, nerving, roweling, or setoning have likewise some adherents, but the evidence indicates that they have neither curative nor preventive value and therefore should be discarded for the method of vaccination which has been thoroughly tried out and proved to be efficacious in preventing the disease.

Prevention.—The various means suggested under Anthrax to prevent the spread or recurrence of this disease are equally applicable to blackleg, and hence do not need to be repeated here in full. They consist of the removal of the animals from the infected pasture to a noninfected field, the draining of the swampy ground, the burial or burning of the carcasses to prevent the dissemination of the germs over vast areas through the agency of dogs, wolves, buzzards, and crows, the disinfection of the stables and the ground where the animals lay at the time of death, and, if possible, the destruction of the germs on the infected pastures. One of the most effective methods for freeing an infected pasture from blackleg is to allow the grass to grow up high, and, when sufficiently dry, to burn it off. One burning off, however, is not sufficient to redeem an infected pasture, but the process should be repeated several years in succession. This method, however, is in many instances impracticable, as few cattle owners can afford to practice it, and the only means left for the protection of the animals is vaccination.

Immunization by Vaccination.—Three French Veterinarians, Arloing, Cornevin, and Thomas, were the first to discover that cattle may be protected against blackleg by inoculation with virulent material obtained from animals which have died of this disease. Later they devised a method of inoculation with the attenuated or weakened blackleg spores which produced immunity from natural or artificial inoculation of virulent blackleg germs. Their method has undergone various modifications both in regard to the manufacture of the vaccine and in the mode of its application. Kitt, a German scientist, modified the method so that but one inoculation of the vaccine was required instead of two, as was the case with that made by the French investigators. The vaccine prepared and distributed by the Bureau of Animal Industry combines the principle of Arloing, Cornevin, and Thomas and the modification of Kitt.

By vaccination we understand the injection into the system of a minute amount of attenuated—that is, artificially weakened—blackleg virus. This virus is obtained from animals which have died from blackleg, by securing the affected muscles, cutting them into strips, and drying them in the air. When they are perfectly dry they are pulverized and mixed with water to form a paste, smeared in a thin layer on flat dishes, placed in an oven, and heated for six hours at a temperature close to that of boiling water. The paste is then transformed into a hard crust, which is pulverized and sifted and distributed in packages containing either 10 or 25 doses. This constitutes the vaccine, the strength of which is thoroughly tested on experiment animals before it is distributed among the cattle owners. This vaccine, which is in the form of a brownish dry powder, is mixed with definite quantities of sterile water, filtered, and the filtrate injected by means of a hypodermic syringe under the skin in front of the shoulder of the animal to be vaccinated. The inoculation is usually followed by insignificant symptoms. In a few cases there is a slight rise of temperature, and by close observation a minute swelling may be noted at the point of inoculation. The immunity conferred in this way may last for eighteen months, but animals vaccinated before they are 6 months old and those in badly infected districts should be revaccinated before the following blackleg season.

The effect of the vaccine prepared by this Bureau in preventing outbreaks of the disease and in immediately abating outbreaks already in progress has been highly satisfactory, and it is not to be doubted that thousands of young cattle have been saved to the stock owners during the six and a half years in which the vaccine has been distributed. More than 7,700,000 doses have been sent out during this period, and from reports received it is safe to conclude that more than one-half of this quantity has actually been injected, whereby the percentage of loss from blackleg has been reduced from 10, 15, or 20 per cent, which annually occurred before using, to less than 1 per cent per annum. With these figures before us it is plain that the general introduction of preventive vaccination must be of material benefit to the cattle raisers in the infected districts. Moreover, there is every reason to believe that with the continued use of blackleg vaccine in all districts where the disease is known to occur and an earnest effort on the part of the stock owners to prevent the reinfection of their pastures by following the direction given, blackleg may be kept in check and gradually eradicated.

CALF DIPHTHERIA (NECROTIC STOMATITIS).

Necrotic stomatitis is an acute, specific, highly contagious inflammation of the mouth, occurring in young cattle and characterized, locally, by the formation of ulcers and caseo-necrotic patches and by constitutional symptoms, chiefly toxic.

This disease has also been termed calf diphtheria, gangrenous stomatitis, ulcerative stomatitis, malignant stomatitis, tubercular stomatitis, and diphtheric patches of the oral mucous membrane.

History.—During the last few years farmers and cattlemen in this country, especially in Colorado, Texas, and South Dakota, have increasingly noted the occurrence of enzootics of sore mouth among the young animals of their herds. Instead of healing, like the usual forms, of themselves, these cases, if untreated, die. Careful study of some of them has resulted in their identification with cases reported in 1877 by Dammann, from the shore of the Baltic; in 1878 by Blazekowic, in Slavonia; in 1879 by Vollers, in Holstein; in 1880 by Lenglen, in France; in 1881 by Macgillivray, in England, and in 1884 by Löffler, who isolated and described the micro-organism which produces the disease. Bang obtained this organism from the diphtheretic lesions of calves in 1890, and Kitt likewise recovered the bacillus from similar lesions of the larynx and pharynx of calves and pigs in 1893.

Etiology.—The cause of necrotic stomatitis, as demonstrated by Löffler and since confirmed by other investigators, is *Bacillus necrophorus*, often spoken of as the bacillus of necrosis. This organism varies in form from a coccoid rod to long, wavy filaments, which may reach a length of 100 μ; the width varies from 0.75 μ to 1 μ. Hence it is described as polymorphic. It does not stain by Gram, but takes the ordinary aniline dyes, often presenting, especially the longer forms, a beaded appearance. A characteristic of the organism, of great moment when we come to treatment, is that it grows only in the absence of oxygen, from which fact it is described as an obligate anaerobe.

Very few organisms exhibit a wider range of pathogenesis. According to clinical observation up to the present time, *Bacillus necrophorus* is pathogenic for cattle, horses, hogs, sheep, reindeer, kangaroos, antelope, and rabbits. Experimentally it has been proved pathogenic for rabbits and white mice. The dog, cat, guinea pig, pigeon, and chicken appear to be absolutely immune. It is not pathogenic for man.

The importance of this bacillus is far beyond even its relation to necrotic stomatitis. Besides this disease it has been demonstrated as the causative factor in foot rot, multiple liver abscesses, disseminated liver necrosis, embolic necrosis of the lungs, necrosis of the heart, in cattle; gangrenous pox of the teats, diphtheria of the uterus and vagina, in cows; diphtheritic inflammation of the small intestine of calves. Among horses it is the agent in the production of necrotic malanders, quittor, and diphtheritic inflammation of the large intestine. In hogs it has caused necrotic or diphtheritic processes in the mucous membrane of the mouth, necrosis of the anterior wall of the nasal septum, and pulmonary and intestinal necrosis, accompanying hog cholera. Abscesses of the liver, gangrenous processes of the lips and nose, and gangrenous affections of the hoof have all been caused in sheep by this organism.

Pathology.—The principal lesions in necrotic stomatitis occur in the mucous membrane of the mouth and pharynx. The alterations may extend to the nasal cavities, the larynx, the trachea, the lung, the esophagus, the intestines, and to the hoof. The oral surfaces affected are, in the order of frequency, tongue, cheeks, hard palate, gums, lips, and pharynx. In the majority of cases the primary infection seems to occur in the tongue.

Infection takes place by inoculation. Some abrasion or break in the continuity of the mucous membrane of the mouth occurs. Very likely the origin may be connected with the eruption of the first teeth after birth, or, in animals somewhat older, the entrance of a sharp-pointed particle of food. Gaining an entrance at this point, the bacilli begin to multiply. During their development they elaborate a toxin, or poisonous substance, which causes the death, or necrosis, of the epithelial, or superficial, layer of the mucous membrane and also of the white blood cells which have sallied forth through the vessel walls to the defense of the tissues against the bacillary attack. This destruction of the surface epithelium seems to be the essential factor in the production of the caseous patch, often called the false membrane. From the connective tissue framework below is poured forth an inflammatory exudate highly albuminous or rich in fibrin-forming elements. When this exudate and the necrosed cellular elements come in contact, the latter furnish a fibrin ferment which transforms the exudate into a fibrinous mass. This process is known as coagulation necrosis, and the resulting fibroid mass, containing in its meshes the necrosed and degenerated epithelium and leucocytes, constitutes the diphtheric or false membrane. Did the process cease at this point it would be properly called a diphtheric inflammation. But it does not. A caseating ferment is supplied by the bacilli, and this, acting upon the fibroid patch, transforms it into a dry, finely granular, yellowish mass of tissue detritus resembling cheese.

Frequently this caseous inflammation results in the formation of one or more ulcers with thickened, slightly reddened borders, surmounted by several layers of this necrosed tissue. The floor of the ulcer is formed by a grayish yellow, corroded surface, under which the tissue is transformed into a dry friable or firm cheesy mass. In the tongue this may progress to two fingers' thickness into the muscular portion; in the cheek it may form an external opening, permitting fluids to escape from the mouth; upon the palate it frequently reaches and includes the bone in its destructive course; upon the gums it has produced necrosis of the tooth sockets, causing loss of the teeth. In the advanced forms, caseous foci may be seen in the lung and in the liver and necrotic patches observed on the mucous membrane of the gastro-intestinal tract.

Symptoms.—Necrotic stomatitis is both a local and a systemic affection. Primarily it is local. The local lesion is the caseo-necrotic patch or ulcer developed as a result of the multiplication of the bacilli at the point of inoculation. The general affection is an intoxication, or poisoning, of the whole system produced by a soluble toxin elaborated by the bacilli.

The stage of incubation is from three to five days. The first symptoms noted are a disinclination to take nourishment, some drooling from the mouth, and an examination of the mouth will show on some portion of its mucous membrane a circumscribed area of infiltration and redness, possibly an erosion. The latter gradually extends in size and depth, forming a sharply circumscribed area of necrotic inflammation. It may measure anywhere from the size of a five-cent piece to that of a dollar or even larger. It has the appearance of a corroded surface, under which the mucous membrane or muscular tissue seems transformed into a dry friable or firm cheesy mass. It is grayish yellow in color and is bordered by a zone of thickened tissue slightly reddened and somewhat granulated. The necrotic tissue is very adherent and can be only partially peeled off. It is homogeneous, cheesy, and may extend two fingers' depth into the tissues beneath. The general symptoms are languor, weakness, and slight fever. In spite of plenty of good food the calf is seen to be failing. It stops sucking, or, if older, altogether refuses to eat. The temperature at this time may be from 104° to 107° F. The slabber becomes profuse, swallowing very difficult, opening the mouth quite painful, and a most offensive odor is exhaled. The tongue is swollen and its motion greatly impaired. Sometimes the mouth is kept open, permitting the tumefied tongue to protrude. One or more of the above symptoms direct the attention to the mouth as the seat of disease; or, having noticed the debility and disinclination to eat, an examination of the animal may show a lump under the neck or swelling of the throat or head. The following extract from a letter is characteristic:

I noticed my calves beginning to fail about the first week in December, but could not account for it, as they were getting plenty of grain and hay. My attention was first attracted by a swelling under the neck of one of the calves. I cast the animal and found it was food that had collected and the animal couldn't swallow it. I removed it, and in so doing noticed a large ulcer on the tongue and a very offensive odor. This was the first knowledge I had of anything being wrong with the calves' mouths. They may have been sick for some time before this.

Out of a herd of 100 belonging to this man, 70 were affected, and the latter emphasizes the insidious character of the onset.

The general affection at this time manifests itself by dejectedness, extreme weakness and emaciation, constant lying down, with stiffness and marked difficulty in standing.

The disease frequently extends to the nasal cavities, producing a thin, yellowish or greenish yellow, sticky discharge which adheres closely to the borders of the nostrils. Their edges also show caseous patches similar to those in the mouth. Sometimes the nasal passage is obstructed by great masses of the necrosed exudate, thus causing extreme difficulty in breathing. When the caseous process involves the larynx and trachea there result cough, wheezing, and dyspnea, together with a yellowish mucopurulent expectoration.

When life is prolonged three or four weeks, caseous foci may be established in the lung, giving rise to all signs of a bronchopneumonia. Many of these cases are associated with a fibrinous pleurisy. The invasion of the gastrointestinal tract is announced by diarrheal symptoms. This disease principally attacks sucklings not over 6 weeks of age, but calves 8 and 10 months old are frequently affected, and several cases in adult cattle have been reported to this office.

In its very acute form many of the cases run their course in from five to eight days. In these the local lesions are not strongly marked, and death seems due to an acute intoxication. In other enzootics the majority of the affected animals live from three to five weeks. These are the cases that occasionally present the pulmonary and intestinal symptoms, and sometimes develop also caseonecrotic lesions in the liver.

Ordinarily cases show no tendency to spontaneous cure. Left to themselves they die. On the contrary, if taken in hand early the disease is readily amenable to treatment. In the latter event the prospects of recovery are excellent.

Differential Diagnosis.—Necrotic stomatitis may be differentiated from foot-and-mouth disease by the fact that in the latter disease there is a rapid infection of the entire herd, including the adult cattle, as well as the infection of hogs and sheep. The characteristic lesion of foot-and-mouth disease is the appearance of vesicles containing a serous fluid upon the mucous membrane of the mouth and upon the udder, teats, and feet of the affected animals. In necrotic stomatitis vesicles are never formed, necrosis occurring from the beginning and followed by the formation of yellowish cheesy patches principally found in the mouth. Mycotic stomatitis occurs in only a few animals of the herd, chiefly the adult cattle, and the lesions produced consist of an inflammation of the mouth and lips and of the thin skin between the toes, followed in a few days by small irregular ulcers in the mouth. This disease appears sporadically, usually in the early fall after a dry summer, does not run a regular course, and can not be inoculated.

Prevention.—Prophylaxis should be carried out along three lines:

(1) Separation of the sick from the healthy animals.

(2) Close scrutiny and thorough disinfection once or twice daily for five days of the mouths and nasal passages of those animals that have been exposed.

(3) Complete disinfection of all stalls and sheds. The disease appears to break out in winter and hold over to spring. It is conceivable that exposure to cold might so disturb the normal circulation of the oral tissues as to make the mucous membrane an excellent location for the causative factor of the disease. There is another possibility, however, which bears on the third line of prophylaxis. The so-called diphtheric inflammations of the vagina and uterus in cows are caused by the same organism that induces necrotic stomatitis. A recent European writer has pointed out the almost constant relation of such attacks to previous occurrences of foul foot or foot rot in the same or other cattle on the place.

In all likelihood the stalls and sheds are the harborers, in such cases, of this germ. It is possible that many of these outbreaks of necrotic stomatitis have some relation to preceding cases of the above-mentioned diseases and the greater use in winter of the stalls and sheds, thus harboring the *Bacillus necrophorus.*

Treatment.—The treatment consists almost solely in careful and extensive cleansing and disinfection of the mouth and other affected surfaces. The mucous membrane of the mouth should be copiously irrigated with a 2 per cent solution of creolin in warm water. This should be performed at least twice daily. Since exposure to oxygen kills the bacilli, one need have no fear about disturbing or tearing off the caseous patches or necrotic tissue during irrigation. The irrigation of the sores should then be followed by the application with a brush or rag on a stick of a paste made with 1 part of salicylic acid and 10 parts of water, or the affected areas may be painted with Lugol's solution of iodin (iodin, 1; potassium iodid, 5; water, 200). Frequent injections into the mouth of 1 per cent carbolic-acid solution make an excellent treatment. The internal administration of 2 grams of salicylic acid and 3 grams of chlorate of potash three times a day has also proved very beneficial when accompanied by local antiseptic treatment.

MALIGNANT CATARRH.

Malignant catarrh, or infectious catarrhal fever, is an acute infectious disease of cattle pre-eminently involving the respiratory and digestive tracts, although the sinuses of the head, the eyes, and the urinary and sexual organs are very frequently affected. It is relatively rare in this country, being more common on the continent of Europe. Outbreaks have occurred, however, in Minnesota, New York, and New Jersey. The causal agent of the disease has as yet never been isolated, and inoculation experiments with the view of artificially reproducing the disease have proven negative in every case. In

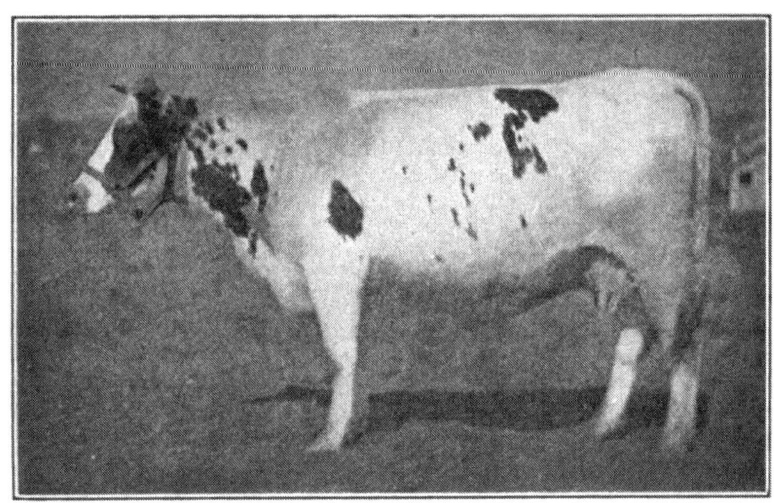

A Tuberculous Cow. Year Book, 1908. (This Animal at the Time Her Picture was Taken, was an Unusually Dangerous Source of Tuberculosis. Because of the Exceptionally Large Number of Tubercle Bacilli Expelled from Her Body.)

A Dangerously Tuberculous Cow. Dept. of Agr. 1908.

spite of the foregoing statements the consensus of opinion of eminent investigators points to malignant catarrh as being of specific origin; that is, due to some form of micro-organism the contagious character of which is poorly developed. This accounts for the slow transmissibility of the disease from one animal to another. In fact, malignant catarrh is a type of that class of affections which are scientifically known as miasmatic diseases; that is, they remain stationary in stables with damp floors, low ceilings, poor ventilation, and bad sanitary conditions in general. Such places furnish a favorable seat of propagation for the infective material, and it will remain active for a long period of time, causing the loss of a few animals each year. One European veterinarian reports an instance where this disease remained for twenty-five years on the same farm, attacking in all 225 animals, with a mortality of about 98 per cent.

The disease is most common in late winter and early spring, at all altitudes, and has a special preference for young, well-nourished cattle, although older animals are not immune. The time elapsing between the entrance of the infective principle into the body of the animal and the appearance of the first symptoms is relatively very long and, according to German investigators, averages from twenty to thirty days. Fortunately, it is not a disease which spreads to any great extent, or which causes severe losses, and hence legislative enactments do not seem to be necessary for its restriction.

Symptoms.—These are extremely variable according to the point of localization of the lesions. It is usually ushered in with a chill, followed by a marked rise of temperature (104° to 107° F.). The head droops, the skin is hot and dry, and the coat staring. Quivering of the muscles in various parts of the body is frequently observed. Marked dullness of the animal passing, according to some observers, into an almost stupefied condition later on, is quite common. The secretion of milk stops in the beginning of the disease, and loss of flesh, invariably associated with the disease, is extremely marked and rapid. The lesions of the eyes may best be likened to moon blindness (periodic ophthalmia) in horses.

There is first an abundant secretion of tears, which run down over the face. The lids are swollen and inflamed, and indeed this may be so marked as to cause involuntary eversion, exposing the reddened conjunctiva to view. Sunlight is painful, as is shown by the fact that the animal keeps the eyes continuously closed. This inflammation may extend to the cornea, causing it to assume a slight clouded appearance in mild cases or a chalky whiteness in more severe affections. Cases of ulceration of the cornea followed by perforation and subsequent escape of the aqueous humor, leading to shrinking of the eyeball and permanent loss of sight, have been recorded; but these are relatively rare, although slight inflammation of the deeper structures of the eye (iris) are more frequent. This inflammation may undergo complete resolution in mild cases, but more frequently permanent cloudiness of the cornea either diffuse or in spots (leucoma) is the result. The mucous membrane of the mouth, nose, sinuses of the head, throat, and lower respiratory passages are also involved. It is first catarrhal in character, but soon a false or diphtheritic membrane is formed, with the production of shallow ulcers. There is dribbling of saliva from the mouth and discharge from the nose, which is at first watery, becoming thicker and mixed with blood and small masses of cast-off croupous membrane, causing a very fetid odor. These croupous areas when they form in the throat, larynx, or windpipe may lead to narrowing of these passages, with consequent difficult breathing and even suffocation. Various respiratory murmurs may also be heard, caused by the to-and-fro movement of mucus and inflammatory deposits along the air passages. There is also inflammation of the horn core with consequent loosening of the horn shell, and the horns are thus readily knocked off by the uneasy, blind sufferer. The animal may refuse all food from the time of the initial rise of temperature, or in less severe cases, and especially when the lesions of the digestive tract are not so marked, the appetite may remain until the disease is well advanced. Constipation is quite common at the commencement of the attack, followed by diarrhea and severe straining, the evacuations becoming very soft, fetid, and streaked with blood. Cases have been reported of the evacuation of desquamated patches of diphtheritic membrane from the intestinal mucosa 6 to 9 feet in length. The kidneys and bladder are usually inflamed, the urine being voided with difficulty and the animal evincing signs of pain. Inflammatory elements, as albumen, casts, etc., may be seen on examination of the urine. In cows the mucous membrane of the vestibule is congested, swollen, and may contain ulcers and an excessive quantity of mucus. Abortion is not infrequent, following a severe attack during advanced pregnancy. In connection with these various symptoms there may be much uneasiness on the part of the animal, leading in some cases to madness and furious delirium, in others to spasms and convulsions or paralysis. A vesicular eruption of the skin may occur, seen principally between the toes and on the inside of the flank and in the armpits, with subsequent loss of hair and epidermis.

Like other infectious diseases, malignant catarrh pursues a longer or shorter course in accordance with the severity of the attack. In acute cases death is said to take place three to seven days after the appearance of symptoms. Recovery, if it occurs, may take three or four weeks. According to statistics, from 50 to 90 per cent of the affected animals die.

If animals which have died of this disease be examined, there will be occasionally found, in addition to the changes of the mucous membrane of mouth and nasal cavities referred to above, shallow ulcers in these situations. These necrotic processes may pass beneath the mucous membrane and even involve the underlying bony structure. In severe cases membranous (croupous) deposits are found in the throat. Similar deposits have been found upon the mucous membrane of the fourth stomach and intestine, which is always inflamed. There is more or less inflammation of the membranes of the brain, kidneys, liver, and some fatty degeneration of the voluntary muscles. In countries where rinderpest occasionally appears it may be difficult to distinguish between it and malignant catarrh, owing to a general similarity of the symptoms. The principal points to be observed in differentiating between the two diseases are the very slight transmissibility of the latter as compared with the intense contagiousness of the former, and the tendency of malignant catarrh to run a more chronic course than rinderpest, which usually results fatally in a very few days. Only a trained veterinarian who takes into consideration all the different symptoms and lesions of both diseases should decide in such cases.

Treatment.—There is no specific treatment for this affection. However, copious blood letting in the earliest stages has been highly recommended, as this has a tendency to deplete the system and lessen the exudation of inflammatory products. Antiseptic washes, as creolin, 2 to 4 per cent solution, or lysol, 5 per cent solution, applied to the nose, eyes, and mouth with ice poultices over the crest of the head and frontal region have also proved efficacious. Calomel should also be given in 1-dram doses twice a day for three days, and in severe cases, involving the respiratory tract, a powder containing ferrous sulphate, quinine, and subnitrate of bismuth, given twice a day, will be found beneficial. At the same time it must be remembered that much greater success is to be looked for in the preventive treatment. This consists in the removal of the healthy from the infected animals (not vice versa) and thorough cleaning and disinfecting of the contaminated stables. If the floors are low and damp, they should be raised and made dry. If this can not be done, place a layer of cement under the stable floor to prevent water from entering from below. The stable should be well ventilated and the soil in the pastures thoroughly drained. If this is carefully carried out, the contagion should be destroyed and the danger of the reappearance of the disease in a great measure lessened.

MALIGNANT EDEMA.

Malignant edema, also termed gangrenous septicemia, is an acute inflammatory disease of domestic and wild animals, resulting from the introduction of a specific organism into the deep connective tissues of a susceptible animal and proving fatal in many instances within twenty-four to forty-eight hours. The disease may be inoculated from one animal to another, but only by inserting the virus deeply below the skin. It is infrequently met with in cattle, but may follow operating wounds, as roweling, castration, and phlebotomy, which have become infected with septic matter, soil, or unclean instruments. The organism has also been obtained in this laboratory from the infected muscles of a calf that was supposed to have died of blackleg, and, as a result, all blackleg virus is thoroughly tested before it is made into blackleg vaccine in order to exclude the malignant edema organism. The essential cause of malignant edema is a long, slender, motile, spore-bearing bacillus, resembling the bacillus of blackleg, and which can only develop in the absence of the atmosphere. Unlike the bacilli of anthrax and blackleg, which are confined to certain districts, this organism is widely distributed and found in ordinary garden soil, foul water, and in the normal intestinal tract of the herbivora. It may be brought to the surface of the soil by growing plants, rains, winds, or burrowing insects and rodents. In animals that have succumbed to the disease the germ is confined to the seat of infection, but a few hours after death it may migrate to other parts of the body through the blood channels. The bacillus may attack man, horses, asses, goats, sheep, pigs, cats, dogs, and poultry. Adult cattle, although refractory to experimental inoculation, suffer from natural infection, while calves are susceptible to both of these methods of exposure. (Kitt.) The introducti n of the bacillus into abrasions of the skin and superficial sores rarely does any harm, because the germ is quickly destroyed by contact with air. If, however, the organisms are inserted deeply into the subcutaneous tissues of susceptible animals, they quickly develop, producing a soluble poison, which is the fatal agent.

In lamb-shearing season, or after docking or castration, the mortality is higher among these animals because of wounds inflicted at such times. The application of antiseptics to wounds thus made will reduce the percentage of deaths to a minimum.

Symptoms.—Usually the first symptoms are overlooked. In the early stages the animal appears listless, disinclined to move about, and seeks the shady and quiet places to lie down. If forced to move about, the hind legs are drawn forward with a peculiar stiff dragging movement and there may be slight muscular trembling all over the body, which becomes more intense as the disease progresses. When driven, the animal shows signs of fatigue, ultimately dropping to the ground completely exhausted. Breathing becomes fast and painful, with frequent spasmodic jerks.

The pulse is quick and weak and the temperature is 106° to 107° F. An edematous, doughy, and painful swelling appears at the point of infection. This tumefaction spreads more and more and will crackle on pressure. In case of an open wound a fetid, liquid, and frothy discharge is observed. The center of the swelling may appear soft and jelly-like, while the margin is tense, hot, and painful. The symptoms increase rapidly, resulting in coma and death.

Lesions.—After death the fat and subcutaneous tissues surrounding the infected area are infiltrated with a yellow gelatinous material containing an orange-colored foam, due to the presence of gas bubbles. The muscles at this point are friable, spongy, and of a uniform brownish tint, disassociated by gas and a blood-tinged exudate. This gangrenous tissue, when present before death, can be removed without pain to the animal. The intestines are generally normal, but they, together with the peritoneum, may be inflamed, and the lungs are usually the seat of an edema. The spleen, liver, and kidneys retain their normal appearance, in marked contrast with anthrax.

Differential Diagnosis.—Unlike blackleg this disease never appears as an epizootic but in isolated cases. It may also be differentiated from the former by the history of a recent parturition or surgical operation, by the presence of an external injury at the site of the swelling accompanied by a fetid liquid discharge, and the gangrenous appearance of the tumefaction. Man is susceptible to malignant edema but not to blackleg. Malignant edema may also be easily differentiated from anthrax in that the blood and spleen are normal in appearance, while in the latter disease the blood is dark and of a tarlike consistency and the spleen appears swollen, injected, and softened. The local tumor in malignant edema contains gas bubbles, while in anthrax swellings these are absent. Inoculation experiments of guinea pigs, rabbits, and chickens will also disclose the differences among the above three diseases, since all of these species are killed by the germ of malignant edema, only the first two species by the anthrax bacillus, while the guinea pigs alone will succumb to the blackleg infection.

Treatment.—Treatment is chiefly surgical and consists in laying the infected areas wide open by free incision, followed by a liberal application of a 30 per cent solution of hydrogen dioxide and subsequently a 5 per cent solution of carbolic acid. Usually the disease when observed has advanced to such an extent that medicinal interference is without avail. Preventive treatment is by far the most desirable, and consists, essentially, in a thorough disinfection of all accidental and surgical wounds, the cleansing of the skin, and the exclusion of soil, filth, and bacteria during surgical operations of any nature. Sheds, barns, and stables should receive a thorough application of quicklime or crude carbolic-acid wash after all rubbish has been removed and burned. All animals should be burned or deeply buried and covered well with quicklime.

SOUTHERN CATTLE FEVER (TEXAS FEVER).

This disease, which is more commonly known as splenetic, or Texas, fever, is a specific fever communicated by cattle which have recently been moved northward from the infected district, or which is contracted by cattle taken into the infected district from other parts of the world. It is characterized by the peculiarity among animal diseases that the animals which disseminate the infection are apparently in good health, while those which sicken and die from it do not, as a rule, infect others.

It is accompanied by high fever, greatly enlarged spleen, destruction of the red-blood corpuscles, escape of the coloring matter of the blood through the kidneys, giving the urine a deep-red color, by a yellowness of the mucous membranes and fat, which is seen more especially in fat cattle, by a rapid loss of strength, and by fatal results in a large proportion of cases.

This disease has various names in different sections of the country where it frequently appears. It is often called Spanish fever, acclimation fever, red water, black water, distemper, murrain, dry murrain, yellow murrain, bloody murrain, Australian tick fever, and tristeza of South America.

The earliest accounts we have of this disease date dack to 1814, when it was stated by Dr. James Mease, before the Philadelphia Society for Promoting Agriculture, that the cattle from a certain district in South Carolina so certainly disease all others with which they mix in their progress to the North that they are prohibited by the people of Virginia from passing through the State; that these cattle infect others while they themselves are in perfect health, and that cattle from Europe or the interior taken to the vicinity of the sea are attacked by a disease that generally proves fatal. Similar observations have been made in regard to a district in the southern part of the United States. The northern limits of this area are changed yearly as a result of the dissemination or eradication of the cattle tick along the border, but the infected area has gradually decreased, owing to the successful endeavors pushed forward to eliminate the ticks.

It was the frequent and severe losses following the driving of cattle from the infected district in Texas into and across the Western States and Territories which led to the disease being denominated Texas fever. It is now known, however, that the infection is not peculiar to Texas or even to the United States, but that it also exists in southern Europe, Central and South America, Australia, South Africa, and the West Indies.

When cattle from other sections of the country are taken into the infected district they contract this disease usually during the first summer, and if they are adult animals, particularly milch cows or fat cattle, nearly all die. Calves are much more likely to survive. The disease is one from which immunity is acquired, and therefore calves which recover are not again attacked, as a rule, even after they become adult.

When the infection is disseminated beyond the permanently infected district, the roads, pastures, pens, and other inclosures are dangerous for susceptible animals until freezing weather. The infection then disappears, and cattle may be driven over the grounds or kept in the inclosures the succeeding summer and the disease will not reappear. There are some exceptions to this rule in the section just north of the boundary line of the infected district. In this locality the infection sometimes resists the winters, especially when these are mild.

In regard to the manner in which the disease is communicated, experience shows that this does not occur by animals coming near or in contact with each other. It is an indirect infection. The cattle from the infected district first infect the pastures, roads, pens, cars, etc., and the susceptible cattle obtain the virus second hand from these. Usually animals do not contract this disease when separated from infected pastures by a fence. If, however, there is any drainage or washing by rains across the line of fence this rule does not hold good.

The investigations made by the Bureau of Animal Industry demonstrate that the ticks which adhere to cattle from the infected district are the only known means of conveying the infection to the bodies of susceptible cattle. The infection is not spread by the saliva, the urine, or the manure of cattle from the infected district. In studying the causation and prevention of this disease, attention must therefore be largely given to the ticks, and it now seems apparent that if cattle could be freed from this parasite when leaving the infected district they would not be able to cause the malady. The discovery of the connection of the ticks with the production of the disease has played a very important part in determining the methods that should be adopted in preventing its spread. It established an essential point and indicated many lines of investigation which have yielded and are still likely to yield very important results.

Nature of the Disease.—Texas fever is caused by an organism which lives within the red-blood corpuscles and breaks them up. It is therefore simply a blood disease. The organism does not belong to the bacteria but to the protozoa. It is not, in other words, a microscopic plant, but it belongs to the lowest forms of the animal kingdom. This very minute organism multiplies very rapidly in the body of the infected animal, and in acute cases causes an enormous destruction of red corpuscles in a few days. How it gets into the red corpuscle it is not possible to state, but it appears that it enters as an exceedingly minute body, probably endowed with motion, and only after it has succeeded in entering the corpuscle does it begin to enlarge. The body is, as a rule, situated near the edge of the corpuscle. There are usually two bodies in a corpuscle. These bodies are in general pear-shaped. The narrow ends are always toward each other when two are present in the same corpuscle. If we bear in mind that the average diameter of the red-blood corpuscles of cattle is from 1/4000 to 1/5000 inch, the size of the contained parasite may be at once appreciated by a glance at the figures referred to.

The various disease processes which go on in Texas fever, and which we may observe by examining the organs after death, all result from the destruction of the red corpuscles. This destruction may be extremely rapid or slow. When it is rapid we have the acute, usually fatal, type of Texas fever, which is always witnessed in the height of the Texas-fever season; that is, during the latter weeks of August and the early weeks of September. When the destruction of corpuscles is slower, a mild, usually nonfatal, type of the disease is called forth, which is only witnessed late in autumn or more rarely in July and the early part of August. Cases of the mild type occurring thus early usually become acute later on and terminate fatally.

The acute disease is fatal in most cases, and the fatality is due not so much to the loss of blood corpuscles as to the difficulty which the organs have in getting rid of the waste products arising from this wholesale destruction. How great this may be a simple calculation will serve to illustrate. If we take a steer weighing 1,000 pounds, the blood in its body will amount to about 50 pounds, if we assume that the blood represents one-twentieth of the weight of the body, a rather low estimate. According to experimental determination at the Bureau Station, which consists in counting the number of blood corpuscles in a given quantity of blood from day to day in such an animal, the corpuscles contained in from 5 to 10 pounds of blood may be destroyed within twenty-four hours. The remains of these corpuscles and the coloring matter in them must either be converted into bile or excreted unchanged. The result of this effort on the part of the liver causes extensive disease of this organ. The bile secreted by the liver cells contains so much solid material that it stagnates in the finest bile canals and chokes these up completely. This in

turn interferes with the nutrition of the liver cells and they undergo
fatty degeneration and perish. The functions of the liver are thereby
completely suspended and death is the result. This enormous destruction of corpuscles takes place to a large extent in the kidneys,
where a great number of corpuscles containing the parasites are always found in acute cases. This accounts largely for the blood-col-
ored urine or red water which is such a characteristic feature of
Texas fever. The corpuscles themselves are not found in the urine;
it is the red coloring matter, or hemoglobin, which leaves them when
they break up and passes into the urine.

Symptoms.—After a period of exposure to infected soil, which
may vary from thirteen to ninety days, and which will be more fully
discussed further on under the subject of cattle ticks as bearers of
the Texas-fever parasite, the disease first shows itself in dullness, loss
of appetite, and a tendency to leave the herd and stand or lie down
alone. A few days before these symptoms appear the presence of a
high fever may be detected by the clinical thermometer. The temperature rises from a normal of 101° to 103° F. to 106° and 107°
F. There seems to be little or no change in temperature until recovery or death ensues. The period of high temperature or fever varies
considerably. As it indicates the intensity of the disease process
going on within, the higher it is the more rapid the fatal end. When
it does not rise above 104° F. the disease is milder and more prolonged. The bowels are mostly constipated during the fever; near the
end the feces may become softer and rather deeply tinged with bile.
The urine shows nothing abnormal during the course of the disease
until near the fatal termination, when it may be deeply stained with
the coloring matter of the blood. (Hemoglobinuria.) Although
this symptom is occasionally observed in animals which recover, yet
it may generally be regarded as an indication of approaching death.
The pulse and respiration are usually much more rapid than during
health.

Other symptoms in addition to those mentioned have been described by observers, but they do not seem to be constant, and only
the above are nearly always present. As the end approaches emaciation becomes very marked, the blood is very thin and watery, and the
closing of any wound of the skin by clots is retarded. The animal
manifests increasing stupor and may lie down much of the time.
Signs of delirium have been observed in some cases. Death occurs
most frequently in the night.

The course of the disease is very variable in duration. Death
may ensue in from three days to several weeks after the beginning of
the fever. Those that recover ultimately do so very slowly, owing to
the great poverty of the blood in red corpuscles. The flesh is re-
gained but very gradually, and the animal may be subjected to a
second though mild attack later on in the autumn, which pushes the
full recovery onward to the beginning of winter.

In the mild type of the disease, which occurs in October and November, symptoms of disease are well-nigh absent. There is little if
any fever, and if it were not for loss of flesh and more or less dull-

"Knud Lombjerge," Red Danish Bull.   Dept. of Agr.

Red Danish Cow. Dept. of Agr.

ness the disease might pass unnoticed, as it undoubtedly does in a majority of cases. If, however, the blood corpuscles be counted from time to time a gradually diminishing number will be found, and after several weeks only about one-fifth or one-sixth of the normal number are present. It is, indeed, surprising how little impression upon the animal this very impoverished condition of the blood appears to make. It is probable, however, that if two animals kept under the same conditions, one healthy and the other at the end of one of these mild attacks, be weighed, the difference would be plainly shown.

Pathological Changes Observable After Death.—In the preceding pages some of these have already been referred to in describing the nature of the disease. It is very important at times to determine whether a certain disease is Texas fever or some other disease, like anthrax, for example. This fact can, as a rule, be determined at once by a thorough microscopic examination of the blood. The necessary apparatus and the requisite qualifications for this task leave this method entirely in the hands of experts. There is, however, a considerable number of changes caused by this disease which may be detected by the naked eye when the body has been opened. These, put together, make a mistake quite impossible. The presence of small ticks on the skin of the escutcheon, the thighs, and the udder is a very important sign in herds north of the Texas-fever line, as it indicates that they have been brought in some manner from the South and carried the disease with them, as will be explained later. Another very important sign is the thin, watery condition of the blood, either just before death or when the fever has been present for four or five days. A little incision into the skin will enable anyone to determine this point. Frequently the skin is so poor in blood that it may require several incisions to draw a drop or more.

The changes in the internal organs, as found on postmortem examinations are briefly as follows: The spleen, or milt, is much larger than in healthy animals. It may weigh three or four times as much. When it is incised the contents or pulp is blackish, and may even swell out as a disintegrated mass. The markings of the healthy spleen are all effaced by the enormous number of blood corpuscles which have collected in the spleen and to which the enlargement is due. Next to the spleen the liver will arouse our attention. It is larger than in the healthy state, has lost its natural brownish color, and now has on the surface a paler yellowish hue. When it is incised this yellowish tinge or mahogany color, as it has been called by some, is still more prominent. This is due to the large amount of bile in the finest bile capillaries, and as these are not uniformly filled with it the cut surface has a more or less mottled appearance. This bile injection causes in many cases a fatty degeneration of the liver cells, which makes the organ appear still lighter in color.

In all cases the gall bladder should be examined. This is distended with bile, which holds in suspension a large quantity of yellow flakes, so that when it is poured into a tall bottle to settle fully one-half or more of the column of fluid will be occupied by a layer of flakes. If mucus is present at the same time, the bile may become so viscid that when it is poured from one glass to another it forms long bands. The bile in health is a limpid fluid containing no solid particles.

If the animal has not been observed during life to pass urine colored with blood or red water, the bladder should be opened. This quite invariably, in acute cases, contains urine which varies in color from a deep port wine to a light claret. In many cases the color is so dense that light will not pass through even a thin layer. The kidneys are always found congested in the acute attack. The disease exerts but little effect on the stomach and intestines beyond more or less reddening of the mucous membrane; hence an examination of these may be safely omitted. The lungs are, as a rule, not diseased. The heart usually shows patches of blood extravasation on the inside (left ventricle), and less markedly on the outer surface.

We have observed jaundice of the various tissues but very rarely. It has been observed by some quite regularly, however.

During the hot season about 90 per cent of the susceptible mature animals from a noninfected district die, but later, in the cool weather, the disease assumes a milder type, with a consequent decrease in the number of deaths.

The Cattle Tick, Margaropus Annulatus, as the Carrier of Texas Fever.—The cattle tick is, as its name indicates, a parasite of cattle in the southern part of the United States. It belongs to the group of *Arthropoda* and to the genus *Margaropus* (*Boophilus*), which is included in the order *Acarina*. Its life history is quite simple and easily traced from one generation to another. It is essentially a parasite, attaching itself to the skin and drawing the blood of its host. It is unable to come to maturity and reproduce its kind unless it becomes attached to the skin of cattle, whence it may obtain its food.

The eggs laid on the ground after the female has dropped from the host begin to develop at once. When the embryo is fully formed within the shell it ruptures this and gains its freedom. The time required from the laying of the eggs to their hatching varies considerably, according to the temperature. In the laboratory in the heat of midsummer this was accomplished in about thirteen days. In the late fall, under the same conditions, it required from four to six weeks. The larva after emerging from the egg is very minute, six-legged, and just visible to the naked eye. If these larvæ be kept on a layer of moist sand or earth in a covered dish, they may remain alive for months, but there is no appreciable increase in size. As soon, however, as they are placed upon cattle growth begins.

On pastures these little creatures soon find their way onto cattle. They attach themselves by preference to the tender skin on the escutcheon, the inside of the thighs, and on the base of the udder. Yet when they are very numerous they may be found in small numbers on the various parts of the body, such as the neck, the chest, and the ears.

The changes which they undergo during their parasitic existence were first studied by Dr. Cooper Curtice in 1889. The young tick within a week molts, and the second or nymphal stage of the parasite's life is thus ushered in. After this change it has four pairs of legs. Within another week another molt takes place by which the tick passes from the nymphal to the sexual, or adult, stage. Impregnation now takes place, and, with the development of the ova in the body, the animal takes an increased quantity of blood, so that it becomes very much larger in a few days. That the rapid growth is due to the blood taken in may be easily proved by crushing one. The intestine is distended with a thick, tarry mass composed of partly digested blood. When the female has reached a certain stage of maturity she drops to the ground and begins to lay a large number of eggs, which hatch in the time given above.

The life of the cattle tick is thus spent largely on cattle, and although the young, or larvæ, may live for a long time on the ground in the summer season, they can not mature excepting as parasites on cattle and horses. We have purposely omitted various details of the life history, including that of the male, as they are not necessary to an understanding of our present subject—Texas fever. How this is transmitted we will proceed to consider.

Southern cattle sent North during the spring and summer months carry on their bodies large numbers of the cattle tick. These when matured drop off and lay their eggs on Northern pastures. These hatch, and the young tick soon gets upon any Northern cattle which happen to be on the pasture. As soon as they have attached themselves to the skin they inoculate the cattle, and Texas fever breaks out a week or more thereafter. For many years there had been a growing suspicion that the cattle tick was in some way concerned in the spread of Texas fever, and the facts which supported this supposition finally became so numerous and convincing that a series of experiments were inaugurated by the Bureau of Animal Industry which served to show that the tick was abundantly able to carry the disease to a herd of healthy cattle, and in fact was probably the only agent concerned in the transmission of the disease from Southern cattle to susceptible Northern animals.

The regulations which have been enacted by the Department of Agriculture for the control of cattle shipments from the infected districts have for their initial purpose the prevention of the transportation of cattle ticks from infected regions to those that are noninfected, either upon cattle or in stock cars or other conveyer, and the exclusion of these parasites from noninfected territory has in every instance been found a certain method of excluding Texas fever.

INJURIOUS EFFECTS OF CATTLE TICKS.

Many cattle owners who have always been accustomed to see both ticks and ticky cattle on their farms are unfortunately not inclined to attach much importance to cattle ticks, and, as a rule, through lack of appreciation of their damaging effects, placidly consider them as of little consequence. That ticks may be detrimental to their hosts in several ways has probably not suggested itself to these stockmen, who are most vitally affected, and it therefore seems necessary to emphasize the fact that, in addition to their relation to

Texas fever, they may also be injurious to cattle as external parasites. While the power of transmitting Texas fever is undoubtedly the most dangerous property possessed by the cattle tick and is the principal cause for adopting stringent measures in securing its complete eradication, nevertheless there still remain other good reasons for the accomplishment of this achievement. These secondary objections to the presence of ticks on cattle consist in the physical harm they do to the host aside from the production of the specific disease of Texas fever. True, a few parasites may remain on cattle indefinitely without causing any noticeable effect, but it is not uncommon to notice bovine animals on pastures with their hides heavily infested with these pests. In such cases it can readily be seen that the continuous sucking of blood causes more or less impoverishment of the circulation. The animal must therefore be fed heavier in order to meet the demands of the parasites in addition to the ordinary needs of the host. If the ticks be removed from the body, the bites inflicted are often distinguished by small inflamed or reddened areas somewhat swollen, with perforations of the skin which may allow the entrance of various kinds of disease germs, and showing that more or less irritation of the hide is produced by these parasites. This condition, together with the loss of blood, frequently induces an irritable state and evidences of uneasiness commonly known as tick worry, which results in the loss of energy and other derangements of the animal's health. It may in some cases become so pronounced, especially in hot weather, that the animal will lose flesh in spite of good pasturing, thereby reducing the vitality and rendering it more susceptible to the inroads of disease. Moreover, if the infestation of ticks is not controlled, the cattle may be so reduced in condition that growth is retarded, and, in the case of young animals, they may never become fully developed, but remain thin, weak, and stunted—a condition that has been termed tick poverty— and easily succumb to other diseases as a result of lowered vitality. In milch cows this debilitating influence of the numerous ticks is shown in a greatly reduced milk supply. This should not appear strange when it is considered that some animals harbor several thousand of these blood-sucking parasites. If these parasites are crushed, it will be found that their intestines are completely filled with a dark, thick mass of blood abstracted from the animal host and containing nutriment that should go to the formation of milk, flesh, and the laying on of fat. In some rare cases the large number of bites over a limited area of skin may be followed by infection with pus-producing organisms, giving rise to small abscesses which may terminate in ulcers. The discharge from such sores, or in some cases the mere oozing of blood serum through the incision made by the mouth parts of the ticks, keeps the hair moist and matted together, and the laying and hatching of fly eggs in these areas give rise to infestation with destructive maggots, causing ulcers and other complications that require medical treatment. These statements regarding the secondary injurious effects of cattle ticks also apply to those ticks which have been previously spoken of as harmless in so far as Texas fever is concerned, and, in fact, to all external parasites. Therefore, it is just as important to eradicate the cattle ticks for reasons other than those associated with Texas fever as it is to exterminate lice, fleas, and other vermin. Furthermore, cattle ticks, aside from the losses sustained by their purely parasitic effects, are the greatest menace to the profitable raising and feeding of cattle in the South, because they are an obstacle to cattle traffic between the infected and noninfected districts.

The So-called Period of Incubation.—After the young ticks have attached themselves to cattle the fever appears about ten days thereafter, in midsummer. When the weather is cool, as in autumn, this period may be a little longer. The actual period of incubation may be shorter than this, for if blood from a case of Texas fever be injected into the blood vessels of healthy cattle the fever may appear within five days. When cattle graze upon pastures over which southern cattle have passed, the time when the disease appears varies within wide limits. When the animals have been put upon pastures immediately after southern cattle have infected them with ticks it may take from thirty to sixty days, or even longer, before the disease appears. This will be readily understood when we recall the life history of ticks. The southern cattle leave only matured ticks which have dropped from them. These must lay their eggs and the latter be hatched before any ticks can get upon native cattle. The shortest period is thus not less than thirty days if we include ten days for the period of incubation after the young tick has attached itself to native cattle. When the infection of pastures with ticks has taken place early in the season, or when this is cold, the period will be much longer, because it takes longer for the eggs to hatch.

If native cattle are placed upon pastures which have been infected some time before with ticks, the disease will appear so much sooner, because the young ticks may be already hatched and attack the cattle at once. It will be evident, therefore, that the length of time elapsing between the exposure of native cattle on infected fields and the appearance of the disease will depend on the date of original infection, and on the weather, whether cold or hot. When native cattle are placed upon fields on which young ticks are already present, they will show the fever in thirteen to fifteen days if the season be hot.

The fever appears before the ticks have matured. In fact, they are still small enough to be overlooked. In any case very careful search should be made for them in those places upon which they prefer to locate—the thighs, escutcheon, and udder. After the acute stage of the fever has passed by, the ticks begin to swell up and show very plainly.

Prevention.—It is generally accepted that if southern cattle are entirely free from that species of tick known as *Margaropus (Boophilus) annulatus,* they can be allowed to mingle with the most susceptible animals without danger. Furthermore, it has been learned from the study of the life history of the cattle tick and from the fact that this tick infests pastures only transiently, never permanently, and will not mature except upon cattle or equines, that its extermination is possible, and that the disease it causes may be prevented. The various methods with these results in view should be directed toward the destruction of ticks on cattle as well as their eradication from the pastures.

How to Free Cattle of Ticks.—Among the most important measures to be adopted in eradicating these parasites from cattle in the infested districts may be mentioned: (1) Picking or brushing them off; (2) smearing or spraying the animals with a disinfecting solution, and (3) dipping the "ticky" animals in a vat containing a solution capable of killing the ticks without injury to the cattle.

The systematic application of one or more of these methods, together with appropriate measures for eradicating or destroying the cattle ticks upon pastures, has been successfully adopted in certain sections, and has thus diminished the area of the infested district.

Picking or Brushing Ticks Off Cattle.—Where the herd is small a very effective but laborious method is to pick off these parasites by hand or to scrape them off with a dull knife or a currycomb. This should be done at least three times a week in order to find all the adults before they mature and fall off, as by this system the smaller ticks which at first escaped detection will be found before they are fully developed. After removing the ticks they should be destroyed, preferably by burning. Care should be taken to go over all parts of the animal frequented by the ticks, especially under the belly, around the tail and udder, and inside the legs. After the ticks are picked or brushed off, the cattle should not be neglected, but should be carefully examined later for the presence of ticks which have been picked up in the meantime. If this work is thoroughly performed and no ticks are allowed to fall off and lay eggs from June 1 to the end of November, the cattle will be free of ticks, and the pastures will have had an opportunity of becoming cleaned.

Smearing or Spraying Cattle with a Disinfecting Solution.—Greasing the legs and sides of cattle with cotton-seed oil, fish oil, or Beaumont crude petroleum will assist in preventing the ticks from crawling up on the body. In small herds, smearing the cattle with a mixture of 1 gallon of kerosene, 1 gallon of cotton-seed oil, and 1 pound of sulphur, or with a mixture composed of equal parts of cotton-seed oil and crude petroleum, or with Beaumont crude oil alone, has proved efficacious when applied to the skin two or three times weekly during the tick season. For this purpose sponges, syringes, brushes, mops, or brooms may be used. This method not only kills the older ticks on the cattle by mechanically plugging up their breathing pores, but also makes the legs so slippery that the seed ticks are unable to get a foothold in order to crawl up on the cattle. Where a large number of animals are to be treated, but not sufficient to make it advisable to construct a dipping vat, spraying the infested animals has given very favorable results. The animals should be placed in a chute or stall, or tied to a tree, and then sprayed with Beaumont oil or a 5 per cent solution of any of the standard coal-tar dips. The solution may be applied by means of a force pump, such as is used by orchardists to spray fruit trees, or by placing the solution in a barrel upon a wagon or on a platform above the animals and allowing the fluid to gravitate through a hose, to the end of which is attached an ordinary sprinkling nozzle. The solution is then allowed to flow over the skin of the animal, especially upon the legs and under portions of the body. If the cattle are on tick-infested pastures, this treatment—either smearing or spraying—must be continued through the whole season, and if thoroughly done it will leave the fields free from ticks the following year.

Dipping in a Vat.—Many efforts have been made to discover a practical method for dipping cattle to destroy ticks without injury to the cattle, and the bureau has experimented for years with this object in view. Numerous kinds of dips have been used and many failures have been recorded, but apparently a successful one has been found in the crude oil—so-called Beaumont oil—obtained from certain Texas wells. This oil has now been used on a rather large scale, and it has been very successful in killing ticks without at the same time materially affecting the health of the cattle when the proper precautions have been observed. In fact, it is distinctly superior to any of the other dips that have been tested. In these experiments it was found that a light oil heavily charged with sulphur is the most desirable for dipping cattle, as the heavy oils injure the animals dipped in them. An oil with 40 per cent of its bulk capable of boiling between 200° and 300° C., having a specific gravity between $22\frac{1}{2}$° and $24\frac{1}{2}$° Beaumé, and containing $1\frac{1}{4}$ to $1\frac{1}{2}$ per cent of sulphur is most desirable, and these requirements should be stipulated before purchase. In a recent dipping of 57,000 head of cattle on the Kansas and Osage Indian reservations the results were very highly satisfactory, both as regards the eradication of the cattle tick and the after results of the dipping, since the loss from all causes was less than 0.75 per cent. This loss represented in dollars and cents would amount to a very small portion (about one-twelfth) of the loss incurred by the sale of these animals as ticky cattle in the stock yards of the North. Other cattle dipped in the same oil, but under conditions that can not be considered parallel, suffered more severely. In order to obtain the best results, the animals, after dipping, should not be unduly exposed to the hot sun nor driven any considerable distance, but should receive plenty of food and good water. They should be allowed to stand for four or more days after dipping and prior to shipment. Dipping should not be attempted until after they shall have shed their winter coats, as a large percentage of all cattle dipped before the heavy coat is lost suffer from a severe irritation of the skin. The method usually adopted in dipping cattle is to construct a narrow swimming tank with a chute at one end for the entrance of the cattle and a sloping exit at the other end where the cattle emerge after getting a uniform coating of oil in passing through the vat. A drip chute is connected with the exit where the excess of oil is allowed to drip off the animals and to drain into the vat. It is relatively more expensive to dip cattle in the South, where the farms and plantations contain a small number of cattle, than in the range country of the Southwest, where this method of eradicating ticks becomes not only plausible and practicable, but also economical. When cattle have been properly dipped in Beaumont crude petroleum or any other approved petroleum under the supervision of a veterinary inspector and by him found free of infection, they may be shipped to any point above the quarantine line, subject only to such restrictions as may be imposed at the point of destination. Such cattle must be shipped in clean, disinfected cars, and must not be driven through the quarantined area or be unloaded therein, except at those points designated by the Secretary of Agriculture. It is earnestly recommended that such shipments shall not occur earlier than four to eight days after the dipping is performed.

By the Soiling Method.—This method of freeing cattle of ticks was suggested by Curtice. It is based upon a knowledge of the life history of these parasites. The time required for the female tick to lay eggs and the latter to hatch—in other words, the time spent on the ground—is rarely less than three weeks, and the period required by the seed ticks to molt and mature—or the time spent on the cattle—is usually from twenty to forty-five days. When cattle infested with ticks are to be cleaned for any reason—as, for instance, before being placed on noninfested pastures—it is recommended that the cattle be kept in a small tick-free inclosure for three weeks, when many of the ticks will have fallen off. They should then be removed and placed in a similar paddock for another three weeks. At this time the cattle should be examined, and if found free from ticks they may be placed in the noninfested pasture at once. On the other hand if any ticks are observed the cattle should be placed in a third pen for two weeks more. By this time even the youngest ticks that were on the cattle at the start will have matured and dropped off; and as the animals are removed from each pen before they could possibly become reinfested with the seed ticks that hatch from the eggs of the females that fell off, they are now tick free. The same pens can not be used repeatedly for this purpose without thorough disinfection, as they become infested with young ticks, which will at once attack cattle if given an opportunity to do so. Care should be taken that hay fed the animals in these pens is from noninfested fields.

How to Free Pastures of Ticks.—How to rid pastures of ticks without destroying the vegetation on them was for a long time a problem. While this may be impossible on large ranches, it has been successfully accomplished on small farms by systematic efforts based upon a knowledge of the life history and the habits of the cattle ticks. The most satisfactory as well as the most practicable methods have been found to be as follows:

By Excluding Cattle for a Definite Period.—The removal of animals from an infested pasture for a stated period will cause all ticks present therein to starve, and the pasture will thus become tick-free. One method of accomplishing this result is to divide the pasture into two parts by a double line of fence. This fence should be board-tight at the bottom to prevent ticks from crawling out, and there should be a 10-foot space between the two lines so that the ticks would be unable to crawl across to the opposite pasture if they should perchance get out. One of these pastures is then kept free from cattle, horses, mules, and asses from spring to late fall, or, better, until January. By this time it will be free of ticks and ready for tick-free cattle that have been cleaned by any of the methods above described; then the other pasture is abandoned for the same period of time.

Butler states that the pasture may be kept free of ticky animals for a shorter period with equally beneficial results, and recommends the following method:

The tick-infested cattle should be removed from their pasture on September 1, cleaned of ticks by any of the methods previously mentioned, and placed in a cultivated field or pasture where no ticky animals have been for at least six months and where they can not come in contact with ticky animals or ticky soil. The original pasture should not be restocked until the following spring (April), at which time all the eggs laid there before September 1 will have hatched, the seed ticks will have starved, and the pasture will be free of ticks. It may then be used for cattle that have no ticks upon them. In case the cattle are not free of ticks when placed in the cultivated field or noninfested pasture on September 1, they will infect this field and will carry ticks to the original pasture if placed there in the spring.

By Cultivation.—Another method of destroying ticks on pastures is to cultivate the soil for a year without permitting any ticky cattle, horses, or mules on the ground during this period. After this treatment the field will be without any Texas-fever ticks and may be restocked with cattle not infested with these parasites.

By Burning Off the Grass.—Pastures that are too large to be disinfected by the above measures or those grazing lands that are open and can not be inclosed, or ranches where a division of the pasture is impracticable, may be freed from ticks by burning them off in the spring or fall and then keeping tick-infested animals from the land. It is advisable to burn off the grass in the spring when practicable, as this permits the pasture to recover quickly and to supply feed in several weeks.

How to Free Cattle and Pastures of Ticks at the Same Time.—The feed-lot method has been recently recommended by Morgan after conducting field experiments in Louisiana and has for its object the ridding at the same time of pastures and cattle of the fever tick. This plan, like the "soiling" method, suggested by Curtice, is based upon the length of time the tick lives upon cattle and the period required for the eggs to be laid and hatched and the seed ticks to attach themselves to their host. For carrying out this idea take a field which has been sown to corn, millet, sorghum, or other forage and fence off three lots within such a field, in one of which the ticky cattle are placed on June 1 by removal from their custom-

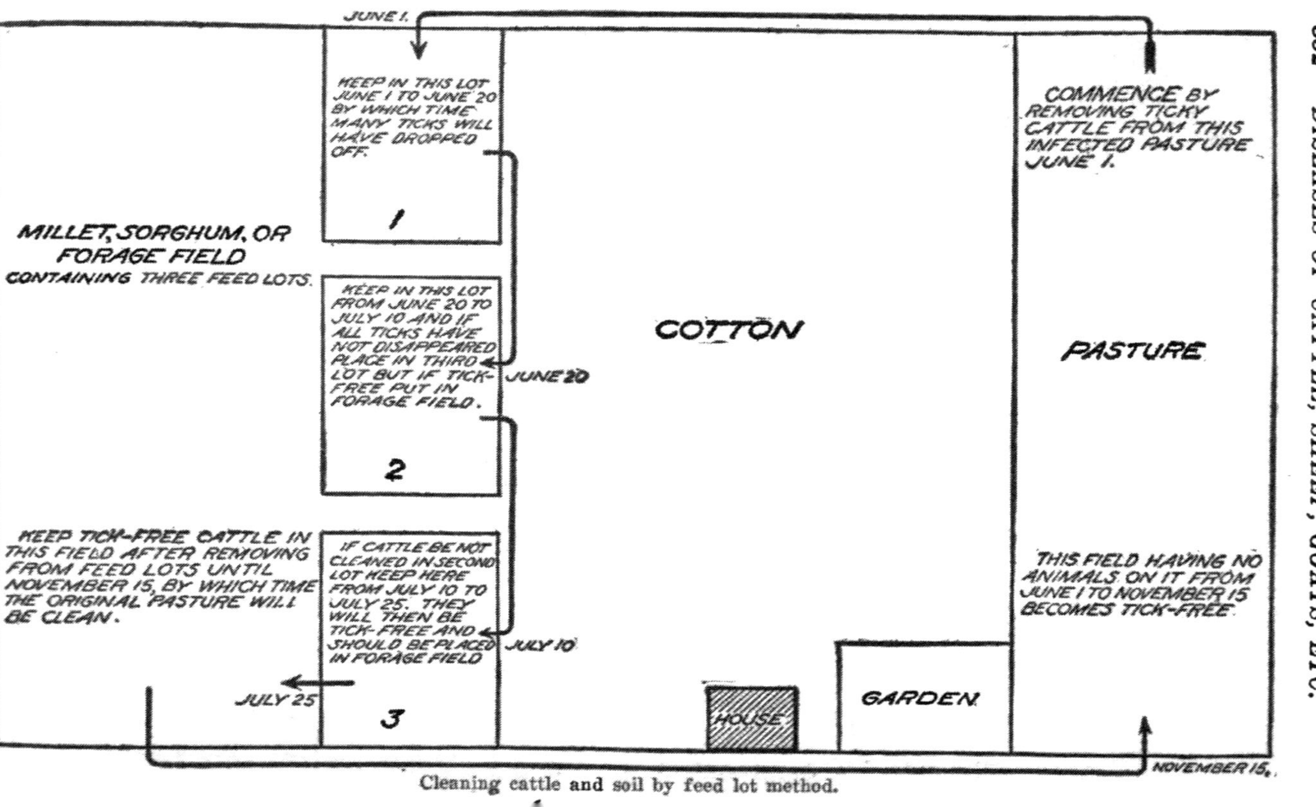

Cleaning cattle and soil by feed lot method.

ary pasture.* In the first feed lot the greater number of ticks drop off and lay eggs. After an interval of twenty days and before these eggs have had time to hatch, the cattle are moved to the second inclosure, where they are kept another twenty days, when they will in many instances be free of ticks and can be turned into the forage field. However, in case ticks are still present, the cattle should be placed in a third paddock for fifteen days longer. All the ticks that were on the animals when placed in the feed lots will have dropped off now, and, as the cattle leave each feed lot before they can become reinfested by the seed ticks which hatch from the eggs of the ticks that fall off, they will be clean and safe. These tick-free cattle are then pastured in the sorghum, corn, or millet field containing the feed lots and the latter are plowed immediately after the cattle are taken out, their edges are sprayed with Beaumont oil, petroleum, or other disinfectant substances, and the soil is cultivated. The cattle are kept in the forage field until November 15, or even later, when all the ticks on the regular pasture will have died of starvation from the exclusion of cattle since June 1, and the tick-free animals can then be replaced on this tick-free pasture. In adopting this method it is essential that the feed lots be inclosed by a fence which is board-tight along the ground, and that this fence be watched carefully and disinfected occasionally to prevent the ticks from getting into the forage field; a single furrow could be thrown up on both sides of the fence for the same purpose. These feed lots should be situated along the edge of the field in order that the cattle in changing from one lot to the other may pass, as directly as possible, through a portion of an adjoining cultivated or tick-free field, so that if the ticks fall off during this drive they will not infest the forage field and later the cattle when pastured therein. The cattle should be fed on the annual crops while in these lots, but never upon crops obtained from infested pastures, as such food may contain seed ticks. Water may be supplied by piping from a well, spring, or creek, by carting it to the feed lots in barrels, or by placing the fence so as to include a spring or portion of a creek, provided the latter does not flow through an infected pasture a short distance above.

By Pasture Rotation.—A very satisfactory method for freeing cattle as well as pastures of the cattle tick is by pasture rotation, which combines the suggestions of Curtice, Butler, and Morgan. It is based upon the knowledge that by severing the relations of the fever ticks and the animals upon which they develop these ticks will perish. To adopt this plan first divide the infected pasture into two parts, which is best accomplished by a double line of fence with a 10-foot space between the lines to prevent ticks crossing from one pasture to another. Further, in order to observe all possible precautions, this fence should have either a furrow thrown up against it or a board or rail placed tightly along the bottom to help keep the ticks within. All animals that carry the cattle tick are excluded from

---

*From our experience the two lots recommended by Morgan would not be sufficient under all conditions.

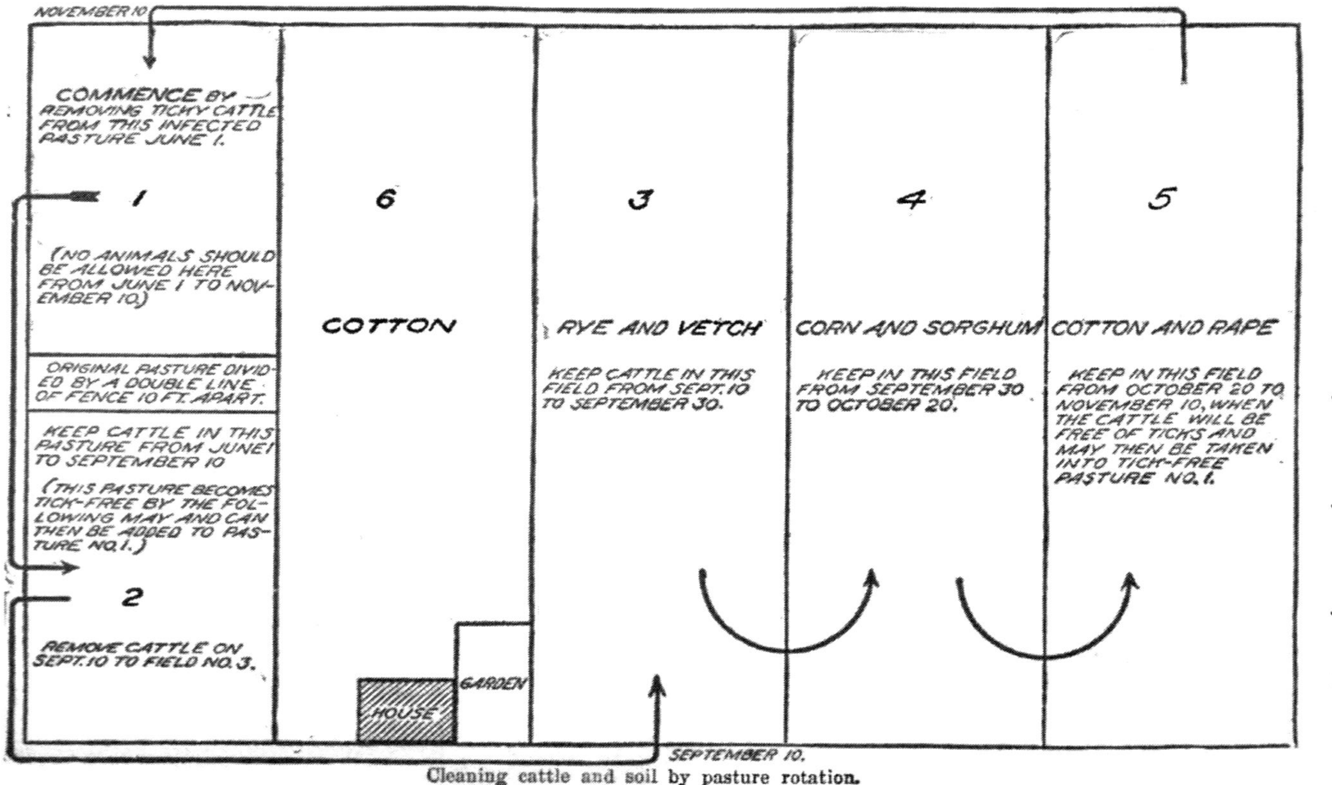

Cleaning cattle and soil by pasture rotation.

the first half of the pasture, which may be termed pasture No. 1, from June 1 until November 10, at which time all the ticks that were there will have perished from want of a host and the field will be ready for receiving tick-free cattle. The ticky cattle, on being removed from pasture No. 1 on June 1, are placed in the other half of the original pasture, which may be called pasture No. 2, where they are kept from June 1 to September 10. They may now be partly cleaned of ticks by placing them at the latter date (September 10) in a cultivated field—for instance, a rye or vetch or wheat and vetch field—and by keeping them therein for twenty days, when a large number of ticks will have fallen off. The partly cleaned cattle may then be removed on September 30 to a field sown to corn and sorghum, corn and cowpeas, or a combination of corn, sorghum, and cowpeas, or other forage crops.

In this field most of the remaining ticks, if not all of them, will have dropped from the animals within twenty days, but in a few instances the cattle may still be infested, so the animals should be moved on October 20 to a cotton field in which rape or crimson clover had been sown at the last cultivation for the purpose of furnishing food for the cattle while there. The crops should have been gathered from all these fields before turning in the cattle. Here they are kept for another twenty days (to November 10), not because they would not be free of ticks at an earlier date, but on account of the desire to keep cattle away from pasture No. 1 until November 10. On this date these clean cattle are returned to pasture No. 1, which will now be tick-free as a result of the exclusion of animals since June 1. These cattle should be kept in this pasture until May, by which time the ticks in pasture No. 2 will have starved owing to the absence of animals therefrom since September 10. Both the cattle and pastures will now be tick-free and the double line of fence between the two fields can be removed and the original pasture restored. This plan, as represented by the diagram, is merely a suggestion of arrangement and may easily be varied with regard to the selection of crops and the location of pastures to suit the demands of individual farms. To prevent ticks from crawling under either of the fences between fields 3 and 4 and fields 4 and 5 it is necessary to have a board or rail placed tightly on the ground along these lines of fence, or to throw up a single furrow along both sides of the fences. To avoid the danger of infestation from the outside, care should be taken to feed the animals, in those cases where the pastures or fields are overstocked, on hay cut from tick-free fields, and to keep out work oxen, mules, and horses that may harbor fever ticks, thus preventing reinfestation of the pasture. When the cultivated fields are on a slope it is advisable to use the lowest field first, in order that the ticks dropped within may not be washed by drainage upon the adjoining fields which are later to hold the cattle. For the same reason, where a stream runs through the fields upon which the cattle are to be placed, the field farthest removed from the head water should be used first. Where an endeavor is made to rid a farm of ticks, it is essential that the work animals (oxen, mules, and horses) used in cultivating the fields be curried to keep off the ticks and prevent the latter from being carried into these fields. Cats should also be kept from the pastures and fields; for, although they do not harbor the mature ticks, seed ticks have been found on them, and while these seed ticks remain only for a short period, this time may be sufficient to allow them to be carried into the disinfected pastures, where they may fall off and reinfest the soil. If a farm or plantation consists of a pasture and but one field under cultivation, the above plan can be made applicable by fencing off three inclosures in the latter and by rotating the cattle in them every twenty days in the manner just described. The same precautions should be observed in changing the cattle from one lot to another and in preventing ticks from getting into the cultivated field as are mentioned above.

IMMUNIZATION OF SUSCEPTIBLE CATTLE.

By Blood Inoculation.—It is often desirable to ship well-bred cattle into infested districts, that they may be used to improve the quality of the native cattle already there. Previous to the discovery of the cause of Texas fever it was found to be well-nigh impossible to introduce pure bred cattle from the North into any of the infected regions without suffering great loss—sometimes as high as 90 per cent—within a few months of their arrival at their southern destination. At first it was thought that the fatalities were due to climatic changes, but later the discovery was made that Texas fever was causing these numerous deaths.

It has now been found practicable to immunize this class of cattle so perfectly that the losses which follow their transportation to a tick-infested region are reduced to a minimum. Young animals six to fifteen months old should, as far as possible, be selected for this purpose, as they are more readily immunized than adults, are more easily handled, and the dangers which may arise from pregnancy while undergoing the immunizing treatment are thus avoided.

Immunity in these cattle is obtained by introducing the microparasite of the blood into their systems. It may be done by direct artificial inoculation or by placing virulent young ticks upon the animals and allowing them to perform the inoculation in the natural manner. The subcutaneous injection of a small amount of defibrinated virulent blood has been found, by means of prolonged experiment, the preferable method, as the number of micro-organisms introduced can be more accurately gauged from the syringe than by allowing the infection to be produced by bites of ticks. Two or three inoculations, if repeated at proper intervals, are accomplished with greater safety to the animal than would be possible by means of a single inoculation. The amount first injected should be small and then gradually increased in the succeeding treatments.

The inoculation always results in a more or less serious attack of Texas fever. Besides having a fever, there is great diminution of red blood corpuscles, and in about 3 per cent of the cases a fatal termination; but the proportion of deaths resulting from the inoculation is small when compared with the fatalities among untreated animals taken into infested districts. To this number should be added those animals (less than 7 per cent) that do not receive sufficient immunity by this method and which succumb when exposed to infested pastures. Combining these failures it will be seen that by this method of immunization, instead of a loss of 90 per cent among breeding stock taken South more than 90 per cent can be saved. The animals should be carefully nursed through the attack and their symptoms treated.

Immunizing inoculations are now being made by the veterinarians of most of the agricultural experiment stations of the Southern States without cost for the services rendered, a charge being made merely for the actual value of food consumed and attendants' wages. These veterinarians have also issued station bulletins which describe fully the necessary steps to be taken in securing the blood and injecting it into the animals to be immunized, so that the stock ownei can follow the instructions with prospects of getting good results.

This operation is not a difficult one, and excellent results will follow where absolute cleanliness and ordinary care have been used, but undoubtedly the best results will be obtained by those who have thoroughly familiarized themselves with the nature of the disease and are experienced in extracting blood from animals. Two methods are in use and will be described separately. One consists in drawing the blood from the jugular vein of an immune animal and immediately injecting it into the cattle to be immunized. It is comparatively simple, requires few instruments, and can be satisfactorily carried out where a small number of animals are to be immunized and if a suitable immune animal is close at hand. First, select an immune animal which is in good health and which is infested with fever ticks or had them the preceding year. Fasten the animal securely, either by tying, throwing, or by placing in a chute. Clip the hair from a space about 4 inches in diameter over the jugular vein on the upper third of the neck, wash the skin thoroughly with a 5 per cent solution of carbolic acid, and then fasten a strap or rope around the neck below the hairless area and draw it tight in order that the blood in the vein will be stopped, causing distension. With a large hypodermic syringe needle, previously sterilized in a 5 per cent carbolic-acid solution, puncture the vein at a slight angle, directing the point forward. When the needle enters the vein the point can be rotated freely in contrast to the restricted movements if still in the tissues, and the blood will either drop or flow from the opening in the needle. Attach the disinfected syringe to the needle with piston in and gradually draw out the poison until the chamber of the syringe is full of blood, when the needle is withdrawn. The blood, before it has had time to clot, is immediately injected into the animals to be immunized and which have been previously tied or restrained, the hair clipped, and the skin disinfected at the seat of injection in the region of the shoulder. Inject then from 1 to 3 c. c., according to the age of the animal, under the skin of each animal until the blood is exhausted. When more animals are to be inoculated than one syringeful will inject, the operation may be repeated in the same manner. The only objection to this method is the possibility of the blood clotting in the syringe, but with practice and promptness this can be easily overcome.

The second method is better suited for the inoculation of a large number of cattle or where the immune animal is at a distance from the cattle to be immunized.

The preliminary steps—the clipping of the hair, disinfection of the skin, placing the rope around the neck to distend the jugular vein, and restraining the animal—are the same as for the first method. In puncturing the vein it is advisable to use a small trocar and canula after sterilization in a 5 per cent carbolic-acid solution, and, when the vein has been entered, to draw out the trocar, allowing the blood to flow through the canula into a perfectly clean and sterile vessel. After sufficient blood has been drawn for the animals to be injected, a clean stick, previously sterilized by boiling in water, is placed in the vessel containing the blood and the latter is stirred for ten minutes or so or until the fibrin in the blood is whipped out. The remaining blood, known as defibrinated blood, is then inoculated under the disinfected skin of the animals to be immunized, as in the first method. This blood should be used as early as possible after drawing, to prevent it from becoming contaminated and decomposed. The place where this injection is made is immaterial, but for convenience a point just behind the shoulder is usually chosen. The dose and number of injections vary with the individual animals. As a rule, it may be stated that 1 cubic centimeter should be injected into an old animal coming into the infested district, 2 cubic centimeters for a 2-year-old, and 3 cubic centimeters for an animal 9 to 15 months old. It will be observed that, unlike the usual custom of applying a treatment, the older animals take less than the young ones owing to their greater susceptibility to the disease. Where an animal has reacted well to a first injection and shows a very high temperature, great reduction of red blood cells, or other symptoms indicative of reaction, it will not be necessary to repeat the injection, but in those cases where the reaction is slight, a second injection should follow after an interval of forty days, and, if need be, a third injection after a similar lapse of time, always increasing the size of dose 50 per cent. A thermometer, to indicate the course and severity of the disease, is indispensable in this work. Usually, after three to ten days, sometimes longer, the inoculated animals show a mild type of Texas fever, which runs a course of from six to eight days and is followed in about thirty days after the injection with a second attack of a milder character than the first. After forty days, when the animal has entirely recovered from the inoculation, a second injection may be given to increase its immunity. In some cases a very severe type of fever follows the first inoculation, requiring careful nursing and treatment, as suggested above. A second, milder attack follows usually in about thirty to forty days, after which the animal need have no further inoculations. It is advisable to prevent any ticks from getting on the cattle until sixty days after their inoculation or until they have fully recovered, at which time a few ticks may be placed upon them in order to re-enforce their immunity.

Bull "Elkjaer Hovding." 4½ Years Old. Jutland Breed. Dept. of Agr.

Jutland Cow. Dept. of Agr.

Naturally this time varies according to the type of the attack. As the best results with these immunizing experiments have been obtained in cool weather and with young cattle, it is recommended that animals from 6 to 15 months old be selected for inoculation, and that they be immunized during the late fall or winter months, in order that they may enter tick-infested pastures in the spring without danger.

By Infesting with Ticks.—Immunity may also be induced in susceptible animals by placing a limited number of fever ticks upon their bodies in order to produce the disease naturally. For this purpose only animals less than 1 year of age should be used, as the method is not applicable for older and more susceptible animals. Upon the bodies of these young cattle from twenty-five to fifty seed ticks should be placed, which in the course of about ten days will occasion a rise of temperature and a mild form of Texas fever. When the animal has entirely recovered from this attack, a second crop—double the number first used—should be applied to the animal in order to increase its power of resistance when pastured on infested soil. In order to carry out this method successfully, a constant supply of seed ticks must be at hand. This can be accomplished by placing the mature females in a Mason fruit jar among some dirt and leaves and keeping them in a warm place. In a few weeks the eggs will have been laid and hatched, and a number of seed ticks will be present for use in infesting the cattle to be immunized. By placing a few adult females in the jar every two months there will always be a supply of these young ticks. This method of producing immunity by controlled tick infestation is not so safe as blood inoculation, since the quantity of germs injected can be more accurately regulated by means of a syringe.

Treatment.—When the disease has broken out, all animals, the sick as well as the healthy, should at once be removed to another noninfected pasture. While this may not cut short the disease, it may save the lives of some by removing them from the possibility of being attacked by more young ticks. Removal from infected pastures likewise prevents a second later attack in October or early in November, which is caused by another generation of ticks. It is true that sick natives infect with a new generation of ticks the pasture to which they are removed, but these usually appear so late that they have but little opportunity to do any damage. Hence, sick natives do not, as a rule, cause visible disease in other natives.

It is of importance to remove all ticks, as far as this is possible, from sick animals, since they abstract a considerable amount of blood and thereby retard the final recovery.

Medical treatment of the sick has generally been unsatisfactory, although in chronic cases and those occurring late in the fall beneficial results have followed. If the animal is constipated, a drench containing 1 pound of Epsom salts dissolved in 1 quart of water should be administered, followed by the sulphate of quinine in doses of 30 to 90 grains, according to the size of the animal, four times a day until the system is well saturated with it. Tincture of digitalis one-half ounce and whisky or alcohol 2 ounces may be combined with the quinine, according to indications of individual cases. An iron tonic containing reduced iron 2 ounces, powdered gentian 4 ounces, powdered nux vomica 2 ounces, powdered rhubarb 2 ounces, and potassium nitrate 6 ounces will be found beneficial in the convalescent stage when the fever has run its course. This tonic should be given in heaping tablespoonful doses three times a day in the food. Good nursing is essential in treating these cases, and the animal should be given a nutritious laxative diet with plenty of clean and cool drinking water, and allowed to rest in a quiet place. If the stable or pasture is infested with ticks the animal should be placed in a tick-free inclosure to prevent additional infestation with these parasites and the introduction of fresh infection into the blood. Furthermore, remove from the sick cattle all ticks that can be seen, as they keep weakening the animal by withdrawing a considerable quantity of blood, and thereby retard recovery.

The sanitary regulations which have been enacted by the Department of Agriculture for the control of the cattle shipments from the infected districts have for their initial purpose the prevention of the transportation of cattle ticks from infected regions to those that are not infected, either upon cattle or in stock cars or other conveyer, during the season of the year when infection is possible. They are based upon the fact that Texas fever is carried north only by the cattle tick, and the exclusion of this parasite from the noninfected territory has in every instance been found a certain method of excluding Texas fever. The regulations governing the movement of cattle from below the quarantine line are made yearly by the Secretary of Agriculture, and they define the boundary of infected districts. The infected area as now determined includes the territory south of an imaginary line which commences in North Carolina, on the Atlantic coast, and passes in a westerly direction through a few counties in the middle of Virginia, North Carolina, Georgia, southern portion of Tennessee, along the northern border of Arkansas, the middle of Oklahoma, and the western part of Texas to the Rio Grande and the Mexican border, whence it passes along the southern boundary of New Mexico and Arizona and across the lower portion of California, to the Pacific slope.

During the months of January and February, the first fifteen days of March, and the last sixteen days of December in each year, cattle of the quarantined area of any State or Territory may be moved interstate, therefrom for purposes other than immediate slaughter under the above-mentioned restrictions into those portions of the States of Virginia and North Carolina not included in the quarantined area. During the month of January and the last seventeen days of December in each year cattle of the quarantined area of any State or Territory may be moved interstate therefrom for purposes other than immediate slaughter under the above-mentioned restrictions into that portion of the State of Oklahoma not included in the quarantined area.

All cattle from the quarantined district destined to points outside of the States and Territories above named may be shipped without inspection between November 1 and January 31, inclusive (the open season), without restrictions other than may be enforced by local regulations at the point of destination. At the present time no cattle may go out of quarantine, except for immediate slaughter, during that portion of the year included between the dates of February 1 and October 31, and known as the closed season. These cattle must be slaughtered after arrival at their destination, and the regulations of the Secretary of Agriculture concerning their handling and movement shall be enforced.

Cattle may be shipped interstate into points outside the quarantined area for purposes other than immediate slaughter, provided they are first examined and certified by an inspector of the Bureau of Animal Industry to be free from infection, but cattle from the quarantined area may enter only for immediate slaughter or during the open season. The following is an abstract of the regulations in force March 20, 1908.

Cattle coming from the infected districts during the closed season can not be driven, but must be conveyed in cars or boats placarded as containing Southern cattle, and bills of lading, waybills, and conductors' manifests shall have this information written upon them. When the cattle are unloaded for feeding, watering, or other purpose, they must be placed in pens reserved for such animals only, in which native stock is not allowed, and a large sign with the words Quarantine pens or Quarantine yards must be conspicuously placed on all such inclosures. On unloading at their destination, only the chutes, alleyways, and pens reserved for southern cattle shall be used. Before the cars or boats which carried these animals are again used their entire interior must be thoroughly washed with water after the removal of all litter and manure and then disinfected with a mixture made of 1½ pounds of lime and one-fourth pound of 100 per cent carbolic acid to each gallon of water, or with any coal-tar creosote dip permitted in the official dipping of sheep for scabies, provided the same is used at one-fifth the maximum dilution (five times the minimum strength) specified for dipping sheep. The litter and manure may be disinfected as above, or, if not disinfected, it shall be stored away where cattle can not reach it during the period from February 1 to October 31 of each year. All chutes, alleyways, and pens used en route and at destination but not reserved for the exclusive use of southern cattle shall be similarly disinfected. Where these animals are yarded adjacent to cattle from above the line at least a 10-foot space not occupied by cattle must be left between, on the inside of which shall be a tight board fence not less than 6 feet high, and on the outside a similar fence not less than 5 feet high. The yards or portions of yards reserved for cattle of the quarantined area shall be so located, or such drainage facilities shall be provided therefor, that water therefrom will not flow on to the adjacent property. Furthermore, provision has been made for noninfected animals to come out of the infested area at any season of the year, but like the ticky cattle they are subject to the restriction that they be dipped in Beaumont crude petroleum or other crude oil to prevent them from becoming infested in passing through the quarantined district. And they must also be shipped in clean, disinfected cars, and must not be driven through the infected area or unloaded therein except at points designated by this department.

In consequence of the enforcement of these quarantine regulations, Texas fever has been practically prevented in the noninfected districts during the last several years, and little or no hardship has been caused to those stockmen handling cattle from the infected areas. Previous to their adoption the tick-infested district was rapidly extending northward, but since the quarantine line was established and rational regulations enforced it has gradually been moved farther south. This problem of still further reducing the infected area is of the greatest importance to the cattlemen of the South—in fact, to those on both sides of the line—and one which is receiving special consideration by this department as well as by many of the interested States.

As an indication of what may be accomplished by hearty co-operation between the State and Federal Governments, it is only necessary to mention that as a result of a Congressional appropriation of $82,500 in 1906 and $150,000 in 1907, the Bureau of Animal Industry, co-operating with the local authorities, succeeded in cleaning up a large number of counties in several States, and has released from quarantine the following areas from July 11, 1906, to June 30, 1908:

State.	Whole counties.	Fractional counties.	Area in square miles.
Virginia	17	....	7,626
North Carolina	19	1	8,655
Tennessee	11	8	6,022
Kentucky	2	....	841
Arkansas	4	....	2,482
Oklahoma	2	4	2,612
Texas	1	....	660
California	5	2	27,630
Total	61	15	56,528

The amount thus released covers 56,528 square miles, an area larger than the entire State of Virginia.

Congress again this year has shown its desire to sustain adequately these operations by an appropriation of $250,000, so if the States will do their part in appropriating money and enforcing satisfactory laws in the infected districts, it would become merely a matter of a relatively short period of time before the fever tick would be exterminated and southern cattle permitted to reach the more favorable markets of the North at any time of the year without restraint. Prices would then be higher, the demand greater, and the odium attached to ticky cattle at the stock yards removed. Purebred northern cattle could then be brought into the South to improve the native breed without danger of death from Texas fever, southern animals could enter the show rings of the North without restriction, and the total cost of tick extermination would be far less than the amount saved in the first year after it had been accomplished. However, much co-operation must be had between the farmer and the State and Federal Governments before such a desirable result is possible. And in the meantime, with such conditions attainable, laxity should not be allowed in enforcing the present regulations, national, state, and local, and equal care should be taken to enlighten the stock raisers of the infected district as to the benefits which will follow their thorough understanding of Texas fever and their intelligent assistance in its eradication.

CHRONIC BACTERIAL DYSENTERY.

Chronic bacterial dysentery is a chronic infectious disease of bovines caused by an acid-fast bacillus simulating the tubercle bacillus and characterized by marked diarrhea, anemia, and emaciation, terminating in death.

Recently this disease has been observed in the United States for the first time by Pearson in Pennsylvania cattle, and later by Mohler in Virginia cattle, and in an imported heifer from the island of Jersey at the Athenia quarantine station of the Bureau of Animal Industry.

The former has proposed the name chronic bacterial dysentery for this affection, and it has also been termed Johne's disease, chronic bacterial enteritis, chronic hypertrophic enteritis, and chronic bovine pseudotuberculosis enteritis by various European investigators. The disease was first studied in 1895 by Johne and Frothingham in Dresden, but they were inclined to attribute the cause of the peculiar lesions of enteritis which they observed to the avian tubercle bacillus. In 1904 Markus reported this disease in Holland, and subsequently it was observed in Belgium, Switzerland, Denmark, and Great Britain.

Cause.—The bacillus, which has been invariably demonstrated in the intestinal lesions and mesenteric lymph glands in this disease, is a rod about 2 to 3 microns long and 0.5 microns wide. It stains more or less irregularly like the tubercle bacillus, and moreover the similarity goes further in that the organism is also strongly acid-fast, which facts led Johne and Frothingham to surmise that the disease was caused by avian tubercle bacilli. However, it has now been plainly demonstrated that the bacillus of chronic bacterial dysentery is readily distinguished from the latter organisms, for while it resembles the tubercle bacillus in form and staining qualities, no one has succeeded in growing it in culture media or in reproducing the disease by injecting experiment animals.

Symptoms.—Probably the first symptom noticed is that the animal is losing condition despite the fact that its appetite is good and the food nourishing. This is soon followed by a diarrhea which, while moderate at first, soon becomes excessive and may be either irregular or persistent, the feces being of the consistency of molasses and passed frequently. In the meantime the hair becomes dry and harsh and the animal falls off considerably in weight. The temperature, however, remains about normal. The appetite does not seem to be greatly impaired until the last few weeks of life, but nevertheless emaciation continues, the animal becomes more and more anemic, great muscular weakness and exhaustion are manifested, and death follows, apparently as the result of the persistent diarrhea and great emaciation. The disease may continue for four or five weeks or may last for a year or even longer before death intervenes.

Lesions.—The lesions observed on post-mortem are remarkably slight and out of all proportion to the severity of the symptoms manifested. The disease appears to start in the small intestines, especially in the lower portion, where the lesions are usually the most marked, but it also involves the large intestines, including the rectum. The mucous membrane may alone be affected, although usually in the long-standing cases the submucosa is also invaded and the entire intestinal wall is then much thicker than normal and the tissue infiltrated with an inflammatory exudate. The mucous membrane or inside lining membrane is markedly wrinkled or corrugated, showing large coarse folds with more or less reddening or hemorrhagic patches or spots on the summits of the ridges, especially noticeable in the large intestines. The mesenteric lymph glands are usually somewhat enlarged and appear watery on section. The other organs do not appear to be affected except from the anemia present in the later stages of the disease.

Differential Diagnosis.—The principal disease with which bacterial dysentery may be confused is tuberculosis, but the application of the tuberculin test will readily diagnose the latter disease, while no reaction will be noted in case the injected animal is suffering with the former affection. The disease may also be mistaken for the parasitic affections resulting from stomach worms (verminous gastritis) and intestinal parasites, especially uncinariasis, but a microscopic examination of the feces is necessary in order to establish definitely the diagnosis.

Treatment.—As with all other forms of infectious disease, it is advisable to separate immediately the diseased and suspected cattle from the healthy animals. The feces passed by the former animals should be placed on cultivated soil where healthy cattle would not be exposed to them, as the bacilli producing the disease are readily found in such manure. The stalls, stables, and barnyards should also be thoroughly disinfected, as has been described under Tuberculosis, in this chapter, special attention being given to those places which have been soiled by feces. The administration of medicines has thus far been quite unsatisfactory, although treatment should be directed toward disinfecting the intestines with intestinal antiseptics, such as creolin in 2 teaspoonful doses twice daily or tannopin in 1 dram doses twice daily, and strengthening the animal by the use of stimulants such as strychnin in half-grain doses given twice daily hypodermically. Salol, turpentine, or subnitrate of bismuth in a starch or wheat-flour gruel may also give temporary relief, but the diarrhea is likely to reappear and cause the death of the animal. In all cases the food must be carefully selected to assure good quality, and should consist preferably of nutritious dry feed.

NAGANA.

Nagana, also called tsetse fly disease, is an infectious fever occurring chiefly in horses and cattle, characterized by alternating paroxysms and intermissions and produced by a specific flagellate protozoan (*Trypanosoma Brucei*) in the blood. It is probably transmitted from animal to animal solely by the bites of the tsetse fly. This insect is something like a large house fly, and when it settles on a diseased animal sucks the blood and infects its proboscis, it is enabled on biting a second animal to infect the latter by direct inoculation. This disease is found throughout a large portion of central and southern Africa, along the low-lying and swampy valleys. It has never occurred in the United States, nor is it known to be present in the Philippines, but its relation to surra and the possibility of its appearance in one of our island dependencies are the reasons for including a few remarks at this time.

Symptoms.—The chief symptoms in addition to the fever, which is usually about 104° to 105° F., are the muscular wasting, progressive anemia, and loss of power, together with the edema most marked about the head, legs, abdomen, and genital organs. The urine is yellow and turbid, and occasionally contains albumen and blood. There is paralysis of one or both of the hind legs, difficult urination and defecation, labored breathing, discharge from the eyes and nose, extreme thirst, and gradual extension of paralysis to other parts of the body. The disease runs a chronic course, lasting from three to six weeks in horses, and from one to six months in cattle. Besides these animals, the mule, ass, buffalo, antelope, hyena, camel, and dog contract the disease naturally, and sheep, goats, cats, and small laboratory animals succumb to artificial inoculation.

Lesions.—The spleen and lymphatic glands are enlarged. There are sero-fibrinous exudates in the body cavities, the liver is enlarged and engorged, heart flabby, and a catarrhal condition is present in the respiratory passages. Pathological changes occur in the spinal cord. The finding of the trypanosoma by microscopic examination of the blood will be conclusive evidence for diagnosis.

Treatment.—Treatment has not proved satisfactory. Quinine, arsenic, methylene blue, and other drugs have been used, but without success. Endeavors thus far made to produce immunity from this disease have likewise been unavailing.

CATTLE FARCY.

This is a chronic disease of cattle occurring in France and the island of Guadeloupe, West Indies. It is characterized by caseating nodular swellings, first of the skin and afterwards of the superficial lymphatic vessels and glands, finally proving fatal within a year by extension to the viscera. The swellings rupture and discharge a purulent yellowish fluid, which contains the causative organism. This affection, called *farcin du boeuf* by the French, resembles cutaneous glanders or farcy of horses, but is caused by an entirely different organism, the streptothrix of Nocard. Moreover, cattle are immune from glanders and for this reason the name unfortunately applied to this disease, should not lead to any confusion with the cutaneous glanders or farcy of horses. Although the disease has only been described as occurring in Guadeloupe and France, the possibility of its occurence in our new possessions warrants its mention in this chapter.

Treatment.—Treatment consists in making incisions into the swellings and syringing them out with 5 per cent creolin or carbolic acid. The cavities may then be packed with cotton soaked in 5 per cent zinc chlorid solution. The swollen lymphatics may also be bathed or covered with cloths wrung out in this solution.—(Va. Exp. Sta. Bul. 108, 1900.)

PARASITIC DISEASES.

ANIMAL PARASITES.

Many of the insects in the external media surrounding animals have been known and studied for centuries, while others have but recently been studied, or are practically unknown. And science is daily adding to this list forms of organisms which have formerly escaped attention. As scientific knowledge advances along this line many diseases of both man and the lower animals, heretofore imperfectly understood, are found to be the direct result of some form of insect life. In the world of living matter representing organic life the conditions are so framed that the aliment is organic matter. The majority feed on lifeless matter, but there are many which prefer living upon living matter, and so obtain a living during the whole or a part of their life. When the relations between size and strength are such that the consumer is inferior to its victim, the former becomes a parasite of the latter.

A parasite, then, is an organism which, during a portion or the whole of its life, lives within or on the surface of an animal for the purpose of existence, and from which it receives its nutrition, either directly or indirectly.

Parasites are vegetable and animal. The vegetable parasites are termed Phytoparasites and are all fungi, and include moulds and bacteria. The animal parasites are termed Zooparasites, and include the lice, worms, ticks, etc.

In the animal parasites but three sections of the animal Kingdom are represented, viz: Protozoa, Worms, and Arthropodes. The protozoa are small, usually microscopical, organisms formed of a single cell and possess neither differential organs nor tissue. Their reproduction is by direct division, budding, or the formation of spores, in which the male and female organs are not required. They are, in most cases, provided with amœboid movement, and, hence, are seen to assume various forms even in a very short space of time. The micro-organisms of malaria and Texas cattle fever belong to this class.

Animal Too Weak to Stand Unaided. Loco Weed Disease. Dept. of Agr.

Lifting Foot Unnecessarily High. Loco Weed Disease. Dept. of Agr.

A Locoed Lamb. Dept. of Agr.

The Worms are invertebrates with a soft contractile body, nonarticulated or markedly divided into a number of transverse rings. They are always destitute of limbs and usually inhabit the hollow organs of the body, although the larval stage of different species may be found in almost all of the tissues of the body. This section contains a vast group, only one of which is of special importance from a parasitical standpoint. These are the Helminths, designated in many works as Entozoa, intestinal worms, etc., although found in various organs. They are divided into two classes: Plathelminths, with bodies usually flat, and Nemathelminths, with bodies, usually cylindrical. The platheminths are nearly all hermaphrodites, i. e., the male and female organs being present in the same individual, and comprise three orders, viz: Cestodes, Trematodes, and Turbellaries, the first two of which furnish a large number of parasites to man and the lower animals.

The cestodes are represented by the numerous species of tapeworms. Their bodies are flat, ribbon-shaped and nude in the adult form, segmented and provided at one extremity with organs of fixation in the form of suckers or hooks. They have no digestive apparatus, and in the adult form live in the intestinal canal of animals and man. In the larval form, however, they pass through certain transformations and migrate to organs very remote from the intestinal tract, and in different hosts.

The trematodes are represented by the various species of flukes, one of which causes the so-called liver-rot of sheep. Their bodies are soft, nude, and non-segmented and furnished with one or more suckers. They have a digestive canal with but one opening—that of the mouth. Those which act as parasites live in the interior of the body and are characterized by having not more than two suckers, of which the anterior is oral. The turbellaries furnish no parasites, so need not be discussed here. The nemathelminths are round worms in which the sexes are nearly always separate. They comprise two orders, Acanthocephali and Nematodes.

The acanthocephali have no digestive canal and have a protractile proboscis armed with hooks. Only one species is found as a parasite—the Echinorhynchus, which, in the adult stage, lives in the intestines. The nematodes, as a rule, have a complete digestive canal with two openings. They are elongated, slender worms and inhabit all the organs of the body except the bones and nervous system. They furnish a large number of species, some of which give rise to serious trouble and cause the loss of many animals.

The arthropodes are invertebrates, always provided with articulate limbs. They comprise four classes, only two of which contain species which are parasitic in the domestic animals, viz: Arachnidæ and Insects.

The Arachnidæ are air breathing arthropodes. The head is usually fixed to the thorax; there are two pairs of masticatory appendages, fours pairs of feet, no wings and an apodous abdomen. They are divided into ten orders, only two of which furnish parasites to the warm blooded animals—the *Linguatulidæ* and the *Acari*. The adult forms of the first live in the air passages, but in the larval stage infest the internal organs. The acari are not all parasitic Those which are, however, almost invariably inhabit the surface of the body. The order includes the ticks.

The insects are air-breathing and are provided with a trachea. Their bodies are divided into three distinct parts—the head, thorax and abdomen. The head is provided with a pair of antennæ, the thorax with three pairs of limbs and frequently with two pairs of wings. The order includes seven or eight sub-orders, only two of which furnish parasites—the *Dipteria* and *Hemipteria*—nearly all the species of which spend the most of their life on the surface, or within the substance of the skin; at least in their adult stage.

Parasites live on the surface of the body or in organs. The first are called *ectoparasites* and the second *endoparasites*. Each division will be discussed in its order.

The life history of parasites in general is quite simple, but when the life history of those which act as parasites during but a portion of their life is considered, we meet with a variety of habits. Some are parasitic only in the adult stage, and even in this stage may spend all or only a portion of the time on the host. Others are parasitic only in the larval stage, during which time it is a constant parasite, leaving its host only to enter the pupa stage. For example, the mosquito, horse flies, and gnats are parasitic only in the adult form, the gnat and mosquito passing the larval and pupa stages in moist places or in water. On the other hand, the larvæ of the screw worm fly and bot-fly are parasitic, while the adult is not. The time required for the different species of parasites to pass through the different stages of their life varies with each family or species. Some require months, while others require but a few days. In a very large number of animal parasites their entire life is passed upon, or within, the host. Of the internal parasites, the larvæ are frequently migratory and inhabit organs or tissues very remote from those in which the adult is found, and in different species of animals. For instance, the larvæ of a common tape-worm of man are found in the flesh of cattle, and another in the flesh of swine, in the latter constituting the so-called pork measles.

It has been argued by some that insects which now act as parasites have been forced to do so by chance, or certain circumstances, and, although now parasitical, are the descendants of non-parasitic insects. There are numerous facts upon which deductions are founded, especially from a biological standpoint, and by which the theory of evolution must be accepted to a certain degree, since it is not reasonable to suppose that a given form of parasite existed before the existence of its host. In other words, it must be considered that the force of habit has, in many instances, transformed a non-parasitic insect into a parasitic one, in which certain organs have become more highly developed, while others have degenerated. The natural tendency for an insect once started in a parasitic life is to become more and more parasitic, hence the transformation of organs. In some the wings are lost or, if present, are very rudimentary, while in others the mouth parts are greatly developed for the purpose of biting or piercing the skin. In others the clasping organs are exceedingly well developed for the purpose of holding. The eyes and antennæ are also often greatly modified.

Each group of animals has its particular forms of parasites, and each parasite has its particular host. In fact, there is a form of parasite for every form of animal life, from the highest to the lowest, and each form has its particular group of animals for its host. With reference to the external parasites, a parasite of one species of animal will not survive on a different species. With reference to the internal ones, however, there are many which are more or less cosmopolitan, since several of them are content to gain an existence in the tissues, or organs, of varied hosts, at least during some portion of their life cycle.

The rapidity with which parasites multiply is astounding, and, were it not for the fact that there are numerous causes of destruction surrounding them, animal life would be next to an impossibility. Leuwenhœck calculated that the female louse may become the grandmother of 10,000 lice in eight week's time. Other authors assert that the second generation of a single individual may furnish 2,500 progeny, and the third generation 125,000. Gerlach asserts that a couple of the itchmite of man yield six generations in three months, the last generation comprising 1,500,000 individuals. It is estimated that a tapeworm may throw off in one year 150,000,000 eggs. The state of surroundings in which an animal is kept may, however, hasten or retard the multiplication of parasites. Well kept and regularly groomed animals are less liable to parasitic attacks than poorly kept ones. Certain kinds of parasites are also more numerous during certain seasons of the year. For example, the flies, mosquitoes, ticks, etc., are more numerous during the warm summer months, while lice are in greater evidence in the winter time, when cattle and other animals are crowded together in stables and sheds. Butchers' dogs are more frequently infested with tapeworms than those which have less raw meat in their diet. Certain classes of parasites are also more numerous in some countries than others. The trichina, especially, is more common in Germany, notwithstanding the claims made by the Germans that American pork leads the list in this direction. The influence of parasites on the health of their host has been a subject of more or less dispute, insomuch as some have advanced the theory that the host was not only not injured, but benefited, by the presence of the parasite. Others have claimed, and with good reason, that parasites are not only unnecessary for the health of the host, but actually injure it. It may, however, be stated that certain forms of parasites, when in comparatively small numbers, do no special injury, and are only discovered by accident, or by a most careful examination, or on post-mortem. In one or two instances, it has been stated that a certain parasite (liver fluke of sheep), for a time, improves the condition of the host, since the primary stimulation of the liver by these parasites is said to cause the animal to take on flesh with greater rapidity. On account of this phenomenon, it has been stated that in an early day in European countries sheep, to be fattened quickly, were purposely infested with the liver fluke. Such a practice is extremely dangerous, owing to the great danger of infecting the pastures and other members of the flock.

As previously stated, it has been argued that parasites do not injure the host; but such opinions were offered in an early day, when but little was known of the various forms and degrees of parasitism. It is now a well demonstrated fact that parasites are injurious in at least three ways: First, as direct agents of loss from the animal economy. Second, as carriers of the micro-organisms of contagious and infectious diseases. Third, as carriers of other forms of parasites. In the first instance, must be considered the effect produced by the extraction of nutrition from the animal by the parasite—the loss of vitality by the production of sores, and the loss of energy due to the irritation and worry caused by the parasites. At first thought, it would not seem that the small amount of the animal fluids consumed by these little insects would have any appreciable effect on the host. When we consider, however, the amount of blood consumed by a single mosquito, fly or louse, and then multiply this by thousands, it will be seen that the amount of nourishment extracted by them is enormous. The detrimental effect on the host is all the more apparent when the slowness of preparation of these fluids for the building up of the tissues is taken into consideration, as well as the need of the fluids consumed by the parasite for the growth and strength of the animal, the laying on of fat, etc. It will, therefore, be seen that the drain is immense, and that the presence of parasites is no insignificant matter. The loss by the degeneration of tissues manifested in its formation of sores, ulcers, scabs, etc., making a heavy drain on the animal economy, is also of great importance, and is a source of heavy drain on the animal, in addition to the loss of nutrition. The irritation caused by parasites, especially on nervous animals, or on sensitive parts of the animal, is often of great injury, as is illustrated in the attacks of the botflies of the horse, sheep and ox. The irritating effect of the common horse and horn flies upon horses and cattle in pastures in the summer time is often an important factor in the prevention of the laying on of flesh.

It has been stated that as the biting lice live on the cast off scales of the skin, hair, or feathers of fowls, they are an advantage rather than a disadvantage. The irritation these parasites cause by crawling about the skin is frequently considerable, as indicated by the host scratching and rubbing itself on the fence, posts, etc., and in the case of fowls dusting themselves in ashes or dust.

As carriers of contagious and infectious diseases, parasites play an important part. Although comparatively little is known on this point, enough information is at hand to justify the statement that in all probability a large number of contagious diseases are contracted and disseminated through the medium of parasites. It is now known that the micro-organism of malaria is carried by the mosquito, and that various forms of pathegenic bacteria are scattered far and wide by the fly. The micro-organism of Texas cattle fever is known beyond a doubt to be carried by the cattle tick.

As carriers of other parasites, the flea and louse of the dog are known to carry the larval form of one or more of the species of the tapeworm of the dog. The dog, in licking, or biting itself to destroy the parasites, or to relieve himself of the irritation, swallows some of them, and the result is the development of an adult tapeworm in the digestive tract.

The losses due to parasites can not be estimated with any degree of accuracy. As a rule, no notice is taken of their presence until the animal begins to lose flesh, yet during all this while a greater quantity of blood has been necessary to supply the parasite with nourishment and to supply the animal with a sufficient quantity to compensate the tissues for that which has been extracted by the parasite.

Considering all classes of parasites, the deaths therefrom are numerous, especially in sheep, in reference to which it may be stated that three-fourths of the deaths are due to some form of parasitism. In some parts of the South, especially in the lower Mississippi valley, the loss from the buffalo gnat has been enormous. Osborn states that in a single county in Tennessee the loss from this cause in 1874 was $500,000.

It is a popular notion that only poor animals are infested with parasites and that the fat animal is exempt. Such a notion has probably gained credence because parasites are not suspected, or looked for, until the animal is noticed to be in an unthrifty condition. It is a fact, however, that the fattest animal may be infested with lice when a poor animal in the same herd may be free from them. It should be remembered that lice seldom attract attention until they become so numerous that the animals begin to lose flesh. Another idea is that white cattle are most frequently infested with lice. Such is probably not the case, but owing to the fact that lice are more easily seen among the hair of a white animal than on those of other colors, attention may more frequently be attracted to the white animal. It is, however, asserted by a number of observant stock men that animals of a certain color are more frequently attacked by lice. This may be true to a certain extent, and, if true, the reason can not at this time be explained except that the skin of certain individuals of certain color may be thinner and more easily penetrated by the biting or sucking mouth parts of the lice. It is hardly reasonable to suppose, however, that if a louse cast its lot on the skin of one individual he will perish, or leave his host in search of a more tender one. It is a well known fact, however, that certain individuals among the human family are almost entirely exempt from attacks of harvest mites, or giggers, while others are greatly annoyed by them; which in all probability is due to some peculiar condition of the skin or its secretion.

The fact that certain species of lice, and other parasites, will only infest certain species of animals is due no doubt to some difference in the skin of the animal, its secretions, body fluids, character of food, and habits.

It must be remembered that certain species of lice have, through a long course of evolution, adapted themselves to certain species of animals and that they adhere closely to the habits for which such a long course of evolution has adapted them.

From a practical standpoint, it is necessary for the stock owner to know to what extent a certain parasite is capable of injuring his stock, the time and mode of its attack, the species of animal it may affect, and the best method to be adopted for its eradication. In the majority of insects acting as parasites a general treatment may be prescribed, but in certain others a knowledge of the complete life history is necessary in order that they may be thoroughly eradicated.

THE ANIMAL PARASITES OF CATTLE.

The animal parasites of cattle comprise more than a hundred different species, belonging to various groups of the animal kingdom. Fortunately not all of these parasites occur in this country —many are uncommon, and many are comparatively harmless. Some forms, however, occur frequently, and some are of distinct importance to the American stockman on account of the damage for which they are responsible. It is these parasites particularly which will be considered in the present article, and although some forms are discussed which are rare or apparently of little economic importance, most of the minor and unusual parasites and species not found in this country have been neglected.

*Flies.**—Of the various species of flies which infest cattle some are injurious on account of the annoyance, pain, and loss of blood due to their bites, and sometimes also on account of diseases or parasites which are thus transmitted from the blood of diseased animals to the blood of healthy cattle, while others, which in the winged adult state do not bite, are injurious because they live parasitic in cattle during their larval stages.

Remedies for Flies.—There are various remedies to be had, which are more or less efficient in protecting cattle from the attacks of flies. Most of them have to be applied frequently and few, if any, will keep flies away for more than a day or two following their application. The following mixtures may be made at an average cost of 35 to 50 cents per gallon. The numerous propriety fly repellants to be found on the market are usually more expensive, and often less efficient.

At Minnesota Experiment Station rancid lard, 1 pound, and kerosene, one-half pint, mixed thoroughly until a creamy mass forms, was found to give excellent results as a fly repellant, lasting for two or three days, when rubbed not too thickly over the backs of cows with a cloth or with the bare hand. Similar good results were obtained by applying a mixture of three parts of fish oil and one of kerosene, with a small spray pump. A mixture of two parts of crude cotton-seed oil

---

*Further information may be found in a very full report on "Insects Affecting Domestic Animals," issued as Bulletin 5, new series, of the Bureau of Entomology, U. S. Dept. Agr.

or fish oil, with one part of pine tar, applied with a large paint brush, was found to be very successful at the Mississippi Experiment Station, the effects persisting for several days. A mixture of one part of crude carbolic acid to about ten parts of fish oil will repel flies for two or three days when applied by means of a cloth or sponge dipped into the liquid, squeezed partly dry and passed lightly over the hair. It should not be rubbed in, as it is liable in that case to cause blistering.

The following mixture proved the most useful fly repellant of any tried at the South Dakota Experiment Station: Fish oil, 100 parts; oil of tar, 50 parts; crude carbolic acid, 1 part. This was applied by means of a small hand spray pump. One application proved efficient for two days.

The Stable Fly (Stomoxys Calcitrans).—This fly very closely resembles the house fly, but unlike the latter it is a biting fly. It is common about stables and often enters dwellings, especially in cloudy weather. It is the agent of transmission of a parasitic roundworm of cattle (*Filaria labiato-papillosa*). This species has also been accused of transmitting anthrax from diseased to healthy animals, and there is some evidence to show that it may transmit surra, a disease due to blood parasite which affects horses, cattle, and other live stock.

The annoyance suffered by cattle and horses from stable flies is much lessened if the stables are darkened. This fly breeds in manure, especially fresh horse manure. By promptly disposing of manure dropped in stables and barnyards the number of stable flies about the premises can be greatly reduced.

The Hornfly (Hæmetobia Serrata).—This fly, now found nearly everywhere in the United States, was introduced into this country from Europe about the year 1885. Hornflies have the habit of clustering about the base of the horn, whence the name by which they are popularly known. They do not damage the horn and congregate there only to rest. They are frequently seen in a resting position on other parts of the body as well. When resting, their wings are held down close to the body when feeding, their wings are held out nearly at right angles ready for flight. They puncture the skin and suck blood, usually attacking the upper parts of the body, particularly those parts which are out of reach of the animal's head or tail. Unlike most flies, they remain on the animal more or less constantly day and night. Due probably to the irritation and annoyance caused by these hornflies, cattle often do not thrive as they should during seasons when hornflies are numerous. The hornfly has also been charged with transmitting diseases, such as anthrax.

The fly lays its eggs in freshly dropped cow manure. They hatch in about twenty-four hours, and the larvæ or maggots in four or five days develop to the pupal stage, which lasts a week or ten days. From the pupal stage the mature fly emerges. The entire process of development from the deposition of the egg to the appearance of the mature fly therefore requires on an average about two weeks. To protect cattle from the attacks of the hornfly they may be treated with one of the remedies mentioned above. Scattering the droppings of cattle with a shovel, or with brush dragged over pastures, in order to insure the rapid drying of the manure and consequent destruction of the larvæ, is, when practicable, an efficient means of reducing the number of these flies.

Buffalo Gnats.—These small flies, also known as black flies, are about one-eighth of an inch long and have a characteristic humped back. They breed in running water and appear in swarms during spring and summer, often in enormous numbers, causing great annoyance to stock and human beings, on account of their bites and their entrance into the eyes, nose, mouth, and other openings of the body. Their bites appear to be poisonous and in seasons especially favorable to the gnats heavy losses of horses and cattle often occur.

Buffalo gnats are more troublesome in bright, sunny weather than when it is cloudy, and animals which have not shed their winter coats suffer more from their attacks than those with smooth coats. Cattle kept in darkened stables are not molested. The application of one of the fly repellants already mentioned will help to protect animals from buffalo gnats. The burning of smudges is also a useful means of protecting stock from the attacks of these flies.

Screw Worms.—Screw worms are the maggots of a fly (*Chrysomyia macellaria*), so called from their fancied resemblance to a screw. The adult fly is about one-third of an inch long, with a bluish-green body, red eyes, and with three dark longitudinal stripes on the back (thorax). Attracted by odors of decay it deposits its eggs, 300 to 400 at a time, in cuts, sores, castration wounds, etc. The bursting of a tick on the skin commonly results in screw-worm infection at that point. The eggs hatch in a few hours and the larvæ or maggots, or so-called screw worms, begin to burrow into the flesh and continue burrowing and feeding from four to six days, after which they leave the wound and crawl into the 'earth, there transforming into the quiescent pupal stage. After this stage has lasted for one to two weeks, the mature fly appears. .From two to three weeks are therefore required for the entire life cycle.

Besides cattle, the screw worm fly attacks sheep, horses, hogs, and man. In the case of hogs it is generally the ears which are affected. The fly also breeds in dead animals, and all carcasses should therefore be buried deeply or burned.

For proper treatment an animal suffering from screw worms should be caught and thrown. Pour chloroform into the wound, taking care that it penetrates thoroughly into all the burrows of the screw worms, if necessary using a slender stick or a small bunch of twisted hay as a probe. The animal should be held for several minutes in order to insure the continued action of the chloroform. Finally the wound should be dressed with a carbolic or cresylic ointment to promote healing and thus prevent further infection, or the wound may be painted with pine tar.

Grubs, Warbles, Bots.—The common parasites known as grubs, warbles, bots, etc., found under the skin of the backs of cattle, where they form more or less conspicuous lumps during the latter part of

Jersey Bull in Service. Dept. of Ag.

winter and spring, are the larvæ of a fly known as the heel fly or warble fly. This fly (*Hypoderma lineata*) is about one-half inch long, very hairy, and somewhat resembles a small black bee in appearance. The flies appear early in the summer and are more or less prevalent until the beginning of cold weather. They deposit their eggs on the skin of cattle, fastening them to the hairs. Many eggs are deposited on the heels above the hoofs, hence the namo heel fly.

Although the flies are unable to bite, cattle seem to be much afraid of them and apparently are sometimes stampeded by them. Either the eggs or the tiny maggots hatching from them are carried into the mouth by the cattle licking themselves. In the former event the eggs hatch in the mouth or in the paunch. In either case the maggots or larvæ migrate into the esophagus, or gullet, and penetrate into its walls, where they undergo a portion of their development. From the esophagus the larvæ migrate through the tissues of the body toward the back, and according to one investigator enter the spinal canal, where they spend a certain period. Finally they appear about January beneath the skin of the back, forming the well-known swellings. The posterior end of the grub is near the small opening in the hide, through which the grub breathes and discharges its excrement, and through which, when its development is complete, it finally escapes. The anterior end of the grub is at the bottom of the tumor, where the mucous collects upon which it feeds. By spring or early summer the grub is full grown and forces its way out of the skin, falling to the ground into which it burrows for a short distance and transforms into the pupal stage. In about a month the mature fly emerges.

Grubs weaken cattle, cause them to fall off in flesh and milk, and decrease the value of the hide. The beef in the immediate vicinity of a grub becomes slimy and of a greenish color, and is known to the butchers as licked beef. The total loss to this country on account of the warble fly is estimated at $35,000,000 to $50,000,000 a year.

Treatment for Warbles.—During the winter press out the grubs and destroy them, using a knife if necessary to enlarge the opening; or inject a few drops of kerosene into the swelling through the opening, using a machinist's oil can for the purpose. To keep off the flies during the summer, the cattle may be frequently treated with one of the fly repellants already mentioned.

Lice.—Three species of lice, two of them sucking lice (*Hæmatopinus eurysternus*, the short-nosed cattle louse, and *H. vituli*, the long-nosed cattle louse), commonly known as blue lice, and one biting louse (*Trichodectes scalaris*), commonly known as red louse, affect cattle.

The blue lice suck the blood of cattle and are more injurious than the red lice. Unless very abundant the latter cause little injury. If numerous they irritate and worry their host probably more by their sharp claws than by their bites, as their food seems to consist entirely of particles of hair and dead skin.

Cattle lice reproduce by means of eggs or nits which they fasten to the hair. The blue lice infest chiefly the neck and shoulders; red lice, when present, may be found almost anywhere on the body, but are usually most numerous on neck, shoulders, and at the root of the tail.

On account of the itching due to the lice, infested cattle rub against posts, trees, etc., and lick themselves, the hair sometimes coming out and the skin becoming thickened so that mange may be suspected.

Cattle infested with lice should be dipped in the spring and again in the fall, using a coal-tar or tobacco dip, or Beaumont oil emulsion. If only a few cattle are to be treated the dip may be applied with a brush or cloth, or with a small spray pump, or a mixture of kerosene one-half pint and lard 1 pound may be smeared on the body.

Mange, Itch, Scab.—Cattle are subject to four kinds of mange, of which common mange or psoroptic mange is the most important.

Psoroptic mange of cattle is caused by a species of small mites which multiply rapidly and are spread from diseased to healthy cattle by bodily contact, or by pens, stables, railroad cars, etc., recently occupied by mangy cattle. The mites attack the skin and cause it to become thickened and covered with crusts and scabs, with a consequent loss of hair. Intense itching accompanies the disease and affected cattle are more or less constantly rubbing and licking themselves. Psoroptic mange commences at the root of the tail, or on the neck, or withers, and gradually extends over the back up to the head, over the sides, and may finally affect nearly the entire body except the legs. In serious cases the skin may become ulcerated; the animals become greatly weakened and emaciated, and finally die. By taking scrapings from the edges of scabby patches and placing them on a piece of black paper in a warm place the mites may be seen as tiny white objects crawling over the paper, more distinctly if a magnifying glass is used. Mange may be confused with lousiness, ringworm, or with any condition in which there is itching or loss of hair, but if mites are found there is no question of the diagnosis. The disease is worse during cold, wet weather. Mangy cattle when on good pasture during the summer often seem to recover, but in the fall the disease again reappears in a severe form.

The most generally used and most satisfactory method of treating cattle mange consists in dipping the animals in a vat filled with a liquid of such a nature that it will kill the parasites without injuring the cattle. Vats for dipping cattle are built of wood, stone, or concrete, and vary in length from 30 to 100 feet or more. They vary in width from 4 to 7 feet at the top, and 2 to 3 feet at the bottom, and the depth may be from 7 to 10 feet. A narrow chute through which the cattle are driven leads up to one end of the vat, where a steep slide pitches the cattle into the dipping fluid, through which they swim, and climb out of the vat at the other end, which is built sloping and provided with cross cleats to give the animals a foot hold. A draining pen with floor sloping back toward the vat is generally provided. The dip should be used warm, 100° to 110° F., and the cattle should be held in the vat for two minutes to insure thorough action of the dip. The head of each animal should be ducked at least once. Care should be taken that the vat contains a sufficient depth of fluid to swim the animals to be dipped. The dipping fluid may be heated from a steam boiler by pipes or hose, or water heated in large iron cauldrons or tanks may be used for charging the vat, and hot water with a proper quantity of dip added from time to time as the dipping fluid becomes cool.

If Beaumont oil emulsion be used one treatment will be sufficient. With other dips two treatments are required, the second treatment being given ten days after the first. The second treatment is necessary to kill the few parasites which sometimes escape at the first treatment, either in the egg stage or as fecundated females.

The following dips are approved by the Department of Agriculture for dipping mangy cattle which are to enter interstate commerce:

Lime-and-Sulphur Dip.—The lime-and-sulphur dip is made in the proportion of 12 pounds of unslaked lime, 24 pounds of the flowers of sulphur, and 100 gallons of water.

Directions for Preparing 100 Gallons of Dip.—Weigh out the lime, 12 pounds and sulphur, 24 pounds. Place the unslaked lime in a shallow, water-tight box similar to a mortar box, or some suitable vessel, and add enough water to slake the lime and form a lime paste or lime putty. Sift into this lime paste the flowers of sulphur and stir well; then place the lime-and-sulphur paste in a kettle, boiler, or tank containing 30 gallons of water, the water being first heated nearly to the boiling point. Boil the mixture for two hours at least, stirring frequently; add water occasionally to maintain the original quantity. Allow the mixture to settle in the tank or draw the entire contents of the kettle or boiling tank into a large tub or barrel placed near the dipping vat and provided with a bunghole about 4 inches from the bottom, and then allow ample time to settle —from two to three hours or more if necessary. When fully settled, draw off the clear liquid into the dipping vat, taking care not to allow any of the sediment to accompany it, as the sediment will injure the wool. The clear liquid thus obtained only requires the addition of sufficient clear warm water to bring the total up to 100 gallons. Flowers of sulphur must be used, and the lime must be of good quality.

Tobacco-and-Sulphur Dip.—The tobacco-and-sulphur dip is made with sufficient extract of tobacco, or nicotine solution, to give a mixture containing not less than five one-hundredths of 1 per cent of nicotine and 2 per cent flowers of sulphur. Sufficient nicotine would therefore be furnished for 96 gallons (about 800 pounds) of dip by 1 pound of a 40 per cent solution of nicotine. The formula for this dip would be: Nicotine, four-tenths of a pound; flowers of sulphur, 16 pounds; water 96 gallons.

To calculate how much nicotine solution or extract of tobacco should be used for 96 gallons of water, divide the quantity of nicotine required in the dip by the proportion of nicotine in the extract. For example, suppose the nicotine solution contains 25 per cent nicotine, we have 0.40÷0.25=1.6. Therefore in this case it would require 1.6 pounds of nicotine solution for the 96 gallons of dip. Or, if a tobacco extract is used, having for example 2.4 per cent of nicotine, the formula would be as follows: 0.40÷0.024=16.66, and therefore 16.66 pounds would be required for 96 gallons of dip. Do not use any preparation the strength of which is not given on the outside of the package. In preparing these dips the tobacco solution and sulphur should be mixed together with water before adding them to the water in the dipping vat. The dip should on no account be heated above 110° F. after the nicotine solution is added, as heat is liable to evaporate the nicotine and weaken the dip.

Beaumont Oil Emulsion.—Directions for making 100 gallons. —Dissolve with the aid of heat 5 pounds of hard soap (ordinary laundry soaps are satisfactory) in 5 gallons of soft water; to this solution add 20 gallons of Beaumont crude petroleum or a similar oil which may or may not contain sulphur, mixing with a spray pump, or otherwise, in a thorough manner. To this concentrated emulsion add sufficient soft water to bring the total up to 100 gallons, keeping the whole mass thoroughly agitated.

When properly prepared the concentrated emulsion will stand indefinitely without any tendency toward a separation of the oil and water, and can be diluted in any proportion with cold soft water.

Chorioptic mange, due to a different species of mite from that causing common cattle mange, is confined almost entirely to the region at the root of the tail and may persist for years if not treated. The treatment is the same as for psoroptic mange.

Demodectic mange, which is due to a small parasite that lives in the hair follicles, causing pustules, especially on the neck and shoulders, occurs occasionally among cattle in this country and is of importance on account of the injury to the hide. When tanned, hides infested by this parasite are pitted, the pits, in some cases, being so deep that they form holes. No practicable treatment is known for this disease.

TICKS.

About 10 species of ticks have been reported as parasites of cattle in the United States. The most common and the most important is the species known as *Margaropus annulatus*, which transmits Texas fever. Information concerning this tick and Texas fever has been given elsewhere in this volume.

The ear tick (*Ornithodoros megnini*) is frequently found in the ears of cattle in the western United States.

Treatment for Ear Ticks.—On account of their protected location ear ticks are not affected by dipping or spraying. Ear ticks are very difficult to kill, and remedies strong enough for this purpose are liable to injure the cattle, but the parasites may be expelled by pouring into the ear noninjurious substances such as cotton-seed oil, linseed oil, 20 per cent emulsion of crude petroleum, or almost any stock dip diluted as for use in dipping.

BLOODSUCKERS OR LEECHES.

These worms are sometimes taken up by cattle when drinking from ponds. They may attach themselves to the inner surface of the mouth or nose, and sometimes reach the upper part of the windpipe or of the gullet. Bleeding at the mouth or nose may be noticed, the membranes where the leech is attached are liable to be swollen and congested, and as a result of the loss of blood a condition of anemia may result.

Treatment for Bloodsuckers.—If the worm can be reached it may be destroyed by cutting it in two with a pair of scissors, or it may be removed with forceps or with the fingers after wrapping a towel around the hand so that the worm can be held without slipping. Fumigation with tobacco or tar may cause the worm to release its hold if it can not be removed by other means. Ponds may be rid of infestation with bloodsuckers by the introduction of eels.

PARASITES OF THE STOMACH.

The stomach of cattle consists of four compartments, of which the first and fourth are most likely to be the seat of parasitic infestation. The first stomach, or paunch, contains large numbers of minute parasites known as protozoa, which are too small to be seen with the naked eye. These small organisms apparently are in no way injurious. A species of fluke (*Paramphistomum cervi*) is occasionally found in North American cattle, especially grass-fed cattle, attached to the inner surface of the first stomach. This worm is about one-half inch long, and somewhat conical in shape, hence the name, conical fluke, by which it is sometimes known. Although this parasite has been accused of producing serious effects, it is generally considered harmless. Several species of roundworms may occur in the fourth stomach. Two of these are of special importance.

THE TWISTED STOMACH WORM (HAEMONCHUS CONTORTUS).

The twisted stomach worm (*Hæmonchus contortus*) is sometimes found in enormous numbers in the fourth stomach of cattle. Sheep, goats, and other ruminants may also be infested with it. Among the symptoms caused by this parasite may be mentioned anemia, loss of flesh, general weakness, dullness, capricious appetite, excessive thirst, and diarrhea. The anemic condition is seen in the paleness of the skin and mucous membranes of the mouth and eye, and in the watery swellings which often develop under the lower jaw (poverty jaw). If the fourth stomach of a dead animal be cut open and the contents carefully examined, the parasites, which are from one-half inch to 1¼ inches in length and about as thick as an ordinary pin, may be seen, if present in any considerable number, actively wriggling about like little snakes.

Cattle become infected with these parasites by grazing on pastures on which infested cattle, sheep, or goats have grazed and scattered their droppings. The worms in the stomach produce a multitude of eggs of microscopic size, which pass out of the body in the feces. In warm weather these eggs hatch in a few hours. If the temperature is below 40° F. they remain dormant, and if below freezing they soon die. The eggs are also killed by dryness, moisture on the other hand favoring their development. The embryos which hatch from the eggs are microscopic in size, and like the eggs are susceptible to freezing and drying. In very warm weather the embryos complete their development, so far as they are able to develop outside the body, in two or three days. In cooler weather the time required for this development is longer, and at temperatures below 70° F. ten days to several weeks may be necessary. The embryos are then ready to be taken into the body. The eggs and early stages of the embryos apparently do not develop if swallowed, hence only this latter stage seems to be infectious. In this stage they migrate up grass stalks or other objects, showing activity whenever the air is saturated with moisture; that is, during rains, fogs, and dews. When the air becomes dry and the moisture evaporates from the grass the young worms cease their activity, resuming their migrations when the air again becomes overladen with moisture. Embryos which have developed to the infectious stage, unlike the eggs and earlier embryonic stages, are able to survive long periods of freezing and dryness. In two weeks to a month after the embryos are swallowed they reach maturity and begin producing eggs.

Treatment for Twisted Stomach Worms.—Preventive measures are important. As moisture favors the development of the embryos, high sloping ground is preferable for pastures. If low ground is used it should be properly drained. Do not overlook pastures. Burning over the pasture will destroy most of the young worms on the grass and on the ground, and, if possible, this means of disinfection should be used at least once a year. Change the herd to fresh pasture as often as possible. Cattle should be supplied with water from wells, springs, or flowing streams, preferably in tanks or troughs raised above the ground. To a slight degree, salt serves to protect cattle against infection with internal parasites, and plenty of it should therefore be kept accessible.

Medicinal Treatment.—Among the remedies used to remove stomach worms may be mentioned coal-tar creosote, bluestone, and gasoline. It is advisable to treat not only the animals which are seriously affected, but the rest of the herd as well, since the parasites with which they are infested will remain as a source of reinfection to the others. The cattle should be removed to fresh pasture after treatment, if possible.

The animals to be treated should be deprived of feed for twelve to sixteen or even twenty-four hours before they are dosed, and if bluestone is used should receive no water on the day they are dosed, either before or after dosing. In drenching, a long-necked bottle or a drenching tube may be used. In case a bottle is used the dose to be given may be first measured off, poured into the bottle, and the point marked on the outside of the bottle with a file, so that subsequent doses may be measured in the bottle itself. A simple form of drenching tube consists of a piece of rubber tubing about 3 feet long and one-half inch in diameter, with an ordinary tin funnel inserted in one end and a piece of brass or iron tubing 4 to 6 inches long and of suitable diameter inserted in the other end. In use the metal tube is placed in the animal's mouth between the back teeth, and the dose is poured into the funnel, which is either held by an assistant or fastened to a post. The flow of liquid through the tube is controlled by pinching the rubber tubing near the point of union with the metal tube. It is important not to raise the animal's head too high on account of the danger of the dose entering the lungs. The nose should not be raised higher than the level of the eyes. The animal may be dosed either standing on all fours or lying on the side. It has been found by experiment that if the dose is taken quietly most of it will pass directly to the fourth stomach when the animal is dosed in a standing position, and that when the animal is dosed lying down little or none of the dose passes immediately to the fourth stomach. From this it is evident that the position on all fours is preferable, as more of the dose passes to the place where its action is required.

Great care should be used not only in dosing to avoid the entrance of the liquid into the lungs, but also in the preparation and administration of the remedy so that the solution may not be too strong or the dose too large.

Coal-tar Creosote.—Good results have been obtained from a single dose of a 1 per cent solution of a coal-tar creosote. This solution is made by shaking together 1 ounce of coal-tar creosote and 99 ounces (6 pints 3 ounces) of water. The doses of this 1 per cent mixture are as follows:

Calves 3 to 8 months old.............. 5 to 10 ounces.
Yearling steers .... 1 pint.
Two-year-olds and above .... 1 quart.

Serious objections to the use of coal-tar creosote have been found in that the substance known by this name varies considerably in composition and in that some trouble is often experienced in obtaining it in many parts of the country. Complaints have been made that the substance dispensed by some druggists as coal-tar creosote has failed to give satisfactory results.

Bluestone.—Bluestone, or copper sulphate, has been extensively used in South Africa in the treatment of sheep and cattle for stomach worms and is recommended by the colonial veterinary surgeon of Cape Colony as the best and safest remedy. To prepare the solution take 1 pound (avoirdupois) of pure bluestone, powder it fine and dissolve in 9½ gallons of warm water. It is better to first dissolve the bluestone in 2 or 3 quarts of boiling water, then add the remaining quantity of cold water, and mix thoroughly. This solution may be given to cattle in the following-sized doses:

Calves .... 3½ to 4 ounces.
Yearlings .... 6 ounces.
Two-year-olds and above .... 12 to 16 ounces.

In making up the solution only clear blue crystals of bluestone should be used. Bluestone with white patches or crusts should be rejected. It is especially important that the bluestone and water be accurately weighed and measured, and that the size of the dose be graduated according to the age of the animal.

Gasoline.—Gasoline is one of the most popular remedies for stomach worms which have been used in this country, and has the particular advantage of being readily obtained. It is important to repeat the dose if the gasoline treatment is employed, and it is usual to administer the treatment on three successive days, as follows:

The evening before the first treatment is to be given the animals are shut up without feed or water and are dosed about 10 o'clock the next morning. Three hours later they are allowed feed and water, and at night they are again shut up without feed or water. The next morning the second dose is given, and the third morning the third dose, the treatment before and after dosing being the same in each case. The sizes of the doses are as follows:

Calves .... ½ ounce.
Yearling steers .... 1 ounce.

The dose for each animal is measured and mixed separately in linseed oil, milk, or flaxseed tea and administered by means of a bottle or drenching tube. Gasoline should not be given in water.

Other Remedies.—Many other remedies in addition to those mentioned here have been used in the treatment of stomach-worm disease with more or less success. Several of the coal-tar dips on the market are recommended by the manufacturers for the treatment of worms, and the action of some of them is much the same as that of coal-tar creosote.

It is not the policy of the department to recommend the use of any particular proprietary remedy, and as the action of some such agents is very uncertain it is suggested that, if it is desired to use them, they be used with caution and only in accordance with the printed directions on the package. Whatever remedy is used it is wise to test it on two or three animals before the entire herd is dosed.

THE ENCYSTED STOMACH WORM (OSTERTAGIA OSTERTAGI).

This parasite is as thick as a fine hair and less than half an inch in length. It lives in small cysts in the wall of the fourth stomach and is also found free in the cavity of the stomach. When numerous, these parasites cause a thickening of the stomach wall and disturb its digestive functions. The symptoms caused by this parasite are very similar to those produced by the twisted stomach worm. The life history of the encysted stomach worm is not known in detail, but it is undoubtedly very much the same as that of the twisted stomach worm. The same measures as recommended above for preventing infection with the twisted stomach worm should be employed. Medicinal treatment is of little use, owing to the protected position in which the parasite occurs.

INTESTINAL PARASITES.
TAPEWORMS.

Two species of tapeworms are known to occur in the small intestine of American cattle. They sometimes grow to a length of several yards and to a breadth of three-fourths of an inch. Small portions of tapeworms, consisting of one or more segments, are occasionally seen in the droppings of infested cattle. The life history is not known, but the infectious stage is undoubtedly taken in with the food or water, infection being spread by the eggs of the parasite contained in the feces of infested animals. The eggs perhaps are swallowed by some small creature (an insect, worm, or snail) which acts as an intermediate host, and which when swallowed accidentally by a cow while grazing or drinking carries with it into the cow's stomach the infectious stage of the tapeworm.

Adult cattle do not seem to suffer much from infestation with tapeworms, but in calves these parasites may cause scouring and emaciation.

Treatment for Tapeworms.—Medical treatment for tapeworms in cattle is usually unsatisfactory, but the bluestone treatment used for stomach worms and mentioned above may be tried. Arsenic in doses of 1½ to 3 grains has been claimed to give good results in the treatment of calves for tapeworms.

ROUNDWORMS.

A large roundworm (*Ascaris vitulorum*) measuring 6 to 12 inches in length sometimes found in the intestine of cattle, especially calves, may cause inflammation and occasionally rupture of the intestine. Infection occurs through the swallowing of the eggs of the parasite in food or water which has been contaminated with the feces of infested cattle.

A number of species of small roundworms, varying in size from an eighth of an inch to an inch or more in length, occur in the intestines. Of these may be mentioned the hook worm (*Monodontus phlebotomus*) and the nodular worms (*Œsophagostomum columbianum* and *O. radiatum*). The former is about an inch long and is found in the small intestine. The latter are somewhat smaller and are found in the cecum and large intestine. Hook worms, when numerous, may cause anemia and other symptoms similar to those caused by stomach worms. The injury to the mucous lining of the intestine from the bites of hook worms may cause severe inflammation, and affords an avenue of infection with the germs of various diseases. The adult nodular worms apparently do not attack the wall of the intestine, but derive their nourishment from the intestinal contents. Several species of small, very slender roundworms (*Trichostrongylus*), less than a quarter of an inch in length, sometimes occur in the small intestine and fourth stomach, and severe gastro-enteritis, or inflammation of the stomach and intestines, has been attributed to them.

Nodular disease of the intestine, due to young hook worms, and nodular worms which burrow in the intestinal wall, as a rule seems to have little effect on the health of infested animals, but often renders the intestine unfit for use as sausage casings. As nodular disease is widely prevalent among cattle, the loss from this source is considerable. The greenish or yellowish nodules with cheesy contents are frequently mistaken by the inexperienced for lesions of tuberculosis.

The life histories of the various small roundworms occurring in the intestines of cattle have not been worked out, but in general they are very likely similar to that of the twisted stomach worm as described above.

Treatment for Intestinal Roundworms.—The preventive measures are similar to those recommended in the case of the twisted stomach worm (p. 363). Medicinal treatment is generally not very satisfactory. Powdered thymol, in doses of 200 grains or more, has been recommended, but it often fails to have the desired result. It is claimed by one author that 2 to 3 drams of rectified empyreumatic oil in a mucilaginous emulsion, followed the next morning with a purgative of 1 to 1½ pounds of sulphate of soda, will expel the large roundworms (*Ascaris vitulorum*).

PROTOZOA.

A number of species of protozoa have been reported as parasites of the intestines of cattle. To one species has been attributed a serious disease of cattle in Switzerland known as red dysentery, but as yet no cases of this disease in American cattle have been reported.

FLUKES IN LIVER AND LUNGS.

Two species of flukes occurring in the liver and lungs are known to affect cattle of the United States. These parasites are flat leaf-like-worms; one of them, the common liver fluke (*Fasciola hepatica*), is less than an inch in length, while the other, the large American fluke (*Fasciola magna*), is considerably larger when full grown. In their life history these flukes depend on snails as intermediate hosts. At a certain stage of development the young flukes leave the snails, become encysted on stalks of grass, and finally may be swallowed by grazing cattle. Stiles states that flukes may produce a serious, often fatal disease, more especially in younger animals. The symptoms are somewhat similar to those produced by worms in the stomach. The first symptoms are generally overlooked, the disease not attracting attention until the appetite is diminished; rumination becomes irregular, the animals become hide-bound, and the coat dull and staring. The staring coat is due to the contraction of the muscles of the hair follicles. The visible mucous membranes become pale, eyes become dull, there is running at the eyes, and the animal gradually becomes emaciated. As the disease advances the milk supply is lessened, fever appears, there is generally great thirst, but the appetite almost ceases; edematous swellings appear on the belly, breast, etc.; diarrhea at first alternates with constipation, but finally becomes continuous. The disease lasts from two to five months, when the most extreme cases succumb.

Most of the German cattle are said to be infested with liver flukes, but even when a large number are present the nourishment of the cattle is not disturbed. Thickening of the gall ducts, so that a so-called Medusa's head forms on the surface of the liver toward the stomach, appears in even well-nourished animals; even in cases of a cirrhosis of the liver it is seldom that any effect upon the cattle's health can be noticed, and so long as a portion of the liver tissue about twice the size of the first remains intact, the nourishment of the animal may be comparatively good. It is rare that one sees a generalized edema in slaughtered cattle as a result of fluke invasion, and even in the heaviest infections of young cattle only emaciation is noticed.

Treatment.—Medicinal treatment is unsatisfactory. The disease may be prevented to a considerable extent by giving animals plenty of salt, and by introducing carp, frogs, and toads into streams and pools in infected districts; these animals destroy the young stages of the parasite and feed upon the snails which serve as intermediate hosts.

TAPEWORM CYSTS OF LIVER AND OTHER VISCERA.

Three kinds of tapeworm cysts are found in the viscera of cattle. One of these (*Multiceps socialis,* or *Cœnurus cerebralis*) will be further referred to in the discussion of gid. All of these are the intermediate stages of tapeworms which live when mature in the intestines of dogs, wolves, and other canines. The eggs of the tapeworms are scattered over the fields in the droppings of infested dogs or wolves, and these when swallowed in food or water by cattle hatch out and the embryos migrate to the liver, mesentery, lungs, brain, or other organ, where they develop into cysts, variously known as hydatids, bladder worms, water balls, etc. When organs of cattle thus infested are eaten by dogs or wolves the cystic worms are also likely to be swallowed and then develop into mature tapeworms. To prevent cattle from infection with these parasites stray dogs, wolves, and coyotes should be killed wherever found, and dogs too valuable to kill should be kept free from tapeworms. As a precaution against infection with tapeworms, the viscera of cattle, sheep, or hogs should not be fed to dogs unless cooked.

Hydatids (*Echinococcus granulosus*) form tumors of varying size (sometimes as large as 6 inches in diameter) in the liver, lungs, and other organs. Their contents are liquid, resembling water. The presence of these parasites can not be detected in the living animal and there is no medicinal treatment for them. Organs containing hydatids should be destroyed by burning in order to prevent their being eaten by dogs. This is especially important, as dogs infested with the tapeworm stage of this parasite are a menace to human beings on account of the danger of infecting them with hydatids, which develop in man if the eggs of the hydatid tapeworm are swallowed.

Thin-necked bladder worms (*Tænia hydatigena*) are most commonly found attached to the mesentery and omentum. There is no medicinal treatment.

TAPEWORM CYSTS IN THE MUSCLES, BEEF MEASLES.

Small tapeworm cysts (*Tænia saginata*), about the size of a pea, found in the muscles of cattle are the larvæ of the common tapeworm of man. Cattle become infected from feed or water which has been contaminated by the feces of persons harboring the adult tapeworms, and human beings in turn become infected by eating raw or rare beef infested with the larval stage (measly beef).

To prevent cattle from becoming infested with this parasite care should be taken that human feces are not placed where they will contaminate the feed or drinking water.

GID.

Bladder worms (*Multiceps socialis*, or *Cœnurus cerebralis*) which are occasionally found in the brain of cattle, and cause gid, turnsick, or staggers, deserve mention, as they are rather common among sheep in the Northwest. As already alluded to, these worms are the intermediate stage of a tapeworm found in dogs, and their life history and the means of preventing infection have been briefly discussed above.

Cattle harboring this parasite show symptoms indicating an affection of the brain, walking or turning in circles, dizziness, uneven gait, impaired vision, etc.

Treatment consists in trephining the skull and removing the parasite, an operation which requires a skillful operator and is frequently unsuccessful. Unless the parasite is removed affected cattle almost invariably die.

THREAD WORMS IN THE ABDOMINAL CAVITY.

Thread worms (*Filaria labiato papillosa*) 2 to 4 inches long are frequently found in the abdominal cavity. They seem to cause little or no trouble. The embryos produced by these worms enter the blood vessels. Stable flies while sucking blood take up these embryos, which undergo a certain amount of development in the body of the flies. These flies, again biting cattle, introduce the partially developed worms with which they are infested into the circulation, whence the worms migrate to the abdominal cavity and there develop to maturity. The roundworms found occasionally in the anterior chamber of the eye are perhaps immature forms of this species which have reached this location during their migration.

LUNG WORMS. (See Verminous Bronchitis.)

PARASITES OF THE BLOOD.

A species of fluke (*Schistosoma bovis*) which lives in the blood vessels (the large veins) of cattle in tropical and subtropical countries causes bloody urine, and a condition of the rectum somewhat resembling piles. The embryos of *Filaria labiato-papillosa* which occur in the blood may be found by microscopical examination. They apparently cause no trouble. The organism which causes Texas fever is a protozoan parasite *(Piroplasma bigeminum)* of microscopic size, which lives in the blood and attacks the red blood corpuscles. Other parasites which live in the blood cause serious diseases known as surra and nagana, but as yet neither of these diseases has gained a foothold in the United States.

PARASITES OF THE EYE.

Roundworms sometimes seen swimming about in the anterior chamber of the eye (snakes in the eye) are supposed to be immature stages of *Filaria labiato-papillosa*. Their location in the eye is possibly due to their going astray from the normal course of their migration. Treatment for these worms is surgical. They often disappear without treatment.

A species of slender roundworm, one-half an inch to an inch in length, has been described, under the name of *Filaria lachrymalis*, as a parasite of cattle found in summer and fall beneath the eyelids and on the surface of the eyeball, causing an inflammation of the eyes. The worms may be removed by washing out the eyes with an antiseptic, such as a weak solution of coal-tar stock dip, after which iodoform ointment may be applied if the condition is severe.

HOOK-WORM DISEASE OF CATTLE.

This disease, also referred to as bovine uncinariasis and salt sickness, has been reported from Texas, Florida, and South Carolina, and is probably widely distributed throughout the Southern States. C. F. Dawson, of the Florida Station, reports it as the most common disease of cattle. Investigations by A. F. Conradi and E. Barnett, at the South Carolina Station, have shown cattle to be seriously infested with the hook worm, which is frequently associated with other intestinal parasites, including the twisted wireworm or stomach worm, the inflated bowel worm, and the hair worm. The disease as described by Doctor Dawson is an acute or chronic parasitic disease manifested at first by low fever, diarrhea, loss of appetite, soon becoming chronic, with continuance of low fever, constipation, loss of appetite, progressive emaciation, and pronounced anemia, which, in many cases, terminates fatally.

Young animals are more susceptible than older ones, but all ages may be affected. The nematode or roundworm (*Monodontus phlebotomus*), formerly described as *Uncinaria radiata*, is the exciting cause of the disease. These worms, found principally in the duodenum or first division of the small intestine, are provided with an armature of sharp teeth, by means of which they pierce the lining of the intestines and suck the blood, moving from place to place. Other species of hook worm which affect sheep, dogs, cats, foxes, man, and other animals should not be confounded with the species that affects cattle.

The adult worm is from one-half to five-eighths inch in length and of the thickness of an ordinary pin. The eggs are deposited in the intestinal tract and are discharged in the feces, through an examination of which the extent of infestation can be determined. Conradi and Barnett have observed a gorged female whose oviduct contained more than 1,500 eggs, 17 of which were deposited in one hour. At a temperature ranging from 48° to 60° F. forty-one days are required for the eggs to hatch. The life history and habits of the worm have been studied by Conradi and Barnett.

Upon hatching, the young hook worms are very minute, but can easily be seen with the aid of a hand lens when crawling on the glass walls of the breeding jars. They have a tendency to congregate, and these clusters can be easily recognized with the unaided eye. In this stage, as well as in the egg stage, they are very susceptible to heat or cold, being easily killed. Drought is also fatal, the worms dying in a few minutes. They feed on the fecal matter about them. In the second stage they are but slightly hardier. After several days the body wall becomes thicker and more rigid, and soon they pass to the final larval stage.

The larvæ that were hatched from eggs, gathered from fresh feces on February 26, and hatched February 28, had mostly passed to the final larval stage on March 15. In this stage they are protected by a resistant covering called "sheath." Worms kept in the laboratory during January and February, the temperature varying from 48 to 60° F., passed to the final larval stage in forty-one days. While active they were able to continue feeding through the aperture in the front end of the sheath. They move up and down on any near-by moist object, whether it is earth, grass, leaves, or weeds. They finally become quiescent in some elevated position, discontinue feeding, and are then greatly resistant to heat, cold, and drought. This habit of rising appears to be advantageous, as, we believe, the principal method of host infestation is through the mouth.

That part of the life history from egg to larval stage is very probably completed in a few days during the warm weather of summer.

The eggs and young worms require moisture. It seems quite probable that little development takes place in feces dropped on a hill during the drought of summer. There is said to be little danger from infestation in running water.

At present the outlook for a cure for this disease is not very encouraging. Thymol has given good results in the treatment of the disease in man, and has been recommended by some authorities for the disease in cattle and sheep, but we believe it is far from being a specific. Certainly, in the case above referred to, with a dose of 150 grains, it could not be noticed that the worms had been in the least affected three days later. However, further experiments with this drug will be made as opportunity presents itself. Even if drugs such as thymol were effective in expelling worms, the animal, if still pasturing on infested land, would continue to reinfest itself, so that the problem resolves itself into a question of prevention rather than treatment, the outlook for which is more encouraging.

When it is remembered that the disease occurs chiefly, or altogether, on low, wet lands, and that in dry seasons it is less severe, it would appear that much could be done by avoiding such places as pastures for at least one year. The land should be thoroughly drained, and it would be well to liberally apply air-slaked lime to accelerate drying. If in hook-worm infested lots the droppings are gathered every day, it will decrease the infestation.

Plowing, undoubtedly, also reduces the dangers of infestation, as heavily infested material buried 3 inches in loose, pulverulent, moist soil in the laboratory showed that a little over one-third as many larvæ ascended on the glass wall of the breeding jar as in the jar used as a check where an equal amount of material from the same droppings was left on the surface of the moist soil.

It is recommended that on hook-worm infested farms annual crop rotation be practiced as far as possible. The manure should be removed from stables occupied by infested animals daily and air-slaked lime used liberally to dry up the floors. The greatest precaution should be exercised to prevent the spread of this parasite into localities where it does not yet occur, either by shipments of infested cattle or otherwise.

Where it is desirable to eradicate this pest from a lot previous to putting in animals that are not infested, it may be accomplished by burning. For this purpose one should have a good substantial spray pump fitted with hose, extension rod, and a fine nozzle. Either kerosene or gas oil may be used. After the pump is filled and set in operation the spray is ignited near the nozzle. The present price of kerosene, however, would make this operation too expensive over large areas.

MANGE, ITCH, SCAB OF CATTLE.
SCABIES.

Scabies of cattle is also known as range itch, cattle itch, and cattle mange; the last is the correct name, the disease being mange, or scabies. This disease has prevailed to a considerable extent among the range cattle of the West and Northwest, and has been heard of in other portions of the country.

Cause of Scabies, or Mange.—Scabies, or mange, of the ox is a contagious disease caused by a parasitic mite. Cattle are chiefly affected with but two varieties of these parasites, or mites, which belong to the class Arachnoidea. These are, first, the *Psoroptes;* second, the *Symbiotes.* The first is the one which most frequently affects them. It lives on the surface of the skin and by its biting gives rise to great irritation and itching. It is most frequent upon the sides of the neck and shoulders, at the base of the horns, and at the root of the tail. From these points it spreads to the back and sides, and may invade nearly the entire body. Its principal manifestations are more or less numerous pimples, exudation, and abundant scaling off of the skin, falling out of the hair, and the formation of dry, gray-brownish scabs. In the course of time the skin becomes thickened, stiff, wrinkled, and acquires the consistence of leather. When mange has spread over a large surface of the body, the animals lose flesh and become weak and anemic, rendering them constitutionally less able to withstand or combat the effects of the mites. At the same time the decreased vigor and lessened vitality of the affected animals favor more rapid multiplication of the mites and the further extension and intensification of the disease. Thus we have cause and effect working together, with the result that scabies, or mange, of cattle may in some cases prove fatal; especially are fatal terminations likely to occur in the latter part of a severe winter among immature and growing animals, or those of adult and full age when in an unthrifty condition at the time of becoming affected. Variations in the progress of the disease have been noticed depending upon the season of the year, aggravation in winter alternating with improvement in summer.

The mite which causes cattle itch, or mange, is closely related to the mite which causes sheep scab; both belong to the same genus and species, but are different varieties. The sheep-scab mite will not attack cattle, nor will the cattle mite attack sheep or other animals. The itch mites are found to be very numerous upon affected cattle, and a very small quantity of debris from an actively infested area of the skin will often reveal a surprisingly large number of the parasites. These mites may be removed from an animal and retain their vitality for a long time. Specimens have been collected and kept in small glass bottles in the laboratory at the ordinary temperature of the room during the winter months, carrying from 45° F. during the night to 80° F. during the day, which would live and remain active from eight to eleven days. Exposure to bright sunlight, however, would kill most of the mites in a few hours.

Scabies does not appear to affect cattle while they are doing well on grass, nor to attack those in good condition over three years old. The animals which suffer most are calves, yearlings, and two-year-olds, and those in poor condition. The first symptom of the disease is usually an intense itching of the skin about the neck or shoulders, which extends more or less rapidly, depending largely upon the health and vigor of the animal, along the back and sides and down the outside of the legs, but does not usually affect the inside of the legs nor the skin of the abdomen.

The other variety of this parasite which produces mange in cattle is the *Symbiotes*. This is known as Symbiotic mange, or tail mange. It remains generally localized upon the depressions on the back part of the croup and at the base of the tail. It may, however, extend over the whole surface of the body if the treatment of the disease and care of the affected animal are neglected. These cases, however, are rare. Foot mange is also exceptional in cattle. Tail mange has almost no spreading tendency, and its contagiousness is hardly noticeable. It yields readily to treatment, and any remedy that will destroy the activity of the parasite producing the Psoroptic, or common form of mange, will readily kill that causing the Symbiotic, or tail mange. It is possible for the different morbid conditions produced by these two varieties of parasites to exist in the same animal at the same time.

Form and Life History of the Scab Parasite.—The *Psoroptes*, the first variety referred to, live upon the surface of the skin, adhere

FINE DAIRY COW IN CLEAN CONDITION. DEPT. OF AGR.

PRIZE DAIRY COW, RED DANISH BREED. YEAR BOOK, 1902.

to it, and suck the blood and lymph of the skin by means of their mouth organs, producing a more or less intense inflammation through the numerous stings which they inflict. This species is characterized by its relatively greater size. Its general form is rounded or egg-shaped. It can be seen with the naked eye upon dark surfaces, and is very easily seen with the help of a magnifying glass. The head is elongated and pointed. The jaws are long, straight, and stinging. The legs are very long. The sucking cups, which are tulip or trumpet-shaped, are carried on the legs. In the male they are seen on the four pairs of legs; in the female, upon the first, second, and fourth pairs only. In the immature form the *Psoroptes* or common mange mites have three pairs of legs, while in the adult state they possess four. The latter with five joints are fitted with suction cups covered with fine hair and armed with claws or hooks. The head, thorax, and abdomen are not separated. The mouth parts are represented by mandibles or jaws. The skin surface is covered with scales, hair, spikes, or silky hair, etc.

Females, which are larger than males, lay from 20 to 24 eggs; at the end of 4 to 7 days the larvæ come out and, after having undergone 3 or 4 changes, arrive at the stage of reproduction from the fourteenth to the seventeenth day. If exposed to damp air, or placed upon wet manure, the mange mites continue to live from 6 to 8 weeks. Upon damp ground the eggs remain alive from two to four weeks. In a dry place they lose their vitality after 4 to 6 days. Moderate heat is favorable to their vitality and to the hatching of the mites.

In warm places under cover, and during the summer, their movements are more active and they multiply more rapidly than under the opposite condition. It has been estimated that one female alone may produce 1,500,000 individuals in 90 days. Each animal species has its specific mange parasites, or mites; consequently the expression "mange" must necessarily be incomplete unless the variety of the parasite is indicated. Thus, of the Psoroptic variety, we have the ox mange mites, the horse mange mites, and the sheep mange mites.

In each of these animals we also have the Symbiotic, or tail, mange, and in each the variety would be designated as in the case of the Psoroptic or common form; but in neither variety is the contagion transmitted from one species of animal to the other. The tail-mange mites live especially upon the surface of the skin of the extremities, and exist in scabs in the outer layer of the skin. Their outlines are visible to the naked eye. The head is short and wider than it is long. The body is slightly egg-shaped and notched upon the outer edge. The legs are long and the sucking cups are shaped like a Roman shield, and are distributed in both the male and female, as in the case of the same organs on the legs of the common mange mites.

Sarcoptic mange is a more serious disease than either of those already described, but is not common to cattle. It would not, therefore, seem important to refer to this form of mange parasite and occupy space in this work except by a reference to the serious disease which is produced by this variety of mite through certain characteristics natural to it. We find Sarcoptic mange in the following domesticated animals: Horse, sheep, goat, dog, cat, and pig.

This variety dig galleries under the outer layer of the skin and live on the cells of the middle layer of the skin. They multiply in these galleries and occasion a very intense inflammation of the skin. Because of the depth to which the *Sarcoptes* burrow Sarcoptic mange is exceedingly hard to eradicate. It would, therefore, seem fortunate that this form of the disease is not common to cattle. It is rebellious to all medication, and very frequently recurrences of the disease are seen after treatment which has been prolonged for months.

Transmissibility of Mange.—Concerning the transmissibility of the different manges to animals and man, we find that all *Sarcoptes* may live for a considerable period upon man's skin, but the common mange mites, the first variety described, and the tail-mange mites, the second variety described, die very rapidly and occasion but slight irritations. The horse may contract Sarcoptic mange of the sheep, pig, dog, and cat. The ox takes the *Sarcoptes* of the horse, sheep, goat, and cat. The sheep contracts Sarcoptic mange of the goat. The dog takes the *Sarcoptes* of man, pig, cat, sheep, and goat. The pig contracts Sarcoptic mange of the goat. From this it will be seen that Sarcoptic mange, unlike the common and tail manges, is transmissible from one species of animal to another.

Mange is never developed except by contagion. The period of incubation—that is, the interval that elapses between the moment when the mites are deposited upon the surface of the body and the appearance of the disease on the skin—varies according to the number of mites transmitted. When in small numbers, the first manifestations of mange are sometimes seen as late as four to six weeks, while at other times the disease may be clearly apparent at the end of 15 days. Contamination takes place either by direct contact—that is, immediate, as on pasture, at the stable, etc.—or by intermediary agents.

Disinfection.—What has already been said with regard to the contagious character of scabies in cattle—of the number of scab mites which may be found in a small quantity of the debris of the skin and their ability to live and remain active for a considerable length of time under unfavorable conditions—will indicate the importance of the thorough disinfection of corrals, sheds, or other buildings in which affected cattle may have been kept. It is therefore necessary, in order to attain success in the treatment of this disease, to destroy parasites which have fallen off or have been dislodged from the animals, as well as those that are upon them; otherwise there is danger of their becoming reinfected from the premises after the effects of the remedy applied to the animals have disappeared.

Treatment.—Methods in operation for the treatment of scabies in sheep have become more or less familiar to all people interested in sheep husbandry, and it may be said that the same treatment so successfully applied in ridding sheep of scabies has been found equally efficacious in the treatment of scabies of cattle.

In 1898 the Bureau of Animal Industry issued Bulletin No. 21, entitled Sheep Scab: Its Nature and Treatment, which gives a description of this disease in sheep, its cause and treatment, with numerous formulas for the preparation of dips, and illustrations of the methods of applying them, together with directions for their use on both a large and small scale. The treatment of such large animals as cattle, which are difficult to handle, because of their size and the conditions under which they live—the latter making them more or less intractable—would require a considerable amount of any preparation to wet thoroughly all parts of their bodies. Next to effectiveness, therefore, small expense is the first object that must be considered. In the treatment of cattle for scabies, it seems fortunate that the dips of lime and sulphur, both of which are inexpensive, have proved effective and entirely satisfactory.

The dip previously used contained an excess of lime, and frequently proved quite irritating to the eyes and tender parts of the skin; hence the lime-and-sulphur dip now adopted and recommended for the treatment of scabies of cattle is made with the following ingredients:

Flowers of sulphur........................ 24 pounds
Unslaked lime .... 12 pounds
Water ....100 gallons

Place the unslaked lime in a mortar box or some suitable vessel and add enough water to slake it and form a lime paste or lime putty. Sift into this lime paste the flowers of sulphur and stir the mixture well. Be sure to weigh both the lime and the sulphur, and do not trust to measure them in a bucket or guess at the weight. Place the sulphur and lime paste in a kettle or boiler with about 25 or 30 gallons of boiling water, and boil the mixture for two hours at least, stirring the liquid and sediment. The boiling should be continued until the sulphur disappears, or almost disappears, from the surface. The solution is then of a chocolate or liver color. The longer the solution boils the more the sulphur is dissolved, and the less caustic the ooze becomes. Some writers advise boiling from thirty to forty minutes, but this is not sufficient; a good ooze can be obtained only by boiling from two to three hours, adding water when necessary. Pour the mixture and sediment into a large tub or barrel, placed near the dipping vat and provided with a bung-hole about 4 inches from the bottom, and allow it ample time (from two to three hours or more if necessary) to settle.

The use of some kind of a settling tank provided with a bung-hole is an absolute necessity, unless the boiler is so arranged that it may be used for both boiling and settling. An ordinary kerosene oil barrel will answer very well as a small settling tank. To insert a spigot about 3 to 4 inches from the bottom is an easy matter. Draining off the liquid through a spigot has a great advantage over dipping it out because less commotion occurs in the liquid, which therefore remains freer from sediment. When fully settled, draw off the clear liquid into the dipping vat and add enough warm water to make 100 gallons. But under no circumstances should the sediment in the barrel be used for dipping purposes. A double precaution against allowing the sediment to enter the vat is to strain the liquid through ordinary bagging as it is drawn from the barrel or settling tank.

The above directions are for the quantity of dip given in the preceding formula. Any multiple of the constituents may be used, depending upon the capacity of the boiler, vessels, and tank to be filled, but let it be repeated that there should be no guessing about the proportions; that the directions for the preparation of the dip as here given should be closely followed, care being taken that boiling be continued for the full time recommended.

Another good method for making this dip, highly recommended by experienced inspectors, is to mix the lime and sulphur in a mortar box, then slake the lime thoroughly and put the mixture in the cooking tank (which should contain one-fifth the total quantity of water required for the dip), after the water in the cooking tank is nearly boiling. If the mortar box is not at hand the lime and sulphur may be mixed and slaked in the cooking vat and the water then added for cooking. The mixture must be boiled for at least two hours, stirring often. Then add enough water to replace that which has boiled away, so as to have the original proportion of water. Allow to settle two hours, or longer if possible, and draw off the clear liquid for use in dipping.

The liquid obtained by these processes contains calcium sulphides in solution and now only requires the addition of sufficient clear water to reduce to the proper strength for dipping. Flowers of sulphur must be used and the lime must be of good quality.

General Directions.—Soft water is better than hard water for dipping, but if it can not be obtained the hard water may be softened by adding potash or lye, but no more should be added than sufficient to cut the water.

The average depth of the liquid used in a dipping vat is from 5½ to 6 feet, and the amount of dip necessary to obtain that depth should be ascertained before preparing the dip, in order that the requisite amount of the liquid may be prepared.

In 1 gallon there are 231 cubic inches. In order to find the number of gallons contained in a dipping vat multiply together, in inches, the average length, the average breadth, and the depth, and divide by 231, and the result will be the number of gallons. To obtain the average length of vat, add the length at the bottom to the length at the top of dip—or water line—and divide by 2; obtain the average width in the same manner. The depth should be taken at the center of vat, and should be from the bottom to water or dip line.

Be sure to measure only the space filled by the dip, and not above that line. The cooking vat should also be measured. It is convenient to have rods marked, showing the number of gallons at various depths.

Mix the dip thoroughly in the dipping vat by stirring length-
ise in the vat, also from top to bottom. A large hoe is a good in-
rument to use in stirring. After the dip is thoroughly mixed, take
e temperature at different parts of the vat; see that it is uniform,
nd, if too hot or too cold, add hot or cold water with proper pro-
ortion of dip until the right temperature is obtained; be careful to
ave all well mixed. The temperature of the dip when used should
e from 102° to 110° F.

To ascertain the temperature, take some of the dip out of the
at in a bucket, hold the thermometer in it, and read the tempera-
ire while it is in the fluid. The dip must be changed as soon as it
ecomes filthy, regardless of the number of cattle dipped in it, and
n no case should it be used when more than ten days old. When
ere is any doubt as to the good quality and proper strength of
e dip, or if it seems to have deteriorated by standing, by freezing,
r by being fouled by use, do not depend upon it, but throw it away,
ean out the dipping vat, and make new dip. In emptying the vat
e entire contents must be removed, including all sediment and
roppings and other foreign matter.

In order to attain success in the treatment of mange, care and
oroughness of method must be observed. Animals that have been
xposed should be dipped as well as those that show distinct evi-
ences of the disease. After the lapse of ten days or two weeks fol-
wing the first dipping, the animals should be subjected to a second
ipping, in order that parasites which may have survived the first
eatment, or which may have gotten on the animals from corrals,
eds, buildings, or elsewhere, may be destroyed. Careful examina-
ons of thousands of cattle, thirty to forty days after being put
rough the dip for the second time, have failed to reveal evidences
f scabies on any of them.

The dip liquid in the tanks during the whole dipping process
ould be kept at the temperature before stated—from 102° to 110°
. Each animal should be kept two minutes in the dip, and be put
mpletely under twice during that time. All bad cases should be
and-rubbed and kept in the dip four minutes.

Pregnant cows have been treated, as well as cattle of all ages,
om calves to full-grown steers, with the loss of but one animal in
ne of the swimming tanks. This was a steer which for some un-
nown reason seemed to be unable to swim and was drowned. It
ould appear that the dipping of cows, when proper care is taken—
pecially to prevent crowding in the chutes—has no appreciable
fect upon abortions, as a comparison with previous years showed
at the dipping had not increased the average number of abortions
gularly occurring among these herds before dips were used.

SMALL DIPPING PLANTS.

Of the various dipping plants in use, there are probably three
at need description: (1) The small dipping plant, with cage for
wering cattle into dipping tank, which is inexpensive and suitable
r use by a community of farmers; (2) the larger dipping plant
ith swimming tank, such as will be needed if large numbers of

range cattle are to be treated; (3) and a small or medium-sized plant with swimming tank. A suitable plant for a community of farmers has been built for $150, while a large swimming tank will cost about $350.

Such plants as those in operation 18 miles north of Steele, N. Dak., known as the Langedahl, and the William Nelson plant at Menoken, Burleigh County, N. Dak., would seem to be admirable examples of the smaller kind. The former plant, with the exception of the tank, was built by farmers. A thrashing engine may be used for heating purposes by connecting a 1¼-inch pipe to the whistle intake, the whistle being removed, and the pipe joined to the union. These plants have a capacity of 200 head per day. The cost, without engine or labor, excepting the labor to build the tank or vat, was about $150. One person can easily lower the loaded cage by taking a hitch around a post, and it may be raised either with engine or with horses.

Materials for Small Plants.—The list of materials for small plants, the tank of which may be filled with suitable dip, includes several important things, all of which will cost about $7.50. Among the objects and articles needed are sliding and roller gates hung at the ends of the alley or chute at both the entrance and exit of the cage. The animal is made to enter and leave by easy stages, thus avoiding sudden plunges and frights. This is thought to be a decided improvement over having the gates hung by hinges at either end of the cage. Barn-door rollers may be used. The rope from the hoist works over a drum, with a brake, and may be drawn by horses or a stationary engine, so the cage can be lowered by the same man who operates the front gate.

Advantages of the Small Dipping Plant.—A plant of this capacity will answer very well in a community where various owners have bunches of cattle ranging from 80 to 100 head or less. Among its chief advantages over the larger swimming tank are cheapness in construction, because of its size, and proportionately smaller expense in operating; the dip can be kept at the required temperature with facility, because of its lesser volume, and the submersion of the animals, as well as the length of time it is desired to keep them in the dip, can be more easily regulated.

In communities where mange does not exist, and where numbers of small herds are infested with lice, a plant of this character might be constructed and used with profit to the cattlemen. Many of the cattle that were dipped during the past year because of having been exposed to mange, or scabies, by being herded with those affected, showed much improvement in condition soon after dipping, although they had not shown distinct evidence of being affected with mange.

Tank with Heating Appliance.—In some localities where steam for heating the liquid in the dipping tank is not readily available, an oblong radiator made of heavy galvanized iron, set inside of the tank 1 inch from the side, is successfully used. This radiator, or heater, should be set so that the dip may circulate around it. The furnace is made of stone and should be 26 inches wide inside and 8 feet long. On top a cooking vat is placed, made of 14-inch plank on the sides and a galvanized iron bottom 30 inches wide. The cooking vat is 8 feet long by 14 inches high and 30 inches wide. The radiator is connected with the furnace by a 6-inch pipe. Heat circulation is established by means of a stack leading out and up from near the farther end of the radiator. Galvanized stovepipe may be used for the stack. The cage is made of the usual width—3 feet 6 inches wide outside—and the tank 8 inches wider than when steam heat is used, so that space may be allowed for the radiator. The radiator must be protected by guides or standards—guides in the middle or, preferably, standards in the corners of the tank.

LARGE DIPPING PLANT WITH SWIMMING TANK.

The following suggestions are for the construction of a swimming tank where large numbers of cattle are to be dipped. These are in accordance with drawings and notes received from Dr. Louis A. Klein, inspector, Fort Worth, Tex., through the courtesy of Mr. K. Roby, engineer of the Fort Worth Stock Yards Company, and Dr. R. H. Treacy, inspector, Bismarck, N. Dak.

Suggestions as to Labor Required.—Excavate for the vat to the proper depth; level the bottom of the pit for the sills of the vat. After the vat is completed and the outside has been coated with coal tar, fill in around the vat, using the surplus earth to grade the sides of the vat a little above the natural grade, sloping slightly from the vat. Dig all holes required for the gate and fence posts.

Carpenter Work.—All work should be done in a skillful and workmanlike manner; the framework of the vat to be bolted and spiked together; the plank of sides, ends, and bottom of the vat and dripping floor to have edges beveled for the calking as per detail, well driven together and well spiked with 20d. wire nails, using 40d. nails on the 3-inch plank. Calk all seams with oakum, well driven in with a calking iron, and pitched. The exit, or inclined end, of the vat to have a 3-inch bottom plank; all other planks of the vat and dipping floor to be 2 inches thick. Sides of vat to be braced with anchor braces extending back 6 feet from each upright as in smaller swimming tank. The exit end of vat and dripping floor to be cleated with 1½x3 inch strips, well nailed to floor and bottom, or with 4 inch x 4 inch cut diagonal.

Gates and Fence.—The gate post should be set 4 feet in the ground and the fence post 3 feet 6 inches. Set all posts plumb and to a line; well and thoroughly tamp the earth around the posts. The bottom of all posts should be coated with coal tar before being set. Gate posts, 8x8 inches, with 6x8 inch tie framed and drift-bolted to the posts. Fence posts, 6x6 inches. The gates should be bolted and spiked together and braced. Hang with ½x3x36 inch strap eye-and-bolt hinges.

POISONS AND POISONING.

To clearly define the meaning of the word poison would be somewhat difficult. (Even in law the word has never been defined, and when a definition is attempted we are apt to include either too much or too little.) The following is perhaps as satisfactory a definition as may be given: A poison is a chemical substance having an inherent deleterious property rendering it capable in small quantities of producing serious functional disturbances upon gaining access to the system by the usual channels; or it is a substance which, when introduced into the system or applied externally, injures health or destroys life irrespective of mechanical means or thermal changes. The common conception of a poison is any substance which, in small quantity, will destroy life, excepting such as act by purely mechanical means, as, for example, powdered glass.

Some substances that are not usually looked upon as poisons may destroy life if given in large doses, such as common salt. Other substances which are perfectly harmless when taken into the body in the usual way are poisons if injected into the circulation, such as distilled water, milk, or glycerine. Living organisms are not chemical substances, and are not considered in this connection.

SOURCES OF POISONING.

Poisoning may come from many causes, among the chief of which are the following:

(1) Errors in medication.—By using the wrong substance or too large dose an animal may be poisoned.

(2) The exposure of poisons used for horticultural, technical, or other legitimate purposes.—Poisons used for spraying plants, disinfecting, poisoning vermin, dipping sheep, painting, smelting, dyeing, or other purposes, may be so handled as to come within the reach of animals.

(3) Damaged food.—Food that has undergone putrefaction or certain kinds of fermentation or heating, or food that is infested with insects, may have become poisonous, producing forage poisoning, meat poisoning, cheese poisoning, etc.

(4) Poisonous plants in the pasture or forage.

(5) The bite or sting of a poisonous insect or the bite of an animal.

(6) Malicious poisoning.

THE ACTION OF POISONS.

This may be either local, and exerted directly on the tissues with which they come in contact, or remote, acting through the circulation or the nervous system, or both local and remote action may be exerted by the same drug. Poisons which act locally generally either destroy by corrosion the tissues with which they come in contact or by inhalation set up acute inflammation. When any corrosive agent is taken into the stomach in poisonous quantities, a group of symptoms is developed which is common to all. The tissues with which the agent comes in contact are destroyed, sloughing and acute inflammation of the surrounding structures take place; intense pain in the abdomen and death ensue. In a like manner, but with less rapidity, the same result is reached if the agent used be not of a sufficiently corrosive nature to destroy the tissues, but sufficiently irritating to set up acute inflammation of the mucous membrane of the digestive tract. If the poison exerts a remote influence alone, the action is quite different, little or no local effect being produced upon the digestive organs.

To produce an effect on some part of the body distant from the channel of entrance, a poison must have been absorbed and carried in the blood to the central nervous system or other region involved. The poisonous effect of any substance is modified by the quantity used; by its chemical combinations; by the part of the animal structure with which it comes in contact; by the physical condition of the subject; and also by the rapidity with which the poison is excreted. As an illustration, opium may be given with safety in much larger doses to an animal suffering from acute pain than to one free from pain, and to an adult animal with greater safety than to a young one. The rapidity with which the poison is absorbed, owing to the part of the body with which it is brought in contact, is also an important factor. So marked is this quality that some agents which have the power of destroying life with almost absolute certainty when introduced beneath the skin, may be taken into the stomach without causing inconvenience, as curara, the arrow poison, or the venomous secretion of the snake. Other agents in chemical combination may tend to intensify, lessen, or wholly neutralize the poisonous effect. For example, arsenic in itself has well-marked poisonous properties, but when brought in contact with dialyzed iron it forms an insoluble compound and becomes innocuous. Idiosyncrasies are not so noticeable in cattle practice as in practice among human beings, but the uncertainty with which some drugs exert their influence would lead us to believe that well-marked differences in susceptibility exist. Even in some cases a tolerance for poison is engendered, so that in a herd of animals equally exposed injurious or fatal effects do not appear with uniformity. For example, among cattle that are compelled to drink water holding in solution a salt of lead the effects of the poisoning will be found varying all the way from fatality to imperceptibility.

GENERAL SYMPTOMS OF POISONING.

It is not always easy to differentiate between poisoning and some disease. Indeed, examination during the life of the animal is sometimes wholly inadequate to the formation of an opinion as to whether the case is one of poisoning or, if it is, as to what the poison may be. A chemical and physical examination after the death of the animal may be necessary to clear up the doubt. On the other hand, the symptoms may be of such a nature as to point unmistakably to poisoning with a certain agent. In general, the following classes of symptoms may be regarded as indicative of poisoning: Sudden onset of the disease without visible cause, a number of animals similarly affected at once, severe gastro-intestinal disorder or derangement of the nervous system, or both. Sudden alteration of heart action in relation to frequency, force, or rhythm. Local irritation, dyspnœa, or change in the urine or urination.

After death lesions of the greatest variety may be found, and it is necessary for one to be skilled in anatomy and pathology to determine their significance. Oftentimes the stomach and intestines are red, have thick walls, and contain blood. This signifies a severe irritant, such as arsenic or corrosive sublimate. Other alterations sometimes found are inflammation of the kidneys or bladder, points of hemorrhage in various organs, changes in the blood, congestion of the lungs, and certain microscopic changes.

General Treatment.—The treatment of animals suffering from poison must vary according to the nature of the toxic agent. There are a few general plans of action, however, which should be followed so far as possible. In man and in some of the smaller animals it is possible to eliminate unabsorbed poison by the use of the stomach pump or by causing vomiting. These proceedings are impracticable in cattle. It is well, therefore, in many cases to endeavor to expel the unabsorbed poison by emptying the digestive tract, so far as may be, with a non-irritating purge. Castor oil in doses of 1 pint to 2 quarts is best adapted to this purpose. If the poison is known to be nonirritant—as a narcotic plant—from 10 to 20 drops of croton oil may be given with a quart of castor oil. To protect the mucous membrane from the action of strong irritants one may give flaxseed tea, barley water, the whites of eggs, milk, butter, olive oil, or fresh lard. Chemical antidotes may sometimes be used for special poisons, as advised below. In general, if an acid has been taken it may be neutralized with an alkali, such as chalk, magnesia, bicarbonate of soda (baking soda), ammonia (diluted), or soap. If the poison is an alkali, such as caustic soda or potash (lye), or ammonia, an acid, such as diluted (1 per cent) sulphuric acid or vinegar, may be administered. Special treatments and antidotes are considered below.

A poisonous agent may be so gradually introduced into the system as to slowly develop the power of resistance against its own action. In other cases, where the poison is introduced slowly, the poisonous action becomes cumulative, and although there is no increase in the quantity taken, violent symptoms are suddenly developed, as if the whole amount, the consumption of which may have extended over a considerable period, had been given in one dose. Other agents, poisonous in their nature, tend to deteriorate some of the important organs and, interfering with their natural functions, are productive of conditions of ill health which, although not necessarily fatal, are important. Such a class might properly be called chronic poisons. Poisons of themselves dangerous when administered in large doses are used medicinally for curative purposes, and a very large percentage of the pharmaceutical preparations used in the practice of medicine if given in excessive quantities might produce serious results. In the administration of medicines, therefore, care should be exercised not only that the animal is not poisoned by the administration of an excessive dose, but that injury is not done by continued treatment with medicines the administration of which is not called for.

MINERAL POISONS.

Arsenic Poisoning.—Of the common irritant and corrosive poisons, arsenic, especially one of its compounds (Paris green, Scheel's green, or cobalt), is likely to be the most dangerous to our class of patients. The common practice of using Paris green as an

insecticide for the destruction of potato beetle and other insect ene-
mies of the farmer and fruit grower has had the effect of introducing
it into almost all farming establishments.   White arsenic is also a
principal ingredient in many of the popular sheep-dipping preparations, and poisoning from this source occasionally takes place when,
after dipping, the flock are allowed to run in a yard in which there
is loose fodder.   The drippings from the wool of the sheep falling on
the fodder render it poisonous, and dangerous to animal life if eaten.
Familiarity with its use has in many instances tended to breed con-
tempt for its potency as a poison.   Rat poisons often contain arsenic.
The excessive use of arsenic as a tonic, or of condition powders containing arsenic, has been the means of poisoning many animals.
This is the common poison used by malicious persons with criminal
intent.   The poison may also be absorbed through wounds or through
the skin if used as a dip or bath.

If a large dose is given, at once acute poisoning is produced;'
if repeated small doses are given, chronic poisoning may result.   The
poisonous dose for an ox is from 3 drams to 1 ounce.

The symptoms of acute poisoning first appear as those of colic;
the animal is restless, stamping with the feet, lying down and getting
up.   There is tenderness on pressure over the abdomen.   The acute
symptoms increase; in a few hours violent diarrhea is developed; in
many cases blood and shreds of detached mucous membrane are
mixed with the evacuations.   There is irregular and feeble pulse and
respiration, and death is likely to supervene between the eighteenth
hour and the third day.   If the latter period is passed, there is a reasonable hope of recovery.

In chronic poisoning the symptoms are similar to those of
chronic gastro-intestinal catarrh, with indigestion, diarrhea, and
general weakness and loss of condition.

The antidote for arsenic is a solution of hydrated oxid of iron
in water.   It should be prepared fresh by mixing a solution of sulphate of iron, made by dissolving 4 ounces of sulphate of iron in one
half pint of water with a suspension of 1 ounce of magnesia in one-
half pint of water.   This quantity is sufficient for one dose for a cow
and may be repeated in an hour, if much arsenic was taken.   A solution of calcined magnesia or powdered iron or iron filings or iron scale
from a blacksmith's forge may be given in the absence of other remedies.   Powdered sulphur is of some value as an antidote.   One must
also administer protectives, such as linseed tea, barley water, whites
of eggs, etc.

Lead Poisoning.—Lead poisoning of cattle usually comes from
their having licked freshly painted surfaces, and thus swallowing
compounds containing white lead.   In several instances cattle have
been poisoned by silage from a silo painted inside with lead paint
shortly before filling.   Sugar of lead has been administered by mistake for Glauber's salts.   Lead poisoning may be acute or chronic.
The fatal dose of sugar of lead is from 1 to 4 ounces.   Water drawn
from lead pipes or held in a lead-lined tank may cause poisoning.

Symptoms are generally dullness, lying down with the head turned toward the flank, colic, rumbling in the abdomen, loss of control of the limbs when walking, twitching, champing of the jaws, moving in a circle, convulsions, delirium, violent bellowing, followed by stupor and death. The symptoms generally extend over considerable time, but may end in death after twenty-four hours.

The treatment should first be directed toward removing the cause. A large dose of purgative medicine should be given, and the brain symptoms be relieved by giving bromid of potassium in half-ounce doses every four or five hours, and the application of cold water to the head. Dilute sulphuric acid in half-ounce doses should be given with the purgative medicine. In this case sulphate of magnesia (Epsom salts) is the best purgative, and it may be given in doses of from 1 to 2 pounds dissolved in warm water. After the acute symptoms have abated, iodide of potassium may be given, in doses of 2 drams each, three times a day for a week.

Chronic lead poisoning occasionally occurs in districts where lead mining is the principal industry. The waste products of the mine thrown into streams contaminate the water supply, so that the mineral is taken into the system gradually, and a very small per cent of any of the salts taken into the system in this way is pernicious. Water which contains any salt of lead to the extent of more than one-tenth of a grain to the gallon is unfit to drink. Such water when used continually is likely to produce colic from the resulting intestinal irritation, and in aggravated cases paralysis more or less severe is likely to be developed. A blue line on the margin of the gums, the last symptom, is regarded as diagnostic and its presence as conclusive evidence of the nature of the disorder. The free use of purgatives is indicated with iodid of potassium. No treatment is likely to be of avail until the cause is removed.

Copper Poisoning.—The soluble salts of copper, though used as a tonic in the medicinal treatment of cattle, are poisonous when taken in large quantities. Like lead and arsenic, they have an irritant effect upon the mucous membrane with which they come in contact in a concentrated form. Cattle are not very likely to be poisoned from this cause unless through carelessness. The salts of copper—the most common of which is the sulphate of copper, commonly called blue vitriol—is occasionally used for disinfecting and cleansing stables, where it might inadvertently be mixed with the food. It is also used largely for making the Bordeaux mixture used in spraying fruit trees. The general symptoms produced are those of intestinal irritation, short breathing, stamping, and tender abdomen.

Give powdered iron, or iron reduced by hydrogen, or calcined magnesia. Sulphur may be used. This should be followed by a liberal supply of demulcents, linseed infusion, boiled starch, whites of eggs, etc.

Zinc Poisoning.—Several of the soluble salts of zinc are irritant poisons. The chlorid and sulphate are those in most common use. In animals which have power to vomit they are emetic in their action. In others, when retained in the stomach, they set up more or less irritation of the mucous membrane and obdominal pain, producing symptoms already described in the action of other poisons which produce the same result.' The treatment should be the same as for copper poisoning.

Phosphorus Poisoning.—Only one of the forms of phosphorus in common use—the ordinary yellow—is poisonous. Phosphorus in this form is used for the destruction of rats and mice and other vermin, and is largely used in the manufacture of matches.

The symptoms are loss of appetite, colic, diarrhea, irritation of the mouth and throat, and paralysis of the throat. There is also weakness, difficult breathing, and rapid pulse. The course of the poisoning is usually rapid, terminating in either recovery or death within three days. The toxic dose for cattle is from 5 to 30 grains. If taken in large quantities, the excreta are occasionally noticed to be luminous when examined in the dark.

Turpentine given in an emulsion with flaxseed tea in a single dose of from 2 to 8 ounces is beneficial. Permanganate of potash may be given in a one-fourth of 1 per cent solution. Stimulants, such as alcohol and ether, should be administered. Oils and milk must not be given.

Mercury Poisoning.—Mercury poisoning is not rare in cattle from the fact that these animals have a special susceptibility to the action of this substance. Antiseptic washes or injections containing the bichloride of mercury (corrosive subimate) must be used on cattle with great care. Mercurial disinfecting solutions or salves must be used cautiously. Calomel can not be given freely to cattle.

The symptoms are salivation, sore mouth, indigestion, diarrhea, skin eruption, paralysis of local groups of muscles, and nephritis. The treatment consists in administering sulphur in large doses (2 to 4 ounces) or iron powder. Both make insoluble compounds with mercury. Follow with the whites of eggs mixed with water and with linseed tea. If the case does not terminate promptly, give iodid of potash in 1 dram doses twice daily.

Poisoning by Acids.—The mineral acids—nitric, sulphuric, hydrochloric, etc.—when used in a concentrated form, destroy the animal tissues with which they come in contact, and in this respect differ from most of the poisons previously described. When taken into the stomach the mucous membrane of the mouth, pharynx, esophagus, and stomach is apt to be more or less completely destroyed. If taken in large quantities death is likely to result so speedily that nothing can be done to relieve the patient, and even if time is allowed and the action of the acid can be arrested it can not be done until considerable and, perhaps, irreparable damage has been done. The mucous membrane with which the acid has come in contact in the esophagus may be destroyed by its corrosive action and carried away, leaving the muscular tissues exposed. The raw surface heals irregularly, the cicatrice contracting causes stricture, and an animal so injured is likely to die of starvation. In the stomach even greater damage is likely to be done. The peristaltic action of the esophagus carries the irritant along quickly, but here it remains quiet in contact with one surface, destroying it. It is likely to perforate the organ, and coming in contact with the abdominal lining or other organ of digestion soon sets up a condition that is beyond repair. In a less concentrated form, when the acid is not sufficiently strong to be corrosive, it exerts an irritant effect. In this form it may not do much harm unless taken in considerable quantity. When it is, the mucous membrane of the stomach and intestines becomes inflamed; pain and diarrhea are likely to result.

Any of the alkalies may be used as an antidote. Most convenient of these are chalk, baking soda, marble dust, magnesia, lime, soap, or plaster from a wall. Mucilaginous drinks should be given in large quantities.

Oxalic acid in particular is corrosive in its action when taken in concentrated solution, losing its corrosive effect and becoming irritant when more dilute. It also exerts a specific effect on the heart, frequently causing death from syncope. Taken in the form either of the crystals or solution, it is likely to cause death in a very short time. Failure of heart action and attendant small pulse, weakness, staggering, and convulsions are the more noticeable symptoms. Limewater or lime or plaster should be given promptly. Acetic acid is irritant to the gastro-intestinal tract, and may cause sudden paralysis of the heart. It should be counteracted by the use of alkalies, as advised above, by protectives to the digestive tract, and by stimulants.

POISONING BY ALKALIES.

The carbonates of potash and soda and the alkalies themselves in concentrated form cause symptoms of intestinal irritation similar to those produced by mineral acids. Ammonia, caustic soda, and caustic potash (lye) are those to which animals are most exposed. The degree of their caustic irritant effects depends on their degree of concentration. When they reach the stomach the symptoms are nearly as well marked as in the case of the acids. The irritation is even more noticeable, and purgation is likely to be a more prominent symptom. If death is not caused soon, the irritation of the gastrointestinal tract and malnutrition will last for a long time. Treatment consists in neutralizing the alkali by an acid, such as dilute sulphuric acid (1 per cent) or strong vinegar. The administration of such an antidote and its action must be carefully watched during administration. In the chemical change which takes place when the acid and alkali are combined, carbonic-acid gas is liberated, which may be to an extent sufficient to cause considerable distention of the abdomen, even to asphyxia from pressure forward on the diaphragm. Should this danger present itself, it may be averted by opening the left flank, permitting the gas to escape. (See Acute Tympanites, or Bloating.)

Flaxseed or slippery-elm decoction must be given to soothe the inflamed mucous surface. Opium may be used to allay pain.

COAL-OIL POISONING.

Coal oil is sometimes administered empirically as a treatment for intestinal parasites. If given in large doses it produces poisonous effects, which are likely to be manifest some time after the administration. It acts as an irritant to the digestive tract, causing dribbling of ropy saliva from the mouth, diarrhea, tenesmus, and loss of appetite, with increased temperature and cold extremities. Visible mucous membranes are injected, pupils of the eyes contracted, watery discharge from the eyes and nostrils. Remotely it exerts a depressing influence on the functions of the brain and slight coma, and occasionally convulsions, from which the animal is easily aroused. The kidneys also suffer. The urine is dark colored and has the charactertistic odor of coal oil. Death may result from gastro-enteritis or convulsions.

The patient's strength should be fostered by the frequent administration of mild stimulants, of which aromatic spirits of ammonia is perhaps the best. The animal should be encouraged to eat soft food and given mucilaginous drinks.

Crude coal oil is sometimes applied to the skin to kill parasites. If too much is used, especially in hot weather, great weakness and depression may be caused and in some cases death may result.

<h3 style="text-align:center">CARBOLIC-ACID POISONING.</h3>

Although one of the most valuable antiseptic remedies, carbolic acid in a concentrated form, when taken internally or used over a large surface externally, is likely to produce poisonous effects. It causes whitening, shrinking, and numbness of the structures with which it comes in contact, and, besides its irritant effect, exerts a powerful influence on the nervous system. Being readily absorbed, it produces its effect whether swallowed, injected into the rectum, inhaled, or applied to wounds, or even to a large tract of unbroken skin. Used extensively as a dressing, it may produce nausea, dizziness, and smoky or blackish colored urine. The last symptom is nearly always noticeable where the poisonous effect is produced. In more concentrated form, or used in larger quantities, convulsions, followed by fatal coma, are likely to take place. Even in smaller quantities, dullness, trembling, and disinclination for food often continues for several days. In a tolerably concentrated solution it coagulates albumen and acts as an astringent.

As an antidote internally, a solution of sulphate of soda or sulphate of magnesia (Glauber's or Epsom salts) may be given. The white of an egg is also useful. Stimulants may be given if needed. When the poisoning occurs through too extensive applications to wounds or the skin, as in treatment of mange, cold water should be freely applied so as to wash off any of the acid that may still remain unabsorbed. As a surgical dressing a 3 per cent solution is strong enough for ordinary purposes. Water will not hold more than 5 per cent in permanent solution. No preparation stronger than the saturated solution should be used medicinally under any circumstances.

<h3 style="text-align:center">SALTPETER POISONING.</h3>

Both nitrate of soda and nitrate of potash are poisonous to cattle. These substances are used for manure and for preserving meats. They may be administered in a drench by error in place of Glauber's salts, or they may be exposed within reach of cattle and thus be eaten. The toxic dose depends upon the condition of fullness of the stomach.

If in solution and given on an empty stomach, as little as 3 ounces of saltpeter (nitrate of potash) may be fatal to a cow. More of the Chile saltpeter (nitrate of soda) is required to cause serious trouble. Symptoms are severe gastro-enteritis, colic, tympanites, diarrhea, excessive urination, weakness, trembling, convulsions, collapse. The treatment same as for poisoning by common salt.

POISONING BY COMMON SALT.

A few pounds (3 to 5) of common salt will produce well-marked signs of poisoning in cattle. So much salt as this will not be taken by cattle except under unusual conditions. If the food is poor in salt, and if none has been given for a long time, an intense salt hunger may occur that may lead an animal to eat a poisonous quantity if it is not restricted; or an overdose of salt may be given by error as a drench.

Herring and mackerel brine and pork pickle are also poisonous, and are especially dangerous for hogs. In these substances there are, in addition to salt, certain products extracted from the fish or meat which undergo change and add to the toxicity of the solution. Sometimes saltpeter is present in such brines.

The symptoms are great thirst, abdominal pain, diarrhea, poor appetite, redness and dryness of the mouth, increased urination, paralysis of the hind legs, weak pulse, general paralysis, coma, and death in from six to eight hours.

Allow as much warm water as the animal will drink. Give protectives, such as linseed tea, etc. Linseed or olive oil may be given. To keep up the heart action give ether, alcohol, camphor, digitalis, or coffee. To allay pain, give opium.

VEGETABLE POISONS.

These may be divided into two classes—those that are likely to be administered to the animal as medicine and those that may be taken in the food, either in the shape of poisonous plants, or as plants or foods of vegetable origin that have been damaged by fungi or by bacterial action, producing fermentation or putrefaction.

VEGETABLE POISONS USED AS MEDICINE.

Opium Poisoning.—Opium and its alkaloid, morphia, are so commonly used in the practice of medicine that the poisonous result of an overdose is not uncommon. The common preparations are gum opium, the inspissated juice of the poppy; powdered opium, made from the gum; tincture of opium, commonly called laudanum, and the alkaloid or active principle, morphia. Laudanum has about one-eighth the strength of the gum or powder. Morphia is present in good opium to the extent of about 10 per cent. In medicine it is a most useful agent in allaying pain. It has an effect of first producing a stimulating action, which is followed by drowsiness, a disposition to sleep or complete anesthesia, depending on the quantity of the drug used. In poisonous doses a state of exhilaration is well marked at first. This is particularly noticeable in cattle and in horses. The animal becomes much excited, and this stage does not pass into insensibility unless an enormous dose has been given. If the dose is large enough, a second stage sometimes supervenes, in which the symptoms

An Ontario Farm Herd. Dept. of Agr.

are those of congestion of the brain. The visible membranes have a blueish tint (cyanotic) from interference with the air supply. The breathing is slow, labored, and later noisy; the pupils of the eyes are very much contracted; the skin dry and warm. Gas accumulates in the stomach, so that tympanites is a prominent symptom. The patient may be aroused by great noise or the infliction of sharp pain, when the breathing becomes more natural. A relapse into the comatose condition takes place when the excitement ceases. Later, there is perfect coma and the patient can no longer be aroused from the insensible condition. The contraction of the pupil becomes more marked, the breathing intermittent and slower, there is perspiration, the pulse more feeble and rapid, till death takes place. Poisoning of cattle with opium or its products rarely goes beyond the stage of excitement, because the quantity of the drug required for the later effects is so great. Seventy-five grains of morphia administered subcutaneously has sufficed merely to excite for twelve hours.

As an antidote give strong coffee, to 4 quarts, aromatic spirits of ammonia or carbonate of ammonia. Atropia is the physiological antidote.

Strychnine Poisoning.—Strychnine is a very concentrated poison and produces its effect very quickly, usually only a few minutes being necessary if given in sufficient dose and in such a way that it will be at once absorbed. The first noticeable symptom is evidence of unrest or mental excitement, at the same time the muscles over the shoulder and croup may be seen to quiver or twitch and later there occurs a more or less well-marked convulsion; the head is jerked back, the back arched and legs extended, the eyes drawn. The spasm continues for only a few minutes, when it relaxes and another occurs in a short time. The return is hastened by excitement and in a short time again disappears, continuing to disappear and reappear until death results. As the poisonous effect advances the intervals between the spasms become shorter and less marked and the spasms more severe until the animal dies in violent struggles.

The best method of treatment is to put the patient under the influence of chloral, chloroform, or ether, and keep it there continuously until the effect of the poison has passed off. Alcohol may be given in large doses.

Aconite Poisoning.—In recent years tincture of aconite has for some unknown reason become a popular stable remedy. In the hands of some breeders it seems to be used as a panacea for all the ills flesh is heir to. If an animal is ailing, aconite is given whether indicated or not. Fortunately the dose used is generally small, and for this reason the damage done is much less than it would otherwise be. Aconite is one of the most deadly poisons known. It produces paralysis of motion and sensation, depresses the heart's action, and causes death by paralysis of respiration. In large doses it causes profuse salivation, champing of the jaws, and attempts at swallowing. If not sufficient to cause death, there is impaired appetite with more or less nausea for some time after. In poisonous doses it causes the animal to tremble violently, to lose power to support itself, and it brings on slight convulsions, with perspiration. The pulse is depressed, irregular, and afterwards intermittent.

The chemical antidote is tannic acid, which forms an insoluble compound with the aconitin. The depressing effect on the heart should be counteracted by the use of ammonia, digitalis, alcohol, camphor, or other diffusible stimulants, which have a physiological effect opposite to aconite.

Turpentine Poisoning.—Many conifers, but especially some species of pines, contain turpentine. In the winter and early spring the ends of the branches of such trees may be eaten by cattle. If a sufficient quantity is consumed, poisoning may result.

The symptoms signify more or less severe irritation of the digestive and urinary tracts. There is poor appetite, abdominal pain, emaciation, dark urine, which may contain blood, difficulty in passing urine, constrained attitude, and sensitiveness to pressure over the loins. Later there may be excitation followed by depression of the nervous system.

Change food. Give linseed tea, barley· gruel, or slippery-elm bark infusion. For the excitement give chloral hydrate or bromid of potash.

Dietetic Poisons.—A small but important group of poisons may be classed under this head. In some cases it is poison naturally belonging to the plant; in other cases the poisonous principle is developed in what would otherwise be harmless plants as a plant disease, or as a fermentation or putrefaction due to bacterial growth and observed in forage, grain, or meal that has heated, become damaged, or "spoilt."

Loco Weed Poisoning.—The "loco weed" is a term applied to leguminous plants of several genera, all of which are supposed to have certain similar effects on horses and cattle. It is found on the Plains and in the natural pastures of some of our Western States and Territories. The plant grows on high, gravelly, or sandy soil. It has a rather attractive appearance, and retains its soft, pale green color all winter. Of one of the most common species (*Astragallus mollissimus*) it may be said that a mass of leaves 4 to 10 inches high grow from the very short stem. The leaves are pinnate, similar in form to those of a locust tree, with ten pairs of leaflets and an odd terminal one. The flower scape grows from the center of the plant. The flowers, shaped like pea blossoms, appear in June or July, and are yellow tinted with violet. The seeds are contained in a pod about half an inch long. It is said that a stalk-boring larva has attacked the plant and seems to be doing much toward eradicating it.

Horses and cattle seem to acquire a taste for loco weeds, although it is not a plant that would be considered as a food or that would be eaten with a relish the first time. In the early spring, when herbage is scarce, its green appearance may attract the animal, and the habit of eating it be thus acquired. Its effect is not noticeable till a considerable quantity has been eaten. It seems to exert its influence on the nervous system. The gait is slow and measured, the step high, the eyes glassy and staring, the vision defective. Sudden excitement will frequently produce convulsions, which, if the disease is well advanced, have a temporarily prostrating effect upon the animal. Although loco poisoning is a nervous affection, emaciation is one of the most noticeable symptoms. The taste for the weed becomes stronger, the victim preferring it to other food. When it is taken in large quantities delirium is produced and the animal becomes vicious. If the cause be removed before too much injury is done, recovery is likely to take place.

Medicinal treatment seems to be of little avail. Comfortable stabling, quiet, and a liberal supply of wholesome food tend to counteract the poisonous effect of the plant and build up the depleted forces.

Laurel Poisoning.—The mountain laurel, the rhododendron, and the bay tree are poisonous for cattle. The foliage of these plants is most likely to be eaten in the late winter or spring, when there is little forage available. The effect is to cause great mental excitement, salivation, retching, colic, diarrhea, nerve exhaustion, and paralysis.

The treatment consists in administering protectives to soothe the gastro-intestinal mucous membrane, and stimulants to keep up the action of the heart and general strength. For this purpose one may use coffee, whisky, or ammonia.

COTTON SEED POISONING.

Up to the present time it can be said that the toxic principle of cotton seed is known only by its effects on live stock when fed in undue amount. Its study is rendered more difficult by the variability which has been often noticed in the effects on animals consuming similar amounts of cotton seed meal and apparently under similar conditions, also by its slowness of action, which calls for prolonged feeding tests before its effects are exhibited. The effects also are not always sufficiently plain or uniform to give much exactness to this experimental mode of studying the question. It has not been found possible to obtain from cotton seed any substance in concentrated form capable of causing acute poisoning in single doses. Nor can cotton seed meal be fed to any class of animals in sufficient amount to produce obvious toxic effects (other than intestinal derangement) except after prolonged feeding. The most characteristic effects and those most quickly produced, have been observed in pigs where lethal poisoning may occur in three to four weeks. Growing and fattening cattle tolerate high feeding with cotton seed or meal for 60 to 90 days before showing effects attributable to the cumulative action of the poison, although digestive derangement may occur at an early stage. On other kinds of stock fewer observations have been made, but in poultry no uniform symptoms occur, according to our experience, although they do not do well on this feed.

The most notable variation in the effects of cotton seed on live stock is seen in the case of milch cows during lactation as compared with growing and fattening cattle. This relative immunity is possessed also by other kinds of stock during lactation.

Lactation.—The influence of lactation in preventing the toxic action of cotton seed, illustrated by the relative immunity of milch cows as compared with growing and fattening cattle, may be attributed to the constant elimination in the milk of some toxic principle derived from the cotton seed directly or formed in the system from substances contained in cotton seed. (The assumption being that in dry animals this accumulates in the system). That such an immunity exists is shown by the frequency of cotton seed poisoning in beef cattle fatted at the oil mills in the south, as compared with the apparent exemption from this trouble in dairy farms where cotton seed meal is quite generally fed in all sections of the country.*

Other Poisonous Plants.—Other poisonous plants are the box, water hemlock, equisetum, lupine (under special conditions), tobacco, green acorns (when eaten in excessive quantities by horses or cattle), green sorghum and Kafir corn forage (when stunted or frosted), lily of the valley, aconite oleander, jimson weed, green potatoes and potato sprouts, and poison rye grass (*Lolium temulentum.*)

Ergotism.—The poisonous effects of ergot appear chiefly in the winter and spring of the year and among cattle. It is developed among grasses grown on rich soil in hot, damp seasons. Rye seems more liable to ergot than any of our other crops. Of the grasses which enter into the composition of hay, bluegrass is the most likely to become affected. Ergot may also affect redtop, oats, grasses, and grains. On the plant the fungus manifests itself on the seeds, where it is easily recognized when the hay is examined in the mow. The ergotized seeds are several times larger than the natural seeds—hard, black, and generally curved in shape.

The effect of the protracted use of ergot in the food is pretty well understood to be that of producing a degeneration and obstruction of the smaller arterial branches. The result is to shut off the blood supply to the distal parts of the body, where the circulation is weakest, and thus to produce a mummification or dry gangrene of the extremities, as the ears, tail, feet, etc. Cattle seem to be more susceptible than other animals to the influence of ergot, possibly on account of the slowness of the heart's action. When the effect of the poison has become sufficient to entirely arrest the circulation in any part, the structures soon die. The disorder manifests itself as lameness in one or more limbs; swelling about the ankle which may result in only a small slough or the loss of a toe, but it may circumscribe the limb at any point below the knee or hock by an indented ring, below which the tissues become dead. The indentation soon changes to a crack, which, like it, extends completely round the limb, forming the line of separation between the dead and living structures. The crack deepens till the parts below drop off without loss of blood, and frequently with very little pus. Ergot may cause serious irritation of the digestive tract, or by acting upon the nervous system it may

---

*It is assumed that milking cows do not suffer from cotton seed poisoning because instances of such poisoning have not been recorded, but it is quite probable that such cases do occur, their true nature not being recognized. It seems improbable that a complete immunity can exist.

cause lethargy or paralysis. It also operates to cause contraction of the uterus, and may thus cause abortion.

Treatment.—Regarding the treatment, change of food and local antiseptics are, of course, indicated. The former may be useful as a preventive, but when the symptoms have appeared the animal is necessarily so completely saturated that recovery is likely to be tedious. Tannin may be given internally in doses of one-half dram twice daily for a few days to neutralize the unabsorbed alkaloids of the ergot. At the same time give castor oil. To dilate the blood vessels give chloral hydrate. Bathe the affected parts with hot water. If sloughing has gone far, amputation must be resorted to.

Other Poisonous Fungi.—Many other fungi poison herbivora. In some instances, however, where fungi are blamed for causing disease their presence on the foodstuff or herbage is but coincidental with some other and more potent disease-producing factor. For example, if the conditions are favorable to the growth of fungi they are also favorable to the growth of bacteria, and bacteria may produce poisons in foods. In general it may be said that any food that is moldy, musty, or putrid is possibly dangerous. Silage, properly cured, does not belong to this class, because the curing of silage is not a bacterial process. But spoiled silage and silage matted with mold is dangerous and should not be fed.

POISONING BY BITES AND STINGS.

Snake Bites.—The poison contained in the tooth glands of certain venomous reptiles, particularly some of the snakes, which is injected into or under the skin of an animal bitten by the reptile, is a very powerful agent. It is likely to produce a serious local irritation, and in the case of the more poisonous snakes serious constitutional disturbances, even to causing death, which it may do in either of two ways. First, when very strong, by exerting a narcotic influence similar to that of some of the powerful poisons, checking heart action. Second, by diffused inflammation of the areolar tissue, gangrene, and extensive sloughing. The symptoms of snake bite are a local swelling caused by an intense local inflammation, pricks showing where the fangs penetrated, depression, weakness, feeble pulse, difficult breathing, bluish discoloration of the visible mucous membranes, stupor, or convulsions. If the poison is not powerful or plentiful enough to produce death, it is, at any rate, likely to cause severe local abscesses or sloughs.

The treatment may be divided into local and general. Locally every effort should be made to prevent absorption of the poison. If discovered at once the bitten part had better be excised. If that is impracticable and a ligature can be applied, as in the case of a bite to one of the limbs, no time should be lost in applying it above the injury. It should be made sufficiently tight to so far as possible arrest circulation in the bitten part. The wound should be freely incised, so that it will bleed freely, and the poison should be extracted by cupping or pressed out by squeezing with the fingers. Permanganate of potash in 5 per cent solution should be applied to and injected into the wound. The depressing effect of the poison on the general system should be counteracted by liberal drenching with stimulants, such as alcohol, coffee, digitalis, or the aromatic spirits or carbonate of ammonia. In animal practice the alcoholic stimulants and local treatment above described are likely to meet with best success. A special antitoxin for use in treating snake bite is now prepared and may be had from the leading druggists. It is quite effective if used promptly.

WASP AND BEE STINGS.

Wasps and bees secrete a poisonous substance which they are able to insert through the skin of an animal by the aid of their sharp stings. This poison is a severe local irritant, and may even cause local gangrene. It also has a depressing effect upon the central nervous system, and destroys the red-blood corpuscles. To produce these general effects it must be introduced in very large quantities, as when an animal is stung by a swarm of bees or wasps.

The treatment is to wash the parts with diluted ammonia or permanganate of potash solution and to give stimulants internally. If there is so much swelling about the head and nostrils as to interfere with breathing, tracheotomy may be necessary.

POISONING BY INSECTS ON THE FORAGE.

Cattle grazing on forage heavily infested with caterpillars have been known to develop acute indigestion, colic, and, in a few cases, to die as a result of this poisoning. Plant lice cause irritation of the mouth and throat if eaten in large numbers. Some insects secrete a chemical poison which, taken in this way, causes serious digestive disturbance.

POISONING WITH SPANISH FLY.

Spanish fly, in the form of powdered cantharides, may be given in an overdose, or when applied as a blister to too large a surface of skin enough may be absorbed to poison. If given by the mouth it causes severe irritation of the gastro-intestinal tract, shown by salivation, sore throat, colic, bloody diarrhea, etc. It also produces, whether given by the mouth or absorbed through the skin, irritation of the urinary tract, as shown by frequent and painful urination. If death results, it is due to respiratory paralysis. Give protectives and the white of egg, with opium. Do not give oils or alcohol.

LIST OF PLANTS KNOWN TO BE POISONOUS TO STOCK.

Ergot, *Claviceps purpurea* (Fr.) Tul.
Clathrus, *Clathrus columnatus* Bosc.
Fly poison, *Chrosperma muscætoxicum* (Walt.) Kuntze.
American white hellebore, *Veratrum viride* Ait.
Slender nettle, *Urtica gracilis* Ait.
Pokeweed, *Phytolacca decandra* L.
Corncockle, *Agrostemma githago* L.
Aconite, *Aconitum napellus* L.
Western aconite, *Aconitum columbianum* Nutt.
Dwarf larkspur, *Delphinium tricorne* Michx.
Field larkspur, *Delphinium consolida* L.
Purple larkspur, *Delphinium menziesii* DC.
Wyoming larkspur, *Delphinium geyeri* Greene.

Green hellebore, *Helleborus viridis* L.
Cursed crowfoot, *Ranunculus sceleratus* L.
Celandine, *Chelidonium majus* L.
Opium poppy, *Papaver somniferum* L.
Field poppy, *Papaver rhœas* L.
Laurel cherry, *Prunus caroliniana* (Mill.) Ait.
Wild black cherry, *Prunus serotina* Ehrh.
Rattlebox, *Crotalaria sagittalis* L.
Locust tree, *Robinia pseudacacia* L.
Coral bean, *Sophora secundiflora* (Cav.) DC.
Chinese umbrella tree, *Melia azedarach* L.
Spurge nettle, *Jatropha stimulosa* Michx.
Castor oil plant, *Ricinus communis* L.
Box, *Buxus sempervirens* L.
Staff vine, *Celastrus scandens* L.
Common St. John's-wort, *Hypericum perforatum* L.
Water hemlock, *Cicuta maculata* L.
Oregon water hemlock, *Cicuta vagans* Greene.
Poison hemlock, *Conium maculatum* L.
California azalea, *Azalea occidentalis* Torr. and Gray.
Narrow-leaf laurel, *Kalmia angustifolia* L.
Broad-leaf laurel, *Kalmia latifolia* L.
Branch ivy, *Leucothoë catesbæi* (Walt.) A. Gray.
Swamp leucothoë, *Leucothoë racemosa* (L.) A. Gray.
Mountain fetter bush, *Pieris floribunda* (Pursh.) Benth and
Hook.
Stagger bush, *Pieris mariana* (L.) Benth and Hook.
California rhododendron, *Rhododendron californicum* Hook.
Great laurel, *Rhododendron maximum* L.
Oleander, *Nerium oleander* L.
Milkweed, *Asclepias eriocarpa* Benth.
Milkweed, *Asclepias syriaca* L.
Jimson weed, *Datura stramonium* L.
Jimson weed, *Datura tatula* L.
Black henbane, *Hyoscyamus niger* L.
Tobacco, *Nicotiana tabacum* L.
Black nightshade, *Solanum nigrum* L.
Spreading nightshade, *Solanum triflorum* Nutt.
Purple foxglove, *Digitalis purpurea* L.
Sneezeweed, *Helenium autumnale* L.

LIST OF PLANTS PROBABLY POISONOUS TO STOCK.*
Mold, *Aspergillus glaucous* (L.) Link.
Fly amanita, *Amanita muscaria* (L.) Fr.

---

*The list as given is provisional for some species, as the reports upon which their reputation is founded are very meager and sometimes even contradictory. . . . They are here enumerated, not necessarily because it is believed that they are poisonous, but with the view to eliciting more positive evidence either for or against them. Although comprehensive, the list is incomplete, for experience is constantly adding to the number already known or suspected to be poisonous.

Bracken fern, *Pteris acquilina* L.
Yew, *Taxus minor* (Michx.) Britton.
Darnel, *Lolium temulentum* L.
California false hellebore, *Veratrum californicum* **Durand.**
Death camas, *Zygadenus venenosus* Wats.
Alkali grass, *Zygadenus elegans* Pursh.
Lily-of-the-Valley, *Convallaria majalis* L.
Red-root, *Gyrotheca capitata* (Walt.) Morong.
White baneberry, *Actæa alba* (L.) Mill.
Red baneberry, *Actæa rubra* (Ait.) Willd.
Wind flower, *Anemone quinquefolia* L.
Larkspur, *Delphinium recurvatum* Greene.
Mountain larkspur, *Delphinium scopulorum* **Gray.**
Cow poison, *Delphinium trolliifolium* Gray.
Bulbous crowfoot, *Ranunculus bulbosus* L.
Tall crowfoot, *Ranunculus acris* L.
Calycanthus, *Butneria fertilis* (Walt.) Kearney.
Mexican poppy, *Argemone mexicana* L.
Lupine, *Lupinus leucophyllus* Dougl.
Silky sophora, *Sophora sericea* Nutt.
Large-flowered yellow flax, *Linum rigidum* Pursh.
Spurge, *Euphorbia* sp.
California buckeye, *Æsculus californica* (Spach) Nutt.
Ohio buckeye, *Æsculus glabra* Willd.
Horse chestnut, *Æsculus hippocastanum* L.
Red buckeye, *Æsculus Pavia* L.
Spotted St. John's-wort, *Hypericum maculatum* Walt.
Cowbane, *Oxypolis rigidis* (L.) Britton.
Hemlock water parsnip, *Sium cicutæfolium* Gmel.
Wild rosemary, *Andromeda polifolia* L.
Pimpernel, *Anagallis arvensis* L.
Milkweed, *Asclepias mexicana* Cav.
Potato, *Solanum tuberosum* L.
Fine-leaf sneezeweed, *Helenium tenuifolium* Nutt.
Tansy ragwort, *Senecio jacobæ* L.
Spring clotbur, *Xanthium spinosum* L.
Broad cocklebur, *Xanthium strumarium* L.

LIST OF PLANTS SUSPECTED OF BEING POISONOUS TO STOCK.*
Cornsmut, *Ustilago maydis* Corda.
Golden rod rust, *Coleosporium solidaginis* (Schw.) Theum.
Field horsetail, *Equisetum arvense* L.
Sleepy grass, *Stipa robusta* (Vasey) Nash.
Leucocrinum, *Leucocrinum montanum* Nutt.

---

*The list as given is provisional for some species, as the reports upon which
their reputation is founded are very meager and sometimes even contradictory.
. . . They are here enumerated, not necessarily because it is believed that they
are poisonous, but with the view to eliciting more positive evidence either for or
against them. Although comprehensive, the list is incomplete, for experience is
constantly adding to the number already known or suspected to be poisonous.

Crow poison, *Nothoscordum bivalve* (L.) Britton.
Atamasco lily, *Atamasco atamasco* (L.) Greene.
Oak, *Quercus* sp.
Black greasewood, *Sarcobatus vermiculatus* (Hook.) **Torr.**
Sleepy catchfly, *Silene antirrhina* L.
Anise tree, *Illicium floridanum* Ellis.
Mandrake, *Podophyllum peltatum* L.
Lambert loco weed, *Aragallus lambertii* (Pursh.) Greene.
Woolly loco weed, *Astragalus mollissimus* Torr.
Loco weed, *Astragalus bigelovii* A. Gray.
Loco weed, *Astragalus hornii* A. Gray.
Loco weed, *Astragalus pattersoni* A. Gray.
Sesban, *Sesbania vesicaria* Ell.
Prairie thermopsis, *Thermopsis rhombifolia* (Nutt.) Richards.
Trailing arbutus, *Epigæa repens* L.
California Labrador tea, *Ledum glandulosum* Nutt.
Labrador tea, *Ledum grœnlandicum* Oeder.
Privet, *Ligustrum vulgare* L.
Spreading dogbane, *Apocynum androsæmifolium* **L.**
Indian hemp, *Apocynum cannabinum* L.
Butterfly weed, *Asclepias tuberosa* L.
Bittersweet, *Solanum dulcamara* L.
Slender gerardia, *Gerardia tenuifolia* Vahl.
Hedge hyssop, *Gratiola officinalis* L.
Lousewort, *Pedicularis* sp.
Downingia, *Bolelia* sp.
Indian tobacco, *Lobelia inflata* L.
Brook lobelia, *Lobelia kalmii* L.
Pale-spiked lobelia, *Lobelia spicata* Lam.
Great lobelia, *Lobelia syphilitica* L.
Golden-rod, *Solidago* sp.
American cocklebur, *Xanthium canadense* Mill.

LIST OF PUBLICATIONS CONSULTED AND ABRIDGED ABOVE.

Hemorrhagic Septicæmia: Minn. Agr. Ex. S. Bul. 82.

Foot-and-Mouth Disease: U. S. Bureau of Animal Ind. Cir. 141; U. S. Bureau of Animal Ind. Ann. Rept., 1910; U. S. Bureau of Animal Ind. Cir. 147.

Rabies: Mass. Agr. E. S. Bul. 27; Kan. Agr. E. S. Cir. 9; U. S. Bureau of Animal Ind. Cir. 129; Farmer's Bul. U. S. Dept. Agr. 449; Col. Agr. E. S. Bul. 162; U. S. Bureau of Animal Ind. Cir. 54; Year-Book of the U. S. Dept. of Agr., 1900.

Tuberculosis: Year-Book of the Dept. of Agr. 1910; Md. Agr. E. S. Bul. 145; U. S. Bureau of Animal Ind. Cir. 143; U. S. Bureau of Animal Ind. Cir. 70; U. S. Bureau of Animal Ind. Cir. 114; U. S. Bureau of Animal Ind. Cir. 118; U. S. Bureau of Animal Ind. Cir. 127; U. S. Bureau of Animal Ind. Cir. 153; U. S. Bureau of Animal Ind. Cir. 175; U. S. Bureau of Animal Ind. Bul. 32; U. S. Bureau of Animal Ind. Bul. 38; U. S. Bureau of Animal Ind. Bul. 98; U. S. Bureau of Animal Ind. Bul. 96; Farmer's Bul. Dept. Agr. 351; Twenty-third Ann. Rept. U. S. Bu. An. Ind. 1906; Twenty-fifth

Ann. Rept. U. S. Bu. An. Ind. 1908; Year-Book of the Dept. of Agr. 1898; Year-Book of the Dept. of Agr. 1906; Ala. Agr. E. S. Bul. 67 and 125; Ark. Agr. E. S. Bul. 35 and 57; Col. Agr. E. S. Bul. 66; Conn. Agr. E. S. Bul. 19, 23 and 24; Del. Agr. E. S. Bul. 43; Ga. Agr. E. S. Bul. 60; Ill. Agr. E. S. Bul. 128 and 149; Ind. Agr. E. S. Bul. 63 and 113; Iowa Agr. E. S. Bul. 29 and 107; Kan. Agr. E. S. Bul. 69 and 79; La. Agr. E. S. Bul. 43 and 64; Mass. Agr. E. S. Bul. 3, 27 and 41; Mich. Agr. E. S. Bul. 29, 133, 159, 173 and Circular 8; Minn. Agr. E. S. Bul. 51 and 103; New Hamp. Agr. E. S. Bul. 78; New Jer. Agr. E. S. Bul. 101 and 118; New Mex. Agr. E. S. Bul. 55; New York (Geneva) S. Bul. 277; New York (Cornell) S. Bul. 65, 82, 150, 225, 250 and 299; North Dak. S. Bul. 14 and 77; Ohio S. Bul. 95 and 108; Penn. S. Bul. 21 and 29; Tex. S. Bul. 30; Utah S. Bul. 41; Vt. S. Bul. 42; Vir. S. Bul. 3 Vol. II and 4 Vol. III; Wis. S. Bul. 40, 84, 126 and 143; Ontario Canada Exp. Farm Bul. 20.

Actinomycosis, Lump Jaw: Kan. Agr. E. S. Bul. 16; Tex. Agr. E. S. Bul. 30; S. Dak. E. S. Bul. 36.

Anthrax: Miss. Agr. E. S. Bul. 72; S. Dak. Agr. E. S. Bul. 36; Del. Agr. E. S. Bul. 37; Ark. Agr. E. S. Bul. 97; La. Agr. E. S. Bul. 60 and 64 (second series) 109; U. S. Bureau of An. Ind. Bul. 137; Farmers' Bulletin, U. S. Dept. Agr. 439.

Black Leg, or Symptomatic Anthrax: Col. Agr. E. S. Bul. 137; La. Agr. E. S. Bul. 60 (second series) and 109; Kan. Agr. E. S. Bul. 69, 105 and 122; Okla. Agr. E. S. Bul. 27 and 57; Vir. Agr. E. S. Bul. 4, 8 and 10; U. S. Bureau of Animal Ind. Cir. 31 (revised); Mo. Agr. E. S. Bul. 12.

Necrotic Stomatitis: U. S. Bureau of Animal Ind. Cir. 91; U. S. Bureau of Animal Ind. Bul. 67.

Cattle Distemper, or Malignant Catarrh: Va. Agr. E. S. Bul. 12 (new series); Kan. Agr. E. S. Press Bul. 104.

Chronic Bacterial Dysentery: U. S. Bureau of Animal Ind. Cir. 156.

Texas Fever: Ala. Agr. E. S. Bul. 116 and 141; Ark. Agr. E. S. Bul. 101; Del. Agr. E. S. Bul. 23; Fla. Agr. E. S. Bul. 64; Ga. Agr. E. S. Bul. 64; Kan. Agr. E. S. Bul. 69; La. Agr. E. S. Bul. 51, 56, 64, 82 and 84; Miss. E. S. Bul. 42, 69 and 73; Mo. E. S. Bul. 11, 37 and 48; Mont. E. S. Bul. 85; Nev. E. S. Bul. 31; N. Car. State Board of Agr. Bul. Vol. 24, No. 5; Okla. Agr. E. S. Bul. 27, 39 and 81; S. Car. E. S. Bul. 72, 90 and 130; Tenn. E. S. Bul., Vol. 18, No. 1, and Bul. No. 81; Tex. E. S. Bul. 24, 30 and 111; Vir. E. S. Bul (new series) 2, 3, 5, 9; U. S. Dept. Agr. Bureau of Animal Ind. Ann. Rept. 1899; U. S. Dept. Agr. Bureau of Animal Ind. Ann. Rept. 1905; U. S. Dept. Agr. Bureau of Animal Ind. Bul. 130; U. S. Dept. of Agr. Bureau of Animal Ind. Cir. 97, 148 and 174; U. S. Dept. of Agr. Bureau of Ent. Bul. 72; U. S. Dept. of Agr. E. S. Work, Vol. II, No. 13; U. S. Dept. of Agr. Farmer's Bul. 258 and 261.

Poisons, Poisonous Plants and Poisoning: Ariz. Agr. E. S. Bul. 59; Ark. Agr. E. S. Bul. 108; Idaho Agr. E. S. Bul. 37; Kan. Agr. E. S. Bul. 49 and 58; Mass. E. S. Bul. 27; Neb. E. S. Press Bul. 23;

Neb. E. S. Bul. 52, 63 and 77; New Hamp. E. S. Bul. 56; N. Dak.
E. S. Bul. 44 and 58; Ind. E. S. Cir. No. 3.

Parasites Affecting Cattle: Special Rept. on Disease of Cattle
U. S. Dept. of Agr.; Vir. A. E. S. Bul. 112 and 113; New Hamp. E.
S. Bul. 28; Okla. E. S. Bul. 53 and 72; Miss. E. S. Bul. 28; Vir.
E. S. Bul. 108, 109 and 114; Kan. E. S. Bul. 69, 86 and 136; La.
E. S. Bul. (second series) No. 2; S. Car. E. S. Bul. 142; U. S. Dept.
Agr. Div. of Ent. "Insect Life," Vol. IV. Nos. 9 and 10; Iowa Agr.
E. S. Bul. 116; Texas Agr. E. S. Bul. 12 and 18; S. Dak. E. S. Bul.
131; S. Car. E. S. Bul. 114; Neb. E. S. Bul. 74; Ark. E. S. Bul. 20;
Fla. E. S. Bul. 28; Kan. E. S. Press Bul. 30 and 118; U. S. Bureau
of Animal Ind. Bul. 127.

DISEASES OF THE SKIN.

ITCHING PRURITIS.

It is best to consider pruritis first as a distinct subject. It is not
a disease, only a sensation, and therefore a symptom. It is one of the
symptoms accompanying the majority of the diseases which we will
consider in this chapter. It is, then, a functional affection produced
by slight irritation from without or by an internal cause acting upon
the sensory nerves of the skin. Nothing characteristic is seen except
the secondary lesions, produced mechanically by scratching or
rubbing.

There are various forms of itching, the result of specific skin diseases, where the pruritis is a secondary symptom. In such cases it
should not be regarded as an independent affection.

Causes.—Many causes may induce the condition which we recognize here as pruritis. The most common one is dirt on the skin,
resulting from insufficient care. If the ceiling of the stable is open,
so that dust and straw may fall down, the skin is irritated and pruritis results. It also occurs in some forms of indigestion. The parts
of the body most exposed to this condition are the croup, the back, the
top of the neck, and the root of the tail.

Another cause is found in affections of the liver and of the kidneys, when an increase of effete material has to be thrown off by the
skin. Morbid materials circulating in the blood may produce a tickling or smarting sensation of the skin in their passage from the blood
to the free surface of the skin. Certain irritating substances when
eaten may be excreted by the skin, and coming thus in direct contact
with the sensory nerves produce itching, or may go further and cause
distinct inflammation of the skin. In another class of cases the pruritis may be due to an atrophy, contraction, or hardening of the skin,
when the nerves become irritated by the pressure. These conditions
may be so slightly marked in a thick skin like that of the ox that they
can not be recognized. It is frequently noticed that cattle will rub
themselves as soon as they pass from the stable into the open air—
changing from a warm to a cold atmosphere. Again, we may find an
animal which does all its rubbing in the stall. We may look for lice,
but fail to find them. These conditions are generally attributable to
high feeding and to too close confinement. They may be associated

with inflammatory irritation or not; certainly we fail to discover any morbid changes in the skin. There is to some extent a delightful sensation produced by rubbing, and it may partly become a habit of pleasure.

Treatment.—We must place our chief reliance upon a change of food, plenty of exercise, and in most cases the administration of an active cathartic—1 to 1½ pounds of Epsom salts, a handful of common salt, a tablespoonful of ginger or pepper, mixed with 2 quarts of water, all of which is to be given at one dose. Afterwards half an ounce of hyposulphite of soda may be given twice a day for a week, mixed with the feed. For an external application, when the skin is abraded or thickened from rubbing, a solution of borax, 4 ounces to the quart of water, may be used. Carbolic acid, ½ ounce to a quart of water, will give relief in some cases.

ERYTHEMA.

This is the simplest form of inflammation of the skin. It consists of an increased redness, which may occur in patches or involve considerable surface. The red coloration disappears when pressed upon by the finger, but soon returns after the pressure is removed. There is seldom much swelling of the affected part, though often a glutinous discharge may be noticed, which dries and mats the hair or forms a thin scale upon the skin. In simple erythema the epidermis alone is affected; when it becomes chronic, fissures form, which extend into the corium, or true skin.

Causes.—Simple erythema, consisting of an inflammatory irritation, is witnessed in very young calves, in which the navel leaks. The discharge being urine, it causes an irritation of the surrounding skin. Chafing, which is another form of erythema, is occasionally seen on the udder of cows from rubbing by the legs; chafing between the legs is not uncommon among fat steers. Chronic erythema is found in the form of chapped teats of cows and chapped lips in sucking calves. It frequently occurs in cows when they are turned out in winter directly after milking, and in others from chafing by the calf in sucking. Some cows are peculiarly subject to sore teats. The fissures when neglected in the early stage of formation become deep, very painful, often bleeding at the slightest touch, and cause the animal to become a kicker when milked in that condition. Occasionally the lower portions of the legs become irritated and chapped when cattle are fed in a muddy or wet yard in winter, or if they are compelled to wade through water in frosty weather. Another form of erythema occurs in young cattle highly fed and closely stabled for a long winter. The erythema appears in patches, and as it is most common near the end of the winter it is known as the "spring eruption" or "spring itch."

Treatment.—In ordinary cases of erythema the removal of the cause and the application of benzoated oxide of zinc ointment, carbolized cosmoline, or a mixture of creolin, 1 ounce to a pint of water, applied a few times, will restore the skin to a healthy condition. When there are fissures the zinc ointment is the best. If at the teats, a milk siphon should be used instead of milking by hand, and the calf, if there is one suckled, should be taken away. When the calf's mouth is affected it should be fed by hand. When the legs are irritated or chapped, dry stabling for a few days and the application of tar ointment will soon heal them.

URTICARIA (NETTLE RASH, OR SURFEIT).

This is a mild inflammatory affection of the skin, characterized by sudden development of patches of various sizes, from that of a nickel to one as large as the hand. The patches of raised skin are marked by an abrupt border and are irregular in form. All the swelling may disappear in a few hours, or it may go away in one place and reappear on another part of the body. It is always accompanied by a great desire to rub the affected part. In its simplest type, as just described, it is never followed by any serious exudation or eruptions, unless the surface of the skin becomes abraded from scratching or rubbing.

Causes.—Derangements of the digestive organs are the most common causes, such as overloading the stomach when the animal is turned out to graze in the spring, certain constituents of food, and high feeding among fattening stock. When the kidneys are functionally deranged, urticaria may appear. Spinal irritation and other nervous affections may cause it. The disease consists in a paralysis of the nerve ends that control the volume of the capillary vessels in certain areas of skin, thus permitting the vessels to expand, their contents in part to exude, and thus produce a soft, circumscribed swelling.

Treatment.—Administer a full dose of Epsom salts. Give soft, easily digested food, and wash the affected parts with a solution of bicarbonate of soda—common baking soda—8 ounces to the gallon of water twice a day, or diluted glycerin may be applied to the skin. If it assumes a persistent tendency, give a tablespoonful of the following powder in the feed three times a day: Cream of tartar, sulphur, and nitrate of potash, equal parts by weight; mix.

ECZEMA.

Eczema is a noncontagious inflammation of the skin, characterized by any or all of the results of inflammation at once or in succession, such as erythema, vesicles, or pustules, accompanied by more or less infiltration and itching, terminating in a watery discharge, with the formation of crusts or in scaling off. The disease may run an acute course and then disappear, or it may become chronic; therefore, two varieties are recognized, vesicular, or pustular, and chronic eczema.

Causes.—Eczema is not so common among cattle as in horses and in dogs, in which it is the most common of all skin diseases. Among cattle it is occasionally observed under systems of bad hygiene, filthiness, lousiness, overcrowding, overfeeding, excessively damp or too warm stables. It is found to develop now and then in cattle that are fed upon sour substances, distillery swill, house or garden garbage, etc. Localized eczema may be caused by irritant substances applied to the skin—turpentine, ammonia, the essential oils, mustard, Spanish fly ointment, etc. Occasionally an eruption with vesiculation of the skin has been induced by the excessive use of mercurial preparations for the destruction of lice. It is evident that eczema may arise from local irritation to the skin or from an auto-intoxication. Cattle fed on the refuse from potato-starch factories develop a most obstinate and widespread eczema, beginning on the legs.

Symptoms.—In accordance with the variety of symptoms during the progress of the disease we may divide it into different stages or periods: (1) Swelling and increased heat of the skin; the formation of vesicles, which are circumscribed, rounded elevations of the epidermis, varying in size from a pin head to a split pea, containing a clear, watery fluid; (2) exudation of a watery, glutinous fluid, formation of crusts, and sometimes suppuration, or the formation of vesicles containing pus (pustules); (3) scaling off (desquamation), with redness, and thickening of the skin. From the very beginning of the disease the animal will commence to rub the affected parts; hence the various stages may not always be easily recognized, as the rubbing will produce more or less abrasion, thus leaving the skin raw—sometimes bleeding. Neither do these symptoms always occur in regular succession, for in some cases the exudation will be most prominent, being very profuse, and serve to spread the disorder over a large surface. In other cases the formation of incrustations, or rawness of the skin, will be the most striking feature. The disease may be limited to certain small areas, or it may be diffused over the greater part of the body; the vesicles or pustules, may be scattered in small clusters, or a large number run together. The chronic form is really only a prolongation of the disease, successive crops of pustules appearing on various portions of the body, frequently invading fresh sections of the skin, while the older surfaces form scabs, or crusts, upon the raw, indurated skin.

In old standing cases the skin will break, forming fissures, especially on portions of the body that bend—the neck and limbs. Thus the disease may be prolonged indefinitely. When eczema reaches its latest period, either acute or chronic, desquamation of the affected parts is the most prominent feature. The formation and shedding of these successive crops of scales constitute the character of the disease frequently denominated psoriasis.

Treatment.—The treatment of eczema is often anything but a pleasant task. There is no one method of treatment which will always prove successful, no matter how early it is begun or how small an area is involved. We must endeavor to remove the cause by giving attention to the general health of the animal and to its environment. Feeding should be moderate in quantity and not too stimulating in character—green feed, bran mashes, ground oats, clean hay, plenty of salt. If the animal has been fed too high, give an active purgative—Epsom salts preferred—once a week, if necessary, and half an ounce of acetate or nitrate of potash may be given in the feed twice a day. If the animal is in poor condition and debilitated, give a tablespoonful of the following mixture in feed twice a day: Powdered copperas, gentian, sulphur, and sassafras bark, equal parts by weight. If the animal is lousy, the parasite must be destroyed before the eczema can be cured. The external treatment must vary with the character of the lesions; no irritating application is to be made while the disease is in its acute vesicular, or pustular, stage, and, in the chronic stage, active stimulants must be used. Much washing is harmful, yet crusts and scales must be removed in order to obtain satisfactory results from the external applications. Both objects, however, can be attained by judiciously combining the curative agents with such substances as will at the same time cleanse the parts.

In the vesicular stage, when the skin is feverish and the epidermis peeling off, exposing the exuding dermis, an application of boracic acid solution, 2 drams of the acid to 8 ounces of water, will often relieve the smarting or itching, and also serve to check the exudation and dry the surface. If this fails to have the desired effect, use creolin, 1 ounce to a quart of water, as a wash. Either of these washes may be used several times a day until incrustation is well established. Then use creolin, 1 ounce to a pint of sweet oil, or the benzoated oxid of zinc ointment, giving the affected surfaces a thorough application once a day. When the eczema is not the result of an external irritant, it takes usually from one to two weeks before the healing is completed.

In chronic eczema, where there is a succession of scabs, or scales, indolent sores or fissures, the white precipitate ointment, nitrate of mercury ointment, or blue ointment, mixed with equal parts of cosmoline or fresh lard, may be applied every second day, taking care to protect the parts so anointed that the animal can not lick it off.

In some cases the use of the following mixture will do well: Oil of tar one-half ounce, glycerin 1 ounce, alcohol 1 pint. Rub this in after cleansing the parts with warm water and soap. The internal administration of arsenic often yields excellent results in chronic eczema. Take 1 dram of arsenic, 1 dram of carbonate of potash, 1 pint of boiling water, and give 1 ounce of this twice a day in water, after feeding. An alkali internally may be of service. As such, one may give 2 ounces of bicarbonate of soda twice daily. Sublimed sulphur may also be tried in ounce doses twice daily.

PUSTULES (IMPETIGO).

Impetigo is an inflammatory disease of the skin, characterized by the formation of distinct pustules, about the size of a pea or a bean, unattended by itching. The pustules develop from the papular layer of the skin, and contain a yellowish white pus. After reaching maturity they remain stationary for a few days, then they disappear by absorption and dry up into crusts. Later the crusts drop off, leaving upon the skin a red spot which soon disappears. Occasionally the crusts remain firmly adherent for a long time, or they may be raised and loosened by the formation of matter underneath. The dry crusts usually have a brown or black appearance.

Causes.—Impetigo affects sucking calves, in which the disease appears upon the lips, nostrils, and face. It is attributed to some irritant substance contained in the mother's milk. Impetigo is also witnessed among grazing animals, regardless of age, and it especially attacks animals with white hair and skin. The mouth, face, and limbs become covered with pustules, which may rupture in a few hours, followed by rapid and successive incrustations; the scabs frequently coalesce, covering a large surface; pus may form under them, and the whole thickness of the skin become involved in the morbid process. This form of the disease is attributed to the local irritant properties of plants growing in the pasture, such as St. John's wort (*Hypericum perforatum*), smartweed (*Polygonum hydropiper*), vetches, honeydew, etc. Buckwheat, at the time the seeds become ripe, is said to have caused it, also bedding with buckwheat straw.

Treatment.—Sucking calves should be removed from their mother, and the latter should have a purgative to divert the poisonous substance secreted with the milk. When the more formidable disease among grazing cattle appears, the pasturage should be changed, and the affected parts of the animal thoroughly anointed once a day with sweet oil containing 2 drams of carbolic acid to the pint. This should be continued until the crusts soften and begin to drop off, then the parts may be cleansed thoroughly with warm water and soap. Subsequently apply the white precipitate ointment or carbolized cosmoline daily until the parts are healed.

PEMPHIGUS (WATER BLISTERS).

This is an inflammatory disease of the skin, characterized by successive formations of rounded, irregularly shaped water blisters, varying in size from a pea to a hen's egg. The causes are obscure.

Symptoms.—The formation of a blister is preceded by a congestion or swelling of the skin. Yellowish colored water collects beneath the cuticle, which raises the latter from its bed in the form of a blister. The blisters appear in a succession of crops; as soon as one crop disappears another forms. They usually occur in clusters, each one being distinct, or they may coalesce. Each crop usually runs its course in a week. Itching or burning sensations attend this disease which cause the animal to rub, thereby frequently producing excoriations and formation of crust on the affected region.

Treatment.—Give a tablespoonful of the following mixture in feed twice a day: Saltpeter, cream of tartar, and sulphur, equal parts by weight. The blisters should be opened as soon as formed, to allow the escape of the serum, then apply a wash composed of chlorid of zinc, 1 dram to 15 ounces of water. When there is any formation of crusts, apply carbolized cosmoline.

FURUNCULUS (BOILS).

This is an acute affection of the skin, usually involving its whole thickness, characterized by the formation of one or more abscesses, originating generally in a sebaceous gland, sweat gland, or hair follicle. They usually terminate by absorption, or by the formation of a central core, which sloughs out, leaving a deep, round cavity that soon heals.

Causes.—Impoverished state of the blood, the result of kidney diseases, or of local friction or contusions.

Symptoms.—Boils in cattle usually appear singly, not in clusters; they may attain the size of a hen's egg. The abscess begins as a small round nodule, painful to pressure, gradually increases in size

View of a High Class Chicago Milk-Bottling Plant.   Dept. of Agr.

until death of the central portion takes place, then the surface of the skin gives way to internal pressure, and the core is released and expelled. Constitutional symptoms are generally absent, unless the boils occur in considerable numbers, or by their size involve a great amount of tissue.

Treatment.—Poulticing to ripen the abscess. If this can not be done, apply camphorated oil two or three times a day until the core is formed. As soon as the central or most prominent part becomes soft, the abscess should be opened to release the core. Then use carbolized cosmoline once a day until the healing is completed. If the animal is in poor condition, give tonics—copperas, gentian, ginger, and sulphur, equal parts by weight, 1 tablespoonful twice a day. If the animal manifests a feverish condition of the system, administer half an ounce of saltpeter twice a day, continuing it several days or a week.

PITYRIASIS (SEBORRHEA, DANDRUFF, OR SCURF).

This is a condition characterized by an excessive secretion of sebaceous matter, forming upon the skin in small crusts, or scales.

Causes.—It is due to a functional derangement of the sebaceous glands, usually accompanied by dryness and loss of pliancy of the skin. The animal is hidebound, as it is commonly termed, thin in flesh, inclined to rub, and very frequently lousy. The condition is observed most often toward the spring of the year. Animals that are continually housed, and the skins of which receive no cleaning, generally present a coat filled with fine scales, composed of epithelium from the epidermis and dried sebaceous matter. This, however, is a physiological condition, and compatible with perfect health.

Symptoms.—Pityriasis may affect the greater portion of the body, though usually only certain parts are affected—the ears, neck, rump, etc. The skin becomes scurfy, the hairy coat filled with bran-like gray or whitish scales.

Treatment.—Nutritious food, such as oil-cake meal, bran, ground oats, and clean hay. In the spring the disease generally disappears after the animal is turned out to pasture. When lice are present they should be destroyed.

ELEPHANTIASIS (SCLERODERMA).

This condition consists in a chronic thickening of the skin, which may affect one or more limbs, or involve the whole integument. It is characterized by recurrent attacks of swelling of the skin and subcutaneous areolar tissue. After each attack the affected parts remain infiltrated to a larger extent than before, until finally the skin may attain a thickness of an inch, become wrinkled and fissured. In cattle this disease is confined to hot climates. The predisposing cause is unknown.

EDEMA (ANASARCA OF THE SKIN).

This is a dropsical condition of the skin and subcutaneous areolar tissue, characterized by pitting under pressure, the fingers leaving a dent which remains a short time.

Causes.—Edema generally results from a weakened state of the system, arising from previous disease. It may also be dependent upon a functional derangement of the kidneys, upon weak circulation, or obstruction to the flow of blood through the lungs. In debilitated animals and in some animals heavily infested with parasites there is swelling of the dewlap or of the fold of skin between the jaws.

Symptoms.—Painless swelling of a limb, udder, lower surface of abdomen, or lower jaw becomes apparent. This may increase in dimensions for several days, or may attain its maximum in less than twenty-four hours. Unless complicated with some acute disease of a specific character, there is not much, if any, constitutional disturbance. The deep layer of the skin is infiltrated with serum, which gives it the characteristic condition of pitting under pressure.

Treatment.—When the cause can be ascertained and removed, we will have a reasonable expectation of seeing the edema disappear. When no direct specific cause can be discovered and the animal is debilitated, give general tonic. If, on the contrary, it is in good flesh, give a purgative, followed by half an ounce of acetate of potash twice a day. External applications are useless. Edema may be distinguished from erysipelas or anthrax by the absence of pain and fever.

DERMOID AND SEBACEOUS CYSTS (WENS).

A dermoid cyst is formed by an involution of the skin, with a growth of hair on the inner wall of the sac. It may become embedded deeply in the tissues subcutaneously, or may just penetrate the thickness of the skin, where it is movable and painless. They are generally found within the ear or at its base, although they may form on any part of the body. Usually they have a small opening, from which a thick, cheesy matter can be squeezed out. The rational treatment is to dissect them out.

Sebaceous cysts appear not unlike the former. They are formed by a dilatation of the hair follicle and sebaceous duct within the skin, and contain a gray or yellowish sebaceous mass. The tumor may attain the size of a cherry stone or a walnut. Generally they are round, movable, and painless, soft or doughy in consistency, and covered with skin and hair. They develop slowly. The best treatment is to dissect out the sac with contents entire.

VERRUCA (WARTS).

Cattle are affected with two varieties of warts. One, the *verruca vulgaris*, is composed of a cluster of enlarged papillæ, covered with a thickened epidermis, the number of papillæ determining the breadth and their length its height. They are generally circular in figure, slightly roughened on the surface, and spring from the skin by a broad base. Occasionally large numbers of very thin, long, pedunculated warts grow from the skin of the ear, lips, about the eyes, and vulva. Another variety, the *verruca acuminata*, sometimes erroneously denominated epithelial cancers, are irregularly shaped elevations, tufted or club-shaped, occasionally existing as thick, short, fleshy excrescences, giving the growth the appearance of granulation tissue. Their color is red or purplish, and oftentimes by friction they become raw and bleeding, emitting then a very offensive odor. They usually grow in clusters and their development is rapid.

Causes.—An abnormal nutrition of the skin, determined by increased energy of growth operating upon a healthy skin; at other times, upon a weak or impoverished skin.

Treatment.—When they are small and pedunculated they may be snipped off with the shears, and the stump touched with nitrate of silver. When they are broad and flattened they can be dissected out, and the wound cauterized, if necessary. If they are large and very vascular, they may be ligated, one by one, by taking a strong cord and tying it as firmly around the base as possible. They will then shrivel, die, and drop off. If there is a tendency to grow again, apply a red-hot iron, or nitric acid with a glass rod. Very often warts will quickly disappear if they are kept soft by daily applications of sweet or olive oil.

KELIS.

Kelis is an irregularly shaped flat tumor of the skin, resulting from hypertrophy—increased growth of the fibrous tissue of the corium, producing absorption of the papillary layer.

Causes.—It may arise spontaneously, or follow a scar after an injury.

Symptoms.—Kelis generally appears below the knee or hock. It may occur singly or in numbers. There are no constitutional symptoms. Its growth is very slow and seldom causes any inconvenience. It appears as a flattened, irregular, or spreading growth within the substance of the skin, is hard to the touch, and is especially characterized by divergent branches or roots, resembling the claws of a crab, and hence the name. Occasionally some part of it may soften and result in an abscess. It may grow several inches in length and encircle the whole limb.

Treatment.—So long as it causes the animal no inconvenience it is best not to meddle with it; when it does, the animal ought to be fattened for beef, the meat being perfectly harmless to the consumer.

PARASITIC DISEASES OF THE SKIN.
MANGE, ITCH, SCAB.
[See discussion in chapter on "The animal parasites of cattle."]
LOUSINESS.
[See discussion of lice in chapter on "The animal parasites of cattle."]
WARBLES, OR GRUB IN THE SKIN.
[See discussion in chapter on "The animal parasites of cattle."]
BUFFALO GNATS.
[See discussion of these parasites in chapter on "The animal parasites of cattle."]

HORN FLY (HAEMATOBIA SERRATA).

[See discussion of this parasite in chapter on "The animal parasites of cattle."]

TICKS.

[See discussion of these parasites in chapter on "The animal parasites of cattle."]

FLIES.

[See discussion of these parasites in chapter on "The animal parasites of cattle."]

RINGWORM (TINEA TONSURANS AND TINEA FAVOSA).

Ringworm is an affection of the skin, due to a vegetable parasite. Tinea tonsurans is due to the presence of a minute or microscopic fungus—the *Trichophyton tonsurans*. It affects the hair and the epidermic layer of the skin, and is highly contagious, being readily transmitted from one animal to another. This fungus consists of spores and filaments. The spores, being the most numerous, are round, nucleated, and seldom vary much in size. They are very abundant in the hair follicle. The filaments are articulated, waving, and contain granules. This disease is productive of changes in the root and shaft of the hair, rendering it brittle and easily broken off.

Symptoms.—This disease becomes manifest by the formation of circular patches on the skin, which soon become denuded of hair. The cuticular layer of the skin is slightly inflamed, and vesication with exudation occurs, followed by the formation of scaly, brittle crusts. The patches appear silvery gray when incrusted, and are mostly confined to the head and neck. It is a common disease among young cattle in the winter and spring. Very early in the development of the patches the hairs split, twist, and break off close to the skin. This disease is attended with more or less itching. It is communicable to man.

Tinea favosa is due to another fungus, the *Achorion schönleinii*. This enters the hair follicle and involves the cuticle surrounding it, small crusts form which increase in diameter and thickness and then become elevated at their margin, forming a cup-shaped scab, the favus cup, which gives the disease its distinctive character. The number of these cups varies from a few to many hundreds. The hairs involved become brittle and broken, fall off with the crusts, leaving small bald patches. The crusts are of a pale or sulphur-yellow color at first; as they grow older they turn darker, or to a brown color. This form of ringworm has a peculiar odor, resembling that of mice or musty straw. It is occasionally communicated to cattle by man, mice, cats, etc., all being subject to this disease.

Sanitary Measures and Treatment.—The first and most important point in this connection is the early recognition of the disease, so that preventive measures may be adopted before it spreads through the herd, and possibly extends to other species of animals. An animal which is found to be suffering from ringworm ought at once to be separated from the others and treated according to the directions given below. We do not know that ringworm always originates by contagion between diseased and unaffected animals. It is possible that the *Trichophyton* may be a facultative parasite, that is, may in general lead a non-parasitic life, with the power, however, under suitable conditions, especially indicated by an altered or unclean condition of the skin, of adapting itself to a parasitic existence. (According to Grawitz the fungus grows at summer temperature,— best about 30° C.—on acid artificial culture media without losing its faculty for parasitic growth on the skin.)

However this may be, it is certain that when once established the disease is spread by contagion in animals as well as in the human race. Other cattle or horses should not be groomed with any brushes or combs which have been used on diseased cattle. Where it occurs among stabled cattle thorough cleaning and whitewashing of the stable is indicated as well as burning of the bedding and disinfection of halters. Individual animals are best treated in the following way:

The hair is clipped close for some distance around the diseased patch, and the latter well soaked and washed with hot water and soft soap. To prevent dissemination of living spores the water ought to contain some fungicide. (Equal parts of water and 1/500 solution of corrosive sublimate is applicable for this purpose, remembering always that this solution is a poison). After the scales have been removed by this means, apply over the diseased part an antiparasitic remedy. Among the remedies recommended for the purpose are tincture of iodine, iodine ointment, citrine ointment, solutions of corrosive sublimate, carbolic acid and sodium sulphite. All of these and many others are effective when thoroughly and frequently enough applied. When mild remedies are desired, I have found the iodine ointment or tincture most suitable, and recommend these for use when the disease is situated above or close around the eye. The tincture is best applied with a small brush or sponge fastened to the end of a short stick of wood, while the ointment may be rubbed in with the fingers. Both preparations must be thoroughly rubbed into the diseased part and also some distance around it, and the application repeated daily for a week or more.

In other situations a more prompt cure may be expected from the use of stronger preparation, such as citrine ointment (nitrate of mercury ointment), or, in my experience, still better, a blistering ointment composed of red iodide of mercury one part to six of lard, and a few drops of croton oil. One application of this last remedy will effect a cure wherever applied, but it should not be used over too great a surface nor in the neighborhood of the eye, nor should it be re-applied to the same place. All remedies may be washed off twenty-four hours after being applied. In horses the iodine ointment, nitrate of mercury ointment and carbolic solution (20 per cent in glycerine) are suitable; they must be repeated, and if necessary changed or combined until recovery is obtained.

Harness which has been in contact with diseased patches here require attention also. Thorough cleansing by scraping and washing, and then soaking with the disinfecting solution are the means to be pursued to prevent extension of the disease in this way.

In both cattle and horses I would recommend when possible, a change of diet, especially to good pasture. Beside this, there is no special diet which in animals can be said to be antagonistic to ringworm, although in *tinea tonsurans* of children, fatty articles of diet are recommended by all authorities.

In the way of internal medicinal remedies, there is nothing which can be recommended for all cases. Where there is manifest digestive disorder, this will require treatment according to the symptoms presented, but preparations of arsenic, etc., which are often given in skin diseases, should not be used except under skilled supervision, and therefore are not recommended here.

WOUNDS OF THE SKIN.
SNAKE BITES AND VENOMOUS STINGS.
[See pages 68 and 399.]

BURNS AND SCALDS.

This is a rare accident among cattle, yet in cases of fire it may occur. The application of heat, whether dry or moist, unless sufficient instantly to destroy the life of a part, is always followed by the development of vesicles, or blisters, which contain a thin, watery fluid. The blisters may be isolated and not very large, or one blister may cover a very large surface. When the burn is very severe the skin may be wholly devitalized, or the injury may extend into the deeper structures beneath the skin. Then sloughs will occur, followed by a contraction of the parts in healing; if on a limb, this may render the animal stiff. When the burn or scald has been a severe one, the resulting pain is great and the constitutional disturbance very marked.

Treatment.—For a superficial burn use a mixture of equal parts of limewater and linseed oil, or common white paint—white lead ground in oil. This will exclude the atmosphere and protect the inflamed skin. If it is not convenient to obtain this, chimney soot, flour, or starch may be spread on the wound (dry), and covered with cotton batting and light bandage if possible. The blisters should be opened to let the contained fluid escape, but do not pull off the thin cuticle which has been raised by the blister. When the burn is extensive and deep sloughing occurs, the parts should be treated, like other deep wounds, by poulticing, astringent washes, etc. When the system has sustained much shock, stimulants may be required internally, such as 4 ounces of whisky or 2 drams of carbonate of ammonia every hour until the animal rallies. When the pain is very great, hypodermic injections of 6 grains of morphia may be administered every six hours. Frostbite on any portion of the body may be treated as recommended in the article on diseases of the ears.

EMPHYSEMA (AIR OR GAS UNDER THE SKIN).

Emphysema of the skin is not a true disease of the skin, but we shall mention it as a pathological condition. It is characterized by a distention of the skin with air or gas contained in the subcutaneous areolar tissue. It may depend upon a septic condition of the blood, as in anthrax or blackleg; or air may be forced under the skin about the head, neck, and shoulders, as a result of rupture of the windpipe. It occurs in the region of the chest and shoulders from penetrating wounds of the chest and lung, and occasionally follows puncture of the rumen, when the escaping gas is retained under the skin.

Symptoms.—The skin is enormously distended over a greater or less portion of the body; thus any region of the body may lose its natural contour and appear like a monstrosity. There is a peculiar crackling beneath the skin when the hand is passed over it, and on tapping it with the fingers a resonant drum-like sound is elicited.

Treatment.—Puncture the distended skin with a clean broadbladed knife and press out the contained air. Further treatment must be directed with a view to the removal of the cause.

DISEASES OF THE EYE.

CONJUNCTIVITIS (SIMPLE OPHTHALMIA).

This is an inflammation of the conjunctival mucous membrane of the eyeball and lids; in severe cases the deeper coats of the eye become involved, seriously complicating the attack.

Causes.—It may result from a bruise of the eyelid; from the introduction of foreign matters into the eye, such as chaff, hayseed, dust, gnats, etc.; from exposure to cold; poisonous or irritating vapors arising from filthiness of stable. Dust, cinders, or sand blown into the eyes during transportation frequently induce conjunctivitis.

Symptoms.—A profuse flow of tears, closure of the eyelids from intolerance of light, retraction of the eyeball and corresponding protrusion of the haw, disinclination to move, diminution of milk secretion, etc. On parting the lids the lining membrane is found injected with an excess of blood, giving to it a red and swollen appearance; the sclerotic, or white of the eye, is bloodshot and the cornea may be cloudy. If the disease advances, keratitis results.

Treatment.—Careful examination should be made to discover particles of chaff, etc., which may have lodged in the eye, and upon the discovery of such a cause prompt removal is indicated. This may be accomplished by flushing the eye with warm water by means of a syringe, or, if the foreign substance is adherent to the eyeball or lid, it may be scooped out with the handle of a teaspoon or some other blunt instrument. To relieve the congestion and local irritation, a wash composed of boracic acid in freshly boiled water, 20 grains to the ounce, or acetate of zinc, 5 grains to the ounce of pure soft water, may be used, to which may be added 20 drops of laudanum. A few drops of this should be placed in the eye with a camel's-hair pencil or soft feather three or four times daily. The animal should be placed in a cool, darkened stable, and then a cloth folded into several thicknesses should be fastened to the horns in such a manner as to reach below the eyes. This should be kept wet with cold water during the day and removed at night. If there is much fever and constitutional disturbance it becomes advisable to administer 1 pound of Epsom salts dissolved in 1 quart of water.

CONTAGIOUS SORE EYES (INFECTIOUS CATARRHAL CONJUNCTIVITIS, SPECIFIC OPHTHALMIA).

This generally appears in an enzootic or epizootic form, and affects quite a number in the herd. It is distinctly a contagious disease and may be brought into a previously healthy herd by one animal with sore eyes. It may continue in a herd for a season or for several years, affecting all newly purchased animals. It is seldom seen in the winter months. It affects old and young animals alike.

Causes.—The cause of the disease has not been discovered, although it is believed to be due to a germ. The manner in which the disease is spread from one animal to another is little understood, although flies are believed to play an important part. The disease, however, also spreads during the winter, when there are no flies about. Direct contact seems to be a means of spreading the disease. There is a popular idea that pollen and dust cause the disease. They undoubtedly aggravate it, but the disease must be introduced into a locality by an affected animal.

Symptoms.—The first symptom usually noticed is a profuse discharge of tears from one eye, that run down over the face. Dust and dirt often adhere to the moist hair and a dirty streak is observed, especially in white-faced cattle, extending from the inner corner of the eye downward across the face. The disease usually begins in one eye, and later attacks the other eye. In some cases both eyes may be attacked at the same time. Associated with a discharge of tears is a swelling of the eyelids, which are nearly closed, partly from the swelling, but principally to keep the light from the eye, as bright light seems to increase the pain. The front part of the eyeball becomes milky white in appearance and one spot, usually near the center, red or copper-colored. At this point an abscess or small gathering usually forms, and looks to be a reddish, fleshy mass. It breaks, and discharges a small amount of pus or matter that escapes with the tears. As the animal recovers and the eye returns to its normal condition a white speck remains on the eyeball for a time as a scar, showing where the abscess existed. In a few cases this abscess weakens the front of the eye to such an extent that it bursts, and allows the contents of the anterior chamber of the eye to escape. A few of the cases where the eye bursts will heal and the animal will recover the sight, but in a majority of the cases the animal will be permanently blind in that eye. A few cases are reported where both eyes have burst and the animal was permanently blind in both eyes. During the acute stages of the disease, if both eyes are affected at the same time, the inflammation may be so severe as to cause a temporary blindness, the animals being unable to see at all, and it is necessary to feed and water them to prevent them falling away rapidly in flesh. If the animal has the disease in an acute form there is often some fever associated with the disease, and in practically all cases the cattle cease to ruminate, and will stand about with ears lopped and eyes closed, exhibiting all symptoms of severe suffering. Milch cows usually fall away in the amount of milk secreted, or in severe cases it may be stopped entirely. Owing to a closing of the eyes, together with the pain, animals do not eat well, especially while at pasture, and as a result fall away in flesh.

Since practically no animals die from the effects of this disease, and only a few are permanently affected by the loss of sight, the greatest loss is in the shrinkage of flesh that follows an attack of this disease.

Treatment.—If possible the disease should be prevented by keeping infected animals away from the healthy. After the disease is once introduced among a bunch of cattle, by separating and iso' lating the affected animals as soon as the first symptoms are shown, the disease can be checked. It is not practicable to attempt to treat a large number of animals, unless they should be especially valuable or suffer from the disease in a severe form. When it is advisable to treat an animal, it should be placed in a darkened stable, the eyes thoroughly washed with cold water, all secretions removed, and a solution of boric acid, twenty grains dissolved in an ounce of water, should be applied. A little ointment made by mixing one part of finely pulverized iodoform with twelve parts of fresh lard or vaseline, can be applied directly to the eyeball, by putting it on the inside of the eyelid, and gently rubbing it over the surface. Cloths wet with cold water and kept over the eyes are useful in reducing the inflammation. Practically all animals make a good recovery in three to four weeks.

Prevention.—Whenever this affection appears in a herd all the unaffected animals should be moved to another locality—that is, to fields which possess a different character of soil and feed. The water should also be changed, especially if they have been obtaining their drinking water from a stagnant pond.

KERATITIS (CORNEITIS).

This is an inflammation of the cornea proper, although the sclerotica at the corneal border becomes involved to some extent. It may be divided into diffuse and suppurative.

Causes.—The cornea constitutes the most prominent portion of the eyeball, hence it is subject to a variety of injuries—scratches, pricks, contusions, lacerations, etc. Inflammation of the cornea may also be due to the extension of catarrhal conjunctivitis or intraocular disease, and it may occasionally occur without any perceptible cause.

Symptoms.—Diffuse keratitis is characterized by an exudation into and an opacity of the cornea. The swelling of the anterior part of the eyeball may be of an irregular form, in points resembling small bladders, or it may commence at the periphery of the cornea by an abrupt thickening, which gradually diminishes as it approaches the center. If the whole cornea is affected it has a uniform gray or grayish white appearance. The flow of tears is not so marked as in conjunctivitis, nor is the suffering so acute, though both conditions often exist together. Both eyes usually become affected, unless it is due to an external injury.

In favorable cases the exudate within the cornea begins to disappear within a week or ten days, the eye becomes clearer, and regains its transparency, until it eventually is fully restored. In unfavorable cases blood vessels form and are seen to traverse the affected part from periphery to center, vision becomes entirely lost, and permanent opacity *(albugo* or *leucoma)* remains. When it arises from constitutional causes recurrence is frequent, leaving the corneal membrane more cloudy after each attack, until the sight is permanently lost.

Suppurative keratitis may be a sequel of diffuse keratitis; more commonly, however, it abruptly becomes manifest by a raised swelling on or near the center of the cornea that very soon assumes a yellow, turbid color, while the periphery of the swelling fades into an opaque ring. Suppurative keratitis is seldom noticed for the first day or two—not until distinct pus formation has occurred. When it is the result of diffuse keratitis, ulceration and the escape of the contained pus is inevitable; otherwise the pus may be absorbed. When the deeper membranes covering the anterior chamber of the eye become involved, the contents of this chamber may be evacuated and the sight permanently lost.

Treatment.—Place the animal in a darkened stable, give green or sloppy food, and administer 4 ounces of Glauber's salts (sulphate of soda) dissolved in a quart of water once a day. If the animal is debilitated a tablespoonful of tonic powder should be mixed with the feed three times a day. This may be composed of equal parts by weight of powdered copperas (sulphate of iron), gentian, and ginger. As an application for the eye nitrate of silver, 3 grains to the ounce of soft water, with the addition of 1 grain sulphate of morphia, may be used several times a day. If ulceration occurs, it is well to dust powdered calomel into the eye twice daily, or to the eyelids apply a salve of yellow oxide of mercury, 5 per cent in lanolin. Some of this may go onto the cornea and beneath the lids. Apply twice daily. (See below, Ulcers of the Cornea.)

To remove opacity, after the inflammation has subsided, apply a few drops of the following solution twice a day: Iodide of potassium, 15 grains; tincture sanguinaria, 20 drops; distilled water, 2 ounces; mix. Sometimes keratitis exists in a herd as a transmissible disease, spreading like infectious conjunctivitis. Calomel, applied to the eye, is especially useful in such cases.

ULCERS OF THE CORNEA.

An ulcer comes from erosion or is the consequence of the bursting of a small abscess, which may have formed beneath the delicate layer of the conjunctiva, continued over the cornea; or, in the very substance of the cornea itself, after violent keratitis, or catarrhal conjunctivitis. At other times the ulcer is produced by bruises, scratches, and other direct injury of the cornea.

Symptoms.—The ulcer is generally at first of a pale gray color, with its edges high and irregular, discharges instead of pus an acrid watery substance, and has a tendency to spread widely and deeply. If it spreads superficially upon the cornea, the transparency of this membrane is lost; if it proceeds deeply and penetrates the anterior chamber of the aqueous humor, this fluid escapes, the iris may prolapse, and the lens and the vitreous humor become expelled, thus producing a destruction of the whole organ.

Treatment.—It is of the greatest importance, as soon as an ulcer appears upon the cornea, to prevent its growing larger. The corroding process must be converted into a healthy one. For this purpose nothing is more reliable than the use of solid nitrate of silver. A stick of nitrate of silver should be scraped to a point; the animal's head should be firmly secured; an assistant should part the lids; if necessary the haw must be secured within the corner of the eye and then all parts of the ulcer should be lightly touched with the silver. After waiting a few minutes the eye should be thoroughly washed out with a very weak solution of common salt. This operation generally has to be repeated once more at the end of three or four days. If healthy action succeeds, the ulcer assumes a delicate fleshy tint, and the former redness around the ulcer disappears in proportion as the ulcer heals.

In superficial abrasions of the cornea, where there is no distinct excavation, this caustic treatment is not needed. The eye should be bathed with sulphate of zinc, 30 grains to half a pint of soft water, several times a day, and protected against exposure to cold air and sunlight. Excessive ulceration sometimes assumes the form of fungous excrescence upon the cornea, appearing to derive its nourishment from loops of blood vessels of the conjunctiva. Under these circumstances the fungoid mass must be cut away, and the wound cauterized with the nitrate of silver, or else the eye will soon be destroyed. When ulcers of the cornea appear indolent, with a tenency to slough, in addition to the treatment already prescribed, tonic powders should be given twice a day mixed with the feed; powdered copperas, gentian, and ginger, equal parts by weight. Dose, one tablespoonful.

CATARACT.

In cataract the crystalline lens becomes opaque and loses its transparency, the power of refraction is lost—the animal can not see.

Causes.—Cataract generally arises from a diminution (atrophy) or other change in the nutrition of the lens; it may occur as a result of inflammation of the deep structures of the eye. Cataract may be simple, or complicated with amaurosis, adhesions, etc.

Symptoms.—It is known by the whiteness or loss of transparency of the lens, although the pupil dilates and contracts. Sight may be totally lost; however, evidence is usually manifested that the animal distinguishes light when brought out of a darkened stable. For the most part the formation of cataract takes place slowly, the cases in which it originates very quickly being but few.

Treatment.—There is only one method for the treatment of cataract—a surgical operation for the removal of the lens; but this is not advisable, for the sight can not be perfectly restored, and objects would be seen imperfectly without the aid of glasses.

AMAUROSIS.

A paralysis of the nerve of sight or the expansion of the retina.

Causes.—This is the result of concussion from a blow upon the forehead, fracture of bone over the eye (causing downward pressure), rheumatic inflammation of the optic nerve, or from extension of deep inflammation of the eye involving the retina. It sometimes occurs as the result of excessive loss of blood or of great debility.

Symptoms.—In this disease seldom any observation is made until the animal in its gait and by its action indicates blindness. Generally both eyes are affected. The eyeball remains clear, and the pupil permanently dilated. No response to light is manifested.

Treatment.—If due to debility, loss of blood, or associated with rheumatism, general blood tonics may be given in the feed, namely, powdered sulphate of iron, 1 dram; gentian, 2 drams; nux vomica, one-half dram; to be given twice a day. In cases of rheumatism, one-half ounce of saltpeter may be added.

FILARIA OCULI (WORM IN THE EYE).

Filaria oculi (provisionally taken as the larva of *F. cervina*).— This is a small white worm, and is found in the eye, swimming in the aqueous fluid in the anterior chamber. It may be apparently harmless for a long time, but will eventually induce keratitis with inflammatory exudations.

Treatment.—The cornea may be punctured at its upper and outer margin, and the worm squeezed out with the aqueous humor. The latter will be formed again. This operation will result disastrously unless the greatest care and skill are employed.

TUMORS OF THE EYELIDS.

Occasionally tumors form upon or within the substance of the eyelid. These may be of a fibroid nature, and arise from the follicles of the hair as sebaceous tumors, or may be in the form of an abscess. In debilitating diseases the lids sometimes become swollen and puffy, a condition which might possibly be taken for the growth of a tumor. This generally disappears with the improvement of the health of the animal. Warts not uncommonly appear on or about the eyelids of cattle.

Treatment.—The removal of a tumor in the vicinity of so delicate an organ as the eye should not be attempted by anyone not qualified for the operation.

LACERATION OF THE EYELID.

This accident is not uncommon where cattle are fenced in by barbed wire; an animal may be caught under the eyelid by the horn of another; it may occur in the stable by means of a projecting nail or splinter of wood.

Treatment.—The edges of the wound should be brought together closely and correctly, by means of pins pushed through very nearly the whole thickness of the lid, extending through each lip of the torn part; then a waxed silk or linen thread must be wound over each end of the pin, crossing the torn line in the form of the figure

8; the pins should be placed about three-eighths of an inch apart. The projecting ends of the pins should be cut off close to the ligature, and the parts kept anointed with vaseline, to which has been added 5 per cent of creolin. In place of a pin suture, silver wire, catgut, or strong linen thread may be used in the way of an ordinary suture.

FOREIGN BODIES IN THE EYE.

Splinters of wood, hedge thorns, pieces of cornstalk or leaves, stems of hay or straw, twigs of trees, or weeds may penetrate into the eye, break off and remain, causing inflammation, blindness, abscess, etc. These substances may penetrate the eyeball, but more frequently they glide off and enter between the eye and the ocular sheath.

Treatment.—Their removal becomes often a very difficult task, from the fact that the organ is so extremely sensitive, and the retracting power so strong as to necessitate casting the animal, or even the administration of sufficient chloroform to render it completely insensible. The removal, however, is of paramount importance, and the after treatment depends upon the extent and location of the injury—cold water compress over the injured eye, the application of mild astringent and cooling washes, such as acetate or sulphate of zinc, 5 grains to the ounce of water. When there is extreme suffering from pain a 5 per cent solution of atropia or morphia, 5 grains to the ounce of water, may be dropped into the eye, alternating with the cooling wash several times a day. When abscesses form within the orbit a free opening must be maintained for the discharge of pus. In deep penetrating wounds of the eye there is a great tendency to the formation of a fungus growth, which often necessitates the enucleation of the whole eyeball.

FRACTURE OF THE ORBIT.

This accident occasionally occurs among belligerent animals, or as the result of blows delivered by brutal attendants. The orbital process above the eye may be entirely crushed in, pressing down upon the eyeball. In such an event the depressed bone should be elevated into its proper place, and if it fails to unite it may have to be removed with saw or chisel. This margin of the orbit may be crushed at any point and cause periorbital abscess, or necrosis may result from the presence of a splinter or bone or the excessive destruction of the bone. In all cases of fracture the animal should be taken out of the herd and kept by itself until the injured part heals.

DISLOCATION OF THE EYEBALL.

The eyeball may be torn out of its socket by the horns of another animal in a fight, or it may be crowded out with the blunt end of a club, cane, or probe in the hands of a brutal attendant.

Treatment.—When the optic nerve is not lacerated and the retractor muscles at the back of the eye are intact, an attempt at reduction is advisable. This, however, must follow very soon after the injury—before swelling takes place. Divide the outer corner of the eyelid to enlarge the orifice, then by pressure with the fingers of both hands placed upon the sides of the eye the ball may be put back into its place. Apply a firm compress over the injured eye and keep it constantly wet with cold water containing 1 dram of sugar of lead to each quart.

If the attempt at reduction proves unsuccessful the artery at the back of the eye should be ligated, and then the whole mass cut off as deep within the orbit as possible. The orbital cavity should be packed daily with fresh absorbent cotton after washing it out with a 3 per cent solution of carbolic acid or 10 cent dilution of creolin.

INFLAMMATION AND ENLARGEMENT OF THE HAW.

The haw, or membrana nictitans, is subject to inflammation and swelling from the extension of conjunctivitis, or direct injury by foreign substances. It presents a red, swollen appearance, accompanied by considerable pain and a profuse flow of tears. A slight scarification with a sharp knife and the application of a cooling lotion, such as recommended for conjunctivitis, will soon reduce the swelling and restore it to its normal function.

There is, however, a tendency for an inflammation of this membrane to take on a chronic character, which may eventually result in a permanent enlargement, resembling a tumor. When it attains sufficient size to protrude itself permanently over the eye, or project between the lids so as to obstruct the sight, its removal may become necessary. A threaded needle is passed through the body of the enlarged mass, by which the membrane is drawn out as far as possible, then with a blunt pair of scissors it may be dissected away from its attachments. The eye is afterwards treated with simple cooling lotions.

THE EAR AND ITS DISEASES.

Diseases of the ears of cattle are not very common, for the reasons, probably, that they are not subjected to the brutality of drivers so much as horses and that the horns to a great extent protect them against external violence.

OTITIS (INFLAMMATION OF THE INTERNAL EAR).

Inflammation of the deep part of the ear is often difficult to recognize in cattle. It may be caused by disease of bone in that region, from blows inflicted by drivers, or from injury by other cattle. Occasionally the ear becomes involved in actinomycosis, or the inflammation may be the result of a tuberculous affection.

Symptoms.—The animal will hold its head to one side, or shake it, while the ear itself is held immovable. The movement of the jaws in eating usually gives rise to a manifestation of pain; the base of the ear may be feverish and swollen, and very sensitive to the touch. If the inflammation has advanced to the suppurative stage, matter will flow from the ear, which generally emits a very offensive odor.

Treatment.—At first hot fomentations to reduce pain and fever, followed by a sharp blister below the ear. Laudanum, 1 part to 10 parts of sweet oil, may be injected into the ear to relieve pain and to soften the secretions. If there is a discharge from the ear, it should be washed thoroughly out by injecting warm soapsuds until all the matter has been washed away; then inject the following mixture twice a day: Sulphate of morphia, 20 grains; water, 1 pint; glycerin, 4 ounces.

ABSCESS.

Abscesses sometimes form about the base of the ear, either inside or outside, caused by contusions. A serous cyst is found occasionally between the cartilage and the skin on the base of the ear, which may be due to a similar cause.

Treatment.—Make a free incision with the knife into the most prominent part of the abscess or cyst, then wash out the sac with carbolized water, using a syringe for the purpose. If the abscess recurs, open it again, wash it out, and inject tincture of iodin, or fill it with iodoform.

FUNGOID GROWTHS.

As a result of laceration or wound of any kind, fungous growths may develop on the ear, characterized by a raw, bleeding, granulating surface, with a tendency to become pendulous.

Treatment.—The whole tumor or diseased structure should be cut away, and the wound treated daily with a dressing of carbolized cosmoline or turpentine and sweet oil, 1 part of the former to 4 of the latter.

FOREIGN BODIES IN THE EAR.

Bugs have been known to gain entrance into the ear of an animal. I once removed an acorn from the ear of a cow that had been roaming in the woods. Accidentally, pieces of wood from a stanchion may become lodged in the ear.

Symptoms.—A continuous uneasiness or frequent shaking of the head, occasionally the manifestations of exceeding great pains. The animal may rub the head and ear against trees or other objects in an endeavor to dislodge the offending body.

Treatment.—A careful examination will reveal the offending cause, which may be removed with a pair of forceps or scraped out with a hairpin or piece of wire bent at one end. If much inflammation exists, the ear may be swollen so that the foreign substance will be hidden from sight; then a probe may be inserted to feel for the object, which, when located, should be removed, even if it becomes necessary to split the ear at the base to do so. Afterwards treat the ear with frequent warm water fomentations and the injection of soapy water or oil and water.

SCURFY EARS.

Cattle are subject to scurfy ears, which may be due to a general morbid condition of the skin, or may be confined to the ears alone. The affected animal shows an inclination to rub the ear; thick scales of scurf collect on it, which sometimes have the appearance of hard, dry, horny scales. This condition is chiefly due to a faulty secretion of the sebaceous glands of the ear. Thoroughly clean the ear with a stiff brush, then anoint it, so far as affected, with vaseline 4 parts to 1 part of white precipitate ointment. If the scurfy ears are only a part of general scurfiness of the skin, the condition of the animal needs attention. (See Pityriasis, page 413.)

FROSTBITE.

It is not uncommon among young cattle which are poorly nourished and exposed outdoors to storms and extreme cold to suffer frostbite of the ear, which may constitute actual freezing of the part.

Symptoms.—Frostbite presents naturally every degree of severity from the mere chilling of the tip of the ear to positive freezing and death of a portion. In a day or two after the freezing has occurred the ear will become swollen and very painful; the dead part will remain cold and begin to shrivel; a line of separation then forms between the inflamed and the dead or dying portion, and finally the piece destroyed drops off, leaving a raw healing surface. When the ear is only slightly affected by the cold, an excoriation or peeling off of superficial skin takes place, accompanied by some pain and itching.

Treatment.—A good liniment for frozen ears will be found in a mixture of turpentine, ammonia, and chloroform, of each 1 part, added to 6 parts of sweet oil. Rub this on the ear several times a day. It will relieve pain and stimulate the circulation, thus favoring a recovery of the injured structures.

LACERATIONS OF THE EAR.

Aggressive dogs are the most frequent cause of lacerated ear, generally leaving a torn, ragged edge and bruised cartilage.

Treatment.—If the wound is extensive a trimming of the ragged edges becomes necessary; then fasten the edges together with silver wire, catgut, or strong, thick, linen thread, taking a deep hold. Apply pine tar.

DISEASE OF THE CARTILAGE AND NECROSIS.

Occasionally the cartilages of the ear become affected, usually the result of a deep bruise; pus forms, which burrows under the skin, and may find a discharge from any part of the ear more or less distant from the seat of the disease. When the cartilage has been extensively injured, pieces of it may become dead (necrosed) and dissolve, to be carried away with the pus, or it may lead to extensive sloughing and the formation of numerous running sores. In the disease of the cartilage there is seldom much swelling or great pain. The discharge is usually very offensive, and occasionally streaked with blood. Whenever there is a long-continued, persistent discharge from one or more openings in the ear, disease of the cartilage may be suspected.

Treatment.—The sinus formed by the passage of matter should be probed and searched to the bottom for the presence of a foreign substance or the evidence of decaying cartilage. When the probe touches necrosed cartilage it will feel like the presence of a piece of dry leather or partially softened wood. A counter opening must then be made at this place, and all diseased cartilage cut away with the knife. The subsequent treatment consists in keeping the artificial wound open for the discharge of pus, and the injection of chloride of zinc, 5 grains to the ounce of water, once or twice a day, until the wound is healed.

ENCHONDROMA OF THE EAR.

This is an excessive growth of cartilage, found at the base of the ear in the form of a hard, painless tumor, firmly attached to the mov-

Texas Cattle. B. A. I. 1899.

able ear. The only recourse for its removal is the knife in the hands of one acquainted with the anatomy of the part involved in the operation.

TUMORS AFFECTING CATTLE.

[*Synonyms:* New growth, neoplasm, neoformation, pseudoplasm, swelling, and hyperplasia.]

Definition.—Tumors* are abnormal masses of tissue, noninflammatory and independent in character, arising, without obvious cause, from cells of pre-existent tissue, possessing no physiologic function, and characteristically unrestrained in growth and structure.

Tumors are abnormal masses of tissue. The application of the term "tumor" is directly connected with the fact that they produce local enlargement. They are noninflammatory; that is, the process of inflammation is not directly the cause or accompaniment of them. An inflammatory new growth tends to disappear upon the subsidence of the inflammatory process, while spontaneous disappearance of a tumor is comparatively rare.

Tumors are independent. For instance, their nutrition bears no relation to the nutrition of the body. A lipoma, or fatty tumor, in the subcutaneous tissue may go on increasing to huge bulk while the body is steadily emaciating. Again, the tissues of the aged gradually undergo atrophy, yet cancers arise at this time and grow rapidly. They are unrestrained in growth and structure. In the development of an animal we know at what period of its existence the mass of tissue called liver will develop—what its site, structure, and size will be. We know that it will remain only in that locality, and not, as it were, colonize throughout the system. With tumors it is different; there are no laws by which we can forecast the time, place, nature, or size of development of them. There is no cartilage in the kidney or parotid gland, yet a chondroma, or cartilage tumor, may develop in either. Even when a new growth of tissue is started by an injury and consequent inflammation—as, for instance, proud flesh—there is a limitation of its size. But the controlling influences which govern the size of an organ or normal mass of tissue and limit the extent of an inflammatory overgrowth are all absent in the case of tumors.

Tumors arise without obvious cause. Concerning the ultimate cause of tumor formation we are absolutely ignorant. Various theories have been advanced from time to time, but none of them have been applicable to more than a limited number of cases.

Diagnosis.—In the diagnosis of tumors note is taken of clinical history and examination of the tumor.

---

*The term "tumor" literally means a swelling, and thus has been applied to the prominence caused by an overdistended bladder, to the enlargement of pregnancy, to the swelling produced by an abscess, to the overgrowth of tissue (hyperplasia) associated with injury and consequent inflammation, and to numerous other phases of tissue enlargement directly connected with recognized disease processes. For this reason it is becoming more common for scientists to apply the word "neoplasm" to the new growths described in this chapter. Because of the still popular use of the word "tumor," it is retained in this chapter for the designation of those new growths to which the sevenfold characterization of our descriptive definition applies.

Clinical History.—Circumstances connected with the origin of the tumor and its rapidity of growth may point to an inflammatory swelling rather than a tumor. The location of the tumor at its commencement is important, as, for instance, in diagnosing between lipoma and carcinoma, the former being more or less movable under the skin, while a carcinoma develops in the skin. While tenderness on pressure may be caused by compression of a sensitive nerve by a tumor or by tumors of the nerve or nerve sheaths, as a rule this symptom is indicative of inflammatory swelling rather than the existence of a tumor.

Direct Examination of the Tumor.—In the application of this diagnosis the trained observer will note color, size, shape, and surface structure, transmission of light, movableness, consistence, resistance, pulsation, and crepitation. Percussion, auscultation, and exploration are also available methods. Finally, microscopic examination of the growing portions of the tumor by a pathologist will be found most satisfactory.

GENERAL TREATMENT OF TUMORS.

For benign tumors treatment is required only when it damages the animal's value or when merely for sake of appearance. When it is possible, the removal of the tumor by an operation is indicated. If the tumor has a small constricted base, remove by tortion, ligation, or with an écraseur. Ligation following the incision of the skin with a knife avoids the pain of pressing on the sensitive nerves of the skin and is suitable for tumors of broad base and small bodies. A firing iron, such as is used in line or feather firing, may also be used in removing tumors with small attachments. This not only stops the bleeding, but forms a firm scab under which healing may occur rapidly. Those tumors that can not be removed by the above methods may be treated with caustics or acids, such as sulphuric acid, hydrochloric acid, caustic potash, arsenic, silver nitrate, or chromic acid, but it is difficult to limit the action of these drugs. The injection into the tumor of certain chemicals, such as analine dyes, alcohol, acetic acid, citric acid, or ergotine is of doubtful value, as is also the injection of the germs of erysipelas—thought by some to be a specific. Certain specific tumors, such as actinomycosis and botryomycosis, may be successfully treated by the internal administration of potassium iodid, together with the injection into the tumor or the painting of its surface with Lugol's solution or the tincture of iodin. The most reliable means of treating tumors is by extirpation with cutting instruments. Dissect the tumor from the surrounding tissue, ligating all the larger blood vessels, and tearing the tissues with the fingers rather than cutting with a knife. The bleeding may be stopped with a hot iron. The after-treatment is the same as for any ordinary wound of similar size.

BONES: DISEASES AND ACCIDENTS.

Some knowledge of the skeleton is advisable to facilitate the study of diseases of bones and the accidental injuries to which they are exposed. The skeleton of the adult ox is made up of the following number of bones:

Spinal column	45	
Head	28	
Chest	27	
Shoulder	2—	1 on each side.
Arm	2—	1 on each side.
Fore arm	4—	2 on each side.
Fore foot	40—	20 on each side.
Pelvis	2—	1 on each side.
Thigh	2—	1 on each side.
Leg	6—	3 on each side.
Hind foot	38—	19 on each side.
Total	196	

Without attempting to burden the reader with the technical names and a scientific classification of each, it appears desirable to describe some of the characteristics of forms in general, and of a few classes into which they may be divided. In the early fetal life the place of bone is supplied by temporary cartilage, which gradually changes to bone. For convenience of study, bones may be said to be composed of a dense form of connective tissue impregnated with lime salts and contain two elementary constituents—the organic, or animal, and the inorganic, or earthy. In young animals the former predominates; with increasing years the relative proportions of the two change, so that when advanced age is reached the proportion of inorganic far exceeds the organic. The gradual change with advancing years from organic to inorganic has the effect of rendering the bone harder and more brittle, and though it is stronger the reparative process is slower when injury does occur.

The bones are nourished in two ways: First, from the outside through their covering, called the periosteum—the thin, strong membrane that covers every part of the bone except the articular surface of the joints—and, second, from within through the minute branches of blood vessels which pass into the bones through holes (foramen) on their surface and are distributed in the soft structure (medulla) of the inside. The structure of the bone is divided into two parts—the compact or hard material of the outside, which gives strength and is more abundant in the shafts of long bones, and the cancellated softer tissue of the inside, which affords accommodation to the blood vessels necessary for the nourishment of that part of the structure.

In shape bones are divided into three classes—long, flat, and short. The long bones are the ribs and those mostly found in the limbs; the flat bones are found in the head, the shoulder, and the pelvis; and the short bones in the spinal column and in the lower portions of the limbs. With this little introduction, which seems almost indispensable, we will proceed at once to the consideration of diseases of bones, for they undergo diseased processes like any other living tissue.

OSTEITIS.

Inflammation of the compact structure of bones (osteitis) may be either acute or chronic, and may involve the whole extent of the bone affected or may be confined to only a portion of it. This inflammation results from injury, such as concussion, laceration, or a crushing bruise; also from specific influences, as in actinomycosis or cases of foul foot. The latter affection frequently involves the bones, and for this reason the pastern is the most frequent seat of osteitis. There is dull pain on pressure and a painful swelling of bone when pus is present. Suppuration may involve the overlying soft tissues, causing an abscess, which may finally break through the skin. The inflammatory condition sometimes assumes an ulcerated form (caries) or from interrupted nutrition of the part deprived of the blood necessary to its nourishment may cause death of a large section of bone (necrosis), and this dead fragment (sequestrum), becoming separated from the main portion of bone, acts as a foreign body.

Treatment.—This consists in resting the affected part and in giving vent at the earliest possible moment to whatever pus may be present. Free drainage should then be maintained. Apply dressings of lactic acid or inject with 5 per cent zinc chloride solution and pack with tampons of cotton soaked in antiseptic solutions. A laxative is the only internal treatment necessary.

PERIOSTITIS.

This disease is an inflammation of the external covering of bone (periosteum) and is usually produced by wounds, pressure, or crushing of the part. The periosteum is well supplied with sensitive nerve endings and when inflamed is very sensitive to pressure and may cause lameness. This condition is often difficult to determine, and even an acute observer may fail to locate the point of its existence. There are three forms of periostitis—aseptic, purulent, and fibrous.

ASEPTIC PERIOSTITIS.

Aseptic periostitis when it becomes chronic causes such a bony enlargement (exostosis) as is seen in the callous formation following the fracture of a bone. The formation of such a tumor or enlargement on the surface of a bone is liable to occur in any part of the bone covered with periosteum, and when found in the neighborhood of a joint involving two or more bones it is likely to result in their union (anchylosis).

Treatment.—Applications of cold water to check the inflammatory processes are indicated for the first few days in aseptic periostitis, followed by hot fomentations to hurry resorption of fluids. Massage should then be given with camphor ointment, mercurial ointment, soap liniment, or Lugol's solution. In the chronic form point firing or a biniodide of mercury blister will be found beneficial.

PURULENT PERIOSTITIS.

Purulent periostitis follows wounds which reach the periosteum and become infected, as observed in compound fractures, or it may result from advancing purulent conditions in neighboring structures, as in foul foot. It may also occur in the course of an infectious disease, when small abscesses are formed under the periosteum (subperiosteal abscess). It may lead to necrosis of the bone or a fistulous track from the bone to the surface. There is usually much pain and fever present, and the odor from the wound is offensive.

Treatment.—In this form of periostitis the periosteum should be freely incised, followed either by continuous irrigation or frequent injection of the wound with antiseptic solutions.

FIBROUS PERIOSTITIS.

This form of the disease consists in the thickening of the outer layer of the periosteum from the inflammation reaching it from neighboring structures. This newly formed fibrous tissue may become ossified or may transmit the inflammation to the deeper bony structures. It is frequently seen in cases where there has been an intense inflammation of the skin close to an underlying bone.

Treatment.—The treatment should follow that recommended for aseptic periostitis.

RICKETS.

This disease, also called rachitis, is an inflammatory affection of young, growing bones, and involves the ribs and long bones of the legs mostly. It consists in a failure of the organism to deposit lime salts in bone, and for this reason the bones do not ossify as rapidly as they should. The cartilaginous ends of the bones grow rapidly, but ossification does not keep pace with it. The bones become long and their ends bend at the joints, the legs become crooked, and the joints are large and irregular. All the bones affected with this disease are thicker than normal, and the gait of the animal is stiff and painful. A row of bony enlargements may be found where the ribs articulate with the cartilages connecting them with the breastbone and is called the beaded line. A catarrhal condition of the digestive tract is usually observed. The disease may result from an inherited weakness of constitution, poor hygienic surroundings, or improper diet. Calves and foals are less frequently affected with rickets than dogs and pigs.

Treatment.—The affected animal should be given nourishing food containing a proper amount of lime salts. Outdoor exercise and plenty of fresh air are indispensable. Limewater should be given once daily for drinking purposes and ground bone meal mixed with the food. Phosphorus, one-fortieth of a grain, and calcium phosphate, 1 dram, given twice daily to a 2-months-old calf, and proportionally increased for older animals, has proved efficacious in this disease. In some cases the long bones of the limbs are too weak at birth to support the weight of the animal and temporary splints, carefully padded and wrapped on with some soft bandages, become necessary.

OSTEOMALACIA (CREEPS).

This is a condition of bone brittleness or softening of bone found usually in adult life. It consists of the decalcification of mature bone, with the advancing diminution of the compact portion of bone by absorption. The periosteum strips very easily from the bone. This disease is seen in milch cows during the period of heavy lactation or in the later stages of pregnancy, and the greater the yield of milk the more rapid the progress of the disease. Heifers with their first calf are frequently affected, as these animals require a considerable quantity of animal salts for their own growth and for the nourishment of their calves.

Symptoms.—In marked cases there is a gradual emaciation and symptoms of gastro-intestinal catarrh, with depraved appetite, the animal eating manure, decayed wood, dirt, leather, etc. Muscular weakness is prominent, together with muscle tremors, which simulate chills, but are not accompanied by any rise of temperature. The animal has a stiff, laborious gait, there is pain and swelling of the joints, and a constant shifting of the weight from one leg to another. The restricted movements of the joints are frequently accompanied by a crackling sound, which has caused the name of creeps to be applied to the disease. The coat is dull and rough and the skin dry and hidebound. The animal is subject to frequent sprains or fracture of bones without apparent cause, as in lying down or turning around, and when such fractures occur they are difficult to unite. The bones principally involved are the upper bones of the legs, the haunch bone, and the middle bones of the spinal column. The disease in this country is confined to localized areas in the Southwest, known as the alkali districts, and in the old dairy sections of New York. The cause of this affection is the insufficiency or total absence of lime salts in the food, also to feeding hay of low, damp pastures, kitchen slops, and potatoes, or to overstocking lands. It occurs on old, worn-out soil devoid of lime salts, and has also been observed to follow a dry season.

Treatment.—This should consist in a change of food and the artificial feeding of lime salts, such as magnesium and sodium phosphate. Foods containing mineral salts may be given, such as beans, cowpeas, oats, cotton-seed meal, or wheat bran. Cotton-seed meal is one of the best foods for this purpose, but it should be fed carefully, as too large quantities are injurious to cows. Phosphorus may also be given in one-fourth grain doses twice daily, together with a tablespoonful of powdered bone meal or crude calcium phosphate at each meal. Ordinary lime dissolved in drinking water (limewater) will also be found efficacious in combating this disease, and can be provided at slight expense. A change of pasture to a locality where the disease is unknown and a free supply of common salt and bone meal will be the most convenient method of treating range cattle.

SPRAINS.

The most common accident occurring to bones and joints is a sprain of the ligaments uniting the bones, or the tendons uniting the muscles and bones. A sprain is the result of a sudden forcing of a joint in an unnatural direction; or, if in a natural direction, beyond the power of the ligament or tendon to restrain it properly, so that part of the fibers of either are ruptured. When such an accident occurs pain is immediately inflicted, varying in degree with the extent of the injury, which is soon followed by swelling, with more or less heat and tenderness. If the seat of the injury be in any of the limbs, lameness is likely to result. Of the causes of sprain, slipping on ice or a wet floor, playing, or fighting with another animal are the most common.

SPRAIN OF THE SHOULDER JOINT.

This is likely to occur from any of the causes mentioned above or from the animal slipping suddenly into a rut or hole. When such an accident occurs, sudden lameness will attract attention. The animal will be noticed to drag the leg when walking and to carry it in a circular direction, outward and forward, at each step. The leg should be carefully examined, pressure over the joint causing the animal to evince pain. If the person making the examination is in doubt, it is well to make a comparison between the shoulders by pressing first on one and then the other. After such an accident the animal should be tied up so as to limit so far as possible the use of the injured joint. Soft food should be given with a view to keeping the bowels acting freely.

Treatment.—During the first three days the treatment should consist of cold-water irrigation to check the inflammation and relieve the pain. Hot fomentations may then be applied to hasten the absorption of the inflammatory fluids. When the pain has somewhat abated, equal parts of mercurial ointment and green soap may be rubbed into the swollen tissue. Should lameness continue after the tenth day, good results will be obtained from the application of a blister. This may be done by carefully clipping the hair off over a joint, including a surface of 4 or 5 inches in circumference, and rubbing in the following preparation:

Powdered cantharides	dram..	1
Biniodide of mercury	dram..	1
Vaseline	ounce..	1

The animal's head should be carefully tied until the third day, to prevent its licking the blister. The blistered surface should then be smeared with lard or vaseline every other day until the scabs fall off. Gentle exercise should be allowed after the fourth or fifth day from the application of the blister. If the lameness still remains the blister may be repeated in three weeks or a month.

SPRAIN OF THE FETLOCK.

This may occur from misstep when the animal is moving rapidly, and the twisting or wrenching of the foot is sufficient to rupture partially the ligaments which bind the bones together at that part. Such an accident also frequently occurs by the foot becoming fastened in a hole in the floor, and the wrenching is the result of the animal's attempt to liberate it. Lameness, followed by swelling of the joint and pain when it is handled, or when the animal moves the joint, and heat, are the more noticeable symptoms. If the sprain be very severe the animal occasionally does not bear its weight on the limb.

Treatment.—The most important consideration in the treatment of this affection is rest, which is best enforced by keeping the animal in the stall and placing strong muslin bandages about the inflamed joint. As in the sprain of the shoulder, cold water in the form of douches, continuous irrigation with hose or soaking tub, or finely chopped ice poultices is indicated for the first three days. Following this apply a Preissnitz bandage* moderately tight about the joint, which not only conduces to rest, but also favors absorption. Massage later with stimulating liniments, such as soap or camphor.

If the lameness has not disappeared by the tenth day, the blister advised for the sprain of the shoulder should be applied, and the same precautions observed as to tying the animal's head and subsequent smearing with vaseline. When a blister is applied in this locality, the back part of the heel should be first filled with lard or vaseline, and care taken to prevent any of the blistering preparation from coming in contact with the skin of that part. If this precaution is not observed, scratches may ensue and prove troublesome.

SPRAIN OF THE HIP.

This is likely to result from the animal slipping in such a way as to spread the hind feet wide apart. The patient goes stiff with the hind legs, or lame with one hind leg, walking with a straddling gait and swinging the leg outward as it is carried forward. Tenderness may occasionally be detected on pressure, but owing to the heavy covering of muscles outside of the joint this test is not always reliable.

In the acute cases, give rest and cold local application. After the fourth or fifth day the blister mentioned for sprain of the shoulder may be applied with advantage, and if this proves insufficient, we may fire in points over the joint as a last resort.

SPRAIN OF THE BACK.

Sprain of the back, particularly in the region of the loins, is not an uncommon accident among cattle. It is likely to occur from the animal slipping with both hind feet sideways so as to twist the back, or the feet slipping violently backward so that great stress is thrown on the loins. The patient moves with difficulty, using the hind parts in a guarded manner as if afraid of causing severe pain. Occasionally, if the sprain is severe, the animal will rise with difficulty. Pressure on the back in the immediate region of the loins causes pain. Such cases may be mistaken for paralysis, and, in fact, in severe cases, although the nerve supply is not interfered with, the injury to the muscles and resulting pain is so great that the condition is almost equal to paralysis during the early stages of the injury, although likely to be attended with more favorable results. Hot applications, such as blankets wrung out of hot water and changed at short intervals, will be likely to afford relief during the earlier stages. Afterwards the blister mentioned for sprain of the shoulder may be applied with advantage.

---

*A Preissnitz bandage is a dressing which combines the three properties of keeping a part warm, moist, and subjecting it to uniform pressure. It consists of three layers of material. The inner layer is composed of absorbent cotton or some other material which is capable of holding moisture. This is soaked in water and wrapped around the part. The second layer consists of a substance which is impervious to moisture as oiled silk or oiled paper, and is applied about the inner layer to prevent evaporation. The third or outside layer is composed of a flannel or woolen bandage to prevent the radiation of heat and thus keep the moist inner layer at the temperature of the body.

FRACTURES (BROKEN BONES).

Bones may be accidentally broken in many ways and from different causes. Fractures in general are likely to be produced by external force suddenly and violently applied, either directly to the part or at a distance, the force being transmitted through the stronger bones until it expends itself by breaking a weaker one remote from the seat of the injury. Occasionally violent contraction of muscles is sufficient to break a bone. Certain bones, those of the limbs in particular, are more liable to fracture than others, owing to their exposed position. The bones of some animals are more easily fractured than those of others, owing to certain predisposing causes, such as age, habit, or hereditary constitutional weakness. The bones of an animal advanced in years are more subject to fracture because of the preponderance of inorganic matter rendering them more brittle. They are also occasionally rendered liable to fracture by a previously existing diseased condition. Fractures are divided into four classes —partial, simple, compound, and comminuted.

PARTIAL FRACTURES.

Partial fractures are those which are likely to occur in a young animal in which the preponderance of animal matter or the semicartilaginous condition of the bone renders it tough, so that even when considerable force is applied the bone bends, breaking on the side opposite that to which the force was applied, after the manner in which a green stick would bend and break.

SIMPLE FRACTURES.

Simple fracture is one in which the bone is severed in two parts, either transversely, longitudinally, or obliquely, without serious injury to the adjoining structures.

COMPOUND FRACTURES.

Compound fracture is one in which there is an open wound permitting the air to communicate with the ends of the broken bones.

COMMINUTED FRACTURES.

Comminuted fracture is one in which the bone is shattered or divided into a number of fragments.

COMPLICATED FRACTURES.

Complicated fracture is one where other structures surrounding the bones are injured.

GENERAL SYMPTOMS OF FRACTURE.

When a fracture of one or more of the large bones of a limb occurs, symptoms are sure to be well marked. After the accident the animal refuses to touch the foot to the ground and, if compelled to move, does so with great pain and reluctance. There is more or less shortening of the limb, with trembling of the muscles in the vicinity of the injury; deformity, and increased mobility, so that, instead of the natural joints of the limb and the natural muscular control of their motion, a new joint is formed where the fracture occurred, over which the animal has no control. As the leg hangs dependent from the body, shortened by the ends of the bones being forced past one another from the muscular contraction which invariably takes place, it swings in an awkward and unnatural manner, permitting the toe and foot to assume positions in their relations to other parts of the body which otherwise would be impossible. If the fractured bone is so situated that the parts may be moved one upon another, a grating sound, known as crepitus, will be observed.

GENERAL TREATMENT OF FRACTURES.

When a fracture occurs, the advisability of attempting treatment must first be determined. If the animal be young, valuable, and of reasonably quiet temperament, and the fracture not too great in extent, the chances of recovery are fair. On the other hand, if the animal should be of little value, irritable, advanced in years, and the fracture a serious compound or comminuted one, the wiser course would generally be to put the creature out of its misery. Having determined to attempt treatment, no time should be lost in restoring the parts as nearly as possible to their natural position and retaining them there. If the ends of the bones have been drawn past one another, they should, by firm and continuous tension, be drawn out until they again assume the position in which they were before the accident. All this can better be done before the swelling (which is sure to result) takes place. If the swelling has occurred before the injury is noticed, do not attempt to treat it, but proceed at once to treat the fracture as though the swelling were not present, for no step can be taken toward recovery until the ends of the bone have been restored to their proper position. When that is done and proper appliances have been used to prevent them from being again misplaced, the swelling, which is the result of irritation, will be relieved. In selecting the appliances to be used in the treatment of fracture the judgment and ingenuity of the operator are of much importance. Splints, made of wood shaped to fit the limb and padded with soft material where they come in contact with bony prominences, and held in position by means of bandages, are the oldest method, and with some are still the most popular. The fracture pads used in human surgery, and for sale in surgical depots, are very convenient. After being dipped in water they may be molded to fit the limb and be retained by means of bandages. Heavy sole leather is also used after being soaked in warm water and molded to the shape of the limb and holes cut in it to fit over any sharp irregularities in the natural shape of the bones. Gutta-percha sheets are also used and answer well. They are prepared and used in the same way as the leather.

Another and perhaps the simplest of all methods is the application of a plaster of Paris bandage, which is made as follows: Strips of thin cheese cloth 3 inches wide and 8 or 9 feet long are laid flat on a board and on them is spread a layer of plaster of Paris about one-eighth of an inch thick, then, starting at one end, roll carefully so as to gather the plaster in between the layers of the bandage. It is of course important that the cloth be thin and the plaster of Paris fresh and active. After preparing four or five of such bandages the operator is ready to dress the fracture, which, after the parts have been brought into position, should be done by covering all that part of the limb to which the plaster of Paris bandage is to be applied with a single layer of the dry bandage, letting it extend both above and below the part to which the plaster of Paris bandage is to be applied and including under the folds of the dry bandage at each end a layer of absorbent cotton, which is intended to form a pad to prevent the ends of the plaster of Paris bandage from chafing the skin beneath. When this is done one of the plaster of Paris bandages should be placed in a vessel of water and allowed to remain till the air bubbles have ceased to rise from it, which will generally indicate that it is soaked through. Then, taking it in the hand, wind it carefully around and around the limb, unrolling the bandage as it is wound around the limb, occasionally smoothing down the plaster of Paris. Should it form roughly or in ridges, the hand may be dipped in water to impart increased moisture to it. When about finished with one bandage, place another in the water, so that the winding operation may be continued without delay. The bandages should be applied till the cast is from one-half to three-quarters of an inch thick, then gently restrain the animal for one-half or three-quarters of an hour till the plaster is hardened. Any of the appliances used should be so manipulated as to prevent absolutely any motion of the detached parts. If the fracture is near a joint, it is generally best to include the joint in the appliance. The part of the limb below the bandage should be carefully and firmly wrapped with an ordinary cotton bandage all the way from the plaster bandage down to the hoof. This last bandage will tend to prevent swelling, which is likely to occur, the result of the dependent position in which the animal is forced by nature to keep the injured limb.

When plaster of Paris bandages are applied to a compound fracture, the injured part may be previously dressed with a small, thick pad of cotton immediately over the wound. In applying the bandage the operator may with a little care so arrange it as to keep the folds of the bandages off the cotton, or have only a thin layer over it, which may be easily cut out and the cotton removed, leaving a convenient opening through which to dress the wound without removing the bandage. The ends of the bandage or other appliance should be carefully watched to see that the skin does not become chafed, particularly at the lower end. If the bandage should become weak or broken at any part, it may be strengthened without removal by applying other bandages immediately over it. If swelling has taken place before the bandage has been applied, there is likely to be some loosening as it disappears, and even without the swelling there is likely to be a tendency of the bandage to slide downward. This may be overcome by fastening it to a suspender attached to a surcingle or passed over the body and attached to the opposite leg. If the looseness can not be overcome in this way, the space may be filled by pouring in a thin paste of plaster of Paris. A better method, however, is to remove the bandage and apply another. Owing to the hardness of the bandage it will be removed with some difficulty. A deep groove should be cut down completely through it on the opposite sides. This may be done with a chisel and a small hammer, if the bandage is carefully held by an assistant so that the concussion of the

blows is not transmitted to the injured bones. The patient shoul[d]
have a roomy stall and should be tied by the head to prevent any a[t]-
tempts to move around. In some cases slings have been used. Ord[i]-
narily, however, they are not satisfactory in cattle practice, and if a[p]-
plied should only be for a few days at a time and with a view to lesse[n]
the animal's disposition to lie down, rather than to prevent it. Whe[n]
they are used continuously, the pressure on the abdomen is likely [to]
interfere with digestion and the general health of the animal.

Modes of Union.—The animal should be kept as quiet as poss[i]-
ble and given such food as will have a tendency to keep the bowe[l]
slightly relaxed. The success of the operation will depend chiefly o[n]
the skill of the operator, but not alone in the selection and use of t[he]
appliances; for as much attention must be given to subsequent ma[n]-
agement. The patients are unreasonable, and a single awkward m[o]-
tion may undo the work of weeks so far as the union of the parts [of]
the bone is concerned. Union takes place after the same proces[s]
and, if the conditions are favorable, with greater rapidity than in t[he]
human being. The injury that caused the fracture is almost sure [to]
have extended to some of the adjacent tissues, and, even though t[he]
fracture may be of the simplest type, there is almost sure to be co[n]-
siderable hemorrhage around the ends of the broken bone. Thi[s]
however, is unimportant if the skin remains intact, unless a ver[y]
large vessel should be injured, or the fracture should open some [of]
the important cavities of the body, in which case a fatal hemorrha[ge]
might result. If, on the other hand, the fracture be a compoun[d]
one, the external opening furnishes a fertile field for the lodgment [of]
disease-producing germs.

Unless great care is exercised in such cases a suppurative pr[o]-
cess is likely to be established which will seriously interfere with, [if]
not entirely arrest, the process of union between the bones; or it ma[y]
become so serious as to endanger the general health of the anim[al]
and even be attended with fatal results. This last danger is greate[r]
where the injury has occurred to the bones of the arm or thigh. I[n]
such cases, owing to the dense covering of fascia which ensheath[es]
the muscular covering, pus is likely to be imprisoned, and, burrow[-]
ing downward, saturate the whole structure, not only endangerin[g]
the limb, but, by absorption, may set up blood poisoning and ser[i]-
ously interfere with the general health of the patient, even to causin[g]
death. In order so far as possible to prevent such an unfortunat[e]
complication, the wound should be carefully cleansed with a mil[d]
solution of carbolic acid, then dusted over with iodoform before t[he]
bandages are applied, and cleansed and dressed daily in the sam[e]
way. After dressing always cover with absorbent cotton. In t[he]
early process of union an exudation of lymph takes place, which [is]
at first fluid, gradually becoming thicker and firmer till it forms [a]
callus in the shape of a ring or ferrule surrounding the detached po[r]-
tions of the bone, known as the external or ensheathing callus. It o[c]-
casionally happens that this callus only forms at the ends of th[e]
bones, filling the spaces that exist between them, when it is known a[s]
the intermediate callus. The process of union may be divided int[o]

five stages. In the first stage, including the first eight days, the detached portions of the bone and the sharp projections that are not sufficiently nourished are absorbed; the blood which escaped into the surrounding tissues, the result of the injury, is gradually absorbed, and the effused lymph, which is ultimately to constitute the temporary cartilage, takes its place. In the second stage, from the tenth to the twentieth day, the tumor or callus is formed and fibrocartilage is developed inside and around the exposed end of the bone. In the third stage, extending from the twentieth to the fortieth or fiftieth day, according to the age and strength of the animal, the fibrocartilaginous structure undergoes a change and is gradually converted into bone, forming a ferrule on the outside and a plug on the inside, which serve to hold the part in position. In the fourth stage, extending to about the sixth month, the whole of the new structure is converted into bone. The fifth stage, extending up to the end of the first year, the callus is absorbed, being no longer necessary, and the connection between the cavities of the two bones is again established.

Common Complications.—The process of union just described is healthy and normal. Diseased conditions may at any time supervene during the treatment and render the operation unsuccessful. In the case of compound fracture, the open wound communicating with the ends of the bones, a septic condition is apt to arise which may become so serious as to endanger the animal's life and bring about conditions which in human surgery would indicate amputation. Although that operation is not a general one in veterinary practice, there is no reason why it should not be attempted as a last resort, particularly if the animal be valuable or one whose existence is necessary in order to perpetuate some valuable strain. Even in the simplest form of fracture, if the splints or bandages are improperly applied and the fractured bone left so loosely guarded that the broken ends move one upon another, the formation of the calluses previously described is likely to be interfered with, and in place of a strong, rigid, and healthy union a formation of elastic cartilage is the result. This false structure unites the broken ends of the bones in such a way that they move one upon another, depriving the bone of its stability and usefulness. When once the healthy process of union is interrupted in the manner just described, it is with great difficulty that it can be again established. It no longer does any good to continue the restraining power; in fact, the change of the temporary cartilage into bone is more likely to be re-established if the parts move violently upon one another for a short time so as to set up and renew the process of inflammation. Then if the restraint be again applied there is some chance of union. In order so far as possible to avoid this danger, care should be exercised that the bandage fits closely and that it is kept on till there is no longer any danger but that a perfect union has taken place. It is impossible to say at just what time the splints or bandages can safely be removed. In a young and healthy animal of quiet temperament, where the parts have been firmly held in position throughout the whole time, from thirty to forty days may be regarded as reasonably safe. Under more unfavorable conditions as to age, vitality, and restraint, the period would better be extended up to sixty days if the general condition of the animal is such as to permit of so long a continuance. After the appliance has been removed the animal should be allowed to stand quiet for a few days, then given very gentle exercise, gradually increased over a period of a week or ten days, by which time the patient will be so far recovered as to be placed in pasture. It should, however, be alone for a time, so as not to take any chance of injury from fighting or other accidents that association with other animals might involve.

DISLOCATIONS.

Luxation, or displacement of the bones forming a joint without fracture, is comparatively rare among cattle. It most frequently occurs in the stifle joint, where dislocation of the kneepan (patella) takes place. Such an accident may occur from direct injury or external force, as a blow, or from slipping. When it does occur the symptoms produced are somewhat alarming. The animal is unable to draw the leg forward, and either stands with it thrown back with the toe pointing downward or, if it should succeed in getting its weight upon it, holds it firmly on the ground, fearing to move it. Examination of the outside of the joint will disclose the situation of the patella outside of its proper place. If the operator is not familiar with the normal appearance of the joint, it is well to make a comparison between the injured and the sound one. If compelled to move, the animal does so with great difficulty, jerking the leg which it is unable to bring forward, hopping with the other and partially dragging the injured one.

Treatment.—The treatment is simple. A rope 20 feet long should be applied around the fetlock of the affected leg, passed forward between the front legs and up over the opposite side of the neck, back over the withers, and wrapped once behind the elbow around that portion of the rope which passes between the front legs. The leg is then drawn away from the body and forcibly pushed forward by an assistant, while another person tightens up the slack in the rope until the affected leg is off the ground in front of the supporting leg. The rope is then drawn taut and the assistant grasps the tail and pulls the cow toward the affected side. The animal makes a lurch to keep from falling, contracts the muscles, and the patella slips into place with a sharp click, and the animal walks off as if nothing had happened. If the animal resists this method of handling, it may suffice to manipulate the dislocated kneepan by shoving it inward and forward with the heel of the hand while the affected leg is drawn well forward. Unless some precaution is taken the accident is liable to recur, as the ligaments have been stretched by the dislocation till they no longer hold the bone with that firmness necessary to retain it. The animal should be tied and the foot fastened forward, so that the patient can just stand on it comfortably, by means of a rope or strap around the fetlock carried forward between the front legs around the neck and tied on the breast.

Should this accident occur more than once it is a good practice to apply a blister around the joint, as in the formula recommended for sprain of shoulder, and observe the precautions as to restraint and subsequent treatment there recommended. With this one exception, dislocations in the ox occurring independently of other complications are rare.

Dislocation with fracture may occur in any of the joints, and where one is suspected or discovered, examination should always be made for the other before treatment is applied. When a fracture occurs in the vicinity of a joint the force sufficient to rend the bone is likely to be partly exerted on the immediate tissues, and when the bone gives way the structures of the joints are likely to be seriously injured. It occasionally happens that the injury to the joint becomes the most important complication in the treatment of a fracture. In order clearly to understand the reason for this a few words are necessary in relation to the structure of the joints.

The different pieces constituting the skeleton of the animal body are united in such a manner as to admit of more or less motion one upon another. In some of the more simple joints the bones fitting one into another are held together by the dense structures around them, admitting of very little or no movement at all, as the bones of the head. In other joints the bones are bound together by dense cartilaginous structures, admitting of only limited motion, such as the union of the small bones at the back part of the knee and hock (metacarpal and metatarsal). In the more perfect form of joint the power of motion becomes complete and the structures are more complex. The substance of the bone on its articular surface is not covered with periosteum, but is sheathed in a dense, thin layer of cartilage, shaped to fit the other surfaces with which it comes in contact (articular). This layer is thickest toward its center when covering bony eminences, and is elastic, of a pearly whiteness, and resisting, though soft enough to be easily cut. The bones forming an articulation are bound together by numerous ligaments attached to bony prominences. The whole point is sealed in by a band of ribbon-like ligament (capsular ligament) extending around the joint and attached at the outer edge of the articular surface, uniting the bones and hermetically sealing the cavities of the articulation. This structure and the articular surface of the bone is covered by a thin, delicate membrane, known as the synovial membrane, which secretes the joint oil (synovia). This fluid is viscid and colorless, or slightly yellow, and although it does not possess a large amount of fat, its character somewhat resembles oil, and it serves the same purpose in lubricating the joints that oil does to the friction surface of an engine. Although the tissues of the joint when used in a natural way are able to withstand the effect of great exertion, when unnaturally used, as they are very delicate and complex, they are liable to inflammatory and other changes of a very serious nature. The synovial membrane, and in fact the whole structure of the joint, is susceptible to injury and serious inflammatory derangement, and the capsular ligament is liable to be distended from excessive secretion of synovia. The latter process may be almost noninflammatory, and attended with little inconvenience or importance other than a blemish to the animal, which in cattle is not serious. It may occur on the back part of the leg above the fetlock or on the inner and fore part of the hock, corresponding in its location to windgalls and bog spavin of the horse. Continuous support by bandages will generally force reabsorption, and as the limb is not subjected to violent action, as in the case of the horse, the affection is not so liable to recur.

RHEUMATISM.

Rheumatism is a constitutional disease due to a specific condition of the blood and characterized by inflammation of the fibrous structures of the body. It is usually accompanied by stiffness, lameness, and fever. The parts affected are usually swollen, but swelling may be lacking. The inflammation may be transitory—that is, it changes from place to place. The parts usually affected are the fibrous structures of the joints, tendons, ligaments, and muscles. The serous membranes and heart may also be affected. According to its location, rheumatism is specified as articular or muscular. According to its course, it is designated as acute or chronic.

Cause.—Among the factors which are actively causative of rheumatism may be mentioned exposure to dampness and cold, especially while the animal is perspiring or fatigued after severe physical exertion. Among other causes often mentioned are acidity of the blood, nervous derangement, microbes, and injuries. It occasionally follows another disease, such as pleurisy. The influence of age and heredity may be considered as secondary or predisposing causes. Sometimes the disease appears without any apparent cause. On the whole, it may be said that any of the above-mentioned factors may have more or less influence on the production of rheumatism, but the specific cause is as yet unknown.

Symptoms of Articular Rheumatism.—The symptoms appear suddenly and with varying degrees of severity. The animal presents a downcast appearance, with staring coat, horns and ears cold, and the mouth and muzzle hot and dry. Appetite and rumination may be impaired and followed later or be accompanied at the same time by constipation. Constipation may be followed by impaction of the stomach or bowels. Thirst is increased, but the amount of urine voided is scanty. Respiration and pulse are accelerated, and there is usually a fever, rising sometimes as high as 108° F. The animal prefers to lie down, and when forced to rise stands with its back arched. The movements are stiff and lame and cause great pain. The disease may attack one or more joints at the same time; in fact, it is often symmetrical. One joint may improve while another becomes affected, thus showing the shifting tendency of the inflammation. The affected joints, including their tendons, ligaments, and synovial membranes, may be swollen, hot, and distended with liquid. They are very tender, and, if treated carelessly or injured, may become infected, thus leading to suppuration. While rheumatism attacks perhaps more frequently the knees and fetlocks, it has no special affinity for any joint and may attack the stifle, hip, shoulder, or

Native Method of Milking Maltese Goats.
Dept. of Agr.

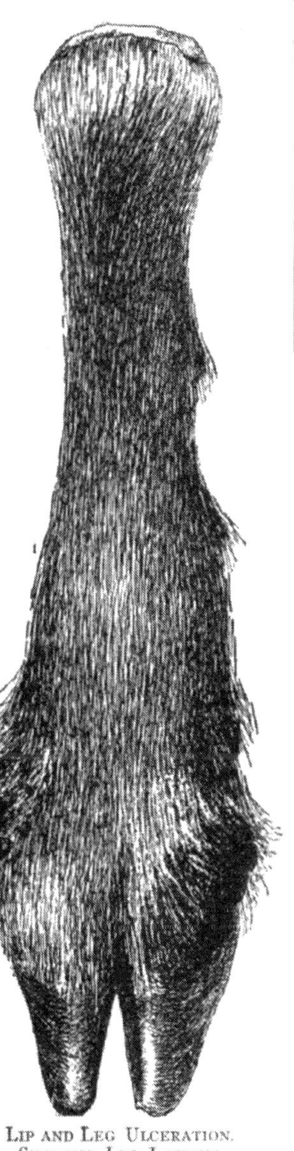

Lip and Leg Ulceration.
Showing Leg Lesions.
Dept. of Agr.

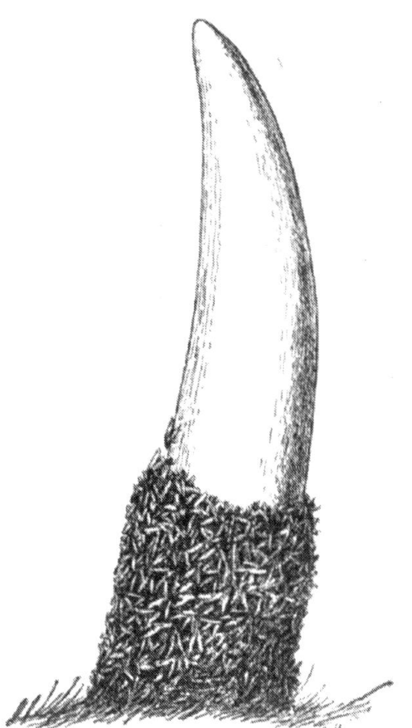

Cow Horn Showing Band of Resting
Horn Flies. Dept. of Agr.

elbow joint. In mild cases of articular rheumatism, the animal may fully recover in a few days.

In chronic articular rheumatism there is less tendency of the disease to shift about, but there is a greater liability of structural change in the affected joints. This change may consist of induration, exostosis, or even anchylosis. These structural changes about the joints may lead to permanent deformity, such as bending of the neck. Fever is not so constant in the chronic form as in the acute, and the latter may lapse into the former.

Symptoms of Muscular Rheumatism.—This form of rheumatism may appear under the same general conditions as the articular form. The general appearance of the animal is the same in both forms. The cow usually assumes a recumbent position, and all the movements made are stiff and lame. The method of rising or of locomotion indicates pain in certain muscles or groups of muscles, as of the croup, shoulder, or neck. As in the case of articular rheumatism, the tendons, ligaments, and sinovial membranes may become involved. The constitutional symptoms in both articular and muscular rheumatism are similar, so that it is often perplexing to differentiate between the two forms.

Prevention.—It is somewhat difficult to procure preventive treatment for cattle, especially when there are large numbers with little or no shelter. In general it is advisable to protect the animals so far as possible from inclement weather conditions, such as cold rains, heavy dews, and frosts. This is more particularly necessary for animals in poor condition, or those which are perspiring or fatigued after long physical exertion. Careful feeding is also essential.

Treatment.—In attempting to treat cattle for rheumatism the first step is to procure proper shelter and environment. The animal should be quartered in a large, clean, dry stall with plenty of light and fresh air, but protected from strong drafts. There should be an abundance of clean, dry bedding. The food should be soft and easily digestible and slightly laxative, and the animal should have access to clean, pure, cool water.

For general or constitutional treatment of acute rheumatism, sodium salicylate is indicated. In order to gain the best results from this drug, it should be administered with the idea of rapidly saturating the system. To cattle it may be given in doses of one-half ounce every two hours for ten hours or until immediate relief is obtained. This drug should not be continued indefinitely, but may be given once a day after immediate relief has been obtained, and this single dose continued daily until permanent relief ensues, when it should be stopped. The use of sodium salicylate in chronic rheumatism is not advisable on account of the danger of depressing the heart, whose action is already somewhat impaired by the lesions which have attacked it. In this case one-half ounce doses of potassium nitrate or bicarbonate may be given three times a day. Besides the constitutional treatment, it may be necessary to give special attention to the bowels in order to relieve constipation. Cattle may be given saline laxatives at the outset, such as 1 pound of Epsom salts for an ordinary-sized cow, and the bowels kept regular by an occasional smaller dose.

In chronic rheumatism the best course of treatment is to give tonics and local treatment. Local treatment may also be advisable in acute rheumatism in addition to the constitutional treatment already prescribed.

External treatment depends solely on the local conditions and should be applied judiciously. Among the various remedies may be mentioned hot or cold moist packs, hot air and vapor baths, friction, etc. Anodynes are often applied locally with good results. Blisters are occasionally indicated. As anodynes may be mentioned liniments and ointments containing salicylic acid or sodium salicylate in combination with laudanum, aconite, or chloral hydrate. Camphorated spirit, soap liniment, and essential oils also afford some relief when applied locally. Of blisters those containing cantharides are most effective.—(B. A. I. Cir. 66; Special Rept. on Diseases of Cattle, U. S. Dept. Agr.)

THE FOOT AND ITS DISEASES.
LAMINITIS (FOUNDER).

Laminitis denotes an active inflammation of the sensitive structures within the wall of the hoof, which may in severe cases result in suppuration and the loss of one or more claws. Owing to the simplicity of the structure of the foot of the ox compared with that of the horse, this disease is rarely seen in an acute form, but a mild form, commonly called foot soreness, is not of infrequent occurrence.

Causes.—Laminitis in cattle may be caused by overfeeding, overheating, continued standing without exercise on a stone or cement floor without sufficient bedding, or by driving long distances over rough or stony soil.

Symptoms.—An unwillingness to maintain the standing position; the animal persists in lying down. The feet will be found unnaturally hot, and frequently some swelling may be noticed above the hoof. Pressure upon the hoof with blacksmiths' hoof-pincers causes pain and pinching. The general body temperature is increased and the breathing accelerated. Ordinarily the animal eats and drinks. When it is made to move excessive tenderness of the feet becomes manifest, as is shown by reluctance to walk and by the very short, hesitating step. Founder affects the hind as well as the fore feet, although the front feet are more often exposed.

Treatment.—Cold packs to the feet, or if the animal can be made to stand in a stream of running water, having a soft bottom, this will often relieve the inflammation without the necessity of any additional treatment. It may be well, however, to give a full dose of Epsom salts, 1 to 1½ pounds, followed by half-ounce doses of saltpeter two or three times a day.

SORENESS (FOOT SORENESS).

Cattle that are driven over stony roads, especially such as have been stabled or pastured on soft ground, soon wear down the soles of their feet and become lame from foot soreness. Draft oxen, for this reason, require to be shod. When the soreness is excessive it may develop into an active inflammation of all the sensitive structures of the foot—laminitis—or into a local bruise commonly called a corn.

Treatment.—Rest, poulticing the feet with moistened clay, followed by astringent washes—strong white-oak bark or alum water.

If the pain and heat last several days, it is probable that pus has formed beneath the wall of the hoof. In this case it is necessary to cut through the wall, usually at the most prominent part of the sole, to allow the accumulation to drain out. The animal should then be caused to stand for several hours daily in a tub containing creolin solution (3 per cent). When not in the creolin solution the foot should be dressed with pine tar and cotton and bandaged with bagging.

LOSS OF HOOF.

Cattle sometimes become fastened between planks or otherwise and pull off the wall of one or both claws in the effort to extricate themselves. The claws of one or more feet may be shed as the result of acute laminitis.

Treatment.—Wash the bleeding surface with an antiseptic and then with an astringent, as a weak solution of alum, then apply a thick coating of pine tar; cover this with a layer of oakum or absorbent cotton; apply another coat of tar over this, and then bandage closely and firmly. This may remain without disturbance until the new growing wall becomes sufficiently strong to sustain the pressure and weight of the animal. If, however, at any time it becomes manifest by oozing or bad smell that pus is forming under this dressing, the bandage should be removed and the suppurating surface freshly cleaned and dressed. This may have to be repeated every few days, and should be continued so long as there is any pus formation. If the loss of hoof is due to suppurative laminitis, the parts denuded of the horny covering must be thoroughly cleansed and disinfected with carbolic acid, creolin, lysol, or other antiseptic. Then apply a moderately thick layer of absorbent cotton, and apply the tar and bandage over this. After this the antiseptic solution may be poured in at the top of the dressing daily. It will thus soak in and saturate the dressing and inflamed tissue. It may become necessary to remove the whole of the dressing at daily or longer intervals to give the parts a fresh cleaning, and then to reapply it.

FOUL IN FOOT (FOOT ROT).

A variety of causes may produce inflammation of the foot between the claws or toes. It may be due to overgrowth of the claws and inward pressure, as in ingrowing nail of man; or it may be caused by the irritation of stable filth, to impaction and hardening of soil between the claws, or to other foreign substances becoming wedged in and causing inflammation and softening or ulceration of the skin in the interdigital space. Under some conditions several cattle in the same herd become affected, and this has led some to think that the disease may be contagious. Occurrences have been reported where foot rot of cattle has appeared within a short time among a large proportion of the cattle in a farming district. This disease is most frequently seen in the hind feet, though all four feet may become affected.

Symptoms.—The animal is observed to limp in walking. On examination of the foot we discover heat, and swelling above the hoof and of the soft parts between the claws which frequently spreads the claws apart to a considerable extent; or the inflammation may have advanced to softening and sloughing of the interdigital membrane. If the disease is neglected at this stage, deep abscesses may form and the pus burrow under the horny wall, or the joint within the hoof may become inflamed and the articular attachments destroyed, in which case the treatment will become difficult and recovery will be very tedious.

Treatment.—In the earlier stages of the disease, before pus burrows beneath the horn, a thorough cleansing and an application of a carbolic-acid solution—1 ounce to a pint of water—clean stabling, and laxative food will usually remedy the evil. Creolin is an excellent remedy at this stage. It should be applied to the suppurating and putrefying tissue between the claws in its pure or undiluted state. It is best applied by means of a cotton swab on a thin stick. Care must be exercised to keep the creolin from contact with the skin about the coronary band or heels. If deep sloughing has taken place the carbolic solution or creolin should be used, and a wad of oakum or cotton smeared with pine tar should be secured firmly in the cleft. This can be done by taking a strip of strong cloth, 2 inches wide, passing the middle between the claws, then tying the ends after winding them in opposite directions above the.hoof. Sometimes warm poulticing with flaxseed meal or bran becomes necessary to relieve excessive fever and pain. If the pus burrows under the horn, its channel must be followed by paring away the horn until the bottom is reached. The after-treatment will be the same as that already recommended. If the joint becomes diseased, an amputation of that toe will be the quickest and surest method to relieve the suffering of the animal, and offers the best chance for an early recovery.

ULCERATION OF THE HEEL.

Occasionally we find ulcers at the junction of the hair with the hoof at the heel, which present an elevated, raw, or ragged surface, and cause considerable lameness. This is generally due to a bruise of the fibrous cushion of the back part of the foot. Subsequent sloughing or necrosis may occur, or pus may form deep down within the wall and gain an exit at the margin of the heel. Sometimes large pieces of skin slough from the heel and pastern from no visible cause. This condition is caused by an infection with certain micro-organisms (streptococci, necrosis bacilli) and may be contagious.

Treatment.—If there is a deep opening, inject carbolic solution once a day until it closes. If the ulcer is only superficial, wash with carbolic or creolin solution and apply a mixture of equal parts of blue vitriol and alum in dry powder.

FISSURE OF THE WALL (SPLIT HOOF).

This is rarely seen among cattle. It may occur in weak walls, in heavy-bodied cattle, by stepping on an uneven surface, especially when the point of the toe is grown out long. One may find the point of the toe broken and the wall split almost up to the hair.

Treatment.—The divided sections may be brought into approximation and held in place by drilling a small hole from one side into and through the other, commencing half an inch back of the fissure on each side; then drive a light horseshoe nail through the hole and clinch it. Pare the injured claw as short as it will bear.

INTERDIGITAL FIBROMA.

Hard, nodular, fibrous tumors sometimes grow in the cleft of the foot, and cause inconvenience, lameness, absorption, or ulceration of the contiguous parts.

Treatment. — They should be dissected out, and the wound dressed with carbolic-acid lotion and pine tar once a day until healing is completed.

DEFORMITIES.

Deformities in the feet of cattle usually consist in overgrowth of horn, generally due to want of wear in animals which are stabled. The hoof may turn inward, outward, or upward, and may give rise to lameness, inability to walk, foul foot, etc. Bulls which are continually stabled and dairy cows very frequently have misshapen feet for want of an occasional trimming, and this deformity may eventually lead to permanent injury.

Treatment.—Cut the superabundant growth of horn down with saw, knife, or rasp, until the foot assumes its natural form.

PRICKS AND WOUNDS.

If an animal suffers with a penetrating wound from prick of fork or nail, the orifice of the wound should be enlarged to perimt a free discharge of pus; then soak the foot in a creolin solution (3 per cent) in a tub, or apply a flaxseed poultice, changing it three times a day until the fever has abated. The foot should be kept bandaged and dressed with pine tar and oakum, and the animal must be kept on a clean floor until the wound is closed and all or nearly all lameness has disappeared.

If an animal is cut in the foot with barbed wire, piece of glass, or any other substance, dress the wound, after proper cleansing, with carbolic-acid solution, 1 ounce to 20 of water. If any uneven edges of horn or skin or lacerated flesh project, trim them off, and in all cases when it can be done a tarred bandage should be applied. This will serve to sustain the cut surfaces in their place, exclude dirt, and protect against flies, maggots, etc.

When the wound has extended into a joint, surgical treatment may become necessary, which will require the services of an educated veterinarian. Occasionally an animal becomes fastened by the foot in some crevice and sustains severe bruising, wrenching, or fracture of some part of the foot. In such cases cold-water packs to the injured member will be of service until the fever and swelling disappear. Afterwards allow the animal rest until the usefulness of the foot is restored. Sometimes such an accident, causing fracture, renders necessary plaster bandages or amputation.

WOUNDS, INJURIES AND SURGICAL OPERATIONS.

Surgery is both a science and an art. The success of surgical operations depends upon the judgment, skill, and dexterity, as well as upon the knowledge, of the operator. The same fundamental principles underlie and govern animal and human surgery, although their applications have a wide range and are very different in many essential particulars. We must not lose sight of the fact that hygiene and sanitation are essential to the best results in veterinary as well as in human surgery.

Asepsis is an ideal condition which, although not always possible in animal surgery, is highly important in connection with the mechanical details of all surgical operations in proportion to the nature and seriousness of the same. Aseptic surgery may be said to be such as is preserved from contamination by poisonous materials, whether such poisons be applied directly to it or be generated in it by the actions of germs that gain access to it and find within it the conditions favorable to their growth. It should be borne in mind that there are three ways that a wound may be kept aseptic; by the protection it receives from the first, at the hands of the surgeon, from the access of septic agents; by the power of living tissue to resist and destroy septic agents, and by application to the wound of substances which destroy them.

Local and general anesthesia should be resorted to in painful and serious surgical operations, as operations upon all living creatures should be humanely performed and all unnecessary pain and suffering avoided. Anesthesia is necessary where absolute immobility of the patient is essential, and where entire muscular relaxation is indispensable. The anesthetic condition is also favorable for the reduction of displaced organs.

Large animals have to be cast and secured before an anesthetic is administered. For complete anesthesia chloroform is generally employed; and sometimes ether and chloroform. A sponge is wet with the anesthetic and placed in a nosebag and the animal allowed to inhale the fumes. The amount of chloroform required to produce insensibility to external impressions varies much in different cases and must be regulated, as well as the admixture of air by a competent assistant.

If the probability of the success of an operation is remote and the animal is in a healthy physical condition, so that its flesh is good for human food, it is more advisable to let the butcher have the animal than to attempt a surgical operation that offers little encouragement to the owner. The best judgment has to be exercised in determining a matter of this kind, for no animal suffering from inflammation or that is in a feverish condition is fit for human food.

All cases of major operative surgery require the skill and dexterity of the experienced veterinary surgeon, and no one else should attempt such an operation, for unnecessary suffering must be prevented as well as the success of the operation attained. Nevertheless, the more knowledge and understanding an owner of animals has of surgical operations and manipulations, the better for all concerned. In the first place, such an owner will appreciate more fully the skill of the qualified veterinarian, and, in the second place, he will be the better prepared and equipped to render assistance to his suffering dumb dependents where no practitioner is accessible and in cases of emergency. There are, moreover, sundry operations upon cattle that the stockman should be able to perform himself.

In the performance of any operation upon an animal of the size and strength of the bull or cow, the first consideration is to secure the animal in such a manner as to preclude the possibility of its injuring either itself or those taking any part in the operation, for two or more are invariably necessary. The nature and time likely to be occupied by an operation must, of course, largely determine the method to be adopted.

The majority of operations with which the present chapter is concerned are usually performed on the animal in a standing position.* To secure the cow in this position, grasp the nose, the finger and thumb being introduced into the nostrils, and press against the cartilage which makes a division between them. If she has horns, grasp one of them with the disengaged hand. If this is insufficient the animal should be secured to a post, the side of a building or put in a stanchion. A very excellent method of restraint is to tie a long rope in a slip noose over the horns, pass it around the chest just behind the fore legs, taking a half hitch on itself, taking another half hitch in front of the hind limbs, passing the free end under the tail, bringing it forward and making it fast either to the head or one of the hitches. The head should be raised to the level of the back before the final knot is tied, so as to render it too serious and painful a matter for her to repeat the first attempt she makes to lower it. Should the nature or extent of the operation be likely to take up a considerable length of time, it is invariably the best plan to throw the animal. In the case of the ox this is very easily done, either by use of horse hobbles, should they be at hand, or by the application of a simple rope. If the horse hobbles are used, they should be fastened on the leg just above the fetlocks (ankle joints), as they are in that position less liable to come off than if placed around the pastern.

Of the many ways of applying the rope for this purpose we will describe two only, which we consider the best and simplest:

First. Take a long, strong rope (one which has been used a few times is more flexible), double it, and at 2 or 3 feet from the doubled end, according to the size of the animal, make a knot and pass the collar thus formed over the animal's head, allowing it to rest on what would be the collar place in a horse. Now pass the ends of

____

*A bull should always be held by a staff attached to the ring in his nose.

the rope between the fore legs, carry one around each hind leg just above the fetlock joint, from outside in, under itself once, and bring the free ends forward, passing each through the collar loop on its own side and bringing the slack back toward and beyond the hind quarters. Two or three stout men should then take hold of each rope and at a given signal pull. The animal's hind legs being drawn forward, the balance is lost, and if the animal does not fall or lie down he can be readily pushed over on his side and secured in the desired position.

Second. The three half hitches. Take a rope 30 or more feet long, make a slip noose at the end and pass it over the animal's horns, leaving the knot in the loop between the horns; then pass the rope backward along the neck to the withers, just in front of which take a half hitch on it, passing it along the back, take one-half hitch just behind the forelegs and a second in front of the hind limbs round the flank. The free end of the rope is taken hold of by one or two assistants while another holds the animal's head. By pulling firmly on the rope, or inducing the animal to make a step or two forward while steady traction is made on the rope, the beast will quietly lie down, when his feet can be secured in the way most convenient for the operator.

There are numerous other methods, involving more or less complete restraint, which may be equally efficacious, but one or other of the ways indicated will doubtless be found to meet fully all ordinary cases.

RINGING THE BULL.

This is usually and ought always to be done before the calf has attained sufficient weight or strength to make his restraint a matter of serious difficulty. An ordinary halter is usually all that is required, the strap being secured to a tree or post. A jointed steel or copper ring is ordinarily used. Those made of the latter metal are preferable.

The common method of punching a round piece out of the nasal septum for the introduction of the ring is open to objection, as portions of the fine nervous filaments are destroyed. The sensibility of the parts is thus lessened and the object of ringing to some extent defeated. The insertion of the ring by means of a trocar and canula is preferable, as the method is not open to this objection.

For some years we have used a little instrument which can be made by any worker in metal, consisting of a steel point riveted into a short canula made to fit on one end of the ring while open. When attached to the ring it is easily and quickly passed through the septum, the half of the ring following as a matter of course. It can then be removed, and the ends of the ring brought together and fastened by means of the screw for that purpose. By this means any animal can readily be ringed by anyone in less time than it takes to describe the process; whereas, by any other method which necessitates first puncturing or piercing the septum and subsequently introducing the ring, the operation is, even when the animal's struggles do not complicate matters, necessarily rendered tedious and uncertain by the fact that the openings through the skin and cartilage are not in apposition.

DEHORNING.

SIMPLE METHOD OF RESTRAINING THE ANIMALS.

The dehorning of cattle can be very satisfactorily performed without other apparatus or instruments than a good strong clothesline and a clean sharp meat saw, or a miter saw with a rigid back. The same simple means for controlling the animal is just as applicable when dehorning clippers are to be used as when the horns are to be removed with the saw. The head of the animal is secured to the horizontal rail or stringer which holds the upper ends of the stanchion boards. The animal is put in the stanchion in the usual manner; then one end of a heavy clothesline is passed around the upper part of the neck and tied in a knot that will not slip, otherwise it will choke the animal. The free end of the rope is now carried between the horns, through the stanchion to the front, up and over the horizontal stanchion rail, then down underneath the neck and up and over the top of the stanchion rail to an assistant, who should hold it firmly. Now open the stanchion, allowing the animal to withdraw its head; then, keeping the rope tight, pass it once around the muzzle, up and over the stanchion rail, and through to the front again to the hands of the assistant, who should stand 3 or 4 feet in front of the animal and hold the rope firmly, but prepared to release it when told to do so by the operator. The animal is now ready for the dehorning operation.

It is necessary that the rope be held by an assistant, as in the event of the animal struggling during the operation so as to throw itself off its feet, or if there appears to be danger of its choking, the rope may be slackened promptly at the word of the operator and the animal partly released. This, however, is rarely necessary, for as soon as the head is secured the operator should be ready, standing at the right shoulder of the animal with his saw, and proceed to saw off first the right and then the left horn. It is a good plan before commencing the real work to experiment upon an animal in the matter of control by tying the head to the stanchion rail as described.

If the stanchion rail is too wide to permit of properly securing the lower part as well as the upper part of the animal's head, the turn of the rope around the muzzle may be omitted and the last lap of the rope carried around the stanchion rail to the front and to the hands of the assistant. Care should be taken that the rope pass each time over the neck of the animal to the stanchion rail between the horns in such a way that it will not interfere with the work of the saw.

WHERE TO CUT THE HORNS.

The horns should be severed from a quarter to a half inch below where the skin joins the base of the horn, cutting from the back toward the front. If the cut is made too high an irregular, gnarly growth of horn is very apt to follow. It will be seen that the point of union of the skin and horn varies in different cattle; hence there can be no rule of measurement, except as the eye becomes trained to see the point or line at which the cut should be made. In the beef breeds fully one-half inch of skin, all around, is usually taken off with the horn.

INSTRUMENTS FOR DEHORNING.

In recent years, since dehorning shears or clippers have come into use, this means of dehorning is considered by some cattle owners to be preferable, especially where large numbers of cattle are to be dehorned. One type of dehorner has a stationary knife blade, with its cutting edge shaped like a very wide V, and opposing this another knife of similar shape, moving in a slide, so that the cutting edges cut the horn from all four sides at once, all the edges passing the center at the same time. Another type has a movable knife with one oblique or one curved edge, and the cutting is done in one direction only. The power for cutting with these instruments is supplied by pulling together two long handles, which, in order to transmit a greater force, are generally so constructed that they act through the medium of a series of cogs.

In dehorning with these instruments the opening between the cutting edges should be slipped down over the horn and the knives closed so that their edges set firmly against the horn in such a position that the cut will be made in the right place and in the right direction. The blades should be kept covered with a thick oil or grease. The handles should be drawn together with a quick, firm, strong pull, so that the horn will be completely severed by the first act and without twisting. Care should be taken to keep the blades sharpened on their original bevel.

Dehorning instruments can be procured of the manufacturers and of dealers in veterinary instruments. In dairy districts adjacent to large cities there are men who go about from farm to farm dehorning animals, charging for their services in some instances as little as 5 cents per horn or 10 cents per animal.

There was published in the report of the New Zealand department of agriculture for 1904 a description of the operation of dehorning cattle by the government veterinarian at New Plymouth, in which it was shown that a cage had been used for the restraint of the animals during the operation, closely resembling the box used for hoisting horses out of ships, this cage being hauled on a wagon from farm to farm as needed. In discussing the various means for the removal of the horns the report was very favorable to the use of the saw in dehorning full-grown cattle. It was stated that in the dehorning of over 10,000 cows with the saw there were no deaths due to the operation, while in cows dehorned by shears there was trouble afterwards in healing of the wounds, due, no doubt, to the crushing, fracturing action which this instrument has upon old horns, where ossification of the cores is advanced. Because of this condition it was recommended that for mature animals a bone saw be used.

TREATMENT AFTER DEHORNING.

It is not usual to apply any preparation after the operation of dehorning to prevent bleeding, as the loss of blood is not sufficient, as a rule, to be of consequence. Care should be taken, however, to prevent substances from getting into the openings left after the horns are removed. The horn cores are elongations of the frontal bones of the skull, and are hollow. They communicate with the frontal sinuses, or air spaces, of the head; therefore foreign substances or fragments of horn which act as an irritant in these cavities are apt to set up an inflammation, resulting in the formation of pus or an abscess, which may prove quite serious. This trouble is of infrequent occurrence, but would appear more liable to happen when the dehorning instruments are used, on account of their tendency to crush, especially in the case of old animals, whereas the saw cuts clean. If proper care is taken, however, such an occurrence following dehorning may, in almost every instance be avoided.

Occasionally animals after being dehorned and turned out of the stable will rub their heads against a dirt or gravel bank or the rough bark of a tree, and foreign material may thus get into the cavities, though usually the soreness of the parts is sufficient to prevent this.

If the animals are dehorned in warm weather, it is well to apply some pine tar with a view to keeping flies from the wounds. Some operators do this in nearly all cases, thinking that it facilitates healing. The dehorning operation should always, when possible, be performed in cool weather, and upon animals which have at least attained the age of two years.

DEHORNING ON THE RANGE.

While the cattle ranchman of the West seems to be equal to every requirement and emergency of his vocation, and is probably informed with regard to the dehorning of his stock, this article would be incomplete without a description of the dehorning operation as practiced in that part of the country.

In the range country of the West dehorning has been extensively practiced for a number of years, and various methods have been used in restraining the animals, as well as in removing their horns. In some instances the methods used are extremely crude, consisting in simply roping and throwing the animal and cutting off the horns with an ax. Most frequently, however, no matter what may be the means of control, either the saw or the dehorning shears are used. As a general thing the corral and chute which form a part of the equipment of every well-appointed cattle ranch are used for this purpose. Dehorning with an ax should never be attempted, as no matter how keen the edge of the ax or how true the aim of the axman, he is working on a living animal, and only a slight movement of the head would result in a deviation of the stroke, and would thus be liable to cause, if nothing more serious, the infliction of unnecessary pain and suffering to the animal.

It is the usual custom in the West to gather the cattle to be dehorned in a corral, either during the early spring, before the fly season begins, or in the fall, after the fly season has passed. At one side of this corral is a gate opening into another smaller inclosure, which is known as the chute pen. The sides of this converge to form an entrance into a narrow chute, which is usually made long enough for about three cattle, though but one is permitted to enter the working ends of the chute at a time, the others being kept back by crossbars. At the front end of this chute is what is known as a squeezer. After the animal enters the squeezer the squeeze gate is pressed close against its side to prevent lateral movement, the stanchion is closed on the neck, and the head is turned and secured to the post by means of a nose clamp and lead rope, first at one side of the chute and then the other, as required for the removal of the horns.

In the construction of these chutes it is usual to have on the side opposite the squeeze gate a movable plank which can be taken out to expose the side of the animal for branding. In the entire construction of such a corral and chute it is best not to economize in lumber or bolts, as it should be strong and durable, so that the animal may be controlled without danger to itself or to the operator.

Another method of restraint is to throw the animal and hold it stretched flat on the ground by means of a rope around its neck held by a man on horseback with a turn around the saddle pommel, a second rope being around the hind feet, similarly held by another man on horseback. In the absence of horses these ropes can be secured by taking a turn around a post. After the animal is thus secured an assistant grasps the nose and upper horn, turning the head so that the lower horn can be removed first. This obviates the danger of fracturing the lower horn, and allows the blood to flow directly on the ground and the head to be held flat for the removal of the upper horn. The dehorning shears are frequently used, but there seems to be a tendency in some localities toward giving preference to the saw.

Many ranchmen apply preparations of pine tar and alcohol, or pine tar and turpentine, after dehorning, to lessen the bleeding and keep the flies away.

TO PREVENT HORNS GROWING ON YOUNG CALVES.

When circumstances are favorable, as in the case of farmers who build up their herds by raising the progeny, the horns may be prevented from growing by a simple and practically painless method, and the custom of preventing the growth of the horns is becoming more popular and more generally practiced under all conditions except in the case of calves dropped on the open range. The calf should be treated not later than one week after its birth, preferably when it is from three to five days old. The agent to be used may be either caustic soda or caustic potash, both of which may be procured in the drug stores in the form of sticks about the thickness of an ordinary lead pencil and 5 inches long. These caustics must be handled with care, as they dissolve the cuticle and may make the hands or fingers sore. The preparation of the calf consists in first clipping the hair from the parts, washing clean with soap and warm water, and thoroughly drying with a cloth or towel. The stick of caustic should be wrapped in a piece of paper to protect the hands and fingers, leaving one end of the stick uncovered.

Moisten the uncovered end slightly and rub it on the horn buttons or little points which may be felt on the calf's head, first on one and then the other, alternately, two or three times on each, allowing the caustic to dry after each application. Be very careful to apply the caustic to the horn button only. If it is brought in contact with the surrounding skin it will cause pain. Be very careful also not to have too much moisture on the stick of caustic, as it will remove the skin if allowed to run down over the face. After treatment, keep the calf protected from rain, as water on the head after the application of caustic will cause it to run down over the face. This must be carefully avoided.

Either caustic soda or caustic potash alone, without the admixture of other substances, answers the purpose satisfactorily. Some years ago, however, certain preparations or "dehorning compounds," composed largely of one or the other of these caustics, were generally used, and as inquiries are still occasionally received concerning such preparations, the following formula is given: Combine in an emulsion 50 per cent of caustic soda, 25 per cent of kerosene, and 25 per cent of water. The caustic soda is dissolved in the water and heated to the boiling point, then removed from the fire, and the kerosene added gradually, while the mixture is vigorously stirred. This emulsion is applied in very much the same manner as the stick caustic, except that it is necessary to employ a short, stiff brush. Sometimes a meat skewer is used, the large end being mashed to form a stubby brush. Two or three applications should be made to each horn button, as in the case of the stick caustic, with intervals to allow it to dry.

In the very young calf the horn button, or point that will ultimately develop into a horn, has scarcely any attachment to the skull, and may be felt as a small button embedded in the skin. In this early stage it may be easily removed with a sharp knife or a pair of curved scissors, but even then caustics should be applied to kill any remaining cell life belonging to this germ point; otherwise there may be some subsequent irregular horn growth, which is more or less of a disfigurement.

BLEEDING (BLOOD-LETTING).

Although nowadays this operation has fortunately become less frequent than when it was generally considered the panacea for all ills, there are beyond doubt some cases in which the operation is admittedly the quickest and surest means of affording relief.

In cattle the operation is usually performed on the left jugular vein, which is large and is easily rendered so prominent as to prevent the possibility of mistake by tying a cord around the neck below the place where the incision is to be made. The rope should be tied in a slip knot, so as to admit of its being easily undone, or a rope used with a loop at one end and a series of good-sized knots at the other, the loop and knots to be used as buttons and button holes. The proper instrument to use is a large-bladed fleam. After the animal is secured the operator stands by the shoulder, holds the fleam in his left hand, the blade just short of touching the skin and parallel to the direction of the vein, and the stick or mallet with which to strike it in his right; one quick, sharp blow should be sufficient. If the hair is long, it is a wise precaution to moisten and smooth it down.

When sufficient blood has been withdrawn the rope is removed and the orifice closed by means of a pin inserted through the lips of the incision *in the skin only,* and a piece of fine string or tow wound either over or under it in the shape of a figure 8, or in a circle between the skin and the pin, the point of which should be clipped off. To prevent the animal from rubbing the part and tearing or dislodging the pin, it is advisable to tie the head up for a couple of days, providing the animal's health will admit of it, after which the pin may be removed and the wound left to heal in the usual manner.

Before leaving the subject it may be well to add that as the good effects derived from bleeding depend more on the quickness with which the blood is drawn than on the quantity extracted, it is of importance that a liberal opening should be made into the blood vessel and the blood allowed to flow until a perceptible impression has been made on the pulse.

SETONING.

Setons are used in cattle for various purposes, of which perhaps the most common is as a preventive in anthrax or blackleg, when a seton is usually inserted in the dewlap. This is not done to afford exit to any poisonous discharge from the system, as is generally supposed, but to cause a sufficient amount of inflammation to increase the coagulating properties of the blood, which in these diseases becomes altered (as described elsewhere), notably losing its viscidity and in consequence oozing through the walls of the blood vessels. For this purpose the seton should be deeply inserted and should be dressed daily with turpentine or common blister.

The ordinary use of a seton is for a different object, as, for instance, to keep up constant drainage from a cavity containing matter, or to act as a stimulant or counterirritant. To insert a seton, the place of entrance and exit having been decided on, with the finger and thumb make a small fold of the skin transverse to the direction the seton is to be inserted, and cut it through, either with a sharp knife or a pair of scissors (this should be done at both the entrance and exit); then with a steady pressure and slight lateral movement insert the seton by means of a seton needle. The seton should consist of a piece of strong tape, varying in breadth according to circumstances, and should be kept in place either by a knot on each end or by tying the ends together.

Setons should be gently moved once a day after suppuration is set up, and they should not be allowed to remain in over three weeks, or a month at the outside.

TRACHEOTOMY.

This operation consists of making an opening in the trachea, or windpipe. It is indicated whenever there is an obstruction from any cause in the upper part of the respiratory tract which threatens the death of the animal by asphyxia (suffocation). The mode of procedure is as follows: Have an assistant extend the animal's head as far as possible to make the trachea tense and prominent; make a longitudinal incision about 2 to 2½ inches long through the skin and deeper tissues and trachea at the most prominent part of the trachea, which is about the middle or upper third, and then insert the tracheotomy tube. The latter should be removed once or twice daily and cleansed, and the wound dressed antiseptically. To ascertain when it is time to discontinue the use of the tube and to allow the wound to close, the hand should be held over the opening, which will necessitate the animal to use its natural passages in breathing. Observe if it is performed in a natural manner; and if so, remove the tube and allow the wound to close. This is the general mode of procedure where the surgeon has all the necessary instruments and a moderate amount of time at his disposal. Often it has to be performed in great haste without the proper instruments and under great disadvantages, the operator having to quickly cut down and open the trachea and spread the parts, using some instrument improvised by him at the time. This operation only gives the animal relief in breathing, and therefore the proper remedial treatment should be adopted at the onset of the attack and continued until the cause (the disease) has been overcome.

CHOKING.

Choking, or the lodging of foreign bodies in the gullet, is divided into pharyngeal, cervical, and thoracic, according to location of the obstruction. The symptoms in general are uneasiness on the part of the patient, involuntary movement of the jaws, grinding of the teeth, a profuse escape of saliva, and tympanites of the rumen. If the obstruction is in the pharynx, the mouth speculum should be introduced and the oiled hand and arm of the operator inserted and an effort made to remove the obstruction. Many cases of choking may be relieved by giving a few ounces of any bland oil at frequent intervals and pulling the gullet on the stretch by forcible extension of the neck. If this should be unsuccessful it will probably be necessary to have recourse to the probang, which should be carefully introduced and the obstruction slowly pushed downward toward the rumen, care being taken not to lacerate the coats of the esophagus. An operation known as esophagotomy may be performed in case the above efforts have failed. I will briefly describe the steps to be taken in such an emergency.

ESOPHAGOTOMY.

In case the obstruction is in the cervical portion of the esophagus, the best procedure is to cut through the skin and subcutaneous muscle of the neck onto, but not into, the esophagus. The foreign body may then be pushed upward until it can be reached and removed through the mouth. The incision should be long; indeed, it may be made the whole length of the neck if necessary, as it is practically but a subcutaneous wound and heals readily.

PUNCTURING THE RUMEN.

This is an operation that when indicated has to be performed at once or the animal may be lost. It is indicated in severe cases of acute tympanites in cattle, commonly known as hoven, which is due to the generation of gas resulting from fermentation. Recurrent attacks of hoven are usually due to tubercular infiltration of the mediastinal and bronchial glands. To relieve this distention an ordinary cattle trocar and canula are inserted into the rumen, the most distended portion of the left side of the animal being the part selected. The trocar is withdrawn and the canula left in until the gas has fully escaped.

Puncturing is not a serious operation in cattle, and in cases of great distention should be performed without hesitancy or delay. Relief is almost instantaneous in many cases. Of course, the proper remedial agents should be administered to arrest further fermentation. (See Tympanites, pages 83-85.)

RUMENOTOMY.

The opening of the paunch, or rumen, in cattle and the removal of a part or the whole of the ingesta through said opening is termed rumenotomy. The operation should be performed in severe cases only, where the rumen is excessively overloaded and distended. The animal is placed with its right side against a wall and firmly held in position by strong assistants. The incision is made in the same place that the trocar is inserted for puncturing the organ in cases of hoven. The opening is increased in size until the operator's hand can be inserted into the rumen. Before any of the contents are removed from that organ a linen cloth should be placed from the outer wound into the rumen in order to prevent any of the ingesta from getting into the abdominal cavity. After removing a portion of the contents of the rumen some practitioners introduce such medicine as may be indicated before closing the wound. Clean the wound and close the opening in the rumen with uninterrupted carbolized catgut sutures. Next close the external wound, consisting of the integument muscle, and peritoneum, with stout, interrupted metallic sutures. No food should be given for several hours after the operation and then gruels only. (See Distention of Rumen with Food, page 85.)

TREATMENT OF ABSCESSES.

An abscess may be detected, if situated externally, by heat, pain, redness, and swelling in the early stages, and, if further developed, by the fluctuation which will be present. When any of these symptoms are absent, the suppuration should be encouraged by the means of hot fomentations and poultices. Care must be taken that the abscess is not opened too soon, or it may to some extent cause it to scatter and the escape of pus will be lessened. The time to open an abscess is just before it is ready to break, and should be done with a sharp lance, a crucial incision sometimes being necessary. The cavity should be syringed out with an antiseptic solution. Care should be taken not to allow the wound to close too rapidly, and to prevent this a tent of lint or oakum should be introduced.

Steer with Chronic Bacterial Dysentery.
Dept. of Agr.

A Tuberculous Bull. Dept. of Agr.

WOUNDS.

It is probably not going too far to say that as a general rule wounds of the bovine species, unless sufficiently serious to endanger the animal's life, are left uncared for. The poor suffering creatures are too often, even in fly time, left to endure untold torture from wounds not at first of much importance, but which, from the constant irritation caused by flies, dirt, etc., often develop into hideous, unhealthy sores, which can not fail, even when they do heal, to leave extensive and lasting blemishes as records of the owner's thriftlessness and inhumanity.

The comparatively low market value of all but the full-blood and pedigreed animal precludes an owner (save in a few exceptional cases, inspired by a higher than ordinary sense of humanity) from entertaining professional assistance. It is more than doubtful whether the suffering creature does not go from bad to worse when its case is made over to the tender mercies of the ignorant local cow-leech, to whom wolf in the tail is a terrifying living presence and hollow horn a solid fact, and whose sole claim to erudition in such matters consists of conceited ability to manufacture on scientific prescriptions an artificial substitute for the cud supposed to be lost.

There is yet another class of owners who entertain a blind belief in liniments and patent nostrums, many of which are not only an unnecessary expense, but may by their very action retard rather than expedite the process by which nature repairs the injured tissues, tendons, and bony structure.

It should always be borne in mind that although some applications are stimulating, and therefore serve as a useful ally in the process of restoration, it is, after all, to nature we must look to renovate the injured parts, and all that the most skillful can do is to aid her intelligently by combating those conditions which are calculated to interfere with her beneficent endeavors. All that the most suitable applications can accomplish in the case of wounds is, in the first place, to prevent the access of those poisonous germs which exist in the surroundings of the animal, such as the soil and the manure, and, in the second place, when the process of repair is for some reason temporarily inactive or altogether arrested, to incite that curative inflammation which is the invariable method by which the cure is effected.

Some owners may urge that it has always been their practice to use some shotgun prescription that has earned for itself a reputation, because it was supposed to have routed a rash on the youngest baby, and proved equally efficacious on a wire cut on the last-dropped calf, without even pausing to think that either case might have done equally well or even better if confided unanointed to the healing hands of Nature. For the purposes of the present work wounds may be divided into three classes: (1) Incised; (2) punctured; (3) lacerated or contused.

Incised Wound.—This is one with clean-cut edges, and may be either superficial or deep. In wounds of all descriptions there is necessarily more or less bleeding, and this is especially liable to be the case in incised wounds, particularly when they penetrate to a considerable depth, or when inflicted on a part where arteries of any size approach the surface. To arrest the hemorrhage must, therefore, be the first consideration. If slight, a generous use of cold water will be all that is necessary, but if one or more vessels of any size have been wounded or entirely severed, they should be taken up and ligated. If the blood flows continuously and is dark in color, it proceeds from a vein, but if bright-colored and jerky in its flow, it is arterial.

There is nothing very formidable or difficult in taking up an artery. It simply means tying up the bleeding vessel, which should be accomplished as follows: To discover the bleeding artery take a sponge, dip it in cold water, and by gentle pressure on the wound clear it of the accumulated blood. The jet of fresh blood reveals the end of the vessel, which is readily recognized by its whitish yellow, or buff, color. It should be seized with a forceps or pincers and slightly drawn clear of the surrounding tissues. Now take the thread and place the middle of it under the artery, fetch up the ends, tie one simple knot tightly, pressing down the thread with the forefinger so as not to include the forceps, then a second one over it, cut off the ends, and the thing is done. The bleeding being arrested, the operator can now carefully clean and inspect the wound, taking care to remove all blood and foreign matters and clip the hair around the edges before proceeding to stitch it up. If the wound is superficial, the lips may be brought together by a series of independent stitches, about three-fourths of an inch to an inch apart. The stitches should not be drawn tightly; it is sufficient to bring the edges of the wound in apposition.

If the wound is deep the needle should be introduced perpendicularly at as great a distance from the lip of the wound as the depth it is to be inserted, so as to give the thread sufficient hold. All the stitches should be as nearly as possible at equal distances from the border of the wound, to prevent unequal strain, and the knots should be made at the side, not over the wound. When the wound is large and deep, care should be taken to have an opening in the lowest part to allow for the escape of the discharges.

In deep wounds which run crosswise of a limb or muscle it will often be advisable to use what is technically known as the "quilled suture." To accomplish this method a curved needle with an eye in the point and a strong double thread should be used. The needle thus threaded is introduced perpendicularly at least an inch from the wound on one side, carried across below and brought out the same distance from the border of the cut on the opposite side, the thread being seized and held in position while the needle is withdrawn, leaving a loop of thread protruding on one side and two loose ends on the other side of each stitch. When a sufficient number of stitches have been made, take a light piece of wood about the size of a lead pencil, corresponding in length to the size of the wound, or slightly longer, and insert it through each of the loops, drawing up the free ends of the threads, which should in turn be tied securely on a similar piece of wood on that side.

Punctured Wounds.—Owing to the uncertainty of their depth and the structures they may involve, punctured wounds are by far the most dangerous and difficult to treat. Not only is the extent of the damage hidden from view, but the very character of the injury, as can be readily understood, implies at least the possibility of deep-seated inflammation and consequent discharge of pus (matter), which, when formed, is kept pent up until it has accumulated to such an extent that it burrows by simple gravity, as no other exit is possible. In this way foreign matters, such as a broken piece of the stake or snag, or whatever caused the wound, may be carried to an indefinite depth, or the cavity of a joint may be invaded and very serious, if not fatal, consequences supervene.

The danger is especially marked when the injury is inflicted on parts liable to frequent and extensive motion, but all cases of punctured wounds should receive unusual care, as no judgment can be accurately formed from the external appearance of the wound. While a probe can ascertain the depth, it throws but little light on the extent or exact nature of the internal injury. For this reason all punctured wounds should invariably be carefully searched by means of a probe or some substitute devised for the occasion, such as a piece of wire with a smooth blunt end, or a piece of hard wood shaped for the purpose. Stitching is not admissible in the case of punctured wounds.

If a punctured wound is not very deep, and when the bruising and laceration are slight, it is possible for healing to take place by adhesion, and this should always be encouraged, as the process of repair by this method is far superior to that by granulation, which will be referred to later. With this object in view, the animal should be kept as quiet as possible. A dose of physic, such as a pound of Glauber's or Epsom salts, should be administered, and warm fomentations or poultices, when this is practicable, applied, the surface of the wound being dressed twice a day with the ordinary white lotion, which is made as follows:

Acetate of lead ....ounce..	1
Sulphate of zinc ....drams..	6
Water ....quart..	1

The lead and zinc should be put in a quart bottle with a pint of rain water and well shaken, when the balance of the water may be added.

In wounds of this description the process of repair may be complicated by the appearance of exuberant granulations, popularly known as proud flesh or dead flesh, but really an overgrowth of new tissue—granulation tissue; but these should not be interfered with unless they should continue after the acute stage of inflammation has been subdued. If, after this, they persist, they may be treated with a solution of sulphate of copper (bluestone) or nitrate of silver (lunar caustic) and water. Irritation, caused by an overinterference with the process of repair, and injudicious bandaging are potent factors in bringing about this condition, and the discontinuance of either or both will often leave no necessity for special treatment.

Contused or Lacerated Wounds.—These are usually caused by a blow with some blunt instrument, by the breaking of the flooring, or when an animal gets one of its limbs through or over the partition between the stalls. The seriousness depends largely on the depth of the injury, and treatment should be directed to allaying the inflammation and preventing the consequent tendency to sloughing. To this end soothing applications, such as fomentations and poultices, are plainly indicated.

Methods of Healing.—Technically these may be divided into a number of distinct processes, but practically we may speak of them as two only, namely, by primary union, or adhesion, and by granulation. As suppuration is not so liable to occur in cattle as in the horse, healing by the former and more speedy process is much more common in the first-named species, more particularly in clean-cut or incised wounds, provided they have been stitched within twelve hours from the time the injury which caused them was inflicted; that they have been kept clean and that the patient has by some means been kept fairly still. This latter stipulation is probably hardest to comply with. Quiet is an important factor in the process of repair among the lower animals as well as their masters, and the rule is none the less good because, unfortunately, it is more frequently honored in the breach than in the observance. Healing by this method is in some cases extraordinarily quick, union between the divided parts having been known to take place as soon as twenty-four hours after their adjustment by the surgeon.

The second method of healing, namely, by granulation, which is, however, the manner in which most wounds in animals heal, takes much longer time. In puncturing wounds of any depth healing necessarily takes place in this way only, and the treatment should be directed largely to alleviating pain and moderating inflammation. The former can be accomplished by opium applied locally in the form of the diluted tincture, or given internally in repeated small doses; and the latter by aconite or fluid extract of gelsemium, 25 to 30 drops of either of which are given in the drinking water or dropped on the tongue at intervals, depending on the severity of the fever.

After-Treatment and Dressing of Wounds.—The dressing of wounds, whether they have been attended to by a veterinarian or not, is a matter which, in case of cattle, invariably devolves upon the owner or his employees. It must not, however, be inferred from this that the matter is of secondary importance. The dressing of wounds is one of the most important branches of veterinary surgery, and one of the most constant difficulties that the practicing veterinarian has to contend with lies in the want of appreciation on the part of owners of the great importance of care and attention in the after treatment of wounds. It is for this reason that the writers are averse to closing this portion of their task without pointedly calling attention to the fact that it is very largely to skillful, patient and careful dressing that satisfactory recovery from most serious accidents is due, and this unswerving vigilance and solicitude we would bespeak not only for the injured parts, but for the general care of the animal and its surroundings.

The first and foremost consideration in the dressing of a wound is the observance of scrupulous cleanliness. The most subtle medicaments and antiseptics are worse than wasted if dirt claims a 50 per cent interest in the business, as is too often the case upon the farm where the care of an animal is relegated to ignorant and thoughtless hired help. Unless an animal is in slings, straw and other foreign bodies as well as blood and necessary discharges usually adhere to a wound when it comes to be dressed. These should be carefully freed from the wound by means of a sponge dipped in a 2 per cent solution of carbolic acid. The sponge should not be brought into actual contact, but should be wrung out just above it, the water being allowed to trickle over the injured part. When the wound and the parts surrounding it have been thoroughly cleansed it may be dressed either with the white lotion, the formula for which has already been given, or with a solution of chlorid of zinc, 1 ounce to a quart of pure cold water. In cold weather the parts may be dressed with the following: Oxid of zinc ointment, 4 ounces; compound tincture of benzoin, 2 drams; mix and keep the box covered.

A single fold of ordinary cotton batting gently pressed over the ointment will cause it to remain adherent to the wounded part. In superficial excoriated wounds in cattle a very excellent first dressing (after thoroughly cleansing the wound) consists of iodoform (a compound of iodin and chloroform) blown on to the wound through a quill or a folded piece of stiff paper. This should be followed by a second dressing of pulverized aloes applied in the same way, which not only forms an artificial scab, but possesses the additional advantage of keeping off flies.

There are several other applications which are efficacious, such as bichlorid of mercury, 1 part to 800 of water; boracic acid, 1 part to 20 parts of water; carbolic acid, 1 part to water 30 parts; but the foregoing will be found as good as any.

No good purpose can be served by applying to healthy wounds irritating mixtures of oils and acids, and an owner may safely make up his mind to the fact that whatever mixtures he may use, no matter how successful it may have been, he is pretty sure to have a neighbor who will want to know the reason why he did not use something else. Whatever antiseptic is used, always recollect that cleanliness, rest, and attention constitute 50 per cent of the contest, and that the other half may safely be left to the restoring touch of Nature.

Barbed-Wire Cuts.—We have specified these simply because there exists in some sections of the country a fixed idea that there is a specific poison in barbed wire, causing injuries which require treatment differing from that which is applicable to ordinary wounds. Barbed-wire cuts differ from ordinary wounds only in the parts being often lacerated and torn, and the treatment already indicated for wounds of that description is applicable to them.

CASTRATION.

Castration consists of the removal of the essential organs of generation. It is performed upon both the male and the female. In the male the organs removed are the testicles and in the female the ovaries. It is performed in the male for several different purposes. It may be necessary, as is the case in certain diseased conditions of the testicles and in strangulated hernia, but the usual object of the operation is to enhance the general value of the animal. For example, if the animal is intended for burden, the operation will better fit him for his work by modifying his temperament and physical condition that he may easily be controlled by his master. Again, if he is merely to be used for beef purposes, the operation will improve the quality of the flesh.

The operation upon the female may be performed on account of diseased conditions, but we may say that the chief object of the operation is to make the animal one of more profit to its owner by altering the lacteal secretion and also the physical condition. Advocates of this operation claim that a spayed cow will milk under favorable conditions for a number of years continuously, and that the milk is greatly increased in richness. Careful tests, however, indicate that the value of this operation with dairy cows has been exaggerated. When the cow is spayed it does away with all trouble attending estrum, or heat, gestation, and parturition with its accidents and ailments. The flesh of the spayed cow is more tender and juicy than that of the entire animal.

The operation upon the male may be either the uncovered or the covered. In the former the incision is made down to the testicle proper, and in the latter the cut is made through the scrotum or the outside covering and through the dartos, or the next coat, care being taken to cut no deeper tissues or coats. The age at which the operation is performed varies, but usually it is performed between the second and third month. If done in early life there is less danger of complications, the organs not being fully developed and in a latent condition. There are many different methods of operating, the principal ones of which we shall mention. In the uncovered operation a good free incision should be made, exposing the testicle completely. Now it may be removed by simply cutting it off. The only danger of doing this is that hemorrhage is likely to follow. To obviate this, before the division of the spermatic cord it should be twisted several times in the following manner: Take hold of the spermatic cord with the left hand, having the cord between the thumb and the index finger. Now twist the free portion several times with the right hand, all the time being careful to push with the left hand toward the body of the animal. In this way the danger of injury to the cord during the animal's struggles will be overcome. The hemorrhage will be none, or very little, if it has been done properly. This is the most simple manner of torsion. There are forceps and other instruments made to perform the operation in this manner. Instead of practicing torsion in any of its ways to prevent hemorrhage, a ligature may be applied either directly to the spermatic artery from which the hemorrhage comes, or to the entire cord. Either a silk or a catgut ligature may be used. The actual cautery is an old method, but we shall not describe it, as we consider that we have better methods now. The next method with the clamps, although extensively used upon the horse, is not practiced to any great extent upon the bovine at the present time. It is a very old method, and is considered very safe. Clamps are used in the covered and uncovered operations.

But more simple and better methods are now known for the castration of the bull. A more modern method is by the ecraseur. The chain of the instrument is placed around the spermatic cord and tightened so as to crush the tissues and thus prevent hemorrhage. The clamp and ligature are the methods principally employed in the covered operation.

The operation of mulling, or crushing, the spermatic cord is an unscientific and barbarous procedure, causing unnecessary pain and suffering.

The above methods apply only to the animal in a normal condition. Before operating always examine and be sure that everything is as it should be. If otherwise, a special operative procedure will be necessary. Whichever mode of operation be adopted from a practical standpoint, the principal precautions to be taken in order to attain success are as follows: First, thorough cleanliness under strict aseptic and antiseptic precautions; second, a free and boldly made incision; third, the avoidance of undue pulling or tension upon the spermatic cord; fourth, free drainage, which can be maintained, provided the original incision has been properly made.

CASTRATION OF THE FEMALE.

Ovariotomy (Spaying).—The operation should be performed when the cow is in her prime and giving her greatest flow of milk, care being taken that she is in good health and moderate condition, not too plethoric; or, on the other hand, she must not be at all anemic, and also that she be not in heat or pregnant. This operation may be performed in one of two ways—namely, by the flank or by the vagina—each operation having its special advantages. In the flank operation the animal may be operated upon either while standing or while in the recumbent position. If standing, she should be placed against a wall or a partition, and her head held by a strong assistant. The legs also must be secured to prevent the animal from kicking. A vertical incision should be made in the left flank, about the middle of the upper portion, care being taken not to make the opening too far down, in order to avoid the division of the circumflex artery which traverses that region. The operator should now make an opening through the peritoneum, which is best done with the fingers. Next introduce the hand and arm into the abdominal cavity and direct the hand backward toward the pelvis, searching for the horns of the uterus. Follow them up and the ovaries will easily be found. They should then be drawn outward, and may be removed either by the écraseur or by torsion. Closing and suturing the wound will complete the operation. An adhesive plaster bandage can be beneficially applied.

The operation by the vagina is more complicated and requires special and expensive instruments. The mode of procedure in brief is as follows: A speculum is introduced into the vagina and an incision is made into the superior wall of that passage about 2 inches from the neck of the uterus, cutting from below upward and from before backward. Make an incision which should not exceed 3½ inches in length. The next step is to get possession of the ovaries. They are situated in a fold of the broad ligament and should be drawn carefully into the vagina through the incision. Now take the long-handled scissors specially made for this purpose, with which the thick border of the broad ligament is divided. The torsion forceps are introduced and applied to the broad ligament above the ovary. The left hand is then introduced and the thumb and the index finger grasp hold of the broad ligament above the forceps. Now commence with the right hand to apply torsion and thus remove the ovary. The other ovary may be removed in the same manner.

The operation of castration is by no means a serious one, and when properly performed there is little danger from complications. Although the danger is trifling, the complications which may arise are sometimes of a serious nature. Hemorrhage, either primary or secondary, tetanus, or lockjaw, abscesses, hernia, or rupture, gangrene, and peritonitis are the most serious complications that follow castration. Whichever complication arises will require its own special treatment, which we will not go into here, as it will be fully dealt with under another heading. We would add, however, that generally speaking, the animal, after being castrated, should either be regularly exercised or be allowed freedom so that it can exercise itself. Drafts of cold air or sudden changes of the temperature are dangerous. The animal should be fed moderately, but of a diet easily digestible. Other surgical operations, not described in this chapter, may be found in other parts of this work by reference to the index.—(Ark. Exp. Sta. Bul. 8; S. Car. Exp. Sta. Bul. 27 (New Series); Virginia Exp. Sta. Bul. 7 (New Series), Vol. I.; Virginia Exp. Sta. Bul. 1 (New Series), Vol. VII.; Georgia Exp. Sta. Bul. 21; Maryland Exp. Sta. Bul. 78.)

LIST OF OTHER PUBLICATIONS CONSULTED AND ABRIDGED ABOVE.

Special Report on Diseases of Cattle: U. S. Dept. of Agriculture, Washington, D. C.

Eye Diseases of the Domestic Animals: Alabama Agr. Exp. Sta. Bulletin 43.

Acute Keratitis (inflammation of the cornea in cattle): California Agr. Exp. Sta. Bulletin 219.

Contagious Sore Eyes of Cattle: Kansas Agr. Exp. Sta. Press Bulletin 115.

Conjunctivitis (simple ophthalmia): U. S. Bureau of Animal Industry Circular 65.

PART II

DISEASES OF SHEEP.

GENERAL CONDITIONS.

SHEEP are subject to as great variety of diseases as most other farm animals. Some of the diseases are much more common than others, and this fact together with the great similarity in the behavior which the animal shows in most diseases, has led flock-masters to think that sheep are subject to few ailments. The similarity in behavior in the early stages makes it difficult to form a diagnosis without a thorough examination of the animal and surroundings.

In examining a sheep, the behavior, appearance, general condition and surroundings must all be taken under consideration. The history should be obtained from the attendant as frequently that is of importance in arriving at a diagnosis and in determining the line of treatment. In none of the domestic animals, can disease be more successfully combatted by prevention than in sheep. It is along this line of treatment that we must direct greatest attention as the animals are not good patients when once attacked.

The symptoms inform us as to the condition of the animal at the onset and during the progress of a disease. Thus we have the symptoms connected with (a) the pulse; (b) the respiration; (c) body temperature; (d) the mucous membrane; (e) surface of the body; (f) secretions and excretions; and (g) nervous system.

The pulse is not as good a guide to the condition of the sheep as in the horse or cow as it is too readily influenced by excitement, by the presence of strangers and unusual handling. We obtain the pulse in sheep by pressing the femoral artery on the inside of the thigh. The pulse in the healthy sheep is subject to considerable variations, from 60 to 80 beats per minute, and when excited or nervous may run considerably above one hundred. The following varieties of pulse are recognized in disease: frequent or infrequent, quick or slow, large or small, hard or soft, and regular or intermittent. The frequency of the pulse has reference to the number of pulsations per minute; quick or slow has reference to the time required for the pulse wave to pass; large or small to the volume of blood that passes; hard or soft to the sense of feeling while passing under the finger; and regular and intermittent to the interval between the beats. There may be a number of beats regular in time and then the missing of one or two, or there may be an acceleration of a few beats. The condition of the circulation may also be judged by placing the hands on each side of the chest as nearly over the heart as possible. This is applicable especially in lambs and sheep thin in flesh.

When the sheep is quiet, the number of respirations will vary from twelve to eighteen per minute; if excited, exercised, or when warm this number will be greatly increased. In most animals there is a comparatively close relationship between the respirations and pulse (1 to 4 or 1 to 5), but in sheep this relationship is not very constant. In disease the respirations may be quickened and their character changed as in fever, pleurisy, peritonitis, etc. In abdominal respiration the movements of the wall of the chest are limited—as occurs in pleurisy, while in thoracic respiration the muscles of the abdomen are held rigid and the walls of the chest make up for the deficiency. This latter condition is seen in peritonitis.

In inflammatory conditions of the air passages, irritation from dust or parasites, the secretions are modified and there is dryness or discharge, and usually sneezing or coughing. There may be modified respiratory sounds that are of value in making a diagnosis.

The normal temperature of the sheep is subject to variation. It is taken per rectum, the ordinary fever thermometer being used. The variations are from 100° to 105° Fahrenheit. During exercise and when the weather or stable is warm and close, the body temperature is elevated; during cold weather or after drinking cold water it will be lowered. In order to get at the normal temperature it is well to take the temperature of several sheep in the flock.

In health the mucous membranes are usually of a pale reddish color. Exercise will cause them to become more vascular. When inflamed they are of a bright-red color. In collapse, internal hemorrhage, impoverished or bloodless conditions they are pale. In chronic indigestion the mouth is foul and soapy; if irritated the mucous membranes are excessively moist, and if feverish they are dry. In some of the parasitic and liver diseases they are yellowish.

The fleece should look smooth and have plenty of yolk; the skin should be of a light pink color. When the animal is diseased or is unthrifty, the wool may become dry and brittle, and the skin pale and rigid. If affected with external parasites, the fleece looks taggy, or the wool lost over large areas, and the skin itself is changed. During febrile diseases the temperature of the skin is not uniformly distributed. If fatally affected the skin feels cold. When debilitated, especially if the debility be due to internal parasites, dropsical swellings may occur under the jaw and in different parts of the body.

The character of the excretions from the kidneys and bowels become modified in disease and should be considered in making a diagnosis of the different diseases. The state of the nervous system is indicated by dullness, excitability, turning the head to one side, walking in a circle, throwing the head back, or by paralysis.

Administration of Medicine.—Drugs may be administered by way of the following channels: (a) by the mouth, (b) by hypodermically injecting into the tissues beneath the skin, (c) through the skin, (d) by way of the air passages and lungs, and (e) per rectum. The most common method of administration is by way of the mouth in the form of a drench. This can be done when the sheep is in the standing position or when thrown on its haunches and held between the knees. The standing position is to be preferred and it is best to give the drench with a small dose syringe. Care should be taken to not throw the head too far back, especially if the drench is bulky or irritating, as a part may get into the air passages and cause serious trouble. If a prompt, energetic effect is desired, and the drug non-irritating, it may be injected into the tissue beneath the skin. In sheep, this method of administration is seldom used.

Liniments, blisters and poultices are applied to the skin for their local effect. Absorption does not readily take place unless considerable friction is used in applying the medicine or the outer layer of skin is removed by blistering or by other means.

Volatile drugs as chloroform, ether, etc., are rapidly absorbed by the enormous vascular surface of the lungs. Anesthetics are seldom used in this class of animals and when medicine is administered by way of the respiratory track it is generally used in different respiratory diseases. This is done by partly filling a pail with boiling water, adding to it an ounce or two of creolin, turpentine or whatever drug is desired and allowing the sheep to inhale the vapors as they rise from the pail. To direct the steam toward the animal's nose, a light stable blanket can be thrown over the head of the sheep and allowed to drop over the sides of the pail.

An enema or clyster is a fluid injection into the rectum and is for the following purposes: (a) to increase the action of a purgative; (b) to stimulate the peristaltic movement of the intestines; (c) for a local effect on the rectum, and (d) to administer medicine and supply food. An injection is generally given for its purgative effect and it is best to allow the fluid to gravitate into the bowels from a height of about two feet. The apparatus needed for this purpose is a funnel and two or three feet of rubber tubing with a nozzle at one end. Before introducing the nozzle into the rectum it should be lubricated with vaseline, In giving a large injection, it is best to elevate the hind parts of the animal.

DISEASES OF THE DIGESTIVE SYSTEM.
STOMATITIS; SORE MOUTH.

Causes.—The lining membrane of the mouth of sheep is rather delicate, but so carefully do they select their feed that it is seldom injured. Stomatitis, or sore mouth, may be seen as a complication in infections and febrile diseases. Young and debilitated lambs when kept in unhygienic quarters (poorly ventilated, filthy, damp stables) are prone to the ulceration form of sore mouth. The disease seems to be communicated from one lamb to the other and is no doubt due to some of the pathogenic germs.

Symptoms.—In simple stomatitis the parts are congested, swollen and inflamed. At first the lining membrane is dry, but in a short time the secretions become excessive and the saliva dribbles from the mouth. The decomposition of the food, etc., going on in the mouth gives rise to a very disagreeable odor. Eating is quite painful and the animal is generally unable to take food. Recovery usually takes place in a few days. In the ulcerative form the gums become dark red, spongy and bleed easily. In a short time a part dies, sloughs out and a deep, ragged looking ulcer forms. The ulcer can be seen on the lips and gums and may become quite extensive, the teeth loosening, dropping out and perforations occurring in the lips. Threads of saliva dribble from the mouth and the breath has a disagreeable odor. The lamb refuses to suckle, becomes weak and may have a foetid diarrhea. This disease frequently results in death in about one or two weeks and if recovery occurs it is very slow. The lining membrane of the fourth stomach may be reddened and the lungs inflamed and the seat of bloody exudations.

Treatment.—In simple stomatitis washing the mouth with antiseptic and astringent washes once a day is all that is necessary. A four per cent watery solution of boric acid can be used. Plenty of this solution should be used and the mouth washed thoroughly. The animal must be fed soft feeds and gruels. In the ulcerative form preventive measures are important. This consists in improving the hygienic conditions and isolating the sick lambs. The quarters should be cleaned and the floors and walls washed with a disinfectant. The local treatment consists in removing the dead tissue from the ulcers, washing the mouth with a two per cent watery solution of creolin and touching the ulcers with lunar caustic.

DEPRAVED APPETITE; WOOL EATING LAMBS.

This disease is more common in lambs than in older animals. The thriftiness of the lamb is interfered with and in a large per cent of cases may prove fatal. The loss due to the injury to the fleeces is of some importance from an economic point of view.

Causes.—By some it is considered to be due to a depraved sense of taste and is classified as a nervous disease. In most cases it seems to result from example and improper food, especially food deficient in saline matter. Sheep shut up during the winter may get into the habit of chewing each other's fleeces. Lambs are especially apt to contract this habit when suckling ewes having long hair on the udder that is soiled with urine and fæces.

Symptoms.—It may be some time before symptoms of unthriftiness are manifested and outside of the loss to the fleece, no symptoms are noticed. Finally the digestive tract becomes involved, due to the irritation from the hair balls that accumulate in the stomach, digestion is deranged and the sheep loose flesh. The animals are sometimes constipated or have a diarrhea. Death may be due to the small hair balls drifting along and obstructing the openings from the different apartments of the stomach, or as a result of the inflammation of the stomach and intestines. The course of the disease varies from a few months to a year.

Treatment.—Avoid keeping sheep in too close quarters and allow plenty of exercise. When the disease occurs on poor pasture a change to a better one and a liberal allowance of salt will prevent it, or a well balanced ration of grain can be added. The long wool on the udder of ewes should be clipped off and if the lambs contract this habit they must be separated from their mothers except when nursing. When indigestion is present the following bitter tonics can be given: bicarbonate of soda (two ounces), powdered gentian (one ounce), sulphate of soda (six ounces); mix and give one teaspoonful in the feed morning and evening.

ACUTE TYMPANITES, BLOATING, HOVEN.

Bloating is more common among cattle than among sheep, but usually when it does occur a number of animals in the flock are affected. The disease is more common during late summer and early fall than at any other season of the year.

Causes.—Diseases of the rumen or any part of the digestive track predisposes sheep to tympanites. When due to these conditions, it usually takes on a chronic form. It may occur as a symptom of choking. A very common cause is succulent foods such as clover, rape, green corn, etc., especially if wet with dew or a light rain and when the animal is not accustomed to eating them. Frozen food and drinking large quantities of cold water after eating may sometimes cause a fermentation of the food in the rumen.

Symptoms.—The abdomen is distended with gas and is larger than normal. The left flank is distended at first but when the gas forms in large amounts the whole abdomen becomes distended. This occurs very quickly, is elastic and resonant. The sheep stop eating and ruminating, look anxious, the eyes are prominent, the mucous membranes are congested and fæces are expelled at irregular intervals. If not relieved the respirations become labored and the pulse weak. Saliva dribbles from the mouth. The animal becomes very stupid and finally sinks to the ground and dies. Death occurs as a result of the absorption by the blood-vessels of a toxic product from the stomach and the interference with the aeration of the blood in the lungs due to the pressure on the air cells by the distended rumen. Acute tympanitis takes a very rapid course. If the gas escapes by way of the gullet or intestines a spontaneous cure may result.

Treatment.—Preventive measures are important. A change to a succulent diet should be made gradually; musty grains, fodders, roots and frosted foods should not be fed to sheep. It is not best to allow a flock to graze in clover or eat any succulent food if wet with dew or light rain. The gas can be removed very quickly by puncturing the rumen with the trocar and canula. The seat of the operation is on the most prominent portion of the left flank. A small sized trocar and canula should be used and to guard against infection, it should be sterilized before using and the skin over the seat of the puncture washed with a disinfectant. The instrument is then plunged through the walls of the abdomen and rumen, the trocar withdrawn and the gas allowed to escape. Before withdrawing the canula the trocar should be replaced. It is always best after using the instrument to boil it in water. This will insure a clean instrument when needed. When a number of sheep in the flock are affected and there is a running stream in the pasture, it is best to drive them into it. The cold water coming in contact with the wall of the abdomen may stimulate the movement of the rumen and the gas will be then worked off by the natural passages. Dipping them into water will have the same effect. To prevent further fermentation, a table-spoonful of turpentine can be given in three or four ounces of lin-seed oil. The following receipt is useful; Glauber salts (half an ounce), powdered gentian (one dram), aromatic spirits of ammonia (two drams), water (six ounces); mix and give as a drench.

CHRONIC TYMPANITES.

Causes.—The chronic form of tympanites is generally due to some chronic diseases of the digestive track. The persistence of some of the causes of the acute form may lead to the conditions becoming chronic.

Symptoms.—The whole digestive system seems to lack tone and vigor. The bowels are irregular and the sheep falls away in condi-tion quite rapidly. Instead of the bloating being severe and inter-mittent as in the acute form it is continuous and the gas does not form rapidly.

Treatment.—The cause should be removed if possible, but in some chronic diseases this cannot be accomplished. The sheep should be fed easily digestible food and have free access to plenty of common salt and pure water. As a laxative, four ounces of sulphate of soda can be given in about ten ounces of water. As a digestive tonic the following can be given: Sulphate of soda (six ounces), powdered gentian (one ounce), and powdered nux vomica (one-half ounce); mix, and give one tablespoonful in the feed morning and evening. Whenever necessary the trocar and canula should be used.

OVERLOADING OF THE RUMEN OR PAUNCH.

Causes.—Overloading of the paunch is generally due to a sud-den change from indifferent or poor food to palatable, succulent food, such as green clover, corn, sorghum, etc., when eaten in excess. If the digestive track is diseased and the movements of the paunch are weak overloading is very apt to occur.

Symptoms.—The animal shows evidence of abdominal pain, does not ruminate or eat and is dull and feverish. The abdomen is distended on the left side, is not elastic as in tympanitis, but feels doughy when pressed on with the fingers. Some gas may form but the distension of the rumen is mostly due to the mass of food. When the disease is acute the symptoms are quite severe, the expression is anxious, the head is extended, eyes prominent and the respirations hurried. Constipation is a prominent symptom. Death may take place in a few hours but generally runs a course of several days. When the symptoms are mild, recovery is complete in a few days.

Treatment.—The proper preventive precautions should be used. The sick animal should be subject to a rigid diet. Exercise and rub-bing of the left flank may restore the normal movements of the paunch. Cold water injections are useful. If gas forms the trocar and canula must be used. As a purgative from four to six ounces of Epsom salts can be given in plenty of water. To excite the move-ments of the paunch four drams of aromatic spirits of ammonia in two ounces of linseed oil can be given every few hours or the follow-ing tonic: Powdered nux vomica (one-half ounce), powdered ginger (one ounce), bicarbonate of soda (two ounces); mix and give a small tablespoonful in a drench morning and evening. Strychnine if given hypodermically in the region of the paunch may stimulate it to contract. Rumenotomy (opening the paunch in the left flank and removing about two-thirds of its contents with the hand) is not followed by as good results as in cattle, and unless the operation is carefully performed will result in the death of the animal.

IMPACTION OF THE THIRD STOMACH; STOMACH STAGGERS.

Causes.—This disease may occur during the course of digestive troubles or febrile diseases. The third stomach may become irritated and inflamed by sudden changes in the diet or by food not prepared for entrance to this apartment, as bran or meal swallowed hastily. Dried and innutritious food when eaten in excess and lack of water, are very common causes of impaction.

Symptoms.—The disease usually develops slowly. The appetite is diminished, rumination occurs at irregular intervals, the sheep is dull and feverish and sometimes its movements are accompanied by a slight groan. Colicky pains and grinding of the teeth are sometimes present. The animal is constipated at first but if recovery occurs it may have a diarrhea. In the acute form nervous symptoms are sometimes manifested. The animal is dull, drowsy and listless and staggers when it walks. At times it becomes delirious, the eyes are prominent, it is restless and runs about coming in contact with whatever is in its way until it becomes exhausted or dies in a convulsion. The acute cases usually run a rapid course but in the chronic form the diseases may last for days.

Lesions.—The third stomach appears larger and harder than normal. When cut into the food lying between the folds of the mucous membrane may be so hard and dry that it can be powdered between the fingers. The lining membrane of the stomach is inflamed and the intestines may be also involved.

Treatment.—The sheep must be subject to a rigid diet and given plenty of water. A purgative of epsom salts (six ounces in plenty of water) or a liberal allowance of flaxseed tea can be given. The action of the purgative should be aided by an injection. It is usually best to give a tonic of powdered nux vomica (one half ounce) and sulphate of soda (four ounces); mix and give one tablespoonful in a drench three times a day. If brain symptoms develop we should prevent the sheep from doing itself harm, and relieve the inflammation as much as possible by applying ice to the head. Irritating purgatives must not be used. When convalescence takes place, the animal should be fed laxative and easily digestible food.

CHOKING.

Causes.—Greedy feeding animals are predisposed to choking. The foreign bodies present in the oesophagus or gullet generally consist of pieces of roots (potatoes, turnips, etc.) hay, grass, or ears of corn. Choking may be due to a diseased condition of the oesophagus as inflammation, paralysis, strictures and dilations,

Symptoms.—The sheep stops feeding, looks anxious and saliva dribbles from the mouth. The respirations are hurried and more or less difficult. Bloating may occur. If the choke is complete the animal is unable to take liquid or solid food and death may occur in a few hours. If incomplete the symptoms are not marked and the accident generally terminates favorably.

Treatment.—If the foreign body is lodged in the back part of the mouth or pharynx it can be removed with a blunt hook or a long iron spoon; if in the neck portion of the oesophagus, it may be worked back into the pharynx by pressure with the thumbs just below the object. If unable to force the object back into the mouth we must then resort to the probang and endeavor to force it on into the stomach. This instrument is several feet in length, hollow and has a bulb at the lower end. A probang for sheep should be half an inch in diameter, flexible and strong. In an emergency a light rod of hickory or elm rounded at both ends, the lower end covered with a piece of chamois firmly fastened, may be used. Heavy walled small rubber tubing will answer for the ordinary case. It is best to drench the sheep with an ounce or two of oil and smear the instrument with oil before passing it. The best position for the sheep is on its rump, the body gripped between the knees and the fore feet held with the hands. The operator should then grasp the tongue with one hand, draw it out of the mouth, rest the end of the probang against the hard palate and pass it rapidly into the oesophagus. It may require considerable pressure with the probang to remove the object, also the exercise of good judgment in doing this or the wall of the oesophagus may be injured.

DYSENTERY IN LAMBS; WHITE SCOURS.

Causes.—This is not an uncommon disease of young lambs. A weak constitution and unhygienic surroundings, damp, dirty, overcrowded, poorly ventilated quarters, are important predisposing causes. Retention of the meconium is at times a cause of scours. The most common causes are too much milk and variations in its character. It may be due to a contagious element that gains entrance to the body by way of the umbilical cord.

Symptoms.—The lamb is dull, depressed, is careless of the teat and refuses to suckle. Constipation may precede the diarrhea. The lamb sometimes shows evidence of abdominal pain by switching the tail and acting uneasy. If fermentation takes place the abdomen is distended. The diarrhea is foul smelling, the tail, hips, and legs soon become soiled, the animal is feverish, extremities cold, and rapidly becomes weak and emaciated. Death may follow as a result of exhaustion. If the cause of the disease is of infectious origin a large per cent of the lambs will die.

Treatment.—This is largely preventive. Dry, well ventilated, clean quarters should be provided and the lamb should be allowed plenty of exercise. If the mother's milk does not agree with the lamb and the fault is in the ration or general management, it should be corrected. If the diarrhea is due to a specific cause, the quarters must be cleaned and disinfected. As soon as the disease

An Advanced Case of Common Scab. B. A. I. 1897.

A Slightly Advanced Case of Common Scab. B. A. I. 1897.

makes its appearance the umbilical cord of all new born should be swabbed with a ten per cent solution of carbolic acid as nearly as possible. At first a laxative of castor oil (two drams), should be given; this can be followed by five or ten drops of laudanum three times a day. If there is much fermentation and the fæces foul smelling the following can be given; subnitrate of bismuth (one dram), salol (one half dram), and bicarbonate of soda (four drams); mix and divide into twelve powders; give one powder in a little milk three times a day. When extremely foetid the following recipe is of more benefit; calomel (one half dram) chalk (six drams); mix and give one teaspoonful in milk three times a day. It is best to diet the lamb and give the irritated stomach and intestines a short rest.

GASTRO-ENTERITIS; INFLAMMATION OF THE FOURTH STOMACH AND THE INTESTINES.

Causes.—Poorly fed, weak and debilitated sheep are predisposed to this disease. Irritating foods, (rich, spoiled, or frosted foods), drinking water swarming with germs, over driving, and over feeding; exposure or anything lessening the resisting powers of the system may cause it. The twisted stomach worm is a common cause of inflammation of the fourth stomach.

Symptoms.—The appetite is poor or lost and the sheep stops ruminating. The pulse and respirations are quickened and the body temperature elevated. Colicky pains may be present and when pressure is made with the hand over the region of the fourth stomach (right hypochrondriac) it will sometimes cause the animal severe pain. At first the bowels are constipated, but this soon changes to a foul smelling diarrhea that is mixed with mucus and sometimes tinged with blood. In severe cases the sheep suffers much pain, grinds its teeth, strains and nervous symptoms are manifested. The general condition of the animal is greatly changed in a short time, becoming poor and weak, and it stands around with the back arched or mopes along after the rest of the flock. Death may occur in a few days or at most a few weeks.

Lesions.—The tissue changes are mostly in the small intestines and fourth stomach. The lining membrane is reddened, thickened and may contain a few ulcers. The walls of the intestines are softened and break when handled.

Treatment.—If due to any mistake in the feeding or handling, it should be corrected at once. Plenty of exercise and access to pure water should be allowed. In summer time it is best to give the sheep the run of a grass lot where there is plenty of shade. In winter time they should be given warm, comfortable quarters. To relieve the constipation and remove the irritation, a laxative should be given; (Epsom salts three to four ounces, or linseed oil five to ten ounces). If the constipation persists this must be supplemented by an injection of warm water and glycerine. If the bowels move too freely and the sheep is in pain a teaspoonful of laudanum can be given two or three times a day or the following prescription can be used: subnitrate of bismuth (one ounce), salol (six drams), and bicarbonate of soda (three ounces); mix and give one teaspoonful every three or four hours. Artificial Carlsbad salts (equal parts of sulphate of soda, bicarbonate of soda, and chloride of soda) can be given. The addition of powdered gentian or nux vomica to the salts will greatly increase their value as a tonic.

INFLAMMATION OF THE LIVER.

PARENCHYMATITIS; HEPATITIS; ACUTE YELLOW ATROPHY OF THE LIVER.

Causes.—This disease is caused by excessive quantities of food, too little exercise, musty, decomposed, irritating fodders, excessive heat, injuries to the liver, and damp swampy pastures. It is frequently seen in contagious diseases and parasitic affections of the liver. This condition is always present in lupinosis.

Symptoms.—At first the symptoms may be obscure. Nothing characteristic is noted. The body temperature is elevated, the pulse is slow, or if the attack is severe, quickened, the appetite is lost or irregular, and the sheep acts dull and stupid. Jaundice may be present. The more characteristic symptoms are as follows: tenderness when pressure is applied over the region of the liver, (right side just back of the last rib); constipation followed by slightly colored, fetid diarrhea; colicky pains and a tendency to stagger. If the disease continues for some time the animal becomes weak and emaciated. Complications may occur, the most common being peritonitis. The prognosis is not favorable in the chronic cases.

Treatment.—Preventive measures must be resorted to. The treatment consists in subjecting the sheep to a spare diet, applying a blister to the right side, giving a purgative of Epsom salts or calomel and repeating it if necessary. Artificial Carlsbad salts (equal parts of sulphate of soda, bicarbonate of soda, and chloride of soda) in teaspoonful doses should be given in the feed two or three times a day. When the acute symptoms have abated the following bitter tonic can be given; powdered gentian (one ounce) potassium chlorate (one ounce) bicarbonate of soda (two ounces); mix and give one teaspoonful in the feed twice a day.

JAUNDICE.

This is not a disease in itself but symptom of disease, and is called jaundice or yellows, because of the yellow color of the mucous membranes, skin and different connective tissues of the body. Jaundice is nearly always present in sheep affected with the liver fluke, is quite common in sheep affected with the twisted stomach worm and is associated with other parasitic diseases. Many cases are seen, too, at slaughter houses the cause of which has not been determined.

Causes.—Any condition that may impede the flow of bile toward the intestines may cause jaundice. Overfeeding, lack of exercise, gall-stones and concretions in the gall duct are common causes. When sheep are allowed to pasture on rich grass lands, the liver sometimes becomes affected and jaundice is seen as a symptom of this condition. The disease has been known to occur among sheep kept in low, damp undrained pastures. Jaundice is a symptom of a disease caused by a toxic substance contained in lupines.

Symptoms.—The different tissues of the body are tinged with yellow, caused by the interference with the secretion of the bile from the liver and its reabsorption by the blood, from which it is deposited in the different connective tissues of the body. In the simplest form, the sheep has a slow pulse, is languid and sleepy, the appetite is irregular and the bowels constipated.

Treatment.—When the disease is caused by faulty hygienic conditions, they should be corrected if possible. A changed diet is always advisable. To cause free movement of the bowel three or four ounces of Epsom salts can be given in a drench, or in chronic cases, calomel in ten grain doses repeated every two or three days if necessary. A liberal allowance of common salt is said to be a preventive. If the sheep is weak a tonic can be given of pow-dered gentian (one ounce), sulphate of soda (two ounces), and bi-carbonate of soda (two ounces); mix and give one teaspoonful in the feed two or three times a day.

PERITONITIS; INFLAMMATION OF THE LINING MEMBRANE OF THE ABDOMEN.

Causes.—Peritonitis may follow as a result of castration. It is not uncommon for it to occur as a complication of a difficult birth or an inflammation of an internal organ. Exposure, poor care, blows or wounds on the abdominal wall, and a rupture of the stomach, intestines or womb may cause this disease.

Symptoms.—The most prominent symptom is pain. The sheep moves stiffly, the hind limbs are dragged, the back arched and the abdominal wall is held as rigid as possible. Pressure on the abdominal wall causes pain. The body temperature will vary. In some cases there is no elevation of temperature in others it is quite high. The sheep may be constipated or have a diarrhea. When fluid is present in the abdominal cavity we can detect it by placing the ear against the wall and listening to the abdominal sounds. The prognosis is not very favorable. The animal may die in a few days. When the disease is prolonged for several weeks it ends in a chronic peritonitis. In favorable cases the symptoms gradually subside and recovery takes place in a week or ten days.

Lesions.—The peritoneum is inflamed and there is an exudate in the abdominal cavity. This may contain fibrin or pus and may have a disagreeable odor. Different internal organs may take part in the inflammation.

Treatment.—Preventive measures consist in using the proper antiseptic precautions when castrating sheep and not operating on the lambs when young. The sheep should be kept as quiet as pos-sible, given good quarters and care and fed nothing but easily di-gestible food. To clean out the intestines and remove the bac-teria which becomes a source of danger, a laxative must be given and injections frequently used. Mucilaginous drinks are advis-able. To relieve the pain the following is useful: laudanum (one ounce) and linseed oil (three ounces); mix and give half a table-spoonful every three or four hours. To relieve the inflammation and lessen the pain, hot water fomentations or ammonia water can be applied to the abdominal wall. In cases having high tempera-tures, it is best to give the following febrifuge; acetanilide (one ounce), quinine sulphate (one ounce), and powdered nux vomica (one half ounce); mix and divide into twelve powders; give one powder every three or four hours. To relieve the diarrhea and fermentation in the intestines the following can be used: subni-trate of bismuth (one ounce) salol (one and one-half ounces), and bicarbonate of soda (three ounces); mix and give in one or two teaspoonful doses every three or four hours.

DISEASES OF THE URINARY ORGANS.

ACUTE CONGESTION OF THE KIDNEYS.

Causes.—During the course of some contagious diseases the kidneys may become the seat of inflammatory process. Food con-taining toxic element, irritating drugs and cold are common causes.

Symptoms.—The sheep lags behind the flock and is often seen lying down. The back is arched, the loins tender, the gait stiff and straddling and frequently it strains and passes bloody colored urine. As the disease advances the animal becomes weak, dull and stupid and when it walks, the gait is uncertain and it frequently stumbles. Death may take place in about a week. If the disease is mild recovery usually occurs in a few days.

Lesions.—The kidneys are reddened and larger than normal; the kidney tissue becomes friable and in some cases almost like pulp.

Treatment.—A sudden change from a dry diet to grass early in the spring should be avoided by feeding the sheep a little rough-ness or grain the first few days they are turned out. Irritating drugs whether applied to the skin or given internally must be used cautiously. After the disease has developed the animal must be given good, nourishing food and comfortable quarters. Plenty of oil or flaxseed meal is a very useful food in this disease. The bowels must be kept loose by feeding laxative food or by frequent doses of castor oil. The following preparation can be given; pow-dered nux vomica (one ounce), sulphate of quinine (one ounce), salol (one half ounce); mix and give in teaspoonful doses three times a day.

INFLAMMATION OF THE KIDNEYS. ACUTE NEPHRITIS. BRIGHT'S DISEASE.

Causes.—Congestion of the kidneys may terminate in an in-flammation. The common causes of nephritis are similar to those causing a congestion of these organs.

Symptoms.—Pain is not as prominent a symptom of this dis-ease in sheep as in other domestic animals. There may be consid-erable fever and a weak pulse. The urine is passed in small amounts and at frequent intervals. Toward the latter stage of the disease, the urine may be tinged with blood and the animal have convulsions. Unless the inflammation terminates in the early stages of the disease, different organs of the body become affected.

Lesions.—The kidneys are enlarged, mottled, of a red or yellowish color. Large abscesses sometimes form in the kidney tissue.

Treatment.—The sick sheep must be given comfortable quarters. Mucilaginous drinks are indicated. Counterirritants in the form of hot compresses to the loins will help in relieving the pain and inflammation. We must help in getting rid of the waste products formed in the body by the use of purgatives and diuretics. As a diuretic, bicarbonate of soda (one teaspoonful) and iodide of potassium (twenty grains) can be given in the drinking water two or three times a day. Castor oil can be given to keep the bowels lax. The same tonic recommended in congestion of the kidneys can be given.

INFLAMMATION OF THE BLADDER.

Causes.—Irritating drugs (cantharides, turpentine, etc.) when given in large doses may be present in the urine in large enough amounts to irritate and inflame the lining membrane of the bladder. Irritation due to retention of the urine and exposure to cold may also cause it.

Symptoms.—The body temperature may be higher than normal. The sheep walks stiffly, strains frequently and passes a small amount of urine. The lining membrane of the bladder is inflamed and thickened. In advanced cases due to the shedding of the epithelium, there may be large raw surfaces of the membrane.

Treatment.—Irritating drugs should not be used in a careless manner. If due to retention of the urine the cause must be removed if possible. The medicinal treatment consists in administering the remedies that will modify the inflammation. Mucilaginous drinks are indicated and the sheep should be kept quiet and the bowels lax. The following can be given: salol (one-half ounce), powdered nux vomica (one ounce), and chlorate of potassium (one and one-half ounces); mix and give in teaspoonful doses, in the feed twice a day.

RETENTION OF URINE.

This is not a disease in itself but a symptom of disease, and is more common in the male than in the female.

Causes.—The causes of retention of the urine are as follows: foreign bodies in the bladder (calculi), sediment in the S curvature of the urethra of the ram, pressure on the urethra by a tumor, inflammation of the sheath, displacement of the uterus, paralysis of the bladder, general weakness and infrequent urination. The feeding of a large ration of roots will also cause the trouble especially in males.

Symptoms.—The sheep refuse to eat, is drowsy and weak. Frequently strains and tries to urinate, but no urine is passed. Sometimes the urine runs off drop by drop. If not relieved the bladder is ruptured, or the blood becomes charged with poisonous substances and the disease terminates fatally, uraemia.

Treatment.—If a calculus is present in the bladder it must be removed if possible. In spasm of the neck of the bladder morphine or belladonna can be given, and when paralyzed, it is necessary to pass the catheter frequently. If due to an inflamed prepuce, the part must be washed with warm water and castile soap, and vaseline applied to the part.

DISEASES OF THE RESPIRATORY ORGANS.
COLD; CATARRH; CORYZA.

Causes.—This affection is due principally to exposure to cold, rainy weather, and in some years is very prevalent. Too early clipping may also be a cause. Confinement in basements of barns without sufficient ventilation will produce it. Coryza is sometimes caused by the larva of the sheep bot fly.

Symptoms.—The membrane lining the anterior air passages is irritated, reddened and inflamed and the sheep sneezes frequently or has a slight cough. During the early stage of the inflammation, the nasal membrane is red and dry. It soon becomes moist, the discharge from the nostrils is watery at first, in a short time may be changed to a heavy white flocculent, purulent fluid. The mucous membrane of the eye may take part in the inflammation; sometimes a slight fever accompanies the cold. If the discharge persists the animal becomes emaciated. If the attack is severe and the exposure continues, the inflammation may extend to other parts of the respiratory tract. The prognosis is usually favorable.

Treatment.—The preventive measures consist in providing the flock with good, clean, dry and well ventilated quarters, when necessary and waiting until a favorable season before clipping them. Usually, good quarters is all the treatment required for the sick animals. Steaming the sheep will relieve the irritated membranes. The steaming should be kept up for about half an hour and repeated two or three times a day. Early in the attack, a laxative can be given, and if necessary, febrifuges. Liquor ammonia acetate is sometimes given in half ounce doses every few hours. A nourishing, easily digested diet will be of much benefit. If due to bot fly larva, the only successful treatment is to trephine into the sinuses of the head and remove the parasites. If the catarrh develops early in the fall and the sheep are in good condition, they may be turned over to the butcher, if in the spring, good food with grain will carry them through until the fly comes away.

INFLAMMATION OF THE LARYNX AND PHARYNX.
SORE THROAT.

Causes.—Sore throat may occur independently of simple catarrh, but more commonly is seen as a complication of that disease. Exposure to frequent colds, changes in climate, wet, chilly weather and such unsanitary surroundings as hot, close, dirty buildings are common causes of sore throat.

Symptoms.—When caused by the inflammation spreading from the nasal cavities to the larynx and throat the early symptoms are the same as described in cold in the head. When the throat becomes inflamed, however, the cough is harder and more troublesome. Pressure over the outside of the region causes the animal pain and provokes coughing. In severe cases the throat is swollen, saliva dribbles from the mouth and the sheep is unable to take food. If the nostrils become plugged by the secretions the animal breathes through its mouth. Ordinarily, recovery occurs in one or two weeks.

Treatment.—The ventilation of the sleeping quarters must be looked after carefully. The sheep house must be kept clean, free from draughts and not overcrowded. The same treatment used in cold in the head is indicated in this disease; easily digested feed, laxatives, hot water inhalations, and febrifuges. After the first few days, the wool on the throat can be clipped off and the following liniment applied: spirits of turpentine, aqua ammonia and linseed oil (equal parts of each); mix and rub on the throat once a day.

BRONCHITIS; INFLAMMATION OF THE BRONCHIAL TUBES.

Causes.—Bronchitis is more often seen in the spring and early fall than at any other season of the year and may exist as a regular enzootic among sheep. The same conditions giving rise to cold in the head and sore throat may cause bronchitis, or it may occur as a complication of some of the infectious diseases.

Symptoms.—The sheep is depressed and feverish, the eyes watery and visible mucous membranes reddened. The cough is hard and dry and usually there is a mucous discharge from the nostrils. If we place the ear to the walls of the chest we hear louder bronchial sounds than normal. In the croupous form of bronchitis the respirations are more noisy and labored and disponea may occur. When the disease is mild the symptoms are not marked, recovery takes place in a few days. Unless complications occur the prognosis is favorable.

Treatment.—The treatment for common cold is usually sufficient. A cathartic of Epsom salts (three or four ounces) can be given. In the early stages of the disease febrifuges and expectorants should be given in order to lower the body temperature and stimulate the secretions of the inflamed mucous membranes. The following can be given: liquor ammonia acetate in half ounce doses every three or four hours; or potassium bicarbonate (seven drams), ammonia carbonate (seven drams), and powdered digitalis (one half dram); mix and divide into eight powders; give one powder three times a day.

CROUPOUS PNEUMONIA.

Causes.—Too warm buildings, heavy fleeces and sudden plethora predispose sheep to pneumonia. It may follow as a complication of bronchitis. A common cause of pneumonia is dipping and shearing during changeable seasons of the year. Catarrhal pneumonia is usually due to the lung worm of sheep.

Symptoms.—The disease generally takes a very acute form. The body temperature is high; the pulse and respirations quickened; nostrils dilated and the breathing labored, causing the flanks to heave. The sheep eats and ruminates irregularly or not at all, has a painful cough and a distressed anxious look. If the disease is going to terminate unfavorably the breathing becomes more difficult, the animal stands in one position with the head extended and the nostrils dilated. When the disease takes an unfavorable turn, the respiratory sounds are deadened and the pulse rapid and almost imperceptible. In sheep pneumonia does not run through the different stages as in some of the other domestic animals. Death sometimes occurs in the first stage, the period of engorgement.

Treatment.—The preventive treatment consists in avoiding such conditions as may cause the disease. When the pneumonia sets in the sick animal must be provided with comfortable, clean, well-ventilated quarters and kept as quiet as possible. As soon as the first symptoms are manifested a laxative of castor oil (two or three ounces), or in strong plethoric animals a purgative of Epsom salts (four ounces in warm gruel) can be given. The diet should be light and easily digested. The following febrifuges can be given: liquor ammonia acetate in half ounce doses every three or four hours; or acetanilid (one and one-half ounces), bicarbonate of soda (one ounce), and powdered nux vomica (two drams); mix and divide into eight powders; one powder can be given in a drench every four hours. As a counterirritant to the walls of the chest aqua ammonia can be used.

PLEURISY, INFLAMMATION OF THE LINING MEMBRANE OF THE CHEST.

Causes.—Pleurisy may occur as a complication of pneumonia, the inflammation extending from the lungs to the pleural membrane. Clipped sheep, or sheep that have lost wool as a result of scab if not sheltered or protected during the changeable seasons of the year are subject to pleurisy. Washing and dipping during the cold weather or injuries to the chest sometimes cause it. Rheumatic affections may be accompanied by pleurisy.

Symptoms.—The general symptoms are as follows: high fever, quick, small pulse, quickened respirations (the expiration being prolonged and the inspiration short and arrested), appetite impaired, rumination suspended. The animal holds the walls of the chest as rigid as possible and when the spaces between the ribs (inter-costal spaces) are pressed upon it causes pain. The cough is short, dry and on account of the pain suffered whenever the ribs are moved, it is suppressed as much as possible. In the first stage of the disease when we listen to the respiratory sounds, friction sounds are heard, due to the dried, inflamed membranes rubbing against each other whenever the animal breathes. Later these sounds disappear and we may be able to detect fluid in the pleural cavity (hydrothorax.)

Treatment.—The same preventive measures and the same general line of treatment laid down in pneumonia is indicated here. After the first day or two, aqua ammonia and linseed oil can be applied to the walls of the chest by parting the wool and applying it in lines. If there is a collection of fluid in the chest cavity and the heart action is weak, the following preparation can be given: tincture of digitalis (one ounce), iodide of potassium (one ounce), and

International Live Stock Exposition. Champion Wether in Competition with All Grade and Crossbred Wethers of the Medium Wool or Down Type Under Two Years Old. Ontario Product. Year Book, 1900.

enough water to make eight ounces. One tablespoonful can be given every four hours. In instances where the sheep cannot receive careful attention a little nitrate of potassium can be given in the drinking water.

HYDROTHORAX. FLUID IN THE CHEST CAVITY.

Causes.—This is a common complication of pleurisy. If the flow of blood in the large veins is impeded or if there is organic heart or chronic kidney trouble present, this disease may occur independently of any inflammation. When this is the case, dropsical swellings are present in different parts of the body.

Symptoms.—In pleurisy, when the acute symptoms subside quickly, it indicates a collection of fluid in the chest cavity. If but a small collection of fluid is present the pain is lessened, but if it forms in large amounts it presses on the lungs and heart, seriously interfering with the functions of these organs. By placing the ear to the side of the chest the fluid can be detected. When the ear is applied to the lower part of the chest walls no respiratory sounds are heard, but if applied high up the sounds may be normal. The exudate in the thoracic cavity is not always the same in character. It may be of yellow, citron, or red color, grayish or muddy if it contains pus or fibrin, and clear, limpid, or transparent if a true dropsical effusion. Dropsical swellings may be present in different parts of the body.

Treatment.—The sheep must be given good care. Counter-irritation to the chest walls, as in pleurisy, is indicated. If constipated, a cathartic must be given. To help get rid of the effusion, the following prescription may be given: tincture of digitalis (one ounce), iodide of potassium (one ounce), fluid extract of gentian (one ounce), and enough water to make eight ounces; mix and give one tablespoonful three times a day. When the sheep begins to improve one teaspoonful of iron sulphate can be given in the feed two or three times a day. In bad cases, tapping the chest and drawing off the fluid by means of the trocar and canula is the only successful treatment.

DISEASES OF THE CIRCULATORY SYSTEM.

INFLAMMATION OF THE HEART AND ITS MEMBRANES.

Causes.—Sharp objects as needles, wire, nails, etc., that are taken into the stomach along with the food and finally pass through the walls of the stomach and injure the heart and its coverings are common causes. Pericarditis (an inflammation of the coverings of the heart) and endocarditis (an inflammation of the lining membrane of the heart) are sometimes seen in rheumatic diseases. Pericarditis may occur as a complication of pleurisy, the inflammation extending from the pleural membrane to the pericardium.

Symptoms.—When cause by foreign bodies penetrating the pericardial sack from the stomach, symptoms of indigestion may precede the cardiac symptoms. The most prominent symptom is pain. The pulse beats are irregular, the temperature elevated, and the sheep weak. The expression is anxious and denotes suffering, the animal does not lie down and may remain in one position for some time. By placing the ear just over the region of the heart we may be able to detect the heart sounds. If no fluid is present in the pericardial sac we sometimes hear friction sounds; if fluid is present fluid sounds. In endocarditis we may hear a blowing sound. In the beginning of the disease the heart beats are strong, palpitating and bounding and the breathing is difficult and distressed. The general condition is soon changed and the sheep becomes thin and weak. The prognosis is very unfavorable.

Treatment.—When the disease is due to the presence of foreign bodies no curative treatment can be given. The sheep should be given a cathartic of Epsom salts (three ounces). To regulate the action of the heart belladonna or digitalis can be given at short intervals and when recovery begins, bitter tonics. The animal must be kept quiet and as comfortable as possible.

PALPITATION; THUMPS.

Causes.—Palpitation is generally seen in animals that are in a weak, anaemic, bloodless condition and appears under the slightest exciting circumstances. In acute inflammatory diseases of the heart or its membranes, palpitation is generally a prominent symptom.

Symptoms.—When the palpitation is due to a weak anaemic condition, the animal is emaciated, the skin and mucous membranes pale and there may be local dropsical effusions in different parts of the body. In these cases the palpitation depends on some excitement and is regular, the jerking of the muscles in the region of the flank corresponding as a rule to the heart beat. Abnormal heart sounds are absent.

Treatment.—Keep the sheep quiet and avoid exciting it. When associated with anaemia, bitter tonics should be given along with good nourishing food. One teaspoonful of iron sulphate can be given in the feed twice a day. The following prescription is useful: fluid extract of gentian (one ounce), tincture of digitalis (two drams), and enough water to make eight ounces; mix and give one tablespoonful three times a day.

ORGANIC DISEASES OF THE HEART.

The short term of life and the method of handling sheep make such organic heart troubles as fatty degeneration, enlargement, dilation and valvular diseases of the heart quite rare. In old overfed, pampered sheep, and those fitted for show purposes the fat may accumulate in and around the heart muscles, replacing the muscular tissue and interfering with the action of the organ. Dilation of one or both sides of the heart may accompany fatty degeneration. In these cases the sheep should be kept quiet and the forcing system of feeding abandoned or the animal sold to the butcher as soon as possible.

DISEASES OF THE NERVOUS SYSTEM.

ENCEPHALITIS; INFLAMMATION OF THE BRAIN.

Causes.—Injuries to the brain due to blows on the head from a whip or club, or to the sheep fighting among themselves may cause it. Overfeeding with grains or feeds rich in albumenoids or proteids (peas, beans, cotton seed, gluten, oil meal, etc.) unhygienic surroundings (close, damp, poorly ventilated quarters) and violent exertion during the hot weather are common causes. Spoiled fodders and grains that are mouldy, or contain smut and microbes are probable factors in inflammation of the brain. Certain substances, containing narcotic substances, as intoxicating rye grass, will sometimes cause it. The larva of the oestrus ovis or grub of sheep will when present in or on the surface of the brain irritate and inflame it.

Symptoms.—The sheep is often drowsy, stupid and disinclined to move, the head is hot, carried upwards or to one side, the eyes fixed, rolled up and reddened, the pupils dilated and the gait stiff and staggering. The sheep may be excited, charge objects, work the jaws, froth at the mouth and bleat. When excited the respirations and pulse are usually rapid. Sometimes it is seen with its head pushed against the wall or lying by itself with the head low or turned backwards. Finally paralysis sets in. The prognosis is very unfavorable.

Treatment.—If the disease is due to unhygienic conditions, spoiled foods, or a faulty ration, the cause must be removed or a number of the flock may become affected. As soon as any of their number take sick, a purgative of Epsom salts (from four to six ounces) should be given to the whole flock. The sick animal or animals must be kept in a cool, quiet place, and cold in the form of wet cloths or ice applied to the head as long as it feels hot. When excited and feverish, acetanilid in one dram doses should be given, or chloral hydrate in one or two dram doses every four hours. As soon as possible, in order to restore tone to the nervous tissue the following can be given: iodide of potassium (one ounce), fluid extract of nux vomica (six drams), and enough water to make eight ounces; mix and give half an ounce three times a day. When sick and during the convalescent stage, the bowels should be kept lax and the animal fed an easily digestible ration.

HYDROCEPHALUS; DROPSY; OR WATER IN THE VENTRICLES OF THE BRAIN.

This disease is frequently seen in lambs, many times they are born with it, the head being so enlarged that delivery is quite difficult. If this is the case the lamb is generally dead, or if alive, rarely lives more than a few days.

Causes.—In-breeding is said to cause it. Its prevalence in some localities would suggest some local influence, as the food and water, as factors in causing the disease.

Symptoms.—The head is large in proportion to the size of the rest of the body. The sheep is lazy, dull, stupid, the gait staggering and uncertain and the animal is not inclined to move. Sometimes the disease is complicated by digestive disorders. Usually the head is twisted on the neck or turned to one side.

Treatment.—If the disease is caused by mistakes in breeding, the management of the flock must be changed. If to local conditions it would be advisable to move the flock to another location. Medicinal treatment is of no use.

CEREBRO-SPINAL MENINGITIS; INFLAMMATION OF THE COVERINGS OF THE BRAIN AND SPINAL CORD.

Causes.—But little is known regarding the cause of this disease. It is probably due to several different toxic principles, but by some it is claimed to be due to a specific cause (a germ). The disease is frequently seen in young animals, generally during the winter and spring.

Symptoms.—The head feels hot, the mucous membranes are congested and the pupils dilated. The animal grinds its teeth, saliva dribbles from the mouth, the lips are contracted, it is weak and dull and shows a tendency to move in a circle. We soon find it stretched upon the ground as if paralyzed, the head thrown back and the muscles of the jaw, neck and back rigid. Sheep in this condition are very sensitive and may have convulsions. Death usually occurs in a few hours, or a few days, but sometimes it lives for several weeks. The prognosis is very unfavorable.

Treatment.—The treatment is the same as that recommended in inflammation of the brain. If mistakes in the care and feeding of the sheep exist, they should be corrected at once. If a number of animals in the flock are affected, the sick should be separated from the healthy ones, and the sheep house and pens cleaned and disinfected.

APOPLEXY; SOFTENING OF THE BRAIN.

Causes.—Any condition increasing blood pressure in the brain may cause this disease. In highly fed, pampered sheep, excitement, extreme heat and over-exertion may produce it. Mechanical injuries may also cause it. If degenerative changes occur in the walls of the cerebral vessels, they become so weak that the slightest increase in blood pressure will rupture them. Floating particles (emboli) in the blood stream may plug a cerebral vessel, cutting off the blood supply to a part, thus bringing about apoplexy, not by pressure on the nerve tissue, but from anaemia.

Symptoms.—As a rule the disease comes on suddenly without our noticing that sheep is sick. In the acute cases it staggers, falls, there is a complete loss of consciousness, convulsive movements of the legs and in a short time the animal dies. In most cases, however, it is dull, unsteady in its gait, or shows a tendency to move in a circle. The pulse is weak, respirations slow, labored, irregular and stertorous, the visible mucous membranes intensely congested, eyes dilated and pupils enlarged, sometimes more in one eye than the other. The paralysis may be general or involve only certain muscular groups.

Treatment.—In acute cases, this is very unsatisfactory. In mild attacks at the outset, cold applications to the head and bleeding can be practiced. The sheep must be kept perfectly quiet. When able to swallow, a purgative of Epsom salts (four to six ounces) can be given. Bromide of potassium should be given in small doses to keep down the force of the circulation. To help absorb the exudate or blood clot that may be present and restore tone to the nerve tissue the following can be given; iodide of potassium (one ounce), powdered nux vomica (six drams) ; mix and divide into twenty powders; give one powder three times a day. A course of vegetable and mineral tonics together with a laxative diet is advisable as soon as the animal shows signs of improvement.

EPILEPSY; FITS.

Causes.—Epilepsy may be due to lesions in the brain, walls of the cranium, or spinal cord. Disorder in the cerebral circulation or such abnormal conditions as are present in uremia, lead poisoning etc., may bring on this condition. In young animals intestinal parasites and irregular management and feeding are common causes.

Symptoms.—Epilepsy will vary in intensity and duration, depending on the cause. The sheep will suddenly stop ruminating or eating, look about in a stupid manner and after turning or staggering, fall to the ground and have violent convulsions. The fit may last but a few seconds or minutes, and the animal will get up and go to feeding as though nothing had happened. Generally, it continues dull and sleepy for some time.

Treatment.—If the cause of the epilepsy is known and can be removed, the treatment must be directed to the cause. When a sheep is in a fit, it should be prevented from injuring itself and cold water dashed on the head. Bromide of potassium is useful in treating epilepsy and should be given in from ten to thirty grain doses in a drench, three or four times a day. Iodide of potassium may also be given. Outdoor life, moderate exercise and bitter or iron tonics are very important.

PARALYSIS.

Causes.—Pressure from diseased vertebrae, tumors or abscesses, and growing parasites on the nerve tissue of the spinal cord or brain, will cause a paralysis of that part of the body that depends on the injured nerve tissue for its nerve supply.

Symptoms.—The paralysis may come on suddenly and the symptoms manifested resemble those seen in inflammation of the spinal cord or brain. Generally, it comes on gradually and may involve a certain set of muscles or organs, or may be general with the special senses clear. The parts affected will point to the seat of the trouble. Sensory troubles, increased sensibility or loss of sensibility, are sometimes present.

Treatment.—The sheep should be made as comfortable as possible and fed easily digested food. To keep the bowels lax, it is advisable to administer a laxative every few days. Nerve tonics such as strychnine (one thirtieth of a grain) or powdered nux vomica (thirty grains) should be given in the feed two or three times a day. Treatment is generally unsuccessful and it is usually advisable to slaughter the animal.

HEAT STROKE; HEAT EXHAUSTION.

Heat exhaustion generally follows violent exertion during the hot weather. The symptoms are as follows: weak, small pulse, general depression, muscular weakness and collapse. The animal soon goes down, is restless and finally dies.

Treatment.—The treatment consists in diffusible stimulants (alcohol in half ounce doses every few hours) tincture of digitalis in teaspoonful doses to sustain the heart and cold douches on the head and fore parts. If the body temperature is sub-normal ward baths can be given.

SUN STROKE.

The cause of sun stroke is exposure to severe summer heat and may occur during or after hard exercise, especially if the sheep is fat or out of condition.

Symptoms.—The symptoms are as follows: rapid breathing, open mouth, reddened, prominent eyes, high temperature, unsteady gait, convulsions and death. Unless the treatment is prompt, the prognosis is unfavorable.

Treatment.—During warm weather conditions that may cause sun stroke should be avoided. When a sheep becomes affected, place it in a shady place and apply cold water to the head, neck and entire body. This can be done by placing the sheep in a tub or tank for a few minutes. The medicinal treatment is the same as that used in heat stroke.

DISEASES OF THE REPRODUCTIVE SYSTEM.
ABORTION.

Abortion occurs when the foetus is expelled twenty days before the normal period. It is not a common accident among ewes.

Causes.—Abortion may be due to the following causes: ergotized grass, acrid plants; frozen food or water if taken in large amounts, filthy water, indigestible foods, or food of a bad quality. Injuries to the abdomen, general diseases, excitement, over-exertion and fear or fright produced by dogs. Poorly cared for and neglected ewes may abort as well as extremely fat ones.

Symptoms.—The symptoms will vary and in some cases are so trifling that the accident is not noticed at the time. The ewe may, however, become quite uneasy and bleat continually. The genital organs are enlarged, a glazy like discharge is seen around the lips of the vulva and sometimes a portion of the foetal membrane is visible. Soon after these symptoms are manifested, the foetus is expelled. If the abortion becomes complicated by retention of the foetal membranes, the ewe will remain away from the rest of the flock, is dull, feverish and refuses to eat. If properly treated, these symptoms pass away in a short time. It may terminate in an inflammation of the womb, but this is not common. The lamb is usually dead.

Treatment.—The treatment is mainly preventive and consists in avoiding such conditions as may cause the accident. When the maternal passages are not prepared for the entrance of the foetus, the ewe is in pain and becomes very restless. The pain can be relieved and the parts relaxed somewhat by hot applications to the region of the pelvis. The ewe must be given a good bed and kept in a quiet place away from the rest of the flock. If weak a stimulant (whisky) can be given. If the act of parturition is prolonged, the necessary aid must be given but it is never best to meddle too soon. If the membranes do not come away within a day or two after aborting they must be removed with the hand and the uterus and maternal passages washed with a watery solution of creolin (two parts of creolin to ninety-eight parts of water). We must not neglect the removal of the afterbirth or its retention will be followed by bad results.

EVERSION OF THE UTERUS AND VAGINA.

Causes.—It consists in a displacement of the parts, in which the uterus and vagina are turned partially or completely inside out, the everted portion of the uterus escaping through the opening of the neck of the womb and projecting like a large tumor from between the lips of the vulva.

Treatment.—The eversion must receive prompt attention or there is danger of the tissues becoming torn, bruised or gangrenous. The parts must be first cleaned and the swelling reduced by washing them with a warm watery solution of creolin. After this has been accomplished, the next step is to replace them. The ewe should be turned on her back and the hind parts elevated and the uterus and vagina returned to their natural positions. Strong stitches should next be taken in the skin on each side of the vulva or through its lips, and crossed in such a way as to prevent the recurrence of the displacement. Care must be taken that the stitches do not interfere with urination. If the uterus is badly lacerated or gangrenous, it can be amputated and the ewe prepared for the butcher.

INFLAMMATION OF THE VAGINA AND UTERUS, VAGINITIS METRITIS.

Causes.—If during labor the walls of the vagina or uterus become torn or bruised, germs may enter and bring about an inflammation of the parts. It may follow retention and decomposition of the foetal membranes. Dirty instruments and dirty hands at the time of birth frequently carry disease producing germs into the uterus. Conditions here are favorable for their development and may result in a fatal inflammation of the parts.

Symptoms.—The ewe is feverish, dull and weak; the appetite is impaired and she frequently strains as if to pass urine. There is more or less discharge from the inflamed parts and the lining membrane of the vulva is red and tumefied. These symptoms may pass off in a few days or become worse. The animal will stand with the abdomen tucked up or lie down most of the time. The ewe may be constipated or have a diarrhea, suffer considerable pain and have a high temperature. The prognosis is generally unfavorable when the disease takes a turn of this kind. In some cases the inflammation becomes chronic. It is then called leucorrhoea, the principal symptom being the discharge from the vagina.

Treatment.—The preventive treatment consists in practicing the proper antiseptic precautions at the time of the birth and removing the foetal membranes before decomposition has occurred. Before assisting in removal of the foetus the hands and instruments must be cleaned by washing the hands and allowing the instruments to lie in a two per cent. watery solution of creolin. The maternal passages and uterus should then be washed with a similar antiseptic solution. If the parts become inflamed, they must be washed daily and when the animal is feverish, the following febrifuge can be given; acetanilid (six drams), quinine sulphate (three drams), calomel (one dram), powdered nux vomica (two drams); mix and divide into eight powders; give one powder in a drench every four hours.

MAMMITIS; INFLAMMATION OF THE UDDER.

Causes.—Congestion of the mammary glands is due to various causes. Exposure to cold, bruises from the head of the lamb, lying on stones or on the ground in damp folds, yards or pastures, and irritation from retained milk, are common causes of inflammation of the udder.

Symptoms.—In most cases the inflammation does not cause the animal much pain and disappears in a few days. It may, however, if neglected, become serious. The udder will then become swollen and painful, the skin covering it red and shiny, and later abscesses may form. The gland secretes but little milk, and it is frequently coagulated or contains pus. The ewe loses flesh, is feverish and has a poor appetite.

Treatment.—In mild cases of mammitis but little treatment is necessary. It is generally advisable, however, to diet the animal. When feverish, a purgative of Epsom salts (three or four ounces) should be given in a drench. The following ointment can be rubbed on the inflamed gland twice a day; vaseline (four ounces), camphor ointment (two ounces), extract of belladonna (one-half ounce); or a liniment of linseed oil (six ounces) and carbolic acid (one dram) can be used. When the milk is clotted or contains pus, it must be drained off with the siphon once or twice a day and a two per cent solution of creolin injected into the gland. A convenient apparatus for this is a teat siphon with about a foot or two of rubber tubing attached and carrying a small glass funnel at one end.

CASTRATION.

Castration of male lambs is best done when the animal is from two to six weeks old and in strong, healthy lambs, the operation may be performed as early as the third day. Flockmasters who allow the lambs to become two or three months old usually suffer some loss, even when the operation is carefully performed.

The operator should provide himself with a table, castrating knife, a pan or pail containing an antiseptic solution and an assistant, to catch and to hold the lambs. When the knife is not in use it should be dropped into the antiseptic solution. The assistant catches the lamb and holds it in a convenient position on the table. The region around the scrotum should be washed with an antiseptic, and if covered with wool, it should be clipped to insure cleanliness. The end of the scrotum is then cut off and each testicle in its turn is drawn out with the thumb and forefinger of the left hand, until the spermatic cord is ruptured. Sometimes it is necessary to pull out the testicle and scrape the cord with the edge of the knife until it breaks off. After removing the testicles if the opening in the scrotum is

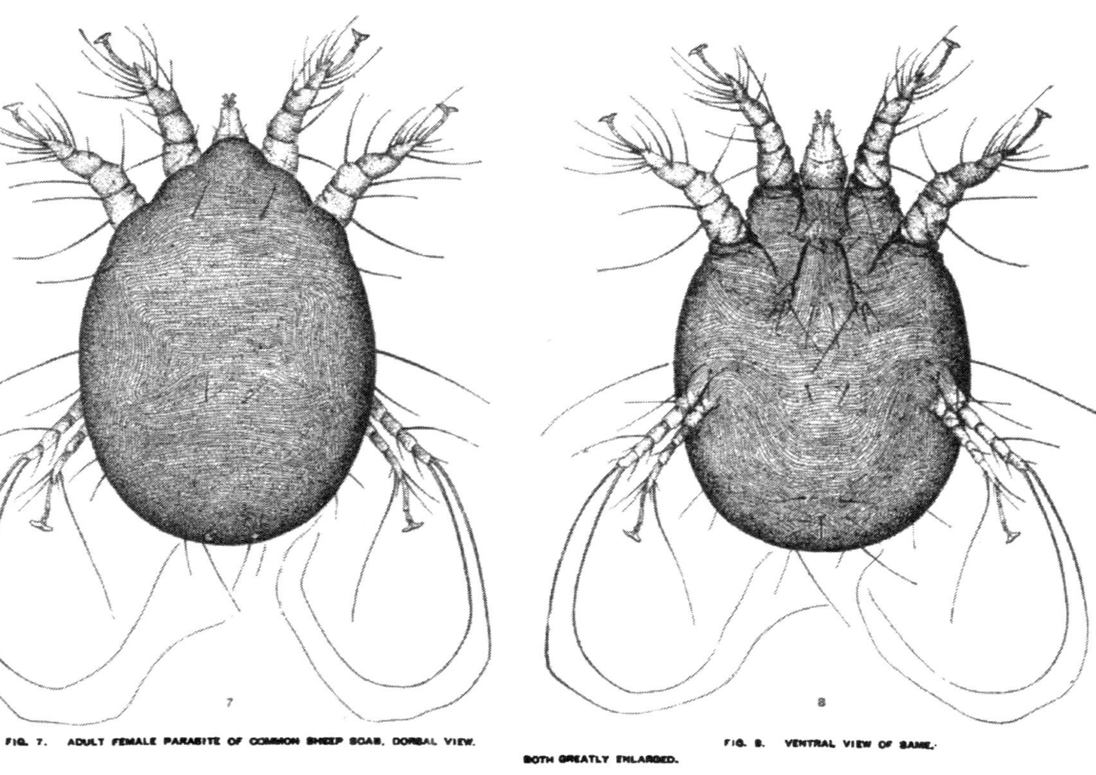

FIG. 7.   ADULT FEMALE PARASITE OF COMMON SHEEP SCAB, DORSAL VIEW.

FIG. 8.   VENTRAL VIEW OF SAME.

BOTH GREATLY ENLARGED.

small, it should be enlarged. This is necessary as there is danger of the margins of the incision adhering before the part is healed, thus interfering with the draining off of the pus and endangering the life of the animal. In castrating a buck it is necessary to confine him in some way. He should be laid on his back on the ground, and the hind legs held by an assistant, or tied in such a way as to prevent his struggling. On account of danger from hemorrhage, it is advisable to scrape the spermatic cord until it breaks or, better, to cut it off with an emasculator. Lambs do better if allowed to run in the pasture. If kept in the sheep house or in a yard, everything should be clean to avoid infection from germs.

DISEASES OF THE EYE.

SIMPLE CONJUNCTIVITIS; SORE EYES.

Causes.—Conjunctivitis is due to irritation from various foreign bodies getting into the eye (dust, seeds, pollen, flies, etc) and injuries of various kinds (blows from a whip, stones, branches of trees, brush, etc.). General diseases, cold winds and wet weather may also cause it.

Symptoms.—The eye is held more or less closed, especially if the light is bright. The discharge is at first watery, but soon becomes heavier and more pus like and adheres to the margins of the lids. The conjunctiva is inflamed, thickened, red and swollen. The cornea usually takes part in the inflammation and when it does, it looks white and opaque and the blood-vessels around its margins often become quite prominent. The inflammation may extend to the deeper layers of the eye. Recovery generally takes place in about a week.

Treatment.—If any foreign body is present, it should be removed and the eye washed with an antiseptic or astringent lotion. If the lids are wounded, it may be necessary to use hot or cold water applications in order to keep down the inflammation. The following eye lotion can be dropped under the lids with a medicine dropper or applied once or twice daily: Boric acid (thirty grains), sulphate of zinc (fifteen grains), and distilled water (three ounces). Equal parts of boracic acid and calomel by weight may be blown into the eye with an insect powder blower.

ENZOOTIC OPHTHALMIA; CONTAGIOUS DISEASES.

Causes.—The direct cause of this disease is not known. By most investigators, it is held to be of an infectious nature, but some attribute it to irritating pollen or soil. The disease is spread by diseased sheep coming in contact with healthy ones and in a short time will affect a large number of animals in a neighborhood. Low, damp, land; and level prairies seem to favor the development of the disease. Dust and pollen may act as carriers of the germ.

Symptoms.—At first the eyes are closed and there is an abundant secretion of tears. This is followed by a heavy pus like secretion. The lids are inflamed, red and swollen, the cornea opaque and thickened. Ulcers may form on the cornea and the eye ball become milky white and hard. Usually at the beginning of the disease the body temperature is elevated and there is a partial or complete loss of appetite. When properly treated but a few of the sheep go blind and recovery occurs in a short time.

Treatment.—It is best to separate the sick from the healthy sheep. The affected sheep should be given cool, dark quarters and the eyes cleaned daily by bathing them with warm water. Following this, calomel and boric acid of equal parts by weight should be blown directly into the eye with a powder blower. If a large number in the flock are affected and suitable quarters cannot be provided, treatment with the powder alone is followed by good results.

ECZEMA.

Eczema, of non-parasitic origin, is not a common disease among sheep, due to the skin being so well protected by the wool and the abundant secretions of the skin. What is commonly known as rain rot may be seen in sheep in poor condition and exposed to heavy cold rains. The rain softens the outer layer of the skin, irritates it and allows the microbes to enter.

Symptoms.—The skin is red and inflamed, and vesicles and pimples form. The skin may become covered by scabs and scruf, and the wool shed in places. When the weather improves and the animals are kept under more favorable conditions, recovery takes place spontaneously.

RHEUMATISM.

Causes.—Rheumatism is more common during the late autumn or early spring than at any other season of the year. Sudden changes in temperature, cold, wet weather, untimely shearing, exposure, draughts, etc., seem to favor the development of the disease. Different theories in regard to its cause are advanced by different authors. The muscles, tendons or joints may be affected.

Symptoms.—Generally the muscles of the back and loins are affected. It may, however, affect the neck or hind quarters. The gait is stiff and the limbs are carried straight and rigid. When the joints are affected, they become swollen, hot and painful and the disease may shift from one to another. In acute cases the body temperature is higher than normal, the respirations quickened and the appetite lost or impaired. When the disease takes on the acute form the animal becomes emaciated and in a short time dies.

Treatment.—The preventive measures consist in keeping the sheep in comfortable, dry quarters, free from draughts. When the rheumatism is localized, local treatment in the form of liniments or blisters can be used. Internally the following can be given: salicylate of soda (one ounce), fluid extract of gentian (one half ounce), and enough water to make eight ounces; mix and give half an ounce in a drench two or three times a day.

INFECTIOUS DISEASES.

ARTHRITIS OF LAMBS (INFLAMMATION OF THE JOINTS).

Causes.—This disease is due to septic substances entering the body by way of the umbilical cord. Filthy quarters and a large umbilical cord that does not dry as soon as ordinary are the predisposing causes.

Symptoms.—These are manifested soon after birth. The lamb is feverish, weak, and careless of the teat. One or more of the joints become enlarged, hot and painful. Constipation is frequently present or it may have a diarrhea. Sometimes the lamb is unable to walk or when it does, it is stiff and lame. Pus sometimes forms in the affected joints, and different internal organs. The disease usually proves fatal and if the lamb does recover it is worthless.

Treatment.—The preventive treatment consists in washing the umbilical cord soon after birth with about a ten per cent. watery solution of carbolic acid. This will cause it to dry and prevent the entrance of germs. The quarters must be dry and clean, and if the disease is present in a flock, the sheep house must be cleaned and disinfected.

MALIGNANT OEDEMA; BLOOD POISONING.

Causes.—Malignant oedema is due to a germ (the bacillus of odema). The germ is present in large numbers in the soil and infection takes place by a wound in the skin becoming contaminated with dirt, faeces, dust, etc.

Symptoms.—A swelling forms in the neighborhood of the infected part. This is at first small but spreads gradually in all directions and feels doughy. The center of the swelling is cold, painless and crackles when pressed on. On the margin it is tense, hot and painful. When cut into it has a disagreeable odor. Pus forming germs are present in the older areas. The general symptoms are loss of appetite, fever, quick, weak pulse, etc. The disease usually terminates fatally in a few days.

Treatment.—The treatment is mainly surgical and consists in making a number of incisions into the oedematous swelling and obtaining drainage as well as admitting air. The part must be washed out with a strong creolin solution two or three times a day. If very weak, stimulants can be given.

RABIES; HYDROPHOBIA.[*]

Rabies is an infectious disease and is caused by the sheep being bitten by a rabid dog. It is not as common a disease of sheep as of cattle, due to their body being so well protected by wool. The period of incubation will vary twenty-five to ninety days.

Symptoms.—The expression of the face is usually staring and when approached the animals may become restless, stamp the foot, bleat, etc. If a stick is held in front of them they will frequently bite at it. On account of the bite itching intensely, the sheep may rub and bite the part. The sexual desire is generally increased and the rabid sheep will crowd and push against the other members of the flock, jumping on them and bleating with a dull, rough voice. Weakness soon sets in and in the latter stage of the disease, when startled, it may drop to the ground, lie still for a time and have difficulty in rising. In some cases the sheep acts dull and does not manifest these rabid symptoms. Death takes place in a few days or a week. When symptoms of rabies are manifested, the sheep should be separated from the rest of the flock or destroyed at once.

---

[*] See also *Rabies* (in dogs), page 644.

VARIOLA; SHEEP POX.

In the early part of the last century, variola was a formidable plague of the flocks of Europe. In 1819 over a million sheep died of this disease in France alone, and in 1823 half a million in Austria. In some European countries it is still prevalent. This disease bears an interesting relation with cow pox in cattle and smallpox in man.

Causes.—Variola is a highly contagious disease, the contagious element being present in the crusts from the pustules on the skin, in the excretions, blood and expired air. It can be carried a long distance. The exact nature of the virus is not known. In sheep sheds, yards, etc., the virus may remain active for a month or six weeks, but is easily destroyed by putrefaction, a high temperature and the ordinary disinfectants. Variola is spread by animals that have had it within a period of a few weeks or a month, by innoculated sheep, wool, dogs, manure, fodder, etc. One attack causes a life-time immunity. The period of incubation is from four to seven days.

Symptoms.—The sheep is depressed, weak, hangs its head, breathes quickly, is feverish and has chills. In a day or two red spots or pimples appear on the skin not covered or incompletely covered with long wool. When the eruptions are close together the skin becomes badly swollen. In about five days the vesicles or pustules form, dry up and scab over, the swelling then disappears and the scabs loosen and drop off leaving a pit in which no wool afterwards grows. As a prevention, healthy animals are given a mild form of the disease by inoculating them on the ear, tail, etc., with a virus obtained from a mild case after it has run for six or eight days.

SYMPTOMATIC ANTHRAX; BLACK LEG.

Causes.—This is not a common disease of sheep. The specific cause is a germ, a bacillus that when conditions are favorable will probably develop in the soil and live for years. The germ gains entrance to the body by some wound on the leg, mouth or body. The period of incubation is from one to five days.

Symptoms.—The tumors may develop on different parts of the body, develop rapidly and are sensitive at first. The skin over the tumor soon becomes gangrenous and cold, and when cut into the tissues are dark colored and a frothy, red liquid together with gas escapes. The general symptoms are loss of appetite, weak pulse, high temperature and finally difficult respiration, violent colic, brain complications, coma, insensibility and death. The disease runs a rapidly fatal course.

Treatment.—This is purely preventive. When the disease is present in a flock, vaccination should be practiced.

ANTHRAX; CHARBON; CARBUNCLE.

Anthrax has been known for centuries, but it has been only within the last fifty years that its true character was discovered. In this country the disease is not very prevalent and is not common among sheep.

Causes.—The specific cause of this disease is a bacillus, the bacillus of anthrax. Outside of the body this germ will grow and multiply whenever the conditions are favorable, and it will resist to a remarkable degree, if spores are formed, germicides, desiccation, high temperature, low temperature and other unfavorable conditions. It develops best in dark soil rich in organic matter, manure, mud, etc. In anthrax countries the overflowing of river bottoms in the spring or a very hot, dry summer will favor the development of the organism and may cause an outbreak of the disease. The germs are taken into the body with the food or by way of a wound in the skin, tongue or mucous membrane of the mouth. When a carcass is not properly disposed of flies and other insects act as carriers of the disease and infect healthy animals. It is not uncommon for the carcass of a sheep or other animal that has died from this disease to be dragged over the pasture, road or street and healthy animals may inhale the germs along with the dust, or take them into the body along with the food. Commercial fertilizers, hides, etc., sometimes act as carriers of the disease.

Symptoms.—Anthrax in sheep generally takes on a very acute form. The animal is suddenly stricken with apoplexy, staggers, falls down, is seized with convulsions and dies in a few minutes. Black blood is discharged from the anus and mouth. When the disease takes on a less acute form the symptoms will differ. The animal may act restless at first. The respirations and pulse are quickened, the mucous membranes are dark colored, it frequently tries to pass faeces, is delirous or dull and finally lies down and dies in a short time.

Treatment.—This is wholly preventive and consists in destroying the carcass by burning or burying deeply at some distance from barns, yards or public highways, and vaccinating all susceptible animals. The dead animals must not be dragged over the ground but disposed of as near the place of death as possible. Disinfectants must be freely used around the place where the animal died.

TUBERCULOSIS; CONSUMPTION.

Tuberculosis is an infectious disease and is caused by a specific germ, the bacillus of tuberculosis. This disease is rarely met with in sheep. Infection is said to take place through being kept with tuberculous cattle and in lambs by drinking of the milk from tuberculous cows.

Symptoms.—The symptoms will depend on the organs involved and the stage of the disease. In the early stages the symptoms are not sufficiently developed to enable us to make a diagnosis, later it can be easily recognized. The sheep may have a slight cough at first or a chronic indigestion. Glands in different parts of the body may become enlarged. In the last stages, the animal is usually emaciated, the fleece ragged, it stands with the back arched, the respirations are rapid, the lung sounds deadened and it breathes through the mouth.

Treatment.—The preventive treatment consists in not exposing the sheep to the disease. When the symptoms are sufficiently developed to enable us to form a diagnosis, the animal should be destroyed and the carcass disposed of in a proper manner.

TETANUS; LOCK JAW.

Causes.—This is an infectious disease and is caused by the bacillus of tetanus, a germ that is present in the soil, especially if rich in organic matter. The disease is more common and takes a more acute form in warm than in cold countries. Infection takes place by dirt containing the bacillus entering a wound. Punctured wounds caused by nails or splinters of wood and contused wounds are most suitable for its development. The disease may follow an operation, especially castration, when performed without proper antiseptic precautions. The period of incubation is short, usually less than a week.

Symptoms.—In this disease the germ remains at the point of inoculation and there manufactures poisonous substances that have an action on the body similar to strychnine. The symptoms are acute. The sheep stands immovable, with all four legs stretched out as if on stilts, the tail is rigid, neck and back stiff and jaws closed. The muscles of the neck and back are hard, the respirations quick and difficult, the pulse weak, and finally it goes down and dies in a short time. In sheep the death rate is very high.

Treatment.—It is important as a preventive measure to treat all wounds properly and to use the necessary antiseptic precautions in performing surgical operations, especially castration. It is only in subacute cases that medicinal treatment is beneficial, and in this disease the administration of medicine is less beneficial than careful nursing. The wound must be cleaned and disinfected, and the sick animal given a quiet, dark stall and made as comfortable as possible. Plenty of fresh water should be provided and if it can eat, soft, sloppy foods or green grass can be given in preference to dry food. If constipated an enema can be given. Chloral hydrate in half dram doses, every hour in the drinking water or feed may relieve the spasms.

INFLUENZA; MALIGNANT CATARRHAL FEVER.

Influenza is an infectious disease the specific cause of which is not known. It is especially prevalent during certain years and when the conditions are favorable may affect a large number of animals in the flock. As in other diseases, age, breed, care, hygienic conditions, etc., will influence the number of animals affected in a flock. Exposure, draughts, confining the flock in too close quarters and poor ventilation are the common predisposing causes.

Symptoms.—The general condition of the sheep is greatly disturbed and the animal presents a droopy, depressed appearance. It is feverish and weak, stands with the back arched and may have a staggering gait. It generally refuses to eat, has a cough and swallows with difficulty. The respiratory mucous membrane is inflamed, the discharge from the nostrils is increased and sometimes swelling appears under the jaw. Diarrhea is sometimes a prominent symptom. When the respiratory apparatus is generally affected the respirations are difficult and rapid. Pneumonia and inflammation of the brain and its coverings are frequent complications. In some cases both the external and internal parts of the eye become inflamed, the lids are swollen, the conjunctival membrane and the eye take on a milky appearance. The duration of the disease is from a few days to several weeks. In mild cases recovery occurs in a few days, but if not cared for properly a relapse may occur. The prognosis is unfavorable in the severe type.

Lesions.—The change in the tissues of the body will vary. In acute cases they are not marked, but when the disease is complicated and the duration a week or more, various tissues and organs are affected. The principal changes are in the respiratory organs. The mucous membrane lining the pharynx, larynx, trachea, and bronchial tubes is red and thickened; that lining the sinuses of the head is also involved and a portion of the lung tissue may be affected by a catarrhal pneumonia. In severe cases the pleural membrane as well as a large portion of the lung is affected. Other lesions are in the brain, stomach, intestines, liver, kidneys, spleen, heart and lymph glands.

Treatment.—The preventive treatment consists in avoiding conditions that will predispose the flock to the disease. If the disease is present in a flock, it should be looked over carefully every day and the sick sheep separated from the healthy ones and given comfortable quarters, good care and good nourishing food. In mild cases this may be all the treatment necessary. In the catarrhal form the following prescription is useful: tincture of belladonna (four drams), tincture of aconite (one-half dram), and sufficient syrup of squills to make a four ounce mixture; mix and give one tablespoonful three times a day. This treatment is best followed by tonics and expectorants. The following recipe can be given: tincture of gentian (four drams), iodide of potassium (two drams), and enough water to make four ounces; mix and give one tablespoonful twice a day. If diarrhea is present one ounce of linseed oil and a dram of tincture of opium given two or three times a day will give good results.

FOOT ROT, INFECTION OF THE GENITAL ORGANS, AND LIP-AND-LEG ULCERATION (NECROBACILLOSIS): CAUSE AND TREATMENT.

This affection, with which every experienced sheep owner is more or less familiar, is designated by various names, such as sore mouth, sore lips, warty mouth, warty nose, impetigo, labialis, erthyma stomatitis, etc. The disease has been observed in this country in both the East and the West as well as in various parts of Europe off and on for the past twenty years, and until quite recently little effort has been made to find the causative agent or to check its spread.

Knowles, in 1907, described very fully and accurately a disease occurring among the sheep of southeastern Montana which affected the lips and legs of the animals. He was the first writer to apply the name infectious lip-and-leg ulceration to this disease, which is quite appropriate, owing to the character and location of the lesions. Knowles found the necrosis bacillus to be the cause of the lesions, and succeeded in transferring the disease from infected to healthy sheep by a series of inoculation experiments.

CHARACTER AND LESIONS.

The characteristic lesions may be found on any part of the exterior of sheep where the bacillus which causes it may gain entrance; but cuts, bruises, abrasions, and exposure to devitalizing processes being less frequent upon parts covered with wool and their contact with infection less likely, it follows that the woolly portions of the body are less subject to lesions than other parts. In this country lesions upon the head, as lips, chin, nose, cheeks, gums, and hard palate, are the most frequent, while much less common are the ulcers on the legs and feet. Shear cuts and the tail stump of docked lambs are at times infected, while slit ears have been more frequently involved. In bucks frequently and in wethers occasionally the sheath is infected. The vulva of ewes has been found ulcerated in a relatively small percentage of cases, while the udder and teats even more rarely have developed the infection, notwithstanding that the sucking lambs showed more or less ulceration and eruptions on the mouth parts. In some cases lesions have appeared in the pharynx and lungs, occasionally in the liver and stomach, and in such instances the disease uniformly results in death.

It may be advisable to arrange these various manifestations of the disease into the following classes, with the statement that further study is required to explain the reason for necrobacillosis in sheep assuming several different forms or types under what appears to be similar environment, as well as for the disease becoming virulently infective in certain cases, while in others, under practically the same conditions, there is a tendency toward latency or even spontaneous recovery.

1. The lip-and-leg form, as the name indicates, attacks the lips or legs, or both. The lesions in some bands are confined very largely to the lips and muzzle, in other bands the lesions are largely confined to the legs, while in still other bands the seat of the lesions is about equally divided between the lips and legs.

The different conditions under which the sheep are kept and the character of the feed may account, in a degree at least, for this difference in the seat of the lesions, and also to some extent for the difference in the spread of the disease, especially within the band. Thus, during the winter, when snow is on the ground and the weather is so cold that the surface of the snow becomes hard and crusted, making grazing very difficult, the chances are that leg lesions would be likely to predominate, owing to the numerous scratches received upon the legs becoming infected with the blood and bits of scab which drop from the infected sheep. On the other hand, if they were fed on a range where cactus and greasewood composed a large part of the feed, the spines of these plants would be likely to wound the lips and nose to such an extent that lip lesions would be apt to predominate. Other sheep ranging over such ground after the infected sheep had passed would under such conditions be very likely to contract the disease.

This form may assume either the active or the inactive stage. The active stage manifests itself in the various locations by inflammation, tumefaction, ulceration, and necrosis, with or without scab formation. There is more or less rapid destruction of the tissue, especially where the lesions are located on the lips or muzzle. Cases are frequently seen where more or less of the lip or the end of the nose has sloughed away as a result of the suppurative inflammation.

The lesions in the early stage usually appear as an acute inflammation of the skin on the outside of the lips. This pimple-like formation is attended with much inflammatory swelling, with a decided

General View of a Lambing Range in Colorado. Dept. of Agr.

Unlambed Ewes Divided into Small Bunches. Dept. of Agr.

tendency toward the formation of pustules. They dry and form crusts of a dark grayish color. The growths extend rapidly and become in the course of a few days confluent, forming a large diffused scab, which when removed is found to cover an ulcerative surface. Simultaneously with this the lips become tumefied, swelling to two or three times their normal thickness. The appetite usually remains good, but the animals feed with difficulty, owing to the sensitiveness of the affected parts. In some cases the lesion extends from the lips up over the cheeks, occasionally involving the eyelids or even the eye itself. At times a mucopurulent nasal discharge appears, which adheres to the nostrils and together with the swollen condition of the surrounding tissues causes a more or less complete occlusion of the air passages, resulting in labored breathing upon exercise. In some cases the lesions extend into the mouth, producing erosions on the inside of the lips, on the gums, and on the dental pad of the hard palate. These lesions, which are of a spongy consistence and present a warty appearance, are especially noticed on the lambs.

Lesions on the legs may coexist with those on the lips. The sheep at this time will show some lameness, especially if the ulcers appear about the coronet, in the fold of the fetlock, or in the vicinity of a joint. The progress and appearance of the ulcers upon the legs are identical with those upon the lips, and they are soon covered by a thick, dry crust which when forcibly removed exposes a granulating surface covered with a tenacious pus.

2. The venereal form, as the name indicates, attacks the genital organs of both sexes. This form is frequently seen in connection with the lip-and-leg form, but it is also observed in some bands that do not present any other lesions.

In bucks the external part of the sheath is affected in most instances, and more infrequently the ulcerations are confined to the penis. The latter condition may be explained by the fact that a buck is liable during copulation to scratch or abrade the membrane covering the penis with burs, etc., in the wool of the ewe, while the sheath may become infected through the use of contaminated bed grounds. In certain sections the erroneous opinion has been held that this form of the disease is syphillis or clap and has nothing to do with lip-and-leg ulceration because it is rightly considered far worse than the latter. It is probable that this form of the disease, which is also known as ulcerated sheath and big pizzle, results in a larger death rate than all the others, and it was reported that in a number of instances quite a percentage of the band, in some cases the entire band of bucks, were destroyed as soon as the disease was discovered because so many of the bucks were rendered useless for breeding through a portion of the penis having sloughed off. Besides, this appears to be the most difficult form to treat, yet good results from treatment were obtained in many cases.

In ewes the lesions are located on the skin or mucous membrane of the vulva, on the under side of the tail, and in the perineal region. In a few cases discharges which collected at the lower angle of the vulva and in the wool adjacent to the perineal region indicated the presence of infection in the vagina.

The sheath form of the disease is characterized by an ulcerated condition of the external part of the sheath without the penis being affected, and is not infrequent among wethers. Constant saturation of the wool around the sheath with urine probably chafes the skin, allowing the entrance of bacilli from infected bed grounds, etc. The first manifestations of this form of the disease are the appearance of one or more very small pale yellow centers within the folds of the sheath at the juncture of the skin and the mucous membrane. Very early there forms at each of these centers an ulcer that extends outward into the skin, but rarely inward. The ulcer or ulcers extend, and frequently coalesce, so that the entire face of the sheath is covered by a single ulcer. During the early stages, in those cases where all or a considerable portion of the face of the sheath is covered with the ulcer, the entire external portion of the sheath will be more or less inflamed and tumefied.

No case of penis infection has been observed in wethers, except a few cases that had been treated by introducing strong caustics within the sheath in contact with the penis. While this condition has been mostly observed in wethers a year or so old, two cases of natural infection were reported in wether lambs not over four months old.

3. The foot-rot form: Owing to the dryness of the soil of a large part of the infected section in the West, this disease probably assumes a somewhat different form from the foot rot of moist localities, though foot lesions were frequently seen in connection with the lip-and-leg forms. In several instances quite a number of sheep in the infected districts presented only foot lesions, while in other instances lesions on the feet were accompanied by ulcers on the lips. The foot lesions may first become visible either at the front or back part of the cleft, but usually the erosions make their first appearance at the heel. The inflammation rapidly penetrates beneath the horny tissue, while from the ulcerous opening there exudes a thin, purulent discharge, possessing an odor pungent and disagreeable but at the same time very characteristic. Sex or age does not appear to have any important influence on the susceptibility of the animal, as the disease manifests itself quite generally in a flock, attacking alike male and female, lambs, yearlings, and aged sheep.

4. The sore-mouth form of the disease is characterized by warty or pustular patches on the lips, covered with slightly elevated brown crusts or scabs, usually seen in lambs during the fall of the year, though it has been observed earlier in the season, both in sucking lambs and in those that had just been weaned.

The disease makes its appearance very quickly, the lips becoming more or less tumefied, with a slight diminution of the appetite, especially in severe cases. In some instances food is taken with difficulty, resulting in unmistakable signs of poor nutrition and the stunting of the animal. At this stage the animal presents a greater or less number of nodules or patches on the lips, most frequently at the junction of the mucous membrane and the hairy portion. In severe cases

hese nodules become confluent, forming large, diffuse, fissured scabs
round the margin of both lips, down on the chin, or up on the nose,
r both, in which case the whole muzzle is affected. The removal of
hese scabs exposes either a purplish-red, easily bleeding surface, or
. pitted, yellowish-white ulcer covered with pus, some of which will
lso be found attached to the under surface of the removed crust. In
ery extensive lesions there may be sufficient pus so that a small
uantity will exude from beneath the crust on pressure. In a few
ases the disease spreads to the mucous membrane of the mouth,
orming small ulcers or fungoid elevations, soft, red, and of a spongy
onsistence. In both corners of the mouth there are usually present
mall yellowish necrotic areas which are generally the last to heal.
. typical, offensive odor, similar to that of Limburg cheese, is given
ff from the infected parts.

In some of the most extensive cases of this form there is a loss of
issue due to ulceration, resembling that seen in the lip-and-leg form.
n these lesions the active, vegetative filaments will be found pene-
rating the healthy tissue. In unmolested cases, except probably the
nore extensive of this form of the disease, the crusts remain intact
ntil the lesions are fully healed, when they drop off, leaving a clean,
ealthy looking surface. In such lesions the quiescent coccoid and
acillary forms of the bacillus will predominate, while only an oc-
asional short filament will be observed.

We have positive proof of numerous cases of the malignant type
f lip-and-leg ulceration developing from the lesions in sore-mouth
ambs.

CAUSE OF THE DISEASE.

There can be little doubt that the disease is primarily the result
f abrasions of the skin and other tissues, allowing the access of the
ausal organism. The latter may be a natural habitant of certain
ocalities or of certain vegetation. One factor that is predisposing in
hese cases is a prolonged drought which renders the feed scarce, in-
ucing the sheep to browse on thistles and roughage which cause the
ecessary abrasions. In fact, it is frequently noted that after rains,
ith the consequent growth of luxuriant feed, the disease becomes
hecked and affected animals rapidly recover. There seems to be
ome connection between dry weather, or rather very dry feed, and
he appearance of the disease. While there are many factors
n dry herbage liable to produce slight abrasions of the lips nec-
ssary for the entrance of germs, in succulent pastures there are few
r none. However, such abrasions by themselves will not produce
he disease, but when they become infected with the germs of necro-
is, lip-and-leg ulceration follows. The necrosis bacillus, which is
ery widely distributed by nature, will not enter a healthy tissue,
equiring, as it does, an abrasion, puncture, or wound through which
o gain access. Of course a spine or prickle, if contaminated with
hese germs at the time of puncture, will act as a direct agent of
ntroduction.

There are several conditions which are responsible as predispos-
ng factors for infection by this organism:

1. Lambs often become affected with sore mouths by coming in contact with the infectious principle. Hard, dry scabs, warty in appearance, are produced frequently, covering the entire lips, and which upon being removed leave a raw, granulated surface with or without an exudate of pus. These lesions may be present in lambs before they are weaned, in those that have been weaned, or in lambs which are forced to the range for hard dry feed after being on succulent forage. It is not, however, the feed or the pasture or the fact that they have just been weaned which of itself causes the lesions; but in addition to these predisposing causes, the necrosis bacillus becomes present and the disease continues to spread.

2. Sheep are sometimes forced to wade through alkali gumbo mud to reach water in the lakes and reservoirs when they become low. This mud becomes matted in the hair and wool of the legs, and becoming dried by the sun and winds may be rubbed off, pulling hair and skin with it, and thus opening the way for the entrance of the necrosis bacillus followed by ulcerations on the legs.

3. In the winter time the tissues, especially of the legs and sheath, may become devitalized as a result of freezing or of frost bites, thus allowing the necrosis bacillus to gain lodgment and develop.

4. Injuries in the region of the legs and feet due to thistles, cacti, briars, bruises, etc., and wounds of the lips as a result of picking up harsh forage or frozen forage or in breaking through crusted snow for feed, provide favorable conditions for the entrance of the bacilli.

The immediate cause of the necrosis is the necrosis bacillus; the remote cause may be any bacterial agent capable of injuring the mucous membrane, or chemical effects connected with the feed—anything, for that matter, that could produce a catarrhal or eroded condition of the intestinal mucosa.

Lodgment in the tissues of the body of a susceptible animal is all the necrosis bacillus requires. Once this is secured where it may develop and throw out its deadly volatile toxin, all tissues with which it comes in contact become alike a prey to its necrosing action. As a result we may have necroses of the skin, muscle, hoof, cartilage, bones, mucous membrane, navel, and internal organs.

ECONOMIC IMPORTANCE OF THE DISEASE.

The importance of this organism is far beyond its relation to lip-and-leg ulceration, since it affects calves, pigs, goats, adult cattle, horses, deer, rabbits, dogs, and chickens, and various forms of necrobacillosis may occur in these animals on premises contaminated with the infectious principle of this disease. Therefore, as a large majority of species of domestic animals are susceptible to this infection, and as a constant relation may exist between an attack of one form of necrobacillosis and the previous occurrence of another type of the infection in the same or another species of animal, it behooves one to prevent any susceptible animal of whatever species from coming in contact with a diseased one, or with such corrals, sheds, manure, and pastures as might be harborers of the contagion.

In whatever part of the animal body the *Bacillus necrophorus* may have instituted the inflammation which characterizes its presence, by whatever name the disease process may be called, be it foot rot, necrotic quittor, necrotic scratches, necrotic vaginitis or metritis, or necrotic stomatitis, there we find a hotbed of infection. Hence, the occupancy of the calving stall by a cow affected with foot rot or by a cow suffering with a vaginitis dependent upon this bacillus is sufficient to insure the development of cases of necrobacillosis. The same principle is involved in the dissemination of the disease through one or more litters of pigs. The very first investigator in this line made the experiment of placing a healthy calf in a stall with two calves affected with sore mouth. The third calf came down in five days with the same malady. The author considered the calves' habit of licking one another as being chargeable with the transmission of the disease.

Necrosis bacilli obtained from lesions of lip-and-leg ulceration will produce similar ulcers in hogs, horses, calves, and chickens which have been artificially infected by them. Moreover, cultures of the necrosis bacillus from warty lips of lambs produced ulcers on the penis of bucks, vulva of ewes, lips of old ewes, and between the claws of adult sheep. On the other hand, cultures from foot rot of sheep and from the testicle of a buck produced lesions on the lips and nostrils of lambs, while bacilli recovered from the liver of a cow caused ulcerations on the lips and mouth of an adult sheep. This transmission of the *Bacillus necrophorus* from one species of animal to another occurs under natural conditions.

On account of the possibility of the wide dissemination of this disease, the loss in condition of the affected animals, the stunting of growth or "setting" of the lambs, and the cost, time, and labor of treating the disease in an affected band, it is evident that the importance of the infection has not been overestimated. Fortunately, if taken in time, the disease in the vast majority of cases responds readily to treatment, the principal requisite being vigilance on the part of the herder to cut out as soon as they occur all cases of the infection, which should be placed in the hospital band for hand treatment.

Flock masters who have experienced an active attack of this disease in their lambs realize its importance and the necessity for drastic measures in holding the disease in check. Other owners, whose sheep have had only a mild attack, scout the seriousness of the disease but may yet learn of its devastating tendency under unfavorable conditions. It is evident that sheep are affected but mildly under favorable climatic conditions and with abundant nutritious feed. When thus affected the animal may quickly and even spontaneously recover. But in fall and winter, when bad weather and poor feed tend to lower the powers of resistance, the disease quickly makes great headway with a greater relative virulence, and in consequence a certain number of animals become so badly affected that no hope of cure at a reasonable cost or in a reasonable time may be entertained.

TREATMENT.

In prevention lies the most important means of keeping the band clean; in treatment lies the only means of making a diseased band healthy. Starting with a clean flock of sheep and wishing to introduce new blood into the band, a quarantine of two weeks is advisable then, if no case of the disease has made its appearance, it will be safe to place the newly arrived sheep with the rest of the flock. A very careful examination of all sheep, especially those intended for breeding purposes, should be made, and in the event of finding any infected sheep in the band these should be cut out, thrown into a hospital band, and treated at once, keeping very close watch on the flock for any new cases that may develop later.

Prevention should therefore be carried out along three lines: (1) Separation of the sick from the healthy animals; (2) close scrutiny of the sheep that have been exposed to infection by contact with affected animals or premises, or otherwise; (3) complete disinfection of all pens, corrals, and sheds, as the necrosis bacilli will retain their virulence under favorable conditions in and around the sheepfold for several years. The walls, racks, and troughs should be sprinkled with a 5 per cent solution of sheep dip or other similar disinfectant. The manure and a portion of the surface soil of the corral should be removed and the ground sprinkled with the disinfectant solution. If possible, the healthy sheep should be taken to new and uninfected bed grounds and pastured on uninfected range. Experience has shown that sound sheep may be safely pastured on land that has been previously occupied by animals suffering from lip-and-leg ulceration if a winter's frosts have been allowed to intervene. The germs of the disease seem to be subdued effectively by this means, and pastures which have become contaminated in one season may be considered safe for their customary usage during the following season. However, the impossibility of changing range in many cases, in some not even temporarily, makes quick eradication the more difficult.

The treatment of these affections occasioned by the presence of necrosis organisms, no matter how many varieties of the disease may make their appearance, can be reduced to a few words, namely, disinfection and cleanliness, or disinfection and prevention. While selecting treatment for that portion of the flock in which the disease has become actually established it should be remembered that the principal requisite is to expose properly the affected surfaces in order that the applied remedy may destroy the infectious matter which has lodged upon them. The remedy which will accomplish this most readily and at the same time without giving rise to harmful secondary conditions is evidently the one that should be given preference.

Treatment of this disease by local antiseptics is very satisfactory if begun in time and applied energetically. It should not be deferred, as better results will be obtained by attacking the outbreak as soon as discovered than can be expected if the disease is permitted to spread among the band or penetrate deeper into the tissues of the affected parts.

In mild, unadvanced cases of the lip and leg form the best results are obtained by removing entirely the scabs and shreds of tissue from the diseased areas by means of a piece of wood sharpened to the proper angle, and applying three or four times weekly a solution of one of the cresol or coal-tar dips, or, what is far better, an emollient dressing containing 5 parts of one of these dips, 10 parts of sublimed sulphur, and 100 parts of mutton tallow, vaseline, or lard. In fact, this form of the disease responds quickly to any of the common antiseptic solutions, and it is astonishing how speedily the majority of these cases improve after careful hand treatment.

In actively progressive cases or in aggravated, chronic forms it is desirable to remove the scabs, scrape all the soft, spongy tissue from the ulcers, and touch the affected area with a 10 per cent solution of zinc chloride or nitric acid in the strength of 1 part to 7 parts of water. Many other remedies have been tried with more or less success, but these two solutions have given the most beneficial results. As these solutions are quite penetrating and extremely caustic in the above strength, they should be handled very carefully and applied to the diseased parts only. Unfortunately, many have used an excessive amount of these very irritating solutions on the principle that if a little is good, more is better. A pointed stick, covered at its point with a piece of cloth or a tag of wool, will answer nicely for making the application of the solution. After using either of these solutions, the subsequent treatment should consist of three applications weekly of the previously mentioned emollient dressing, which is antiseptic but not caustic.

Care must be taken with these caustic solutions, as it is possible to do more harm than good if they are carelessly applied. In fact, the indiscriminate use of strong caustics or the drastic scraping of the ulcers with a sharp knife is detrimental rather than beneficial, as in both cases harm has been done in exposing fresh unprotected surfaces to reinfection.

While a cure of the majority of the chronic and severe cases may be accomplished with four or five weeks of this treatment, the expense of any treatment applied to the small percentage of these cases which resist this method of handling will usually amount to more than the value of the animal when recovered. Therefore, when the number of old cases in the band is small, and the lesions deep, long standing, and resistant to treatment, their destruction is recommended.

Where large numbers of sheep under range conditions become affected and all require hand treatment, the problem is a difficult one. Should the disease attack a large number of animals on the legs and feet, and hand treatment is impracticable, the ulcers may be best treated by causing the affected sheep to pass three times weekly through a shallow trough containing a 5 per cent solution of any of the recognized sheep dips, but care must be taken to insure the fluid coming in direct contact with the sore parts. Those badly infected cases which show a tendency to resist treatment should be hand treated and the affected parts curetted and properly drained. If the lesions are on the coronary band or hoof, all the diseased or loosened portions should be removed with the knife. As in everything else, diligence and careful attention are necessary for successful results in these stubborn cases.

Treatment of the venereal form especially demands this careful handling. The penis of the bucks, if found diseased, should be forced out of the sheath and the necrotic patches cautiously cauterized with the zinc chloride or nitric acid solution previously mentioned, and dressed daily by injecting a 1 per cent sheep-dip solution, a 1 to 500 permanganate of potash solution, or a 25 per cent solution of peroxid of hydrogen into the sheath until cured. If the penis or inner part of the sheath is extremely ulcerated and the prospects of cure is not favorable in a reasonable time the animal should be killed. Lesions on the external part of the sheath are treated like similar lesions on the lips and legs. All the tags of filthy wool should be removed, and if the lesions are mild, treat with mild antiseptics every two or three days; if severe or chronic, cauterize first and then dress with mild antiseptics three times weekly. Care must be observed, however, not to overdo the cauterization on this part, as closure of the orifice of the sheath is liable to occur as a result of too vigorous treatment, and a severe inflammation and swelling of these parts may take place. The same strength injections of sheep dip, peroxid of hydrogen, or potassium permanganate, as above mentioned, may be used in the vagina of the ewes, and the external lesions treated the same way as those on the sheaths of the bucks and wethers.

At times an infection with the necrosis germ is seen in the form of abscesses containing semisolid pus and spoken of by shepherds as boils. These are very easily cured by opening them with a knife, cleaning out the pus, and applying the disinfectant and antiseptic solutions already referred to.

The warty lip form of this disease, as already mentioned, runs a course to recovery under favorable conditions in about three to four weeks, but medicinal treatment will materially aid recovery and prevent some of the cases from becoming malignant or chronic with more or less loss of tissue from ulceration. The application of lard, mutton tallow, or vaseline containing 5 per cent of a recognized sheep dip has been very beneficial after rubbing off the scabs and crusts that form around the margins of the lips and nostrils. The necrosis germ being one which thrives best without oxygen, exposure to the atmosphere will of itself prove beneficial. Pure strength coal-tar dips, peroxid of hydrogen, tincture of iodin, and 1 per cent pyoktannin have all been found efficient, but the milder remedy just before recommended has given the best results. The lesions of the lining membrane of the mouth, which sometimes accompany this disease of lambs, may be satisfactorily treated by washing the mouth with a 2 per cent chlorate of potash solution, a 3 per cent boric acid solution, or a 1 per cent creolin solution.

DIPPING PLANT, B. A. L., 1903

The German treatment, consists in the application of 1 part of creosote and 50 parts of cod-liver, linseed, or castor oil externally, and the administration of 1 tablespoonful of this mixture internally to each lamb twice daily.

As an aid to treatment, as well as a preventive measure, it would be advisable to feed to the sheep salt which contains either sulphur in the proportion of 1 part to 12, or crude carbolic acid 1 part to 100 —that is, about 4 ounces of crude carbolic acid poured upon 12 quarts of ordinary barrel salt and thoroughly mixed.

After the affected sheep have received local treatment and recovered they should be dipped in one of the recognized sheep dips prior to being turned upon uninfected pastures or premises. Recent developments strongly indicate that much territory is infected, and it is difficult to assert that any given range is entirely clean upon which to run the sheep after dipping. While the dips may destroy unprotected bacilli on the body of the sheep, they have less effect upon those germs which are protected by the grease. dirt, and yolk of the wool. Again, it is often difficult to find all infected animals within the band, and the disease appearing in them following dipping reflects unfairly upon the effects of the dip. Certain sheep-dip preparations do not properly emulsify in alkali water, which is the only kind available in many sections, and the results from such dips are not as efficient as they should be. However, one dipping of these recovered cases must be considered from our present view point as a necessary precautionary measure.

The place to suppress this disease is on the range, and if much inconvenience and financial loss is to be avoided in making shipments to noninfected States the individual flock master must battle with it at home, holding back all diseased or recently exposed sheep and shipping only those which remain healthy after they have been removed from infection for at least two weeks.

RULE 8, REVISION 2.—TO PREVENT THE SPREAD OF LIP-AND-LEG ULCERATION (NECROBACILLOSIS) IN SHEEP.

(Effective on and after August 1, 1910).

During the existence of quarantine the interstate transportation, movement, trailing, or driving of sheep, except as hereinafter provided, from the area quarantined is prohibited. Owing to the differences in the manifestations of this disease, the classification of affected and exposed sheep will be designated as follows:

1. Exposed Sheep.—(a) Sheep which are affected with the mild or inactive form of lip-and-leg ulceration, where only one portion of the body is involved without evidence of suppuration, shall be classed as exposed sheep after they have been hand treated under the supervision or direction of an employe of the Bureau of Animal Industry with an emollient dressing containing 5 parts of one of the permitted cresol or coal-tar sheep dips, 10 parts flowers of sulphur, and 100 parts of mutton tallow, vaseline, or lard, and may be shipped interstate when accompanied by a certificate of inspection and treatment issued by an inspector of the Bureau of Animal

Industry, subject to the laws and regulations of the State or Territory to which they are destined.

(*b*) Sheep that are not infected with lip-and-leg ulceration but which have been exposed to sheep showing the disease in the malignant form, or to the contagion of the disease in the malignant form through infected corrals, pens, and chutes used by sheep so affected with the disease, may be shipped interstate in cars placarded as hereinafter provided to a recognized slaughtering center for immediate slaughter, without dipping, or they may be moved interstate for breeding or feeding purposes under the conditions hereinafter provided for such sheep.

(*c*) Sheep that are not visibly diseased with lip-and-leg ulceration but which are part of a band of diseased sheep may be moved interstate from the quarantined area or from public stock yards for breeding purposes, provided they are held seven days for a second inspection before such interstate movement, and further provided that if, upon such second inspection, disease is found, the animals apparently free shall be segregated and properly dipped before their interstate movement is permitted.

(*d*) Sheep that are not diseased with lip-and-leg ulceration but which are part of a band of diseased sheep, or sheep slightly diseased after the hand treatment described in paragraph (*a*), or sheep that have been exposed to the disease through infected corrals, pens, or chutes used by diseased sheep, may, without dipping, be moved interstate from the quarantined area or from public stock yards for feeding or grazing in fenced inclosures, provided permission shall have been obtained in advance of the movement from the proper official of the State or Territory into which the sheep are to be shipped. If the permission of such state or territorial official is not obtained the sheep shall, before being moved interstate, be dipped as hereinafter provided for sheep exposed to disease through infected corrals, pens, or chutes.

2. *Diseased Sheep.*—Sheep affected with lip-and-leg ulceration which show the disease in more than one tissue and show pus formation to a greater extent than indicated for exposed sheep shall be classed as diseased sheep, and shall under no condition be moved interstate from the quarantined area.

3. *Healthy Sheep.*—Sheep that are not affected with lip-and-leg ulceration nor exposed to sheep showing lesions of more than one tissue accompanied by pus formation may be moved interstate when accompanied by a certificate of inspection from an inspector of the Bureau of Animal Industry.

4. *Dipping.*—When it is desired to dip sheep for interstate movement as hereinbefore provided, the dipping shall be done under the supervision of an employee of the Bureau of Animal Industry and in one of the cresol or coal-tar creosote dips permitted by the Department of Agriculture in the official dipping of sheep for scabies, provided the dip is used at a strength specified for use in the dipping of sheep for scabies. The dipping fluid shall be thoroughly mixed before flowing into the vat and also

before the sheep are placed therein. The dip shall be maintained at a temperature of from 85 degrees to 95 degrees Fahrenheit, and the sheep shall be retained therein about one minute. The dipping shall be done carefully and the sheep handled as humanely as possible. The Department disclaims responsibility for any loss or damage resulting from the dipping.

5. Placarding Cars.—When, as hereinbefore provided, exposed sheep or sheep of diseased bands are shipped interstate without dipping for immediate slaughter, the proper officers of the transportation company shall affix to both sides of each car a durable placard not less than 6½ by 10 inches in size, on which shall be printed with permanent black ink in bold-face letters not less than 1½ inches in height the words "Sheep for Slaughter Exposed to Lip-and-Leg Ulceration." These placards shall also show the name of the place from which the shipment was made, the date of the shipment (which must correspond with the date of the waybills and other papers), the name of the transportation company, and the name of the place of destination. Each of the waybills, conductors' manifests, memoranda, and bills of lading pertaining to such shipments by cars or boats shall have the words "Exposed to Lip-and-Leg Ulceration" plainly written or stamped on its face. Whenever such shipment are transferred to another transportation company or into other cars or into other boats, or are rebilled or reconsigned to a point other than the original destination, the cars into which said sheep are transferred and the new waybills, conductors' manifests, memoranda, and bills of lading covering such shipments by cars or boats shall be marked as herein specified for cars first carrying said sheep and for the billing, etc., covering the same. If for any reason the placards herein required are removed from the car or are destroyed or rendered illegible, they shall be immediately replaced by the transportation company or its agents, the intention being that legible placards shall be maintained on the cars from the time of shipment until they arrive at destination and the disposition of the cars is indicated by an inspector of the Bureau of Animal Industry.

6. Disinfection.—All public stock yards, feeding stations and approaches, chutes, alleys, and pens thereof which have contained diseased animals shall, before healthy or nonexposed animals for interstate transportation are placed therein, be cleaned and disinfected as hereinafter provided. Failure to clean and disinfect said places will subject them to quarantine.

Cars and other vehicles, yards, pens, sheds, chutes, alleys, etc., that have contained diseased sheep shall be cleaned and disinfected in the following manner: Remove all litter and manure from all portions of the cars, including the ledges and framework outside, and from the posts, floors, and fences of yards, pens, sheds, chutes, alleys, etc., and empty all troughs, racks, or other feeding or watering facilities; then saturate the entire interior surface of the cars, including the inner surface of the car doors, or the entire surface of the fences, posts, floors, troughs, and racks of the yards, pens, sheds, chutes, alleys, etc., with a 5 per cent solution of pure carbolic acid, or with a 3 per cent solution of liquor cresolis compositus, U. S. P.

7. All sheep originating in any State or Territory and which are unloaded at stock yards where federal inspection is maintained will be inspected and handled in accordance with the regulations contained in this order before being permitted to move interstate.

NOTICE REGARDING THE INTERSTATE MOVEMENT OF CATTLE, SHEEP, AND SWINE WHICH ARE AFFECTED WITH LIP-AND-LEG ULCERATION (NECROBACILLOSIS).

UNITED STATES DEPARTMENT OF AGRICULTURE,
OFFICE OF THE SECRETARY,
Washington, D. C., August 10, 1911.

The attention of managers and agents of railroads and transportation companies, of stockmen, and others interested in the interstate movement of live stock is directed to the provisions of section 6 of the act of Congress approved May 29, 1884, which prohibits the interstate movement of live stock affected with any contagious, infectious, or communicable disease.

Under this section it is a misdemeanor, punishable by fine and imprisonment, for any person or corporation to deliver for transportation, receive for transportation, transport, drive on foot, or otherwise remove from one State or Territory or District of Columbia into another State or Territory or the District of Columbia any cattle, sheep, or swine which are affected with lip-and-leg ulceration (*necrobacillosis*), and which by a physical examination show the disease in more than one tissue or lesions of the disease with pus formation. However, sheep which are affected with the mild or inactive form of lip-and-leg ulceration involving the lips or face without evidence of pus formation may be moved interstate, provided the affected parts are immediately before such movement treated with an emollient dressing containing 100 parts mutton tallow, vaseline, or lard, 10 parts flowers of sulphur, and 5 parts pure carbolic acid. (In lieu of the carbolic acid three parts liquor cresolis compositus, U. S. P., may be used.) When this treatment is given at public stockyards, where Federal inspection is maintained, it should be done under the supervision of an employee of the Bureau of Animal Industry.

JAMES WILSON,
Secretary of Agriculture.

PARASITIC DISEASES.
GRUB IN THE HEAD (OESTRUS OVIS, Linn.)

The parasitic disease of the nostrils of sheep is generally known as grub in the head. The presence of the parasite is not seen from a general examination, only the catarrhal discharge. The grubs are only found on a careful post mortem examination. As a matter of fact, we have very little catarrh of sheep affecting only one side of the nostrils and that usually in late winter and early spring. These supposed catarrhs are nearly always due to the grub stage of the sheep gad fly.

The sheep gad fly is unknown to the sheep breeder in anything except the larval or grub state. The mature fly is like an over-grown house fly of a dullish yellow color so closely covered with small, black spots as to give the whole a brownish appearance. The abdomen consists of five rings, velvety and variegated with brown and straw color. The feet are brown; the wings are transparent and quite large. The head is whitish underneath. There are no mouth parts and the eyes are purplish brown. There are three eyelets on the top of the head. The space between the eyes in the male is very narrow, being less than one-third that of the female. The fly is only obtained by hatching the grub in a cage and watching developments. They are very sluggish and remain in hiding until fully matured and the temperature is sufficiently high. The female rises high and flies swiftly to a flock and deposits an egg containing a developing larvæ. The male never bothers a flock. The female only flies during the hot months and in the middle of the day.

The attack of a flock of sheep by these flies is attended with the same fright as is seen when the horse gad fly strikes the horse's nose. The sheep will push their noses down into the ground between their legs, run, stamp, snort and huddle together, seek the shade of low sheds, or under buildings. The attack seems to strike terror to them. The sheep are not molested during the morning or evening. As the mature fly has no mouth parts or means of feeding, it is evident that its sole mission is to propagate the species.

The young bot begins to make its way up the nasal passage as soon as it is deposited. This is accomplished by means of the hooks and spines. The operation is attended with some tickling or irritation as there is often violent sneezing and snorting but apparently without avail.

The larvæ find their way to the superior part of the nasal cavity, between the turbinate bones, the frontal or facial sinuses, or between the ethmoid cells. Their presence causes some irritation and stimulation of secretion, which they use as food. They live in this location for several months, at least over the winter, and make their escape in the spring. Ordinarily we do not find more than one, two, or three grubs in the head of affected sheep. Occasionally eight or ten will be seen. Some writers record from twelve to twenty grubs in bad cases and there are records of from sixty to eighty. When the number is small there are no serious symptoms. When there are several, there is usually marked catarrhal discharge and we have the thick effusive mucous characteristic of the snotty nose.

Treatment.—This must be preventive as far as possible. The fly does not attack sheep in the shade and only seeks its prey during the middle of the day. A low temporary shed that will afford shade in the pasture will be a great protection. Valuable breeding stock can well be stabled and allowed to graze during the morning and evening. Some resort to putting tar on the noses every few days to prevent attack. This can be done by smearing the sides of a narrow feed trough so that the sheep can not avoid touching in the attempt to get the grain.

The treatment of a sheep already affected is unsatisfactory. Injecting turpentine into the nostril as so often recommended reaches only a few that may not be in the sinus. Trephining or opening the skull is rather theoretical and not practical on large flocks. Occasionally fumigating the stable with turpentine or smoke from tar will palliate the catarrh. If the disease develops in the fall, fatten as fast as possible and dispose of to the butcher. If in the spring use good care and feed to carry the sheep along until the grub comes away.

SHEEP TICK.

The sheep tick as it is commonly called is one of the commonest of the parasites affecting sheep. It is not a true tick but a wingless fly. This parasite is not a native of this country, but has been brought here through importation from Europe. It was first rather confined to the eastern states, but owing to the purchase of breeding stock, and subsequent traffic in sheep, it has been carried to a large percentage of the flocks in this state. The losses occasioned are not from destroying the sheep by killing, but from the lack of thrift occasioned by their irritating and biting the skin. It is difficult to estimate the losses occasioned in a flock by the presence of this parasite, but where they become numerous there can be no doubt but that it amounts to a considerable sum. The state has been called upon to investigate cases of supposed scab that were due to ticks.

The parasite of this disease, *Melophagus ovinus*, Linn, is a wingless fly. It has six well developed legs, a short, flat head set closely upon the body and a large, oval abdomen. Their resemblance to the tick, with its large abdomen, small head and eight slender legs is not so very close when critically examined. The full grown tick is about one-fourth of an inch in length and about one-third as wide as long.

The body is short, flattened above and below, very tough and leathery in character. The color varies from an ashen to reddish gray and quite a bright red, dependent upon the quantity of blood imbibed and the time elapsed since the meal. The head is broad and very flat and somewhat sunken into the thorax. The eyes are small and on about a level with the head. The proboscis is tubular and reinforced at the upper part. Its end is armed with teeth. The thorax is nearly square and bears the strong legs. The abdomen is bag like. The legs are each provided with two sharp claws. The legs and body are covered with bristles. There are no wings but a couple of bristle spots take their place. The sexes may be separated by their size and the form of the sexual apparatus.

The tick being wingless depends wholly upon its ability to crawl for locomotion. It is able to crawl through the wool at quite a lively rate. It bites, and sucks the blood for its food. Formerly it was thought that it lived in part upon the oily matter of the wool and the epidermis of the skin. The fact that the tick soon starves to death even when kept in fresh wool practically settles the matter that it is almost if not wholly dependent upon the blood for its nourishment. The bite at the time of its infliction is not painful, but afterward it becomes reddened and itches even more than that inflicted by the mosquito.

The tick does not reproduce rapidly like the sheep scab mite. Only one egg is laid at a time and not more than eight or nine are produced during the lifetime of the female. A number of observers believe that there are only one or two. The egg is large and resembles a seed. It has a hardened case, having a row of seven dots one on each side. The special peculiarity of the eggs is the fact that they contain half developed pupae at the time they are deposited. The eggs are laid in the wool and a slight waxy substance secures their adhesion. The insect comes out with fully developed characters. The length of time required for the eggs to hatch is variously given at from three to four weeks. A large number of eggs taken by myself from sheep, and placed in wool at body temperature required from 17 to 22 days to develop.

The tick is a true parasite and can not live off the sheep more than a few days. Not being able to fly they must depend upon crawling to infect new stock, and this necessitates close contact, or the use of very recently used pens. The tick may fall upon the bedding and by chance crawl upon another animal. Their slow rate of multiplication prevents them from becoming very numerous except in the spring of the year. At shearing time from fifty to two hundred may be found on badly affected animals. After shearing the tick will migrate to the lamb because of lack of protection and under such circumstances may cause considerable loss.

The means of destroying the tick is by dipping, the same as for scab. The dip used for this purpose need not be more than one-third or one-half as strong as that used for scab. The preferable dips are those containing crude carbolic acid or creolin. The sheep or lamb need not be in the bath more than a few seconds. The sheep become no wetter by continued immersion. Unlike the condition in scab the parasites are all on the outside and readily accessible. Sheep giving evidence of this trouble should be dipped at any time if the weather is favorable. They should be dipped after shearing as the quantity of dip then required is small. Both the old sheep and the lambs should be dipped at the same time. While one dipping will so rid the flock of ticks that they will not again become very numerous during the summer, a second dipping is necessary to completely eradicate them. This should take place about two weeks after the first when the young will have made their appearance and can be destroyed. In the winter when this treatment is not practical the free use of Pyrethrum powder well dusted into the wool will be quite effectual.

After the destruction of the insects on the sheep, it is best to put the flock in new pens until the ticks which may have been dropped about the yards and pens will have died. The shorn wool should also be far enough removed so that the ticks cannot crawl back to their hosts. By exercising vigilant care, a flock can be entirely rid of this pest.

THE SHEEP LOUSE. (TRICHODECTES SPHAEROCPHALUS.)

This louse is exceedingly small and according to reports rarely seen in this country. Prof. Osborn in his work on "Insects Affecting Domestic Animals" states he has found it quite plentiful on sheep coming from Canada. When present in large numbers, it causes severe itching, rendering some remedy necessary. The use of Pyrethrum powder or the regular dips will prove effectual.

SCAB IN SHEEP. (SCABIES).

Introduction.—The disease commonly called sheep scab is one of the oldest known, most prevalent, and most injurious maladies which affect sheep. It is a contagious skin disease caused by a parasitic mite. Investigation has shown that the disease is not hereditary, as the parasites which cause it live on the external surface of the body. It is possible, however, for a lamb to become infected from a scabby mother at the moment of birth or immediately after. The treatment must consist of external applications for the destruction of the parasites and not internal remedies to purify the blood.

The disease is one of the most serious drawbacks to the sheep industry and results in enormous financial losses. The losses are due to the shedding of the wool, failure of condition, and the death of the sheep. Yet, despite its insidious nature, its ease of transmission, its severe effects, and its prevalence in certain localities, it is a disease which yields readily to proper treatment.

Cause of Common Sheep Scab.—Sheep scab is a strictly contagious disease. Common sheep scab is caused by that species of mites technically known as *Psoroptes communis*. Parasites of this species cause scab in horses, cattle, sheep, goats, and rabbits; but for each of these species of animals there appears to be a distinct variety of this parasite. Although it is more or less difficult to distinguish between these varieties, they differ somewhat in size; also it is found that the *Psoroptes communis* of the sheep does not cause scab of the horse, ox, or rabbit; nor, on the other hand, does the *Psoroptes communis* of the horse, ox, or rabbit cause scab of the sheep. Naturalists, therefore, distinguish the parasite of sheep scab by the name *Psoroptes communis* var. *ovis.*

The parasite of this disease is one of the larger mites, and is quite easily seen with the naked eye. The adult female is about one-fortieth inch long and one-sixtieth inch broad; the male is one-fiftieth inch long and one-eightieth inch broad. These mites are discovered more readily and more clearly on a dark than on a light background, and for that reason the crusts from the affected skin are often placed upon black paper and kept in the sunshine for a few minutes in order to reveal the parasites crawling about.

The Psoropt inhabits the regions on the surface of the body which are most thickly covered with wool—that is, the back, the sides, the rump, and the shoulders. Its presence is the cause of the true body scab on sheep, and of all parasitic mites it produces the most serious injuries.

Description of Common Sheep Scab.—The mites of common, or body, scab—that is, the Psoroptes—prick the skin of the animal to obtain their food, and probably insert a poisonous saliva in the wound. Their bites are followed by intense itching, with irritation, formation of papules, inflammation, exudation of serum, and the formation of crusts, or scabs, under and near the edge of which the parasites live. As the parasites multiply they seek the more healthy parts, spreading from the edges of the scab already formed, thus extending the disease. The sheep are restless; they scratch and bite themselves, and rub against posts, fences, or stones, or against other members of the flock. This irritation is particularly noticeable after the animals have been driven, for the itching is more intense when the sheep become heated. The changes in the skin naturally result in the falling of the wool. At first slender tags are noticed; the fleece assumes the condition known as flowering; it looks tufty or matted, and the sheep pulls out portions with its mouth, or leaves tags on the objects against which it rubs. Scabs fall and are replaced by thicker and more adherent crusts. The skin finally becomes more or less bare, parchment-like, greatly thickened, furrowed, and bleeding in the cracks. With shorn sheep, especially, a thick, dry, parchment-like crust covers the greatly tumefied skin. Ewes may abort or bear weak lambs.

PARTS OF BODY AFFECTED BY SCAB.

When sheep are kept in large numbers the chances for infection are naturally greater, and the disease may begin on almost any part of the body. Generally, however, it affects the parts which are covered with wool. When the sheep are fat and the wool has a large amount of yolk, the progress of the disease may be slow; usually beginning on the upper part of the body, withers, and back, it extends slowly, but none the less surely and in ever-increasing areas, to the neck, sides, flanks, rump, etc. In two or three months the entire body may be affected.

CONTAGIOUSNESS OF SCAB.

Common scab is exceedingly contagious from one sheep to another, and may in some cases show itself within about a week after healthy sheep have been exposed to infection. The contagion may be direct, by contact of one sheep with another; or indirect, from tags of wool, or from fences, posts, etc., against which scabby sheep have rubbed, or from the places where the sheep have been bedded down. One attack of scab does not protect sheep from later attacks. Transmitted to man, sheep scab may produce a slight spot on the skin, a point which is sometimes taken advantage of for the purpose of diagnosis. In case of suspected scab, one of the crusts is bound lightly on the arm. After a short time an itching sensation is felt and the mites are found on the skin. Transmitted to horses, cattle, or goats, common sheep scab fails to develop.

Chances for Recovery From Scab.—Cases of apparent spontaneous recovery are rare. Usually when proper methods of treatment are not adopted the disease increases, leads to anæmia, emaciation, exhaustion, and death, and may result in a loss of from 10 to 80 per cent of the flock. Scab is favored by seasons when the wool is longest, and by huddling or overcrowding the animals; also race, energy, temperament, age, state of health, length, fineness, and abundance of wool, and the hygienic conditions of the surroundings influence the course and termination of the disease. Young, weak, closely inbred animals, and those with long, coarse wool will most quickly succumb. Unhealthy localities, damp climate, and poorly ventilated sheds favor the disease. Pure or mixed Merino sheep succumb sooner than certain other breeds. The mortality varies according to conditions, but is highest in autumn and winter. When owners are careless the death rate may be very high; if untreated the sheep may die in two to three months. Hygienic conditions, good food, and cool, dry atmosphere tend to check the disease. Sheep sheds should accordingly be well ventilated and open to light and sunshine. With proper attention to hygienic conditions and thorough dipping, a positive cure can be guaranteed.

Vitality of the Scab Parasite.—Taken from the sheep, the mites possess a remarkable vitality. It is generally stated that, kept at a moderate temperature on portions of scab, the adults may live from four to twenty days, but they will occasionally live much longer; cases are on record where they have lived three, four, or even six weeks when separated from sheep; if the atmosphere is dry they will generally die in about fifteen days; but death is often only apparent, for the mites may sometimes be revived by warmth and moisture even after six or eight weeks; the fecundated females are especially tenacious of life. Various rather contradictory statements may be found regarding their resistance to cold. Krogmann states that they may live at a temperature of $-10°$ C. $(+14°$ F.) for twenty-eight days; other authors claim that the mites die in two hours at $47°$ F.; still other authors, that they die at $50°$ C. $(122°$F.). They are said to have been kept alive in cold water for six days and in warm water for ten days. Several authors admit, however, that the parasites are usually killed by a soaking rain; though it is claimed that in damp, dark stables they may live for months. Experience has shown that in some cases apparently healthy sheep have become infected in places where no sheep have been kept for four, eight, twelve, or even twenty-four months.

All matters connected with the vitality of the scab mite have an important bearing in explaining cases of indirect infection on roads over which scabby sheep have been driven, or in fields and sheds where they have been kept. From the facts now at hand, the following important rules can be presented:

(1) Scabby sheep should never be driven upon a public road; (2) sheds in which scabby sheep have been kept should be thoroughly cleaned, disinfected, and aired, and should be left unused for *at least four weeks* (better two months) before clean sheep are placed in them; (3) fields in which scabby sheep have been kept should stand vacant *at least four weeks* (better six or eight) before being used for clean sheep; (4) a drenching rain will frequently serve to disinfect a pasture, but it is well to whitewash the posts

against which scabby sheep have rubbed. Even after observing the precautions here given it is not possible to absolutely guarantee that there will be no reinfection, but the probabilities are against it.

Life History of the Scab Parasite.—A study of the life history of the scab parasite is necessary in order to determine several important points of practical value, such as the proper time for the second dipping, etc.

The female mite lays about 15 to 24 eggs on the skin, or fastened to the wool near the skin; a six-legged larva is hatched; these larvæ cast their skin and become mature; the mites pair and the females lay their eggs, after which they die. The exact number of days required for each stage varies somewhat, according to the writings of different authors, a fact which is probably to be explained by individual variation, and by the conditions under which the observations and experiments were made. Thus Gerlach, in his well-known work (1857), estimates about fourteen to fifteen days as the period required for a generation of mites from the time of pairing to the maturity of the next generation. He divides this time as follows: Under ordinary conditions the eggs hatch in three to four days, although two authors allow ten to eleven days for the egg stage; three or four days after birth the six-legged larvæ molt and the fourth pair of legs appear; this fourth pair are always present when the mites are two-thirds the size of the adults; when seven to eight days old the mites are mature and ready to pair; several (three or four) days are allowed for pairing; another generation of eggs may be laid fourteen to fifteen days after the laying of the first generation of eggs. Without going into all of the other observations on these points, it may be remarked that the eggs may not hatch for six or seven days; the six-legged larvæ may molt when three to four days old, and become mature; after pairing a second molt takes place, lasting four to five days; a third molt follows immediately, then eggs are laid and the adults die; in some cases there is a fourth molt, but apparently without any further production of eggs. Accepting Gerlach's estimate of fifteen days as an average for each generation of 10 females and 5 males, in three months' time the sixth generation would appear and consist of about 1,000,000 females and 500,000 males.

Several practical lessons are to be drawn from these figures: First, it is seen that the parasites increase very rapidly, so that if scab is discovered in a flock, the diseased sheep should immediately be isolated; second, if new sheep are placed in a flock, they should either first be dipped, as a precautionary measure, or they should at least be kept separate for several weeks to see whether scab develops; third, since the chances for infection are very great, the entire flock should be treated, even in case scab is found only in one or two animals; fourth, as dipping is not certain to kill the eggs, the sheep should be dipped a second time, the time being selected between the moment of the hatching of eggs and the moment the next generation of eggs is laid. As eggs may hatch between three and seven, possibly ten or eleven, days, and as fourteen to fifteen days are required for the entire cycle, the second dipping should take place after the seventh day, but before the fourteenth day; allowing for individual variation and variation of conditions, the tenth, eleventh, or twelfth day will be the best time to repeat the dipping.

Conditions Which May Be Mistaken for Scab.—Any parasite or condition which causes an itching, and thus leads the sheep to scratch themselves, or any abnormal condition of the skin, may be temporarily mistaken for scab; but if the rule is held in mind that no scab is possible without the presence of the specific parasites, it will be easily determined whether scab is present or not. The following are the more important cases to be considered:

(1) Itching due to other parasites; such as the common sheep tick, true ticks, and lice, may be distinguished from scab by finding the parasites. The dipping used for treating scab will also kill sheep ticks and lice.

(2) Inflammation of the sebaceous glands may be mistaken for common scab. It appears most frequently in autumn. There is a severe itching, the skin is red and sensitive, and is covered with a strong-smelling, yellowish, viscid yolk; tufts of wool may be shed. It may be cured, after shearing, with any starchy lotion.

(3) Rain rot—in rainy weather an eruption may appear on the skin which might be mistaken for scab. There is, however, no parasite present; itching is absent, and the trouble disappears when dry weather comes.

Treatment of Scab.—Proper hygienic conditions alone, though of importance in connection with the subject of treatment, can not be relied upon to cure scab. The only rational treatment consists in using some external application which will kill the parasites. Formerly medicines were given internally, and even within a few years past it has been claimed that feeding sulphur to sheep will cure the disease. The statements regarding sulphur were such as to lead the department to try the experiment, which, however, was soon abandoned as unsuccessful. The external application of scab cures is in various ways made known as hand dressing, hand curing, spotting, pouring, smearing, and dipping. Of these methods, dipping is by far the most satisfactory.

Hand Applications.—While common scab is the disease treated in this bulletin, as a matter of information, it may be stated that in case of head scab, or in light cases of foot scab, which appear to be rather rare, hand applications may be resorted to, and will frequently suffice. A nonpoisonous ointment may be made by taking 4 ounces of oil of turpentine, 6 ounces of flowers of sulphur, and 1 pound of lard. Mix the ingredients at a gentle heat, and rub in well with the hands or with a brush at the same time breaking the crusts. The simple sulphur ointment may be made of 1 part of sulphur and 4 parts of lard; one-fourth part of mercurial ointment may be added. Few remedies are so useful in mange in dogs, ringworm, and other itching complaints as sulphur iodide, and it may well be given a trial on head scab. It is prepared as follows: **Mix** in a nonmetallic vessel, as a porcelain mortar, 4 ounces of iodine with 1 ounce of sublimed sulphur, gently heating the mixture until it liquefies; the red-brown liquid upon cooling becomes a gray-black crystalline mass, insoluble in water, but soluble in glycerine and fats, with 8 or 10 parts of which it is mixed for ointments or liniments. An ointment of flowers of sulphur and carbolated vaseline would also probably give good results. One author advises for head scab and foot scab a mixture consisting of 1 part of mercurial ointment and 11 parts of sulphur ointment. Foot scab and head scab would also probably respond to treatment with the various dips used for common scab.

Hand dressing is not recommended for common scab; in fact, it must be looked upon as directly responsible for a considerable amount of the disease, since it is too often relied upon to cure the disease, while in reality it is only a palliative. The only condition under which hand dressings can be advised is in case scab is discovered in one or two sheep of a flock during severe winter weather, when dipping would be impracticable. In that event, the infected sheep should be immediately isolated from the flock; and they might be hand dressed, if desired, in order to hold the disease in check. It can not be too strongly insisted upon that pouring, spotting, etc., are only expensive and temporizing methods of dealing with scab.

Pouring is done as follows: Part the wool on the back by making a furrow with the finger from the head to the tail; furrows are also made along the shoulders and thighs to the legs, and on the sides; pour the ointment or dip in these furrows. A still better plan is to pour the warm dip from a coffeepot or teapot directly on the affected parts, rubbing it well in with the hand, a brush, or a corncob. It must be repeated for emphasis, however, that such treatment can not be relied upon, and should be used only in emergency cases when dipping is impracticable.

A mercurial ointment may be made as follows: (A) Dissolve 1 pound of resin in one-half pint of oil of turpentine; (B) mix 1 pound of mercurial ointment with 6 pounds of lard, with gentle heat; and (C) when cool, mix the two compounds, A and B. It should be remembered that mercurial ointments are not unattended with danger, and on this account it is better to prepare a small amount of dip and pour it on the affected part as described above.

Dipping.—By far the most rational and satisfactory and the cheapest method of curing scab is by dipping the sheep in some liquid which will kill the parasites. The dipping process is as follows:

Shear all the sheep at one time, and immediately after shearing confine them to one-half the farm for two to four weeks. Many persons prefer to dip immediately after shearing.

At the end of this time dip every sheep (and every goat also, if there are any on the farm).

Ten days later dip the entire flock a second time.

Be careful in dipping rams, as they are more likely to be overcome in the dip than are the ewes.

Injury may, however, result to pregnant ewes, which must, on this account, be carefully handled. Some farmers arrange a stage, with sides, to hold the pregnant ewes, which is lowered carefully into the vat, and raised after the proper time.

Use a dip made of lime and sulphur, tobacco and sulphur, or one of the coal tar dips.

Purchase no proprietary dips except those having the approval of the Department of Agriculture, Washington, D. C.

Use all proprietary dips according to directions.

Remove all sediment from the lime and sulphur dip, as it injures the wool.

Tobacco dips should never be boiled.

For a general dip a tobacco or coal tar preparation is to be preferred to lime and sulphur, as a lime and sulphur dip has little effect in destroying the sheep tick or louse.

A fresh solution should be used for the second dipping. This is absolutely essential if the lime and sulphur or the tobacco and sulphur are to be used.

Mix the dip well in the vat.

It is better to use warm water than cold water in dipping sheep, as warm water cuts the grease and allows the dip to get to all parts of the skin of the animal.

The correct temperature for a dip is from 100 to 105 degrees Fahrenheit.

Sheep can be dipped in the winter if warm days are selected for that purpose. If the sheep are badly afflicted with scab, the thick scabs should be softened previous to the dipping of the sheep by pouring some of the dip on these places and rubbing them with some smooth instrument, or the scabs can be softened while the sheep are being dipped, by rubbing the thick scabs with a brush. Care should be taken, however, not to draw blood, as on coagulation it will protect the mite from the dip.

Lambs do not need to be dipped for so long a time as older sheep, as their wool is short. They are also more delicate in constitution, hence can not stand the dipping as well as older sheep.

Always water sheep before dipping, otherwise they may drink the dip which is sometimes found in little puddles in the dripping pens. Each sheep should be held in the dip from two to three minutes, and the head quickly immersed once or twice just before the sheep leaves the vat. A sheep in moderate length of wool and allowed to drip thoroughly after being dipped will carry away from two to three quarts of the dip. A sheep after being shorn will carry away about a quart of the dip. The question should not be, how many sheep can be dipped in a day, but how well can they be dipped.

If scabby sheep are taken from a pasture and dipped, they should not be returned to that place for a period of thirty days. Heavy rains are said, however, to disinfect open fields. If the sheep have been housed in buildings prior to the dipping, these buildings should be disinfected before the sheep are returned to them.

Preliminary Questions in Choosing a Dip.—The homemade dips which are most commonly used have either tobacco or sulphur as their basis, while the prepared dips contain tobacco, sulphur, arsenic, carbolic acid, etc., as curative agents.

In selecting a dip several points should be considered: First of all, the question of expense will naturally arise; next, the question. as to whether or not scab actually exists in the flock to be dipped, or whether or not the dipping is more of a precautionary matter, or for the sake of cleansing the animal's skin. The facilities at hand, the setback to the sheep, and the length of the wool are also matters for consideration, as well as the pastures into which the dipped sheep are to be placed. Notwithstanding statements to the effect that a given dip can be used under all conditions, the above questions are evidently important.

If fuel is very scarce, so that it is impracticable to boil the mixture for at least two hours, the lime-and-sulphur dips should not be selected. A tobacco-and-sulphur dip, as well as many of the better proprietary dips, can be made without the necessity of lengthy boiling, and should be given preference whenever facilities for boiling are not at hand.

In case it is necessary to place the dipped sheep on the same pastures they occupied before being dipped, it is always best to use a dip containing sulphur. If a proprietary dip is selected under those circumstances, it is suggested that sulphur be added, about 1 pound of flowers of sulphur to every 6 gallons of dip. In case it is possible to utilize fresh pastures after dipping, the use of sulphur is not so necessary, but is always advisable. The object in using sulphur is to place in the wool a material which will not evaporate quickly, but will remain there for a longer period of time than the scab parasites ordinarily remain alive away from their hosts. By doing this the sheep are protected against reinfection.

Kinds of Dips.—Sulphur is one of the oldest known remedies for scab. As a scab eradicator it must be placed among the best substances at our disposal. It is one of the constituents of certain proprietary dips, but its use to the farmer is best known in the tobacco-and-sulphur dip and in the lime-and-sulphur dip. These homemade mixtures, as already shown, are the two dips which have played the most important roles in the eradication of scab from certain English colonies, and their use, especially the use, *as well as the abuse,* of lime and sulphur, is quite extensive in this country.

The Tobacco-and-Sulphur Dip.—The formula, as given here and as adopted by the New South Wales sanitary authorities, appears to have been first proposed in 1854 by Mr. John Rutherford.

The proportions adopted by Rutherford, and afterwards made official by the scab sanitary authorities, are:

```
Tobacco leaves.............................pound..1
Flowers of sulphur...........................do....1
Water (original formula, 5 gallons imperial, equivalent
    to 6 United States gallons)................gallons..6
```

The advantage of this dip lies in the fact that two of the best scab remedies, namely, tobacco (nicotine) and sulphur, are used together, both of which kill the parasites, while the sulphur remains in the wool and protects for some time against reinfection. As no caustic is used to soften the scab, heat must be relied on to penetrate the crusts.

Directions for Preparing Tobacco-and-Sulphur Dip.—The tobacco-and-sulphur dip is prepared as follows:

A. Infusing the tobacco: Place 1 pound of good leaf or manufactured tobacco for every 6 gallons of dip desired in a covered boiler of cold or lukewarm water and allow to stand for about twenty-four hours; on the evening before dipping bring the water to near the boiling point (212° F.) for an instant, then remove the fire and allow the infusion to stand over night.

B. Thoroughly mix the sulphur (1 pound to every 6 gallons of dip desired) with the hand in a bucket of water to the consistency of gruel.

C. When ready to dip, thoroughly strain the tobacco infusion (A) from the leaves by pressure, mix the liquid with the sulphur gruel (B), add enough water to make the required amount of dip and thoroughly stir the entire mixture. All things considered, the tobacco-and-sulphur is as good a dip as is known at the present time.

Various Formulas for Lime-and-Sulphur Dips.—Under the term "lime-and-sulphur dips" are included a large number of different formulas requiring lime and sulphur in different proportions. In general practice all of these dips are spoken of as "the lime-and-sulphur dip," but in reality each separate formula represents a separate dip.

To give an idea of the variety of the lime-and-sulphur dips, the following list is quoted, the ingredients being reduced in all cases to avoirdupois pounds and United States gallons:

1. The original "Victorian lime-and-sulphur dip" proposed by Dr. Rowe, adopted as official in Australia:

```
        Flowers of sulphur.....................pounds  20 5-6
        Fresh slaked lime........................do..   10 5-12
        Water ................................gallons 100
```

2. South African (Cape Town) official lime-and-sulphur dip:

```
        Flowers of sulphur (minimum)..........pounds  15
        Unslaked lime............................do..  15
        Water ................................gallons 100
```

3. South African (Cape Town) official lime-and-sulphur dip, February 4, 1897:

```
        Flowers of sulphur.....................pounds  20 5-6
        Unslaked lime............................do..  16 2-3
        Water ................................gallons 100
```

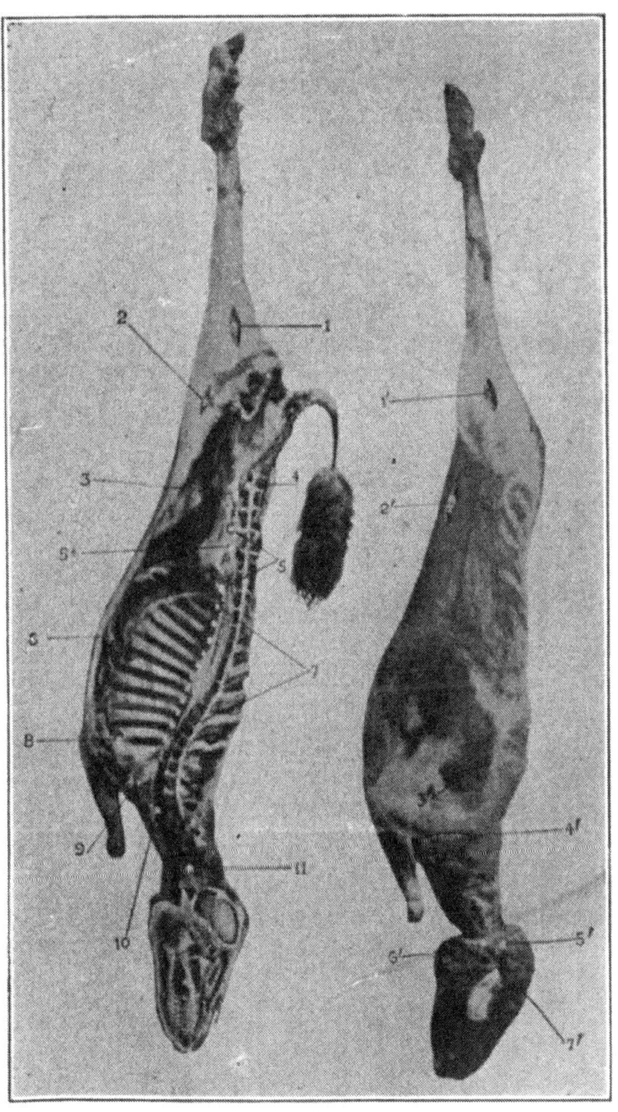

Lympyh Glands in the Sheep. Dept. of Agr.

4. Nevada lime-and-sulphur dip:
   Flowers of sulphur......................pounds 16 2-3
   Lime ....do.. 33
   Water ....gallons 100
5. Fort Collins lime-and-sulphur dip:
   Flowers of sulphur.....................pounds 33
   Unslaked lime..........................do.. 11
   Water ....gallons 100
6. A mixture used extensively and with general satisfaction, contains the same proportions of lime and sulphur (namely 1 to 3) as the Fort Collins dip, but the quantities are reduced to:
   Flowers of sulphur.....................pounds 24
   Unslaked lime..........................do.. 8
   Water ....gallons 100

In case of fresh scab, formula No. 6 will act as efficaciously as the dips with a greater amount of lime, but in cases of very hard scab a stronger dip, as the Fort Collins dip, should be preferred, or, in unusually severe cases, an ooze with more lime in proportion to the amount of sulphur, such as the Victorian (No. 1), the South African (No. 3), or the Nevada (No. 4) dip might be used.

Dangerous Formulas.—Among the dangerous formulas for lime-and-sulphur dips are the following:

   a. California lime-and-sulphur dip:
   Flowers of sulphur......................pounds 100
   Lime ....do.. 25
   Water ....gallons 100

A very dangerous misprinted formula is found in several books and journals, probably due to a typographical error, which specifies a much larger proportion of lime than any of those mentioned above. Thirty-three pounds of lime to 100 gallons of water is the largest proportion admissible under any circumstances, and 16 2-3 pounds is as much as should be used without expert advice and supervision.

All things considered, where it is a choice between sacrificing the weight of sheep, and to some extent the color of the wool, by using tobacco and sulphur, and sacrificing the staple of the wool by using lime and sulphur, the farmer should not hesitate an instant in selecting tobacco in preference to lime. The loss in weight by using tobacco and sulphur is not much greater than the loss in using lime and sulphur, while the loss in staple is of more importance than a slight discoloration.

Preparation of Lime-and-Sulphur Mixture.—Almost as many different methods of preparing the liquid exists as there are different formulas, some of the methods laying great stress upon sifting both the lime and the sulphur, others laying great stress upon allowing the liquid to settle, others leaving out of consideration both of these points. The method which has been found to be the easiest and most satisfactory is as follows:

A. Take 8 to 11 pounds of unslaked lime, place it in a mortar box or a kettle or pail of some kind, and add enough water to slake the lime and form a lime paste or lime putty.

Many persons prefer to slake the lime to a powder, which is to be sifted and mixed with sifted sulphur. One pint of water will slake 3 pounds of lime, if the slaking is performed slowly and carefully. As a rule, however, it is necessary to use more water. This method takes more time and requires more work than the one given above, and does not give any better results. If the boiled solution is allowed to settle the ooze will be equally as safe.

B. Sift into this lime paste three times as many pounds of flowers of sulphur as used of lime, and stir the mixture well.

Be sure to weigh both the lime and the sulphur. Do not trust to measuring them in a bucket or to guessing at the weight.

C. Place the sulphur-lime paste in a kettle or boiler with about 25 to 30 gallons of boiling water, and boil the mixture for two hours at least, stirring the liquid and sediment. The boiling should be continued until the sulphur disappears, or almost disappears, from the surface; the solution is then of a chocolate or liver color. The longer the solution boils the more the sulphur is dissolved, and the less caustic the ooze becomes. Most writers advise boiling from thirty to forty minutes, but the Bureau obtains a much better ooze by boiling from two to three hours, adding water when necessary.

D. Pour the mixture and sediment into a tub or barrel placed near the dipping vat and provided with a bunghole about 4 inches from the bottom and allow ample time (two to three hours, or more if necessary) to settle..

The use of some sort of settling tank provided with a bunghole is an absolute necessity, unless the boiler is so arranged that it may be used both for boiling and settling. An ordinary kerosene oil barrel will answer very well as a small settling tank. To insert a spigot about 3 to 4 inches from the bottom is an easy matter. Draining off the liquid through a spigot has the great advantage over dipping it out, in that less commotion occurs in the liquid, which therefore remains freer from sediment.

E. When fully settled, draw off the clear liquid into the dipping vat and add enough warm water to make 100 gallons. The sediment in the barrel may then be mixed with water and used as a disinfectant, *but under no circumstances should it be used for dipping purposes.*

A double precaution against allowing the sediment to enter the vat is to strain the liquid through ordinary bagging as it is drawn from the barrel.

Position of the Bureau on Lime-and-Sulphur Dips.—To summarize, the position of the Bureau of Animal Industry on the lime-and-sulphur dips is as follows: When properly made and properly used, these dips are second to none and equalled by few as scab eradicators. There is always some injury to the wool resulting from the use of these dips, but when properly made and properly used upon shorn sheep it is believed that this injury is so slight that it need not be considered; on long wool the injury is greater and seems to vary with different wools, being greater on a fine than on a coarse wool. This injury consists chiefly in a change in the microscopic structure of the fiber, caused by the caustic action of the ooze. When improperly made and improperly used the lime-and-sulphur dips are both injurious and dangerous, and in these cases the cheapness of the ingredients does not justify their use. In case scab exists in a flock and the farmer wishes to eradicate it, he can not choose a dip which will bring about a more thorough cure than will lime and sulphur (properly made and properly used), although it will be perfectly possible for the farmer to find several other dips which will, when properly used, be nearly or equally as effectual as any lime-and-sulphur dip. There is no dip to which objections can not be raised.

Tobacco Dips.—The active principle of tobacco, upon which the tobacco dips depend for their action, is a poisonous substance known as nicotine. This poison when applied to animals externally in too strong solutions may cause nausea, fainting, and even death. The dog and the rabbit are particularly susceptible to its effects. Diluted to about thirty-three one-thousandths to sixty one-thousandths of 1 per cent it makes a slow but sure-acting and excellent sheep dip.

Unfortunately the percentage of nicotine varies greatly, not only in different kinds of tobacco, but also in different parts of the plant, in different years, and even in different parts of the same package. There is more nicotine in the leaves, for instance, than in the stems.

On account of the variation in the amount of nicotine in the different samples of tobacco, it is practically impossible for the farmer to make up an exact desired strength of tobacco dip if he prepares his own mixture from the leaves. He can, however, prepare a mixture which will come within the limits suited to kill the scab parasites. If a solution of an exact given strength is desired, it will be necessary to buy prepared nicotine, or prepared tobacco dips of a guaranteed strength, and reduce them to the strength determined upon.

Directions for Preparing the Dip.—For every 100 gallons of dip desired, take 21 pounds of good prepared tobacco leaves; soak the leaves in cold or lukewarm water for twenty-four hours in a covered pot or kettle; then bring the water to near the boiling point for a moment, and, if in the morning, allow the infusion to draw for an hour; if in the evening, allow it to draw over night; the liquid is next strained (pressure being used to extract as much nicotine as possible from the wet leaves) and diluted to 100 gallons per 21 pounds of tobacco. This dip should be used as fresh as possible, as it contains a large amount of organic material which will soon decompose.

The proportions here given—21 pounds of prepared tobacco leaves to 100 gallons of water—have given very satisfactory results, especially in Cape Town colony, where the reports of the scab inspectors accord this homemade tobacco dip third place among the dips officially recognized.

By all means the use of a tobacco dip, or of the tobacco-and-sulphur dip, in preference to the lime-and-sulphur dips is advised in case the sheep to be dipped show no unmistakable signs of scab.

At present most tobacco dips are made either with the extract of tobacco or with nicotine solution, on account of the convenience of mixing these preparations with water. The regulations of the Bureau of Animal Industry call for 0.07 of 1 per cent of nicotine in a tobacco dip.* Sufficient nicotine would therefore be furnished for 100 gallons (about 800 pounds) of dip by 1 pound of a 40 per cent solution of nicotine. The formula for this dip would be:

Nicotine ....pound.. 0.56
Water ....gallons.. 100

The nicotine solution or tobacco extract should not be added to the dip until just before it is ready for use, and then the dip should be thoroughly stirred, so as to secure a uniform mixture. The dip should on no account be heated above 110° F. after the nicotine solution is added, as heat is liable to evaporate the nicotine and weaken the dip. It will be an easy matter to calculate how much nicotine solution or extract of tobacco should be used for 100 gallons of water by dividing the quantity of nicotine required in the dip by the proportion of nicotine in the extract. For example, suppose the nicotine solution contains 25 per cent of nicotine, we have $0.56 \div 0.25 = 2.24$. Therefore in this case it would require 2.24 pounds of nicotine solution for the 100 gallons of dip. Or, if a tobacco extract is used, having, for example, 2.40 per cent of nicotine, the formula would be as follows: $0.56 \div 0.024 = 23.33$, and therefore 23.33 pounds would be required for 100 gallons of dip.

The advantages of the tobacco dip are that it is comparatively cheap, since the farmer can grow his own tobacco; that it is effectual and at the same time not injurious to the wool. The disadvantages of the dip are that it sometimes sickens the sheep; that it also occasionally sickens the persons who use it, especially if they are not smokers; it spoils very rapidly; it causes a greater setback, or shrinkage, than lime and sulphur, but less of a setback than carbolic dips.

Arsenical Dips.—There are both homemade arsenical dips and secret proprietary arsenical dips. It is well to use special precautions with both because of the danger connected with them.

The drawbacks to the use of arsenic may be summed up somewhat as follows: (a) Its danger as a deadly poison. (b) Its drying effect on the wool. (c) Its weakening of the fiber of the wool in one particular part near the skin, where it comes in contact with the tender wool roots at the time of dipping. (d) Its not feeding the wool or stimulating the growth, or increasing the weight of the fleece, as good oleaginous dips do. (e) The danger arising from the sheep pasturing, after coming out of the bath, where the wash may possibly have dripped from the fleece, or where showers of rain,

*See regulation 33, page 551. This order also dispenses with flowers of sulphur in the official tobacco dips.

after the dipping, have washed the dip out of the fleece upon the pasture. (*f*) Its occasionally throwing sheep off their feed for a few days after dipping, and so prejudicing the condition of the sheep. (*g*) Its frequent effect upon the skin of the sheep, causing excoriation, blistering, and hardness, which stiffen and injure the animal, sometimes resulting in death.

It may be said, on the other hand, that arsenic really has excellent scab-curing qualities; it enters into the composition of a number of the secret dipping powders and forms the chief ingredient in one of the oldest secret dips used. This particular dip has been given second place (with some qualifications) among the officially recognized dips in South Africa. In deference to the opinion of those who prefer an arsenical dip several formulas are quoted here.

Formulas for Arsenical Dips.—Finlay Dun recommends the following: Take 3 pounds each of arsenic, soda ash (impure sodium carbonate) or pearl ash (impure potassium carbonate), soft soap, and sulphur. A pint or two of naphtha may be added if desired. The ingredients are best dissolved in 10 to 20 gallons of boiling water and cold water is added to make up 120 (United States) gallons. The head of the sheep must, of course, be kept out of the bath.

A mixture highly indorsed by certain parties consists of the following ingredients:

Commercially pure arsenite of soda.......pounds.. 14
Ground roll sulphur........................do.... 34½
Water ....gallons (U. S.).. 432

The arsenite of soda is thoroughly mixed with the sulphur before being added to the water.

Precautions in Use of Arsenical Mixtures.—Any person using an arsenical dip should bear in mind that he is dealing with a deadly poison. The following precautions should be observed:

(1) Yards into which newly dipped sheep are to be turned should first be cleared of all green food, hay, and even fresh litter; if perfectly empty they are still safer. (2) When the dipping is finished, the yard should be cleaned, washed, and swept, and any unused ooze should at once be poured down a drain which will not contaminate food or premises used by any animals. (3) Dipped sheep should remain in an open, exposed place, as on dry ground. (4) Overcrowding should be avoided, and every facility given for rapid drying, which is greatly facilitated by selecting fine, clear, dry weather for dipping. (5) On no account should sheep be returned to their grazings until they are dry and all risk of dripping is passed.

Suggestion as to Danger.—The arsenical formulas given above are copied from the writings of men who have had wide experience in dipping, but this Department assumes no responsibility for the efficacy of the dips given or for their correct proportions. Furthermore, as long as efficacious nonpoisonous dips are to be had, there is no necessity for running the risks attendant upon the use of poisonous dips.

Carbolic Dips.—A carbolic-acid dip may be made at home or may be purchased as a proprietary article. This class of dips kills the scab mites very quickly, but unfortunately the wash soon leaves the sheep, which is consequently not protected from reinfection in the pastures. If, therefore, a carbolic dip is selected, it is well to add flowers of sulphur (1 pound to every 6 gallons) as a protection against reinfection.

The advantages of carbolic dips are that they act more rapidly than the tobacco or sulphur dips, and that the prepared carbolic dips are very easily mixed in the bath. They also seem, according to Gillette, to have a greater effect on the eggs of the parasites than either the sulphur or the tobacco dips. The great disadvantages of this class of dips are, first, in some of the proprietary dips, that the farmer is uncertain regarding the strength of material he is using; second, the sheep receive a greater setback than they do with either lime and sulphur or tobacco.

If a carbolic dip is used care must be taken that the ingredients form a thorough emulsion; if a scum arises to the top, a softer water should be used.

In justice to this class of dips it is only fair to state that while the views here expressed are entirely in accord with the opinions of some authorities, they do not agree with the views held by others; but they are based upon the material purchased in open market, and probably represent the experience of many who have used these dips. The investigations of the Bureau of Animal Industry certainly show that more tests are necessary before this class of dips can be indorsed. It is hoped that these tests may be made in the near future.

One of the prominent proprietary carbolic dips was formerly recognized as one of the three official dips in New South Wales, but it has now been stricken from the list. In Cape Town carbolic dips are not much used, and in the official reports little is said concerning them.

Setback to the Sheep from Dipping.—Dipping often results in a slight setback. If sheep are weighed immediately before dipping, and again at the same hour the following day, it will be noticed that the weight has changed. There may be a gain, but usually there is a loss varying from ½ to 3½ pounds. The second day there may also be either a gain or loss. As the weight of sheep varies from day to day, from 1 to 5 pounds in loss or gain, due chiefly to the increase or decrease of the amount of fodder and water in the stomach, the effects of dipping can not be estimated in twenty-four or forty-eight hours. In order to meet statements made concerning loss or gain in weight, the Bureau of Animal Industry had sheep dipped at stated intervals and the weights taken from week to week; all the sheep were kept under exactly the same conditions; the dips used were lime and sulphur, tobacco and sulphur, and two proprietary carbolic dips.

In both the Western and the Eastern experiments the sheep treated with lime and sulphur averaged the greatest gain, the sheep treated with tobacco the second highest gain, while the sheep treated with carbolic dip showed the lowest gain.

DIPPING PLANTS.

There are numerous kinds of dipping plants in use, the size and style varying according to the conditions which are to be met and the individual taste of the owner. The farmer who has but a small flock can use a small portable vat for dipping, turning a part of his barn or some shed into a catching pen; by holding the sheep a moment at the top of the incline, as the animals emerge from the vat, and allowing them to drain, he can do away with the necessity of a draining yard.

When large flocks are to be dipped at stated periods it will be economy to build a more permanent plant. Such a plant should consist of (1) collecting and forcing yards, provided with a (2) drive and (3) chute, or slide, into the (4) dipping vat, from which an (5) incline with cross cleats leads to the (6) draining yards.

Heating tanks or boilers are also necessary. For a small vat, any portable caldron with a capacity of 30 to 100 gallons will answer, and the proper temperature may be maintained by pouring fresh hot ooze into the vat as the supply is exhausted by the dipping. In the large permanent plants the temperature can best be regulated by means of a steam pipe or hot water coil close to the floor of the tub.

Thermometers are an absolute necessity. The floating dairy thermometer will be found to be most convenient, and several extra thermometers should be kept on hand to replace broken instruments. The thermometer is dropped into the vat and allowed to float for a short time, then quickly removed and the temperature determined. It is well to make paint marks at the side of the 100° and 110° points.

Building Material.—The yards and vat may be built of wood, concrete, cemented stone, or brick, according to the individual taste of the owner and the facilities at hand.

Dimensions.—The dimensions of the various parts given in the following descriptions may be varied according to the breed and the number of sheep to be dipped. Dipping liquid will be saved by making the tub much narrower on the bottom than at the top. On top, simple oblong dipping tanks vary from 1 foot 9 inches to 3 feet in breadth, 2 feet or 2 feet 6 inches forming a convenient medium. Floors vary from 6 inches to 3 feet in width, 9 inches forming a good working medium. Depth varies from 3 feet to 5 feet 6 inches, 4 feet to 5 feet forming a convenient medium. If calves are to be dipped in the same vat it will be best to make the tub 5 feet or 5 feet 6 inches deep.

In sinking the tub in the ground it is always well to have the top of the tub 9 inches above the ground line. It is also well to sink one end (where the sheep are thrown in) slightly lower than the other end, as this will make it easier to empty and clean the vat.

Crutches, or Forks.—In using large vats, crutches, or dipping forks, are necessary, and even with small vats they are useful.

Crutches should be 5 or 6 feet long. The handle should be strong (rake handles are a little too light). One end is provided with an iron ferrule, into which the bent iron is inserted. The iron should be one-half inch round or three-quarters inch half round.

Gauges.—The capacity of tubs should be plainly marked on the side every 3 or 6 inches, in order to correctly measure the amount of liquid.

Small Portable Vats for Small Flocks.—If no regular dipping vat is at hand, a good-sized tub may be used. Dipping in this manner is slow and tedious, but may be resorted to in case of necessity, as, for instance, when a few sheep are bought from another flock which is not known to be absolutely free from scab. If care is taken to dip thoroughly the dipping may be done as effectually in such a tub as it could be done in a large vat. Recourse to ordinary tubs is not advised, however, when it is possible to use regular dipping vats. Lambs may, in case of necessity, be dipped in troughs.

A small portable vat is suitable for use in dipping small flocks. When not in use this vat may be conveniently stored away. An advantage connected with this vat is that it may be drawn from place to place as desired. The dimensions here given may be varied, according to individual taste, by making the vat longer, broader, or deeper. A convenient size will be 9 feet long by 2½ feet broad at the top, 9 inches broad at the bottom, and 3½ to 5 feet deep; the floor measures 9 inches broad by 4 feet long; from 1 foot above one end of the floor a slant with cross cleats rises to the top and end of the vat. The sheep are dropped in by hand, one at a time, at the deep end, and after being held in the dip for two minutes are allowed to leave the vat at the slanting end. They are held a moment on the slant to allow them to drain off, thus economizing in dip. A gate may be placed at the deeper part of the slant if desired, in order to save labor. This gate should swing toward the exit of the vat. Such a tank may be made of 1½ inch pine boards, with tongue and groove, and should be well pitched or painted.

This plan of vat may be easily modified, if desired, so as to have a small dripping platform attached. In this modified plan an inclined platform is added to the vat and a removable skeleton box is made to fit over it. While one sheep is being dipped another sheep is allowed to ascend the incline into the small dripping pen. When the sheep is sufficiently drained the gate is opened, it leaves the pen, the gate is closed, the sheep in the vat enters the pen, and another sheep is placed in the vat.

DIPPING PLANTS WHICH CAN BE UTILIZED FOR LARGE FLOCKS.

Where large numbers of sheep are to be dipped, receiving pens close to the dipping vat are necessary, and of course the number and size of the pens vary with the number of sheep to be handled. The yards may be either square or oblong, or they may be circular. The square or oblong yards are simple in construction, and need no other description than that furnished by the illustrations.

Dipping Vats.—The dipping vat may be made on several different plans—the single oblong straight vat, the double or triple, with turns at the ends, the square or oblong. For the single oblong dipping we will give details of construction. In the use of this vat, suitable for holding three sheep at once, time will be saved in dipping if a long vat is used, so that the animals may swim directly through without stopping, and then leave the tank. The tank should be made about 2½ feet broad at the top, 9 inches broad at the bottom, and 4 to 5 feet deep. The length may be 20 to 120 feet, as desired. One end (the entrance) should be straight, or with a steep slant, while the last 5 to 14 feet at the other end (exit) should have a gradual slant with cross cleats. Vats are in use varying from 10 to 120 feet long. Naturally, the longer the vat the more building material and ooze will be required.

The Dripping Pens.—There should be two drippings pens, side by side with a swinging gate at the entrance; one pen is filled and the gate is then closed, opening the other pen; when the second pen is filled the first pen is emptied by allowing the sheep to pass out into a large lot; or the pens may be in direct line with the vat.

These pens should have a slight incline toward the tub, so that the dripping ooze will run back to the tub. A good plan is to build the incline from the sides toward the center fence; under the fence build a partially covered gutter inclining to the tub; the cover of the gutter should be removable to allow cleaning; at the end of the gutter nearest the tub place a grating to catch the wool and droppings, thus preventing these materials from being washed into the dip.

The Incline to the Dripping Pens.—At the end of the vat an incline, with cross cleats, is built so that the sheep may leave the dip of their own accord and enter the draining pens. A board fence, 2 feet high above the top of the vat, should run a few feet each side of this incline, to prevent the sheep from escaping. The rise for fat, heavy wool sheep must not be too steep, otherwise the exertion will be too great. Some inclines are 5 feet 9 inches in a surface distance of 14 feet 3 inches.

Much labor will be saved if a hinged or, still better, a sliding gate is placed at the deepest portion of the incline. The sheep may thus be held in the dip as long as desired; when the time is up the gate is opened and the sheep enter the draining pens.

Shelter and Arrangements for Cleaning the Dipping Plant.— The vat, boilers, and dripping pens should be under cover, and it will be well to extend the cover over the drive and the forcing pens.

Cleaning the plant may be facilitated if the following suggestions are observed: It is well to have one end of the vat slightly lower than the other end, so that the ooze will run toward that point when the tub is being emptied. If the entire floor of the collecting pens is made of brick, cement, or boards, and inclines slightly toward one or two points, the yards may be more easily cleaned by means of a hose and stream of water. If this plan is adopted there should be an upright baseboard or a solid wall of concrete or brick a few inches in height running around the edge of the entire pen. If there is direct sewer connection for the vat a trap or manhole should be made to catch the droppings and the tags of wool, otherwise the sewer pipe will become obstructed.

Boiling, Infusing, and Settling Tanks.—The arrangement of the boiling tanks depends upon two factors in particular: First, upon the kind of dip used; second, upon the arrangement adopted for keeping the bath at the proper temperature.

In case a steam pipe is placed near the floor of the dipping vat in order to keep the ooze at its proper temperature while dipping, the vat itself may be used for heating water. Clear water is run into the vat and the steam turned on full force until the proper temperature is obtained. If a carbolic or a prepared tobacco dip is used, the material may then be mixed in the vat if desired. Even in this case, however, it is best to provide a separate boiling tank for heating and preparing fresh ooze to replace the dip as it is used up.

These boiling tubs may be made of wood or iron, according to the facilities at hand. If steam is to be had, the square or round wooden boiling tub may be used, and an open steam pipe run into it to heat the water. If the steam pipe can not be used, either in the vat or in the boiling tanks, iron tanks should be provided. The iron tanks are set in brick or stone frames, with a fireplace below. It is best to have two tanks, each with a capacity of about 400 gallons.

If a homemade tobacco dip is prepared from the leaves there should also be provided two iron infusing caldrons, each with a cover and with a capacity of 80 to 120 gallons. The infusion is prepared in these smaller tanks, while the bulk of the water is heated in the boiling tanks or in the swim itself.

If a lime-and-sulphur dip is used, it is absolutely necessary to provide some means for settling the mixture, in order that the bath may be free from sediment. This may be done in two ways. The better way is to have separate settling tubs provided with bungholes or pipes 3 or 4 inches from the bottom. After the mixture is thoroughly boiled it is pumped into the settling tubs and allowed to remain there until it is perfectly free from sediment; the clear liquid is then run into the dipping vat and diluted with warm water to the proper strength. Or the boiling tanks may also be used as settling vats. A pipe with elbow joint is run into the boiling tank 3 or 4 inches above the bottom; the opening of the pipe should point sidewise, not up. After boiling the proper length of time the fire is removed and the liquid allowed to stand until clear; only the clear ooze is drawn off, the sediment remaining on the floor of the boiling tank.

Measures and Pumps.—The capacity of the vat should be marked at different depths. The capacity of the boilers should also be marked in the same way. If these are marked for every 100, 200, 300, or 500 gallons (according to the amount of dipping to be done), separate measuring tanks will be unnecessary. In case the tanks are not marked a separate measuring tank should be provided.

If a homemade tobacco dip or a lime-and-sulphur dip is used, a set of scales is necessary. To guess at weights in mixing lime and sulphur may result in too strong a dip.   A portable pump will be found of great use in filling and emptying tanks.

FEDERAL LAWS AND REGULATIONS RELATIVE TO SHEEP SCAB.

As the scab of the sheep is unquestionably a contagious disease, it is unlawful to ship sheep so affected from any State, Territory, or the District of Columbia into any other State, Territory, or the District of Columbia.   The penalties for such shipment of diseased sheep are heavy, as will be seen from an examination of sections 6 and 7 of the act approved May 29, 1884, which are as follows:

Section 6.   That no railroad company within the United States or the owners or masters of any steam or sailing or other vessel or boat, shall receive for transportation or transport, from one State or Territory to another, or from any State into the District of Columbia, or from the District into any State, any live stock affected with any contagious, infectious, or communicable disease, and especially the disease known as pleuro-pneumonia; nor shall any person, company, or corporation deliver for such transportation to any railroad company, or master or owner of any boat or vessel, any live stock, knowing them to be affected with any contagious, infectious, or communicable disease; nor shall any person, company, or corporation drive on foot or transport in private conveyance from one State or Territory to another, or from any State into the District of Columbia, or from the District into any State, any live stock, knowing them to be affected with any contagious, infectious, or communicable disease, and especially the disease known as pleuro-pneumonia: *Provided,* That the so-called splenetic or Texas fever shall not be considered a contagious, infectious, or communicable disease within the meaning of sections four, five, six, and seven of this act, as to cattle being transported by rail to market for slaughter, when the same are unloaded only to be fed and watered in lots on the way thereto.

Section 7.   That it shall be the duty of the Commissioner of Agriculture to notify, in writing, the proper officials or agents of any railroad, steamboat, or other transportation company doing business in or through any infected locality, and by publication in such newspapers as he may select, of the existence of said contagion; and any person or persons operating any such railroad, or master or owner of any boat or vessel, or owner or custodian of or person having control over such cattle or other live stock within such infected district, who shall knowingly violate the provisions of section six of this act, shall be guilty of a misdemeanor, and, upon conviction, shall be punished by a fine of not less than one hundred dollars nor more than five thousand dollars, or by imprisonment for not more than one year, or by both such fine and imprisonment.

The provisions of this statute are very specific and clear, and there can be no possible doubt of their application to the disease under consideration.   Congress has, nevertheless, gone still further by way of emphasizing this application, and has particularly directed the attention of the Department of Agriculture to a few important diseases, including sheep scab, by the following clause, which has been repeated in the Appropriation Act for a number of years: * * * and the Secretary of Agriculture is hereby authorized to use any part of this sum he may deem necessary or expedient, and in such manner as he may think best, in the collection of information concerning live stock, dairy, and other animal products, and to prevent the spread of pleuro-pneumonia, tuberculosis, sheep scab, and other diseases of animals, and for this purpose to employ as many persons as he may deem necessary.

Act of February 2, 1903.

Acting in accordance with this legislation, the following orders have been made and promulgated by the Secretary of Agriculture, and are now (1911) in force:

REGULATIONS TO PREVENT THE SPREAD OF SHEEP SCABIES.

Regulation 29.—No sheep which are diseased with scabies shall be shipped, trailed, otherwise removed, or allowed to drift from one State, Territory, or the District of Columbia, into another State, Territory or the District of Columbia, except as hereinafter provided; and no sheep shall be shipped trailed, otherwise removed, or allowed to drift from a State or Territory or portion thereof quarantined for the disease of scabies in sheep into another State, Territory, or the District of Columbia, except as hereinafter provided, until the sheep shall have been inspected by an inspector of the Bureau of Animal Industry, found to be free from the disease and from exposure thereto, and are accompanied by a certificate from the said inspector. All of the sheep in a certain flock or shipment in which the disease is present shall be classed as diseased sheep, and none of them shall be removed or offered for interstate shipment until dipped as hereinafter provided. The practice of picking a flock— *i. e.,* removing sheep which are visibly diseased and then offering any portion of the remaining sheep for either inspection or interstate shipment, or both—is directly and positively prohibited.

Regulation 30.—Healthy sheep in an area not quarantined for the disease of scabies in sheep which have not been exposed to the disease may be shipped or trailed interstate without restriction by the regulations of the Secretary of Agriculture to prevent the spread of scabies in sheep; but if said sheep be unloaded en route or at destination and are placed in infectious premises they shall thereafter be treated as exposed sheep and shall not be forwarded to destination for purposes other than immediate slaughter until they shall have been dipped under the supervision of an inspector of the Bureau of Animal Industry.

Regulation 31.—Sheep that are diseased with scabies and that have been dipped once in one of the approved dips, under the supervision of an inspector of the Bureau of Animal Industry within ten days of date of shipment, may be shipped interstate for immediate slaughter to a recognized slaughtering center, and when so shipped the said sheep shall not be diverted en route and shall be slaughtered within two weeks after arrival at destination. If diseased sheep are to be shipped interstate for stocking or feeding purposes they shall be dipped twice as above indicated, ten days apart, and shall be submitted to inspection before shipment.

Sheep that are not diseased with scabies, but which have been exposed to the contagion of the disease, may be moved interstate for feeding or stocking purposes after one dipping, or they may be shipped interstate by rail or boat to a recognized slaughtering center for immediate slaughter without dipping.

Regulation 32.—When diseased sheep have been dipped once and are shipped interstate for slaughter in accordance with Regulation 31, or when exposed sheep are shipped interstate without dipping for immediate slaughter in accordance with Regulation 31, the proper officers of the transportation company shall affix to both sides of each car a durable placard not less than 5½ by 8 inches in size, on which shall be printed with permanent black ink in bold-face letters not less than 1½ inches in height the words dipped scabby sheep, or exposed sheep for slaughter, as the case may be. These placards shall also show the name of the place from which the shipment was made, the date of the shipment (which must correspond with the date of the waybills and other papers), the name of the transportation company, and the name of the place of destination. Each of the waybills, conductors' manifests, memoranda, and bills of lading pertaining to such shipments by cars or boats shall have the words dipped scabby sheep or exposed sheep for slaughter, as the case may be, written or stamped upon its face. Whenever such shipments are transferred to another transportation company or into other cars or into other boats, or are rebilled or reconsigned to a point other than the original destination the cars into which said sheep are transferred and the new waybills, conductors' manifests, memoranda, and bills of lading covering such shipments by cars or boats shall be marked as herein specified for cars first carrying said sheep and for the billing, etc., covering the same. If for any reason the placards required by this regulation are removed from the car or are destroyed or rendered illegible, they shall be immediately replaced by the transportation company or its agents, the intention being that legible placards shall be maintained on the cars from the time of shipment until they arrive at destination and the disposition of the cars is indicated by an inspector of the Bureau of Animal Industry.

Regulation 33.—The dips now approved are:

(a) The tobacco dip, prepared from tobacco or from suitable tobacco products containing nicotine so as to produce a dipping bath which shall contain not less than seven one-hundredths of 1 per cent of nicotine.

(b) The lime-and-sulphur dip, made by mixing 8 pounds of unslacked lime and 24 pounds of flowers of sulphur and boiling with 30 gallons of water for not less than two hours. All sediment should be allowed to subside before the liquid is placed in the dipping vat. This liquid should be diluted sufficiently to make 100 gallons before use.

And, pending further investigation, the following-described dips;

(c) The cresol dip which consists of a mixture of cresylic acid* set with soap. When diluted ready for use this dip should contain one-half of 1 per cent of cresylic acid.

(d) The coal-tar creosote dip, which is made by mixing coal-tar creosote or coal-tar oils and cresylic acid separately with resin soap in varying proportions. This dip should contain when diluted ready for use not less than 1 per cent by weight of coal-tar oils and cresylic acid. In no case should the diluted dip contain more than four-tenths of 1 per cent nor less than one-tenth of 1 per cent of cresylic acid; but when the proportion of cresylic acid falls below two-tenths of 1 per cent the coal-tar oils should be increased sufficiently to bring the total of the tar oils and the cresylic acid in the diluted dip up to 1.2 per cent by weight.

The cresol dip and the coal-tar creosote dip should always be tested on a small scale with the water and under the conditons to be employed in dipping in order to avoid possible injury to stock. The diluted sample should be allowed to stand for at least an hour. If after this length of time there is a separation of an oily layer, the dip should not be used with that kind of water. Especial care in this connection is necessary where hard water is to be used.

In the undiluted coal-tar creosote dips there may be, in cold weather especially, a separation of naphthalene and other constituents of the dip. Care should therefore be taken to see that the concentrated dip is homogeneous in character before using any portion of it.

Manufacturers who desire the department to approve their dips for official dipping should submit a sample of their product to the Bureau of Animal Industry in Washington and accompany this with the formula used in preparing the dip.

Before a proprietary substance is approved for use in official dipping the manufacturer must agree as follows:

(1) To recommend for sheep scab a dilution of the product, so as to conform to the requirements of the Department of Agriculture.

(2) To maintain said product at a uniform composition.

(3) To place on packages of dips which have been examined and found to conform to the requirements of the department the following statement:

A sample of this product has been submitted to the United States Department of Agriculture for examination. We guarantee the contents of this package to be of the same composition as the sample submitted to the department, and that when diluted according to the directions printed thereon for the treatment of sheep scab it will give a dipping fluid of the composition required of a————†

---

*By the term cresylic acid as used in these regulations is meant cresols and other phenols derived from coal tar, none of which boils below 185° C, nor above 250° C.

†There should be inserted here the name of the class of dips to which the product belongs, such as cresol or lime and sulphur, etc,

dip by the regulations of the Secretary of Agriculture governing sheep scab.

(4)   To have on containers or advertising matter no reference to the United States Government or any of its departments except as provided in the preceding paragraphs, unless such reference has been submitted to and approved by the Department of Agriculture, and to have on containers or advertising matter no false or misleading statement.

Regulation 34.—The dipping shall be done carefully and the sheep handled as humanely as possible.   The Department disclaims responsibility for any loss or damage resulting from the dipping, and those who wish to avoid any risks that may be incident to dipping at the stock yards, as well as to avoid liability to prosecution, should see that their sheep are free from disease before shipping them to market.

Regulation 35.—Sheep shipped interstate under a certificate from an inspector of the Bureau of Animal Industry are not guaranteed uninterrupted transit; for in the event of the discovery of scabies or of exposure thereto en route the sheep shall thereafter be handled as diseased or exposed sheep, as hereinbefore provided, and the cars or other vehicles and the chutes, alleys, and pens which have been occupied by them shall be cleaned and disinfected, as hereinafter provided.

Regulation 36.—Public stock yards shall be considered infectious and the sheep yarded therein as having been exposed to the disease, and no sheep shall be shipped interstate therefrom, except for immediate slaughter, without dipping.   Where, however, a part or all of the stock yards is reserved and set apart for the reception of uninfected shipments of sheep and is kept free of disease, sheep may be shipped interstate from the uninfectious yards or portions thereof without dipping.   If diseased sheep are introduced into the uninfectious yards or portions thereof, they shall be immediately removed therefrom and the chutes, alleys, and pens occupied by the said sheep shall be thoroughly cleaned and disinfected.   No sheep shall be shipped interstate for feeding or stocking purposes from any stock yards where an inspector of the Bureau of Animal Industry is stationed without a certificate of inspection or of dipping issued by the said inspector.

Regulation 37.—Cars and other vehicles, yards, pens, sheds, chutes, etc., that have contained diseased sheep shall be cleaned and disinfected in the following manner.   Remove all litter and manure and then saturate the interior surfaces of the cars and the woodwork, flooring, and ground of the sheds, alleyways, and pens with a solution containing 5 per cent of pure carbolic acid or with a solution containing 2 per cent of cresol.   When cresol is used it must be mixed with soft soap in order to render it easily soluble in cold water.   Cars and premises are not required to be cleaned and disinfected on account of their having contained "dipped scabby sheep" that have been dipped within ten days or sheep that have been exposed to scabies. In determining exposure, all sheep in a flock or shipment in which disease is present shall be classed as diseased.

Instructions have also been issued to inspectors to rigidly enforce the meat-inspection law and regulations relating to scab in sheep. Sheep in an advanced stage of scab are feverish and unfit for food, and their carcasses will be condemned. Shippers who forward animals for slaughter in this condition will be likely to lose heavily upon them, as they will be subject to quarantine and condemnation. This is an additional and important reason for curing affected animals before they leave the feeding place.

The laws and regulations which have been adopted for the control of sheep scab are necessary to prevent the spread of the disease and the losses which result from it. If disregarded they may prove inconvenient and expensive to shippers whose flocks are affected.

SIMPLE METHOD OF TREATING THE ARSENICAL DIPPING SOLUTION.

Previous suggestions as to precautions in the use of arsenic in connection with the dipping of cattle in the standard arsenical solution, more particularly with regard to the safe disposition of the solution remaining in a vat when it is desired to empty the latter for cleaning, have appealed to the writer as scarcely sufficient to insure the greatest safety, especially with reference to the possibility of contamination of the water-supply, both human and animal, on the farm.

For instance, Farmers' Bulletin 378, of the United States Department of Agriculture, commends the following precautions in this connection: "In addition to properly protecting vats containing arsenical dip when not in use, another precaution must be observed when vats are to be emptied for cleaning. The dip should not be poured or allowed to flow on land and vegetation to which cattle or other animals have access. The best plan is to run the dip in a pit properly protected by fences. The dip should not be deposited where it may be carried by seepage into wells or springs which supply water used on the farm."

No bad results have, so far, been called to our attention, and where the disposition of this poisonous solution is directed by intelligent persons who are alive to the risk and who will follow closely the precautions given above, there need be little danger. Still, on account of the present extensive use of the arsenical dip, and the prospect of a still wider adoption of it throughout the South, and also the possibility of the disposal of the solution being delegated to some person, or persons, not sufficiently aware of the risk of water contamination, through ignorance, or otherwise, it occurred to the writer that if some simple, inexpensive, and effective method could be employed to render the arsenic in solution, in the vat, inert, or harmless, it would add considerably to the safety of the solution which had to be disposed of when the cleaning of the vat was undertaken.

Forty gallons of the arsenical dipping solution were taken from the Experiment Station vat and placed in a 50-gallon receptacle. To the 40 gallons of solution were added 3 lbs. of air-slacked lime. The mixture was thoroughly stirred and allowed to stand for

DELAINE MERINO RAM. ANNUAL REPORT, NOVA SCOTIA. 1907.

HOOF OF SHEEP SHOWING EFFECTS OF CHRONIC FOOT-ROT. B. A. I. 1904.

about one hour, after which 3 lbs. of copperas, in warm solution, were added. The clear solution remaining on top in the receptacle was tested about 15 hours later, and with no trace of arsenic whatever.

In order to make the calculation as simple as possible, it may be figured out for each hundred gallons of the arsenical solution left in the dipping vat at the time it is to be cleaned. For this quantity of solution, 6 lbs. each, of air-slacked lime and commercial copperas should be ample, as it was calculated to an excess. Or, in other words, for each 100 gallons of the arsenical solution left in the vat, 6 lbs., each, of air-slacked lime and common commercial copperas should be used.

In building concrete dipping-vats, it would be well to have marks on the inside indicating each one or two hundred gallons, so that a more or less accurate estimate could be made of the remaining solution at any time. Or, when a vat is being filled, the water could be measured as it is put in, and a measuring-stick marked, after each 100 or 200 gallons had been added, which could afterward be used for a similar purpose. Or, the quantity of solution could be ascertained by the use of the following rule:

Measure, in inches, the length at the top of the solution, and also at the bottom of the vat. Add these two numbers together and divide by 2 to get the average length. In the same way measure, in inches, the top width of the solution, and the width of the bottom of the vat, and divide by 2 to get the average width. Then measure the depth of the solution in inches. Multiply the average length by the average width, and multiply the result by the depth. Divide the last result by 231, and the answer will be the number in gallons of solution left in the vat.

Presuming that the quantity of solution left in the vat, including the sediment composed of manure and mud, should be 500 gallons. This would take 30 lbs., each, of air-slacked lime and copperas. After adding the lime, the mixture should be thoroughly agitated, or stirred, and allowed to stand for at least one hour. The copperas should first be dissolved in hot water, and while still hot, should be added, somewhat slowly, to the contents of the vat, and the whole again stirred and then permitted to remain still for ten or twelve hours, or over night. At the expiration of this time, the clear solution on top may be syphoned or pumped to any convenient place without danger, as it should contain no arsenic whatever; and the precipitate, or sediment, afterward removed and buried in a hole or small pit, if thought necessary, although it, too, should be harmless, or inert, as the arsenic has been changed to a condition that is insoluble in water.

SUMMARY.

Unless carefully disposed of, the arsenical dipping solution taken from the vat previous to cleaning the latter may be a source of danger in contaminating the water supply, or vegetation, although, up to the present, accidents from this cause have not been brought to the attention of the writer.

This danger may be minimized, or entirely prevented, by the addition of commercial copperas, after the solution has been rendered excessively alkaline through the addition of air-slacked lime.

The clear solution left on top, after the addition of the copperas solution, should contain no arsenic, and may, with safety, be pumped, or syphoned, to any convenient place; and the sediment remaining buried in a small hole dug for the purpose. Air-slacked lime and copperas are quite inexpensive materials, and easily obtainable by anyone. The amounts suggested of the materials are sufficiently in excess to be effective in any strength of arsenical solution now in use.

This method is simple, effective, and inexpensive, and if adopted, may be the means of preventing casualties from the careless disposal of the poisonous arsenical solution, especially when undertaken, at the time of emptying the dipping-vat for cleaning at the end of the season, or at other times, by those who may not be conversant with its poisonous nature.

INTERNAL PARASITES.

THE BLADDER WORMS (TAENIA MARGINATA; BATSCH).

On dressing sheep and lambs it happens sometimes that the folds of the omentum or caul will contain a number of semi-transparent bladder-like bodies from a half to one inch in diameter. A similar condition may be found on the brain due to another variety of the parasite. These bladders contain a worm known as the bladder worm and are one stage in the development of the tape worm.

The Tænia marginata, Batsch, is the variety affecting the abdominal cavity. In from one to two weeks after sheep ingest the eggs of this parasite, the young will have developed and migrated from the intestinal canal and a favorite place for them is on the surface of the liver. They may migrate from any part of the intestinal tract and therefore may be found at any place along its course. The bladders are composed of a delicate, whitish membrane and when viewed toward the light, one point will appear to be denser than the rest. As these bladders grow this spot becomes thicker and denser. This is the head and the part by which it is attached to the cyst wall. This head is fully developed with hooks and suckers, and when freed becomes the starting point for the development of the mature state in some other animal. The parasite requires about two weeks from the time of the ingestion of the eggs to develop and migrate through the intestinal wall. It requires about eight weeks more to develop into mature cysts, but when matured as cysts they may remain in this condition for a long period of time. This is as far as the parasite ever develops in the sheep. To complete its life cycle the sheep, when it is killed or dies, must be eaten by a dog, wolf or other carnivorous animal, the cyst is ruptured and the head attaches itself to the intestinal wall and begins to develop into the form known as the tapeworm. The tapeworm becomes fully developed in from ten to twelve weeks, and the young worms in the form of eggs, and the segments are discharged with the faeces. These embryos fall upon pasture and are taken up by grazing sheep to run another life cycle.   .

The bladder worms are likely to cause peritonitis when migrating in large numbers from the intestine or liver. The bladder worms that come to the surface of the liver either result in destroying their host or die after a couple of weeks, the location not being favorable for development. Those finding their way into the folds of the omentum seem to cause little inconvenience. The sheep may become infected at any time of the year, preferably during the grazing season, and also from eating hay containing the excreta of dogs. The young sheep are susceptible, but those past five or six years possess a resistance that protects them even against intentional feeding. The diagnosis of the trouble in sheep is difficult to make except by post-mortem. There have been severe losses attributable to this disease, but it is of less importance in this State than in many others.

The treatment may be wholly preventive. When once the cysts have been formed there is no remedy that can reach them. In the dog the tapeworm may be expelled by suitable remedies. The sheep husbandman must therefore treat the dog, keep off all dogs, and burn or bury carcasses of affected sheep so that dogs will not have access to them. Areca nut powdered, two grains for each pound of body weight, or ethereal extract of male shield-fern are suitable remedies for causing their expulsion from the dog.

GID OR TURNSICKNESS.

For over a century claims have been published to the effect that the sheep disease known as gid existed in the United States. Abundance evidence indicates that it certainly has had a foothold in this country for over twenty years. In Montana the range has been infected for at least twenty years, and during that period the infected area has increased until a territory 400 miles long and in places 200 miles wide is infected range.—(Bu. An. Ind. Cir. 165, 1910).

Gid is a disease due to the presence in the brain, or, rarely, in the spinal cord of the sheep of a larval tapeworm parasite having the general appearance of a fish bladder full of water. This parasite is commonly known by the scientific name *Cœnurus cerebralis,* but the correct name is *Multiceps multiceps.* It is translucent and at times larger than a hen's egg. On this bladder are a number of white objects about the size of a grain of wheat and projecting, usually, into the fluid with which the bag is filled. These objects are tapeworm heads. On feeding this bladderworm, as the gid parasite is called, to a dog, the bladder digests, but the tapeworm heads pass on to the intestine, where they add segment after segment back of the head, till in the course of a month or two each head has become the head of one of the familiar segmented tapeworms, the worms in this case becoming 2 or 3 feet long. Having attained this size, the posterior segments, which contain hundreds of very small tapeworm eggs, begin to break off and are passed out onto the range or pasture with the feces.   Under favorable conditions these eggs are washed onto the grass or into standing or running water, and sheep eating grass or drinking water so infected thereby take the eggs into the stomach.   Here the shell digests off and a very small embryo, armed with six hooks, bores its way through the walls of the digestive tract by means of these hooks, gets into the blood vessels, and is swept around till it lodges.   In any location except the brain or spinal cord the parasite may grow to the size of a pea, but at that point or sooner it degenerates and dies.   Those that get to the brain or spinal cord develop into the bladderworm described above.

At the time when the embryos get to the brain and begin to travel on its surface or through its substance there are usually slight symptoms of fever and restlessness, which are easily overlooked. Should the infection be severe enough to kill the sheep at this stage, an examination of the brain will disclose a number of curving channels on its surface.   But as a rule these symptoms abate and there is no further indication of the presence of the parasite until it has grown to the point where the heads form on the bladder and set up the symptoms characteristic of the last stages of gid by projecting out of the bladder and into the brain.   This is accomplished by virtue of the fact that the head is seated at the bottom of a little tubular neck with an opening to the exterior.   Ordinarily this neck projects into the bladder fluid; but the head and neck can be projected through the opening mentioned, the neck turning inside out, just as a glove finger might be turned inside out.   When the head is pushed out it brings the crown of hooks with which it is armed into contact with the brain, and it is to the irritating action of these hooks on the brain that such symptoms as walking in a circle are ascribed.   It seems probable that only such symptoms as circling or running or jumping without apparent cause, which are of an intermittent and occasional sort, should be referred to the action of the tapeworm heads.   Such symptoms as are constant in the last stages of the disease, including blindness, constant carriage of the head to one side, loss of appetite, and the like, should probably be referred to atrophy of the brain due to the pressure of the parasite, and to other nervous disturbances resulting from this pressure.

The final symptoms of gid do not show until seven or eight months after the sheep has become infected, the sheep usually dying about nine months after the time of infection.   This point is important, because the Montana sheepmen, being unacquainted with the true nature of the disease, have been inclined to attribute gid to the nature of the country in which the sheep were feeding at the time of the outbreak, and it is difficult to convince them that the infection was more or less remote from the range where the outbreak occurs.

LIFE HISTORY IN RELATION TO MONTANA CONDITIONS.

The actual history of the disease in most cases in Montana seems to be about as follows: The developed larval parasite, capable of infecting the dog, is found in sheep mostly while on the winter range from December to the end of March, exceptional cases occurring outside of this period. The adult worms develop in dogs, and probably in coyotes and other wolves also, from eating the heads of sheep dying of gid during the months mentioned. These worms require a month or two to develop to the point where the tapeworm eggs are passed with the feces, and eggs from dogs infected at this time are probably being spread over the pasture and range any time after the 1st of February. Up to the time of the spring rains it is unlikely that many sheep become infected. It is likely that up to the time of the rains the eggs generally lie alive and untouched or else perish. It is only as the feces are promptly broken up by water and the eggs released that sheep are liable to become infected. From the time the spring rains set in—usually during May, it is said—the sheep, now on summer range, take up the infection. The beating rain breaks up the dog feces, washes the tapeworm eggs into puddles and reservoirs from which the sheep drink, and splashes them on the grass which the sheep eat. Allowing the usual nine months' period of development, sheep infected in May will die in December. The deaths from January to March, inclusive, indicate that the storms of June, July, and August play a part in the infection of sheep. From this time dry weather apparently saves the sheep from further infection on the summer range, and on removal to winter range cold weather probably serves to keep the feces frozen, and thereby prevents them from breaking up and washing about. The death at this time of sheep infected the previous spring and summer gives opportunity for renewed infection of dogs and probably of other carnivora. Thus the life cycle takes about a year for its completion, and is closely related to weather conditions.

It appears from a study of field conditions that gid is most prevalent in the winters following a spring when the rainfall is abundant, an opinion expressed by many European writers, and in places where the range is most thoroughly carpeted with forage. In parts of the plains country of southeastern Montana where the forage is largely bunch grass, the range has not yet become infected, in spite of giddy sheep brought in from the infected region. The infection seems to persist better in upland valleys. In some of these infected localities the ground is covered with a moss in the spring, and it is said that the sheep are very fond of this. It seems evident that the washing about of feces deposited on such a moss carpet or on a range where the grass grows in a continuous mat would be more certain to leave tapeworm eggs where sheep would get them than feces deposited on the bare ground in a country where they could wash along on the ground between scattered bunches of grass. The necessity of watering sheep on summer ranges at shallow watering places and in reservoirs and ponds in coulees where contamination by dogs is inevitable must also play some part in the infection of sheep.

SYMPTOMS OF GID.

COMPARISON WITH SYMPTOMS OF LOCO POISONING.

In a general way the symptoms of gid in sheep are such that the sheepmen may be pardoned for confusing gid with loco disease, due to eating white loco weed. Close observation, however, will readily distinguish one from the other. Locoed sheep show symptoms of poisoning, while giddy sheep show evidences of brain trouble or more rarely of trouble in the spinal cord. Locoed sheep are nervous, uncertain in their movements, and out of condition, but they never show the regular automatic repetition of some unusual movement that giddy sheep show. Giddy sheep very commonly turn in a circle, a very characteristic symptom. The circle may be relatively large or very small, or the sheep may even pivot in one place. A giddy sheep will sometimes graze for awhile, then raise its head as if it had just thought of something and start off for it, swinging around in a circle and perhaps stopping and beginning to feed in the place from which it started. Later, the sheep will circle for hours without stopping. Less often the sheep will throw the head back and bolt in a straight line as if frightened, or perhaps put the head between the front legs and go stumbling forward. The head is often held to one side and may be raised or lowered.

On the range the first symptom that the herder notices is that giddy sheep become hard to herd. They lag behind the flock, and when the dog is sent to bring them up, instead of running into the flock as normal sheep would, they run away from it. When the rest of the flock is standing quiet, giddy sheep can be seen worming restlessly about in it; and while the others are feeding, giddy sheep will be executing some meaningless maneuver, such as circling or running without any apparent cause.

Locoed sheep when put on alfalfa will nearly always recover; giddy sheep will show no abatement of symptoms and will invariably die unless operated on. When a sheepman has any doubt as to whether his sheep have gid or some disease which merely resembles gid, it will pay to kill a sheep and examine the brain. The developed gid parasite is large and easily recognizable as a bag full of fluid, and its presence is proof that the sheep had gid. It is of course perfectly possible for a sheep to have loco disease and gid simultaneously, though no cases of this sort are known, so far as available records show.

COMPARISON WITH SYMPTOMS OF GRUB IN THE HEAD.

Sheep which are infected with so-called grub in the head (the larva of *Œstrus ovis*, the sheep gadfly) may sometimes be suspected of having gid. However, such sheep are characterized by a catarrh or "snotty nose," due to the irritation caused by the parasite in the nose and frontal sinuses. They do not show the automatic movements of giddy sheep. Grub in the head is rarely fatal, though sheep may die from a massive infection or from the larva or grub penetrating to the brain, a thing which it is claimed may happen in rare cases. The disease may be definitely diagnosed by a post-mortem examination of the back part of the nose and frontal sinuses, where grubs will be found if the disease is grub in the head. This disease is especially common in Sweet Grass County. Gid and grub in the head sometimes occur in the same sheep, at the same time, and a sheep which circles may be suspected of having gid even though the presence of the *Œstrus* larvæ is also indicated.

THE ERADICATION OF GID.

Knowing the life history of the gid parasite, the eradication of the disease becomes a very simple matter. It is only necessary to step in at some point where the parasite is most easily attacked and prevent its further development. This is accomplished in two ways: first, by destroying the heads, or at least the brains, of sheep dying of gid; and second, by keeping sheep dogs or other ranch dogs free of tapeworms. Of these two steps the first is much the more important, for the reason that it is much more practical and effective than the second and also is much easier.

NECESSITY FOR DESTROYING HEADS AND BRAINS.

Claims have been made to the effect that the destruction of the heads of giddy sheep is unnecessary, on the ground that dogs do not eat sheep heads. In a former publication* the writer has shown the unlikelihood of scientists being mistaken as regards the life history of the gid parasite, and has shown by experiments that a dog not only would eat a sheep head, but having once eaten one, would subsequently go for the brains first of all when given a sheep head. It was shown that a dog would at times eat a skull so completely as to leave almost nothing, and at times lick the brains out through the foramen magnum and leave the skull apparently intact; in neither case would there be anything to suggest to the casual observer that a dog had eaten the brains.

The shepherd dog used in the experiment described in the article referred to, was fed an unskinned sheep head after an interval of over nine months since the first experiment. The first day some of the outer parts only were eaten in seven hours. After an interval of a day the head was fed again, and this time it was picked down to the bones, but the brain case was not entered. The remainder of the head was left overnight and the next morning examination showed that the dog, following the method used on the former occasion, had licked out the brain through the foramen magnum, the opening where the spinal cord enters the brain. This opening had been enlarged little, if any, by the dog's teeth. A sheep head fed about a week later was treated the same way. The meat was eaten off the skull the first day and the brain licked out the evening of the second day.

It may safely be asserted that an adult coyote would have as little difficulty in getting at the brains as a dog would. A sheep brain covered with a lime-and-sulphur dip and one covered with a coal-tar dip were fed to the coyotes. Small parts of the brain covered with the lime and sulphur were eaten at once, in seven hours half of it was eaten, and in twenty-four hours it had all been eaten. The brain covered with coal-tar dip had been only partly eaten in the same time. After being fed one regular meal the coyotes were given one sheep brain covered with 40 per cent formaldehyde and one covered with turpentine. Eighteen hours later the coyotes had eaten

---

*Bureau of Animal Industry Circular 159.

both brains and had vomited them, owing to the formaldehyde and turpentine. A brain covered with 50 cubic centimeters of coal oil was eaten within half an hour and one which had been burned with the same amount of oil and some wool was eaten at once.

The evidence that dogs eat sheep brains, even where these are protected by the skull, is not entirely experimental. During the investigation in Montana, the writer asked a large number of sheepmen whether their dogs would eat sheep heads and the answer was never in the negative. Some did not know. Many claimed to have seen dogs eat sheep heads. One sheepman said he had seen a dog eat a sheep head and only leave a few splinters of bone uneaten. Another stated that he had a dog which preferred sheep brains and would break open skulls to get them. Another stated that coyotes are fond of the brains of young sheep, and one man had seen what he took to be fragments of sheep skulls around coyote dens. Such testimony, fitting in, as it does, with the known facts and the experimental indications, must be held to more than offset the negative testimony of those who, in correspondence with the Bureau, claim that they know of no one who has seen dogs eating sheep skulls.

METHODS OF DESTROYING HEADS AND BRAINS.

One method of destroying heads of giddy sheep which the writer has advocated among Montana sheepmen is to burn the sheep head where this is practicable. A plan which is quite as good or perhaps better is to split the head longitudinally with an ax or meat cleaver and get out the brain and burn it. This plan has the advantage that it does not require a quantity of wood, which is a scarce article over a large part of Montana's sheep ranges. The brain can be burned on a forkful of hay or straw and the parasite effectually destroyed. Coal oil in small amounts does not generate enough heat. Burning is practicable where wood or hay is available or where the sheep can be brought up to the home ranch and killed.

These conditions can not be met with in many cases, and the simple procedure advocated in such cases is to have the herder carry, as part of his wagon equipment (since most Montana herders work out from a wagon), an ax or a meat cleaver and a bottle or jug filled with any one of a number of fluids that would serve to kill the gid parasite and to discourage dogs or other carnivora from eating brains which had been covered with such substances. Among other things which a well-fed dog or a hungry and suspicious coyote would usually avoid are 40 per cent formaldehyde, turpentine, or the always available sheep dips of the coal-tar creosote, tobacco, and cresol varieties. Coal oil is too volatile, lacking in penetration, and not sufficiently repellent. The lime-and-sulphur dip might be used, but is not recommended, as it is not as strong or as repellent as the other things. The substances recommended have the advantage of being fatal to tapeworms on contact without being fatal to dogs, a point of interest to the man who must consider the possible danger to his sheep dogs. A dog might eat enough to make himself sick, but could hardly eat enough of such repellent substances to kill him, as vomiting would usually ensue and relieve the stomach. These substances need only be used in small quantities, and hence are easy to carry and inexpensive.

When a sheep becomes hard to herd, circles, or shows other definite signs of gid, it should be marked, a thing easily accomplished by tying a rag or something of the sort to the wool or about the neck, and when the band is brought up to the bedding ground for the night this sheep should be killed and the brain destroyed.

The best way to destroy the brain when it can not be burned is to split the skull longitudinally with an ax or cleaver, scoop out the two halves of the brain, chop them up or crush them, and pour on them turpentine, formaldehyde, or one of the sheep dips mentioned above. This operation takes only a minute or two, and the death of the gid parasite in the brain would follow in a few seconds after the application of the substances mentioned. A cleaver weighing 1½ pounds is heavy enough to split a sheep skull without difficulty. The brains should be completely covered with the turpentine or whatever is used, but even then it only requires a small amount to do the work. Fifty cubic centimeters (less than a tenth of a pint) would be sufficient if carefully applied, and while it would be undesirable to scant the amount, nevertheless a quart bottle would hold an ample supply for one herder for a season under ordinary conditions. Chopping in the top of the skull, and leaving the brains in place after breaking them up and covering with some repellent fluid, is not sufficiently thorough in actual practice. The fluid does not penetrate sufficiently and there is no saving of time. In cases where the heads are to be boiled and fed to the dogs, the boiling should be prolonged and thorough, and the skull should be broken so as to give the hot water free access to the brain.

DISPOSAL OF GIDDY SHEEP.

When a giddy sheep has been killed and the brain disposed of by the method just given, the pelt may be taken and the meat disposed of as desired. The meat is fit for food at the beginning of the last stages of the disease, before neglect of food has starved the animal and brought on a condition of emaciation. At the same time the usual sentiment among sheepmen is that they are too much accustomed to the best mutton to eat sheep that were in any way diseased. The disease occurs mostly in winter, at a time when the sheep are not in condition to market and when none are being marketed. But in case the meat is not to be used for man it can be fed to the herder's dogs, or if the camp tender is around it can be fed to the dogs at the home ranch, or, as one outfit does, to the hogs. Over a large part of Montana when a sheep dies the carcass is allowed to lie where it falls, the pelt being usually, but not always, stripped off. Such a condition aids in spreading a disease like gid. A stream of clear mountain water at the home ranch of one big outfit was defiled by throwing into it the skeletons of sheep after the meat had been fed to the hogs. Big owners with excellent water supplies, amply able to afford concrete watering troughs, preferred to let their sheep drink the water after it had run into a hole in the ground and become converted into a stagnant puddle. Montana sheepmen must come to an appreciation of the fact that clean water it not only wholesome but profitable.

Many sheepmen maintain a hospital band at the home ranch, and the sick, weak, and crippled sheep from all the bands are brought in to this point and given a chance to recuperate. Some outfits kill those sheep which can not keep up, and take the pelt. Others, when a sheep can not keep up, let it drift and take a chance on picking it up again—a very small chance on an open prairie in coyote country.

It is in keeping with the careless practices mentioned above that some sheepmen refuse to bother with a disease like gid, which takes from the flocks from two or three to forty sheep yearly, on the ground that it is too small a matter. Others claim that it is impossible to get sheep herders to do anything more than herd the sheep, which is often true. However, a realization that under some conditions the loss may amount to hundreds of sheep, together with the increasing value of sheep, will probably induce sheepmen to pay more attention to this disease, especially when it is realized that the avoidable neglect of a simple method of prevention endangers not only the flocks of the owner, but also those of his neighbors. As for the herders, it is usually true that the outfits with the hardest working owners and sheep foremen get the best service from their herders.

OPERATION AS A SUBSTITUTE FOR SLAUGHTER.

A number of Montana sheepmen, mostly Scotchmen, who have handled sturdied or giddy sheep in Scotland, prefer to operate for gid instead of killing the sheep and destroying the brain. Of the two operative methods usual elsewhere, the use of the trocar and of the trephine, the trocar method alone is used in Montana so far as the writer learned, although such simple methods as cutting out a piece of bone with a pocketknife and extracting the cyst, or puncturing the cyst with a pocketknife, are more or less common. The writer talked with one man who in addition to these methods had tried boring a hole in the skull with a knife blade and using a rubber syringe to suck out the parasite, and had also tried injecting a half teaspoonful of tincture of iodin and potassium iodid. Some men claim to save 50 per cent of sheep operated on, and claims were made of even higher percentages of success. Others, including one man who claimed to have operated on 50 sheep, had saved none.

It is commonly believed that operating instruments can be obtained only in Scotland or elsewhere in Europe. This is not correct. Trephine outfits can be purchased of any one of a number of makers of surgical instruments in the United States, and can be ordered from almost any druggist. Trocar outfits with cannula and syringe, designed expressly for operating on giddy sheep, can be imported through certain American firms. Such outfits, boxed, will cost up to $9. Nevertheless trocars, cannulas, and syringes can be made to order in this country at a cost of $5 or less. One or two sheep saved will pay for this. When a giddy sheep can not be marketed and will be fed to the dogs in any case, the sheep which die as a result of an operation are no loss, and those which are saved are clear gain.

Only the more favorable cases should be operated on. These are cases where the diagnosis indicates that the parasite is situated on the upper surface of the cerebrum, or large anterior part of the brain, and therefore accessible from an opening in the top of the skull. It is hardly possible always to locate a parasite accurately from the symptoms. The abnormal movements of the sheep are believed to be due to the everted tapeworm heads which irritate such parts of the brain as they come in contact with and thereby set up corresponding reactions. Inasumch as a large cyst will have numerous heads capable of irritating the brain at relatively widely separated points, it will set up correspondingly variable reactions. At the same time certain symptoms will correctly indicate the location of the parasite in the majority of cases. Moreover, if the parasite is located on the upper surface of the brain it not uncommonly causes the formation of a soft spot in the skull just over the cyst, and this can be found by pressing firmly on the skull with the thumb till a place is found where the skull yields a little. As a rule, when such a place is pressed on the sheep will start violently. It may be that this is due to the pressure on the skull being communicated by hydrostatic pressure through the cyst, and thus causing the sudden simultaneous eversion of all or many of the tapeworm heads.

There are some sheep which can not be saved by operation. Some of these have the parasite in an inaccessible location at the base of the brain. Others have several parasites in the brain and their detection and successful removal may be impossible. Still others have the parasite located in the cerebellum, the small posterior part of the brain, or in the spinal cord, and can not be successfully operated on. Finally, the operator will not always be successful and some sheep will die of meningitis or some other complication.

For the purpose of the sheepman who wishes to perform the operation for gid, only those animals that circle should be operated on. In a majority of these cases the parasite will be located in the cerebrum near the surface and on the side toward which the sheep turns. The soft spot in the skull, if present, will usually be found on this side. The sheep will usually have a peculiar stare and will often run into things as if blind.

In any operation avoid the middle line of the skull and operate to one side, as the main blood vessels are located in the middle line. It is advisable to use a local anesthetic, such as cocain, as it not only lessens the suffering of the animal, but also makes the animal easier to handle and operate on as a result of the lessened pain. For the purpose of injecting cocain, a hypodermic syringe, with a capacity of 2 cubic centimeters, can be purchased for a trifling sum.

If a trephine outfit is used the trephine should have about a five-eighths inch cut. Beside the trephine there will be needed a knife or scalpel—an ordinary pocketknife will serve, but is not so easy to sterilize—a pair of fine scissors with the blades bent at an angle to the handle, a pair of forceps, an ordinary pair of shears, a curved surgical needle, and some thread. Sterilize the instruments by boiling at a place convenient to the operation. Operate in a place sheltered, so far as possible, from wind and dust and sun, but with plenty of light to work by. The essential feature of the operation is cleanliness of the hands, of the instruments, and of the site of operation. It is useless to perform an operation of this sort in a careless fashion and with little regard for cleanliness, as the almost inevitable result will be a bacterial infection resulting in the death of the sheep and the loss of the time spent.

Inject 2 cubic centimeters of water with a one-eighth grain tablet of cocain dissolved in it at the site of operation, pushing the needle through the skin and then moving it about so as to distribute the cocain all around the operation area. Shear the wool close over this area and for some distance around. Have the hands and the site of operation thoroughly cleaned with some antiseptic solution, such as 3 per cent carbolic acid solution (about a tablespoonful to the pint), or a solution of 1 to 1,000 potassium permanganate (put the amount of crystals that can be heaped on a quarter into a quart of water). Take the scalpel or knife and make a V-shaped incision with the place to be operated on included between the legs of the V. With the stylet of the trephine pushed out, start to cut, using the stylet to center the trephine. When the cut is started, draw back the stylet and cut till the bone breaks or is sawed through. In animals other than old rams with thick skulls it requires only a few turns of the wrist to accomplish this, and care must be taken not to press too hard. If the piece of bone comes out stuck in the trephine it can be removed with the stylet. If it does not come out, lift it out with the knife, breaking or cutting any unsawed adhesions. When bleeding occurs, sponge the bleeding parts with a piece of cotton batting or gauze moistened in the 3 per cent solution of carbolic acid or the 1 to 1,000 potassium permanganate solution. Make a cross-shaped cut in the hard membranous covering of the brain with the bent scissors, taking care to cut only the covering and not the brain.

If the parasite is located right at this point it will push out, oftentimes breaking, and may be grasped with a pair of forceps and drawn out. If it does not push out it may be sought for by inserting the forefinger, carefully washed in the antiseptic solution, into the opening and feeling around for a soft spot in the brain. If such a spot is found the finger may be drawn back and the parasite will usually follow it, and may be removed with the forceps. According to Pfab (1910), the cavity of the brain from which the parasite was removed should be washed out by means of a syringe until all bleeding stops, even though it takes half an hour for it to stop. A weak antiseptic solution, such as a carbolic acid solution of one-half of 1 per cent, a solution of 1 part of corrosive sublimate to 5,000 parts of water, or a 3 per cent borax solution, would probably be satisfactory for this. Tablets of corrosive sublimate sufficient for making solutions of known strength in given amounts of water can be purchased of druggists. Corrosive sublimate is poisonous and corrodes metal on contact and must be handled accordingly, using glass receptacles and glass or rubber syringes. Boiled normal salt solution (1 teaspoonful of salt to a quart of water) may be used to syringe out the cavity. Inject the solution gently with a large sterilized syringe, then withdraw it, empty the syringe, and repeat with fresh solution.

When the bleeding stops put the V-shaped flap of skin back in place and take a stitch through the tip of the V and a few along the upper side. Leave the other side free, and do not put back the piece of bone. This will give the wound a chance to drain and prevent the animal from dying of a pus accumulation on the brain. Cover the wound with a pad of cotton wrapped in gauze, or of gauze alone, the pad being moistened with 3 per cent carbolic or 1 to 1,000 potassium permanganate solution, and tie this in place with a strip of cloth. Keep the animal quiet and shut up in a darkened shed for a day or two. Should it show signs of fever and nervousness open the flap and syringe out the cavity again, closing the wound as before.

The trephine operation permits the operator to examine the brain more thoroughly and makes the removal of the entire parasite easier and more certain than is the case in the trocar operation. These things and the fact that it is easier to procure suitable instruments in this country make it more suitable for American sheepmen than the trocar operation.

In using the trocar outfit, shear the wool from the area to be operated on, and then shave a small place clean, using an antiseptic solution to disinfect the shaved area. Inject cocain under this. Insert the trocar in the cannula. Drive the trocar and cannula carefully into the skull until it is evident that the skull is penetrated. They will go in very easily if the soft spot is struck. Most cannulas do not have the guard, and care must be taken not to penetrate the brain too far. Withdraw the trocar, leaving the cannula in place. If the parasite is struck a flow of watery fluid should follow the withdrawal of the trocar. Insert the syringe in the cannula, and syringe out the fluid till no more will come. Then take off the syringe and withdraw the cannula. The cannula should have a cleft at the end which is in the skull, and the parasite will often be caught in this. As the cannula is carefully withdrawn the parasite may be grasped with a pair of forceps and carefully drawn through the hole in the skull. Syringe out the cavity with a weak antiseptic solution as above directed till bleeding stops. Cover this hole with a pledget of cotton wrapped or sewed in gauze and soaked in the 3 per cent carbolic or the 1 to 1,000 potassium permanganate solution. Do not use pine tar or similar substances, as they do not permit of drainage. If the parasite is not struck the first time, a second or third spot may be selected and the trocar driven in.

The parasite should be destroyed. Burn it or put it in the strong antiseptic solution or in sheep dip. One sheepman told the writer that in operating on giddy sheep, and he had operated on quite a number, he threw the parasite away. This was almost the worst thing he could have done. The worst would have been to whistle for a sheep dog and feed it to the dog. That would have been only a little surer than throwing the parasite on the ground, as the two to ten sheep dogs around the home ranch of the average Montana sheep outfits would be almost certain to eat the parasite. Dogs sniff at such things out of curiosity, and eat them, perhaps, for the same reason. The writer has never yet seen a dog refuse to eat a bladder worm. In passing, it should be said that all attempts to cure gid by the administration of medicine have proven failures. No cure of the sort is known.

ADMINISTRATION OF TAPEWORM MEDICINE TO DOGS.

As regards the administration of tapeworm medicine to dogs, many sheepmen think this is too much trouble, and many are puzzled by the names of strange medicines and unfamiliar terms of dosage. There are, however, some sheepmen who do give their dogs some tapeworm medicine. The best time to do this is after the outbreak of gid for the year is over and no more giddy sheep heads are available. This will usually be early in April, and in most seasons the dogs can be treated before being sent out on the summer range. This will eliminate the tapeworm before the advent of the rainy season starts the period of infection by washing the eggs onto the grass and into the drinking places. To safeguard against cases of gid which occur later than March, it would be a good idea to administer tapeworm medicine about four times a year, as new tapeworms develop from bladder worms in one or two months. This treatment could hardly be given while the dogs were on the range, and would require the temporary use of other dogs in order not to interfere with the herding. It is necessary that the dogs be tied up or confined while the medicine is given, in order that the tapeworms may be destroyed when passed. The easiest and best way to destroy them is one which is used by a Montana sheepman. It consists in covering the worms and feces with a sufficient amount of hay or straw and burning them. Another way would be to bury the worms and feces with sheep dip, quicklime, or something of the sort. If the worms are put in some antiseptic solution, preferably formaldehyde or corrosive sublimate, and forwarded to the Bureau of Animal Industry, Washington, D. C., they will be identified and the sender notified as to whether they are gid tapeworms.

It is highly desirable that dogs should be treated for tapeworms. Not all dog tapeworms will cause gid in sheep, but they often develop injurious larval forms in man and the domestic animals, and they are injurious to the dog. The fact that the dog belongs to the herder may be only an additional reason for insisting on giving it a dose of tapeworm medicine. The outbreak of gid in New York State was apparently derived from some dogs imported from Scotland, and it is altogether likely that dogs belonging to wandering sheep herders have brought gid from infected areas into many Montana flocks previously uninfected.

The following drugs may be used to rid dogs of tapeworms: *Pelletierine tannate.* Very efficient, safe, and readily retained by the stomach. *Oleoresin of aspidium,* or *ethereal extract of male fern.* Very reliable. *Kamala.* Effective and convenient in that it acts as its own purgative as a rule. Sometimes advisable to follow by one of the purgatives mentioned later in this article. *Koussein, kussein, or brayerin.* Very prompt and safe. Will act as a purgative, but should be followed by one of the purgatives noted below. *Areca nut.* Good when freshly ground.

The dose for each of the above remedies is as follows: Pelletierine tannate, 5 to 15 grains; oleoresin of aspidium, 15 to 40 minims; kamala, 15 to 30 grains; koussein, 15 to 50 grains; areca nut, 20 to 50 grains. A sheep dog, weighing from 30 to 40 pounds, would require approximately the following amounts: Of pelletierine tannate, 10 grains; of oleoresin of aspidium, 30 minims; of kamala, 20 to 25 grains; of koussein, 30 grains; of areca nut, 35 to 40 grains.

For the purpose of the man who is unfamiliar with apothecaries' weights and measures, or who is in no position to weigh and measure in such fashion, the writer suggests that the drug desired, together with a box of No. 00 capsules, be purchased, and the amount of the drug be measured and administered in the capsule. There is a certain amount of variation in the amount of a powdered drug which can be placed in a capsule, owing to variations in the different lots of drugs, to variations of the same lot under varying conditions, and especially to variation in degree of compression. This is not of very great importance, however, as there is also a variation in the response to drugs of different dogs and of the same dog at different times. Give the 30 to 40 pound sheep dog 2 capsules full of pelletierine tannate, or 2 capsules full of oleoresin of aspidium, or 2 to 2½ capsules full of kamala, or 5 capsules full of koussein, or 6 to 7 capsules full of areca nut. In the case of the powdered drugs the powder should be packed in the capsule by repeated tapping.

Where No. 00 capsules are not available when desired, other sizes may be purchased and the dose computed from the number of No. 00 capsules needed. The following table shows the relation of the No. 00 capsule to other capsules as regards capacity:

Number of capsule	00	0	1	2	3	4	5
Relative capacity	12	8	6	4	3	2	1

It is evident from this that it would take 12 times as many No. 5 capsules, 6 times as many No. 4 capsules, etc., of any drug as it would of No. 00 capsules. Drugs should be purchased in small quantities and used while fresh, as they lose in strength and efficiency in most cases as they get older.

The method which the writer commonly employs in administering drugs to dogs is to push the capsule down the throat as far as possible with the right forefinger, working from the right side, while an assistant holds the dog with a piece of board in the left angle of the jaw to keep the dog from biting. Another way is to drop the capsules into the mouth and then hold back the head, keeping the piece of board in the angle of the jaw, and pour water in the mouth, holding the nose till the capsules are swallowed. Where it seems inadvisable to do these things, capsules may be fed in pieces of meat, or the drug may be fed in soup or milk, or in pills made up with honey and meal or molasses and meal.

The dog should be fed nothing but milk or left without food the evening before the medicine is to be given. It is sometimes advisable to give one or two grains of calomel at this time. The next morning administer the tapeworm medicine, but do not feed. Keep the dog shut up or tied up. If tied, it is advisable that a long rope be used, as some dogs object to defecating when tied with a short rope. After a couple of hours administer three to four grains of calomel, or one to two grains of podophyllin, or one to two drams of jalap, or a tablespoonful of magnesium sulphate. The calomel or podophyllin can be purchased in 1-grain pills of any druggist. Castor oil, in doses of an ounce or so, may be used, but is not recommended, for the reason that it appears in some cases to increase the solubility of the tapeworm medicine, all of which medicines are more or less poisonous, and so increases the likelihood of the medicine being taken into the dog's system with harmful or even fatal results.

The feces and worms should be burned with hay or buried with quicklime or sheep dip, as already advised. As has been noted, the coyote probably carries the gid tapeworm. As the coyote can not be treated for tapeworms and is a difficult animal to exterminate, it is evident that the most important measure in the elimination of gid is the destruction of the heads of giddy sheep. In order that efforts at eradication may not be rendered ineffective through the importation of dogs infected with the gid tapeworm, the Secretary of Agriculture has issued an order, under date of November 25, 1910, providing that collie, shepherd, or sheep dogs imported into the United States be subjected to quarantine and inspection until the presence or absence of infection with this tapeworm can be ascertained.

SUMMARY.

Gid has occurred in Montana for over twenty years and causes at times severe losses. It is usually confused with loco disease or other diseases. The losses and the history of the disease here and in Europe warrant prompt efforts at eradication.

The gid parasite occurring as a bladderworm in the brain of the sheep, is transmitted to dogs by the latter eating the heads and brains of sheep dying in the last stages of gid. The heads on the bladderworm develop into tapeworms in the intestines of the dog, and the eggs formed by these tapeworms are passed onto the range or pasture and taken up by sheep in their food or water. From these eggs an embryo gets to the brain of the sheep and forms the gid parasite. There is absolutely no evidence to show that this life history of the gid parasite is incorrect.

The life cycle takes about a year for its completion and appears to be closely related to weather conditions. The weather and the nature of the forage appear to determine to some extent the amount of infection. The symptoms of gid are very striking and readily distinguishable in most cases. The eradication of gid is very easy.

COTSWOLD RAM. DEPT. OF AGR.

LINCOLN RAM (COURTESY FARMERS' ADVOCATE).

Destroy the heads or brains of giddy sheep, and keep sheep dogs and ranch dogs free of tapeworms. The first is the more important of the two.

Destroy the heads by burning, or split the skull, scoop out the brains, chop them up or crush them, and cover with turpentine, formaldehyde, or sheep dip. Ignorance and carelessness, resulting in leaving heads of giddy sheep to be eaten by dogs or coyotes, are responsible for the spread of gid in Montana. Instead of killing giddy sheep and destroying the brain, the more favorable cases may be operated on if desired, taking care to destroy the parasite when it is removed from the brain.

Tapeworm remedies should be administered to dogs at least once a year when the outbreak of gid for the year is over. The medicines may be measured out in capsules in the amounts noted in the text. The tapeworms should be destroyed by burning or burying with quicklime or sheep dip.—(Bu. An. Ind. Cir. 165, 1910.)

THE BROAD TAPE-WORM (TAENIA EXPANSA).

This tape-worm is now one of the most common parasites of sheep. It occurs wherever sheep are kept in this country. On account of its breadth and great length it is easily recognized. The length may exceed five yards and at the broadest part it is from one-half to three-fourths of an inch wide. At the head the width is not so great. This parasite is found in the intestine at all seasons, but becomes numerous in the fall and early winter. The life history of the worm is not clearly understood, but is thought to be quite simple. On reaching maturity a number of segments are shed at one time and the embryos contained in these segments, after reaching the herbage or water, undergo certain changes, and entering the body of another sheep, reach complete development, and again produce embryo, which are shed as before. As the conditions in spring and summer are very favorable for the existence of the embryo outside of the body, sheep may become badly infected at this time, and show symptoms of tape-worm disease in late summer or fall. Low, wet pastures are supposed to be most favorable for producing tape-worm disease, but probably an overcrowded pasture, even if high and dry, is as much to be avoided.

The best evidence of the presence of tape-worm is the finding of the segments in the droppings. Unless a number of the parasites are present, no indication of disease will be observed, but when present in considerable numbers in young lambs, serious trouble often arises. Dr. Curtice mentions finding fourteen adult worms in a lamb four months old, and that the number of individuals present may be from two or three to a hundred. It is seldom, however, that more than five or six are observed. Symptoms of disease do not appear until the parasites reach considerable size, when they partially block up the intestinal tube and probably cause considerable irritation. The affected lamb ceases to thrive, becomes weak and emaciated, and may finally die from exhaustion. In late stages, diarrhœa is a prominent symptom. The mucous membranes are pale, the wool becomes deprived of oil and is easily pulled out, and the appetite, at first good, in later stage becomes impaired. Other diseases may supervene and carry off the already debilitated animal. The appetite of affected animals may for some time continue good, more food and drink being taken than when free from parasites.

A number of correspondents have reported serious loss of lambs from tape-worm diseases, and this, like some of the other parasitical troubles, is, no doubt, becoming more widely disseminated over the State. After the parasites reach the adult stage, the segments are usually soon shed, and the lamb, if not too badly emaciated, may improve and entirely recover.

Prevention consists of providing, if possible, new pastures and a pure water supply. Over-stocking and the use of low, wet pastures should be avoided if possible.

Medicinal treatment is quite effectual if the flock is taken in hand early. No treatment will avail in the late stages of disease, when the animal has become badly debilitated. The treatment should be commenced as soon as tape-worm disease can be detected, and if possible, before actual symptoms of disease appears. For the destruction of this parasite, several preparations are recommended. Before administering the medicine, food and water should be withheld for about twelve hours, and it is advisable to follow the tape-worm remedy in three or four hours with a cathartic. Unless the head of the worm is expelled, the segments will be reproduced and the most successful remedy is one that leads to the expulsion of the entire worm.

Areca nut, powdered, in one to three dram doses, male shield fern in two ounce doses, kousso in one and one-half to two dram doses, and picrate of potash in from six to twenty grain doses, are the preparations most highly recommended. The picrate of potash is said to be very efficient, but if properly administered, no doubt any of the above will give good results. Oil of turpentine is also much used. After using this remedy for the destruction of the stomach worm, I have observed sheep to pass large numbers of tape-worms.

In the treatment of badly affected flocks, the animals should receive the best of care, and in addition to being supplied with nutritious food in liberal quantities, should for a time receive tonic treatment.

LARGE ROUND WORM (ASCARIS LUMBRICOIDES).

This parasite is very common in swine, but is seldom met with in sheep. It is thought that the latter may become infested with the parasite by being pastured with swine. The worm is several inches in length and may be easily recognized. It is found in the small intestine and is most abundant in summer and fall. Any good worm medicine will destroy them.

THE CAECUM WORM (TRICHOCEPHALUS AFFINIS).

This parasite is found in the large intestine of sheep, goats and cattle. It is common in sheep, where it is often found in great numbers. It is a small, whip-like shaped worm. The slim part represents the head extremity which is attached to the mucous membrane. The thick portion or caudal extremity floats freely in the intestinal contents. The life history is simple. The eggs, after passing to the ground and developing to a certain extent, pass with food or water into the intestine again, where they complete their development.

The caecum worm is not thought to be especially harmful, but when present in large numbers alone or in conjunction with other parasites, it may cause serious trouble. The usual worm remedies can be used with a considerable degree of success. After the administration of oil of turpentine these worms are passed in considerable numbers.

THE FRINGED TAPEWORM OF SHEEP (THYSANOSOMA FIMBRIATA).

An adult worm measures from 6 to 12 in. in length. In comparison with other species of tapeworm the head is large, about the size of a pin's head, and provided with four distinct suckers. For the purpose of this report it is deemed neither advisable nor essential to enter into a minute description of the structure of this parasite.

The possession of one peculiar and characteristic feature permits of the ready identification of the fringed tapeworm. The posterior border of each segment of the worm bears a fringe, giving a velvety appearance to the entire animal. If there is any doubt as to the identification, the presence of this fringe can be readily recognized by placing the worm in a small vial of water, thus causing the fringe to float out somewhat from the segments of the body.

Distribution, Mortality and Occurrence.—The tapeworm has been found by Natterer in species of deer in South America. In sheep it is reported from Colorado, Utah, Nebraska (Curtice) ; New Mexico (Cadweiss, Curtice) ; California, Oregon, Utah (Curtice) ; Missouri (Stewart, Curtice) ; Washington, D. C. [in sheep from Colorado (Hassall and Stiles).

Experience shows that even in the best cared for flocks the mortality may run high, and there is truth in the statement of Curtice that it forms at times a veritable scourge to the sheep industry of the western plains.

In the majority of cases this tapeworm is found in the duodenum or first portion of the small intestine. Not infrequently, however, they may be found in the common bile duct from the liver, and also in some cases in the hepatic ducts. Curtice states sometimes they may be found in the ducts of the pancreas, believing that they enter these various channels while young.

Life History.—The exact life history of the fringed tapeworm is unknown. Curtice's experiments in attempting to infest young lambs directly with eggs from the fringed tapeworm proved negative, which suggests that, like many other tapeworms, it must pass through some intermediate host or hosts. Yet this is merely conjecture and, as above stated, its life history has not been fully determined.

Symptoms.—The attention of the owner is probably first attracted to the disease by the fact that lambs which should be doing well are unthrifty, scour and soon begin to gradually die. A more

careful examination will show that the mucous membranes of th
eyes are pale and bloodless; and, as the animal becomes more seri
ously affected, it appears thin and emaciated, and the skin hide
bound. Soft swellings appear under the throat or in the neighborhoo
of the neck, owing to the serous extravasations; the gait becomes fee
ble, the body under-sized, and the head often large. The appearanc
of being foolish and the difficulty in vision, to which Curtice calls at
tention, we have not noticed. A microscopical examination of th
blood shows a large increase in the number of leucocytes. Altogethe
the picture, therefore, is one of cachexia or malnutrition, and so far a
symptoms are concerned there is absolutely nothing which serve
to diagnose this from any other of the parasitic diseases of sheep
A positive diagnosis can only be made by conducting a post morten
examination and recognizing, in the manner already indicated, th
presence of the fringed tapeworm.

Prevention.—While practical efforts to prevent parasitic dis
eases depend upon a complete knowledge of the parasite's life his
tory, and although no established rules can be given, nevertheless
this does not minimize the importance of providing sheep with a
rotation of pastures. No disease results in greater mortality among
sheep in the United States than those of parasitic origin. By run
ning sheep over the same ground, year after year, we are courting
the infestation and reinfestation of each individual in the flock. As
a general rule in the prevention of most parasitic diseases, there car
be no question of the utility of occasionally providing fresh pasture
over which no sheep have ranged for at least one year. The selec
tion of high, sloping ground for a pasture is advisable whenever pos
sible. The animals should be watered from tanks raised above the
ground so that the water does not become contaminated with their
droppings. The fencing off of sloughs, ponds and stagnant pools is
also very important in preventing infection. The burning over of
the pasture will destroy the eggs and young worms on the grass, or
on the droppings. As this malady is more fatal in the young ani
mal, a liberal supply of grain will assist in tiding it over and fur
nish vitality to withstand the disease. They should have free access
to salt at all times.

Treatment.—During the past few years, as opportunities have
been offered, various modes of treatment have been used, including
kamala, kousso, etherial extract of male fern, picric acid, copper
sulphate, etc., as well as some proprietary compounds bought in the
open market. While not recommended as the best, nor as an ideal
form of treatment, nothing has proved so uniformly satisfactory as
Hutcheson's method with copper sulphate. Our experience with this
form of treatment is, therefore, at variance with the results obtained
by Stiles. We are indebted to Bulletin No. 19 of the Bureau of Animal Industry for the following description of the Hutcheson method
of treatment:

(a) To prepare the mixture dissolve one pound avoirdupois
of good commercial powdered blue stone, sulphate of copper, in two
imperial quarts (2 2-5 U. S. qts.) of boiling water. When the blue

stone is thoroughly dissolved, add 6½ imperial gallons (7 4-5 U. S. gals. or 31 1-5 U. S. qts.) of cold water, making in all 7 imperial gallons (8 2-5 U. S. gals.) of water. Use only blue stone of a uniformly blue color. Avoid that which is in conglomerate lumps with white patches and covered with a white crust. The owner is cautioned against guessing at the weights and measures, for this is sure to result in too strong a solution, which will kill his animal, or too weak a solution, which will fail to be effective. If a smaller quantity than the above is desired it can be made up on the proportion of one ounce of copper sulphate to two quarts of water.

(b) *Preparation of the Animal.*—Fast the sheep twenty to twenty-four hours before dosing.

(c) *Size of Dose—*

Age of Animal	Tablespoonfuls	Fluid Ounces
For a lamb 3 months old	1	2-3
For a lamb 6 months old	2	1 1-3
For a sheep 1 year old	3	2
For a sheep 1½ years old	4	2 2-3
For a sheep 2 years old and over	4¼	3

The doses should be measured off in bottles plainly marked with a file, to serve as a graduate.

(d) *Dosing.*—While a drenching tube is more satisfactory, the popular method of drenching is with a long necked bottle. The assistant places the sheep on its haunches, taking its forelegs in the left hand and steadying the head with the right hand. The bottle is then inserted in the sheep's mouth and the solution slowly poured down to prevent choking. For the same reason do not raise the nose above the height of the eyes. In this connection it is of interest to note the results obtained by Stiles in drenching sheep in different positions. If the animal was drenched while standing, almost the entire quantity of the dose went into the fourth or true stomach. If it was placed on its haunches, the fluid passed partly into the fourth stomach and partly into the first. If it was placed on its back, almost the entire dose passed into the first stomach or paunch. These tapeworms being found principally in the intestines, it is quite evident from Stiles' experiments in drenching that the most favorable results are to be expected by drenching the animal in a standing position, inasmuch as that portion of the dose which otherwise passes into the other compartments of the stomach is largely lost. But the most usual method of drenching is as already described.

(e) *Overdose.*—If after dosing, any of the sheep seem to be suffering from an overdose, indicated by lying apart from the flock, not feeding, manifesting a painful excited look and a spasmodic movement in its running, walking with a stiff gait, or purging with a dirty brownish discharge, take the affected animal from the flock to a shady place and dose with laudanum and milk. For a lamb four to six months old give a teaspoonful of laudanum in a tumbler of milk. Repeat half the dose in two or three hours if necessary.

(f) *After Treatment.*—The animals should not be allowed water for several hours after receiving the copper sulphate.

This method of treatment has been followed not only by us personally, but in answer to inquiries it has been recommended during the past two years. So far as information could be obtained the results have been most successful. Of course no treatment succeeds where an animal is already so badly infested as to show marked weakness and emaciation. We have yet to record fatalities from this method of treatment, although some farmers have used larger doses or made a stronger solution than has been recommended. It cannot, however, be too emphatically stated that he who modifies either the size of the dose or the strength of the solution is taking his own risks and at the expense of the flock.

The practice of simply treating those animals in the flock that begin to show signs of parasitism is hardly worthy of notice. The entire flock should be treated at the same time, for while other sheep may be able to withstand the presence of the parasites, they serve as a source of infection. While the tapeworms are being voided the flock should be confined to one place, the droppings with the segments of worms collected and destroyed or removed to a place to which the sheep do not have access, to guard against a recurrence of this disease.

LIVER FLUKE (FASCIOLA HEPATICA; LINN).

The liver fluke is a broad flat worm found in the liver of sheep, goats and cattle. Its life history is one of great interest. The eggs are produced in immense numbers and pass through the gall duct to the intestine and out with the faeces. Those that fall in favorable places as puddles of water escape from the shell. They are very delicate, covered with hair to aid in swimming and have a proboscis to puncture the body of a variety of small snails. It is necessary that it should find a snail in a day or two otherwise it will die. If it should find a snail it punctures the body to the respiratory tract, and becomes encysted. It is here known as the sporocyst and may divide into several bodies, five to eight and these are developed into rediæ. The rediæ are about one-twelfth of an inch long. These rediæ are liberated from the sac and these in turn develop within themselves from fifteen to twenty bodies known as cercariæ and it is these latter that escape from the snail. The cercariæ after some slight change become encysted on grass or wherever it may happen to be. In this stage it will resist drying, temperature changes, etc., and is the form in which it is swallowed by the sheep. The swallowed cyst has the shell digested by the action of the gastric juice and the young soon finds its way to the liver where it becomes an adult and the process is repeated. By some form of migration the flukes may find their way into lungs. The eggs seem to be passed through a period of a month or more during the summer, the first development of the offspring takes place in the summer and the cyst comes on later in the fall.

The symptoms of fluke disease are not all recognized by the stockman. There is a period of migration from the intestine to the liver lasting during the summer that is attended by little disturbance. During the late fall and winter the affected sheep show a lack of thrift, disinclination to eat heartily; a paleness about the eyes and lips, yellow tinge in the skin; there may be fullness between the jaws, the wool is dry, brittle and easily pulled. The third stage follows the second and not easily separated from it. The animal loses flesh rapidly, becomes emaciated, the appetite keeps up but the most marked character is the wasting. The fourth stage is that of natural migration of the parasite late in the spring, and spontaneous recovery. The sheep as a rule die in the second or third stage if badly infected. (For treatment see liver fluke under Diseases of Cattle.)

STOMACH WORMS (HAEMONCHUS CONTORTUS) IN SHEEP.

The stomach worm of sheep, known to zoologists as *Hæmonchus contortus*, is generally recognized as one of the most serious pests with which the sheep raiser has to contend. Sheep of all ages are subject to infection, and cattle and goats as well as various wild ruminants may also harbor the parasite. The most serious effects of stomach-worm infection are seen in lambs, while full-grown sheep, although heavily infested, may show no apparent symptoms of disease. It is from these, however, through the medium of the pasture, that the lambs become infected.

Symptoms and Diagnosis.—Among the symptoms which have been described for stomach-worm disease probably the most frequent are anemia, loss of flesh, general weakness, dullness, capricious appetite, thirst, and diarrhea. The anemic condition is seen in the paleness of the skin and mucous membranes of the mouth and eye, and in the watery swellings which often develop under the lower jaw. A more certain diagnosis may be made by killing one of the flock and opening the fourth stomach. The contents of the fourth stomach are allowed to settle gently, and by carefully watching the liquid the parasites, if present in any considerable numbers, will be seen actively wriggling about like little snakes from one-half to 1¼ inches long and about as thick as an ordinary pin. They are a blood-red color, due to their habit of sucking blood from the sheep.

Life History of the Stomach Worm.—The worms in the stomach produce eggs of microscopic size, which pass out of the body in the droppings and are thus scattered broadcast over the pasture. If the temperature is above 40° to 50° F. the eggs hatch out, requiring from a few hours to two weeks, according as the temperature is high or low. When the temperature is below 40° F. the eggs remain dormant, and in this condition may retain their vitality for two or three months, afterwards hatching out if the weather becomes warmer. Freezing or drying soon kills the unhatched eggs. The tiny worm which hatches from the egg feeds upon the organic matter in the manure, and grows until it is nearly one-thirtieth of an inch in length. Further development then ceases until the worm is swallowed by a sheep or other ruminant, after which it again begins to grow, and reaches maturity in the fourth stomach of its host in two to three weeks. The chances of the young worms being swallowed are greatly increased by the fact that they crawl up blades of grass whenever sufficient moisture—such as dew, rain, or fog—is present, provided also that the temperature is above 40° F. When the temperature is below 40° F. the worms are inactive.

The young worms which have reached the stage when they are ready to be taken into the body are greatly resistant to cold and dryness; they will stand repeated freezing, and have been kept in a dried condition for thirty-five days, afterwards reviving when moisture was added. At a temperature of about 70° F. young worms have been kept alive for as long as six months, and the infection in inclosures (near Washington, D. C.) which had been pastured by infested sheep did not die out in over seven months, including the winter, the inclosures having been left vacant from October 25 to June 16. It is uncertain whether infection in fields from which sheep have been removed will die out more rapidly during warm weather or during cold weather. It is, however, safe to say that a field which has had no sheep, cattle, or goats upon it for a year will be practically free from infection, and fields which have had no sheep or other ruminants upon them following cultivation may also be safely used. The time required for a clean pasture to become infectious after infested sheep are placed upon it depends upon the temperature; that is, the field does not become infectious until the eggs of the parasites contained in the droppings of the sheep have hatched out and the young worms have developed to the final larval stage, and the rapidity of this development depends upon the temperature. It may be stated here that neither the eggs nor the newly hatched worms are infectious, and only those worms which have reached the final larval stage are able to continue their development when swallowed. This final larval stage is reached in three to four days after the eggs have passed out of the body of the host if the temperature remains constantly at about 95° F. At 70° F., six to fourteen days are required, and at 46° to 57° F., averaging about 50° F., three to four weeks are necessary for the eggs to hatch and the young worms to develop to the infectious stage. At temperatures below 40° F., as already stated, the eggs remain dormant.

Methods of Preventing Infection.—It is evident from the foregoing statements that in the northern part of the United States, under usual climatic conditions, infested and noninfested sheep may be placed together in clean fields the last of October or first of November and kept there until March or even later, according to the weather, with little or no danger of the noninfested sheep becoming infected. If moved then to another clean field they may remain there nearly the entire month of April before there is danger of infection. From the first of May on through the summer the pastures become infectious much more quickly after infested sheep are placed upon them, and during May it would be necessary to move the sheep at the end of every two weeks, in June at the end of every ten days, and in July and August at the end of each week, in order to prevent the noninfested sheep from becoming infected from the worms present in the rest of the flock. After the 1st of September the period may again be lengthened. This method of preventing infection in lambs would require a considerable number of small pastures or subdivisions of large pastures, and in many instances could not be profitably employed, but in cases where it could be used it would undoubtedly prove very effective. By the time the next lamb crop appeared the pastures used the year before would have remained vacant long enough for the infection to have disappeared, and would consequently again be ready for use. By continuing this rotation from year to year, not only would each crop of lambs be protected from infection, but as reinfection of the infested ewe flock is prevented at the same time, the parasite would in a few years be entirely eradicated from the flock and pastures.

If such frequent rotation is not possible or practicable, a smaller number of pastures may be utilized, after the ewe flock has been treated with vermifuges. The treatment may be given either before or after the birth of the lambs. If before, the ewes should be treated before pregnancy is too far advanced, in order to avoid possible bad results from the handling necessary in treatment. Probably the best time for treatment is late in the fall or early in the winter. The treated sheep should be placed immediately on clean pasture in order to avoid reinfection. The object of treating the ewes is to get rid of the worms with which they are infested, and thus remove the source from which the pasture becomes contaminated. If it were possible by treatment to free the old sheep entirely from stomach worms, it is evident that the lambs would remain free from infection, provided, of course, that the flock were afterwards kept on clean pasture. Unfortunately, there is no vermifuge known which can always be depended upon to remove all of the worms, but it is possible to get rid of most of them and thus greatly reduce the amount of infection to which the lambs will be exposed. Two other methods may be suggested by which lambs can be kept free from infection with stomach worms.

1. It is assumed that a large pasture is available which has had no sheep, goats, or cattle upon it for a year, if a permanent pasture, or since cultivation, if a seeded pasture. This pasture is subdivided into two by a double line of fence, and a drainage ditch is run along the alley between the two fences. At one end of the alley between the two subdivisions a small yard is constructed, communicating with each of the subdivisions by means of a gate. When the lambs are born they are placed in one of the subdivisions and the ewes are placed in the other. The small yard should be kept free of vegetation and must not drain into the lamb pasture. As often as necessary the lambs are allowed in the small yard with the ewes for sucking. The rest of the time the lambs and ewes are kept separate in their respective pastures. By this arrangement the lambs are exposed to infection only while they are in the small yard, where they may become infected either by embryos of the stomach worm present on the manure-soiled skin of the infested ewes, or by embryos picked up from the ground which has been contaminated by the droppings of the ewes. The chances of infection from the skin of the ewe are so slight that in practice this source of infection need not be considered. The danger of infection from the ground may be

avoided by frequently removing the manure from the yard and keeping the surface sprinkled with lime and salt. The lambs and ewes will soon learn the way to their proper pastures, and after a few days little difficulty will be experienced in separating them each time after the lambs are through suckling.

2. Another plan which may be followed where the climatic conditions are suitable—that is, in regions where there is a cold winter season—is that of having the lambs born at a time of year when there will be no danger of their becoming infected during the suckling period, and weaning and separating them from the rest of the flock before the advent of warm weather. Under the usual climatic conditions of the State of Ohio, for instance, if the lambs are born in the latter part of October or the first of November they may remain with the ewes on fields which have not been previously occupied by sheep, goats, or cattle within a year—or, if cultivated fields, since cultivation—until the following March without danger of becoming infected, since the eggs in the droppings of the infested ewes will not hatch out during this time of year because of the cold weather. The use of fields not previously occupied by sheep, goats, or cattle within a year, or since cultivation, is necessary, since otherwise the fields would be already infected with young worms which had hatched out and reached the infectious stage before the beginning of cold weather, and the lambs would consequently be liable to infection from picking up these young worms, which are not killed by cold weather after they have reached the final stage of larval development. When they are weaned the lambs must, of course, be placed on clean pasture, if they are to continue free from infection. With this method only two clean pastures are necessary, one in which the ewes and lambs are placed in the fall, and another for the lambs when they are weaned in March.

Unfortunately for this scheme, it is not always possible to have lambs born at the beginning of the winter season; but with additional clean pastures a modification of the foregoing method may be used in the case of lambs born toward the end of the winter or in the spring. In the northern United States lambs born the first of February, for example, may be kept with their mothers in a clean field or pasture until the last of March, as in the case of those born at the beginning of winter, but unlike the latter they will not then be old enough to wean. Accordingly they are not separated from the rest of the flock, but the ewes and lambs are moved together to a second clean pasture April 1. May 1 they are moved to a third clean pasture, May 15 they are moved again, and finally the lambs are weaned June 1 at the age of four months, and moved by themselves to a clean pasture. In the case of lambs born the first of March and weaned the first of July three additional clean pastures would be required for use during the month of June, and with later lambs a still greater number of pastures would be necessary.

Treatment for Stomach Worms.—Among the remedies which may be used to remove stomach worms may be mentioned coal-tar creosote, bluestone, and gasoline. The animals to be treated should be deprived of feed for twelve to sixteen or even twenty-four hours before they are dosed, and in case bluestone is used should receive no water on the day they are dosed, either before or after dosing. In drenching, a long-necked bottle or a drenching tube may be used. In case a bottle is used the dose to be given may be first measured off, poured into the bottle, and the point marked on the outside of the bottle with a file, so that subsequent doses may be measured in the bottle itself. A simple form of drenching tube consists of a piece of rubber tubing about 3 feet long and one-half inch in diameter, with an ordinary tin funnel inserted in one end and a piece of brass or iron tubing 4 to 6 inches long and of suitable diameter inserted in the other end. In use the metal tube is placed in the animal's mouth between the back teeth, and the dose is poured into the funnel, which is either held by an assistant or fastened to a post. The flow of liquid through the tube is controlled by pinching the rubber tubing near the point of union with the metal tube. It is important not to raise the animal's head too high on account of the danger of the dose entering the lungs. The nose should not be raised higher than the level of the eyes. The animal may be dosed either standing on all fours or set upon its haunches. It has been found by experiment that if the dose is taken quietly most of it will pass directly to the fourth stomach when the animal is dosed in a standing position, and that when the animal is placed on its haunches only a part of the dose passes immediately to the fourth stomach. From this it is evident that the position on all fours is preferable, as more of the dose passes to the place where its action is required.

Great care should be used not only in dosing to avoid the entrance of the liquid into the lungs, but also in the preparation and administration of the remedy so that the solution may not be too strong or the dose too large.

Good results have been obtained from a single dose of a 1 per cent solution of coal-tar creosote. This solution is made by shaking together 1 ounce of coal-tar creosote and 99 ounces (6 pints 3 ounces) of water. The doses of this 1 per cent mixture recommended by Stiles are as follows:

Lambs 4 to 12 months old	2 to 4 ounces.
Yearling sheep and above	3 to 5 ounces.
Calves 3 to 8 months old	5 to 10 ounces.
Yearling steers	1 pint.
Two-year-olds and above	1 quart.

Serious objections to the use of coal-tar creosote have been found in that the substance known by this name varies considerably in composition and in that some trouble is often experienced in obtaining it in many parts of the country. Complaints have been made that the substance dispensed by some druggists as coal-tar creosote has failed to give satisfactory results.

Bluestone, or copper sulfate, has been extensively used in South Africa in the treatment of sheep for stomach worms and is recommended by the colonial veterinary surgeon of the Cape Colony as the best and safest remedy. His directions are to take 1 pound avoirdupois of pure bluestone, powder it fine, and dissolve in 9½ gallons of warm water. It is better to first dissolve the bluestone in 2 to 4 bottlefuls of boiling water, then add the remaining quantity in cold water, and mix thoroughly. This solution is given in the following-sized doses:

```
Lambs   3 months old....................  ¾  ounce.
Lambs   6 months old.................... 1½  ounces.
Sheep  12 months old.................... 2½  ounces.
Sheep  18 months old.................... 3   ounces.
Sheep  24 months old.................... 3½  ounces.
```

In making up the solution only clear blue crystals of bluestone should be used. Bluestone with white patches or crusts should be rejected. It is especially important that the bluestone and water be accurately weighed and measured, and that the size of the dose be graduated according to the age of the sheep.

Gasoline is one of the most popular remedies for stomach worms which has been used in this country and has the particular advantage of being readily obtained. It is important to repeat the dose if the gasoline treatment is employed, and it is usual to administer the treatment on three successive days, as follows:

The evening before the first treatment is to be given the animals are shut up without feed or water and are dosed about 10 o'clock the next morning. Three hours later they are allowed feed and water, and at night they are again shut up without feed or water. The next morning the second dose is given, and the third morning the third dose, the treatment before and after dosing being the same in each case.

The sizes of the doses are as follows:

```
Lambs .......................................  ¼  ounce.
Sheep .......................................  ½  ounce.
Calves ......................................  ½  ounce.
Yearling steers ............................. 1   ounce.
```

The dose for each animal is measured and mixed separately in linseed oil, milk, or flaxseed tea, and administered by means of a bottle or drenching tube. Gasoline should not be given in water.

Many other remedies in addition to those mentioned here have been used in the treatment of stomach-worm disease with more or less success. Several of the coal-tar dips on the market are recommended by the manufacturers for the treatment of worms, and the action of some of them is much the same as that of coal-tar creosote.

Whatever remedy is used, it is wise to test it on two or three animals before the entire flock is dosed.

Fluid Extract of Kamale, in doses of 1 drachm per 50 pounds of lamb administered in glycerine with 2 or 3 ounces of water, has been recommended.—(B. A. I. "Animal Parasites of Sheep," Circ. S. 93 and 102; 17th and 27th An. Rept. B. A. I.; Va. Bul. 178, and V. X. n. s. No. 7; Okla. Bul. 53; O. Bul. 91 and 117; S. C. Bul. 142 and 114.)

·INTESTINAL WORMS.

NODULE-DISEASE OF THE INTESTINES OF SHEEP (OESOPHAGOSTOMA COLUMBIANUM, CUR.).

There is hardly a State in the Union that can claim freedom from this disease among its flocks. For some time it had been mistaken for tuberculosis, the nodules, or tumors, on the intestines resembling, somewhat, the tubercles of consumption; but later investigation revealed the presence of a very minute round worm as the true cause.

The disease gets its name from the nodulated condition of the intestines, they being, in advanced cases, thickly studded with nodular enlargements all along their course, as far back as the last portion of the bowel (rectum). Everyone who has butchered sheep, in many sections of the country, must be familiar with the appearance, although, perhaps, ignorant of the cause of this condition, known popularly, in some localities, by the term, knotty-guts.

In the adult stage, the worm, or parasite (Oesophagostoma Columbianum) is about one-half an inch in length, and may be found located in the intestines, and more particularly, the large bowel. The immature stages or forms, vary in length from 1-100 to 1-6 of an inch, depending upon age and stage of development. These are found encysted in the nodules. The writer has dissected quite a number of the larger, older, tumors, without finding the parasite in them, and from which we would infer that they had escaped into the intestine. The life-history of this minute worm, so far as appears to be known, from the more recent investigations, is as follows: The mature female lays her eggs in the intestine. The eggs hatch in a short time, and the embryos, or minute immature worms, pass, in some manner, through the mucous, or internal, lining of the bowel, and become encysted or embedded there; and the irritation produced by the worm seems to give rise to the nodules or tumors, which can be seen, of various sizes, projecting from the intestine, sometimes along its entire course.

The tumor consists of a cheesy material, often greenish in color, which, on breaking its outer covering, can be squeezed out. It is thought by Dr. Curtice that the embryos are tho chief cause of the trouble, and that the adult worms produce but very little, as the latter are comparatively few as compared with the number of tumors. Some of the adult parasites, and probably some of the eggs, pass out from the intestines with the manure, and in this way pastures and other feeding quarters are infected; and in turn, shallow and sluggish watering places into which they drain. There is however, a stage in the life cycle of the worm that seems to be still undetermined. That is, from the time it leaves the bowels with the manure until it is again found in the tumors on the intestines.

The symptoms of nodular disease are not very characteristic during life. In fact, there must be thousands of fat sheep slaughtered annually in the abattoirs of the country affected with this ailment, which exhibit no special indications previous to being killed. But in the more advanced stages of the disease, the symptoms resemble those seen in other parasitic troubles, such as general debility and in the most severe cases rapid emaciation, and excessive diarrhoea. A positive diagnosis can only be made by postmortem examination and finding the characteristic nodules on the intestines. The cause of death in acute cases is evidently the interference caused by the tumors to the process of absorption. Or, in other words, the animal is deprived of proper nutrition on account of the function of the intestinal walls being interfered with by the tumors, and the process of absorption of nutrient material thereby lessened. The extent of the derangement may be said to be in direct ratio to the number of tumors present.

The treatment so far suggested is chiefly preventive, although we believe the best results would be obtained from a combination of both preventive and curative, when handling an infected flock. The chief drawback to the desired effects of medicinal treatment is the embedded or encysted position of the parasites in the tumors which seem to be beyond the reach of medicines. Still, as adult worms are found free in the bowels, vermifuge medicines would necessarily have some effect upon those in this situation. The gasoline treatment, used in stomach-worm disease, has been recommended. A weak solution of creolin seems to have given favorable results in the hands of Dr. M. Jacob, of the Tennessee Experiment Station, a report of which he gave in a paper read before the United States Association of Experiment Station Veterinarians, at Atlantic City, N. J., in September, 1901. We quote from his paper the following: "Sheep had been dying at the rate of four or five a week. They had been put in a new field about six weeks previously, but still continued to die until after they had received, daily, about 20 minims of crude creolin per head. This was prepared in the form of a drench by dissolving 5 ounces of creolin in one gallon of water, and giving each sheep about one ounce a day for ten days. This treatment seemed to give pretty fair results, for during the next two or three months the death rate was very markedly decreased." Dr. Jacob thinks the treatment ought to be continued for at least one month. The individual treatment of sheep, where there are large numbers of them, is an undertaking which but few of our sheep owners in the State would attempt, except, perhaps, in the case of the animals being valuable purebreds. Dr. Cooper Curtice also states, however, "that in case medicinal remedies are tried, each animal must be dosed."

Those who are at all familiar with intestinal parasitic diseases are aware that medicinal treatment alone will not yield satisfactory results, but that other measures, outside of the animal, must likewise be adopted. For, to attain our object, we must not only endeavor to destroy the parasites in the animal but we must also treat the infected pastures to destroy or render innocuous the parasites that may be on their surface, and capable of infecting animals (sheep in this case) grazing over them. A combination of both, then, is necessary for the most satisfactory results. Curtice remarks, "that the same care in changing pastures, in providing good drinking water and a plentiful supply of salt, should be observed in this disease as for other parasites. Judicious fall and winter marketing of infected sheep will also tend to lessen the chances of infection. If pastures are known to be permanently infected, then they should be turned over to other stock for a year or two before being again grazed on by sheep. When it is practical, on the smaller farms, the sheep lots should be plowed, and either planted or left fallow. The object of change of pasture and of plowing is nearly the same; in the one case to wait until the parasites have died out; in the other, to bury them beneath several inches of soil, from which the sheep owner may rest assured they will not emerge."

The conclusions deducible from the results of experiments may be stated as follows:

(1). That sheep suffering from Nodular Disease of the Intestines, when placed upon a hitherto clean pasture, transmit infection to it through extrusion of the nodule-worm (Oesophagostoma Columbianum) from their bowels, probably with their droppings.

(2). That when sound lambs are permitted to occupy a pasture so infected, they will contract nodule disease.

(3). That when the surface of an infected pasture is turned under by ploughing, and the land cropped, even for a single season, the infection may be destroyed.

(4). That when sound lambs are allowed to occupy and graze upon a pasture (previously infected) after being cultivated and cropped, as above mentioned, they will remain free from nodule disease.

(5). That lambs, the progeny of ewes affected with nodule disease of the intestines, can be raised free from this disease, provided proper methods are adopted to prevent contamination, and,

(6). That, if an infected pasture is placed in cultivation for a time, to destroy the parasites on it; clean lambs raised, as suggested by the method adopted by us, or purchased and known to be clean, and all affected sheep disposed of for slaughter (this ailment being confined to the intestines mainly, and not rendering the flesh unsafe as an article of human food), the disease may eventually be eradicated from both the land and the flock.

(7). See also treatment for Stomach Worms.

Strongylus Ventricosus, Rud.—This species is found associated with Strongylus filicollis in the upper part of the small intestine. It is generally found in the fall of the year. It is very small and so far as known, of little consequence.

Strongylus Filicollis, Rud.—This is one of the very small worms affecting the intestine of lambs and sheep. Taken by itself it probably does little harm. It may be found in considerable numbers in the fall. It is so delicate that it would escape observation from the ordinary observer.

Dochmius Cernuus, Creplin.—This is a rather stout parasite of the small intestine and may be mistaken for the twisted stomach worm by those not accustomed to examining for parasites. It is fairly stout and is found attached to the mucous wall, as it feeds upon the blood. This worm is rarely found in large numbers, otherwise it might become a serious parasite. It probably causes more losses now than are attributed to it.

Hair Lung Worm (Strongylus Ovis Pulmonalis).—The hair lung worm is the smaller of the two varieties of worms affecting the lungs. It is the one that inhabits the smaller air cells and the disease caused by it is a pneumonia, as distinguished from the large lung worm affecting the bronchi and causing bronchitis or hacking cough.

This lung worm is so small that it escapes the attention of the flock master, and farmer. What he finds upon post-mortem is solidified lung as in pneumonia. The disease is generally referred to as pneumonia, and it is only when a competent observer is employed or that the history of a number of cases is presented, do we get a diagnosis of the parasitic character. The disease is of much more frequent occurrence than is at all suspected.

The complete life history of the worm remains to be determined. The young escape from the lungs during acts of coughing, but what becomes of them from that time until they are again found in the lung has not been determined. It is surmised that they undergo such changes as may be necessary on the pasture or in water and after a short time are again taken into another animal while grazing or with the drink. Whether they find an intermediate host in some insect or low form of animal life is not known. Some observers reasoning from analogy consider that such is a part of the life cycle. Other observers do not consider such to be a necessary part of the life cycle. The disease is only on certain pastures—pastures that have become infected through bringing in some diseased sheep. The disease spreads throughout a flock to greater extent on very wet years than in years of drought. A fairly low pasture used continuously throughout the season is also bad. Its ill effects are most marked upon old sheep.

This parasite penetrates the air passages to its most minute branching. It causes irritation and inflammation of the wall of the air passage and cells and a general breaking down of the tissue. As in all inflammatory processes nature attempts its arrest of extension by walling it off. Each worm then becomes the center of a slight inflammatory area that is walled off and resembles a tubercle. The contents of the inside are broken down and galatinous, outside the capsule is firm and fibrous. These tubercles are about a twentieth of an inch in diameter at first, but in the later stages becomes about an eighth of an inch in diameter. The parasite is always found in the central part surrounded by greenish or yellowish material, thin and pus-like, or may be dry and cheesy. They may become calcareous by lime deposition. These tubercles undergo quite a series of changes from that of a simple blood spot under the pleura to that of a hard grey nodule. When the worm matures it migrates to the bronchia to mate and lay eggs, and these hatch and the young being very active set up an inflammation. If it is severe we have the pneumonia that sickens or kills the sheep. The pneumonic

Virginia Deer in Park Near Saranac, N. Y. Dept. of Agr.

areas are small, limited to the point of parasitic involvement and resembles the ordinary catarrhal form. With the exudate numerous
worms and eggs are thrown off in the act of coughing. The fact
that the worms are present in every stage of development and tubercles show every condition from the hemorrhage to dry caseous
and calcareous infiltration indicates that multiplication may take
place in the lungs as well as from infection from without.

The diagnosis can not be made until the disease has progressed
to the point of producing pneumonia and a post-mortem is made.
The prognosis will depend upon the extent of parasitic invasion. No
medicinal treatment can be given that will secure the expulsion of
the worm.

As a preventive precaution, pastures where the disease has been
known to occur should be abandoned for at least a year. It is desirable that the sheep be pastured upon land that has been under continuous cultivation as that tends to destroy any parasites that may
be present.

THE THREAD LUNG WORM (STRONGYLUS FILARA, RUD).
This is the larger lung worm and is the one generally referred
to by most observers in reporting lung worm disease. It may be
seen on opening the trachea and bronchi and is identical with that
found in calves. Curtice regards this as of being of less frequent
occurrence than the hair worm and that it often occurs that the
lesions found due to the hair worm are erroneously ascribed to this
one.

The complete life cycle of this worm is not fully determined.
The eggs, or rather the embryos, are expelled by the act of coughing
and distributed upon the pasture, the feed, water trough and whatever may be near. How much time is necessary to be spent outside
the body and whether they must pass any part of their existence in
some lower animal is not known. How the parasite finds its way
into the lungs, too, after being taken into the mouth with the food
or water is not clearly demonstrated. The worm develops quite
rapidly in the bronchi and is found to affect principally lambs and
young sheep, thus differing from the hair lung worm. The symptoms of lung worm are those due to the irritation of the bronchial
tubes. The bronchitis differs in no respect from a bronchitis associated with a cold. There are accumulations of mucous, sometimes
of a bloody character, sometimes a cough and expulsion of this mucous. In some cases the cough is the prominent symptom and in
that way gets the name of hoose. With it may be difficulty in
breathing. The general health is impaired. The appetite may remain good, but what is eaten does not seem to do much good. The
wool becomes dry and harsh, without yolk, slips easily, the skin is
thin and tender giving the name of paper skin. There is paleness
of the mucous membranes of the eyes and lips. The animals are
thin and become exhausted easily either from exercise or exposure.
The course extends over a period of three or four months.

The disease is most noticeable in summer, fall and early winter,
begins to wane during the middle of winter and practically disap-

pears in the spring. A damp season favors the development of the worms. When the symptoms develop early there is little chance for recovery, but when they develop late, the chances of recovery are good. When recovery takes place the lamb will always remain dwarfed and there will be loss of flesh and fleece.

As in the case of the hair worm, where the disease develops on a pasture, the same should be abandoned for a year and in its stead fields used that have been in crops. The use of surface water should be avoided.

Medicinal treatment promises more in the case of this parasite than in that of the hair lung worm. These parasites lying free in the bronchial tube may be reached to a limited extent. Internal medicants that may be eliminated through the lungs, inhalation and intra-trachael medication have all been recommended. After reviewing considerable literature upon the subject, it appears that few remedies are better than turpentine. This may be given both internally and by inhalation. If given internally, about a dram may be administered with a little milk or oil to make an emulsion. If given as an inhalation, a couple of ounces may be placed on the surface of a bucket, or kettle of hot water and allowed to diffuse in a small, close stable. Or equally as good, a quantity poured on some hot bricks. Either method will require repetition. Good food and tonic will also be necessary to maintain the general body condition.

PLANT POISONING OF STOCK IN MONTANA.

Losses from poisonous plants are more extensive in the case of sheep than in the case of other stock, and the greater part of this account will be occupied with descriptions of the conditions which lead to such poisoning, the plants concerned, and the methods for preventing serious losses. Sheep raisers, as a rule, are so situated that a part of their grazing range lies on level plains, while another portion extends over foothills and mountains. It should be remembered that many of them control large tracts of country, and that, therefore, large portions of their ranges lie at a considerable distance from the home ranch. The sheep are managed in the way in which they will be able to find the best grazing conditions during the greater part of the year. Most sheep men put up a quantity of hay for the winter, but in ordinary seasons it is expected that the sheep will obtain their sustenance during nearly all the year from the native plants growing upon the ranges. In general, the different bands of sheep, especially the ewe bands, are kept near the home ranch during the winter season and until after the lambing and shearing seasons are past in the early summer—that is, until about the 10th of July. They are then driven away to the summer range, which may be on level plains, but usually lies on the foothills or mountains.

Sheep raisers have long understood the dangers from poisonous plants in the early spring on mountain ranges, and have also understood that it is comparatively safe to allow sheep to graze in such situations from July until October. In connection with this annual change of grazing ground, it is of interest to note that the feeding habits of sheep differ considerably under the different conditions. On the plains sheep eat preferably the short fine grass and avoid weeds, while on the mountain ranges they feed to a great extent upon the native plants other than grasses which grow in such situations. It is a fact, generally observed, that sheep do not take kindly to the tall mature grass which is found on mountain ranges in the month of July. The plants on mountain ranges, which furnish a great part of the forage for sheep, include five-finger, spiræa, golden-rod, wild sunflower, sand vetches, wild licorice, wild geranium, and lupines.

A number of the native plants which are known to be poisonous are so far advanced by the time the sheep are taken to the summer range that they are too coarse and unpalatable to be eaten by sheep. This is especially true of the purple larkspur and death camas, the latter being quite dry and shriveled by the middle of June. The water hemlock is not so common in the mountains as along the small streams of the plains, and in its mature stages is so coarse that it is seldom eaten by sheep. The tall larkspur does not ordinarily grow on the plains, and is too coarse for sheep forage during the season from July to September.

With regard to the mountain ranges of the State, especial mention should be made of the native species of lupines. These plants are apparently poisonous only when containing ripe seeds, and it was observed that sheep seldom eat this plant on the range during mid-summer. After the fall frosts the lupine pods open and the seeds fall out. In this condition it is often eaten in great quantities by sheep, especially after snowstorms, when other forage is covered up.

The effect of alkali upon stock and its possible action predisposing them toward eating poisonous plants is much discussed by stockmen, but not well understood. The belief is gradually gaining ground that sheep are kept in better condition by regular salting, and are less apt to develop a perverted appetite than when left without salt and allowed to seek for alkali as the only possible substitute. The most common forms of alkali found in Montana are sulphate of soda and Epsom salts. It would seem impossible for these substances to take the place of common salt in the physiology of domesticated animals. It must still remain doubtful whether any serious cases of poisoning are to be attributed to the continued eating of alkali or drinking of alkaline water, but in a few instances direct evidence was obtained that the appetite of the sheep was perverted by the use of alkalis, and that more extensive poisoning occurred from eating poisonous plants than in the case of sheep that were regularly salted.

CONDITIONS WHICH FAVOR POISONING.

In discussing the conditions under which poisoning occurs, attention should also be called to the methods of managing sheep which are at present in vogue. The most serious cases of poisoning observed have occurred while sheep were being driven from one point to another at a more rapid rate than would be assumed under normal feeding conditions. The practice of trailing sheep to market renders it necessary to urge sheep forward at a rate of from 6 to 10 miles per day. It is easy to understand that under such circumstances the sheep are forced to grab at any green thing within reach, and can not exercise the same choice of forage which they would if feeding at ease. The same conditions prevail in driving sheep from winter to summer range and often with disastrous consequences.

An obvious method for avoiding the danger from driving or trailing sheep too rapidly consists in detailing two herders with each band, so that one may travel in advance of the sheep and direct the band away from the poisonous areas. The herder in the rear of the band may cooperate with the herder ahead in preventing the sheep from becoming too closely crowded together.

The present practice of the sheep raisers on Western ranges is to keep sheep under the constant care of a herder, in bands of from 2,000 to 2,500. They understand the great differences in the skill with which bands of sheep are managed by different herders. If a band is frequently dogged and urged forward, the inevitable result is to crowd the sheep together and render it impossible for those which happen to be in the center of the band to feed. It is impossible to insist too strongly upon the desirability of interfering as little as possible with the sheep during feeding. All sheep raisers understand that it requires considerable time for a large band to become scattered out after having been rounded up by dogs or by their fright. The time necessary for such redistribution of the band is lost from the feeding time and the sheep become hungry and excited. Under such circumstances it is frequently observed that they are more apt to eat unwholesome plants than when given greater liberty in feeding.

The problem of stock losses from poisonous plants is affected also by the water supply on the range. On ranges where the only water supply in the dry season is found in alkaline lakes, it would seem desirable to build troughs into which spring water is piped. This would enable stock to obtain water more conveniently, and the water would be less alkaline than when allowed to flow into alkaline lakes and gradually become saturated with alkali by evaporation.

It has long been observed that poisoning is especially apt to occur after heavy rains. A number of explanations for this fact have been offered. It has been supposed that certain plants are more poisonous when wet with fresh rains or dew than when dry. The explanation which is most frequently suggested, however, is that after heavy rain-storms the roots of various plants are more easily pulled up than when dry, and it is well known that in the case of many poisonous plants the active principle is chiefly located in the roots. In the case of death camas, the writer attempted to determine the question whether the bulb could ever be pulled up by the stem, and found that under ordinary circumstances this could not be done. After an unusually heavy rainstorm, however, it was found that a considerable proportion of the bulbs could be drawn out of the soil by pulling upon the stem of the plant. This observation is of some importance in connection with the fact that the bulb of death camas is considerably more poisonous than the leaves or stem. Similar statements might be made concerning the larkspurs, loco weeds, and water hemlock. As sheep pull up the bulbs and eat them while grazing after a storm, increased mortality from poison plants results.

A number of serious cases of stock poisoning have occurred after snowstorms. In all cases which were investigated an explanation was found in the fact that other forms of vegetation were covered by the snow and that certain poisonous plants of coarse growth remained standing above the snow. In some of the mountainous basins the tall larkspur grows abundantly and stands at a height of about 2 feet by the 1st of June, when late spring snowstorms are apt to occur. Frequent cases of poisoning in cattle, from eating large quantities of the tall larkspur, have been observed under such conditions. It may be doubted whether this plant would be extensively eaten under any other conditions. An occasion was offered to investigate some extensive cases of poisoning in sheep during autumn, for which lupine was responsible. In these cases the conditions were the same as in that just discussed. Early fall snowstorms had covered other vegetation, and large quantities of the lupines were still standing. Ordinarily the lupines are not poisonous at this time of the year for the reason that the seeds have fallen off, but during some seasons the seeds are retained much longer than usual.

The feeding habits of sheep and other stock are greatly influenced by the full or empty condition of the stomach. It would seem desirable to adopt a general rule never to turn sheep in a starved or unusually hungry condition upon a range which is known to contain poisonous plants in abundance. It requires but a few moments' observation to satisfy one's self that a sheep does not exercise the same care in the choice of forage when very hungry that it does when feeding under ordinary circumstances. The disastrous consequences of neglecting this rule are most frequently experienced while sheep are being shipped long distances by railway. When the sheep are unloaded from the cars at intervals for feeding, they are ravenously hungry and usually unacquainted with the plants which grow at the place where they are unloaded. A number of very extensive cases of poisoning have been observed under such circumstances. In one case 1,000 sheep died from eating lupine in a ripe condition. The sheep came from another state and were unaccustomed to the character of the vegetation where they were feeding.

From observations made on the stock ranges of Montana, it is believed that it is impossible to conclude with certainty that sheep learn to avoid all poisonous plants by long acquaintance with a given range. In general, however, it may be said that on any particular range less extensive poisoning occurs among the sheep which are familiar with the range than among strange sheep. This statement may be accepted as true for all plants except loco. The eating of loco plants seems to be a pernicious habit, which spreads rather than decreases among the sheep which are acquainted with the range.

The actual condition of the vegetation in a given locality also exercises considerable influence upon the extent of poisoning which may occur. If certain poisonous plants start to grow in the early spring before the native grasses and offer a considerable amount of succulent material, sheep and other stock are naturally tempted to eat them, especially if it is difficult to obtain a sufficient quantity of grass. It sometimes happens that poisonous plants closely resemble grasses in general appearance. This is true of death camas before flowering, and since such plants grow mingled with grass it may be possible that they are unintentionally eaten along with the grass. During seasons of great drouth the native grasses mature earlier in the season than usual and soon become dry and unpalatable, while a number of other plants remain green and somewhat succulent for a longer period. This statement is especially true of certain leguminous plants, such as loco weeds and lupines. The loco habit is apt to become established in lambs during dry seasons. Lambs are more affected by drouth than the older sheep, and insist upon having some succulent forage. During dry seasons they may be able to find such forage only in loco weeds and other similar plants.

The stage of growth of the plant determines largely whether it will be eaten at a given time or not. For instance, larkspur and water hemlock become so coarse during their later stages that they are seldom, if ever eaten by sheep; and some plants, as the death camas and purple larkspur, turn yellow and shrivel up very soon after flowering, and in such condition they are not tempting and are seldom eaten.

So far as it has been possible to determine by observation, the taste and smell of poisonous plants have little, if any, influence in determining the extent to which they are eaten. It must, of course, remain entirely doubtful whether plants which have an exceedingly disagreeable taste for us affect stock in the same manner. The taste of larkspurs is disagreeable and even nauseous to man, but they are frequently eaten in large quantities by sheep, cattle, and other animals. The death camas possesses a bitter principle and the juice produces an irritation of the mouth cavity, which persists for an hour or more and causes increased salivation. It was impossible, however, to get any evidence that the bitter taste had any influence upon the frequency with which the plant is eaten by the stock. From a theoretical standpoint it might be plausible that the taste and odor of plants largely determine their use as food by stock, and further observations on this point may lead to some definite conclusions in the matter.

The problem just stated may be somewhat affected by observed variations in feeding habits of stock with reference to poisonous plants. It seems impossible to make any definite statements with regard to this matter, or even to predict from one year's observations what will be the feeding habits of sheep for another season. It is observed that during some seasons the purple larkspur is eaten in large quantities by sheep and other animals with serious consequences, while during other years the same sheep may walk over conspicuous areas of this plant without touching it. A striking variation is also observed in the feeding habits of a single band of sheep. One sheep may feed almost exclusively upon a certain plant which is scrupulously avoided by the others. The habits of sheep vary not only individually, but in the same band as a whole from season to season, and an equally striking variation is noted in the different parts of the State and in different States. An illustration of this variation may be of interest in this connection. The feeding habits of a band of sheep on a foot-hill range, at an altitude of 4,600 feet, were observed. Some of the sheep ate considerable quantities of wild sunflower, a few ate false lupine, some fed largely upon the wild geranium, while others grazed almost exclusively upon sand vetches. Two were seen eating the leaves of lupine, and about 50 ate a few specimens of death camas. The majority of the sheep in this band fed exclusively upon the native grasses. On one range a band of sheep was kept for two months during the spring of 1900 on a range which abounded in death camas without any cases of poisoning occurring. Another band on the same range passed over a conspicuous area of purple larkspur twice daily in going from and coming to the corral, and no evidence was to be obtained that they had touched this plant. The same band, however, on being moved to a locality where they found the death camas, became poisoned, and a number of them died. Nearly all of the band had been affected, showing that the plant was generally and greedily eaten. The arbitrariness of the appetite of sheep exercises a great influence on the occurence and extent of poisoning. Obviouly, poisonous plants do no harm until eaten, and the chief factor in determining the amount of poisoning which is likely to occur on a given range is the extent to which the plant will be eaten by the sheep. This factor can not be estimated with any certainty. It can not be determined by feeding experiments, since it is impossible to reproduce the natural conditions which prevail upon the range. It is manifestly unsafe to assume that an animal is fond of a certain plant because it is eaten in confinement when no other fodder is to be had.

REMEDIAL AND PREVENTIVE MEASURES.

A number of remedial and preventive measures may be suggested from observation and experience. Experiments have been tried on a small scale in various parts of the State in displacing poisonous plants upon the range by the use of aggressive forage plants, such as smooth brome grass and blue joint (*Agropyrum occidentale*). These grasses grow vigorously upon the ranges of the plains and mountains. Naturally the brome grass attains a much greater size and covers the ground more completely in moist than in dry situations. Judging from the present outlook in Montana, it will require several years for the brome grass to form a sod sufficiently thick to displace death camas, larkspur, or loco weeds. The brome grass starts early in the spring and is much sought for by sheep. A native species of brome grass (*Bromus marginatus*) is rapidly spreading in some parts of the State, especially near Augusta and in the Judith Basin, and in the former locality has killed out a few timothy meadows and entirely replaced the timothy. Although it can not be said that experiments have so far demonstrated the possibility of driving out poisonous plants by this method, the habit of starting early in the spring, which is characteristic of brome grass, is very useful, since desirable forage is thus afforded for the sheep at the season when poisonous plants are most often eaten.

It is highly desirable that herders should familiarize themselves with the appearance of the more important poisonous plants in all their stages. They will thus be enabled to recognize such plants at once, and to herd sheep and other stock away from the dangerous areas. A herder who is familiar with the appearance of poisonous plants should be more valuable to the sheep raiser, for the reason that he will be in a position to avoid many serious losses. The number of plants which are of great economic importance from their poisonous principles is not large, and many of them are already thoroughly known by the average herder. In some cases, however, great confusion prevails as to the names of plants, and this confusion can only be avoided by careful study of the characters of the plants. It would seem almost inexcusable to confound death camas and the wild onion, yet such has been the case for a number of years over a large portion of the State. In some localities lupines are known as loco weeds or larkspurs indifferently, and vice versa.

On some portions of the range where death camas grows very abundantly it will probably be found necessary to abandon certain areas during the spring months. Later in the season, as already indicated, the death camas dries up and offers no tempting forage to stock.

The possibility of eradicating a poisonous plant by digging manifestly depends almost entirely upon the extent of its distribution. In the case of the tall larkspur, which usually occurs in well-defined areas, the plant might be dug up at a moderate expenditure. The water hemlock also occurs in well-defined localities along streams and irrigation ditches, and might be exterminated in the same manner. Such plants as the loco weeds, death camas, and purple larkspur, however, grow in too great variety of situations and in too great quantity to be exterminated in this manner. Even cultivation of such areas can not be recommended, since ordinarily difficulty would be experienced in getting water upon the land in sufficient quantity to irrigate, and no cultivated crops could therefore be raised.

In the treatment of poisoned animals serious mistakes are often committed by herders and cowboys. It is frequently assumed that poisoned animals must be kept moving under all circumstances. This may possibly be beneficial in poisoning of a narcotic nature, where the animals become stupefied. In all cases, however, where unusual excitement is manifested, the animal should be left entirely to itself, without any additional cause of fright or excitement. The inevitable result of all unnecessary stimulation of animals which are poisoned upon the range is to exaggerate the effects of the poison and to hasten a fatal result. In general, therefore, it would seem advisable to allow animals to lie down or to move about at will, without any interference. The injurious effects of urging sheep forward, when suffering from larkspur poisoning, have already been described by the writer in Montana Experiment Station Bulletin No. 15. Sheep herders and cowboys have resorted at once to bleeding in all cases of poisoning of animals. Different places for bleeding, which are supposed to have more beneficial effects than any other are the root of the tail, the ear, the inside of the lips, or the roof of the mouth. Bleeding at one or the other of these places is claimed to be almost uniformly efficacious. With regard to this practice, it is obvious that it will have a good or bad effect according to the symptoms of the poisoned animals. If the poisonous plants which have been eaten have a depressant action upon the heart and circulation, the blood pressure would be further lowered by drawing blood, and the practice should not be indulged in. In a case of poisoning, where the chief symptoms are increased blood pressure, accompanied by cerebral excitement and a hard pulse, the bleeding might have a good effect.

Melted lard or fat pork is frequently administered in cases of plant poisoning, especially in "bloat." These substances have a laxative action which may help to eliminate the unabsorbed parts of the stomach contents. The lard may hinder the absorption of the poisonous substances by the formation of an oily coating on the wall of the stomach. Drenches of baking soda (bicarbonate of soda) are frequently given in cases of poisoning where an unusual amount of acid in the stomach is suspected. Soda often has a good effect in the case of bloat from eating large quantities of clover or alfalfa. Vinegar is another much used popular remedy for plant poisoning. It is administered when the stomach contents are believed to be strongly alkaline. One stockman stated that he had frequently administered both soda and vinegar at the same time with beneficial results. It would seem, however, that these substances would naturally neutralize one another in the stomach cavity.

During the season of 1900 the best success in the treatment of animals poisoned with noxious plants was obtained from the use of permanganate of potash. This substance is well known as an antiseptic in surgery, as well as for internal use. Its antiseptic action is due to its great oxidizing power. This substance was used in cases of poisoning for the purpose of destroying such portions of the poisonous alkaloids as still remained in the stomach. It was not supposed that permanganate of potash would exercise any noticeable effect as a physiological antidote of plant poisons; but it was believed, on the other hand, that the pronounced oxidizing power of potassium permanganate would destroy plant alkaloids which had not been absorbed from the stomach, and thus enable the animal to recover, provided a fatal dose of the poison had not already been absorbed. The permanganate of potash was administered in three different ways—as a drench, by allowing the animals to drink it, and as a direct injection through the walls of the stomach. No pronounced advantage was noted in favor of any method. The drenching would perhaps be preferred by stockmen generally as being more simple and convenient of application. The action of the potassium permanganate is perhaps a little more direct and prompt, if a solution is injected directly into the stomach by means of a syringe. This method, however, requires a little more time than drenching, and, although fairly safe in the hands of an intelligent stockman, is not so simple as drenching.

In all experiments a solution was used containing equal weights of potassium permanganate and sulphate of aluminum. The latter substance was added for the purpose of counteracting any alkaline reaction of the water which might be used in making the solution, and for increasing the oxidizing action of the potassium permanganate. From our experiments it seems desirable to recommend that from 5 to 10 grains of each of these compounds be dissolved in water together and given as a drench to adult sheep. A smaller quantity may be given to young lambs. Hogs will take the same dose as sheep, horses from 15 to 20 grains, and cattle from 30 to 50. In dissolving these substances a quantity of water should be taken, which is most convenient for drenching purposes, usually about a pint, but a quart or even more may be taken. In cases where a large number of animals are poisoned at once, it will be found desirable to prepare a large quantity of the solution, containing a thousand or more doses, dissolved in water in such proportions that a convenient quantity of the water, say 1 pint, will contain the desired amount of the potassium permanganate. This substance forms slightly explosive compounds when mixed with sirup or similar organic substances; otherwise no especial precaution is to be observed in its use. When administered to animals it should all be in solution, since the pure salt would irritate the mouth cavity. It will be found to dissolve much more rapidly and surely when pulverized before mixing with water.

The sheep is easily managed, and no method of administering remedies offers any noteworthy difficulties. Convenience and rapidity of application are the chief factors in determining what method shall be adopted. When a thousand or more sheep are poisoned simultaneously, no remedy is practicable which requires any great length of time for its application. Drenching is, perhaps, the most rapid method for this purpose, and long-necked bottles or regular drenching bottles may be used. In drenching, the sheep should be set upright, and care should be exercised that the solution is not wasted. With a little experience the drench may be given rapidly with no danger to the sheep. In cases of poisoning, where the throat is paralyzed and the animal unable to swallow, drenching will be found dangerous or impossible. In such cases the solution may be injected directly into the stomach by means of a large syringe and trochar and canula. The point for inserting the canula should be the same as that which is adopted for paunching in cases of bloat.

BLOATING AND ITS REMEDY.

Stockmen are usually acquainted with the serious or fatal consequences of bloating in cattle and sheep. The plants which most frequently cause bloat are alfalfa and various clovers, but ordinarily only when eaten in a green condition. A few cases are reported, however, from eating alfalfa or clover hay. It is usually asserted by stockmen that the liability of bloating is greater when the alfalfa or clover is moist with rain or dew or after a slight frost. The danger of bloat is certainly much greater in animals which are unaccustomed to this

kind of forage, and gradually disappears after feeding upon green
alfalfa or clover for a long time. A number of cattle and sheep die
every year from this trouble, which becomes quite serious at times.
The remedies in most common use by sheep herders and cowboys for
preventing the fatal effects of bloating are doses of lard and paunching. The usual instrument for making the incision is a long knife
with a blade an inch or more in width. The gases which are formed
in the stomach are thus allowed to escape and the pressure upon the
internal organs is relieved. Many stockmen prefer to use a trochar
and canula, which are especially designed for such cases and are for
sale by dealers in veterinary instruments. The chief advantage in
this instrument is that it is much smaller than the knife and the incision heals more readily, without liability of complications. In in-
cipient bloat the administration of large doses of soda in connection
with cathartics may render this operation unnecessary. Where the
stomach becomes so extended that the animal can not walk, it becomes
necessary to puncture in order to prevent fatal consequences. The
gas pressure within the first stomach may in some cases become so
great as to interfere with respiration and the action of the heart, or
even to rupture the stomach wall and diaphragm. The proper place
for making the incision may be described as being the point upon the
left side of the body equally distant from the last rib, the angle of
the hip bone, and the border of the lumbar vertebræ. At this point
the wall of the stomach and the body wall are in close proximity,
which renders the operation simple and effective.

MOST IMPORTANT POISONOUS PLANTS OF MONTANA.

Death Camas (Zygadenus Venenosus).—This is a smooth,
simple-stemmed perennial, with an onion-like bulb, narrow linear
leaves, and a short terminal cluster of greenish yellow flowers. The
plant abounds everywhere in Montana in moderately moist places in
open ranges. It is frequently called in the State by the misleading
name of wild onion.

The death camas is undoubtedly the most important poisonous
plant in the early spring in Montana. It is found in every county of
the State and on every stock range which the writer visited. It occurs
in great abundance in the localities where it is found, and starts growing very early in the spring, even somewhat in advance of the native
grasses. The leaves of the plant are narrow and resemble grass
leaves, being at the same time somewhat thicker and more succulent
than grass. These facts combine to make the death camas a dangerous enemy to stock. The preferred location in which this plant grows
is the low, shallow coulee, or ravine. It does not grow in the driest
situations on the level plain nor in swampy localities. In Montana, it
grows at altitudes varying from 1,900 to 8,000 feet, or in all altitudes
at which sheep are grazed. A sheep may, in the course of a short
time, eat a sufficient number of death camas plants to cause death. In
collecting the material for feeding experiments, the writer dug up 250
death camas plants in the course of a half hour, and it may be possible for a sheep to collect them even more rapidly where the plant
grows abundantly. It is impossible to state definitely whether the

aerial parts of the plant or the bulbs cause the most poisoning. Feeding experiments showed conclusively that both the leaves and the bulbs are poisonous, but the bulbs could not be obtained by sheep or other animals except after heavy rainstorms, when the ground was thoroughly softened. During the season of 1900, sheep died from eating this plant at various dates in the months of May and June. The earliest date at which sheep were poisoned by this plant was 'April 25.'

A great variation in the death rate was observed in different bands of sheep, and depended apparently upon the amount of poison which they had received. The death rate varied from 5 to 48 per cent in different bands.

From experiments it would appear that the fatal dose of death camas for sheep is between one-half and 1 pound.

The remedies which were tried in the cases of death camas poisoning included hypodermic injections of strychnine in one-twentieth, one-tenth, and one-fifth grain doses, hypodermic injections of atropine in one-sixtieth and one-thirtieth grain doses, and solutions of potassium permanganate made as previously described. The potassium permanganate was given in 4-grain doses as a drench and by means of direct injection through the body wall into the stomach. In a few cases the sheep were allowed to drink the solution.

The symptoms of poisoning from death camas as observed in a large number of cases were rather uniform, and the following description should enable any sheep raiser to recognize them. A certain uneasiness and irregularity in the movements of the sheep are the first signs of poison. These irregularities become more pronounced and are accompanied by spasms and rapid breathing. Sheep become excited under the influence of the poison, but do not exhibit the condition of frenzy. It was observed that ewes were able to recognize their lambs until within a few minutes before death. The later symptoms are those of complete muscular paralysis, combined with a rapid, shallow breathing and a frequent, weak pulse. The duration of the different symptoms varies according to the amount of the plant which the sheep has eaten. When large quantities are eaten the symptoms succeed one another rapidly, the spasms and labored breathing are very noticeable, and death results in from one to three hours. In other cases like those already described the sheep remain in a condition of complete paralysis for a period of twenty-four to forty-eight hours. In such cases the breathing was so shallow as to be scarcely perceivable. A small percentage of sheep recover after being in this condition for a few hours but very few ever recover after being paralyzed for twenty-four hours. Postmortem examinations made on 40 sheep which had died from eating death camas showed the lungs in all instances to be filled with blood. There were no changes in the brain and no marked congestion, except in a few cases of long duration. In adult sheep the effect upon the digestive organs was not marked. There was also an increased amount of saliva and regurgitation through the mouth and nostrils. In lambs these symptoms were present with the addition of pronounced digestive disturbances.

A majority of sheep which were poisoned from death camas, as is the case with other poisonous plants, were yearlings and 2-year-olds. It is possible that more fixed and settled habits of feeding are formed as the animals grow older. There was no indication that ewes with lambs at their side were any more apt to eat death camas than were dry sheep.

It is frequently observed in the study of stock poisoning that a great variation prevails in the time when the first symptoms of poisoning develop. The only explanation for this fact which suggests itself is to be found in the anatomy of ruminants. In one case it may happen that the poisonous substances pass into the fourth stomach and are thus absorbed at once, while in another case poisonous plants may remain in the first stomach, or rumen, with a mass of other forage material and are not absorbed until after some hours. Obviously, a poisonous plant has no effect upon domestic animals until absorption takes place, and the variation of time at which the symptoms are manifested may perhaps be explained by the facts to which attention has just been called.

The evidence establishing the poisonous nature of death camas from observation and with experiments is quite conclusive. Death camas was found to be present in abundance in localities where poisoning occurred. It was found upon examination of the range that this plant had been eaten extensively. Death camas was found in large quantities in the stomachs of sheep which died under such circumstances. Sheep which were seen eating the plant when feeding at leisure upon the range showed within a few hours the symptoms of poisoning as previously described. Besides this evidence obtained under natural conditions, experimental proof was secured by collecting death camas and feeding it to sheep. During extended trips over different parts of the State many localities were examined where it was stated that poisoning uniformly occurred if sheep were allowed to range there during the early spring. Death camas was found to be the only suspected plant which grew in abundance in all such localities.

Tall Larkspur (Delphinium glaucum).—This is the common tall larkspur of Montana, often erroneously called aconite. It is a simple-stemmed perennial, 3 to 6 feet in height, smooth throughout, and covered during its earlier stages with a whitish coating. The basal leaves are long stemmed and form tufts which attain the height of a foot or more by the 1st of June. These lower leaves resemble those of the wild geranium, being circular in outline and divided into a number of broad segments. The upper-stem leaves become gradually narrower with narrowing lance-like segments. The flowers are numerous, pale blue, and in a long terminal raceme. The tall larkspur is most likely to be mistaken for the wild geranium during its younger stages before flowering. After flowering the two species are readily distinguished. A little experience, however, during which special attention is devoted to the leaf characters of the two plants, will enable anyone to note the differences, even at a considerable distance. The leaves of the geranium are always somewhat hairy, while those of the larkspur are smooth.

The preferred habitat of the tall larkspur is in moderately moist shaded localities, especially on foothills and along the mountain sides. It occurs in valleys and up to an altitude of 9,000 feet. At the higher altitudes flowers are often darker blue in color and the height of the plant is somewhat less.

Attention has already been called to the possibility of eradicating poisonous plants by digging. This method is especially applicable to the tall larkspur. To illustrate this point, it may be well to describe briefly the conditions in the lower Gallatin Basin, where cattle have been allowed to graze every season for a number of years. A few animals are poisoned every year by eating the tall larkspur. In 1898 the loss amounted to 40 cattle, while ordinarily the losses are much smaller. In this basin the larkspur is almost entirely confined to a few areas of small size. It is believed that a month's work for one man with a weed digger, designed for cutting off the roots at a short distance below the ground, would exterminate the plant. The expense of this labor would not exceed the value of two cattle, and this number is less than the average annual loss from the tall larkspur on this range. Similar conditions were noted in the vicinity of Deerlodge, Red Lodge, and Bigtimber.

All cases of poisoning from this plant observed in Montana during the season of 1900, as well as in previous years, have been among cattle. Apparently it is not eaten by sheep, partly for the reason that the plant is too coarse by the time the sheep are driven to the summer range. Stockmen occasionally claim that horses and cattle may eat the plant in considerable quantities with impunity, and the observations already made on the tall larkspur indicate a considerable variation in its poisonous properties at different stages of growth. Apparently the plant is uniformly dangerous or fatal when eaten in large quantities in its earlier stages and up to the time of flowering. The root system of the tall larkspur is extensive and the roots are probably never eaten by stock.

The only remedy with which experiments have been made by the writer in treating stock poisoned by this plant is potassium permanganate as a drench. This substance, combined with sulphate of aluminum, was given in doses of 25 grains to 4 cattle, and all of these animals recovered. The remedy was given during the first stages of poisoning and before it was possible to determine whether or not the cattle had eaten a fatal quantity of the larkspur. However, 3 of the cattle, which were poisoned at the same time and were not treated, died within about 6 hours after the first appearance of the symptoms.

The symptoms of poisoning by this plant generally are the same as from an overdose of aconite. There is a more or less pronounced stiffness, accompanied by straddling and irregularity in gait. These symptoms increase in severity until locomotion becomes impossible and the animal falls to the ground. If subsequently excited, the animals may suffer from severe muscular spasms. The special senses are seldom affected, and slightly increased salivation is noted in some cases, though the symptom is never so marked as in poisoning from death camas. The animal is finally attacked with violent convulsions, in which it dies. In this respect, also, the symptoms differ from those of death camas poisoning, which latter are generally quite without spasms. The digestive functions are not noticeably affected by larkspur poisoning. The temperature may be slightly lowered at first, and during the later stages the pulse and breathing become rapid.

Observations thus far made indicate the advisability of administering potassium permanganate and sulphate of aluminum at once, as recommended for death camas poisoning. For counteracting the physiological effects of larkspur, atropine in hypodermic doses of one-half to 1 grain for cattle and horses will give good results. Alcohol and other stimulants may be administered.

The most effective preventive measure consists in determining the exact distribution of this plant upon the range and herding stock away from the dangerous areas during the spring and early summer.

Purple Larkspur (Delphinium bicolor).—This plant is a slightly hairy, tuberous-rooted perennial, 1 to 2 feet in height, with a cluster of divided, long-stemmed root leaves, and dark purple flowers, which appear from May to August, according to the altitude. The purple larkspur is common throughout Montana on moderately moist foothills and mountain ranges at all elevations up to 10,500 feet. Its distribution is much more general and extensive than that of the tall larkspur. In the majority of localities where it grows, it would seem, therefore, impossible to exterminate it by digging or other practicable methods. The purple larkspur often occurs abundantly together with death camas, and its habitat in general seems to be practically the same as death camas. Neither the purple larkspur nor the death camas grows abundantly in localities which are far removed from foothills and mountains. The first green leaves appear during the latter part of April and the earliest flowers are observable about the first of May. A great variety of opinion prevails with respect to the poisonous character of this plant, some stockmen claiming that it is uniformly poisonous and others believing that it may at times be eaten with impunity. The evidence obtained by the writer as a basis for Bulletin 15 of the Montana Station, is believed to be conclusive in proving that the plant is poisonous for sheep in its early stages. The plant was called *Delphinium menziesii,* but recent systematic work on larkspurs indicated that this species is *D. bicolor.* Former experiments by Dr. S. B. Nelson, of the Washington Station, indicated that the true *D. menziesii* in the flowering stage was not poisonous. The apparent discrepancy of results is perhaps explained by the difference in species and the difference in stage of growth of the plant with which experiments were made.

During some seasons the purple larkspur causes extensive losses of sheep and calves in Montana. Cattle and horses eat it less frequently. As already noted, a great variation exists in the appetite of animals with regard to poisonous plants, and it is noteworthy that in the season of 1900 the purple larkspur was eaten very sparingly.

Conclusive evidence against the plant was obtained only in one locality, and this among calves in the Flathead Valley. The symptoms of poisoning in these two cases were similar to those already outlined for poisoning by the tall larkspur in cattle, with the exception of a slight bloating observed in the calves. Respiration and pulse were very rapid, the body temperature was slightly lowered, and a profuse sweating was observed. Death occurred about four hours after the appearance of the first symptoms. In general, the symptoms of poisoning from purple larkspur closely resemble those produced by tall larkspur, and are distinguished from those of death camas by the absence of any regurgitation, which is characteristic of death camas poisoning, and by the presence of violent spasms, which are usually absent in poisoning from death camas.

In treating animals poisoned by this plant it is recommended that the same remedies be applied which were suggested in poisoning by the tall larkspur. In the writer's previous experience with this plant, atropine was found to be effective in counteracting the depressant action of the larkspur.

Western Water Hemlock (Cicuta occidentalis).—This species is a smooth perennial, 2 to 5 feet high, with 3 to 10 elongated fleshy roots clustered at the base of an ascending axis 3 to 5 inches long, with twice decompound leaves and narrow serrate leaflets 2 or 3 inches in length, and flat-topped clusters with greenish white flowers. This plant is commonly known in Montana as wild parsnip, although a number of other plants have also received the same name in the State. It is generally distributed along the banks of streams, irrigation ditches, and marshy localities in the vicinity of ponds. The common name wild parsnip has apparently given rise to a mistaken notion that this plant is identical with the common parsnip of the garden, having established itself outside of cultivation. The two plants should be readily distinguished, the flowers of the garden parnsip being yellow, while those of water hemlock are white; the latter is also a much slenderer and less leafy plant than the former.

During the season of 1900 conclusive evidence was obtained that 36 cattle were poisoned from eating this plant, and of these 30 died. About 105 sheep were poisoned by it during the same year, 80 of which died. The mortality was, therefore, quite high, being 76 per cent for sheep and 87 per cent with cattle. The roots of this plant are occasionally eaten by man, usually with fatal results. During the season of 1900, in Montana, there were 5 cases of poisoning of human beings from eating this plant, resulting in 4 deaths.

The water hemlock, as already indicated, grows in wet places, and, except where grasses have formed a tough sod, the roots may be easily pulled up by the stem. It was not determined to what extent the roots are eaten by stock when pulled up in connection with the stem. In the case of sheep poisoning it was observed that the roots had been eaten and they were found in the stomach of the sheep. In other cases an examination of the place where the poisoning had occurred showed that some of the plants had been pulled with the roots attached and the latter left lying on the ground or that the

SHOWER BATHS FOR CATTLE. DEPT. OF AGR.

CLASS IN LIVE STOCK, STUDYING SHEEP ON A FARM NEAR WATERFORD, PENN. YEAR BOOK, 1905.

plants had been eaten off without disturbing the roots. Observations in the field, which were confirmed by laboratory experiments, showed that during the early stages of growth the leaves and stems of the water hemlock, including the basal portion, contain sufficient poison to produce death. The roots are generally known to contain a virulent poison.

The remedies which were tried in cases of poisoning by water hemlock include morphine and chloral hydrate, combined in a few cases with emptying of the stomach by means of paunching and the use of cathartics. Potassium permanganate was not tried in any case, for the reason that the violent physiological effects of the poison were already manifested and it seemed necessary to counteract these symptoms. Morphine in one-fourth grain doses was given hypodermically to 2 sheep at intervals of five minutes. No decided effects of the morphine were noted until after the third dose, when the sheep became calmer. After receiving five doses both sheep lay down in an apparently stupefied condition, in which they remained for several hours. These sheep recovered after showing the effects of the poison for four or five days. An experiment was tried with chloral hydrate, during which 1 sheep was given one-half ounce in three equal doses at intervals of ten minutes. The effect of this substance was not so immediate, but seemed to be otherwise very similar to that of morphine. The sheep passed into a stupor from which it emerged after two hours. No further violent symptoms were manifested, but the animal did not recover its appetite, and finally died after three days. In another case where 10 cows were poisoned with water hemlock one cow was seen when the first symptoms of poisoning began to appear. The stomach was at once opened at the point where the ordinary operation of "paunching" is performed and the stomach contents removed. Melted lard and an enema of lukewarm water were administered without the addition of direct antidotes. The animal recovered after about two days without further care.

Water hemlock is an especially dangerous plant, since the symptoms of poisoning are so violent and are manifested so quickly. It is apparent that where several hundred animals are poisoned simultaneously and may die, as sometimes occurs, within fifteen minutes, great difficulty is experienced in administering even the simplest treatment to each animal.

The symptoms of poisoning from this plant are signs of acute pain with attempts to run away in any direction in which the animal happens to get started. Cerebral frenzy, accompanied with muscular spasms, are striking features. Respiration is labored and irregular, and the pulse hard and intermittent. Any attempt to manipulate the animal always results in increasing the mental excitement and the violence of the convulsions. In some cases of actual poisoning by this plant animals died within fifteen minutes after the first symptoms appeared. In other cases, both of young sheep and cattle, the animals lived from two to three hours, finally dying in violent spasms.

If the characteristic symptoms of poisoning from this plant have already appeared, chloral hydrate or morphine should be administered at once. If it is believed that a considerable quantity of the plant still remains in the stomach unabsorbed, a drench of potassium permanganate should be administered in order to destroy its poisonous property. A few cases are reported where this plant seemed to cause poisoning in hay. In general, it is advisable to remove specimens of water hemlock from hay before feeding. Since this plant ordinarily has a limited distribution in any locality, it might easily be eradicated by digging, especially along streams and ponds where sheep and other animals are driven for water.

White Loco Weed (Aragallus spicatus).—This is an erect tufted perennial, 4 to 18 inches high, with pinnately divided leaves and spikes of white or cream-colored flowers, shaped like those of the pea. The pod is one-celled, and when shaken produces a rattling sound, which gives the plant the name of rattle weed in some localities. The white loco weed is exceedingly common throughout Montana. It occurs most abundantly on the northern slopes of foothills up to an altitude of about 8,000 feet. Its preferred habitat is for the most part in rather dry situations. The habit of the plant varies in different parts of the State. In some localities the flowers are pure white, while in others they are decidedly yellow.

The loco problem has been an important factor with stock raisers for a number of years. In different parts of the country different plants are considered the chief offenders. In Colorado the plant which is most ordinarily known as loco weed is *Astragalus mollissimus,* while in Montana the species already named is perhaps most important; but there are others which have a rather wide distribution and are known to produce the same effects. Among these may be mentioned *A. splendens, A. lagopus,* and *A. besseyi.*

It is a common belief among a number of stockmen that the eating of large quantities of alkali may produce a locoed condition. There is no other evidence, however, for this belief, and there is considerable evidence to disprove it. On one stock range which was visited in the season of 1900, the loco disease had prevailed for a number of years, and the first cases were observed in sheep which were grazing upon a mountain range where no alkali was to be found in the soil or water. The white loco weed, however, grew in abundance, and sheep ate it in large quantities. After removing this band of sheep to a location on the plains where all the water was strongly alkaline and where the loco weed grew quite sparingly, a great improvement was noted in the sheep. The belief is gaining ground among the more intelligent stockmen that the failure to salt the sheep regularly may in many instances be the cause of sheep developing a perverted appetite, which is manifested by eating loco weeds to the exclusion of other more suitable forage.

The losses caused from the loco disease are very heavy in nearly all the Rocky Mountain States. The locoed condition is so commonly observed among sheep and horses that cases are not reported, and it is practically impossible to learn the exact extent of the disease. In the Judith Basin one prominent stockman was nearly ruined financially by the prevalence for a number of years of the loco habit among his sheep. In another instance the raising of horses was abandoned over a large tract of country on account of the loco weeds. During the season of 1900 about 650 locoed sheep and 150 locoed horses were seen during the writer's field work. The locoed horses were all in one herd, and of the 650 sheep, 500 were in one band and 150 in another. These numbers represent not more than one-fourth of the actual cases. A few locoed sheep and horses were to be seen on nearly every stock range.

The loco disease occurs under two forms—an acute and a chronic. An acute case of loco disease was observed in a 2-year-old ewe with a lamb at her side. The ewe was observed eating large quantities of white loco weed on May 22, 1900. During the afternoon of the same day she became unmanageable, and the lamb was badly affected. An examination of the ewe at this time showed that she was completely blind and was affected with dizziness. She walked around in long circles to the right, and after a short period remained standing for a few moments in a sort of stupor. At the beginning of each attack the head was elevated and drawn to the right; eyelids, lips, and jaws were moved rapidly. Each attack lasted from one to two minutes, and the intervals between the attacks lasted about five minutes. The second day the attacks became more severe and of longer duration, the head being turned more decidedly to the right and the animal sometimes falling upon the ground. Similar symptoms, accompanied by digestive disturbances, were manifested by the lamb during the second day, and it died during the afternoon. On the morning of the third day it was found that the ewe was pushing against the corral, and had apparently been in that position during the greater portion of the night. The animal then began to whirl around to the right. Later she became unable to stand, and the spasmodic movements were largely confined to the legs. On the morning of the fourth day she died. The pupil of the eye was at no time dilated, and the expression was nearly normal. The pulse was at first very irregular, but on the second day became again regular and of normal frequency. The only remedy which was tried was frequent injections of one-quarter grain doses of morphine, but this was without effect. Two other ewes ate smaller quantities of loco weed at the same time and were similarly affected, but less severely. In these cases morphine was tried with better success. The lambs, however, died from the poisonous properties contained in the milk of the mother.

The general symptoms of loco disease are quite familiar to all stock raisers. Perhaps the most characteristic are those of cerebral origin, and are shown in peculiarities of gait and action, which may be compared to a drunken condition. The brain disturbances may consist in impairment of the special senses or in irregular motor impulses, which produce incoherent muscular action. In some cases the animal becomes blind. More frequently the animal makes errors in judgment of the size and distance of objects. These visual disturbances are often quite ludicrous. The animal often takes flight apparently at imaginary objects, or at objects which under ordinary circumstances would cause no alarm. Locoed horses are somewhat dangerous for driving purposes on account of their tendency to run away. Such horses are frequently attacked with kicking fits without any apparent cause. The sense of hearing is often affected, and the response to sounds is irregular and out of proportion to the volume and character of the sound. Irregularities in muscular movements of sheep may assume a variety of forms. The animal may simply carry its head in an extended or otherwise unnatural position. In some cases the back is arched. Trembling is a characteristic symptom. In locoed horses a great difficulty is sometimes experienced in persuading them to go backward. Locoed sheep are exceedingly difficult to manage. The different members of the band may suddenly take a notion to run away in different directions, with the result that it is almost impossible for the herder to prevent their becoming separated. In cattle the disease appears to be rare, although symptoms, so far as observed, are essentially the same as those in sheep and horses. Occasionally locoed cattle manifest dangerous symptoms, and attack men and other animals. The belief is quite general among sheep raisers that one of the effects of eating loco weeds is an elongation and loosening of the teeth. This symptom is ordinarily mentioned as characteristic of the locoed condition. Dr. M. E. Knowles, State veterinarian of Montana, suggested that this was merely the natural process of shedding the teeth, which occurs in sheep at about the age of eighteen months. It hardly seems possible that the loco habit would cause such a peculiar phenomenon.

In chronic cases of loco the animal gradually becomes more emaciated and crazy. In sheep the fleece may be shed in patches or as a whole. The animal becomes unable to care for itself, and is apt to fall into the water while attempting to drink. Fits of trembling are of frequent occurrence, and the animal finally dies of inadequate nutrition and total exhaustion. In chronic cases of loco disease in horses the animal is usually left to its own resources on the range. During the later stages it may remain for weeks at a time upon a small area of ground without taking water. The writer had the opportunity of observing a number of such cases in horses that were almost unable to walk. Under such circumstances the animals seldom or never lie down. One horse which was seen remained for a period of two weeks, in 1897, upon a piece of ground about 150 feet square. During this time the horse had no water.

Numerous autopsies on locoed sheep and horses revealed conditions which, though fairly uniform, do not constitute a well-defined series. A slight congestion of the brain membranes was observed in all cases. The lungs and heart were in normal condition. Fatty tissue was considerably reduced in quantity, and the muscles were paler in color than under normal conditions.

The most serious mistake in connection with loco disease is made in allowing locoed sheep to remain with the rest of the band. The loco habit is apparently learned by imitation of locoed animals, and so long as locoed sheep are allowed to remain with other sheep the loco habit rapidly spreads. On one sheep range the writer found 500 locoed sheep in one band. The owner of this band stated that the number of locoed sheep in the band was constantly increasing, and that at the same time the worst cases were dying from time to time. The habit of eating loco weeds had prevailed on this range for two years, and during the winter of 1899 the owner had lost 700 sheep from loco disease. Another band of sheep belonging to a neighboring sheepman accidentally came in contact with this band during the spring of 1900. In the early part of May the herder of this second band reported two or three cases of locoed sheep in his band. On June 25, when this band of sheep was brought to the shearing shed, the number of locoed sheep was found to be increased to 150. In another part of the State an experienced sheep raiser, after being nearly ruined financially through the loco disease, adopted the method of immediate isolation and the feeding of locoed sheep for mutton. His stock was replaced with sheep that were free from the loco habit, and the trouble has been entirely eradicated from his range.

No specific remedy for the loco disease has been discovered, and in the nature of the case no such remedy is likely to be found. In the present state of knowledge concerning the subject the only rational treatment to be recommended is that of confinement and feeding with a nutritious diet. By separating the locoed sheep at once from other sheep the spreading of the habit will be prevented, and the locoed animals may be fattened and thus prevented from becoming a total loss. A sheep raiser of the Yellowstone Valley in the fall of 1899 discovered 1,200 cases of loco disease among his sheep. These 1,200 were immediately separated from other sheep and put together in the feeding corral along with 1,000 other locoed sheep which were bought from other sheep men. These 2,200 locoed sheep were fed upon alfalfa and roots for a period of two months. At the expiration of this time all the sheep, with the exception of about 50, had apparently made a complete recovery from the loco disease, and were in a good condition for market. Nearly all of the 50 remaining were separated from the band on account of being cripples. Although locoed animals may readily be fattened and sold for mutton, their recovery from the loco habit is apparent only, and is due to their inability to obtain the loco weed. Such animals when allowed to run upon the range again almost invariably return to their old habit of eating loco weed. Animals which have once been locoed are, therefore, unsuitable for stocking the range.

In combating the loco disease the most rational methods include salting of the sheep regularly, the immediate removal of locoed sheep from the band, confining them in a corral, and feeding them upon a nutritious diet. They may thus be fed for market and their pernicious habit will not spread to other sheep. In the case of locoed horses, an apparent recovery takes place if they are confined in a stable and fed on ordinary cultivated forage or allowed to run in pastures where no loco weeds are found. Such horses are always somewhat dangerous and more apt to run away or become unmanageable than horses which have not become affected with this disease.

Lupines (Lupinus leucophyllus L. sericeus, L. Cyaneus).—These plants are commonly known by the names blue pea, blue bean, and wild bean. They are coarse, silky haired perennial herbs, with blue flowers arranged in conspicuous terminal racemes, which blossom in June and July, with long-stemmed leaves which are divided into from 7 to 11 leaflets radiating from a common point. The fruit is a hairy, several-seeded pod, and the seeds are small and somewhat flattened. The three species above mentioned are very similar in general appearance and can only be distinguished by the systematic botanist.

Lupines are generally distributed throughout Montana, and should be readily distinguishable from all native plants on account of the character of the leaves and flower clusters. As a rule these plants do not occur in the flat river bottoms. They occur most abundantly on the foothills and mountain ranges at moderate elevations. In many parts of the State lupines are so abundant in such locations as to cover the ground completely over large areas. In such cases the lupines may be cut for hay, and several thousand tons of such hay are annually cut in Montana.

During the season of 1900 the lupines began to bloom about May 20, and the first full pods were collected on June 5. Lupines are not very extensively eaten by sheep during the spring and summer, except when they are unusually hungry or are being driven from one range to another. Lupines are more often eaten by sheep in summer on the mountain sides and in the fall and early winter after early frosts have opened the pods and the seeds have fallen out. Lupine hay is greedily eaten by all kinds of stock during the winter, and large quantities of this hay have been fed for the past fifteen or twenty years. Lupine hay is cut by different stockmen at different seasons. Where considerable dependence is put upon wild hay, the time of haying depends upon the press of other business. It therefore happens that lupine hay is cut in different years at dates ranging from the first of July to the middle of September. When cut during the first half of July, the newly ripe pods, full of seeds, are secured in the hay. When, however, the harvesting of lupine hay is postponed until September, the pods become ripe and split open, and the majority of seeds fall out. A striking variation in the quantity of pods containing seeds is noted during different years. During seasons in which May and June are wet, the quantity of pods is usually large. When, however, these months are dry, only a few pods are found on each plant and a vast majority of the flowers fail to be fertilized.

The writer has frequently observed that sheep are especially fond of the pods of various leguminous plants before they become mature and while they are still in a succulent condition. In some parts of Montana it was noticed that sheep fed extensively on the pods of lupines and other legumes.

The first case of poisoning from lupines which was brought to the attention of the writer occurred in August, 1896. A band of sheep while being driven from one range to another, in a hungry condition, was allowed to feed upon an area of lupines in a nearly ripe condition. Within two hours the sheep manifested violent symptoms of poisoning, and ultimately 100 out of the band of 200 died. In the winter of 1897 a band of 150 bucks, after having been fed during the winter on cultivated hay, were given a liberal quantity of lupine hay during the afternoon. About three hours after feeding, symptoms of poisoning developed. The sheep were found to be in a frenzied condition, and 90 of them died during the night.

In August, 1898, a horse came under the observation of the writer two hours after having eaten a liberal quantity of lupine hay. The animal showed the usual symptoms of lupine poisoning, but recovered after a period of about three days. In the winter of 1897, three 2-year-old colts were fatally poisoned by feeding with lupine hay. The animals died on the second day after feeding.

During October, 1898, about 2,000 sheep died in various parts of Montana as a result of eating lupine upon the range. During this season the seeds, contrary to the usual occurrence, had been retained until after heavy frosts. An examination of the stomach contents of the poisoned sheep showed that in all cases lupine was almost the only food material. Stems, leaves, and pods of this plant were identified in the stomachs, and the abundance of pods and seeds was especially striking. During the winter of 1898-99 more than 3,600 sheep died from eating lupine hay in Montana. This number of deaths occurred among 7,000 sheep which were affected. The death rate was therefore about 50 per cent. In these cases the lupine had been cut at a much earlier date than usual, and at a period when the pods were full of nearly ripe seeds. The most extensive losses of sheep from feeding lupine hay occurred in the Judith Basin. At one ranch on Sage Creek 2 tons of lupine hay was fed to a band of 2,000 sheep, with the result that 700 died within a period of forty-eight hours. In order to determine the cause of the poisoning, 200 pounds of the lupine was fed to 50 sheep from another band. Some of these sheep died before finishing their meal, and, altogether, 28 died within a period of twenty-four hours. Similar experiences were had during the same winter on a number of other sheep ranges. In the Deer Lodge Valley an experienced sheep raiser, who had for several years fed lupine hay, cut a portion of his hay during the first half of July. Haying was then interrupted until September, when the rest of the lupine was cut, and the stack which had been begun earlier in the season was completed. During the following winter, when this hay was fed, the lupine which was cut late in the season caused no trouble. The first feed, however, which was given from the bottom of the stack of lupine, which was cut in July, caused the death of about 700 sheep. The disastrous result of allowing sheep which are unacquainted with lupine to feed where this plant grows in abundance is well illustrated by the case of a train load of sheep which were unloaded near the Mullen Tunnel, at an altitude of 6,000 feet.

The shipment was made in July, and the sheep were unloaded in a ravenously hungry condition. Since lupine constituted the most conspicuous forage material accessible to the sheep, they ate great quantities of the pods and leaves. Within a few hours a large number of sheep showed signs of poisoning, and 400 died.

The most disastrous case of sheep poisoning which the writer has observed in Montana occurred on June 28, 1900, about 5 miles west of Livingston. Two bands of sheep, each numbering 3,000, had recently been imported from Oregon and were being "trailed" west along the railroad track. The two bands of sheep were driven over parallel but slightly different courses during the day and arrived at the same point at night. One band came in contact with a considerable quantity of lupines (*Lupinus cyaneus*) in a ripe condition and ate large quantities of the pods. The other band followed a course by which no lupines with pods could be obtained. The first band was driven across a small stream, where both were watered, and after crossing the stream found and ate considerable quantities of lupine pods. During the night symptoms of poisoning developed, and ultimately 1,900 out of the 3,000 sheep in the first band died, while none in the other were affected. A preliminary investigation of this case led the writer to suspect malicious poisoning. A subsequent postmortem examination of about 75 sheep showed that all the sheep that died had eaten large quantities of lupine pods in a ripe condition. The symptoms were such as were observed in other cases of lupine poisoning, and the evidence as a whole pointed conclusively to lupine as the cause of death.

The symptoms of lupine poisoning are so well known in Europe that chronic lupine poisoning has been given the name *lupinosis*. In this country the chronic form has not been observed. In cases of lupine poisoning in Montana there was noted an acute cerebral congestion, accompanied with mental excitement. The sheep rushed about in different directions, butting one another and other objects. The first stage of frenzy was soon followed by a second stage, characterized by pronounced irregularity of movement, spasms, and falling fits. In the majority of cases death occurred in from one-half to one and one-half hours. In extensive cases of lupine poisoning it was uniformly observed that a number of the sheep lingered on from two to four days before they died. The muscular convulsions resembled those caused by strychnine. The excretion of the kidneys was much increased and frequently was bloody. Postmortem examinations of sheep poisoned by lupines revealed conditions similar to those in acute forms of loco disease, with the addition of a congested condition of the kidneys.

No remedies have been tried in cases of stock poisoning from American species of lupine. From our general experience with potassium permanganate it seems reasonable to suppose that this substance would probably destroy the lupine alkaloids in the stomach if administered promptly after the first signs of poisoning. In the main, however, reliance should be placed upon prevention. With regard to the use of lupine hay, our experience and observations indicate that this is always dangerous for sheep if cut at a time when the seeds are retained in the hay. Since the limit of the period during which lupines are not poisonous can not be determined for the present with any certainty, it seems advisable to abandon entirely the use of lupine hay for sheep, except after a preliminary test in feeding large quantities of the hay to one or two sheep. If it should prove to be nonpoisonous, it may then, of course, be fed with safety.

The poisonous principle in all plants which have been fully investigated varies in quantity according to the stage of growth of the plant, and is located more abundantly in one part of the plant than in another. These facts seem to be strikingly true of lupine, since, as already indicated, the plants are sometimes eaten in large quantities with impunity, while at other times the plants cause extensive losses, especially among sheep. The evidence thus far collected regarding this matter indicates that the seeds are the most poisonous part of the plant.

LESS IMPORTANT POISONOUS PLANTS AND SUSPECTED PLANTS.

Ergot.—Besides the poisonous plants of more importance, which have already been discussed, there are a number of other species which are known to be poisonous or which are suspected of being poisonous by stockmen. Perhaps especial mention should be made of ergot on account of the great prevalence of this parasitic fungus on a considerable variety of grasses in Montana. Ergot is most abundant on wild-rye grass and bluejoint. The form in which this fungus is most readily seen is that of a black, straight, or slightly curved spur, from one-fourth to one-half inch in length from the fruiting head of the infested grass. Bluejoint and wild-rye grass are extensively cut for hay, and when badly infested with ergot are exceedingly dangerous fodder. In addition to the ordinary form of ergotism, which is well known to cattle raisers, the following case was apparently due to extensive eating of ergot, in which the symptoms were quite unusual. In 6 horses which had been feeding for several weeks on infested bluejoint hay symptoms of paralysis developed, beginning first with the muscles of the throat and gradually extending over the whole body. An attempt was made to counteract these symptoms by alcoholic stimulants and hypodermic injections of strychnine, with success in 2 cases only. The other horses died of general paralysis within from six to eight hours. A number of cases of the ordinary form of ergotism were observed in Montana, and, as attention has already been called in Iowa to the constitutional effects of continued eating of ergot by domestic animals, it seems highly probable that the great prevalence of ergot in Montana may be the cause of many unexplained cases of plant poisoning in the State.

It was learned in conversation with stockmen during the season of 1900 that the ergot spurs are quite generally considered as being the seeds of the grasses which they infest. The difference between ergot spurs and seeds of grasses may be easily learned and should be known by all persons who handle stock.

Swamp Camas (*Zygadenus elegans*).—This species resembles death camas in general habit. It differs from the latter in its greater height, larger flowers, and wider leaves. It grows in more moist situations than death camas. Marsh hay containing a large quantity of swamp camas and cut in the fall of 1899 proved on the first feeding to be poisonous to sheep. An examination of the remaining portion of hay showed that no other plant was present which could be considered poisonous. The seeds of the swamp camas were probably the cause of the poisoning in this case. During the season of 1900 six cattle were poisoned while feeding in a pasture where swamp camas grew in abundance, and two of the animals died. The symptoms of poisoning were nearly identical with those manifested by sheep in poisoning by death camas and postmortem examination revealed a similar anatomical condition. Large quantities of swamp camas were found in the stomachs of the dead animals.

Among the plants in Montana of restricted distribution which are known to be poisonous mention should be made of the California swamp hellebore (*Veratrum californicum*), black henbane (*Hyoscyamus niger*), and spreading nightshade (*Solanum triflorum*).

A large number of plants have been suspected of being poisonous by various stockmen. In some cases the evidence is apparently quite convincing that they are poisonous to a slight extent, while in others there is absolutely no evidence on one side or the other. Many plants belonging to the parsley family have been called indiscriminately by the name wild parsnip, and they have been generally suspected. No definite evidence was obtained against any one of these plants. The false lupine (*Thermopsis rhombifolia*) has been suspected of being poisonous, and in one case, where 100 cattle died on a range near Weibaux during the season of 1900, this plant grew in abundance and had been eaten to some extent. Otherwise, no evidence was obtained against it. This plant is also known by the name of yellow pea among stockmen; it is frequently eaten by sheep without serious effects, and is cut for hay to some extent.

One instance of the apparently poisonous effects of oat smut was observed by the author in Gallatin Valley. A crop of oats which was badly infested with smut was cut before maturing and stored for hay. This hay was fed to a dairy herd in the following winter with the result that 12 cows died of gastritis and frenzy after a period of about twelve hours. On postmortem examination the stomach walls were much congested, showing a decided irritation.

A number of plants have been suspected of being poisonous from fancied resemblance to plants which are known to be poisonous. One curious confusion of species has already been referred to by which a number of stockmen referred to death camas as wild onion and then considered the wild onion as being poisonous. No evidence is obtainable for believing the wild onion to be poisonous. Wild licorice has at times been suspected of causing poisoning, although it is well known that a large quantity of this plant is cut for hay and fed with impunity. The green plants are also frequently eaten by cattle and horses on the range. The wild hyacinth (*Leucocinum montanum*) has been repeatedly sent to the writer with statements concerning its alleged poisonous nature. It has been supposed by some that the seeds or the roots were poisonous; but since the seed capsules are formed under ground and the plant grows in such dry situations that it is practically impossible to pull up the roots, it is difficult to see how stock could ever feed upon these portions of the plant. No evidence whatever has been obtained which could connect this plant with any case of poisoning. The cow parsnip (*Heracleum lanatum*) is occasionally called wild parsnip and consequently considered poisonous. The plant is much coarser than the water hemlock and is known to be harmless. The false mallow (*Malvastrum coccineum*) is well known for its showy, brick-red flowers, which blossom in May and June. This plant has been accused of being poisonous, but it was found during the season of 1900 that it is extensively eaten by sheep on certain ranges and was well known to be a valuable forage crop by Mr. W. C. Gillette, on whose range it had been eaten by sheep for a number of years.

Helenium Autumnale.—False sunflower, sneezewort, sneeze-weed, swamp sunflower, yellow star, ox eye. *Ord Compositæ.* An indigenous herb, with large golden yellow compound flowers which appear in August. All its parts are bitter and somewhat acrid, and when snuffed up the nostrils in powder are powerful sternutatories. Nine different varieties of Helenium have been described, but *H. autumnale, H. parviflorum* and *H. tenuifolium* are the best known; the last two for their peculiar deleterious effects on the nervous system of the lower animals especially.—Dunglison's Medical Dictionary.

The *H. autumnale* injures and kills some of our domestic animals. It is distributed in damp lands from near the great northern lakes to the vicinity of the Gulf of Mexico, and commences blooming late in August and continues till frost. The other species bloom earlier, the entire blooms being bright yellow, while the central portion of this is purplish. While the others are annuals, this is perennial; the root and lower part of the stems survive through the winter. The stems do not branch so near the ground as the others, and the plant is acrid, pungent. In common with the other species, it is also bitter. But the degree of bitterness and acridness is very variable. Within an area of a few square yards plants may be found with these properties very strong, and others in which the bitter is weak and the acridness scarcely perceptible.

In the sheep the spasms in severe cases are epilepti-form and a sheep may have many such convulsions and yet recover without treatment and after many hours rise up and walk.

The horse and mule succumb to the baleful effects of the poison quicker and more completely than other animals. The effect is manifested very soon after ingestion and with great violence. The animal cannot control his motions, plunges about blindly, falls dead or perhaps breaks his neck in falling forward with the head under the body.

An antidote which has proved effective is a pint or two of melted lard poured down the animal's throat. The relief is very prompt. But it must be given before the horse loses control of his limbs, or it cannot be administered at all. The relief is so prompt and complete that it is difficult to believe that it is the direct effect of the lard on the nerve centres, but as a local emollient applied directly to the burning throat and stomach. The local trouble being quickly relieved, the violent reflex effect on the nervous system suddenly ceases.

When we consider the wide distribution of this plant and that in some places it is so abundant as to hide the earth from view over whole acres, it is remarkable that so few poisonings occur. But animals have no special fondness for it. When they have been long on the road and deprived of green food, stopping where this weed is found and other green plants scarce, they are disposed to eat a little of it. It is under such conditions that the plant is most frequently eaten and the poisoning occurs.

Animals, notably sheep, once intoxicated by the plant and recovering, seem to acquire a mania for it, and when finding themselves in localities where it grows, hurry to and devour it.

Woody Aster.—During the past several years thousands of sheep have died in Wyoming through what is supposed to have been the eating of poisonous plants on the range. For the last two or three seasons the losses have occurred, in many instances, in localities where previous losses had been noted, and where a certain plant that later came to be suspected as poisonous was found in enormous numbers. Several different plants have at times been suspected by stock owners, and until very recently the private opinion of those who have ranged stock was the only evidence on which one could base a conclusion as to the nature of the trouble. Under these conditions very little has as yet been done in the way of determining the plant or plants involved, the symptoms produced, etc., all of which must receive careful attention before it will be possible to deal with the question satisfactorily.

A plant commonly known as Woody Aster, which was very abundant in those areas designated by the sheepmen as Poison Patches, has been suspected. It is interesting to note in this connection that sheep commonly refuse to eat this plant on the range when other forage is available, and that poisoning usually occurs either when the hungry animals are driven, after shearing, directly across the Aster patches, or where, for some reason, immediately after a rain or snow storm they purposely eat it. It is under one of these conditions that the most severe losses have occurred.

The plant in question is confined to certain districts characterized by a gumbo clay soil, more or less intermixed with gravel and containing more or less of alkali and other salts. It is a soil in which only the various kinds of alkali-loving plants, such as pig weeds, saltbushes, grease-woods, and this Aster thrive. A fact of interest in this connection is that this particular plant is not only confined to this type of soil, but Wyoming is the center of its distribution. Perhaps more singular yet is the fact that the Aster is almost invariably more or less infected with a fungus (*Puccinia xylorrhizae*). If it should prove to be true that the malady is due to the eating of the Aster then it may be the Aster itself that is the source of the trouble, but the chances are rather better that the specific poisonous qualities are due to the fungus.

Description of the Plant.—To those who are familiar with the range it will be possible to describe the plant so that it can be recognized. It need only be looked for upon gumbo clays, usually on gentle slopes or sometimes on ridges. Often these conditions are met with in the neighborhood of temporary ponds or lakes where the sheep are watered. The plant has a strong woody root, more or less branched just at the surface of the ground. From these woody crowns, tufts of short branches spring. These bear green, narrow leaves, one or two inches long, the whole tuft becoming at length several inches high and finally producing in June, a considerable number of large white daisy-like flowers with a yellow center. If the leaves be examined it will be found that they usually bear a considerable number of yellowish or brownish spots, caused by the fungus previously mentioned.

The time when the foliage first appears will vary with each year. Again, the time of blossoming is a matter of weather conditions. So far as it is known, sheep are the only species susceptible to poisoning by the Woody Aster, and of these the greatest losses are reported in old pregnant ewes in early spring and in lambs late in summer.

In the spring we experience more wet weather and the plants are resultingly more active as well as more inviting in appearance. Over-crowding of the range at this time urges the consumption particularly of the greener, more advanced vegetation over the less matured grasses.

The greatest losses naturally occur after shearing, when the fasted sheep are of necessity driven across patches of the Aster plant. The sheep, having little time to choose their food and urged by hunger, grasp the plants most attainable, *i. e.*, the Aster, since its ranker growth allows it to outstrip and stand above the natural grasses. It is at this time, also, the flowering period of the plant or just previous to it, that the leaves of poisonous plants are considered to be the most active. There can be no doubt but that wet weather favors poisoning by the Aster, just as its toxicity is affected by various stages of its growth, but at present we can only theorize as to the reason.

Puccinia.—That fungi of various kinds are known to be poisonous furnished one reason for suspicion towards the Woody Aster, which has been almost invariably infected and markedly so, by the *Puccinia xylorrhizae.* The occurrence of the fungus on the Aster is a factor of importance in this problem. Even though it might not possess poisonous activity of its own, it is conceivable that the Aster may be sufficiently nitrogenous so that the numerous fungi may occasion a chemical change in the material similar to ptomain production by bacteria in the decomposition of foods of animal origin. As the Aster gives off a pronounced and extremely disagreeable odor as well as possessing, while in a growing stage, a bitter taste, the sheep exhibit aversion towards eating it except under the spur of hunger.

SYMPTOMS OF ASTER POISONING.

Weakness of locomotory muscles with prostration; later weakness extends to the muscles of the neck. Temperature about 103 to 104.5. Pulse very rapid and weak, 92 to over 300.

Respirations dyspneic (labored) with mucous rales.

Tympany (bloat) is generally pronounced. Abdominal pain, evidenced by groaning.

Diuresis (increased secretion of urine). Froth, often sanguinous (bloody), from the air passages.

The mucous membranes vary from anaemic (bloodless) to cyanotic (bluish).

The stools are soft, with mucous, to very soft.

Pupils are sometimes noticeably dilated.

Cerebral symptoms present in a few instances.

Before death complete prostration and apparent unconsciousness.

Course.—Varies from a few hours to three or four days, according to the amount of plant ingested and the condition of the plant.

Treatment.—Co-operation with most of the sheepmen in the vicinity gave H. S. Eakins, field man in charge of the camp, considerable opportunity for trying out experimental treatments.

Tapping was not productive of very good results; some relief, however, being afforded by escape of some of the gas.

Stimulants and carminatives or anti-ferments were chiefly indicated.

AUTOPSIES.

Rumen: Fermentation producing a frothy mass with a small amount of flatus.

Omasum: Slight inflammation with some desquamation (shedding) of epithelium of mucous folds or leaves.

Intestines: Slight enteritis (inflammation of intestine). Colitis (inflammation of colon) and proctitis (inflammation of rectum) sometimes present.

Liver: Passive congestion. Cloudy swelling with focal necrosis (death).

Spleen: Congested.

Pancreas: Slight congestion.

Lymph Glands: Congested.

Kidneys: Acute nephritis—albuminoid degeneration.

Bladder: Generally full, with some cystitis (inflammation).

Lungs: Badly congested (passive), with edema (dropsical swelling) and itis (inflammation). Pleuritic (from pleura) effusion (pouring out of fluid).

Trachea and air passages: Injected.

Heart: Hydro-pericardium (fluid in heart sac); petechia (blood spots) of myocardium (heart muscle) with myocarditis (inflammation of).

Brain: Occasionally slight cerebritis; veins injected.

Peritoneum: Itis; effusion.

Tissues were preserved from all post-mortems; sectioned and studied for the determination of the pathological changes resulting from Aster poisoning. The definite facts obtained from their study will be incorporated in the results obtained from a continuance of the work.

SUMMARY.

1. The Woody Aster has been proven to be poisonous to sheep.

2. The Woody Aster grows only on alkalied gumbo-clay soils, and but for the one recorded season, is always heavily infested with the fungus, *Puccinia xylorrhizae.* The presence of the fungus may add to the poisonous character of the plant.

3. Ninety to one hundred per cent of the animals affected die.

4. Aster poisoning is characterized by lassitude, difficult respiration, muscular weakness, bloat, and final prostration.

5. Duration of illness, from a few hours to several days.

6. *Anatomical Diagnosis.*—Gastro-enteritis due to fermentation of ingesta acting as an irritant. General passive congestion due to weak and impeded heart action; and, in part perhaps, by reason of diaphragmatic pressure on lungs produced by tympany. Albuminoid degeneration of liver and kidney due to precipitation of proteids by toxin or toxins.

7. *Treatment.*—Purely symptomatic and none uniformly successful. Administration of stimulants in small doses as tr. opii., alcohol, and ether; carminatives, gentian, nux vomica, and ginger; antiferments, eucamphol.

8. *Prevention.*—Avoid Aster patches.

LIST OF PUBLICATIONS CONSULTED AND ABRIDGED ABOVE.

The Nodular Diseases of the Intestines of Sheep: Iowa Agr. Exp. Sta. Bul. 35; La. Agr. Exp. Sta. Bul. 64, 79, 83 and 89.

Gid or Grub in the Head of Sheep: Iowa Agr. Exp. Sta. Bul. 35; Bu. of An. Ind., Dept. of Agr., Bul. 66 and 125; Bu. of An. Ind., Dept. of Agr. Cirs. 159 and 165; Va. Agr. Exp. Sta. Bul. 110.

Scab in Sheep: Va. Agr. Exp. Sta. Bul. 124; Wyo. Agr. Exp. Sta. 12th An. Rept.; S. Dak. Agr. Exp. Sta. Bul. 36 and 107; N. Dak. Agr. Exp. Sta. Bul. 61; Ky. Agr. Exp. Sta. Bul. 143 and 157; La. Agr. Exp. Sta. Bul. 132; Iowa Agr. Exp. Sta. Bul. 35; Col. Agr. Exp. Sta. Bul. 38; Ind. Agr. Exp. Sta. Bul. 80; Minn. Agr. Exp. Sta. Bul. 16; Farmers' Bul., Dept. of Agr. 159; Bu. An. Ind., Dept. Agr. Cir. 89.

Ticks Affecting Sheep: Va. Agr. Exp. Sta. Bul. 111; Iowa Agr. Exp. Sta. Bul. 35.

Lice Affecting Sheep: Iowa Agr. Exp. Sta. Bul. 16 and 35; Va. Agr. Exp. Sta. Bul. 112.

Fringed Tapeworm: Kan. Agr. Exp. Sta. Bul. 86; S. Dak. Agr. Exp. Sta. Bul. 78.

Lung Worms in Sheep: Iowa Agr. Exp. Sta. Bul. 35.

Common Parasites of the Domestic Animals: Okl. Agr. Exp. Sta. Bul. 53.

Stomach Worms of Sheep: La. Agr. Exp. Sta. Bul. 95; Ohio Agr. Exp. Sta. Bul. 117 and 91; Iowa Agr. Exp. Sta. Bul. 35; Va. Agr. Exp. Sta. Bul. 64, 128, 178 and 126; S. Car. Agr. Exp. Sta. Bul. 142; W. Va. Agr. Exp. Sta. Bul. 90; Bu. An. Ind. Dept. Agr. Cir. 102; Bul. 127.

Poisonous Plants Affecting Sheep: Mon. Agr. Exp. Sta. Bul. 15; Wash. Agr. Exp. Sta. Bul. 73; Wyo. Agr. Exp. Sta. Bul. 88; An. Rept. Bu. An. Ind., Dept. Agr. 1900; Miss. Agr. Exp. Sta. Bul. 9.

Diseases of Sheep: Ind. Agr. Exp. Sta. Bul. 94.

Food Rot, Infection of the Genitals and Lip-and-Leg Ulceration: Bu. of An. Ind. Cir. 160; Bu. of An. Ind. Cir. 94; Bu. of An. Ind. Bul. 63.

Angora Goat Six Days Before Death from Takosis. B. A. I. 1902.

PART III

DISEASES OF GOATS, DOGS, AND CATS.

GOAT DISEASES.

GOATS are less subject to disease than sheep; but these species are so closely allied that treatment in cases of disease is the same for both. Several accounts have been published in the agricultural press of goats in the Southwest being affected with stomach worms and with grub in the head, the same as sheep are affected in the same localities. There are occasionally outbreaks of disease in certain localities, but these are due to local causes, and generally have not been difficult to overcome.

The treatment recommended for the screw worm is as follows: Add to any one of the carbolic sheep dips 10 per cent of chloroform. Apply this mixture, after thoroughly cleaning the wound, with a wad of cotton. The chloroform immediately destroys the larvæ and the carbolic dip prevents the further blowing of the wound. The stomach worm (*Strongylus contortus*) is the same form as found in sheep, cattle, and deer. The treatment in all cases is the same as for sheep.

Goats have at least two kinds of scab parasites peculiar to their species, but apparently only two kinds of scab develop. Psoroptic scab of sheep does not develop disease upon them, though it can undoubtedly sustain life for a while. Tapeworms of the genus Moniezia are found in goats. In the intestines are also found five round worms, namely, *Strongylus filicollis, Œsophagostoma venulosum, Sclerostoma hypostomum, Uncinaria cernua,* and *Trichocephalus affinis.* Verminous pneumonia of sheep also occurs in goats.

Tuberculosis is so rare in goats that every case discovered has been recorded, the number of such cases being less than a dozen. It may be said, therefore, that they are practically immune from this widespread and insidious disease.

Goats are apt to have foot rot, but a cure is easily effected by the use of sulphate of copper (blue vitriol). It is usually applied by driving the goats through a trough containing a solution of strong blue vitriol. The solution should be about an inch in depth. Oscar Tom, a breeder of much experience, says: Butter of antimony applied with a stiff feather will cure it, or mix 1 ounce of sulphuric acid with 2 ounces of vinegar and apply as above. Go over the whole band. Generally one application cures if well done. Change the range at the same time if you can.

Angoras are frequently affected with lice, which cause a loss of mohair from the rubbing and scratching of the goat. The lice may be exterminated by dipping. The common sheep dips are generally used for the purpose. It is a common practice to dip the goats once a year, and some advise dipping twice a year—in spring just after shearing and again in the fall.

The fact that many plants which are poisonous to sheep and cattle may be eaten with impunity by goats is frequently referred to by writers for the press. It is true, however, that goats sometimes die from eating poisonous plants, especially in the mountainous dis tricts of the Carolinas. It is believed that goats will not eat poisonous plants to an injurious extent unless driven by hunger to do so.

TAKORIS, A CONTAGIOUS DISEASE OF GOATS.

The disease presents many of the symptoms usually accompanying a parasitic invasion and is characterized by great emaciation and weakness, with symptoms of diarrhea and pneumonia. In the early stages of the affection there is usually little to indicate that anything is seriously amiss with the animal. The first observable symptom manifested is the listless and languid appearance of the animal, evidenced by its lagging behind the flock, and is usually accompanied by a drooping of the ears and a drowsy appearance of the eyes. The pulse is slow and feeble and the temperature is elevated slightly at first, but becomes subnormal a few days before death. The highest temperature observed in the natural disease was 104.1°, and the lowest, in a prostrated animal a few hours before death, registered 99.7° F. Snuffling of the nose, as in a case of coryza, with occasional coughing is sometimes in evidence.

As the disease advances the animal moves about in a desultory manner, with back arched, neck drawn down toward the sternum, and with a staggering gait. Rumination is seldom impaired. The appetite, while not so vigorous, is still present, though capricious, and the affected animal shows plainly that the ravages of the disease are rapidly overcoming the restorative elements derived from the food. The fleece is usually of good growth and presents a surprisingly thrifty appearance when the condition of the animal is taken into consideration. All the exposed mucous membranes appear pale and the respirations are accelerated and labored. The goats finally become so weak that they are readily knocked down and trampled upon by their fellows. If picked up they may move off slowly and eat a little, but within a few hours are down again, and in this way linger for several days, shrinking to about half their natural weight, and occasionally bleating or groaning, with head bent around on the side or drawn down to the sternum. A fluid discharge from the bowels of a very offensive odor is usually observed in the last few days of life, but this symptom is not constant.

COURSE AND SUSCEPTIBILITY.

This disease may assume a subacute or chronic type, usually the latter. The animal dies of inanition in from eight days to six or eight weeks. Several owners have reported deaths after only two or three days of illness, but the goats doubtless had been affected for a longer period, although not noticed on account of their mingling in the flock. It is the consensus of opinion among the breeders interviewed that many of the animals succeeded in living for weeks, but gradually became weaker and more debilitated, finally dying in a comatose condition. In no instance have we observed or heard of the natural recovery of an animal after once the symptoms of takosis were noticed. The younger goats seemed to be the most susceptible to the disease, although the old animals were by no means immune.

MORPHOLOGY (*Micrococcus Caprinus*, Sp.).

The specific organism of takosis appears in fresh bouillon cultures as a spherical or oval micrococcus with a diameter of 0.8 to 1μ. In these cultures it is single or in chains of two, three, or four elements, but most frequently is found in pairs, as diplococci, with a diameter transverse to the axis of the chain greater than the longtitudinal diameter. There is quite a variation in the size of the cocci, probably due to the increase in the size of the organism preparatory to the act of fission. As the cultures become older the cocci develop a stronger tendency to form chains, and after remaining in the incubator at $37°$ C. for three or more days chains of four to six elements are at times observed, as are also irregular clumps of cells which collect in masses of varying sizes. When they assume this grouping tendency no oval forms are to be found and each of the organisms is strictly spherical in outline. In the tissues they are frequently seen to deviate from the spherical and assume somewhat of a lancet shape, with the pointed extremities in apposition. This same form has been met in samples of blood freshly drawn from the ear of an affected goat. The elements forming pairs are frequently very unequal in size and are not always of uniform shape.

ECONOMIC IMPORTANCE.

A few years ago the flocks of Angora goats in this country were comparatively unimportant in number, and they were nearly all of them kept in southern latitudes, but during recent years the raising of these animals has received a remarkable impetus. New uses have been discovered for the fleece, they have been widely exploited as brush eradicators, and their flesh has been more readily accepted as a food product, until at present they have reached an established, settled value in many of the larger live-stock markets. As a result of the wide-spread interest thus awakened in them, many stock raisers have made purchases of foundation stock with the intention of establishing therewith a profitable flock. Others have made larger purchases at the start, being unwilling to wait for the slow natural increases in numbers of their animals. By means of numerous transactions the animals have been placed in widely distributed northern localities to which they were formerly strangers, but the serious losses caused to these investors by outbreaks of takosis served as a check to many prospective purchasers, and the Angora goat industry was, in consequence, subjected to a discouraging setback, and has not expanded to the proportions which it would otherwise have reached.

Now that the cause of the trouble has been determined, one may be warranted in claiming that the disastrous effects of all outbreaks up to the present time may in the future be avoided in large measure. The owner of the flock of goats will now see the importance of deciding upon the nature of the ailment affecting them just as soon as any general disease is noticed; and when takosis has appeared and been identified, if he will at once apply the precautionary measures and the course of treatment to be recommended later in this work, he should avoid many of the discouraging experiences of his predecessors.

As has already been stated in this article, the most serious losses that have come to our notice have occurred among goats that were removed from southern localities to new regions far to northward, and that had not become fully acclimated in their new surroundings. In many instances the trouble has appeared very soon after the arrival of the animals at their destination, even before they have recovered fully from the serious strain incident to the long journey by rail.

Another feature of takosis, which is of great economic importance to the breeder of goats, is experienced in the unavoidable tendency to abortion which is manifested by all pregnant females that are affected with the disease. Females of the sheep and goat families will never reproduce in a prolific manner if in a wasted, emaciated condition during the breeding season. Many of them will fail to come in heat, and others, although passing through the period of estrum normally, will fail to conceive. Takosis is essentially a wasting disease, and one of the marked results of its attack upon a flock of breeding goats is seen in the shrunken kid crop of the following season.

It is rare indeed for a pregnant doe to complete her term of gestation if attacked during this period by takosis. Abortion follows almost invariably. As might naturally be expected, the accident of abortion under these circumstances always ends fatally, as the animal is unable, in her already weakened condition, to withstand the shock incident to delivery. Many times the fetus dies in utero, and thus becoming a foreign body to the maternal organism, it but hastens the eventual collapse of the doe. In holding autopsies on the bodies of affected pregnant does, it has been occasionally noted that the death of the fetus preceded that of the mother by a few days, and the fetal decomposition present has indicated that it played a prominent part in causing the death of the adult.

One flock has been brought to our notice which contained about 1,600 does at the commencement of the breeding season in the fall of 1901. They were seriously affected with takosis at this time, and in consequence there were but seventeen living kids produced in the following spring. Another instance is reported where the total increase of a flock of over 1,000 does for the year was limited to eleven living kids.

DIFFERENTIAL DIAGNOSIS.

PARASITISM.

The condition which will most frequently be mistaken for takosis in goats is parasitism. In common with sheep, goats serve as hosts for a formidable array of animal parasites, and the loss directly or indirectly due to parasitic invasions must annually serve as a serious tax upon the goat raisers of the country.

The effects of internal parasites upon the goats are very similar in many of their outward manifestations to the symptoms of takosis. There is a persistent unthriftiness, although the appetite of the animal remains good. The fleece does not retain its proper luster. There may be considerable snuffling of the nose, accompanied by frequent coughing. The animal may become affected with diarrhea, more or less severe, and its accompanying weakness. The eyes lose their brilliance and gradually assume a dull sunken appearance. The formation of an edematous tumor beneath the jaws is frequently noticed during the later stages of a serious invasion. These, in a general way, are the symptoms resulting from an attack by animal parasites, but it must be remembered that there are species of worms that find their natural habitat in some particular organ, and that, in consequence, it is impossible to give an accurate enumeration of the symptoms that may be manifested in any given case under the general heading of parasitism.

The symptoms produced by the local disturbance of the affected part will predominate, while others, frequently caused by parasitic invasion will be entirely lacking. Careful post-mortem examination will quickly disclose the presence of parasites. A differential diagnosis previous to death of the animal may, however, be made by giving due consideration to the various symptoms manifested by these diseases. First of all, the infectious nature of takosis, when compared with the enzootic course of a parasitic invasion, will justify one in making a definite diagnosis. In attacks of takosis, symptoms of pneumonia will be frequently noted, especially labored breathing or rapid respiration. These symptoms are not diagnostic of parasitism. The edematous lump under the jaw, so frequently present in cases of parasitism, fails in takosis. The luster of the fleece is less affected in takosis, while diarrhea is more frequently noted. Continuous coughing and snuffling, while diagnostic of the presence of lung-worms, are not characteristic of takosis and are noted only occasionally in cases of this disease, unless there is a complication with some other affection.

ANEMIA.

In goats this is very rare, and when it does occur it is usually secondary to some previously existing disease, such as chronic pneumonia, peritonitis, or to poor food and starvation. It does not assume an infectious nature, and may be differentiated from the anemic condition accompanying takosis by the absence of the specific organism on microscopic examination.

WATERY CACHEXIA, OR HYDREMIA.

This usually results from poor feeding, innutritious food, or pasturing on low ground. The natural goat pasture is high dry land. The animal is weak, readily exhausted, breathes rapidly, and its heart palpitates. The mucous membranes of the eyes, nose, and mouth are pale and swollen. The edema which is present about the head, neck, and abdomen will serve to differentiate this disease from takosis. This edema of the head disappears when the animal lies down. Icterus may accompany the disease when the discoloration of the mucous membrane easily establishes the nature of the affection. A change of pasture and a more nutritious diet are accompanied by a return of health to the flock.

CONTAGIOUS PNEUMONIA.

There have been several instances recorded in which flocks of goats have been affected with a contagious pneumonia. Hutcheon has met with this epidemic in South Africa; Steel has seen it in East India; and it has also been brought to the attention of French and Italian veterinarians.

Soon after the outbreak of this disease in the flock many of the animals will become affected with a cough. The temperature rapidly rises until occasionally as high as 107° F. is recorded. The appetite becomes disturbed or disappears altogether, and there is slight nasal discharge. The conjunctiva appears brownish or bronzed, the vesicular murmur of the lungs becomes modified, the pulse quickened, and the breathing accelerated, labored, and painful. The affected animals always evince pain when pressure is applied between their ribs.

The post-mortem examination of these cases shows the lesions to be chiefly confined to the thoracic cavity. The visceral pleura is usually adherent to the thoracic walls. The diseased lung is solidified and enlarged throughout one-half to three-fourths of its substance. It is covered with a firm elastic fibrinous membrane.

Respecting the nature of the disease, Dr. Hutcheon writes: It was a specific infectious form of pleuro-pneumonia, affecting goats only, cattle and sheep remaining free from infection, although constantly exposed to it. The disease was introduced into the Cape Colony by a shipment of Angora goats from Asia Minor, where the disease is represented as being indigenous.

At the present time contagious bovine pleuro-pneumonia has no existence among the flocks or herds of America, but since the goats of other countries have been proved susceptible to an analogous disease, the above mention of its leading characteristics may not be out of place.

TREATMENT.

Prevention.—It has been shown that the most destructive outbreaks have occurred among the goats that just previously have been shipped from a southern locality to a more northern latitude, and this fact suggests the need of caution in the removal of animals in this direction. Sudden climatic changes should be avoided so far as possible, and when shipments of goats for breeding purposes are to be made which necessitate their transportation northward over considerable distances the changes should be made during the months of summer or late spring, and not in the fall or winter, when the contrast of temperature will be so much greater.

Earlier writers have called attention to the fact that Angora goats do not take kindly to transportation from one climate to another.   Hobson states that the native proprietors of Angora flocks in Asia Minor unanimously assert that this goat can not be transported from the place where it was born to a neighboring village of a different altitude without suffering a deterioration, and although able to resist both heat and cold they can not withstand much humidity, either in their pastures or folds.

The second precautionary measure is closely allied to the first, namely, Angora goats should be provided with stables that are thoroughly dry, not alone in their ability to shed rain, but on account of being erected upon ground that has perfect natural drainage, and these should be accessible by them at all times, as the effect of rains upon the general health and strength of these animals has been frequently proved to be very disastrous.   So great is their natural aversion to a wetting that they will seldom get caught out in a shower if shelter is within their reach, but will leave their browsing and march under cover before the downpour arrives.   The reason for this is obvious.   Their fleece is wholly lacking in yolk; consequently it will not shed water in the least, and a fall of rain immediately soaks the animal clear to the skin.

As a third measure of prevention may be mentioned careful feeding.   No animal is as well fortified against the attack of an infection when reduced by lack of nourishment as it is when in vigorous, thriving condition.   Among the predisposing causes of disease usually enumerated by general pathologists will be found debility due to insufficient or unsuitable food, and, although the reason for this may not be established beyond the reach of argument, it is pretty generally conceded that the continued lack of proper nourishment establishes in the blood of an animal an abnormal degree of alkalinity which grants an increased susceptibility to the inroads of pathogenic organisms.

Another preventive measure to be mentioned here is one that is applicable only after the disease has made its appearance in the flock.   The segregation or isolation of all affected animals as soon as they evince any symptoms of the disease will be found a most valuable means of protection for those that remain unaffected, and a strict quarantine over all of the diseased members of the flock should be maintained so long as the disease remains upon the premises.

THERAPEUTICS.

Medicinal treatment has proved unsatisfactory in many of the cases of takosis to which it has been applied.   The most pleasing results that have been derived from the use of drugs in our experiments at the laboratory have followed the administration of calomel given alone in 0.10-gram doses twice daily for two days, to be followed by powders composed of arsenic, iron, and quinine, as follows:

Grams.

Arsenious acid.............................. 1.40
Iron, reduced............................... 12.00
Quinine sulphate............................ 6.00

Mix and make into twenty powders, giving one to each adult goat morning and evening at the conclusion of the administration of calomel. After an interval of two days, this treatment is repeated. In case the diarrhea persists, the sulphate of iron has been substituted for the reduced iron, with beneficial effects.

CONCLUSIONS.

As a result of the present preliminary investigation, the following conclusions have been reached:

1. The disease here described as takosis has appeared in many parts of this country, but particularly in the Northern States, where it has caused great loss to many breeders of Angora goats.

2. It is a progressive, debilitative, contagious disease, characterized by great emaciation and weakness, with symptoms of diarrhea and pneumonia, and causes a mortality of 100 per cent of those affected and from 30 to 85 per cent of the whole flock.

3. From the carcasses of numerous animals that have succumbed to this disease a new organism, *Micrococcus caprinus*, has been recovered in purity and is presumably the etiological factor.

4. This micrococcus possesses pathogenic properties for goats, chickens, rabbits, guinea pigs, and white mice, but not for sheep, dogs, or rats.

5. Although the disease has been described before so far as could be ascertained no bacteriological investigations have been previously made.

6. Medicinal treatment was attempted with varying success, while the immunizing experiments thus far conducted (although too few to permit of any conclusive statement or accurate estimate as to their protective value), have shown highly encouraging results. When accompanied with measures of isolation and disinfection, the treatment may prove of great assistance in the suppression and eradication of the disease in an infected flock.

MALTA FEVER.

Microeoccus melitensis, the causal factor of Malta fever, is an aerobic, round or slightly oval micro-organism about 0.4 micron in diameter which usually occurs singly or in pairs, but when cultivated in bouillon appears in short chains. In hanging-drop preparations it shows an active Brownian movement, although according to Gordon this is a true motility due to flagella, which he claims to have stained successfully. The organism is stained by the usual basic aniline dyes, but does not take Gram's stain. Its growth is extremely slow even in the incubator, and it requires a faintly acid medium. In gelatin it grows feebly and without liquefaction. On agar minute transparent or pearly white colonies appear after three or four days, and two days subsequently the growths become amber-colored; later they become more opaque, of a buff color, with granular margins. In bouillon it gives rise to diffuse cloudiness, with a subsequent formation of white flocculent sediment without the formation of a pellicle. In litmus milk the medium is not coagulated, and in ten days to two weeks the milk becomes distinctly alkaline. Indol is not produced. It is pathogenic to monkeys by subcutaneous injection, but, according to Durham, rabbits and guinea pigs are only susceptible to an intracerebral inoculation.

Malta Fever in Man on the Island of Malta.—On the Island of Malta there has been endemic for an indefinite period a febrile disease of the inhabitants termed Malta fever, and also known as Rock, Mediterranean, or undulant fever. It is a specific infectious disease caused by the *Micrococcus melitensis* discovered by Bruce in 1887, and is characterized by an irregular fever of an undulating type, with frequent remissions and relapses, constipation, excessive perspiration, and joint pains, rheumatic in character. It runs a protracted but indefinite course of from three months to a year, with a low rate of mortality of about 2 to 3 per cent.

This disease, which resembles typhoid fever very closely, was so exceedingly prevalent among the British soldiers and sailors stationed on the island that in 1904 a commission was appointed by the English Government, under the supervision of an advisory committee of the British Royal Society, to investigate the possible sources of infection and advise methods for its control. The commission investigated the disease in all of its phases in a most exhaustive manner, and was led to consider that the milk from Maltese goats was an important, if not the main, factor in the dissemination of Malta fever among human beings. The subsequent experiments showed that a large proportion, reaching upward of 50 per cent, of the 20,000 goats on the island were affected with the disease.

Infection by Means of Goats' Milk.—Zammit noted early in 1905 that the Maltese goats were to some extent affected by Malta fever after they had been fed on living cultures of the *Micrococcus melitensis*. This observation was later confirmed by the finding that the goats were not only able to be artificially infected but that about 50 per cent of them acquired the disease naturally, and that the organisms were eliminated in their milk and urine. It was then decided to investigate the milk of such infected though apparently healthy goats with the result that in Malta 10 per cent of the goats were found to be eliminating the specific coccus in the milk, and this milk when fed to monkeys even for a day was able to produce typical attacks of Malta fever which ran a course parallel to that of the disease in man. The only logical conclusion which could be formulated from this work was that the Maltese goats were carriers of the virus of Malta fever and one of the principal means of transmitting the disease to human beings through the ingestion of their milk.

All the available evidence points to contaminated food as the vehicle by which these goats become infected with the virus of Malta fever. It has been definitely established that monkeys and goats may be infected in this manner. Furthermore, it has been shown that the urine of infected goats and of ambulatory cases in man at times contain the *Micrococcus melitensis,* so that goats feeding on material that has come in contact with such urine (which is not at all infrequent by the usual method of handling these animals) are readily infected. Thus the frequency and method of infection in goats are quite readily explained.

Condition of Health of the Infected Animals.—The organism of Malta fever lives a more or less passive existence in the body of the goat, exercising its pathogenic effect when it gains entrance to the human body. The symptoms in those goats are not apparent except in a few cases, and even in these instances it is possible that the symptoms of anorexia, diarrhea, weakness, etc., were the result of one of the several intercurrent diseases with which the goats become affected.

Method of Treating the Goats.—As Malta fever in man is not a highly virulent disease, the mortality being about 2 or 3 per cent, it is consequently fair to presume that as the disease is less virulent in goats these animals would probably be more amenable to treatment than the human, the adult goats were placed on a mixture of 20 grains of potassium iodid and 15 grains of salol per head in their feed twice daily for one month. Quinin was then substituted for the potassium iodid and the treatment continued one month longer. By this system of treatment it was hoped that any latent virus of the disease which might be present in the tissues of the animals would be overcome and destroyed. The results gave little hope of eradicating the infection by drug administration.

CONCLUSIONS.

1. It has been definitely demonstrated that the *Micrococcus melitensis,* the organism of Malta fever, has a more or less passive existence in the body of Maltese goats, exercising its pathogenic effect when it gains entrance to the human body.

2. These goats, when carriers of the virus of Malta fever, are one of the important factors, if not the principal factor, in the dissemination of this disease, through the ingestion of their milk by human beings.

3. Goats infected with Malta fever eliminate the causative agent of the disease in both the milk and the urine.

4. All the available evidence points to contaminated food as the vehicle by which the goats become infected with the organism of Malta fever. The urine of infected goats and of ambulatory cases in man at times contains the *Micrococcus melitensis,* so that normal goats feeding on material which had come in contact with such urine are readily infected. Thus the frequency and the method of infection in goats are quite easily explained. Infection by goats' milk is directly demonstrated when contact infection and other modes of exposure were entirely eliminated.

5. So long as Malta fever remains so prevalent in the Island of Malta, and such a large percentage of the native goats are passive carriers of the *Micrococcus melitensis,* it will be impracticable to attempt to introduce these animals into the United States. Even if they were assuredly free from *Micrococcus melitensis,* it is doubtful,

on account of climatic conditions, whether they could be profitably bred in this country, except in the extreme Southern States.

DISEASES OF DOGS AND CATS.
CANINE DISTEMPER.

Canine distemper is an infectious and contagious disease, characterized by a catarrhal inflammation, individually or collectively, of the various systems and organs of the body. Synonyms.—Canine distemper has been variously termed, Epizootic of Dogs, Canine Plague, Canine Glanders, Typhus, Typhoid, Catarrhal Fever and many others.

Cause.—Canine distemper is caused by a micro-organism and according to Bruo Galli Valerio, this micro-organism is a bacillus whose dimensions vary from 1.25 to 2.5 micromillimeters in length and .31 in breadth. This bacillus is found in the lungs, central nervous system, secretions from the nose and eyes and from the pustules of the skin. It gives characteristic cultures in gelatin at eighteen to twenty degrees Centigrade. The inoculation of a culture from the brain, under the skin of a dog five or six months old, has reproduced the disease with its characteristic pulmonary and cerebro-spinal symptoms. As predisposing cause in delicate animals, exposure to wet and cold is the most important, as it tends to weaken the constitution of the animal as well as, in many cases, to set up a simple catarrh first, which renders a much more suitable means of infection by the distemper bacillus. Another is an old prejudice, which is still common, consisting of the withholding of meat in the food of young dogs, as a vegetable diet determines in time a weakening of the organism of the carnivorous animal. Bischoff and Voit showed in a number of experiments that dogs which were fed exclusively on bread became cachectic, and that cats died.

Animals Affected.—Canine distemper is found in the dog, cat, fox, wolf, hyena, monkey and has been seen in the human family. In the canine species, it exists in a sporadic, enzootic and epizootic state. In large cities, where it exists permanently, the number of cases noticed vary according to the different years; but, with the exception of simple gastro-intestinal catarrh, it is the most frequent affection of the canine species.

Symptoms.—Owing to the fact that the pathological lesions may be localized in one or more of the various systems of the body, and that each system affected will give rise to its respective, peculiar train of symptoms, it is necessary to classify under separate heads the symptoms produced by each individual seat of lesion, in order to give a comprehensive description of this disease. The symptoms will be taken up as they most commonly present themselves, which are: The symptoms of the beginning, ocular symptoms, or symptoms of the eye, symptoms of the digestive apparatus, symptoms of the respiratory apparatus, nervous symptoms, symptoms furnished by the skin, and the general symptoms.

Symptoms of the Beginning.—In its initial stage the disease is marked, as a rule, by general phenomena. Depression, a low-spirited condition, a capricious appetite or anorexia (loss of appetite), fatigue, trembling, chills, erected hair, a dry and hot nose. As a rule, the disease enters on its course with an elevation of temperature (102 to 104 degrees Fahrenheit). In some cases, where the patient is strong, the rise in temperature is not so well marked.

Ocular Symptoms.—In a great majority of cases it is in the eyes that the first local symptoms are observed. They consist of a conjunctivitis, which later becomes purulent; the eye is watery; there is photophobia; the eyelids are injected, the conjunctiva is red and tumefied, the exudate dries and forms crusts on the edges of the eyes during the day, and agglutinates them during the night. The continued inflammation, in addition to mechanical interference (scratching, rubbing, etc.), often causes the formation of true ulcers. In other cases are observed in both eyes a diffuse parenchymatous keratitis (an inflammation of the cornea); giving rise to a milky or cloudy appearance of the cornea. In some cases the eye manifestations are the chief symptoms.

Symptoms of the Digestive Apparatus.—There is generally a capricious appetite or loss of appetite; redness and dryness of the buccal mucous membrane; intense thirst; either constipation or a fetid diarrhea, either mucous, frothy or hemorrhagic. In weak animals and in advanced stages the urine, which is often albuminous, contains coloring matters of the bile. These intestinal symptoms may be the only manifestations of the disease.

Symptoms of the Respiratory Apparatus.—These, which are those of catarrh or inflammation of the mucous membrane lining the nasal cavities, bronchial tubes and air-cells of the lungs, present themselves very suddenly, and are characterized by a serous, mucous or purulent discharge, with sneezing and itching of the nose. Later the discharge becomes yellowish and streaked with blood, with a more or less offensive odor. Small ulcers often appear on the nasal mucous membranes. Accompanying this nasal catarrh a laryngeal catarrh is often seen which is marked by a cough, at first dry and hard, afterwards moist and accompanied by a discharge. This cough often produces vomiting. From the larynx the inflammatory condition extends into the bronchi. Bronchitis is indicated by the increased number of respirations, by a coarse respiratory murmur, and by rales. In bronchiolitis, or an inflammation of the mucous membrane lining the small bronchioles of the lungs, which is frequent in distemper, the breathing is accelerated and quite difficult; a weak, painful cough is heard at the time of percussion of the thorax, also dry and moist rales with fine or coarse bubbles are heard on oscultation. In young and weak animals which do not succeed in expectorating the bronchial exudate, the latter is drawn into the alvioli, and catarrhal pneumonia (an inflammation of the mucous membrane lining the air-cells of the lungs) is developed. These symptoms are accompanied by a rise in temperature, a harsh, roughened and intensified breathing in circumscribed areas of the thorax. Cough is weak and laborious, and the pulse becomes weak and rapid.

Nervous Symptoms.—In weak and anemic subjects serious cerebral symptoms predominate; characterized by stupefaction. In strong animals we notice especially symptoms of active cerebral hyperemia, sparkling eyes, hot head, restlessness, great excitement, followed later by others which are produced by cerebral compression, especially convulsions, which are often limited to one or more members. At certain moments violent epileptiform spasms appear. The animals, which are anxious and over-excited, shake their heads and wander around without aim, or run around as if lost, with a frothy saliva running from the mouth.

The animal falls, utters a cry, loses consciousness, and undergoes generalized tonic or clonic spasms, the rectal and vesical sphincters are paralyzed, and there is expulsion of urine and fecal matter. These phenomena are due to arterial anemia and venous hyperemia of certain regions of the cerebro-spinal center, as well as to the action of the infectious poison on the nervous system. These nervous symptoms are generally followed by either complete or partial paralysis, more commonly of the posterior extremity.

Symptoms Furnished by the Skin.—In nearly half of the cases a peculiar pustular exanthema or eruption is developed upon the inner fascia of the legs and on the abdomen. In mild cases this exanthema only becomes papular and is sometimes the only symptom that is present.

On the surface of the skin very red spots appear which within twenty-four hours are transformed into military pustules surrounded by a red zone. These pustules either dry and form crusts, or burst and form moist wounds which heal in from six to eight days. This eruption may be only in circumscribed areas or it may be distributed over the entire surface of the abdomen.

General Symptoms.—The temperature, as a rule, rises in the beginning, and increases when inflammatory localizations are produced, at the approach of death often dropping considerably below the normal. The course of the fever, however, is generally irregular. As the disease advances, emaciation becomes more and more marked; the abdomen becomes tucked up, the ribs prominent, the hair dull and bristly, the orbits become sunken, the mucous membranes pale, the gait is staggering and weakness is extreme. The animal gives off a fetid odor and is almost always found in a recumbent position and in a deep state of coma.

Course and Prognosis.—Canine distemper offers a great variety of changes. When it is marked by a simple papular or slight pustular exanthema, by a simple inflammation of the conjunctiva, by slightly marked nervous symptoms, by a mild catarrh of the respiratory or digestive mucous membranes, it often runs a rapid and abortive course, and may end in recovery within eight or ten days. Its duration, however, is from three to four weeks. Where marked brain and spinal lesions complicate the disease, it runs a slow course, dragging along for months, unless some vital portion of the brain is involved, or some important function disturbed, in which case, death takes place in a very short time. The average mortality is from fifty to sixty per cent.

The prognosis is unfavorable in young animals, manifesting weakness, when several organs are involved at once, where lobular pneumonia is pronounced, where diarrhea is excessive, where exhaustion is pronounced, where the breath is fetid, and finally, where there is a lowering of the temperature below the normal.

Death is produced by cerebral paralysis, which may end the disease within a few days, or by pulmonary edema, septemia or exhaustion. The prognosis is more favorable where the animal is older and stronger, where the disease runs a mild course and is localized to circumscribed regions.

Differential Diagnosis.—The distinction of this disease from a simple catarrh is sometimes very difficult to make. In general, however, the multiplicity of the catarrhal lesions aid us in our object, such as simultaneous invasion of the several organs, the young age of the affected animals, the marked elevation of temperature, the general progress of the disease, and especially the pustular eruption. Where the symptoms of cerebral excitement are present the so-called hydrophobia is generally thought of; in fact, in the writer's opinion nearly all, if not all, of the mad-dog scares are in reality canine distemper with the nervous symptoms predominating. It is said that in the latter disease, the aggressive tendency (so characteristic of rabies) is absent; but probably the seat of the lesion in the brain has a great deal to do in determining the different symptoms, as in a case where the nervous symptoms followed very closely upon the general catarrhal symptoms of distemper, these nervous symptoms were decidedly of an aggressive nature.

When the exanthema is extensive and covers a large surface of the body it may offer a close resemblance to mange; but in distemper the itching is not so great, and the rapidity with which the exanthema extends, coupled with the other symptoms, as a rule clears up the difficulty. In the early stages it is often very difficult to diagnose distemper from simple catarrhal pneumonia, and at times we are compelled to wait a short while for the other symptoms of distemper to present themselves before we can positively differentiate the two diseases.

Pathological Anatomy.—The air-passages show an inflammatory condition, the mucous membrane, which is sometimes pale, is at other times dark red, tumefied and covered with a purulent, thick, brownish-gray exudate mixed with blood-clots; this exudate is even found in the bony cavities of the nasal sinuses. Sometimes the nasal mucous membrane is covered with small ulcers.

The bronchioles and air-cells of the lungs sometimes only bear evidence of an inflammation of the mucous membrane lining them; at other times the entire cavities of these small tubes and air-cells are filled with inflammatory exudate. The lungs show these inflammatory centers only in spots, while the neighboring air-cells are distended with air. The mucous membrane lining the mouth, pharynx, stomach and intestines is either pale, or red, tumefied and covered with viscous mucus.

The mesenteric lymphatic ganglia are tumefied. The brain shows evidence of cerebral edema, anemia, and softening of the brain and nerve. The convolutions of the brain are soft and flattened; there is a serous exudate in the lateral ventricles and in the sub-arachnoid spaces. The blood vessels of the pia mater are distended, and sometimes a sero-hemorrhagic exudate may be found on this membrane; at times the nerve-cells and ganglia are involved. Changes in the spinal cord are, as a rule, less prominent; there is rarely more than a slight anemia and edema in the lumbar region. Where, however, there are symptoms of acute paralysis, the spinal cord shows marked evidence of intense inflammation, characterized by degenerative changes in the walls of the blood vessels and an albuminous exudate along the blood vessels and in the interstitial connective tissue of the gray substance of the cord.

In chronic distemper, circumscribed areas of true inflammation of the connective tissue of the spinal cord and partial atrophy of the nerve substance have been found. In some cases, the muscle cells of the heart and the cells of the liver and kidneys have been found in a state of fatty degeneration. The lymphatic glands are generally tumefied and edematous, and finally, eschars are generally found upon the elbows and thighs due to the animal assuming a recumbent position so much of the time.

Treatment.—The treatment is in great part symptomatic; our object is to try to destroy the contagious agent (and thus remove the cause), to relieve the unpleasant symptoms as much as possible, to relieve the catarrh of the various organs and to sustain the strength of the patient.

Calomel has given remarkably good results in combating the disease when localized in the digestive tract or when the infectious elements have penetrated that duct. It should here be given in one-grain doses three times a day. Its chief action is that of a good disinfectant. The inhalation of a one per cent. solution of carbolic acid often has a very soothing effect upon the respiratory mucous membranes; also a five per cent. solution of compound tincture of benzoin added to the above.

Treatment of the Ocular Complications.—A one per cent. solution of carbolic acid or a five per cent. solution of boracic acid proves an excellent factor in combating ulcerations of the cornea and purulent conjunctivitis. Also one-half to one per cent. solution of sulphate of zinc. In very obstinate cases, from one-half to a two per cent. solution of nitrate of silver (lunar caustic) acts as a rule very nicely. When the latter is used, the parts should be washed afterwards with a five per cent. solution of common salt so as to render harmless any excess of silver nitrate. Where parenchymatous keratitis (inflammation of the substance of the cornea) is present, a solution containing six grains of the sulphate of atropine to one ounce of water, or, in its place, equal parts of the fluid extract of belladonna is used with good effect, both to keep the iris from becoming adherent to the cornea and also to relieve the inflammatory process. Two or three drops of this solution should be dropped into the eyes two or three times a day. For the itching of the eyes five drops of a two per cent. solution of cocaine dropped into the eyes every three hours generally relieve it. When the lids become granulated they should be cauterized with sulphate of copper or bluestone. Insufflations of calomel often act very nicely in clearing up corneal opacities.

Treatment of the Lesions Localized in the Digestive Apparatus. —Five drops of dilute hydrochloric acid and five drops of tincture of nux vomica added to half a wineglassful of water given three times a day act as a good digestive tonic. For diarrhea one-half grain of salol and one grain of sub-nitrate of bismuth blown into the mouth three times a day generally suffice; but when the diarrhea is persistent two to five drops of the tincture of opium have to be resorted to. For the respiratory localization, the above-mentioned inhalations should be used from the start. Hot applications should be put to the throat and chest. When the cough is troublesome two grains of the compound licorice powder, or one grain of Dover's powder two or three times a day often alleviate the trouble.

Treatment of the Nervous Symptoms.—The spasms originating from the central nervous system should be combated by some nerve sedative and some antispasmodic, as two and one-half drachms of bromide of soda, two drachms of chloral hydrate, and water enough to make a four-ounce mixture. Give one teaspoonful every three or four hours. The above may be alternated with the sulphate of morphine given hypodermically in one-eighth grain doses. Paralytic conditions and weakness should be treated with strong but easily digested food. The sulphate of strychnine, in one-sixtieth grain doses three times a day, makes a very good stimulant tonic.

Treatment of the Fever.—At first, when there is only a slight elevation of temperature, no treatment is necessary, but when the fever begins to rise it should be watched very carefully. Two grains of either phenacetine or acetanilid blown into the mouth every two hours until the temperature begins to drop is as good a method as can be used; but it is well to guard against its depressing effect upon the heart by the use of the strychnine as above mentioned. Alcohol in some form is also a very valuable heart stimulant, when given in teaspoonful doses every two or three hours, according to the strength of the animal.

For the eruption of the skin, the oxide of zinc ointment acts very nicely, or equal parts of sub-nitrate of bismuth, acetanilid and starch make a very nice dressing. In every case of distemper, the animal should be kept in a well-ventilated room, large enough for proper exercise, but free from draughts. It should be .fed with nutritious, but easily digested food, as egg-nog, raw eggs, finely chopped, lean meat, or broths of various sorts.

RABIES.

In the category of infectious diseases rabies stands at the head of those about which the ideas of the general public are most at

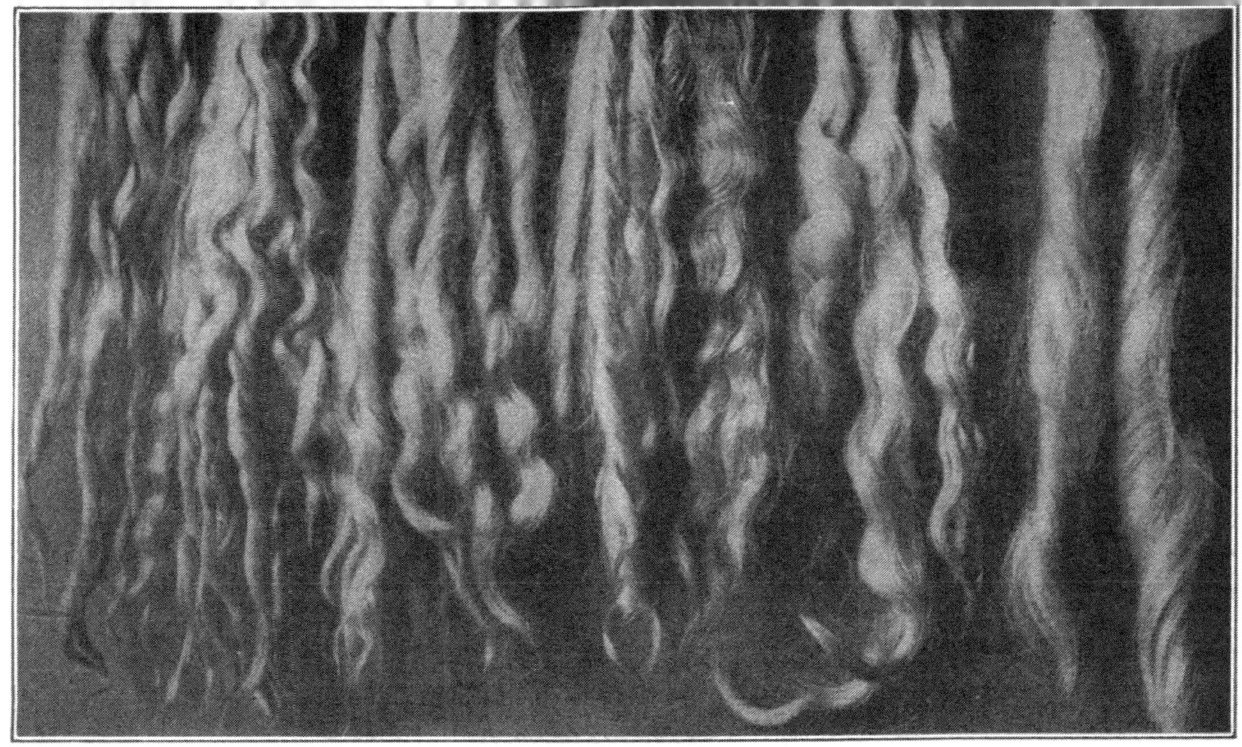

Samples of Mohair. B. A. I. 1000

variance with the actual facts. It is commonly believed that a person bitten by a dog in perfect health is liable to become affected with hydrophobia should the dog develop rabies at any subsequent period, however long afterwards. Consequently believers in this theory are particularly anxious to have the dog killed at once before he has had an opportunity to go mad. Nothing could be more fallacious and at variance with our knowledge of all infectious diseases, and the killing of the dog should always be discouraged.

Until recently it was considered that the dog's saliva became virulent only three days before the appearance of symptoms of rabies. According to some recent experiments by Nicolas it has been found that the saliva may become virulent six or even eight days before the symptoms develop. Therefore in case the animal remains healthy for ten days after it has bitten the person or animal, no danger need be apprehended from that bite even though the dog develop rabies within the next few weeks.

Madstone.—The curative value of the madstone is still devoutly believed in by a great many people in certain sections of the country. Within the last few years a madstone was forwarded to the Department, the owner stating that it had prevented several cases of rabies and he was anxious for it to be tried by the Bureau. Some of these madstones, properly called hair balls, are obtained from the stomachs of various wild and domestic animals. They are in some cases composed of matted hair which the animal has licked from its body and swallowed; but in the majority of cases they consist of masses of vegetable fiber, such as the awns of clover and beards of grain, which have gradually collected over a considerable period of time and are formed into a spherical shape by the contraction of the gastric walls. Gallstones, intestinal calculi, and in fact any porous stones may be used as madstones.

After a person has been bitten the madstone is applied to the wound, and it is believed that the longer it adheres the more sure it is of preventing the disease. Whether it will stick or not depends entirely on the amount of hemorrhage or discharge from the wound. Where this is profuse the blood infiltrates the meshes of the madstone, soon coagulates or dries, and tends to hold it in place, and it adheres for a considerable time under such circumstances. In these cases the virus is supposed to be removed and the treatment is heralded a success. On the other hand, where the wound is small and the discharge slight there is nothing to hold the stone in place and it immediately falls off. Certain of these madstones have been held in families for three or four generations and are guarded as carefully as any heirloom. Cases have been known where people have made long journeys and paid large sums of money to have a madstone applied. Its specific value against rabies is no greater than that of a piece of blotting paper applied in the same manner. The application of madstones gives the unenlightened public a false sense of security, and their use should be discouraged by all possible means.

Rabid Dogs and Water.—It is commonly believed that mad dogs will not go near water, and in case such an animal is seen to ford a creek or lake it is taken as proof that he did not have rabies. This fear of water is a symptom usually marked in human cases, but is never present in the dog at any stage of the disease. Animals in the early stages when running about the country will cross bodies of water without the slightest fear. Even after the throat becomes completely paralyzed the animal will often constantly attempt to drink water from a pail or bucket if placed within its reach, but, owing to the paralysis of the throat muscles, swallowing is impossible.

Dog Days.—The idea is prevalent with many people that dogs are particularly liable to go mad during the so-called dog days, which extend from the first of July to the middle of August. These days are called dog days because they cover the period of time when the dog star Sirius is above the horizon with the sun; they have no connection with the dog. On account of the clemency of the weather dogs probably travel about during this season more than in winter, and hence are slightly more liable to infection. Statistics, however, as well as our own experience about this section of the country, show that the disease is present throughout the year, and seasons have very little if any influence.

Color of the Animal's Mouth.—It frequently occurs after a person is bitten by a dog that some friend will immediately look into the mouth of the animal. In case the mucous membrane is black, he will at once conclude that the bite is dangerous, even though the dog appears perfectly normal; but, if the mouth happens to be red, he thinks there is no danger from the bite. This is entirely erroneous. The black color is due to a normal deposit of pigment in the mucous membrane of the mouth. It is present in a certain percentage of all dogs and has no connection with rabies. In this paragraph the writer is not referring to the so-called black tongue of dogs in the South, which is the vernacular name for dumb rabies, resulting from the swollen, darkened appearance of the tongue following its extrusion from paralysis of the lower jaw. This will be referred to in the section on symptoms.

Lyssophobia.—Many educated men, including some physicians, claim that all cases of hydrophobia in the human family are the result of wrought-up nervous excitement due to fear on the part of the patient. While at times these symptoms, termed lyssophobia, do occur in neurotic individuals who have been bitten by healthy dogs, they are always hysterical in nature, cause no organic lesions, and universally terminate in recovery. Thus lyssophobia is entirely distinct from the real disease, which is universally fatal to the human being.

Spontaneous Rabies.—In many instances the origin of an outbreak of rabies is difficult to trace. This has given rise to the opinion that the disease may appear in the dog spontaneously, that it is an intrinsic part of his being which may crop out at any time under various extraneous conditions. This is as impossible as it would be for typhoid fever, tuberculosis, or any other infectious disease to develop spontaneously. Rabies is an infectious disease and can be produced only by inoculation with the specific virus which causes it. This specific virus is present in the saliva of animals affected with the disease and is transmitted to other animals and persons by the saliva on the teeth of such animals.

Period of Incubation.—The period of incubation of rabies varies within wide limits, being more or less different in the various species of the animals. It also differs in the same species, depending on several important factors, as the location of the bite, the character of the bite, and the amount of the virus injected. Bites about the head, face, and hands in human beings are the most serious because these parts are the most exposed. The clothing on other parts of the body tends to wipe the saliva from the teeth, and thus prevents it from inoculating the wound. Bites about the face and head are also more dangerous than on other parts because they are so thickly supplied with nerves and the distance the virus has to travel to reach the central nervous system is short. Through experimentation it has been pretty definitely proved that the virus travels along the course of the nerves rather than by means of the blood current. Deep, penetrating, or lacerating bites are obviously of greater import than superficial scratches, as more virus enters the former wounds and they are difficult or impossible to cauterize completely. Severe hemorrhage from the wound is favorable, as there is a possibility of part or all of the virus being thus mechanically removed. Infection and suppuration of the wound may also destroy the virus. None of these conditions, however, can be depended upon, but they account for the fact that a considerable proportion of persons and animals bitten do not contract the disease even when no treatment is given.

The shortest period of incubation is six days in the rabbit. This short period can only be obtained with what is known as "fixed virus" obtained in the laboratory by repeated passage of the ordinary virus through a long series of (50) rabbits. The disease as contracted from the bite of a rabid dog requires an incubation period of from fifteen to ninety days. At times this incubation has been prolonged greatly in excess of the above figures. In one case which came under the observation of this laboratory a dog belonging to one of the District fire companies was bitten by a rabid dog which was examined by the Bureau. The animal, being a great pet, was not killed and remained normal for exactly one year, when it came down with a typical case of rabies which was proved by microscopic examination and rabbit inoculations. Such a long incubation period, however, is so extremely rare that it is usually not considered in formulating quarantine laws for the prevention of the disease. Shorter periods of incubation than fifteen days have been reported, but they are very unusual.

Symptoms of Rabies in the Dog.—The symptoms are generally described under two types, the furious or irritable and the dumb or paralytic. The latter type is always seen in the terminal stages of the former; and, when the cases are of the dumb form from the outset, it is probable that the toxemia is overwhelming, and such cases usually run a more rapidly fatal course.

The Furious Type.—In the furious type, following the variable period of incubation, there is first noticed a change in the disposition of the animal, which should at once excite suspicion. Playful animals become morose, and quiet, reserved dogs may become unusually affectionate. The animal is nervous and easily excited, but obeys any command of its owner. In the course of a day or two the nervous condition increases and the animal becomes irritable and may snap if approached suddenly or startled. The bark becomes changed to a long drawn out combination of a whine and a howl, impossible to describe but never forgotten when once heard. Some dog owners speak of it as being somewhat of the nature of the bark of a foxhound while in the hunt, but this does not properly describe it. The animal if loose may pick up and swallow straw, sticks, stones, leather, and other foreign bodies. In some cases there is a tendency to bite parts of the skin, usually at the point where the animal was bitten, and in one case under the writer's observation the animal chewed the skin over the os calcis until the entire head of the bone was exposed to view. This tendency to bite the skin is probably due to an intense localized pruritis.

There is a marked tendency in these early stages for the animal to seek quiet spots and to hide in corners or dark places. If an attempt is made to remove the animal, the person is in great danger of being bitten. The restlessness of the animal becomes more marked. He may stand looking intently into space as if at an imaginary object. There is difficulty in swallowing, and saliva may dribble from the mouth. The irritability increases until the animal becomes furious, biting at a stick or other object thrust toward him. At this stage if the animal is not secured he may leave home and travel for miles. During the long journey he will fight with dogs and attack other animals in his path, but never barks or makes any outcry during these attacks. The animal may go 20 or 25 miles from home, but always returns, if not prevented, in an exhausted condition, covered with wounds and dirt and greatly emaciated. Signs of commencing paralysis now appear, with dropping of the lower jaw, inability to swallow, and irregularity in the pupils. The legs finally become paralyzed and the animal passes into the dumb form of the disease.

Dumb Rabies.—This form of the disease occurs in only a small percentage of the cases. The symptoms are somewhat similar to those of furious rabies except that marked irritability is absent and there is an early appearance of paralysis. This form of the disease, therefore, renders the dog less dangerous than the furious type. The animal lies quietly in some secluded place and appears to be stupid. The paralysis of the jaw comes on early, the tongue protrudes and becomes congested and covered with dirt, giving rise to the term black tongue, which is a bad synonym used in some localities, especially in the South, for this form of the disease. The use of this term to designate dumb rabies should be discouraged, as it tends to confound the disease with dog distemper. The hind legs, trunk, and forelegs become paralyzed, and death usually ensues in about three days, while the furious type lasts from six to eight days. Recovery from rabies in the dog after well-marked symptoms have developed is possible, and authentic cases have been reported by Pasteur, Roux, Babes, Courmont, and Remlinger. This is so rare, however, that it is of little importance.

Summary of Symptoms.—The important symptoms, any one of which when well marked should render the dog suspicious and lead to its being confined, are: (1) Change in disposition; (2) alteration of voice; (3) inability to swallow; (4) leaving home and returning in an exhausted and emaciated condition; (5) paralysis of the jaw; (6) swallowing abnormal substances, as wood, stones, etc.

DISEASES OF CATS.

Cases of rabies are less numerous in cats than in the other domestic animals. This is no doubt due to the dexterity with which they are able to escape from their pursuers, the conditions under which they live, their strong antipathy for dogs, and the fact that they seldom when caught by him escape alive. When, however, infection does take place the disease progresses very rapidly terminating fatally about the third day from the commencement of symptoms. These are frequently not seen, as the infected animal often hides away, and is not found until either death is approaching,·or has taken place. In other cases, the animal is extremely restless and excitable, moves about persistently in an erratic manner, and seldom remains at ease. The eyes assume an unusual brilliancy, the pupils are dilated, resulting in a wild frightened expression. Great thirst is apparent, but there is no desire for food. He shows a tendency, however, to pick up and swallow stones, sticks, and other foreign bodies. The voice rapidly changes to a loud harsh tone. He may run from one secluded spot to another constantly, mewing in a loud, harsh, unnatural, screechy manner. Saliva flows profusely, which with the persistent licking, frequently apparent, soon moistens the coat of the animal, and adds to its dejected appearance. Any noise or excitement may be followed by paroxysms; these may occur frequently or occasionally, during which the animal jumps about furiously, and will attack a dog, or other animal or man, biting and scratching savagely. Emaciation is rapid and complete, paralysis soon takes place, followed quickly by death.

PROPER DISPOSAL OF DOGS AFTER BITING PERSONS.

In many cases in which a person is bitten by a dog there is immediately a great popular clamor to have the animal at once destroyed. This should always be discouraged. The mere fact that a dog inflicts a bite on a human being does not by any means prove that he has rabies. This is the dog's only means of defense and he bites instinctively when harmed.

Therefore, after a person has been bitten, do not kill the dog unless a competent veterinarian has pronounced the disease rabies or the dog is showing well-marked symptoms. Instead, when practicable, the animal should be tied up securely and watched carefully for a week or ten days. In case suspicious symptoms do develop the dog should be examined by a veterinarian familiar with the disease, and if he pronounces the case rabies the animal may then be killed. If the animal is valuable and shows no symptoms of rabies there is no reason for destroying it. In this way valuable dogs can often be saved to their owners.

POST-MORTEM EXAMINATION OF CARCASS.

When a dog suspected of having rabies has died or been killed a post-mortem examination should be made. In rabies there are no absolutely characteristic post-mortem findings. Particular attention should be paid to the stomach. The mucous membrane of this organ is frequently congested, and in some cases a marked hemorrhagic inflammation is present. Foreign bodies, as sticks, straw, stones, coal, dirt, etc., and an absence of food in the stomach are very suspicious indications of rabies. The absence of these conditions, however, does not by any means exclude rabies. Undoubted cases of the disease have frequently been received at this laboratory where a considerable quantity of food was present in the stomach and the mucous membrane was in a normal condition. Redness and congestion of the pharynx and larynx with cerebral and meningeal congestion are also to be found in some cases. A negative post-mortem examination when the animal has died naturally also tends to suggest rabies as the cause of death. From the fact that the pathological alterations are not constant they are not relied upon to any extent in this laboratory. There are cases, however, in which, the microscopic changes being indefinite, we are forced to get all possible information, including history and post-mortem findings, if we are to draw conclusions without waiting for rabbit inoculations to decide definitely the diagnosis.

METHOD OF PREPARING PARTS TO BE FORWARDED TO LABORATORY.

It is only necessary to forward the head to the laboratory after the post-mortem examination has been made. This is removed with the skin intact by cutting through the middle of the cervical vertebræ. It should then be wrapped in dry cheese cloth or other material and forwarded by express. During very warm weather the head, after being wrapped, should be placed in a tin receptacle and packed in a wooden box containing chopped ice. By removing the head at the middle of the cervical vertebræ the plexiform ganglia are left intact, and upon arrival at the laboratory they can be removed and examined microscopically for the lesions described by Van Gehuchten and Nelis, and a diagnosis can be made within twenty-four hours.

This plan is not practicable in summer when several days are required for the head to reach the laboratory, as the brain undergoes softening, becomes invaded with bacteria, and the experimental rabbits inoculated are liable to death from septicemia. Putrefactive changes are also liable to occur in the ganglia, and thus render the conclusions from their examination indefinite. In case the time required to reach the laboratory is considerable and the weather warm, the brain, including the medulla oblongata, should be removed as carefully as possible in one piece, immersed in two or three times its volume of pure neutral glycerin, and sent in this manner. In large animals one cerebral hemisphere and the medulla are sufficient. In some cases even with this method the Negri bodies can be demonstrated in the large nerve cells of the hippocampus major, and thus a diagnosis can be made in a few hours without waiting for the rabbits to develop the disease, which requires from two to three weeks.

It must be remembered, however, that to get the best results with the rapid methods of diagnosis it is essential that the animal be allowed to die naturally from the disease or that it be destroyed only after symptoms are well advanced. When the animal is killed in the early stages the changes in the nervous system have frequently not developed sufficiently to be recognized.

THE PASTEUR TREATMENT AND ITS RESULTS.

The preventive treatment of rabies devised and perfected by Pasteur has done much to strip this dread disease of its mortality among human beings. It was first advocated by Pasteur in 1885 after thorough experimentation on the lower animals. In 1886 the original Pasteur Institute was opened in Paris. The first Pasteur Institute in the United States was opened in New York City in 1890, and was followed by a similar institution in Chicago in July of the same year.

The frequency of the disease throughout the country and the number of people consequently applying for treatment has led to the foundation of a number of Pasteur institutes. Besides those already mentioned there are others at Pittsburg, Ann Arbor, St. Paul, New Orleans, St. Louis, Houston, Baltimore, Richmond, and Atlanta.

METHOD OF THE PASTEUR TREATMENT.

The principle on which the treatment is based consists in the production of an active immunity by means of repeated injections with an emulsion of spinal cords of rabbits dead from inoculation with fixed virus, which cords have been attenuated to various degrees by drying.

Rabbits inoculated with fixed virus die in from six to seven days. Their spinal cords are removed aseptically and dried in bell jars over sodium hydrate. Fifteen days of such drying renders the cord harmless, and such a cord is emulsified with normal salt solution and 2 or 3 c.c. of the emulsion is injected beneath the skin, constituting the first inoculation. Cords dried fourteen, thirteen, twelve, eleven, ten days, etc., are used for the subsequent injections, until finally an emulsion of a cord dried only three days, which contains practically all its virulence, is injected. The injections are made daily for a period covering fifteen to twenty-one days. The cost of the treatment is from $100 to $150 including board and room at the institute. The New York board of health has on several occasions prepared the material and sent the requisite dose each day by mail to physicians and veterinarians in other cities at the rate of $25 for each course of treatment.

The treatment is not harmful except for the slight pain caused by the hypodermic injections. Patients are not required to remain in the institute constantly during the treatment, it only being necessary for them to present themselves each morning to have the injections made.

VALUE OF THE TREATMENT.

The value of the Pasteur treatment can not be overestimated. In 1896, nine years after the parent institution in Paris was founded, there were still many who doubted its value. In this year a commission was appointed by the House of Commons of England, consisting of Paget, Brunton, Fleming, Lister, Quain, Roscoe, Sanderson and Horsley, to ascertain the value of the treatment. After exhaustive investigation this commission reported that Pasteur's inoculations were as valuable against rabies as Jenner's vaccination was against smallpox. The statistics of the large number of Pasteur institutes during the past ten years are alone sufficient to prove that this was one of the greatest of Pasteur's discoveries. Without the treatment the mortality ranges from 10 to 80 per cent of the persons bitten. With the treatment the mortality statistics covering thousands of cases is always less than 1 per cent, and during recent years has been reduced to from 0.3 to 0.5 per cent. The observations of Brawner, of Georgia, noted above, are very convincing in this connection.

ERADICATION OF THE DISEASE.

If eradication were once accomplished all that has been said about treatment would be rendered unnecessary. Furthermore, rabies is one of the most easily eradicated of all infectious diseases. The factor of success in the undertaking can be summed up in three words, namely, muzzling all dogs. Could this be efficiently carried out in the United States for a few years rabies would be entirely eradicated, as has been demonstrated by the experience of other countries. Other domestic animals have the disease, it is true, but its transmission by these animals is rare and need not be considered. Wild animals as a factor in its spread may require consideration in a few localized sections of the country.

When the muzzling of dogs is suggested, however, the sanitarian meets with many obstacles. Many dog lovers can not appreciate, or are indifferent to the anxiety, mental terror, and suffering of several thousand human beings in our country yearly, and the actual death of from 100 to 300 yearly, not to mention the suffering and death of countless dumb brutes. But once a dog-muzzling law is passed dog owners are up in arms, using their time, influence, and money to secure its repeal or prevent its enforcement on the ground of alleged cruelty. In reality there is no cruelty whatever inflicted on a dog by causing it to wear a muzzle when in public places or running at large. The animals soon become used to it and manifest not the slightest inconvenience.

In the absence of muzzling the disease will continue year by year, causing constantly increasing suffering, financial loss, and death. The greater freedom of movement which the dog enjoys over all other domestic animals, except possibly the cat, makes it difficult or impracticable to control the disease by any other means than general

muzzling. How is this to be accomplished? This question seems to
be almost insurmountable. A national dog-muzzling law is sometimes proposed as a solution, but the power of the Federal Government in dog muzzling, as in other matters, would be confined to
those cases where the interstate dissemination of the disease is involved. The Secretary of Agriculture under present law could
quarantine States where the disease exists, but it can readily be seen
that it would be impracticable to enforce such a quarantine further
than to require that all dogs transported interstate by common carriers should be muzzled. This, however, would have no material influence in the eradication of the disease. Practically all the States
are infected, and the great majority of the serious outbreaks of rabies
are entirely within the confines of particular States.

It is necessary, therefore, for the States and municipalities to
take action and for the public to be educated to the importance of the
disease and the value of dog muzzling. Dog-pound service should be
increased in all the large cities. This results in the.destruction of a
large percentage of homeless and ownerless dogs, which class of animals are mainly responsible for keeping the infection of rabies alive.
The importance of this service is shown by the effect which it had in
Washington in 1900, when 2,771 more dogs were impounded than
during the previous year, with an immediate and marked decrease in
the frequency of the disease during the following year.

To secure individual State legislation in regard to dog muzzling,
Federal co-operation, and the equally important education of the
public will require concerted and unceasing action on the part of
professional men and sanitarians, with the co-operation of the general
public and the press. With such State legislation, the Bureau of
Animal Industry could co-operate with the State authorities by placing officers within the confines of a State in case of an outbreak
where the disease was spreading beyond the control of the State authorities. A large percentage of homeless and ownerless dogs could
be impounded and humanely destroyed. No dog would be seen on
the streets of cities or loose in the country without a muzzle. Animals
developing the disease would be unable to transmit it, because they
would be either muzzled or confined. Financial loss, suffering, and
death due to this disease would rapidly decrease from the beginning,
and in a few years' time rabies would be unknown in this country.

Once our country becomes free from the disease, we could easily
prevent its reappearance by enforcing a prolonged quarantine of all
dogs coming into the United States from foreign countries where the
disease prevails.

RESULTS OF MUZZLING DOGS IN OTHER COUNTRIES.

To prove the practical value of these repressive measures we have
only to observe the results obtained in foreign countries. Prior to
1875 rabies had been prevalent in Berlin for many years. In that
year a law was enacted, including the whole of Prussia, which provided for the killing of dogs suspected of having rabies, and the
muzzling and leading of all dogs when in public places. This led to

the complete eradication of the disease, and no case has occurred in Berlin since 1883.

In Holland in 1875, rabies being quite prevalent, dog muzzling was established. The disease immediately began to disappear, and in 1879 only 3 cases were reported, since which time the country has been free from the disease, except along the Belgian border.

In Great Britain the value of muzzling, which was enforced in spite of great public opposition, has been admirably demonstrated. In 1889 it was first adopted, and the disease had almost disappeared by 1892, when the muzzling was stopped on account of the determined opposition. The disease immediately began to increase, and in 1895 muzzling was again enforced. The decrease in rabies was immediate and marked, and since November, 1899, the country has been entirely free from the disease.

In Sweden the value of muzzling has also been demonstrated. In fact, in all cases where this measure has been effectually carried out the disease has been completely controlled.

The disease has never been known in Australia. This is due to the fact that the infectious agent never gained a foothold in that country, and for a number of years the government has wisely prevented such an unfortunate occurrence by laws which absolutely exclude the importation of dogs into that country.

In countries where steps have been taken to exterminate rabid dogs—Holland, Sweden, Norway, and Germany—rabies in man has almost disappeared. In England, where the disease in dogs has been eradicated, and in Australia, where the affection has not been allowed to enter, the disease among the residents is unknown.

DOMINION OF CANADA.
REGULATIONS RELATING TO RABIES.
By Order in Council Dated 10th August, 1905.

1. No dog or other animal which is affected with or has been exposed to the infection of rabies, shall be permitted to run at large, or to come in contact with other animals.

2. Any Veterinary Inspector may declare to be an infected place within the meaning of 'The Animal Contagious Diseases Act, 1903, R. S. C., 1906,' any place or premises where the infection of rabies is known or suspected to exist.

3. Veterinary Inspectors are hereby authorized to order the slaughter of any dog or other animal affected with rabies, or suspected of being so affected, and to order the disposition of the carcass of such animal.

4. Veterinary Inspectors are hereby authorized to order dogs or other animals which have been exposed to the infection of rabies to be detained, isolated or muzzled.

5. No dog or other animal, nor any part thereof, shall be removed out of an infected place without a license signed by an inspector.

6. Every yard, stable or outhouse, or other place or premises, and every wagon, cart, carriage, car or other vehicle, and every vessel

and every utensil or other thing infected or suspected of being infected with rabies, shall be thoroughly cleansed and disinfected by and at the expense of the owner or occupier in a manner satisfactory to a Veterinary Inspector.

7. On receiving the report of an Inspector to the effect that rabies is known or suspected to exist in any locality, the Minister of Agriculture may order that all dogs, or other animals, within such an area as he may determine or describe, shall be detained, isolated or muzzled in such manner and during such period as he may see fit.

J. G. RUTHERFORD,
Veterinary Director General.

HEALTH OF ANIMALS BRANCH,
DEPARTMENT OF AGRICULTURE,
OTTAWA.

PARASITES OF DOGS AND CATS.

THE SUCKING DOG-LOUSE (HŒMATOPINUS PILIFERUS).

Although the dog has been the closest companion of man among the domestic animals from very early times, and consequently this parasite in all probability well known to keepers of dogs, it was not technically described until about the year 1838.

It does not appear to have been a very numerous or injurious parasite, apparently much less so than the *Trichodectes latus* infesting the same animal, and less annoying than either ticks or fleas. Denny says (Monog. Anop. Brit., p. 29), "I have found it upon dogs two or three times, but it is by no means of common occurrence." Denny says (loc. cit.), "I also received specimens from the ferret." It can hardly be inferred, however, that this animal is a normal host of the species, as such an instance might occur entirely from accident, the louse having been transferred from some dog to a ferret associated with it.

This species is somewhat smaller than the lice infesting most of the larger mammals, the full-grown individuals being nearly one-tenth of an inch long. It is described generally as of a light-red or ashy flesh color, but evidently varies as the other species, according to condition of the body as well as age of specimens. In preserved specimens these colors become lighter, assuming a yellowish hue, the abdomen, except where darkened by the intestine and its contents, appearing a shade lighter than the front part of the body. The abdomen is thickly covered with fine hairs and minute warty eminences, these latter when magnified about 300 diameters appearing like the scales of a lizard or fish. Specimens from different breeds of dogs do not appear to have been noticed as different, though a form described as *H. bicolor* by Lucas may perhaps be found to present race characteristics.

THE BITING LOUSE OF THE DOG (TRICHODECTES LATUS).

Something over a century ago DeGeer mentioned a species of parasite on the dog under the name of *Ricinus canis*, which probably referred to this species, and another mentioned by Olfers under the name of *Pediculus setosus* probably preceded the description by Nitzsch under the name which the insect has borne since 1818.

Probably every one who has had much to do with dogs is aware to what an extent this parasite may multiply and how troublesome it is to this friend of man. It is generally believed that the lice are more troublesome to puppies than to old dogs, and it is not at all unlikely that the insects migrate when possible from older to younger animals.

In color this species agrees pretty closely with the other species and it is of about the same length as the cat louse, a little more than one millimetre, but it is much broader in proportion, being more than half as wide as long, and the head is short and the front but slightly curved.

THE LOUSE OF THE CAT (TRICHODECTES SUBROSTRATUS).

While it is possible that this parasite was referred to by Otto Fabricius about the year 1780 under the name of *Pediculus canis*, the first certain reference to it appears to have been the description by Nitzsch in 1818. Since that time it has been referred to by nearly all writers on the common parasites of animals, but so far as we know there has been no special description of the different stages, and we must assume that there is no important departure from the habits of species that are more thoroughly known.

It is a little more than a millimetre in length and has much the appearance of the species occurring on other domestic animals, but is distinguished particularly by the form of the head, which is quite pointed, and the under part of the front of the head is hollowed out in a furrow about the size of a hair. The insect will often be found adhering by the mouth parts with a hair so closely held in this groove that it is somewhat difficult to tell where the hair begins as separate from the insect.

There is no record that we have seen that indicates its presence on any other animal than the domestic cat, and, it is only occasionally that cats become infested with it. When they do the usual remedies may be administered, especially a washing with kerosene emulsion, after which the animal should be allowed to dry in a warm place, as the fur is so fine that they dry slowly.

ORDER PROVIDING FOR THE INSPECTION AND QUARANTINE OF COLLIE, SHEPHERD, OR SHEEP DOGS IMPORTED INTO THE UNITED STATES, OR THE TERRITORIES THEREOF, FROM ANY COUNTRY OF THE WORLD EXCEPT NORTH AMERICA.

[Refer to Gid or Turnsickness, under Diseases of Sheep.]

U. S. DEPARTMENT OF AGRICULTURE,
BUREAU OF ANIMAL INDUSTRY,
Washington, D. C., November 25, 1910.

The fact has been determined by the Secretary of Agriculture that collie, shepherd, or sheep dogs are subject to the infection of tapeworm *(Tænia cœnurus)*, the infective element causing gid, sturdy, or staggers in sheep, through the invasion of the brain and spinal canal of these animals by the cystic form of this parasite *(Cœnurus cerebralis)*:

Now, therefore, I, JAMES WILSON, under authority conferred by section 2 of the act of Congress approved February 2, 1903 (33 Stat., 791), do hereby order, and notice is hereby given to the owners, officers, and agents of all steamers and other vessels of all descriptions, plying between any foreign country, except the countries of North America, and the United States or the Territories thereof, and to all stockmen and all other persons concerned in any way or manner in the importation of, or traffic in, collies, shepherd, or sheep dogs, that all such dogs entering the United States or the Territories thereof shall be subjected to quarantine for a period not to exceed two weeks, or until it can be determined by inspection or examination by an inspector of the Bureau of Animal Industry, as to whether such dogs are the hosts of *Tænia cœnurus.* In the event it is found by such inspection or examination that such animals are so infected, they must be medically treated under the supervision of an inspector of the Bureau of Animal Industry and held in quarantine until it can be definitely determined that they are free from such infection before being allowed to be imported into the United States or to mingle with sheep or other live stock in the United States.

The ports of entry for such dogs are limited to the ports designated in the regulations of this Department for the entry of animals which are subject to both inspection and quarantine, viz: On the Atlantic seaboard, Boston, Mass.; New York, N. Y.; and Baltimore, Md. On the Pacific seaboard, San Francisco and San Diego, Cal., and Port Townsend, Wash.

This order will take effect immediately and will continue in force until otherwise ordered.

JAMES WILSON,
Secretary of Agriculture.

AUTHORITIES ON DISEASES OF GOATS CONSULTED ABOVE.

Takosis, A Contagious Disease of Goats: Bu. of An. Ind. Bul. 45.

Malta Fever: Bu. of An. Ind. Ann. Rept. 1908.

The Angora Goat: Farmer's Bul. Dept. Agr. 137.

AUTHORITIES ON DISEASES OF DOGS AND CATS CONSULTED ABOVE.

Canine Distemper: Va. Agr. Exp. Sta. Bul. 87.

Rabies: Rept. of the Vet. Dir.-Gen. and Live-Stock Com. of Canada, for the years, 1909, 1910 and 1911; Farmer's Bulletin 449; Bu. of An. Ind. Cir. 129.

Lice Affecting the Domestic Animals: Iowa Agr. Exp. Sta. Bul. 16.

The Sucking Dog Louse: Va. Agr. Exp. Sta. Bul. 112.

The Dog and Cat Flea: Va. Agr. Exp. Sta. Bul. 112.

THE COUNTRY LIFE PRESS
GARDEN CITY, N. Y.